Windows NT®
Power Toolkit

Other Books By New Riders Publishing

Planning for Windows 2000
Eric Cone, Jon Boggs, and Sergio Perez
ISBN: 0-7357-0048-6

Windows NT DNS
Michael Masterson, Herman Kneif, Scott Vinick, and Eric Roul
ISBN: 1-56205-943-2

Windows NT Network Management:
Reducing Total Cost of Ownership
Anil Desai
ISBN: 1-56205-946-7

Windows NT Performance
Monitoring, Benchmarking, and Tuning
Mark Edmead and Paul Hinsburg
ISBN: 1-56205-942-4

Windows NT Registry
Sandra Osborne
ISBN: 1-56205-941-6

Windows NT TCP/IP
Karanjit Siyan
ISBN 1-56205-887-8

Windows NT Terminal Server and
Citrix MetaFrame
Ted Harwood
ISBN: 1-56205-931-9

Cisco Router Configuration and
Troubleshooting
Mark Tripod
ISBN: 1-56205-944-0

Exchange System Administration
Janice Rice Howd
ISBN: 0-7357-0081-8

Implementing Exchange Server
Doug Hauger, Marywynne Leon, and William C. Wade III
ISBN: 0-7357-0024-9

Network Intrusion Detection: An
Analyst's Handbook
Stephen Northcutt
ISBN: 0-7357-0868-1

Understanding Data Communications,
Sixth Edition
Gilbert Held
ISBN: 0-7357-0036-2

Windows NT® Power Toolkit

New Riders

201 West 103rd Street,
Indianapolis, Indiana 46290

Stu Sjouwerman
Ed Tittel

Windows NT Power Toolkit

Stu Sjouwerman and Ed Tittel

Copyright © 1999 by New Riders Publishing

International Standard Book Number: 0-7357-0922-x

Library of Congress Catalog Card Number: 99-65207

Printed in the United States of America

First Printing: September, 1999

03 02 01 00 99   7 6 5 4 3 2

Interpretation of the printing code: The rightmost double-digit number is the year of the book's printing; the rightmost single-digit number is the number of the book's printing. For example, the printing code 99-1 shows that the first printing of the book occurred in 1999.

Trademarks

Warning and Disclaimer

Publisher
David Dwyer

Executive Editor
Al Valvano

Development Editor
Katherine Pendergast

Managing Editor
Gina Brown

Project Editor
Alissa Cayton

Copy Editors
Daryl Kessler
Amy Lepore
Audra McFarland

Indexers
Kevin Fulcher

Technical Reviewers
Steve Crandall
Tim Crosby
Ken Forester
Neil Kemp
Todd Klindt

Layout
Amy Parker
Ron Wise
Caroline Wise

About the Authors

Stu Sjouwerman has been in computing since 1979. He is executive vice president of Sunbelt Software, Inc., the world's largest distributor of Windows NT system management utilities. Stu is the editor of Sunbelt's *NTools* E-News, which goes to over 300,000 NT administrators, and he has spent more time rooting around with Windows NT than he would really like to admit.

Apart from his many hours playing businessman, Stu is an avid reader of science fiction. He always has the latest "hot-rod" Windows NT machines at home, rollerblades about 20 miles a week, and is an admitted "X-Files" groupie. You can reach Stu at `stus@sunbelt-software.com` or via his Web page at `http://www.sunbelt-software.com/ntnews.htm`.

Ed Tittel is an 18-year computer industry veteran with an interesting background. A former anthropologist, Ed switched his academic focus in the late 1970s from that field to computer science so he could stay in his adopted hometown of Austin, TX. For the first half-dozen years of his career, Ed wrote code primarily aimed at databases, management tools, and project management. In the late 1980s, Ed changed his focus from programming to the people side of the business, when he became a systems engineer for Novell, Inc. By 1993, Ed had become Novell's director of technical marketing, responsible for technical content in the company's trade shows and developer conferences. In 1994, when Novell announced its intentions to close its Austin offices, Ed got the impetus to start his own business.

Today, Ed runs LANWrights, Inc., a seven-person research, training, and writing company that specializes in Microsoft and Novell software, and in Web technologies. The author of over 100 computer trade books and hundreds of magazine articles, Ed helped dream up the idea that led to this book. In his spare time, Ed likes to play with his trusty Labrador puppy, Blackie, shoot pool, and travel, and keeps trying to perfect his chicken stock recipe. You can reach Ed via email at `etittel@lanw.com`.

About the Technical Reviewers

Steve Crandall is a technology consultant in Cleveland, OH. During his 20 years in the industry, Steve has held positions in systems engineering, technical marketing, and technical management. He is currently a graduate student in the history of technology and science at Case Western Reserve University.

Tim Crosby is a network support specialist for a software development company in Indianapolis, IN. Previously Tim has worked in various technical support roles in the computer industry. He received his undergraduate degree in management information systems from the University of Southern Mississippi and his graduate degree from Indiana University. He is currently an MCP in Windows NT Server and Windows Workstation 4.0, and is pursuing his MCSE certification in Windows NT 4.0.

Ken Forster is an enterprise architect for a major food manufacturer. In his past lives, he has been on the founding team of two successful software companies and was a winner of Microsoft's Windows World Open for the best manufacturing application. Ken has a lovely bride, Diane, and three wonderful children: Amber, Stephanie, and Alex. You can reach Ken at `ken@forsters.org`.

Neil Kemp is a senior systems engineer and has been working in the IT industry for the past 12 years. He holds an MCSE accreditation, as well as professional qualifications in NetWare, Compaq, and HP. Neil started out in the industry working for a small firm in the UK, servicing, repairing, and upgrading the Commodore range of PCs and home computers. He then moved on to various programming roles—most recently installing, troubleshooting, and commissioning company networking and infrastructure. This involves anything from peer-to-peer workgroups, to complete NT Domain models with other OS integration. Most recently he has been involved with piloting and deploying Windows Terminal Server and Windows 2000 Server. Neil lives in Stevenage, a small town in Hertfordshire, UK. He enjoys swimming, movies, and frequenting the local gym.

Todd Klindt started his professional career in August of 1996 working as a system administrator for the state headquarters of the Iowa National Guard. In December of 1996, he was offered a position with one of Iowa's leading computer network integrators, Century Systems. In April 1997, Todd took his first Microsoft Certification test, Networking Essentials. By August of 1997 he was an MCSE, and by December of 1997 he had taken and passed nine Microsoft exams. Todd is also a NetWare CNA. In July of 1998, Todd started working at Engineering Animation, Inc., and now provides support for internal Windows and UNIX users.

To Vic, who taught me that language is art.
Stu Sjouwerman

Acknowledgments

This book results from the hard labor of many individuals whose names don't appear on its cover. In particular, I'd like to thank my co-author, Stu Sjouwerman, for helping us bring this project to fruition. I'd also like to thank my friends and colleagues, James Michael Stewart and Dawn Rader, without whose hard work and tireless effort this book simply couldn't have been completed. Michael contributed over half the content for this volume, while Dawn edited, worked, and reworked its contents several times along the way to publication. Other people who contributed content to this book include Gary Novosel, Barry Shilmover, Lee Scales, George Turnbull, and Kofi Adumata. I'd also like to thank the LANWrights support staff for this project, which includes the wise and wonderful Louise Leahy, our rewrite expert; Todd Klindt, our sagacious technical editor; and Kyle Findlay, who ran down the permissions for the software that appears on the CD that accompanies this book. Also, thanks to Mary Burmeister, our "Jill of all trades" for pitching in to help, wherever that help was needed. If I've left anybody out, that doesn't mean I don't appreciate your efforts, it only means that my memory isn't what it once was, and that I couldn't find you in my notes.

On the New Riders side, we'd like to thank our executive and development editors Al Valvano and Katie Pendergast; our team coordinator, Ann Quinn; and our production team: Alissa Cayton, Daryl Kessler, Amy Lepore, Audra McFarland, Kevin Fulcher, Amy Parker, Ron Wise, and Caroline Wise. Without their help, patience, and understanding, we would never have been able to publish this book. So please accept my fervent thanks to one and all for helping us turn a good idea into what we hope will be an equally good book!

Contents

Your Feedback Is Valuable

As the reader of this book, *you* are our most important critic and commentator. We value your opinion and want to know what we're doing right, what we could do better, what areas you'd like to see us publish in, and any other words of wisdom you're willing to pass our way.

As the executive editor for the Networking team at New Riders Publishing, I welcome your comments. You can fax, email, or write me directly to let me know what you did or didn't like about this book—as well as what we can do to make our books stronger.

Please note that I cannot help you with technical problems related to the topic of this book, and that due to the high volume of mail I receive, I might not be able to reply to every message.

When you write, please be sure to include this book's title and author, as well as your name and phone or fax number. I will carefully review your comments and share them with the authors and editors who worked on the book.

Fax: 317-581-4663
Email: newriders@mcp.com
Mail: Al Valvano
          Executive Editor
          New Riders Publishing
          201 West 103rd Street
          Indianapolis, IN 46290 USA

Introduction

Welcome to the *Windows NT Power Toolkit*, a book designed to help Windows NT users at all levels—from novice to expert—function like a power user on steroids! We've designed this book to be easy to read, easy to use, and a great source of tips, tools, and techniques to enhance your Windows NT user experience, especially for Windows NT Workstation.

Who This Book Is For

If you use Windows NT as a desktop operating system, either full or part time, this book is for you. By and large, this book is not aimed at the types of problems and topics that network or system administrators must solve on a day-to-day basis (but even those folks should find it useful).

Rather, this book is aimed at helping those people who must work with Windows NT to get their work done on a day-in, day-out basis. Thus, it provides information about what Windows NT is, how it works, and how to get the best use out of your system as an end user.

But whether you're a seasoned professional or a newbie, you'll find a lot to help you improve your productivity in this book, including the following:

- Lots of useful overview and orientation information
- Windows NT hardware and software management advice
- Useful Windows NT Registry tweaks
- Networking tips and tricks
- Advice for making the most of Windows NT's file systems and utilities
- Everyday task scripting and automation
- Recommendations for tweaking and tuning Windows NT for maximum performance
- And (as the proverbial saying goes) "much, much more!"

What's in This Book

Each chapter is designed to provide useful coverage of some topic or technique related to Windows NT, from the fundamentals of its architecture to the ins and outs of remote access, printing, protocols, and system security. Throughout the book, in nearly every chapter, you'll also find pointers to built-in Windows NT software, Resource Kit utilities, and third-party software products designed to improve your abilities to get your work done using Windows NT. Whenever possible and practical, you'll find copies of this software on the CD that accompanies this book.

To help organize the voluminous material that this book contains, it's organized into six parts, as follows:

Part I: Windows NT Overview

The first part of the book contains three chapters that together provide an overview of Windows NT's capabilities and a roadmap to its visible contents. Chapter 1 covers a bit of Windows NT history, compares various versions of the software, and discusses upgrade and migration issues. Chapter 2 covers Windows NT's basic administrative utilities, and Chapter 3 provides a roadmap to various Windows NT directory structures, files, elements, and explains how to live with the routine of change so common on modern systems.

Part II: Nuts and Bolts of Windows NT

This part of the book contains six chapters. The first three of these chapters discuss how Windows NT interacts with hardware, how Windows NT boots itself during startup, and the various Windows NT Control Panel utilities that help you to control and configure your system. The remaining three chapters focus on that all-important Windows data repository—namely, the Registry—including an overview of its structures and functions, safe editing techniques to manipulate Registry contents, and a slew of details about important Registry keys and values.

Part III: Networking Windows NT

Part III contains seven chapters, beginning with a Windows NT networking overview in Chapter 10. Chapter 11 follows with a discussion of Windows NT networking models, which is followed in turn by coverage of TCP/IP in Chapter 12, NetBEUI in Chapter 13, and NWLink in Chapter 14. In Chapter 15, issues related to Windows NT-UNIX integration are addressed, and Chapter 16 covers Dial-Up Networking (DUN) and the Remote Access Service (RAS).

Part IV: Managing Your Windows NT Systems

This part of the book also contains seven chapters, starting with coverage of Windows NT's file systems and storage capabilities in Chapter 17. Chapter 18 covers Windows NT backup hardware, software, and recommended backup methods and techniques. Chapter 19 includes a discussion of Windows NT's built-in scripting facilities, along with batch files and commands and third-party automation alternatives to help you turn rote work over to your computer rather than doing things by hand repeatedly. Chapter 20 covers tuning and optimizing Windows NT, while Chapter 21 explains what's involved in managing newer 32-bit applications along with older, 16-bit applications in a Windows NT environment. Chapter 22 surveys printing in the Windows NT environment, starting with an overview of the Windows NT print architecture and moving on to installing, configuring, and updating printers on a Windows NT system. Part IV concludes with Chapter 23, a discussion of Windows NT security tips and tricks that documents well-known holes and backdoors in the system, and explains how to close them for good!

Part V: Windows NT Goes Online: Internet or Intranet Access

Part V covers the software components included with Windows NT that support Internet or intranet access and services. Chapter 24 documents Windows NT's capabilities as a Web client, primarily using Internet Explorer. Chapter 25 switches its focus to Windows NT's abilities as an email client, primarily using Outlook 2000. Chapters 26 and 27 survey Windows NT's Web-serving software, including the Personal Web Server (PWS) included in Windows NT Workstation, the Internet Information Server (IIS) included in Windows NT Server, and the many tools and utilities that accompany these components in their respective environments. Chapter 28, the final chapter of this book, discusses other Windows NT Internet services not mentioned elsewhere, including FTP, Gopher, and more, to round out coverage of Internet utilities and services.

Appendixes

Although these are not official chapters of the book, these nine elements offer a variety of useful explanatory and supplementary information related to Windows NT. Appendix A provides a concise but useful compendium of Windows NT information resources, both on- and offline. Appendix B compares Windows NT Workstation to Windows NT Server. Appendix C provides an overview of the features and functions that Microsoft has announced for Windows 2000, the successor to Windows NT. Appendix D provides a comprehensive list of Performance Monitor objects and counters, and Appendix E explains where to find information about readying Windows NT machines for the year 2000. Appendix F describes important Windows NT keyboard commands, shortcuts, and their equivalents, and Appendix G documents the contents of the Windows NT boot partition. In Appendix H, you'll find an overview of Windows NT's latest service pack: SP 5. And finally, in Appendix I, you'll find a list of all the software and information that's included on the CD-ROM that accompanies this book.

All in all, there's a tremendous amount of information herein, along with a great collection of tools and utilities to help you use what you learn in this book.

How to Use This Book

You can use this book in any of a variety of ways. If you're a relative newcomer to Windows NT, you'll probably benefit from reading the book in sequence—part by part, and chapter by chapter. If you're an intermediate user, look for chapters on topics of interest and tackle them as you please. Just remember that for some topics—such as the Windows NT Registry covered in Chapters 7, 8, and 9—you may have to read more than one chapter to cover the ground. If you're a Windows NT expert, we recommend that you use the book's index and table of contents to point your reading to more precise topics. But no matter what your level of expertise, we also suggest that you investigate the contents of the CD that accompanies the book, simply because you'll find so much "good stuff" on it.

So roll up your sleeves, curl up in your favorite reading chair, and get down to it. Also, please feel free to share your comments with the authors. Send your comments, suggestions, questions, and criticisms to `NTpower@lanw.com`; we'll do our best to answer all email. Thanks for buying our book and enjoy your reading experience!

I

Windows NT Overview

1

Introducing Windows NT

THIS CHAPTER LAYS THE GROUNDWORK for the rest of the book. It begins with an overview of the history and origins of Microsoft Windows NT, and continues with an analysis of its structure and components. It concludes with a discussion of how to get from other versions of Microsoft Windows to Windows NT 4.0, the software that serves as the focus for this book.

In its relatively short life, Windows NT has seen some major internal modifications, as well as external changes. Although Windows NT has yet to attain perfection, it has come a long way in a short time. Microsoft Windows 2000, the next-generation product that will replace Windows NT 4.0, should propel the Windows NT 32-bit, high-performance, high-security operating system into the twenty-first century.

Windows NT History and Description

Computer networks are a normal part of any advanced computer user's working environment. Most of us use a computer network every day without even thinking twice about it. But computer networks have not been around very long.

Before the wonderful features of today's networks were so broadly available, most users relied on a networking technology known as "sneakernet." Sneakernet was a great invention. It almost never failed, was easy to upgrade, and was extremely scalable. Every time you added a computer system to your organization, that machine automatically joined your current network and configured itself likewise.

In case you haven't already guessed, using sneakernet meant copying the information you needed to transfer to a floppy disk, taking that floppy disk to the destination computer, and copying the information onto that system. The key mode of transportation for this network was its users' shoes, hence the name "sneakernet." To some users, sneakernet is a fond memory; to others, it's a relic of a bygone era; to a surprising number, it's still business as usual.

The first commercially available local area network was the Attached Resource Computer Network (ARCNet) architecture from Datapoint Corporation, developed in 1977. It was based upon a scheme of "file processors" and "application processors"—servers and clients. More than 500,000 ARCNet systems were in use before Ethernet was a commercial product.

The first commercially successful network operating system was Novell's NetWare, which hit the streets in 1984. Because of its success, many believe that Novell was the first company to offer a system that allowed users to share information and resources across a network. Not to be outdone, Microsoft released its first version of a network operating system in early 1985 under the name MS-NET. MS-NET worked hand-in-hand with MS-DOS 3.10. When MS-NET was released, Microsoft was still a relatively small company and did not choose to market the software aggressively. It did, however, establish a relationship with IBM that helped to move the MS-NET networking software into the marketplace. In 1985, there were really only two mainstream options for organizations that wanted to implement PC-based networks: MS-NET and NetWare. Unfortunately for Microsoft, although MS-NET was inexpensive and easy to implement, NetWare outperformed MS-NET and offered corporate users more powerful file and print services. In this first networking encounter between the two companies, Novell carried the day.

Microsoft realized that it needed to close the gap between its products and Novell's if it was to succeed in the networking market. To try to accomplish this goal, the company designed a second-generation network operating system based on the OS/2 1.0 operating system. This network operating system, called Microsoft LAN Manager, involved extensive collaboration with the networking giant 3Com Corporation.

As with MS-NET, Microsoft did not intend to market LAN Manager directly, but hoped that IBM and other partners would sell the product. Although IBM did sell LAN Manager, some of those other partners (including Compaq Computer Corporation) decided not to participate in this venture. This prompted Microsoft to enter the marketplace directly to market and sell LAN Manager itself.

Unfortunately, NetWare had a head start on LAN Manager and continued to outperform this product, as it did its predecessor. But when Microsoft released LAN Manager version 2, the new product further closed the gap between the two network operating systems.

While working on the OS/2 operating system with IBM, Microsoft was developing a new operating system that was intended to replace LAN Manager. This new operating system was initially designed to run on the OS/2 operating system. It was

Microsoft's intention to develop this new operating system to make it processor-independent. Processor independence would allow this new operating system to venture into the UNIX world and permit it to run on processors that, until then, could run only UNIX.

In October of 1988, Microsoft hired a gentleman by the name of David Cutler. David Cutler was an operating system guru who had worked for Digital Equipment Corporation and had helped that company develop its VMS operating system. Microsoft decided to call this project their "New Technology" operating system project (although there is some debate about how this name was really chosen; see the accompanying sidebar on this subject).

The product's original name was to be OS/2 NT. In early 1990, however, Microsoft decided that it would base the interface for this operating system on its current desktop operating system, Microsoft Windows 3.0 instead of on OS/2. Because Windows 3.0 gained a large installed base rather quickly, we can only speculate that they wanted to leverage the success of that product with the introduction of the new product.

In early 1991, IBM learned that Microsoft was planning to base its new operating system on Windows rather than on OS/2, and withdrew from its development. IBM continued to work on the OS/2 operating system for several years and ultimately developed the OS/2 Warp product family before switching its focus to Windows NT in 1997 and 1998.

Finally, on July 17, 1993, Microsoft released LAN Manager NT, calling it Windows NT Advanced Server. Although this was a new operating system, Microsoft marketed this product as version 3.1. Two powerful factors helped to motivate this strategy. First, Microsoft was already marketing its Microsoft Windows 3.1 desktop operating system at that time and felt that users might not adopt Windows NT Advanced Server if it had a 1.0 version number. Second, NetWare was already on version 3.11 and Microsoft's marketing wizards believed that people might assume Windows NT Advanced Server was an inferior product, due solely to its lower-numbered version designator.

In September of 1994, Microsoft released a new version of the Windows NT operating system and dropped the word "Advanced" from its name (although this is not the last you will see of Windows Advanced Server). This new version was called Microsoft Windows NT 3.5 and was a tuned-up version of 3.1. Windows NT 3.5 required less memory, included built-in NetWare and TCP/IP connectivity, and was separated into Server and Workstation versions. Windows NT 3.5 also included new administration tools that could be executed from a Microsoft Windows for Workgroups (version 3.11) system. (We discuss Server and Workstation versions in the section titled "Differences Between Windows NT Workstation and Windows NT Server" later in the chapter.)

In 1995, Microsoft released Microsoft Windows NT 3.51, which fixed some bugs from the previous version and also added new functions that included file and directory compression, plus support for new hardware. Version 3.51 also represented a turning point for Windows NT's sales and marketplace acceptance and marked the beginning of its incredible ramp up to the market share that Windows NT enjoys today.

The version of Windows NT that is being used and sold today is version 4.0. When this product was released, many people believed that it was simply version 3.51 with the Windows 95 interface grafted on. Nothing could be further from the truth: Windows NT 4.0 added significant functionality to its predecessor, including Dynamic Host Configuration Protocol (DHCP) services, and its graphics-handling architecture was modified to increase overall performance.

As we write this book, the world is waiting for further news about the release of Windows 2000, formerly known as Windows NT 5.0. At present, Windows 2000 is in beta 3. Windows 2000 differs from Windows NT 4.0 more than it is similar to it. In fact, Windows 2000 is almost as different from Windows NT 4.0 as Windows 95 is different from Windows 3.x. Windows 2000 will add major new functionality, including the following features:

- Active Directory (a data structure that allows any network object to be tracked)
- Plug and Play support
- COM+, which provides a major improvement to Microsoft's Component Object Model
- File system improvements including disk quotas and defragmentation capabilities
- FAT32 support (FAT stands for File Allocation Table)
- An upgrade path from Windows 95

What's In a Name?

There is some discussion as to how the name "New Technology" was derived. Some think that Microsoft (and David Cutler) decided on the name and called it Windows NT (WNT). Others believe that the initials WNT were decided on first and that "Windows New Technology" was derived from the initials. Here's one explanation we find interesting, be it gospel truth or imaginative fiction.

Anyone who has seen the movie *2001: A Space Odyssey* can't help but remember that one of the main characters in the movie is named HAL. Many people wonder where that name came from. But if you take each of the letters in that name and increase its letter value by one, you will see immediately where the name comes from. That is, the next letter after H is I, the next letter after A is B, and the next letter after L is M.

You can apply the same technique to the Windows NT characters, WNT. The next letters in this sequence are VMS. And VMS, of course, is the operating system that David Cutler worked on when he was with Digital Equipment Corporation.

Conspiracy theorists are welcome to find significance here! We simply find it amusing.

With Windows 2000, the term "workstation" is no longer used. Instead, the following names have been assigned to the different flavors of Windows:

- Windows NT Workstation is now known as Windows 2000 Professional.
- Windows NT Server is now known as Windows 2000 Server.
- Windows NT Server Enterprise edition is now known as Windows 2000 Advanced Server.

Microsoft has also created a new category of the server operating system, called Windows 2000 Datacenter Server. This will become Microsoft's high-end server product and will support up to 32 processors simultaneously in a system along with 64GB of RAM.

If you're interested in learning more about the Windows 2000 product line, visit the Web sites listed in the "For More Information" section at the end of this chapter.

Windows NT Architecture

To understand how and why Windows NT operates the way it does, you must understand its architecture. Knowing the "lay of the land" also allows you to understand why some programs run better than others do on Windows NT and why some applications do not run at all. This section covers the Windows NT architecture in detail.

Windows NT is designed around a modular architecture, which means that this architecture incorporates a collection of separate and distinct components. This separation of components allows the operating system to be ported from one processor platform to another without requiring its developers to rewrite or recompile the entire system.

The Windows NT architecture can be divided into two main components: the Kernel mode and the User mode. Figure 1.1 illustrates the Windows NT 4.0 architecture.

The Kernel mode represents a highly privileged mode of system operation. Components that run in this mode have direct access to all hardware components and memory on the system. This includes all address spaces for all User mode processes. A large portion of the Kernel mode is known as the Windows NT Executive. The Windows NT Executive includes the Hardware Abstraction Layer, the Microkernel, and the Executive Services. The following sections describe these elements in detail.

The User mode is a less privileged mode that has no direct access to hardware. Components that run within this mode can access only whatever address space is assigned to them. But to access even their own assigned address space, components need to request access from the Kernel mode. When the User mode requires access to system resources, it uses operating system application program interfaces (APIs) to request them and waits for those APIs to grant (or deny) their requests.

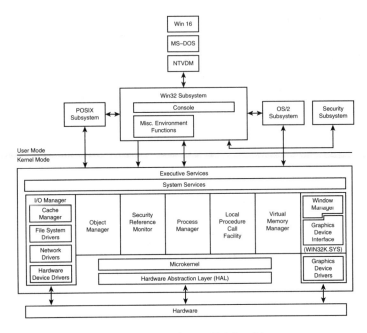

Figure 1.1 The Windows NT 4.0 architecture.

These two modes can be described as being similar to a bank. Everything behind the bank counter represents the Kernel mode, whereas everything in front of the counter represents the User mode. Assuming that you have an account at a bank, you can access any information about your account, but you must ask a bank teller to access the bank's systems on your behalf. Just being a client of the bank does not give you access to any other clients' information. Tellers operate in Kernel mode. They can access information about any bank client, handle funds for deposits and withdrawals, and transfer funds between accounts. We examine the Kernel and User modes in more detail in the following sections.

Kernel Mode

The primary component of the Kernel mode is the Windows NT Executive. The Executive is further divided into three major components:

- Hardware Abstraction Layer (HAL)
- Microkernel
- Executive Services

It is important that you understand these three components, what they enable Windows NT to accomplish, and how they communicate with one another.

Hardware Abstraction Layer

The Hardware Abstraction Layer, or HAL (no relationship to that loveable computer in *2001*), is the component that makes Windows NT a truly portable operating system. By portable, we do not mean that it runs on a laptop computer, but that it can be easily translated, or *ported*, to operate on a variety of processor platforms.

In fact, the HAL is simply a library of routines that enables Windows NT services to access and manipulate a system's primary hardware component: its central processing unit, or CPU. Windows NT is also able to operate on systems with more than one CPU, again by invoking a special version of the HAL and the Microkernel. The library of routines that makes up the HAL is provided by Microsoft and is installed during the Windows NT setup process. The HAL lies at the bottom of the Windows NT Executive between the physical hardware and the operating system.

HAL gets its name from the fact that it hides, or *abstracts*, the physical characteristics of the processor platform behind a standard interface. This standard interface allows the Windows NT Executive to make calls to the hardware without any need to know about the specifics of the hardware it's addressing. The Executive simply makes a call, and the HAL translates it to match the characteristics of whatever hardware is in use and then passes this information to that hardware.

The HAL allows the same operating system to run different processor platforms (such as Alpha or Intel) without having to be completely recompiled. That's because the HAL for the Intel x86 CPU family is different from the HAL for the Alpha AXP processor family, but both HALs share a common interface to the rest of the Windows NT Executive, so the rest of the system can remain oblivious to CPU differences.

As we mentioned, the HAL is installed during the setup process. It is rare that you will need to change the HAL, but such modification is required in some cases. For example, if you are running Windows NT on a single processor system and then upgrade that machine to a multiple processor system, the HAL will probably need to be replaced to recognize the presence of one or more new CPUs.

Microkernel

The Microkernel is the heart and soul of Windows NT. It lies just above the HAL and operates in close cooperation with the HAL. The Microkernel schedules all threads—a *thread* is a unit of processor execution—in the system and takes care of all interrupts and exceptions. The Microkernel really starts to earn its keep in multiple processor systems. In such systems, the Microkernel schedules and synchronizes activity between all available processors.

The Microkernel operates like a dispatcher at a trucking office. It's up to the dispatcher to ensure that all truckers are kept busy. If one trucker is constantly working while others sit idle, the organization suffers. The same is true with a multiple processor system. If a single processor is utilized while others stay idle, the system's resources are not being used to their maximum potential.

When threads are ready to be executed by the processor, the Microkernel schedules them based on their dynamic priority. Dynamic priority is a numerical value that ranges from 1 to 31. This number relates to the importance of a thread, where 1 is the lowest importance and 31 is the highest. Threads that are assigned with the highest priority always run first on the processor. This is true even if a thread with a lower priority must be interrupted so that the higher-priority thread can execute.

Under Windows NT, most user applications are assigned Normal priority (set between 6 and 10). User mode priorities generally occur in the range of 1 to 15; Kernel mode priorities generally occur in the range of 16 to 31. Among other things, this means that User mode execution invariably takes a back seat to Kernel mode execution. The priorities for Windows NT are listed in Table 1.1.

Table 1.1 **Windows NT Thread Priorities**

Priority	Priority Class	Thread Priority
1	Idle	Idle
2	Idle	Lowest
3	Idle	Below normal
4	Idle	Normal
5	Idle	Above normal
6	Idle/Normal	Highest/lowest
7	Normal	Below normal
8	Normal	Normal
9	Normal	Above normal
10	Normal	Highest
11	High	Lowest
12	High	Below normal
13	High	Normal
14	High	Above normal
15	High	Highest/time critical
16	Real-Time	Idle
22	Real-Time	Lowest
23	Real-Time	Below normal
24	Real-Time	Normal
25	Real-Time	Above normal
26	Real-Time	Highest
31	Real-Time	Time critical

Priorities

It's important to note that setting the priority for an application too high could render your system unusable for the remainder of that session. In addition, these settings affect only the current session. When you reboot the computer, the system default settings are re-established.

You can use several tools to modify an application's priority. The tool that you should use most often to control priority settings is the Windows NT Task Manager. To modify an application's priority, in this case EXPLORER.EXE, follow these steps:

1. To run the Windows NT Task Manager, press Ctrl+Alt+Delete simultaneously, and then click the Task Manager button. Alternatively, you can right-click on the taskbar and choose Task Manager from the popup menu.

2. Click the Processes tab.

3. Select the process whose priority you wish to change, and then right-click its entry in the list. (In this case, it appears as EXPLORER.EXE.)

4. Choose the desired priority from the Set Priority option. You can select from Real-time, High, Normal, and Low. (Real-time is available only if you log on with administrative privileges.)

Windows NT Executive Services

The Windows NT Executive Services are really a collection of services that can be invoked by any operating system component. These services include the following:

- **I/O Manager.** This provides a consistent interface for the majority of I/O operations on a Windows NT computer (except for screen and keyboard or mouse-related I/O, which is handled by the GDI).

- **Object Manager.** This provides a set of protocols by which objects are named, retained, and protected.

- **Security Reference Monitor.** This fields all requests for system objects or resources from other Windows NT processes, regardless of whether they are in User or Kernel mode.

- **Process Manager.** This creates and deletes processes, tracks process and thread objects, and provides services for creating processes and threads.

- **Local Procedure Call Facility.** This acts as a message delivery subsystem for User-mode processes.

- **Virtual Memory Manager.** This maps virtual addresses on a process's 4GB address space (2GB for the process's use and 2GB for system use).

- **Window Manager.** This handles user interaction with the Windows NT GUI, moving and resizing windows, selecting icons, and moving the cursor.

- **Graphics Device Interface.** This provides a set of standard interfaces that applications can use to communicate with graphical output devices such as printers and monitors without knowing anything about them.

- **Graphics Device Drivers.** This supplies the necessary software that permits the operating system (and by extensions) to communicate with hardware.

Situated just above these service groups are the System Services. These services act as the interface between User and Kernel mode components.

User Mode

When Microsoft created the Windows NT operating system, it knew that the only way the computer and networking market would embrace this new operating system was if a large software base existed. The company had two primary options it could adopt: It could work with independent software vendors (ISVs) to build applications for release with the operating system, or it could make Windows NT as compatible with previous operating systems as possible. For obvious reasons, Microsoft chose both options: It encouraged developers to build native 32-bit multi-threaded applications that could take full advantage of Windows NT, but it also chose to support as much backward compatibility with 16-bit Windows and DOS applications as possible.

When Windows NT was released, organizations could leverage their existing software base with this new operating system. This not only saved the huge costs involved with purchasing and installing new software, but it also saved the costs of training users to use such new applications. Over time, most such organizations have slowly migrated to take advantage of the performance and functionality gains that Windows NT can deliver, but the pursuit of both options has allowed them to do this on their own time.

Microsoft accomplished its goal of supporting modern 32-bit applications alongside legacy 16-bit applications by creating User mode components named *environment subsystems*. These components allow different applications to run seamlessly on the same desktop. In fact, Windows NT can run multiple instances of applications that are written for the following operating systems:

- MS-DOS
- OS/2 1.x (but only with limitations)
- Windows 3.x
- POSIX (but only with limitations)
- Win32

Because these subsystems emulate different operating systems, they allow Windows NT to support a variety of runtime environments. This section describes the various subsystems that coexist within the Windows NT User mode.

One of the best features of this model is that each of these subsystems runs in its own "playground." Thus, each application runs in its own space on the system. This separation protects each of the subsystems from being shut down as a result of a misbehaving application in another subsystem.

For applications written for older Microsoft operating systems (such as MS-DOS and Windows 3.x), Windows NT creates what is known as a Virtual DOS Machine (VDM). Windows NT provides the following protected subsystems and VDMs:

- MS-DOS NTVDM
- Win16 NTVDM
- OS/2 subsystem

- POSIX subsystem
- Win32 subsystem

These systems are covered in detail in the following sections.

The MS-DOS Environment

When MS-DOS applications execute on a Windows NT system, a process called the Windows NT Virtual DOS Machine (NTVDM) is created. The NTVDM is simply an application that emulates the environment an MS-DOS application would experience on an Intel 486-based system.

In native MS-DOS, you are limited to running one application at a time (excluding Terminate and Stay Resident applications). When MS-DOS applications run under Windows NT, this limitation is eliminated because each MS-DOS application runs in its own separate NTVDM. As stated earlier, each of these NTVDMs emulates an Intel 486-based system.

Likewise, because each NTVDM is assigned its own virtual address space, whichever MS-DOS application occupies that NTVDM believes it is running on its own Intel 486-based system. This protects each MS-DOS application from other such applications, while protecting the operating system from corruption or damage.

The number of NTVDMs that can run on a Windows NT system at any one time is limited only by the system's hardware. If this limit is ever reached (which we believe is unlikely on most modern Pentium or better systems), you can simply upgrade the CPU or install more memory.

The Win16 Environment

Like MS-DOS applications, 16-bit Windows applications also run in an NTVDM. The main difference lies in the way these applications execute. Because most 16-bit Windows applications are better behaved than MS-DOS applications (mostly because they are somewhat aware of one another), Windows NT runs them within a single NTVDM process with a shared address space. Another name for the Win16 NTVDM is WOW, which is an acronym for Windows-on-Windows (or Win16-on-Win32). When you run a Win16 application within a NTVDM, the process name wowexec.exe shows up beneath that instance of NTVDM.EXE in Task Manager.

Direct Hardware Access

Windows NT isolates programs from resources, such as the display adapter, printers, and COM ports, and programs written to take direct control of such resources will not work under Windows NT. Only programs that use standard APIs to communicate with resources will run properly.

NTVDM Names

Although each MS-DOS application runs in its own NTVDM, all active NTVDMs appear as NTVDM.EXE in Task Manager.

Once in a while, you will run into a Win16 application that does not want to play nicely. Because all Win16 applications share the same address space by default, a badly behaved application can shut down the rest of the Win16 applications running within that NTVDM. For this reason, Microsoft implemented an option that allows you to run such applications in their own address spaces. To run a Win16 application in its own address space, you must perform the following steps:

1. Click Start and then Run.

2. Type the name of the Win16 application you would like to run in its own address space. Windows NT automatically detects whether the application is a Win16 application. If it is, the Run in Separate Memory Space option appears.

3. Select Run in Separate Memory Space.

4. Click OK.

The OS/2 Subsystem

The OS/2 subsystem supports character-based applications written for the OS/2 1.x operating system. Unfortunately, this works only on Intel-based systems and not on RISC-based systems. OS/2 real-mode applications will, however, run on a RISC-based system in the MS-DOS environment. To execute these applications, simply run them as you would any other application.

Windows NT 3.51 and earlier versions supported a file system known as the High Performance File System (HPFS). HPFS is the file system that OS/2 1.x uses. In Windows NT 4.0, however, this file system is no longer supported. If you are upgrading from a previous version of Windows NT that had HPFS volumes, you must back up the data, reformat the hard drive as either FAT or NTFS (New Technology File System), and restore the data from backup. If you're running Windows NT 3.51, you might want to use its CONVERT.EXE utility to convert HPFS volumes to NTFS because the CONVERT.EXE utility in Windows NT 4.0 does not support this functionality.

The Two OS/2s

You will see two types of OS/2 applications: character-based and graphical applications. *Character-based applications* are programs that do not utilize graphics—only text characters. *Graphical applications* use graphics when running. The OS/2 subsystem in Windows NT cannot handle graphical OS/2 applications without add-on software, and such add-ons do not give this subsystem general OS/2 capabilities. With the declining popularity of OS/2, this is not likely to pose problems for many users, but it isn't wise to assume that Windows NT can run any OS/2 application, especially newer graphical ones.

The POSIX Subsystem

Windows NT includes a subsystem that will run POSIX (Portable Operating System Interface for Computing Environments) applications and meet all basic requirements for POSIX. This subsystem is known as the POSIX subsystem. POSIX is a set of standards that defines the different components of an operating system. These definitions include security, networking, and graphical interfaces. Currently, the only standard that has been adopted as an industry standard is the POSIX 1 standard.

POSIX's roots derive from the UNIX world. For this reason, it is a case-sensitive operating system. POSIX also supports multiple names for a single file, known as *hard links*. Because of these requirements, POSIX applications can be executed only on Windows NT systems running NTFS. It's important to remember to use POSIX-aware applications and utilities to manage POSIX-compliant files, because although native Windows NT applications and utilities preserve case in filenames, they are otherwise indifferent to case in filenames.

The Win32 Subsystem

The Win32 subsystem is the system Windows NT uses when it runs native applications. In earlier versions of Windows NT, the Win32 subsystem also included windows, graphics, and messaging support. With Windows NT 4.0, these services have moved into the Kernel mode, or, more specifically, into the Executive Services.

Win32 has two primary built-in functions:

- **Console.** The console simply gives Windows NT the capability to handle hard errors and shutdowns, and to support text windows.
- **Miscellaneous environment functions.** The Miscellaneous environment functions support highly specialized functions that let 32-bit Windows NT applications create and delete processes.

Differences Between Windows NT Workstation and Windows NT Server

It is a common misconception that Windows NT Server and Windows NT Workstation are exactly the same. Although these two products have many similarities, their differences set them apart as completely different operating systems. Windows NT Workstation is optimized as a client operating system, whereas Windows NT Server is designed as a network operating system.

Windows NT Workstation is Microsoft's desktop operating system. It is geared mostly toward organizations instead of toward individuals using their systems at home. To give Microsoft credit where such credit is due, Windows NT Workstation is more stable than Windows 95 or 98. It will also outperform both of these "home" operating systems on the same hardware, with the exception of graphics display.

If it's running games on your computer that you desire most ardently, Windows NT Workstation is probably not for you. If, however, you are searching for a fast, stable, and secure operating system, Windows NT Workstation should definitely meet your needs.

Windows NT Server is designed as a network server operating system. Although it looks and feels like Windows NT Workstation or Windows 95, it is not designed as such. Its Windows 95–like interface is a double-edged sword. On one hand, it makes Windows NT Server easier for administrators to configure and manage. On the other, to an inexperienced user, it looks like a Windows 95 system and might invite them to make mischief. That's probably why the default is to deny ordinary users the right to log on locally to a Windows NT Server machine.

Before we look at the differences between Windows NT Server and Windows NT Workstation, let's look at their similarities. Table 1.2 outlines the similarities between these two operating systems.

Table 1.2 **Similarities Between Windows NT Server and Windows NT Workstation**

Feature	Benefits
Multiple platform support	Both Windows NT Server and Windows NT Workstation run on the Intel platform (486 and beyond), as well as RISC-based systems (namely Alpha, MIPS, and PowerPC—although MIPS and PowerPC are no longer supported).
Multitasking and multithreading	Both have multitasking capabilities, which means that multiple applications can execute simultaneously. Multiple threads in applications can also operate at the same time.
Security	Both require mandatory logons by default. Other features include discretionary access controls, auditing, and memory protection.
Foreign operating system support	Both support MS-DOS, Win16, OS/2 1.x, and Win32 applications.
Networking	Both contain several built-in networking protocol stacks and utilities.
Storage	Both provide support for up to 4GB of memory and 16 Exabytes of disk space.
File systems	Both provide support for FAT, NTFS, and CD-ROM File System (CDFS).

Table 1.3 lists the differences between the two operating systems.

Table 1.3   **Differences Between Windows NT Server and Windows NT Workstation**

Feature	Windows NT Workstation	Windows NT Server
Connections	10 inbound, unlimited outbound	Unlimited inbound and outbound
Symmetric multiprocessing	Up to two processors	Up to four processors out of the box (can support more than four processors but OEM versions of Windows NT Server are required)
Remote Access Service connections	1 session	256 sessions
Directory replication	Import only	Import and export
Primary or backup domain controller role	No	Yes
Services for Macintosh	No	Yes
Hard disk fault tolerance	No	Yes
DHCP Services	Client only	Client and server
DNS (Domain Name System) Services	Client only	Client and server
WINS (Windows Internet Name Service) Services	Client only	Client and server
NetWare connectivity	Client Services for NetWare (CSNW)	Gateway (and Client) Services for NetWare (GSNW)
Extra features		NetWare Migration tools; Clustering capabilities (Enterprise Edition only)

Upgrade from Earlier Versions of Windows NT

Fortunately, the upgrade path from previous versions of Windows NT to version 4.0 is relatively smooth. The Windows NT Setup program automatically detects any previously installed version of Windows NT. Upon finding an existing installation, the Windows NT Setup program gives you the options of either upgrading the existing installation or installing a new copy.

If you choose to install a new copy of Windows NT, you must be aware of several issues. First, if you install Windows NT in the same directory as an existing installation, the Windows NT Setup program will attempt to upgrade the system (even though you have instructed it otherwise). Second, if you choose to install Windows NT into a different directory, you will be required to reinstall all applications, re-create all user and group accounts, and reconfigure all security information on the new system. This is because the Windows NT Setup program does not migrate any old settings when a new installation is performed.

There is also one instance in which an upgrade will not work directly. Until the release of Windows NT 4.0, all prior versions of Windows NT supported HPFS, which was used primarily in OS/2. In Windows NT 4.0, HPFS is no longer supported. If you upgrade an existing Windows NT installation that controls HPFS volumes, these volumes will no longer be available under the new installation. To allow Windows NT 4.0 to access data stored on an HPFS volume, you must first complete the following steps. You must complete these steps before you upgrade to Windows NT 4.0.

1. Boot the existing version of Windows NT.

2. To convert HPFS volumes to NTFS, use the CONVERT.EXE utility. To convert HPFS volumes to FAT, complete steps 3 through 6. Otherwise, jump straight to step 6.

3. Back up all data stored on the HPFS volumes.

4. Re-create the HPFS partitions using FAT.

5. Restore the data from backup to the newly created FAT partitions.

6. Upgrade the Windows NT installation using the Windows NT Setup program.

Upgrade or Migrate from Other Windows Versions

Before you upgrade from an older version of Windows, you must be aware of some limitations inherent in the upgrade process. The upgrade or migration path you take will depend on which Windows operating system is currently installed. These operating systems fall into two categories: upgrading or migrating from a Microsoft operating system that's neither Windows 95 nor Windows 98, and upgrading or migrating from a Windows 95 or 98 system.

The upgrade path from systems running a Microsoft operating system that's neither Windows 95 nor Windows 98 is simple. These operating systems include MS-DOS 6.x, Windows 3.x, and Windows for Workgroups 3.x. The Windows NT Setup program automatically detects the existing operating system, upgrades it, and migrates all meaningful user and application information to the new installation of Windows NT.

When upgrading a system from Windows 95 or 98, however, you must be sensitive to some special issues involved in such a maneuver. Those issues are discussed in the following section.

Windows 95 and Windows 98 Issues

The Windows 95 (or Windows 98) Registry is vastly different from the Registry in Windows NT. For this reason, there is currently no automatic upgrade path from Windows 95 or Windows 98 to Windows NT. Therefore, you must perform such an upgrade manually. To do so, follow these steps:

1. Check the Hardware Compatibility List (HCL) to ensure that all the hardware currently installed on your system functions with Windows NT.

2. Install Windows NT Workstation into a separate directory. This will create a dual-boot configuration for your system.

3. Reinstall all your applications. If you would like to continue to dual boot your system, install those applications into different directories from the ones where they currently reside. However, if you plan to remove the Windows 95 or 98 installation, you can install these applications into the same directories where they currently reside.

4. If you decide not to dual boot Windows 95 or Windows 98 and Windows NT, you must manually delete the Windows 95 or Windows 98 directory.

When performing an upgrade from Windows 98 to Windows NT, you must attend to all the issues presented in the previous section. Another thing you must watch for when performing an upgrade from Windows 98 (or when upgrading from Windows 95 version B, also known as OSR2) is related to the file system. Both Windows 95 OSR2 and Windows 98 support a file system known as FAT32. The issue is that Windows NT 4.0 does not currently recognize this file system. If you attempt to install Windows NT on a partition that is formatted with FAT32, that installation will fail.

The HCL Online

Due to the size of the HCL and the rate at which new hardware appears on it, Microsoft has set up an online searchable version of the HCL. It resides at **http://www.microsoft.com/hwtest/hcl**.

Migrate from Other Operating Systems

Microsoft has included tools in Windows NT Server to ease migration from a
NetWare server to a Windows NT Server environment. In this section, we briefly discuss the components that need to be installed for such a migration to occur and
describe the types of information that can move from a NetWare server to a Windows
NT Server.

The Migration Tool for NetWare (NWCONV.EXE) ships with Windows NT
Server 4.0. Before you can migrate any information from the NetWare Server successfully, you must install and configure the Gateway Services for NetWare on your
Windows NT Server system. After GSNW is installed and configured, you can use the
Migration Tool for NetWare to transfer NetWare accounts, plus files and directories
from the NetWare volumes to a Windows NT Server. This migration can occur only
between a NetWare server and a Windows NT domain controller.

Microsoft recommends that you perform such a migration in two steps. First,
migrate all the user accounts to the Windows NT Server. By default, the Migration
Tool for NetWare automatically transfers all user security information to the Windows
NT Server. Second, migrate all relevant files and directories to the Windows NT
Server. If you migrate files and directories from the NetWare Server to a Windows
NT Server that is using an NTFS partition, the Migration Tool for NetWare automati-
cally transfers all meaningful file and directory permissions.

Before you start any NetWare to Windows NT migration, be sure to perform a
trial migration first, and then study the log files for any errors that might result. (This
operation simulates a migration without actually moving or changing anything on the
Windows NT side.) A trial migration allows you to catch any problems that might
occur during an actual migration before resulting changes become permanent.

For More Information

For more information about Windows NT architecture and Windows NT 2000,
consult the following references:

- Solomon, David A. *Inside Windows NT*. Microsoft Press, May 1999.
  ISBN: 1572316772.

- TechNet: A monthly, CD-based technical subscription service from Microsoft
  that includes most Resource Kits and related software, service packs, a
  Knowledge Base, and a great deal more useful information. For information
  about obtaining a subscription and access to online information, register for the
  TechNet Subscription CD online at **http://technet.microsoft.com/**.

- Microsoft Knowledge Base: A compilation of questions to and answers from the
  Microsoft technical support operation. This is available online at **http://
  support.microsoft.com/**, but is also included on CD with a TechNet
  subscription.

- Microsoft Windows 2000 Professional: **http://www.microsoft.com/windows/ professional**.

- Microsoft Windows 2000 Server: **http://www.microsoft.com/windows/server**.

2

Common Windows NT Administrative Utilities

MICROSOFT WINDOWS NT WORKSTATION includes several utilities to aid system configuration and administration. All of these tools are accessed via the Start menu, in the Programs, Administrative Tools section. This chapter takes a look at those tools, as well as several third-party tools that can make maintaining a Windows NT system a little easier.

What Administration Really Means

Keeping a Windows NT network functioning encompasses many activities. Such activities range from maintaining user accounts to configuring security, monitoring network traffic, correcting system problems, and enabling local and remote access. The size and complexity of a network is directly related to the number of tasks to be performed to keep it up and running. The larger the network, the more details there are to juggle.

The range of tasks required to sustain a network varies considerably from network to network. Most networks require managing user accounts, applying security controls, and backing up data. Other networks may also require remote access management, performance monitoring, and error tracking.

Administration really means planning out the network, mapping out configurations, implementing decisions, and monitoring the activity of the network over time. As the network grows, you need to adjust your settings and configurations to support the changes. You may find that your original decisions sustain a growing network adequately, or you may need to change things on the fly. In either case, vigilance is your primary asset to sustaining the network. When things go wrong, the users will blame you, no matter where the fault actually lies.

To avoid downtime, you must foresee problems that are likely to occur and correct problems when they do occur. That's why it's so important to learn your system, understand your tools, and plan out your attack. Otherwise, you may find yourself working over the weekend or pulling an all-nighter to get things running smoothly again.

Windows NT System Administration

Windows NT system administration is a task-based responsibility that requires you to rely upon the tools and utilities at your disposal. If you are unfamiliar with your tools, you can't perform the required tasks. Just as a handyman needs the right tool for a particular job, you need to know which tools can perform which functions. In the following sections, we walk through the administrative, management, monitoring, and related tools included with Windows NT Workstation. In addition to reviewing the discussion in this chapter, you should take the time to work with the tools themselves. Hands-on experience is invaluable and cannot be substituted. Plus, you may want to review the online help documentation included in the tools, as well as materials from the *Windows NT Workstation 4.0* and *Windows NT Server 4.0 Resource Kits*, and TechNet (discussed in the following sidebar).

Microsoft Resources

In our experience, the resources that Microsoft provides are among the best for product documentation, troubleshooting information, and general, all-around information. The two items we can't live without are the following:

- **Microsoft Technical Information Network (TechNet).** A monthly CD-based publication that delivers numerous electronic titles on Windows NT. Its offerings include all the Microsoft Resource Kits (see next bullet), product facts, technical notes, tools and utilities, the entire Microsoft Knowledge Base, as well as service packs, drivers, and patches. A single user license to TechNet costs $299 per year, but it is well worth the price. Visit **www.microsoft.com/technet/** and check out the information under the TechNet Subscription menu entry for more details.

- **Microsoft Resource Kits.** Available on nearly all major products from Microsoft. The *Microsoft Windows NT 4.0 Server Resource Kit* and the *Microsoft Windows NT Workstation 4.0 Resource Kit* are essential references for Windows NT information. Both book sets come with CD-ROMs that contain useful tools. Visit **mspress.microsoft.com** for additional information on the Resource Kits.

A number of other resources that provide additional information about Windows NT are available. For instance, a quick search at **www.amazon.com** using the phrase "Windows NT" turns up a list of over 600 additional references on this subject.

User Manager (With and Without Domains)

User Manager is the administration tool you can use to perform the following functions:

- Manage user accounts
- Manage groups
- Manage policies: accounts, user rights, and auditing
- Manage trust relationships (Microsoft Windows NT Server only)

User Manager (see Figure 2.1) has slightly different capabilities on Windows NT Workstation than on Windows NT Server. For example, the Windows NT Server version, called User Manager for Domains, creates domain user accounts as well as local user accounts, plus it creates and manages global groups and local groups. User Manager on Windows NT Workstation creates only local users and local groups.

Local groups are used for access to local resources. Global groups are used for accessing information across domain boundaries. Obviously, if you have a domain-based network, you'll need the Windows NT Server User Manager for domains. However, for workgroup-based networks, the Workstation version of User Manager and local groups should suffice.

Global groups can be added to local groups, but new global groups cannot be created or their membership changed from User Manager on Windows NT Workstation. The changes made to policies in User Manager on Windows NT Workstation apply only to the local user accounts, whereas those changes made with User Manager for Domains on a Windows NT Server apply to the entire domain. In addition, User Manager for Domains can create trust relationships between domains. Otherwise, the operation of User Manager and User Manager for Domains is the same.

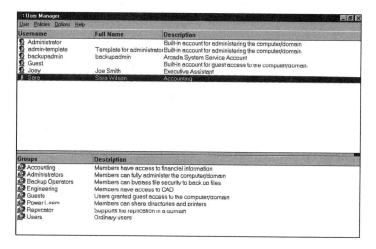

Figure 2.1   Windows NT Workstation's User Manager.

You should already be familiar with basic user account and local group creation and management. If not, consult the online help documentation, the *Microsoft Windows NT Workstation 4.0 Resource Kit*, and TechNet.

Establishing, Copying, and Removing User Accounts

In addition to the basic functions of User Manager, there are a few shortcuts and caveats of which you need to be aware. One of the most useful features of User Manager is the capability to copy existing user accounts. If you need to create several accounts with the same base settings, you can save time by copying an existing account with the desired settings and duplicating it for each new user. By copying an account in this way, you have a basic, or template, account that you can then tweak to match the new user's access requirements. You can copy an account to use as a template by performing the following steps:

1. In User Manager, highlight the account to be copied.
2. Select Copy from the User menu.
3. Fill in the Username, Full Name, Description, Password, and Confirm Password fields.
4. Select appropriate settings for the account, and then click OK.

Keep in mind that any user account that is copied retains the group assignments and permissions of the original account. Be sure that any new account you create requires the settings that match the original copied account. Otherwise, you could open up the system to a potential security risk.

When you are in a quandary about what to do with old user accounts, we recommend disabling rather than deleting them. Deleting a user account completely removes it from the system. This means that it never existed, according to Windows NT. Even if you created another account with the same name and permissions, it would still have a different SID and be considered a different account by Windows NT. In addition, if you need to perform a security audit or create a duplicate account, you'll be unable to do so. However, by disabling the account, you not only remove it from use, but you retain it for security audits and to be used as a template if duplicates are required.

When giving a user account membership in a group, be sure to think about the results of multi-group membership. In some cases, you might overlap group purposes, which can result in granting some users too much access. Plus, if you actually use the No Access setting, you may end up blocking access to someone who legitimately needs it.

Determining User Access

If you have difficulty figuring out which group or user is granted access to a specific resource, you may want to use Somarsoft's DumpACL. *DumpACL* is a security tool that inspects the Access Control Lists (ACLs) of files and folders to create an easy to understand list of resources, groups, and access levels. But it just doesn't stop at file resources. It can also inspect printers, the Registry, and shares for security settings. This invaluable tool is available free of charge from the Somarsoft Web site at **www.somarsoft.com/**.

Home directories help keep all user files in a single location. This makes the location of files easier for users and makes backing up user files possible. To create a home directory automatically for each new user, you should employ the template user copy procedure described earlier in this section. Specify for the template account a home directory of D:\users\%username% or whatever the path needs to be (see Figure 2.2). Using the variable %username% causes Windows NT to automatically create a directory named after the account name and to configure the user account to use that directory as its home directory.

If you allow dial-up access to your system, you can opt to grant remote access only to specific users. The Dialin button on each user account's Properties dialog box is where dial-up access is granted. By default, users do not have the capability to connect over a dial-up link. After dial-up access is granted, you should also decide whether to use call-back security. Call-back security begins with a user dialing up the RAS server. After logon, the user is disconnected; the RAS server then calls the user back, the user logs on again, and then network communication commences. Call-back security is secure only when a predefined number is used. Allowing the caller to define the call-back number doesn't add any security. The ability of the caller to define the call-back number does, however, cause the RAS server side of the connection, rather than the travelling user, to pay for long distance charges.

For details about system policies (account, user rights, and audit), see Chapter 23, "Managing Windows NT System Security," which discusses these items with regard to security.

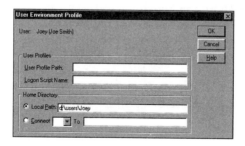

Figure 2.2   Defining a home directory for a new user.

Backup Utilities

Windows NT Workstation includes a built-in backup tool. Microsoft Windows NT *Backup* is similar in function to Seagate Software's Backup Exec for Windows NT. Although it is a functional backup utility, the following list describes some problems with Windows NT Backup:

- Backups are restricted to local tape devices.
- Scheduling of backups is not supported within the application.
- Remote Registry backup is not supported.
- Remote files are accessible only if a drive is mapped to a local drive letter.

Scheduling backups with the native backup utility requires the use of the Windows NT *Scheduler* service. This service is enabled through the Services applet in the Control Panel. You'll need to set its startup parameters to Automatic. Use the command from the command prompt to configure scheduled operations. Windows NT Backup Help includes details on the syntax employed to schedule backups. You can also use the WinAT tool from the *Windows NT Workstation 4.0 Resource Kit* CD, which provides a graphical interface to the Scheduler.

We provide pointers to a number of excellent third-party backup utilities at the end of the chapter in the "For More Information" section.

When selecting a backup solution, make sure the solution exhibits the following features:

- Must back up to tape, disk, floppy, and other media types
- Must back up and restore local and network resources
- Must back up and restore local and remote Registries
- Must include internal automation and scheduling of backups
- Must fully support Windows NT security
- Must support backup tape locking, encryption, or other media security features

With these requirements, you are sure to find a backup product that meets your needs and can keep up with an expanding network. Note that many backup solutions are rated as "enterprise" solutions. This is often a term used to indicate that the product can support a large network. You'll also notice that these products have a price tag of over $1,000. This doesn't mean that you'll have to shell out a grand to obtain good backup software, but you should take the time to shop around. For example, Backup Exec from Veritas has a desktop version available online for under $100.

Disk Administrator

Disk Administrator (see Figure 2.3) is the primary tool used to manage partitions. When you add a new hard drive to your computer, use Disk Administrator to create primary and extended partitions and logical drives, plus assign drive letters. You can also use Disk Administrator to create volume sets and stripe sets. The Windows NT Workstation version of Disk Administrator cannot create fault-tolerant disk configurations. Only the Windows NT Server version can create disk mirrors, disk duplexing, and disk striping with parity.

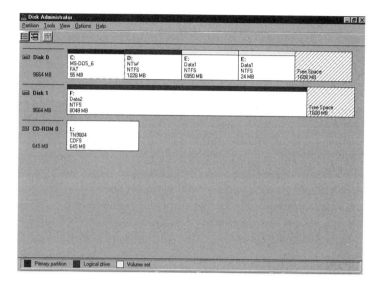

Figure 2.3   Windows NT Workstation's Disk Administrator.

You cannot alter the boot or system partitions with Disk Administrator. If you try to format or delete the partition where key Windows NT files reside, the tool displays an error and will not allow the operation to take place. However, there is no such protection for other partitions. So be careful not to destroy partitions that contain important data.

Disk Administrator is a powerful disk management tool, but it lacks a key feature: defragmentation. Windows NT 4.0 does not include a disk defragmentation tool. We provide references at the end of this chapter for a couple of good disk defragmenters for Windows NT. *Defragmentation* is important because it reduces the chance of data corruption due to read/write errors. NTFS drives are less prone to problems than FAT drives, but the occurrence of defragmentation is the same. After significant sections of contiguous free space are scarce, Windows NT begins to fragment files across a drive by employing smaller chunks of empty space. On active drives (drives on which the frequency of write, change, and delete operations are high), fragmentation occurs quickly, drive performance begins to suffer, and the possibility of corrupt files increases.

According to Microsoft, NTFS partitions are not accessible from MS-DOS or non-Windows NT operating systems. However, several third-party utilities and file drivers are available that make such access possible. Reading data from NTFS partitions was previously restricted to Windows NT. Now, with NTFSDOS from System Internals, you can read, rename, and even copy over files from an NTFS partition (providing the new file is exactly the same size) using MS-DOS. You can grab this tool from the System Internals Web site at `http:www.sysinternals.com/`.

In addition, you can now access NTFS partitions from LINUX. The tool that enables this access was created by Martin von Löwis, and can be found at `http://www.informatik.hu-berlin.de/~loewis/e_index.html`.

Another problem with Windows NT Workstation's Disk Administrator is that the MS-DOS FDISK utility cannot manage NTFS logical drives in an extended partition in any way. However, the DELPART utility from the *Windows NT Server 3.1 Resource Kit* can. This tool was not included on later releases of the Resource Kit, but it still exists on the Internet. Its primary feature is the ability to delete any partition or logical drive on a hard disk. We found the tool at `www.platinumed.com/util/ntindex.htm`. If this link fails you, you can find it elsewhere with a little searching skill using the keyword "delpart" at `www.metacrawler.com/` or using the WebFerret tool from FerretSoft at `www.ferretsoft.com/`.

Security Breach!

It is important to note that use of these tools opens up a potential security risk. Both tools allow you, or any other user, to bypass the security on NTFS files.

Tools from System Internals

In addition to NTFSDOS, System Internals offers many other great tools as well. You should take the time to review this site and all the great utility offerings there. One utility that stands out is Undelete for Windows NT. This is an enhancement to the Windows NT Recycle Bin. You may have noticed that files deleted from command prompts and applications are not captured by the Recycle Bin. This Undelete utility monitors for these types of deletions and protects the files by adding them to the Recycle Bin. If you rely on the Recycle Bin to save you when files are deleted, this tool will provide a larger security blanket. As mentioned earlier, the System Internal's Web site is at `http://www.sysinternals.com/`.

Event Viewer

Event Viewer (see Figure 2.4) is where Windows NT records information about various occurrences within the system. Event Viewer hosts three log files: System, Application, and Security. The System log file records events related to system operation, most often associated with device drivers and services. The Application log file records events related to applications, programs, and utilities, not native Windows NT tools. The Security log file records events related to security and auditing. The Security log will not record any information until the audit policy is enabled.

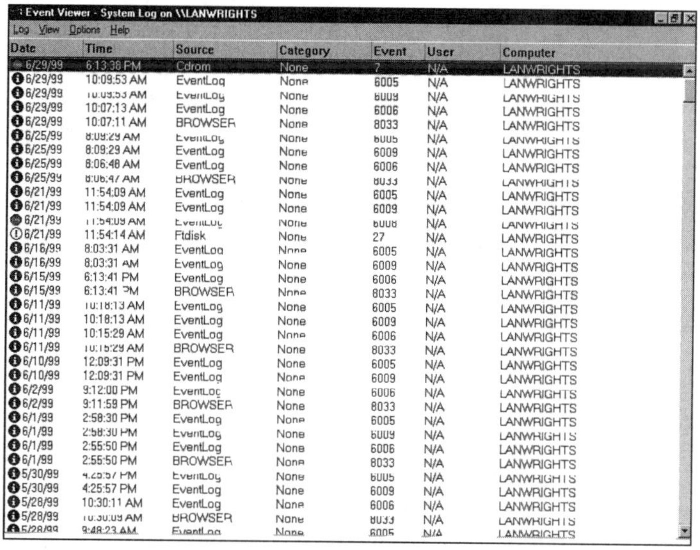

Figure 2.4   Windows NT's Event Viewer.

The System and Application logs can be viewed by anyone. The Security log is restricted to administrators. The viewed log file is selected from the Log menu bar command.

The default settings for the logs restrict each log file to a maximum of 512KB and a time length of seven days. When the fixed file size is reached, the log file is closed. The log file must be cleared before you are able to log in to that file again. Events older than the specified day length are overwritten by new events. If your log files close, you lose some information, so you need to either increase the file size or decrease the day limit. If you need to retain events for longer time periods, you should increase the file size and the day limit. You can change these options through the Log Settings menu command, accessed from the Log menu. Each log file has its own size and day limit settings.

You can view the log files from a remote system on your network using the Select Computer command from the Log menu. This feature simplifies administrative tasks by allowing you to diagnose a system via Event Viewer remotely rather than requiring that you sit at its keyboard.

You can save logs to a file to store or use them with other applications. You can load the .EVT file type into another Event Viewer. The log's .TXT file can be in standard monospace-columned or in comma-delimited format.

Use the Filter command from the View menu to quickly locate events of a certain type or pertaining to a particular source, category, user, computer, or event ID. Use the Find command from the View menu to search through the contents of the selected log for an event by keywords.

Somarsoft offers a utility for dumping Event Viewer logs into a format suitable for most databases. *DumpEvt* is a sophisticated version of DUMPEL from the *Windows NT Server 4.0 Resource Kit* CD. This utility is available from the Somarsoft Web site at **www.somarsoft.com/**.

Event Viewer can record a significant amount of useful, if not vital, information, but extracting or even locating the data within the log files can be a daunting task. You may want to invest in an Intrusion Detection solution that can automatically and semi-intelligently scan Event Viewer. These tools look for patterns of failure, intrusion, or degradation of the system, then report the findings to you in a concise format. Please look for recommendations in the "For More Information" section at the end of this chapter.

Performance Monitor

Performance Monitor is a tool no system administrator can live without. However, this tool is discussed in depth elsewhere in this book. So, instead of including the same discussion twice, please see Chapter 20, "Tuning and Optimizing Windows NT," for complete details.

Windows NT Diagnostics

Windows NT Diagnostics is a read-only window into the hardware and environmental configuration of your Windows NT systems. This nine-tabbed dialog box reveals a plethora of data regarding the state of your operating system. The tabs and the details they offer are shown in Table 2.1.

Table 2.1 **Windows NT Diagnostics Tabs and Details**

Tab Name	Details Provided
Version	OS name, version, build, service pack level, CPU type, OS serial number, and registered user.
System	HAL version type, BIOS information, and CPU numbers, types, and speeds.

Tab Name	Details Provided
Display	The video card's BIOS version and type, screen resolution and depth settings, video card memory installed, and details about the video driver in use.
Drives	The floppy, hard drive, and CD-type drives installed on the system. Double-clicking a drive reveals a Properties dialog box where disk-specific details are listed: serial number, bytes per sector, sectors per cluster, free and used space, file system format, and more.
Memory	The current state of memory. These details are much the same as found in Task Manager. (See Chapter 20.) This tab also displays details about the page file, its use levels, and its host drive.
Services	Installed services and whether they are running or stopped. Clicking the Devices button displays the installed device drivers and their status. Double-clicking a service or driver opens an object-specific properties dialog box where further details are revealed.
Resources	Used and free system resources for IRQ assignments, I/O port addresses, DMA settings, memory addresses, and a list of devices. This is a great tab to view before installing new hardware, especially manually configured devices, to determine free resources.
Environment	Currently defined environmental variables and their values for both the system and the current local user.
Network	General information about the network, such as workgroup name, domain name, network OS version, total number of logged on users, and the names of the hosts where the users are connected. The Transports button lists the installed transport protocols. The Settings button lists all of the network specific Registry defined settings. The Statistics button lists a wide range of network counters and statistics.

You cannot use Windows NT Diagnostics to change or modify any of the settings it displays, but simply being able to view these items can help sidestep mistakes or quickly locate problems.

The *Windows NT Server 4.0 Resource Kit* CD provides a handful of tools that you may find useful in determining the state of your system. These diagnostic tools include the following:

- **DEPENDS.** Inspects files and determines what files it depends on, such as .DLL, .SYS, and .INI files.
- **ENUMPRN.** Lists the installed printer drivers by name, version, and platform.

- **NTMSG.HLP.** Lists most of the error and system messages issued by Windows NT with expanded explanations and information about their meanings, causes, and solutions.
- **TLIST.** Lists all of the active tasks or processes on a system.
- **PULIST.** Does basically the same thing as TLIST, but also tells you who owns a task. In addition, it also lets you view the processes on a remote machine.
- **SCLIST.** Tells you the states of your services.
- **SRVINFO.** Provides exhaustive details about your server.

Complete details on syntax and use of these tools is included with the *Windows NT Server 4.0 Resource Kit.*

Remote Access Administration

Remote Access Administration is used only on a system acting as a dial-up server. For Windows NT Workstation systems, you can host only one inbound connection at once due to the limitations of the license agreement. The Remote Access Admin tool is used to view the status of the dial-up connections. You can view the connections by port, domain, or server. From the list of users, you can view user account information, disconnect users, or send messages to one or more users. This tool also allows you to grant or revoke dial-up access (and call-back settings) in a single sweeping command rather than only on a user-by-user basis through User Manager.

A few *Windows NT Server 4.0 Resource Kit* tools are associated with Remote Access. The most useful tool is RASUSERS. This tool lists all users who have been granted dial-up access permission. This tool is on the Windows NT Server version of the Resource Kit only, but it can be used on Windows NT Workstation.

For More Information

If the information about Windows NT native administration tools presented in this chapter has increased your desire to learn more, here are some resources you can research to obtain more knowledge:

- Frish, Aeleen. *Essential Windows NT System Administration.* O'Reilly and Associates, 1998. ISBN: 1565922743.
- *Microsoft Windows NT Workstation 4.0 Resource Kit.* Microsoft Press, 1996. ISBN: 1572313439.
- Microsoft TechNet: **www.microsoft.com/technet/**

We recommend the following backup software:

- Veritas's Backup Exec: **www.veritas.com**/
- Computer Associate's ARCserve: **www.cai.com**

You can locate other selections by searching with the keyword "backup" at:

- **www.serverextras.com**/
- **www.bhs.com**/
- **www.computeresp.com**/
- **www.beyond.com**/

For performing disk defragmentation in Windows NT 4.0, we recommend the following:

- Executive Software's Diskeeper: **www.execsoft.com**/
- Symantec's SpeedDisk: **www.symantec.com**/

Here are several tools you can examine in the area of security auditing and intrusion detection software:

- TIS (Haystack Labs) WebStalker-Pro: **http://www.tis.com/prodserv/ stalkerproducts/webstalker/index/html**
- Internet Security Systems' Web, Intranet, and Firewall scanners: **http://www.iss.net**
- Harris Corporation's STAT: **http://www.sunbelt-software.com/stat.htm**
- Blue Lance's LT Auditor+: **http://www.bluelance.com**/
- Palo Verde's NT Spectre: **http://www.netspectre.com**/
- Centrax's Entrax: **http://www.centraxcorp.com**/

3

The Windows NT
Layout

Whr COMPARED TO OTHER MICROSOFT operating systems, Windows NT has
many important differences. These range from capabilities to functions and security.
But one rarely discussed area is the layout of Windows NT files and components. In
this chapter, we look at the file and directory structure created by a Windows NT
installation, provide a roadmap for the important programs, and discuss other issues
related to file structure and layout.

Windows NT Directory Structures

The Windows NT Workstation installation routine makes several changes to your hard
drives. At a minimum, two partitions are created—a system partition and a boot partition. Unfortunately, the way these terms are used is backwards from common sense
usage. The *system* partition is the partition that contains the initial bootstrap components and the boot menu. The *boot* partition is the partition that hosts the main
Windows NT directory and all the operational drivers and files.

The boot and system partition files can be located on the same partition, on different partitions, or even on different hard drives. However, the system partition must
always be on the first hard drive in the system and must be an active primary partition. The boot partition can be either a primary partition or a logical drive within an
extended partition.

System Partition

Table 3.1 shows the files contained on the system partition for an x86 computer.

Table 3.1   **Files Located on the System Partition for an x86 Computer**

File	Description
NTLDR	Controls the operating system boot selection process and hardware detection before the actual Windows NT kernel is launched. It requires that BOOT.INI, NTDETECT.COM, BOOTSECT.DOS (if dual booting), and NTBOOTDD.SYS (if booting on a non–BIOS enabled SCSI drive; that is, scsi() is used instead of multi() in the ARC name in BOOT.INI) exist in the root system partition.
BOOT.INI	Contains the contents of the boot menu displayed by NTLDR. This file contains the default operating system selection, the time out period for the selection, and an ARC name or pathname for each listed operating system boot selection. For more information on the BOOT.INI file, see Chapter 5, "Booting Windows NT."
NTDETECT.COM	Detects the major components of the computer before NTLDR selects a configuration and loads the kernel.
BOOTSECT.DOS	Present only on dual-boot systems. This file is used by NTLDR when the selected operating system is not Windows NT. BOOTSECT.DOS in turn seeks out the OS-specific operating system loader file, such as IO.SYS for MS-DOS or OS2LDR.EXE for OS/2.
NTBOOTDD.SYS	Used only on systems with SCSI drives that do not have on-board BIOS translation enabled. It is a copy of the device driver for your particular SCSI drive.

Table 3.2 lists the files located on the system partition for a RISC computer.

Table 3.2   **Files Located on the System Partition for a RISC Computer**

File	Description
OSLOADER.EXE	This file performs the same functions on a RISC computer that NTLDR, NTDETECT.COM, and BOOTSECT.DOS perform on an x86 system.
HAL.DLL	This is the platform-specific driver file built by the installation routine for the current computer system. This file is loaded by OSLOADER.EXE.
.PAL	These files appear only on Alpha systems. They are collections of special drivers required to boot Windows NT. These files are loaded by OSLOADER.EXE.

Other files may appear in the system partition on x86 dual-boot and multi-boot systems. The addition of these files does not affect the function or capabilities of the required Windows NT boot files present in the system partition. Installing multiple operating systems on a single computer with Windows NT Workstation (or Server) often requires a specific installation order or manual post-installation configuration changes. Both the *Microsoft Windows NT Workstation 4.0 Resource Kit* and TechNet include detailed articles on performing multi-boot setups with Windows NT Workstation, Windows NT Server, Windows 95, Windows 98, MS-DOS, and OS/2.

Multi-booting Windows NT with non-Microsoft operating systems, such as Linux, often requires third-party boot and partition managers. For popular tools, see the "For More Information" section at the end of this chapter.

The system partition does not include any folders (also called *directories*). It exists as a root directory only with three or more files. The presence of additional directories in the system partition does not affect the operation of boot files.

You might notice that the files found in the system partition are among the files found on an Emergency Repair Disk (ERD). This should not be surprising, because an ERD is used to restore files to the system partition if these files are corrupted, deleted, or otherwise destroyed.

Boot Partition

The directory structure and subsequent files installed into the boot partition are quite a bit more complex than those of the system partition. Table 3.3 describes the four directories created in the root directory of the boot partition during the installation of Windows NT.

Table 3.3 **The Directories Created by Windows NT Workstation in the Root Directory of the Boot Partition**

Directory	Description
Program Files	This directory is the default installation location for Windows applications.
Temp	This directory is used to store temporary files. Its path is associated with the Environment tab of the System applet with the TEMP and TMP variables.
Recycler	This is not a true directory; instead, it is the system-controlled temporary repository for deleted files. You can access its contents by launching the Recycle Bin tool from the desktop.
Winnt	This is the main directory that contains all the Windows NT system files.

The root of the boot partition is also the default location for PAGEFILE.SYS, which is the paging file used by Windows NT's virtual memory system. We discuss how to tune Windows NT's performance through placement and configuration of the paging file in Chapter 20, "Tuning and Optimizing Windows NT."

The Program Files directory is home to two subdirectories: Plus! and Windows NT. The Plus! directory derives its name from the software extension package originally created for Windows 95. On Windows NT Workstation (and Windows NT Server), this directory contains Microsoft Internet Explorer, the only application stored in this directory ported over to Windows NT. The Microsoft Internet subfolder of Plus! contains the Internet Explorer executable and related files.

Source for File and Folder Structure

The file and folder structure discussed in this chapter is derived from a fresh installation of Windows NT Workstation on an x86 desktop system. The Custom installation was chosen and all options were selected. No other applications from Microsoft or any third-party vendor were present on the system. This means that no additional services or applications were installed from the Windows NT distribution CD, no service packs or hot fixes were applied, and Internet Explorer was not updated. An exhaustive list of the files found on the system partition is included in Appendix G, "An Exhaustive Review of the Boot Partition".

Terminology

The terms *folder* and *directory* are synonymous. Microsoft typically prefers to use the term folder. This falls in line with Microsoft's endeavor to simplify computing for non-technical users who may more readily understand the concepts of files and folders (like a filing cabinet) rather than files and directories.

The Windows NT subfolder contains three additional subfolders. The Accessories subfolder contains the executable and associated files for WordPad. WordPad is a text editor that offers more features and capabilities than Notepad, but far less than Microsoft Word. The Windows NT subfolder hosts another subfolder, called ImageVue. This folder contains the executable and associated files for Imaging for Windows NT. Imaging is a basic scanning and editing utility developed by Wang Laboratories. The Windows NT subfolder also hosts the Pinball and the Windows Messaging folders as well as the Dialer (DIALER.EXE) and Hyper Terminal (HYPERTRM.EXE) executables. The Windows Messaging folder is home to the Inbox Exchange client (EXCHNG32.EXE), the Exchange client Registry registration tool (MLSET32.EXE), and the Inbox Repair Tool Scanner (SCANPST.EXE) executables and related files.

The Temp folder contains no permanent files. It is a storage area for transient files created by the Windows NT core system, its related utilities, and installed applications.

The Recycler folder is the system-controlled temporary storage directory for deleted files. The actual contents of the Recycle Bin can be viewed only by launching the Recycle Bin utility from the desktop. Attempting to view the contents from Windows NT Explorer or My Computer will be unsuccessful. The Recycler directory is not created by the installation procedure; it is created when a file on the respective partition is deleted.

The Winnt root-level folder is the main repository of all of the files required to launch and operate Windows NT. This folder contains an extensive subfolder hierarchy. The following files are among those stored in the Winnt folder:

- Screen savers (.SCR)
- Wallpaper and tiling images (.BMP)
- Native Windows NT application executables (.EXE)
- Initialization and configuration files for various utilities and applications (.INI)
- Readme, log, and documentation files (.TXT, .LOG, .WRI)

The important files located in the root Winnt folder and other Winnt subfolders are listed here and discussed in more detail throughout this chapter.

- **Config.** Contains configuration .IDF files used by the MIDI sound system.
- **Cursors.** Contains static and animated cursor files. You can use these by configuring the Mouse applet.
- **Fonts.** Contains all installed fonts.
- **Forms.** Contains forms and other configuration items for the Microsoft Exchange client.
- **Help.** Contains some of the help files used by the help system for Windows NT and all of its native utilities. The rest are stored in the System32 subfolder.
- **Inf.** Contains the .INF (system information) files used to install software components.

- **Media.** Contains media files (sound and video) used by sound themes.
- **Profiles.** Contains the user profile directories. Each user profile directory contains data specific to the user environment, including history lists, favorites, desktop icons, and Start menu layout.
- **Repair.** Contains some of the files used to create the ERD. Compressed versions of the Registry keys are stored here. The command `rdisk /s` updates this directory.
- **ShellNew.** Contains document templates used when new files are created using the right-click, New selection from Windows NT Explorer, or the desktop.
- **System.** Contains 16-bit versions of protected and real mode drivers and .DLL files used by applications. These files are provided for backward-compatibility with older applications. Additional 16-bit driver files can be stored in this directory.
- **System32.** Contains a wide variety of system files and subfolder trees.

The first level of subfolders under the Winnt main folder are described in the following list and shown in Figure 3.1

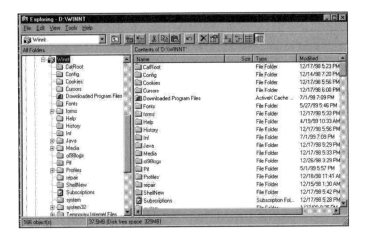

Figure 3.1 Windows NT Explorer displaying the default directory structure of the main Winnt folder.

The System32 subfolder contains most of the files used by Windows NT. This is the primary storage location for DLLs, Control Panel applets (.CPL), device drivers (.DRV), help files (.HLP and .CNT), MS-DOS utilities (.COM), language support files (.NLS), screen savers (.SCR), setup information files (.INF), and a handful of other files used for support, configuration, or operation.

The subfolder structure beneath Winnt\System32 is described in the following list:

- **Config.** Contains the Registry files used during bootup and is the storage location for the system log files viewed through Event Viewer.

- **DHCP.** Used only on Windows NT Server when it serves as a Dynamic Host Configuration Protocol (DHCP) server.

- **Drivers.** Contains driver files (.SYS); the \etc folder contains sample copies of the HOSTS and LMHOSTS files.

- **Os2.** Contains drivers used by the OS/2 subsystem.

- **Ras.** Contains the default scripts used by Dial-Up Networking.

- **Repl.** Contains the folders distributed by the replicator service. Because Windows NT Workstation cannot be an export server, the Export subdirectory is not used. However, the Import subdirectory can accept data, such as system policies, from an export server elsewhere on the network.

- **Spool.** Used by the printing system to store spooled print jobs and related files. The Printers subfolder is used to store spool files. The other folders found here vary based on printer drivers and configuration.

- **Viewers.** Contains the QuickView application and its related DLLs.

- **Wins.** Used only on Windows NT Server when it serves as a Windows Internet Name Service (WINS) server.

As you can see, the directory structure created by the Windows NT Workstation setup process is quite extensive. If you add additional services and applications from the Windows NT distribution CD, install service packs and hotfixes, upgrade Internet Explorer, add Microsoft Outlook Express, or install other Microsoft and third-party applications, this directory structure increases in depth and complexity.

Key Windows NT Executables

The range and number of files included in the Windows NT directory structure is enormous. Most of these files are drivers, DLLs, or some type of configuration storage. Driver, configuration, and DLL files provide you, the user, with little other than sustaining and enabling the operating environment. However, most of the executable (.EXE) files and the MS-DOS utilities (.COM) are quite useful. You can launch them from the Start menu or other standard GUI launch site (when applicable) or you can launch them from Windows NT Explorer, My Computer, a command prompt, or by selecting the Run command from the Start menu. The following sections list the names of files that you can launch manually and provide you with a brief description of each utility or application.

Main Winnt Root Directory

The following executables reside in the main Winnt root directory:

- **EXPLORER.EXE (Windows NT Explorer).** Used to interact with the file systems hosted by Windows NT. It is also the program responsible for creating the Start button and associated objects. If you ever lose the desktop, the Start button and the taskbar, you can usually restore them by pressing Ctrl+Alt+Delete, selecting Task Manager from the pop-up menu, and starting Explorer back up with the Run command (accessed by selecting the New Task (Run) option from the File menu).

- **NOTEPAD.EXE (Notepad).** Used to edit text files.

- **REGEDIT.EXE (Registry Editor).** A 16-bit Registry editing tool that you can use to search the entire Registry at one time.

- **TASKMAN.EXE (Task Manager).** Used to view active applications and processes, as well as view the performance of the CPU and memory.

- **WELCOME.EXE (Welcome).** A Welcome screen that can display tips and other information each time you log in to Windows NT.

- **WINHELP.EXE (Windows Help).** A 16-bit Windows help reader.

- **WINHLP32.EXE (Windows Help).** A 32-bit Windows help reader.

Winnt\System32

The following list of executables resides in the Winnt\System32 directory:

- **APPEND.EXE (Append).** Allows applications to open or access files in directories other than the current working, or active, directory by appending the path parameter. This utility is from MS-DOS 5.0.

- **ARP.EXE (ARP).** The Address Resolution Protocol command line utility used to manage the ARP cache on TCP/IP systems.

- **AT.EXE (AT).** Used to schedule tasks to occur at a specific time and date. It requires that the Scheduler service be running.

- **ATSVC.EXE (Scheduler).** A Scheduler service used by Windows NT to execute tasks at specified times.

- **ATTRIB.EXE (Attributes).** Displays or changes the attributes (read-only, archive, hidden, or system) of files.

- **AUTOCHK.EXE (Auto Check Disk).** Launches automatically during Windows NT bootup if a volume is marked as dirty (has bad clusters, has error blocks, or is otherwise damaged).

- **AUTOCONV.EXE (Auto Convert).** Used by the Windows NT setup routine to convert a FAT volume to NTFS.

- **AUTOLFN.EXE (Auto Long Filenames).** Used by the Windows NT setup routine to repair, copy, or enable long filenames on drives that have been converted from another file system (usually FAT) to NTFS.

- **BACKUP.EXE (Backup).** A command line backup tool from MS-DOS 5.0 used to back up files from one drive to another.

- **BOOTOK.EXE (Boot Acceptance).** Used with the Last Known Good Configuration process to save the configuration parameters after a successful logon.

- **BOOTVRFY.EXE (Boot Verify).** Used with the Last Known Good Configuration process to verify a boot selection.

- **CACLS.EXE (Change ACLs).** A command line utility used to change or edit the permissions for files and folders.

- **CALC.EXE (Calculator).** A GUI calculator that can act as a standard or a scientific calculator.

- **CDPLAYER.EXE (CD Player).** A CD Player GUI used to control the playback of audio CDs.

- **CHARMAP.EXE (Character Map).** A GUI utility that displays the characters contained in each font installed on the system.

- **CHKDSK.EXE (Check Disk).** A disk inspection tool that can search for and repair disk errors.

- **CLIPBRD.EXE (Clipboard Viewer).** Used to view the contents of the object or data currently copied into memory (also known as the Clipboard).

- **CLIPSRV.EXE (Clipboard Server).** The network DDE clipboard service used by the Clipboard Viewer to access the objects or data copied into memory.

- **CLOCK.EXE (Clock).** A GUI clock that can display analog or digital time in a floating window.

- **CMD.EXE (Command Prompt).** An executable that provides the command prompt (MS-DOS shell interpreter) for Windows NT.

- **COMP.EXE (Compare).** An MS-DOS utility used to compare the contents of two files or sets of files.

- **COMPACT.EXE (Compact).** A command line utility used to compress individual files or directories on an NTFS volume.

- **CONTROL.EXE (Control Panel).** Provides the Control Panel window where all Control Panel applets are displayed.

- **CONVERT.EXE (Convert).** Used to convert partitions from FAT to NTFS.

- **CSRSS.EXE (Client–Server Runtime Server Subsystem).** Used to maintain the Win32 system environment console and other essential functions.

- **DCOMCNFG.EXE (DCOM Configuration).** Used to display and configure DCOM settings and configuration.

- **DDESHARE.EXE (DDE Share).** Displays the active DDE shares and enables property editing for these shares.

- **DDHELP.EXE.** The Direct Draw Helper.

- **DEBUG.EXE (Debugger).** A command line debugging tool.

- **DISKPERF.EXE (Disk Performance Counters).** Used to switch on and off the performance counters for the disk subsystem.

- **DOSKEY.EXE (DOS Keyboard).** An MS-DOS 5.0 keyboard history utility that provides a history of command line executions and macros.

- **DOSX.EXE (DOS Extender).** A VDM (virtual DOS machine) MS-DOS extender for standard mode.

- **DRWATSON.EXE (Dr. Watson).** A 16-bit GUI application failure-detection and fault-logging utility that watches over the Win16 subsystem.

- **DRWTSN32.EXE (Dr. Watson 32).** A 32-bit GUI application failure-detection and fault-logging utility that watches over the Win32 subsystem and native Windows NT applications.

- **EDLIN.EXE (Edit Line).** An MS-DOS–based line editor.

- **EVENTVWR.EXE (Event Viewer).** The executable for the Event Viewer.

- **EXE2BIN.EXE (Executable to Binary).** A programmers' tool from MS-DOS used to convert .EXE files to .BIN files.

- **EXPAND.EXE (Expand).** A command line utility used to decompress individual files or directories on an NTFS volume.

- **FASTOPEN.EXE (Fast Open).** An MS-DOS utility that improves performance on systems that have large directories by decreasing the time it takes to open frequently accessed files.

- **FC.EXE (File Comparison).** An MS-DOS utility that compares files or sets of files to reveal their differences.

- **FIND.EXE (Find).** A command line utility used to search for a string of characters in a file or files.

- **FINDSTR.EXE (Find String).** A command line utility used to search for a string of characters in a file or files.

- **FINGER.EXE (Finger).** A TCP/IP utility used to obtain information about a user account via a remote system.

- **FONTVIEW.EXE (Font View).** A command line utility that displays a sample output for a font in a printable GUI window.

- **FORCEDOS.EXE (Force DOS).** Instructs Windows NT to launch an application as an MS-DOS utility when it contains the code for both OS/2 and MS-DOS.

- **FREECELL.EXE (Free Cell).** A GUI card game.

- **FTP.EXE (FTP).** A TCP/IP command line File Transfer Protocol utility used to transfer files between the local system and a remote FTP server.

- **GDI.EXE (Graphical Device Interface).** A core system component that provides the Win16 Graphical Device Interface API library for backward-compatibility with Win16 applications.

- **GRPCONV.EXE (Group Convert).** Converts Microsoft Windows 3.x and Microsoft Windows for Workgroups Program Manager groups into Start menu items.

- **HELP.EXE (Help).** Displays basic and general help information about many Windows NT commands.

- **HOSTNAME.EXE (Hostname).** A TCP/IP command line utility that displays the hostname of the current system.

- **INETINS.EXE (IIS Install).** The installation tool for Microsoft Internet Information Server, which is included on the Windows NT distribution CD.

- **INTERNAT.EXE (International Language).** Enables the Windows NT system to support (and switch between) multiple languages for keyboard settings and applications.

- **IPCONFIG.EXE (IP Configuration).** A TCP/IP command line tool that displays the IP configuration for all installed interfaces and can be used to renew and release DHCP leases.

- **KRNL386.EXE (Kernel 386).** Contains the core kernel routines for Win16 enhanced mode functionality.

- **LABEL.EXE (Label Drive).** A command line tool used to display, edit, or change the volume label of a drive.

- **LIGHTS.EXE.** Provides the settings for modem status lights in Windows 95 and Windows 98 by monitoring the COM ports.

- **LMREPL.EXE (LAN Manager Replicator).** The LAN Manager Replicator service.

- **LOCATOR.EXE (Locator).** Adds support for Remote Procedure Calls (RPCs) to the Windows NT environment.

- **LODCTR.EXE (Load Counters).** Used to add new counters to Performance Monitor.

- **LSASS.EXE (LSA Security Service).** The Local Security Authority server process.

- **MAPISP32.EXE (MAPI 32-bit Spooler).** The Exchange client's 32-bit spooler service for sending and receiving email.

- **MAPISRVR.EXE (MAPI Server).** The Exchange client's mail server process.

- **MDISP32.EXE (MAPI OLE Automation Server).** The Exchange client's email OLE automation server process.

- **MEM.EXE (Memory).** A command line utility that displays the current state of memory.

- **ML3XEC16.EXE (Microsoft Mail 3.x for Windows 16-bit Extensions).** Used by the Exchange client for 16-bit backward compatibility.

- **MPLAY32.EXE (Multimedia Player).** A GUI multimedia player.

- **MPNOTIFY.EXE (Multiple Provider Notify).** Used by the WinLogon service to notify non-Microsoft network servers about security events.

- **MSCDEXNT.EXE (Microsoft CD-ROM Extensions).** Provides CD-ROM extensions for the Windows NT environment, enabling data CDs to be accessed just like hard drives.

- **MSPAINT.EXE (Microsoft Paint).** A basic graphics creation and viewing tool.

- **MUSRMGR.EXE (User Manager).** The User Manager executable. This tool manages users, groups, and system policies (and should not be confused with USRMGR.EXE, which is the executable for the User Manager for Domains).

- **NBTSTAT.EXE (NBT Statistics).** Displays NetBIOS over TCP/IP statistics.

- **NDDEAGNT.EXE (Network DDE Agent).** Manages DDE services over a network.

- **NDDEAPIR.EXE.** The server-side application programming interface (API) for the Network DDE Agent.

- **NET.EXE (Network).** Used to manage, configure, and view network-related controls, such as net use, net print, net user, and so on.

- **NET1.EXE (Network).** Another network command utility that performs the same functions as NET.EXE.

- **NETDDE.EXE (Network DDE).** A background network DDE provider.

- **NETSTAT.EXE (Network Statistics).** Displays TCP/IP network statistics.

- **NLSFUNC.EXE (National Language Support Function).** Used to load country-specific language support.

- **NOTEPAD.EXE (Notepad).** The Notepad text editing utility.

- **NSLOOKUP.EXE (Name Server Lookup).** Used to display the diagnostic and statistical information from DNS servers.

- **NTBACKUP.EXE (Windows NT Backup).** The Windows NT Backup executable.

- **NTOSKRNL.EXE (NT Operating System Kernel).** The Windows NT operating system kernel.

- **NTVDM.EXE (NT Virtual DOS Machine).** An executable that provides the VDM used to host MS-DOS applications and Windows on Windows (WOW—support for Win16).

- **OS2.EXE (OS/2 Environment).** An executable that provides the OS/2 operating system emulation environment for OS/2 1.x character mode applications.

- **OS2SRV.EXE (OS/2 Server).** The OS/2 subsystem server, used in the OS/2 emulation environment.

- **OS2SS.EXE (OS/2 System).** The OS/2 system server, used in the OS/2 emulation environment.

- **PACKAGER.EXE (Object Packager).** Used to create icon links to embedded data for use in documents.

- **PAX.EXE (POSIX Tape Archive).** A POSIX tape backup utility.

- **PBRUSH.EXE (Paintbrush).** A basic graphics creation and viewing tool. This program is just a stub that launches MSPAINT.EXE. It will not work if MSPAINT.EXE is missing, but MSPAINT.EXE will work if PBRUSH.EXE is missing. If you run PBRUSH.EXE and check the running tasks, it is not listed, but MSPAINT.EXE is.

- **PENTNT.EXE (NT Pentium Test).** A command line tool that tests the system for the Pentium floating point error.

- **PERFMON.EXE (Performance Monitor).** The Performance Monitor executable.

- **PING.EXE (PING).** A TCP/IP utility used to test the existence of or the ability to communicate with remote systems.

- **PORTUAS.EXE (Port User Account Service).** A utility to port the OS/2 LAN Manager User Account service to Windows NT.

- **POSIX.EXE (POXIS).** A POSIX.1 subsystem provider.

- **PRINT.EXE (Print).** A command line print utility used to send print jobs to a port.

- **PROGMAN.EXE (Program Manager).** An alternate shell that can be used in place of Windows NT Explorer. It is the main interface used in Windows 3.x, Windows for Workgroups, and Windows NT 3.51.

- **PSXSS.EXE (POSIX Subsystem server).** A POSIX system server, used in the POSIX emulation environment.

- **QBASIC.EXE (Quick Basic).** The MS-DOS 5.0 Quick Basic interpreter.

- **RASADMIN.EXE (RAS Admin).** The Remote Access Admin executable.

- **RASMON.EXE (RAS Monitor).** The RAS Monitor executable.
- **RASPHONE.EXE (RAS Phone).** The Dial-Up Networking Phonebook application.
- **RCP.EXE (Remote Copy).** A TCP/IP utility used to copy files between the current system and a remote RSHD (Remote Shell) server.
- **RDISK.EXE (Repair Disk).** Used to update the \winnt\repair directory and create ERDs.
- **RECOVER.EXE (Recover).** A command line utility to recover readable data from a defective drive.
- **REDIR.EXE (Redirector).** A Win16 network redirector.
- **REGEDT32.EXE (Registry Editor).** A 32-bit Registry editing tool that can set security permissions on Registry keys and values.
- **REPLACE.EXE (Replace).** A command line tool used to replace files.
- **RESTORE.EXE (Restore).** A command line tool used to restore files from backups made with the BACKUP.EXE utility.
- **REXEC.EXE (Remote Execute).** Used to execute commands on remote systems running the REXECD service.
- **ROUTE.EXE (Route).** Used to view and edit the local routing table.
- **RPCSS.EXE (RPC Subsystem).** A remote procedure call subsystem.
- **RSH.EXE (Remote Shell).** Executes commands on remote systems running the RSH service.
- **RUNDLL32.EXE (Run DLL).** Used to execute DLL files from a command line.
- **RUNONCE.EXE (Run Once).** Used to execute tasks as defined in the runonce Registry key.
- **SAVEDUMP.EXE (Save Dump).** Saves the contents of memory to a dump file in the occurrence of a STOP error.
- **SERVICES.EXE (Services).** Used by Windows NT to manage services.
- **SETUP.EXE (Setup).** The Windows NT setup tool.
- **SETVER.EXE (Set Version).** Used to define the version of MS-DOS reported to an application.
- **SHARE.EXE (Share).** An MS-DOS utility used to enable two applications to use the same file.
- **SHMGRATE.EXE.** A Windows NT user data migration tool.
- **SKEYS.EXE (Serial Keys).** A system service that adds support for the SerialKeys feature.
- **SMSS.EXE (Session Manager).** A session manager that is used to establish the Windows NT environment during bootup.

- **SNDREC32.EXE (Sound Records).** A Sound Recorder application.
- **SNDVOL32.EXE (Sound Volume).** A GUI volume application.
- **SOL.EXE (Solitaire).** A GUI solitaire card game.
- **SORT.EXE (Sort).** A command line utility that sorts input and writes the results to a file or the screen.
- **SPINIT.EXE.** An initialization file for downloading software from trusted providers.
- **SPOOLSS.EXE (Spooler Service).** The spooler service for the print subsystem.
- **SPRESTRT.EXE.** Used to restore the Registry to restart the GUI-mode portion of the setup application.
- **SUBST.EXE (Substitute).** An MS-DOS command used to associate a path with a drive letter.
- **SYNCAPP.EXE (Synchronize Application).** A tool used by the Briefcase to synchronize contained files.
- **SYSEDIT.EXE (System Edit).** A system file editing utility that opens the SYSTEM.INI, WIN.INI, CONFIG.SYS, and AUTOEXEC.BAT files in one editor window.
- **SYSTRAY.EXE (System Tray).** The system tray provider. It controls the taskbar and icon tray.
- **TAPISRV.EXE (TAPI Server).** The Telephony API (TAPI) server used by the RAS subsystem.
- **TASKMAN.EXE (Task Manager).** Used for backward-compatibility with older non-Windows NT software instead of actually providing access to the Task Manager.
- **TASKMGR.EXE (Task Manager).** The Task Manager application.
- **TCPSVCS.EXE (TCP Services).** The TCP Services provider.
- **TELNET.EXE (Telnet).** A telnet client used to access remote telnet server systems.
- **TFTP.EXE (Trivial FTP).** An alternate FTP program for use over the User Datagram Protocol (UDP).
- **TRACERT.EXE (Traceroute).** Used to identify the route between the local system and a remote system on a TCP/IP network.
- **UNLODCTR.EXE (Unload Counter).** Used to unload Performance Monitor counters.
- **UPS.EXE (UPS Service).** The uninterruptible power supply service.
- **USER.EXE (Win16 User).** A utility used for Win16 compatibility.
- **USERINIT.EXE (User Initialization).** Used to establish the operating environment for a user after logon.

- **WINCHAT.EXE (Windows Chat).** A chat tool.
- **WINDISK.EXE (Disk Administrator).** The Disk Administrator application.
- **WINFILE.EXE (Windows File Manager).** An alternate file management tool from Windows 3.x, Windows for Workgroups, and Windows NT 3.51.
- **WINHLP32.EXE (Windows Help).** The 32-bit Windows Help tool.
- **WINLOGON.EXE (Windows Logon).** The Windows Logon service.
- **WINMINE.EXE (Mine Sweeper).** The mine sweeper game.
- **WINMSD.EXE (Windows NT Diagnostics).** The Windows NT Diagnostics application.
- **WINSPOOL.EXE (WOW Spooler).** The printer spooler service for WOW (the Win16 subsystem).
- **WINVER.EXE (Windows Version).** Displays the current Windows version.
- **WOWDEB.EXE (WOW Debugger).** The WOW debugger.
- **WOWEXEC.EXE (WOW Execute).** Executes Win16 applications for Win32 applications.
- **WRITE.EXE (Write).** A text and rich-text document editing tool.
- **XCOPY.EXE (Extended Copy).** A command line utility used to copy files and directories.

MS-DOS.COM Files in the Main Winnt Root Directory

The following list of MS-DOS .COM files resides in the main Winnt root directory:

- **CHCP.COM (Change Code Page).** Sets or displays the code page (character set) number currently active. Code 437 is for the United States.
- **COMMAND.COM (Command Interpreter).** Launches a new instance of the MS-DOS command interpreter.
- **DISKCOMP.COM (Disk Compare).** Compares the contents of two floppy disks using a track-by-track comparison.
- **DISKCOPY.COM (Disk Copy).** Copies the contents of one floppy to another.
- **EDIT.COM (Edit).** A text editor.
- **FORMAT.COM (Format).** Formats floppy drives and disk partitions with NTFS or FAT.
- **GRAFTABL.COM (Graphics Enable).** Sets Windows NT to display an extended character set in graphics mode.
- **GRAPHICS.COM (Print Graphics).** Allows MS-DOS applications to print graphics.

- **KB16.COM (Keyboard).** Configures the keyboard for a specific language layout for Win16 applications.

- **KEYB.COM (Keyboard).** Configures the keyboard for a specific language layout for 32-bit applications.

- **LOADFIX.COM (Load Above Fix).** Loads MS-DOS applications into memory above the first 64 KB.

- **MODE.COM (Device Mode).** Used to manage the mode of peripheral devices (such as modems, printers, and fax devices).

- **MORE.COM (More).** A display tool that limits scrolling output to a single screen at a time.

- **TREE.COM (Directory Tree).** Displays the directory tree hierarchy in a graphical manner.

- **WIN.COM (Windows Loaders).** A backward-compatible Win16 application loader.

The Windows NT Workstation Distribution CD

The Windows NT Workstation distribution CD contains more than just the files used to install Windows NT Workstation. In addition to the main installation files, there are collections of additional drivers, language support, and extra tools.

The root directory of the distribution CD hosts seven subfolders. Four of these are the installation directories for the four platform types—x86 systems (\i386), Alpha systems (\Alpha), MIPS systems (\Mips), and Power PC systems (\Ppc).

The \Langpack subfolder contains several additional language drivers that can be added to your system. Just right-click an .INF file and select Install from the pop-up menu.

The \Drvlib subfolder contains a wide range of additional hardware device drivers, including drivers for multimedia, communication, networks, printing, and video devices. The drivers are separated into subfolders by general device type, model name or reference name, and platform. Be sure to install the drivers for the correct platform type.

The \Support subfolder contains five subfolders and a version of the Hardware Compatibility List (HCL) file that is dated August 9, 1996 (we recommend pulling the latest version of this file from the Microsoft Web site). The \Support\Books folder contains WordPad versions of the Windows NT Startup manual. The \Support\Debug folder contains a variety of debugging tools. These tools are described in the following list:

- **I386KD.EXE, ALPHAKD.EXE, MIPSKD.EXE, and PPCKD.EXE.** Debugging tools for each platform. They can be used locally or remotely.

- **APIMON.EXE.** An API monitor used to trace API calls.

- **CDB.EXE.** A User Mode Debugging tool.

- **DUMPCHK.EXE, DUMPEXAM.EXE, and DUMPFLOP.EXE.** Tools that can be used to examine the contents of a STOP error crash dump file.
- **IAMGECFG.EXE, SETNT351.CMD, and SETWIN95.CMD.** Tools used to verify version problems in applications.
- **NTSD.EXE.** Windows NT's software debugger.
- **PCMCMD.EXE.** Reads PC Card BIOS configuration information, which can be dumped into a file.
- **PMON.EXE.** A text-display Performance Monitor.
- **POOLMON.EXE.** A memory pool monitoring tool.
- **PSTAT.** Displays process thread statistics.
- ***EXTS.DLL.** Several debugger extension files.

These are advanced programming and debugging tools. If you need details on how to use these tools, please consult the *Microsoft Windows NT Workstation 4.0 Resource Kit* and TechNet.

The \Support\Deptools folder contains the deployment tools described in the following list:

- **SETUPMGR.EXE (Setup Manager).** Used to create automated installation scripts.
- **SYSDIFF.EXE (System Difference).** Used to create system snapshots for bulk installations.
- **ROLLBACK.EXE (Rollback).** Should not be used because it destroys the Registry instead of returning the system to a preconfiguration state.

The \Support\Hqtool folder contains the hardware qualifier disk. This disk is used to test a system for HCL compliance. However, the HCL used by this tool is from August 1996 and no update is available for the application.

The \Support\Scsitool folder contains the SCSI drive interrogation tool. This tool is used to verify that the SCSI subsystem can support Windows NT. This tool may not be 100% accurate because new drivers can enable Windows NT to access or support SCSI devices and functions not included in the original release of Windows NT.

Installing a Program

Installing software can cause drastic changes to your Windows NT system, depending on what the software is and what installation utility you use. Some software packages install themselves into a single directory and make no changes to your system other than adding a Start menu item. Other software packages install parts of themselves throughout your system, place driver files in the main Windows folder tree, alter Registry settings, and more.

The only real 100% protection from software installation is to not install the soft-ware. However, because this is often unavoidable, you have a few other options. First, always back up your system and update your Emergency Repair Disk before installing new software. This ensures that you can return to a pre-software-installation state if things do not go as planned. Second, use a software installation monitoring tool. There are some examples of these in the "For More Information" section at the end of this chapter.

A third option is to rely upon the software's own uninstall capabilities. Unfortunately, you often don't know if a software product even has an uninstall option until you complete the installation. A final option is to rely upon Windows NT's installation shield to detect, monitor, and record software installation. In some cases this is adequate; but once again, you won't know what your uninstallation options are until after you've performed the installation.

For More Information

If the information about Windows NT hardware issues presented in this chapter has increased your desire to learn more, here are some resources you can research to obtain more knowledge:

- Microsoft Windows NT Workstation 4.0 Resource Kit. Microsoft Press, 1996. ISBN: 1572313439.

- Microsoft TechNet: `http://www.microsoft.com/technet`

Following are two popular tools for multi-booting Windows NT with non-Microsoft operating systems:

- V Communications' System and Partition Commander, located at `http://www.v-com.com/`

- PowerQuest's Partition Magic, located at `http://www.powerquest.com/`

For more information about the tools and utilities found in the main Winnt root directory, you can take the following action:

- Use the `help <name>` command from a command prompt.
- Look through the Windows Help system. (Select Help from the Start menu.)
- Use the `/?` parameter after the utility name from a command prompt.
- Execute or launch the program, then look for help information.
- Review the *Microsoft Windows NT Workstation 4.0 Resource Kit.*
- Consult the TechNet CD-ROM.
- Search the Microsoft Web site: `http://www.microsoft.com/support/`.

The following tools monitor your system for changes, especially during software installation. You can use the recorded changes to uninstall software and return your system to its previous state:

- Norton Uninstall Deluxe: **http://www.symantec.com/**
- Quarterdeck's Cleansweep Deluxe: **http://www.quarterdeck.com/**
- Cybermedia's Uninstaller: **http://www.cybermedia.com/**
- IMSI Software's WinDelete: **http://www.imsisoft.com/**

II

Nuts and Bolts of Windows NT

4

Windows NT and Hardware

THE WINDOWS NT WORKSTATION NETWORK client operating system has specific system requirements for it to function properly. In this chapter, we discuss the hardware requirements for running Windows NT Workstation. In addition, we explore adding new hardware to an existing Windows NT system, and we examine several tools you can use to inspect, configure, and troubleshoot hardware.

Windows NT Hardware 101

Although Windows NT is a powerful network operating system, not all hardware can be used with it. These hardware restrictions are based on several aspects, including the following:

- Windows NT is a complex program that requires robust hardware.
- Windows NT is security-oriented and requires securable hardware.

Windows NT was not designed with most entertainment or personal uses in mind, such as gaming, full-screen videos, graphical design, and music editing. Therefore, Windows NT doesn't have built-in support for such hardware.

These limitations are important for several reasons. First, if you attempt to install Windows NT on unsupported hardware, the installation may fail. Second, if you are able to get Windows NT to function on unsupported hardware, you might not be eligible for Microsoft technical support. Third, Windows NT might function for a while on unsupported hardware, but applying new or updated drivers or service packs may render the system unusable. Hardware that once worked could cease to function because service packs make these types of system changes.

To help you determine what hardware is supported, Microsoft has compiled and maintained a list of compatible devices. This list is known as the Hardware Compatibility List (HCL). It is included on the Windows NT CD and the TechNet CD-ROM, and it is available online at `http://www.microsoft.com/hwtest/hcl/`. This list focuses on the fundamental hardware components supported by Windows NT, and is not exhaustive of all available components on the market. The HCL lists information about device types, some of which are shown in the following list. (To view a complete listing, download the HCL from the Microsoft Web site.)

- CPU (single and multiple)
- System (motherboards)
- Storage devices (hard drive, CD, tape, and so on)
- Storage controllers (IDE, SCSI, RAID, and so on)
- Network devices and interfaces
- Video (cards and monitors)
- Input devices (keyboard, mouse, and so on)
- Modems
- Printers
- Audio
- UPS
- International devices

The HCL indicates whether a listed device is fully supported, partially supported, or not supported. Furthermore, it indicates whether the device drivers are included on the Windows NT Workstation CD, are available from Microsoft, or are available from the device's manufacturer or vendor.

What's in a Service Pack?

A *service pack* is a collection of code replacements, patches, error corrections, new applications, version improvements, and service-specific configuration settings that correct or replace problems in the original release of a product.

Installing Non-HCL Devices

If you want to throw caution to the wind and install devices not listed on the HCL, be sure to search the manufacturer's or vendor's Web site to see whether the device is compatible with Windows NT. In some cases, new hardware is supported by Windows NT (via a compatible driver on the Windows NT Workstation CD or a new driver from the vendor) that has yet to be added to the HCL. If the device is supported in Windows NT, you may be able to obtain technical support from the equipment manufacturer or Microsoft.

Always make sure that your core system components are on the HCL. The core components are the CPU, motherboard, memory, storage devices, and storage controllers. Typically, if you employ a supported CPU, you'll be forced into using a supported motherboard and memory. But take the time to verify those, too, just in case. Other items, such as the keyboard, mouse, video card, and monitor don't necessarily need to be fully compatible, but you should have fully compatible spares handy in case the components cannot be used with Windows NT.

If you are using storage devices or storage controllers that are supported, but for which drivers are not included on the Windows NT Workstation CD, the default method of installing Windows NT, which attempts to install the storage drivers automatically, may not be successful. Instead, you should choose to install the vendor-supplied storage drivers manually. We recently purchased a new dual-CPU system with an embedded Adaptec AIC-7895P Ultra and Ultra Wide SCSI on the motherboard. When the installation started to switch into GUI mode, a STOP error occurred. We skipped auto storage detection and manually specified the drivers, and then the installation was completed successfully.

Checking Hardware for NT Compatibility

Another important step is to make sure your hardware is Windows NT compatible. If your hardware is older than August 1996, you can use the Windows NT Hardware Qualifier (NTHQ) to verify hardware compatibility. The NTHQ is an automatic inspection tool used to inspect a computer system for HCL compatibility. It is found on the Windows NT Workstation CD in the \Support\Hqtool folder. However, if you have hardware that is newer than the NTHQ, the tool becomes useless because Microsoft has not offered an updated version of the NTHQ. If you use the version from the Windows NT Workstation CD, you'll only verify that your system was compatible as of August, 1996. Because more than two years of technology advancement has occurred since that time, you'd just be wasting your time. The only method currently available to check for HCL compatibility is to manually check your hardware against the HCL.

Fortunately, most non-custom, pre-built systems from big-name manufacturers (such as those from Dell, Compaq, HP, and Micron) are certified as Windows NT compatible. You should have no problem installing Windows NT onto these systems right out of the box. However, custom-built systems (whether they're built in-house or from a local vendor) offer less security of HCL compatibility. If a component is not supported or causes Windows NT to fail, you'll be responsible for returning to the vendor to purchase replacement parts instead of getting the vendor to perform the replacement under warranty (that is, if the system is labeled as Windows NT compatible).

In a production environment, HCL compatibility is of premium importance. Having to fight with components to maintain a functioning system is expensive in terms of time and productivity. Outside of critical production, such as on test, personal, or home systems, HCL deviancy is not as detrimental. We recommend that you stick with components listed on the HCL in any situation in which a downed system can cost you money or customers. You'll need to be the judge of your own time and sanity regarding whether HCL compatibility on non-critical systems is worthwhile. We've spent so many sleepless nights and lost so many weekends to messing with non-HCL devices that we don't even think twice anymore. If it's not on the HCL, it's not going into a Windows NT system.

Minimal Hardware Requirements

In addition to making sure that all your hardware is compatible with Windows NT, you need to make sure that your system meets a few minimum requirements before installing Windows NT. Table 4.1 lists the minimum hardware requirements (according to the Windows NT Workstation 4.0 documentation) and recommended hardware requirements (according to industry professionals) for installing Windows NT Workstation 4.0 on a PC.

Table 4.1 **Windows NT Workstation Minimum and Recommended Hardware Requirements**

Item	Minimum	Recommended
Processor	x86 33Mhz	Pentium or higher
RAM	12MB	16MB or more
Display adapter	VGA	VGA or better
Hard disk space	117MB	120MB or more
Additional drives	3.5-inch disk drive and CD-ROM	3.5-inch disk drive and CD-ROM

The Roles Drivers Play

Windows NT relies on device drivers to provide system-level control over hardware components. A device driver is a low-level software component that provides an interface between the language and control mechanisms of the operating system with the functions and capabilities of the device. Every device that can be accessed, controlled, or used by the Windows NT system has an associated driver loaded into active memory.

The Devices applet in the Control Panel lists the installed drivers, their status, and their startup value (see Figure 4.1). The list of drivers includes all the generic drivers for each type of core system component, as well as any special or custom installed drivers. Only about half the drivers actually installed are ever active. This is due to duplicate drivers (such as device-specific drivers and generic drivers for video cards) and drivers without matching hardware (such as the PCMCIA driver). The status of a driver indicates whether the driver is loaded and active (started) or not loaded (blank). The startup parameter defines how the driver is activated. Possible values are listed here:

- **Boot.** Drivers set to Boot are loaded when the system starts and before other drivers are loaded. This setting is used for drivers critical to initial system operation.

- **System.** Drivers set to System are loaded when the system starts and after all Boot drivers are loaded. This setting is used for drivers critical to general system operation.

- **Automatic.** Drivers set to Automatic are loaded when the system starts and after all Boot and System drivers are loaded. This setting is used for required drivers not essential to system operation.

- **Manual.** Drivers set to Manual are not loaded when the system starts, but can be loaded manually by clicking the Startup button in the Devices applet or started automatically by a dependent device.

- **Disabled.** Drivers set to Disabled are not loaded at system startup, and users are prevented from starting the device. However, the system can still start Disabled devices if necessary.

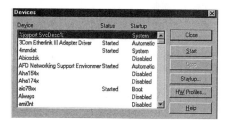

Figure 4.1   The Devices applet in the Control Panel.

You can also use the Devices applet to configure hardware profiles. A *hardware profile* is a collection of drivers specific to a hardware configuration. Hardware profiles are most often used on portable or notebook computers that can be attached to a network, use a modem, have a docking station, have swappable drives, or use PCMCIA cards or PC cards. A hardware profile is used for each different component configuration so only those drivers needed for the present devices are loaded. This not only speeds the system by not loading unused drivers, it also reduces system errors by not loading drivers when the associated hardware is not present or active.

You can also use hardware profiles to disable devices even when they are present. For example, a notebook computer that gains Internet access via a modem when on the road and via the company LAN when in the office may use one hardware profile to disable the modem when connected to the LAN and another to disable the NIC when travelling. The modem would still work when the computer is at the office, but because the modem would be disabled, the system would always use the LAN to connect to the Internet instead of attempting to dial the modem.

You initially create hardware profiles through the System applet on the Hardware Profiles tab (see Figure 4.2). Simply select an existing profile and click Copy. After copying the profile, make any necessary changes for that profile and save it under a new name. When two or more profiles exist on a system, you'll be prompted upon each bootup to select the profile you want to use for that session. You can select which drivers are enabled and disabled for each profile through the Devices applet.

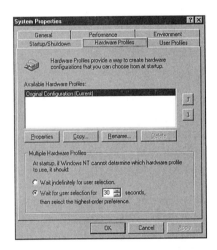

Figure 4.2   The System applet.

From within the Devices applet, select the driver to manage from the list, and then click the HW Profiles button. This displays the Device dialog box, where the status of the selected driver is listed for each existing hardware profile. Select a profile and click Enable or Disable to change its status. The changes you make to a profile will not take effect until the next time the system is booted with that profile.

Document Your Current Hardware Configuration

Knowing your system's components is an important part of maintaining a functioning environment. Just as a surgeon can't aid you if he doesn't know anatomy, neither can you administer a system without knowing the devices within it. It is important that you maintain an accurate account of the devices, configurations, drivers, and other related items. Having documentation at hand can save time and effort when you're configuring or troubleshooting.

Windows NT does not include an exhaustive inventory utility that can print a complete list of your system components. However, a few tools can offer you some insight to expound on your own exploration. First, you need to create a list of the hardware components manually. You need to know the type, make, model, and general specifications of each piece of hardware. Be sure to collect this data for every device inside of or connected to your computer, including the following:

- CPU
- Motherboard
- Memory
- Storage controllers
- Storage devices (hard disk drives, floppy drives, CD-ROM drives, tape drives, and so on)
- Video card, monitor
- Sound card, speakers
- Network interface card, network media (cable)
- Modem
- Printer
- Keyboard, mouse

Having done that, you need to add information about where you obtained drivers for each device: from the Windows NT Workstation CD, a manufacturer-supplied disk, or a file from a Web or FTP site.

Next, list all details about the hardware- or software-based configuration for each device. Include items such as to which bus port it is connected, any jumper or dip switch settings, connected cables (both internal and external), existence or absence of terminators and other device-specific settings, and any software-controlled BIOS settings. Some devices require that you boot into MS-DOS (whether on a dual-boot system or from a floppy) and then use an MS-DOS configuration tool to set BIOS settings (some 3Com NICs are this way). The more data you collect and record, the less you'll need to search for it later during a crisis. It's a good idea to have all of this information in one place; that way, when you're troubleshooting, you know where to go to look for such information.

This information is the start of an ever-expanding collection of data about your computer system. We like to call this collection of data a *computer information file* (CIF). In addition to a device inventory and configuration details, you need to include copies of all drivers, device manuals, and a maintenance log for every device in your CIF. Anything and everything that's ever used to install, configure, decipher, explain, research, or troubleshoot any component or aspect of your computer system should be included in the CIF.

Within Windows NT, you can employ a few tools to extract some configuration data from the Windows NT environment. The most obvious of these tools is the Windows NT Diagnostics (WINMSD.EXE) tool (discussed in Chapter 2). The data from this utility can be printed out or saved to a file using the Print Report or Save Report command from the File menu. Several Control Panel applets (such as Keyboard, Modems, Display, Mouse, Multimedia, Network, PC Card, Ports, Printers, SCSI Adapters, Tape Devices, Telephony, and UPS) offer information about hardware. In general, these applets will help you discover the installed drivers, BIOS version, and current settings. For further information on the Control Panel applets, refer to Chapter 6 "Windows NT Control Panel Utilities."

If you want to avoid writing out the hardware inventory by hand or even creating your own database to organize the details, you can employ Hardware Organizer from PrimaSoft (shown in Figure 4.3). This tool is designed to help you maintain an exhaustive inventory of every component within your system. It includes fields for nearly everything you could ever think of recording. Not only can you create a well-organized database of information with this tool, but you can export that data into Web-ready HTML documents, easy-to-read reports, or informational labels. The templates provided that store data are fully customizable. In addition, this tool is Internet-enhanced to give you immediate access to online resources for drivers, documentation, and troubleshooting tips. If you're interested, you can download a trial version from the PrimaSoft PC Software Web site at **http://www.primasoft.com/32org/32hdo.htm**.

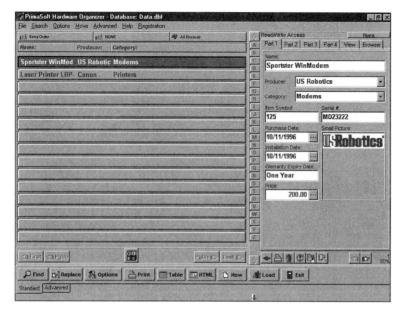

Figure 4.3   Hardware Organizer from PrimaSoft.

Adding New Hardware

Windows NT provides only two options for installing new hardware. Either Windows NT provides a Control Panel applet for the device type, or the manufacturer provides a Windows NT installation utility. Unlike Windows 95 and Windows 98, Windows NT does not include an Add New Hardware applet.

Windows NT makes provisions for installation of the following types of devices into an existing system using the Control Panel applets:

- Video cards and monitors
- Keyboards
- Modems
- Mice and other pointing devices
- Multimedia components (audio, video, joysticks, and so on)
- Network adapters, protocols, and services
- PC cards
- Printers
- SCSI adapters and controllers
- Tape devices
- UPSs

For devices not listed previously, such as a specialty hard drive, a CD-ROM or other optical drive, or a SCSI device (hard drive, CD-ROM, scanner, and so on), you'll need to use a manufacturer-supplied installation utility. Even if Windows NT includes a related applet for installation, many devices can be installed successfully using only the manufacturer's installation utility. When in doubt, seek out the manufacturer for installation instructions and, when available, their own installation utility. In most cases, you'll have fewer problems with the vendor's installation than if you try to force the limited Windows NT applets into performing installations they aren't quite capable of.

Removing the Old Drivers

Windows NT is a bit adverse to changes in the composition of the hardware on its host system. In other words, removing old drivers from Windows NT is nearly impossible, and adding new devices is often difficult. The Devices applet does not offer a remove or uninstall function. Your only recourse is to set the Startup value to Disabled or Manual to prevent the driver from loading during startup.

Some of you may think that you can get around this limitation by deleting the driver files and hacking the Registry. If you are so bold, go for it. But we strongly caution against such action. Driver files are not always labeled clearly, nor can you be positive that some other device or service does not require the file. Plus, how can you be sure that you've removed all the related files for a particular device? In addition, the driver-related items in the Registry are not all located in the same areas and are not stored under "device" or "driver" labeled keys. Undertaking a search and destroy mission in the Registry is often dangerous.

In most cases, old drivers will just sit on your system unused. In a few situations, drivers can be removed if the vendor provided an installation routine that records an installation log and includes an uninstall option. The uninstall routine can appear as an item in the Start menu or as an entry in the Add/Remove Programs applet in the Control Panel. Otherwise, you should simply disable the driver rather than attempting to extradite it from the system.

Adding new hardware to an existing system can be tricky. As with adding new devices to any computer system, you first need to verify that the new component will not cause resource conflicts before you physically install it. This means checking requirements for IRQ, I/O address, DMA, and memory. The Windows NT Diagnostics tool's Resources tab is a great place to check for available (free or unused) system resources (see Figure 4.4).

Next, you need to locate the drivers for the device. This is actually where adding new hardware can become a problem.

Figure 4.4   The Windows NT Diagnostics tool's Resources tab.

Adding New Drivers

Windows NT is not perfect right out of the box. In the two plus years since its release, several updates to the base network operating system have been distributed. These are known as service packs and hotfixes (see Chapter 23 for details). These update patches change core components of the operating system as well as the device drivers it uses. Windows NT configures its HAL (Hardware Abstraction Layer) during initial installation based on the presence of the core system hardware components. Changing these base system components (such as CPU type or number, BIOS version, and motherboard speed) usually results in an nonviable operating system.

After you install a service pack, you should use only drivers from that service pack for installing new hardware devices. Attempting to use drivers released before the service pack or on the Windows NT Workstation CD can result in device inoperability, intermittent failure, or system level STOP errors. When you add new devices to a Windows NT system, always visit the device manufacturer's or the vendor's Internet site to look for new or updated drivers for Windows NT. If no drivers are found, attempt to pull drivers from the installed service pack and then from the Windows NT Workstation CD.

To pull a driver from a service pack, you must extract all the files from the service pack file. To do so, you issue the command **nt4sp4.exe -x** (or a similar command based on the actual filename of the service pack) from a command prompt or using the Run command from the Start menu. The **-x** parameter instructs the setup routine to request an extraction directory and then extract all files into that directory without launching the installation procedure. When the files are extracted, you can specify the extraction directory in any dialog box that requests files from the Windows NT Workstation CD. If the file is not found, you can specify the Windows NT Workstation CD.

After you install a new driver, you should reboot immediately. This causes Windows NT to attempt to load the new driver. If startup fails, you can employ the Last Known Good Configuration (LKGC) boot option by pressing the spacebar when prompted. This should return your system to the state of the last successful logon. If you are able to log on to the system but the driver does not enable the device, the LKGC will not be useful because the LKGC is overwritten each time a logon is successful. Always reboot after adding a new driver or changing a driver configuration. Another tip is to make only a single change each time. Otherwise, you will not know what change to your system caused any problems that might occur.

You may also want to take extra precautions when adding new drivers to your system. Backing up data on drives that may be affected by the driver change is wise. Also, updating your Emergency Repair Disk (ERD) by issuing the `rdisk /s` command gives you a way out if your startup files are damaged. Finally, backing up the Registry may prove useful if you need to repair, replace, or restore a segment of the Registry that's damaged or changed by the driver installation process. Keep in mind that the most often recommended troubleshooting solution for Windows NT is reinstallation. So, taking every precaution to avoid that unpleasantry is a mark of an intelligent administrator.

Windows NT and Plug and Play

You need to be aware of two other issues when working with hardware under Windows NT: Plug and Play and BIOS configuration. Windows NT does not support the Plug and Play model. Plug and Play is a technology used to detect and configure hardware devices automatically during bootup. However, because there are so many Plug and Play devices on the market, Microsoft included a workaround for those willing to handle the problems that can arise when installing Plug and Play hardware in Windows NT.

Pulling drivers

Always be sure to pull drivers from the same release number, security bit length, and language version of the service pack that is installed on the system. Doing otherwise can result in problems with no resolution.

The workaround is a Plug and Play driver that enables Windows NT to read the BIOS of Plug and Play devices, but not configure them automatically. This improves the range of devices that can be installed under Windows NT. You can find the Plug and Play (PnP) driver on the original Windows NT installation CD in the \Drvlib\Plug and Playisa\x86 folder. It's called PNPISA.SYS. However, if you have applied a service pack, you should use the Plug and Play driver from the extracted service pack files. To install the Plug and Play driver, right-click the PLUG AND PLAYISA.INF file accompanying the .SYS file, and then select Install from the pop-up menu. Be sure to reboot immediately after installation.

Repeated Prompts

You'll need to know how to deal with a few quirks related to the Plug and Play driver. The driver will scan the system for unknown or new devices during each startup. If a device is found, Windows NT attempts to apply existing (already installed) drivers to the device. If that fails, you'll be prompted to provide drivers from the Windows NT Workstation CD or from a manufacturer-provided disk. You also have the options of telling Windows NT to skip driver installation this time and prompt at the next startup, or to completely ignore the device and never prompt again. When prompted for driver files, you should first attempt to use manufacturer-provided files. If those don't work or exist, you should try the extracted service pack files or, finally, try the Windows NT Workstation CD.

In most cases, after the driver is installed, you'll never see the prompt again. However, we've experienced several problems with notebook displays that caused the Plug and Play driver prompt to occur every time the system booted. We disabled the driver through the Devices applet by changing its setting to Disabled. This stopped the annoying prompt, but it stopped the autodetection of new Plug and Play devices as well. A second problem is that the driver is not perfect. Often, it discovers devices that are purposely dormant, such as a bus mouse connector on a motherboard when a serial mouse is in use, or it will not discover other devices, such as external modems.

When nonexistent or unnecessary devices are detected, you should either instruct the system to not prompt you again or disable the Plug and Play driver. If real Plug and Play devices are not detected, you'll need to perform driver installation through normal means. A final problem with the Plug and Play driver is that it still does not add the capability to configure Plug and Play BIOS settings—which returns us to the second hardware issue we mentioned earlier.

Problems with BIOS Configuration

The Plug and Play driver for Windows NT may pose problems for devices that are BIOS configurable. These devices do not have physical switches or settings, but rely on a chip to perform all configuration settings. These BIOS settings can be changed only through a configuration tool. When Plug and Play is involved, these settings are automatically set by the Plug and Play–compliant operating system. When Windows NT and the Plug and Play driver are present, the first possible configuration settings are used whether they cause conflicts or not. Windows NT is not able to alter the BIOS settings of devices due to its built-in hardware security restrictions.

Working around this limitation can be difficult. First, you need to determine the initial default settings of the device. Then determine if these settings can be retained by changing the settings of other devices (although this moves the configuration problem to another device, another device may have physical controls instead of BIOS only). If not, you need to locate an MS-DOS-based configuration tool from the manufacturer. One device type we've performed this on over and over again is the 3Com network interface card. The driver disk includes a great MS-DOS configuration tool that can be used to set the BIOS as well as perform diagnostics on the device. You should look for this type of tool for every device that has BIOS configurations.

If you are unable to move other devices and no MS-DOS configuration utility is available, you still have one final option. First, disable the Plug and Play driver, and then power down the Windows NT system. Locate a Windows 95 or Windows 98 system. Install the device in the Windows 95/98 system in the same position (bus slot, SCSI order, and so on) as it would be in the Windows NT system. This works best on a dual-boot system, but it can work when two separate machines are used. In the case of a dual-boot system, you don't need to move the card because it will already be physically installed. Boot the system, and then allow Windows 95/98 to install the device. On the Windows 95/98 system, select the Device Manager tab (shown in Figure 4.5) from the System applet, locate the device in the list, open its Properties dialog box, and select its Resources tab. Deselect the Use Automatic Settings check box, and then modify the settings to match those needed on the Windows NT system. When you finish changing the settings, power down the system and move the device back into the Windows NT system (or, in a dual-boot configuration, reboot into Windows NT). The device should then work fine in Windows NT.

Some of the Control Panel applets, such as the Multimedia applet, allow you to open a Settings or Resources dialog box for a device. You can change the settings displayed in these dialog boxes. However, changing them changes only the Windows NT system; it does not modify the BIOS settings. The ability to change the settings through these dialog boxes is for the purpose of matching the Windows NT system's driver interface with the actual device settings.

Figure 4.5   The Device Manager tab of the System applet from Windows 98.

Video Driver

Windows NT's video system can be a bit troublesome. During the initial installation, the default drivers for standard VGA are used. This results in a display area of 640×480 or 800×600 with only 16 colors. Although this may be fine for installation, it is typically not very conducive to ongoing human interaction with the system. Therefore, you'll need to install additional video drivers to obtain better resolutions and color depth. How video drivers are actually installed is different for each video card vendor. You would think they would all comply with Windows NT's standard method of installation via the Settings tab of the Display applet, but they don't. You need to read the documentation that accompanies the video card to determine how the drivers should be installed. If the documentation fails to mention Windows NT, you need to visit the vendor's Web site or contact them by phone. We are amazed at how many video cards require special installation instructions for Windows NT.

Installation

There are typically two methods of installing video drivers. It is important to use only the method prescribed by the vendor; otherwise, you never correctly install the driver. We've had to reinstall Windows NT to correct video driver problems before, so take our advice—look for documentation first. No matter which installation method you use, you should always set the system to standard VGA (VGA compatible display drivers) first, before attempting to install new drivers. As always, reboot before installing new drivers.

The two methods for installing video drivers are:

- Use the Display applet's Settings tab
- Use a manufacturer-supplied installation utility

In most cases, the video cards you are using are newer than Windows NT. This means that the drivers included on the Windows NT Workstation CD are not designed for your video cards. Thus, you should always seek out new or updated drivers before attempting to use the old drivers from the Windows NT Workstation CD. This is especially true if you have already applied a service pack.

When you're installing from the Display applet, don't use the Detect button unless the video card's documentation specifically instructs you to do so. Instead, use the Change button and specify the disk or the service pack expanded file directory. After the drivers are installed, be sure to reboot.

If the vendor provides an installation routine, attempting to install the driver via the Display applet will often fail. Be sure all programs are closed before you launch the installation utility. Some of these tools simply automate the Display applet configuration, whereas others perform a system level installation with direct Registry changes. Either way, let the tool perform its work to completion unhindered, and then reboot.

If you are working with a Plug and Play video card designed for Windows 95 or 98, you may experience difficulties installing the driver on Windows NT. Sometimes, just trying the recommended installation process a second or third time resolves the problem. If not, you need to attempt the Plug and Play configuration solutions mentioned earlier to alter the resource settings in the BIOS. If the video drivers still fail to load, you'll need to contact the vendor for further instructions or try reinstalling Windows NT with the new hardware in place.

Video Driver Tools

Tools for working with video drivers are fairly scarce and are typically available only for a specific video card and driver pair. This means you need to check the vendor's Web site for utilities to enhance your video experience.

As for generic utilities, you can find screen savers, wallpaper images, movie players, and even video conferencing software just by looking at any of our favorite shareware and software sites:

- `http://www.bhs.com/`
- `http://www.32bit.com/`
- `http://www.shareware.com/`
- `http://www.slaughterhouse.com/`

Working with the Display

The Windows NT Display applet has four tabs in addition to the Settings tab: Background, Screen Saver, Appearance, and Plus! Use of these tabs is fairly straightforward, and you are probably already thoroughly familiar with them. If not, check the online Help, the *Microsoft Windows NT Workstation 4.0 Resource Kit*, or TechNet. However, you need to keep the following things in mind when working with the Display applet:

- A solid background color uses less video resources than a pattern, which uses less video resources than wallpaper. For systems with an older video card or low video memory (fewer than 2MB), try to stick with solid color backgrounds.

- Screen savers should be employed only on systems that do not perform tasks when in sleep mode. If your Windows NT system hosts Web pages or an FTP site, performs a backup, runs a defragmentation program, or even downloads files from the Internet automatically, avoid using graphic-intensive screen savers. The Open GL 3-D screen savers included with Windows NT can tax the CPU up to 90 percent, causing background tasks to effectively operate at roughly 1/20th their normal speed.

- The Plus! options all require more video resources and some CPU cycles to function. Use the visual settings sparingly on low-end systems.

- Unless required, try to stick to 256KB or 65KB colors instead of True Color (16.7 million) or greater color depth. The higher the color depth, the less resolution can be obtained and the more video resources are used. On video cards with 8MB of onboard RAM, this may not be much of a problem.

- When selecting refresh frequencies, always use the Test button to verify that your selections will function. You should also check the monitor's documentation to discover what frequencies are supported. On some monitors, using the wrong frequency can damage the electronics of the display.

- The List All Modes button on the Settings tab lists all of the combinations of resolution, color depth, and frequency supported by the video card and driver combo, but this does not mean they are supported by your monitor. Always check the monitor's documentation and test the settings before you accept them.

In case you make a change to the Display applet (whether to the video driver, color scheme, wallpaper, or whatever) and it results in an unintelligible display, there is a recovery method. You'll need to reboot by either resetting the power (not recommended) or using the keyboard to instruct the system to shutdown and restart. Two key sequences work for this:

- Ctrl+Esc, Up Arrow, Enter, Alt+R, Enter
- Ctrl+Alt+Delete, S, R, Enter

When the system starts to reboot, watch for the boot menu. Select the menu item labeled Windows NT Workstation Version 4.00 [VGA mode]. This boots the system using the default VGA compatible driver. You'll see a display of 640×480 resolution and 256 color depth. From the VGA mode boot, you can reset the video settings or install a new driver.

Audio Card Installation

Windows NT was not really designed with multimedia, specifically audio, in mind. Windows NT is a work-oriented network operating system that's not intended for desktop audio. However, it offers enough of a multimedia support structure that it is possible to get Windows NT to perform most multimedia and audio functions. The real trick is finding the right drivers and getting them installed.

We've had the most success with the Creative Labs line of Sound Blaster products under Windows NT. Other vendors' audio products can work under Windows NT, but we've learned to stick with what works rather than going out exploring. In any case, you should always visit the vendor's Web site for updated drivers and installation instructions.

Most audio cards are Plug and Play. Thus, you'll need to install the PLUG AND PLAYISA.SYS driver (described earlier in this chapter in the section "Windows NT and Plug and Play") before installing the drivers for the card. But, before you do this, be sure to have the audio card's extracted drivers on hand, because when the system reboots, it will detect the card and request drivers.

If your audio card is not detected automatically, you still have two options for installing the drivers. Some manufacturers provide an installation utility; if they do, get it and use it. Otherwise, you'll need to use the Multimedia applet's Devices tab (see Figure 4.6) to install the drivers. The Add button displays a list of the known supported media devices from August 1996. If you select one of these, be sure to provide the path to the extracted service pack files in the Install Driver dialog box. From the list of devices, you can select "Unlisted or Updated Driver" to use newly obtained drivers. Once again, be sure you've already extracted the files supplied by the manufacturer before starting the installation process.

Figure 4.6   The Devices tab of the Multimedia applet.

Storage Devices

Storage devices are a key component of a functioning operating system. They host not only the operating system itself, but all your data files. Understanding your storage system and its limitations is an important element in administration. The Disk Administrator is the primary tool by which storage devices are managed (see Chapter 2). Windows NT Explorer and My Computer offer some storage device management functions, but these focus on operations within existing parameters, such as formatting, working with directories, and moving, copying, and deleting files. In addition to these basic operations, you need to be familiar with several underlying issues to properly manage your storage subsystems.

The SCSI Adapters applet is the tool used to install drivers for storage device controller cards. You install both SCSI and ATI (IDE, UDMA, and EIDE) type controller cards through this applet. The Drivers tab offers an Add button that reveals a list of supported adapters. Drivers released since August 1996 can be installed via the Have Disk button.

In most cases, hard drives attached to a properly installed controller card will function without additional drivers (assuming that their jumpers are set properly). However, some specialty drives with advanced features (encryption, RAID, buffering, and so on) require drivers that can be installed only using a vendor-supplied installation utility. Other types of storage devices (CD-ROM drives, tape drives, optical drives, and other removable media drives) require drivers, and these can be installed only using a vendor-supplied installation utility.

Installing New Drives

Installing new drives can cause problems. For example, adding a new SCSI drive to an existing SCSI chain of drives can offset the ARC names of those drives. Windows NT counts drives in a SCSI chain in the order of their SCSI ID numbers (0 through 7 or 0 through 14, depending on the SCSI controller card) not their attached sequence. This means that adding a new SCSI drive with an ID between two existing drives will change the drive letters of existing drives. This can cause drive lettering changes. If the bumped drives host Windows NT system files, you'll need to modify the BOOT.INI file's Advanced RISC Computer (ARC) name to reflect the change. (The BOOT.INI file and ARC names are discussed in detail in Chapter 5.)

It is good practice to set the IDs of SCSI devices in sequential order without skipping any number, using the values starting with 0 and continuing through 6. The SCSI adapter itself is often set with an ID of 7 by default. Setting SCSI IDs in sequential order will prevent the domino effect from occurring when new drives are added. If you add an IDE drive to a system that uses only SCSI drives, the system might not boot. Computers in the x86 family almost always attempt to boot from IDE drives first and then from SCSI. If you need additional drive space on a SCSI system, stick with SCSI drives or you may be forced to completely reconfigure or reinstall the operating system.

Creating Partitions

When you install a new hard drive, you must partition it before data can be stored on it. Most often, you will use Disk Administrator to partition drives. Keep in mind that primary partitions take priority in automatic drive letter assignment over logical drives in extended partitions. When you install a new drive and decide to partition it, you may want to use an extended partition instead of a primary to reduce the drive letter shuffling. In any case, it is always best to assign the drive letters instead of letting Windows NT automatically deal out letters. After you assign a drive letter (even if this means assigning the letter that Windows NT already gave the partition by default), Windows NT will not change it if you create new partitions.

If you change the partitioning on an existing drive, especially on the drive hosting the boot and system partitions for Windows NT, you'll change the ARC path for that partition. Fortunately, Disk Administrator will warn you and instruct you exactly how to change the BOOT.INI file to correct for this. Be sure to follow the Disk Administrator's warning before you restart the system, or you will not be able to boot.

> #### Editing BOOT.INI
> Remember to open the BOOT.INI properties and deselect Read Only before attempting to edit the BOOT.INI file. We discuss the BOOT.INI file in detail in Chapter 5.

When you first configure your system to install Windows NT, create a boot partition (the partition where the main Windows NT system files will be stored) of at least 1GB. In our network environment, we've discovered that a boot partition of 512MB or less quickly results in lots of out of drive space errors. We also recommend moving the paging file to a different partition (preferably on a different physical drive—see Chapter 20) and moving the print spooler directory (discussed in Chapter 22). You can use FDISK (an MS-DOS application) or the Windows NT setup routine to create the partition for the system files. Note that FDISK is not able to create partitions greater than 2GB in size.

Support for New Interfaces

Windows NT 4.0 does not include support for IrDA (Infrared Data Association's IR communications standards), USB (Universal Serial Bus), or FireWire (IEEE 1394). If you purchase a computer that includes hardware with these technologies, either Windows NT will not recognize them and function normally, or it will misconfigure them and cause operating problems. Windows NT should be installed on systems that are made up of HCL-compatible components only.

If Windows NT attempts to install drivers for these unsupported technologies, you can try to disable them through the Devices or Services applet. But the best solution is to either remove the non-compatible technology device or move to a fully compliant system.

Support for IrSA, USB, and FireWire are slated for inclusion in Windows 2000 (previously known as Windows NT 5.0). Some vendors may release drivers for these technologies for Windows NT 4.0, but using them may remove you from Microsoft's support coverage. Be sure to check the use license and contact the vendor regarding support.

Windows NT for Laptops

If you want to install Windows NT on a laptop or notebook computer, you should contact the vendor of the notebook computer before attempting the installation. In some cases, successful installation requires special CMOS settings, drive configuration tools, or system drivers. The manuals included with the purchase of a notebook computer usually do not address these issues.

Windows NT on a laptop can present you with interesting difficulties. Windows NT does not support power management features found on most portable computers. You must turn off all power-saving features by editing the CMOS before you install Windows NT. This greatly reduces the length of time you can operate your laptop on battery power.

Windows NT does not support hot-swappable PCMCIA cards or PC cards. You must restart the system each time you want to switch cards. In fact, you should create a unique hardware profile for each PC card configuration. The PC Card applet cannot be used to switch PC cards; rather, it is used to inspect the drivers and settings of the cards that are currently present.

Multiple CPUs and Windows NT

Windows NT Workstation can support one or two CPUs right out of the box. Windows NT Server can support up to four CPUs right out of the box and includes support for up to 32 CPUs in special OEM versions.

If you upgrade your system from a single CPU to multiple CPUs, you must reinstall Windows NT. Actually, any modification in the number of CPUs in a system requires reinstallation. You must rebuild the HAL in order to accommodate the change in the number of CPUs.

A tool named UPTOMP.EXE on the *Microsoft Windows NT Workstation 4.0 Resource Kit* CD is used to upgrade an existing x86 installation from supporting a single CPU to multiple CPUs. However, it works only on systems that have not been upgraded with a service pack or hotfix. If you have applied any service packs or hotfixes to your system, you must reconfigure the system to support additional CPUs. A few Knowledge Base articles cover this process in detail. We recommend articles Q156358, Q124541, Q142660, and Q148245.

After you reconfigure your system to use multiple CPUs, Windows NT automatically balances the workload among them. Only in special Enterprise OEM editions of Windows NT do you have any control over what processes are distributed to a CPU.

Adding multiple CPUs to a single computer is not the only way to improve the computing power on a Windows NT system. A new technology called *clustering* can network multiple individual computers in such a way that they all can work on a single task.

The Microsoft Knowledge Base

The Microsoft Knowledge Base is just what the name implies: a repository of vast amounts of information about Microsoft products. Knowledge Base articles come from a variety of experts, and each article is classified by an index number that begins with the letter "Q." The Knowledge Base can be found on the TechNet CD-ROM as well as the Microsoft Web site at **http://www.microsoft.com/NTServer/ Support/searchkb/default.asp**.

Third-Party Hardware Utilities

There are only a few useful hardware utilities around. We've scoured the Internet to find these.

SmartLine Vision's DeviceLock is a tool you can use to add security to any device in the same manner you add security to drive shares. Now you can secure CD-ROMs, floppies, RAM drives, removable media disks, and serial and parallel ports. DeviceLock also includes a cache flush to force storage devices to clean out their buffers before the storage devices go offline. Also included is a remote control utility to manage DeviceLock from another Windows NT system or even from a Windows 95/98 client. You can find more information and a trial download at `http://www.protect-me.com/dl/`.

If you often find yourself unable to locate that key piece of information to configure a device, resolve a problem, or perform critical troubleshooting, you may want to check out SupportSource. This is a subscription service accessed from an easy-to-use Windows NT application interface. With a customizable layout, a powerful query engine, a Web-enabled interface, component-level diagrams, and detailed hardware specification documents, this service may help you out of a jam. For more information, a download trial, and subscription and purchase details, visit the SupportSource Web site at `http://www.supportsource.com/`.

System Internals has a nifty tool for recovering data from drives on non-bootable systems through a serial port; it's called NTRecover. We can't begin to explain how this works, but it is a great recovery tool if you can no longer boot a system that hosts critical data files. The damaged system is booted with a floppy that loads the NTRecover driver files, a serial cable is used to connect the damaged system with a functioning system, and the NTRecover host tool is launched on the functioning system. With a fully registered version, not only can you read data from the damaged system, but you can write to the drives and perform disk repair functions as well. For more information and to obtain a downloadable trial (limited to read-only access), visit the System Internals Web site at `http://www.sysinternals.com/`.

For More Information

If the information about Windows NT hardware issues presented in this chapter has increased your desire to learn more, here are a few resources you can research to obtain more knowledge.

- Parlante, John. *Windows NT Hardware Companion*. Macmillan, 1998. ISBN: 157870079.

- *Microsoft Windows NT Workstation 4.0 Resource Kit*. Microsoft Press, 1996. ISBN: 1572313439.

- Microsoft TechNet: `http://www.microsoft.com/technet/`

- For more information on Microsoft's inclusion of new hardware technologies in its operating systems, check the Driver and Hardware Development Web site at `http://www.microsoft.com/hwdev/`.
- For more information on Windows NT clustering, visit the Microsoft Cluster Server Web at `http://www.microsoft.com/ntserver/ntserverenterprise/exec/overview/Clustering.asp`.

If this chapter hasn't provided enough detail on the third-party utilities to satisfy you, try searching on your own at one of these software sites:

- `http://www.bhs.com/`
- `http://www.32bit.com/`
- `http://www.serverextras.com/`
- `http://www.tucows.com/`
- `http://www.slaughterhouse.com/`
- `http://www.shareware.com/`
- `http://filepile.com`
- `http://www.sunbelt-software.com`

Keywords of *hardware*, *driver*, *device*, or a specific type or name of device should help you locate additional utilities.

5

Booting Windows NT

AFTER WORKING WITH WINDOWS NT WORKSTATION (and Server, for that matter)
for a short period of time, you will realize that many of the failures and crashes you
encounter occur during the boot process. Although the boot process looks very simple
on the surface, it is actually quite complex. In this chapter, we describe the steps that
Windows NT takes from the time you initially turn on your computer to when you
are given the login prompt.

In addition, we examine some of the tools available to you (from both Microsoft
and third-party vendors) for the recovery of a failed Windows NT Workstation system,
including the Windows NT boot disk and the emergency repair disk.

System and Boot Partitions

When Windows NT was written, Microsoft made decisions that, to this day, we still
shake our heads and try to figure out. The distinction between the System and Boot
partitions is one of these decisions. Common sense tells us that the Boot partition
should contain the boot files, and the System partition should contain the system files.

Well, who needs common sense anyway? In the Windows NT world, the opposite is true. As a rule, boot files reside on the System partition, and system files are on the Boot partition. Just remember that it's opposite of common sense, and you'll do just fine.

To properly boot an OS (Windows NT included), you must have at least one system partition configured; this is also known as an active partition. There are two main ways to select and configure an active partition. The first is to use a DOS-based utility such as FDISK. The second is to use Windows NT's Disk Administrator. To use FDISK, follow these steps:

1. Boot your system using a bootable DOS disk that contains a copy of FDISK.EXE. The version of FDISK on that disk must be the same version of DOS as the COMMAND.COM on the boot floppy.

2. From the DOS prompt, type **FDISK**.

3. Enter the number of the partition you want to make active. The letter "A" appears in the Status column of that partition. The selected partition is now active.

4. Reboot the system to put these changes into effect.

To use Windows NT Disk Administrator, follow these steps:

1. Execute the Disk Administrator program by selecting Start, Programs, Administrative Tools (Common), Disk Administrator. Or go to Start, Run, and type **windisk**.

2. Select either a primary partition or a logical drive by clicking it, and then choose the Make Active option from the Partition menu. A dialog box appears, stating the following: **The requested partition has been marked active. When you reboot your computer the operating system on that partition will be started.**

Active Partition Bar

The active partition is marked with a small "x" in the left side of the colored bar above the partition or drive. By default, the bar is a dark blue color and will most likely hide the "x." However, you can change the color of this bar so it is easier to see.

A Recipe to Boot

Although the Windows NT boot process is lengthy and complex, it follows a very distinct and logical path. Knowing the steps that Windows NT takes during its initialization stages will assist you in troubleshooting exactly where the boot process might be failing.

The Windows NT boot process can be divided into nine parts:

1. Power On Self Test (POST)

2. Initializing the system

3. Booting the system

4. Choosing the operating system

5. Detecting the hardware

6. Choosing the boot configuration

7. Loading the kernel

8. Initializing the kernel

9. Logging into the system

Microsoft currently supports Windows NT Workstation on either the Intel x86 processor or the Compaq Alpha processor. Due to the differences between these two processor architectures, the steps Windows NT takes differ slightly for each platform. We will look at how the Intel platform boots. Before we can examine how Windows NT boots, we need to know the files involved in this process.

Intel and Windows NT

The Windows NT boot process uses several files. Some of these files exist in all circumstances, whereas others exist only if certain conditions are met. We will discuss the roles that these files play in the boot process in future sections. The following is a list of the most commonly used files:

- BOOT.INI
- NTLDR
- NTDETECT.COM
- BOOTSECT.DOS
- NTOSKRNL.EXE
- HAL.DLL
- NTBOOTDD.SYS
- Power On Self Test (POST)

One of the first tasks any Intel-based computer will perform is known as the Power On Self Test, or POST. POST is a set of tests that your computer executes to check up on itself. It would be impossible to cover all the tests that are performed because the available tests vary greatly depending on the BIOS version that is installed in the system. Some of the most common tests include checking the hard drives, the memory, the video card, and the keyboard.

Although most people assume that only computers run a POST, some adapter cards execute their own POSTs (based on the information stored in their BIOS). One of the most common types of adapter cards that perform this task is a SCSI card. In most cases, a SCSI card can run tests to check its configuration and to detect any devices that might be connected to the system. A SCSI card that can accomplish this task is known as a SCSI Adapter with the BIOS-enabled, which we'll explain in further detail later in this chapter.

When POST runs into a problem, it usually notifies you, the user, either by displaying an error message on the screen or by sounding a preset series of beeps (this is the most common method of notifying you of errors). The number, the length, and the sequence of beeps that sound depend on the BIOS itself. At first, it might seem kind of weird that the system would beep instead of displaying an error message, but when you think about it, it does make sense. How else would you know there is a problem with the video card if the system could not display the message on the screen (due to the problem with the video card)?

When the POST is finished, the system moves into the next phase of its startup process, initializing the system.

Initializing the System

The machine must now find a way to boot the operating system (OS). To accomplish this task, and because each OS boots differently, it must find information on how to pass control to the OS. If the startup detects a floppy disk in the drive, it will search the first sector of that disk for the Partition Boot Sector. If one is found, it will treat that floppy as a startup disk and pass control to it. If a floppy is detected in the drive but is determined to be a non-system disk, a message similar to the following will appear:

```
Non-System disk or disk error
Replace and press any key when ready
```

Beeping Errors

If your system is one that informs you of errors by sounding a sequence of beeps, you can "break" the code by checking out the FAQ at the *PC Guide* Web site. The *PC Guide*'s code page on troubleshooting BIOS beeps can be found at

http://www.pcguide.com/ts/x/sys/beep/index.htm.

In addition, be sure to review the documentation that came with your motherboard. It will contain the most useful information for your particular system. Also, check the Web site of your motherboard's manufacturer as additional information might be listed there.

If, however, the floppy disk is deemed to be a bootable disk, the Partition Boot Sector will be loaded into memory. The Partition Boot Sector contains information on how to pass control to the OS present on that disk. After this information is gathered, all control will be transferred to the OS.

If the system either detects a bootable floppy in the drive or does not detect a floppy disk at all, it checks the next device to see if it is bootable. With most systems, the next available device is a hard drive. The first area on a hard drive is known as the Master Boot Record (MBR).

If the system does not find an MBR on the hard drive, you will get the following message:

```
Missing operating system
```

If the system finds a Master Boot Record on the hard drive, it loads it into memory, processes it, and passes control to the OS as outlined in that MBR. The BIOS now steps into the background and is not used again.

Booting the System

At this point, the operating system boot process has begun. Control is now passed to a Windows NT file known as NTLDR. This files and displays the Boot menu, detects the hardware, and initializes any adapters that might be used to boot the system.

As soon as the screen that says `OS Loader V4.01` appears, NTLDR has executed. The version number that appears on the screen is dependent on the version of Windows NT that is installed. In this example, the version number is 4.01 for Windows NT 4.0. In contrast, the version number for Windows 2000 (formerly known as Windows NT 5.0) is 5.0.

NTLDR then detects the file system with which the hard drive is formatted (FAT or NTFS) and loads the appropriate driver so it can continue to read information off the hard drive. Next, it loads the BOOT.INI file into memory, processes it, and then displays the Windows NT Boot menu. (See the sidebar titled "Choosing the Operating System" later in this chapter.)

If you select a non-Windows NT or a previously installed OS, NTLDR will find the BOOTSECT.DOS file. This file contains the Master Boot Record as it existed before being replaced with the Windows NT version of the MBR. NTLDR loads this file, executes it as if the MBR is being read, and passes control to it. At this point, Windows NT is out of the picture and has no say in how the OS is booted.

Detection Order of Bootable Devices

With the advent of bootable CD-ROMs, ZIP disks, and other forms of media, BIOS manufacturers have changed the way the BIOS detects bootable devices. You can select the order in which the system will attempt to detect bootable devices on most new computers. Because of this, the previously described boot order may not occur on your system. Due to the large number of combinations and boot device orders, we won't cover each of the bootable devices.

If you select a Windows NT installation, NTLDR locates and executes the NTDETECT.COM file. This file detects and gathers information about the hardware installed in your system. When you see the message *ntdetect v4.0*, you know that NTLDR has executed the NTDETECT.COM program.

After NTDETECT.COM successfully detects and gathers information about your system's hardware configuration, you are given the option of placing Windows NT startup into what is known as the Hardware Profile/Last Known Good menu. As you may already know, Windows NT has the ability to boot into several different hardware configurations. You will find this feature handy if you are running a notebook that has a docking station. When the notebook is "docked," Windows NT has access to several hardware components that are not available when the notebook is "undocked," such as SCSI controllers, high-speed networking devices, and directly connected printers. Use this menu option to select the preferred configuration.

The Last Known Good (LKG) menu is a great recovery feature that is built into Windows NT. Whenever you make a configuration change to Windows NT that requires you to reboot (such as changing the video driver), Windows will not only modify the current Registry, but it will back up the old one. When you reboot the system, if the configuration is wrong and causes Windows NT to display a STOP error (also know as the "Blue Screen Of Death"), or if it is loaded into an unusable state (in which it is unable to see anything on the screen, for example), you can simply recover the old configuration by using the LKG feature. However, if you are able to boot the machine but the configuration change creates problems, you cannot use the LKG feature, because it is rewritten upon each successful boot. When the `Press The Spacebar NOW To Invoke Hardware Profile/Last Known Good Menu` message appears, simply press the spacebar to enter the Hardware Profile/Last Known Good menu. This option is displayed for only about five seconds before Windows NT continues with its initialization.

The final task NTLDR performs is loading the Windows NT Kernel (NTOSKRNL.EXE) and its execution. After executing the Kernel, NTLDR passes all the information it received from NTDETECT.COM, passes all control to the Kernel, and terminates.

Understanding the BOOT.INI File

An important part of booting and troubleshooting Windows NT is understanding how the BOOT.INI file works. When you fully understand how NTLDR uses the information stored within the BOOT.INI file, you will be well on your way to troubleshooting most Windows NT boot problems.

Choosing the Operating System

In the previous section, we mentioned that NTLDR displays a boot menu that allows you to choose the OS the system should boot. One of the items on the boot menu will always be highlighted. This is the default operating system. Also, notice there is a countdown timer at the bottom of the menu (on the right side). When the timer reaches zero, it automatically boots the default OS. This feature allows Windows NT to automatically reboot itself without having a user present.

When you install Windows NT, the setup program automatically creates a `BOOT.INI` file and stores it in the root folder of the startup disk. If you run the Windows NT installation program after Windows NT is installed and you choose to install another copy of Windows NT, the setup program appends the BOOT.INI file that already exists and makes the latest installation the default boot option. When you boot Windows NT, NTLDR uses the information stored in the BOOT.INI to display and execute the boot loader menu.

Assuming that a single copy of Windows NT Workstation is installed over an existing Windows 95 installation, a default BOOT.INI file might look like this:

```
[boot loader]
timeout=30
default=multi(0)disk(0)rdisk(0)partition(1)\WINNT
[operating systems]
multi(0)disk(0)rdisk(0)partition(1)\WINNT="Windows NT Workstation Version 4.0"
multi(0)disk(0)rdisk(0)partition(1)\WINNT="Windows NT Workstation Version 4.0
➥[VGA mode]" /basevideo /sos
C:\="Windows 95"
```

The `BOOT.INI` file can be broken down into two separate, yet very important, sections:

- The [operating systems] section
- The [boot loader] section

Two variables are set in the boot loader section of the BOOT.INI file. The first, time-out=, is the amount of time (measured in seconds) that the user has to select an OS before NTLDR automatically starts the default OS. The default value for the timeout variable is 30 seconds. If you set the value to zero, NTLDR will automatically start the default OS without showing the boot loader menu.

If you set the timeout value to minus one (–1), NTLDR will display the boot menu without counting down the time. In other words, it will wait indefinitely for you to make a selection. This can also be achieved by pressing any key except Enter while the boot menu is displayed and counting down.

The second variable, default=, defines which OS is booted by default. The default variable is simply a link to the [operating systems] menu and gets its boot information from there.

The [operating systems] Section

This section of the BOOT.INI file contains a list of operating systems that are available to boot. Each entry contains the path to where NTLDR can find the OS system files, the string to display in the boot loader menu, and an optional switch that controls how Windows NT boots up.

This section allows you to define multiple operating systems, as well as the options for booting the same OS with different switches enabled. The path for each OS is defined using the industry standard Advanced RISC Computing (ARC) naming convention. ARC naming enables you to define the location of the OS files regardless of the type of controller, the physical hard drive, or the partition. It is written according to the following formula:

```
Controller(w)drive(x)drive(y)partition(z)\%systemroot%
```

Two different ARC statements can be used in the BOOT.INI file:

- `Multi(w)disk(x)rdisk(y)partition(z)\%systemroot%`

- `Scsi(w)disk(x)rdisk(y)partition(z)\%systemroot%`

The `multi` option can be used for either IDE controllers or SCSI controllers that have the BIOS enabled (meaning that they can detect and mount the SCSI drives). The `SCSI` option is used for SCSI controllers that have the BIOS disabled. This option requires the NTBOOTDD.SYS file (the SCSI controller driver) to load the SCSI controller so NTLDR can access the drives. The value of the variable w is the number of the controller installed in the system (in the case where there are multiple controllers). The first controller is given a value of 0, the second a value of 1, and so on.

The `disk` variable is used to define which hard drive is to be accessed on a SCSI controller with the BIOS disabled. As with the controllers, the first drive on the controller is given a value of 0, the second a value of 1, and so on. The `SCSI` and `disk` variables work together to define the controller and the hard drive where the OS files reside. If `multi` is used, disk will always be 0.

The `rdisk` variable is used to define which hard drive is to be accessed on either an IDE controller or a SCSI controller with the BIOS enabled. Again, the first drive on the controller is assigned a value of 0, the second a value of 1, and so on. The `multi` and `rdisk` variables work together to define which controller and drive are used to store the OS files. If `SCSI` is used, RDISK will always be 0.

Next, the `partition` variable is used to define which partition on the hard drive stores the OS files. Unlike the other variables in the ARC naming convention, the first partition on the hard drive is given a value of 1, the second a value of 2, and so on.

Finally, the `%systemroot%` variable defines the folder in which the OS files are stored. The default, when you install Windows NT, is the WINNT folder.

For example, assumeing that you have a system with two IDE controllers, with three hard drives on each controller and two partitions on each hard drive. Assume also that the Windows NT system files are located in the \WINNT folder on the second partition, which is on the third hard drive that is connected to the first controller. The ARC statement as it would appear in the BOOT.INI file would be as follows:

`Multi(0)disk(0)rdisk(2)partition(2)\WINNT`

The information that appears in the quotes at the end of the ARC statement is what will appear as the menu entry for this statement. Finally, you can add one or more switches. When you install Windows NT, the Windows NT setup program creates two different boot entries. The first simply boots Windows NT normally; the second boots it with the `/sos` and `/basevideo` switches. Definitions of the BOOT.INI switches are given in the next section.

The BOOT.INI Switches

As has already been stated, several switches can be added to the end of Windows NT ARC statements in the [operating systems] section of the BOOT.INI files. They are not case sensitive and are listed in Table 5.1.

Table 5.1   **The BOOT.INI Switches**

BOOT.INI Switch	Description
/BASEVIDEO	This switch boots Windows NT using a standard VGA video driver. This driver is compatible with every VGA video card. Use this switch if you have installed a new video driver and Windows NT will not boot properly. You will then be able to change the video driver to one that will work. This switch is used in conjunction with the **/SOS** switch in the default ARC statement in the BOOT.INI file.
/BAUDRATE=**XXXX**	This switch allows you to select the baud rate to use when debugging the system. If you do not select a value, the value of 9600 will be used by default when a modem is installed. This switch automatically enables the /DEBUG switch.
/CRASHDEBUG	When you enable this switch, it loads the Windows NT debugger. Unless a Kernel error occurs, however, the debugger is inactive. The Windows NT debugger is useful if your system is experiencing Kernel errors.
/DEBUG	This switch enables the debugger when Windows NT is loaded. /DEBUG allows you to start the debugger using a host debugger that is connected to the computer. Use this switch if your errors are easily reproducible.
/DEBUGPORT=com**X**	This switch designates the serial port to be used for communication with the host debugger. Like the /BAUDRATE switch, this switch starts the /DEBUG switch automatically.
/MAXMEM:**X**	The /MAXMEM switch allows you to limit the amount of memory Window NT can use.
/NODEBUG	This switch tells the system not to use the debug information.
/NOSERIALMICE=[COM **X** | COM**X,Y,Z**...]	This switch turns off automatic detection of the serial mouse on the ports specified. This is very useful if you have an uninterruptible power supply (UPS) connected to your system. Many UPSs will be disabled when Windows NT attempts to detect a mouse on the port upon which they are communicating.

continues

Table 5.1 **Continued**

BOOT.INI Switch	Description
/numproc=	This switch allows you to specify how many processors in a multi-processor machine are to be used.
/SOS	This switch displays device driver names and locations as it is loaded. Use this switch if you suspect that a device driver is corrupt or missing. This switch is used in conjunction with the /BASEVIDEO switch in the default ARC statement in the BOOT.INI file.

Detecting the Hardware

NTLDR calls NTDETECT.COM, which detects your video card, keyboard, mouse, drive controllers, CPU, and communication ports.

Kernel Loading

After the hardware has been successfully detected and the Hardware Profile/Last Known Good menu has been completed, the system loads the Windows NT Kernel. During this phase, you will see several periods ("dots") on the third line. Each period represents a service that is being loaded, the most important being the Windows NT Kernel (NTOSKRNL.EXE) and the Hardware Abstraction Layer (HAL.DLL). Although the system loads these two key services, they are not actually executed until the next phase of the boot process.

Next, the system checks the Registry and determines which services need to be started for the system to complete its boot process. Then, the services are executed.

Kernel Initialization

When all the services have been loaded into memory, it is time to initialize the Kernel. You can tell that the Kernel has been initialized when the boot screen switches from a black background (as it was up to this point) to a blue background. This background color change is the first task the Kernel performs. Do not confuse this blue screen with the infamous Blue Screen of Death (BSOD). Luckily, the two are completely different.

Any services that were not initialized during the Kernel loading phase will then be started. Four services that must be executed for Windows NT to complete the startup process:

- BootExecute Data Item
- Memory Management key
- DOS Devices key
- Subsystems key

Logging In to the System

The last phase of the boot process initializes the logon subsystem (WinLogon) and passes control to it. Windows NT will displays the initial logon screen. It is important to note that, although you can now begin the logon process, Windows NT may not be completely initialized. It has initialized only the components that must be in place for the logon to take place. Any non-dependent services, such as Peer Web Services, will be executed after the logon dialog box appears.

Building Boot Disks and ERDs

This section details how to create and use both boot disks and the emergency repair disk (ERD). A boot disk allows you to boot a machine into MS-DOS to run diagnostic software to determine why Windows NT won't boot. The ERD, on the other hand, allows you to fix problems with the Registry if the LKG menu cannot be used.

Building Boot Disks

Because of the overhead needed to boot Windows NT, there is no way to boot a copy of Windows NT using floppy disks. It would just require too many disks. If you recall, when you installed Windows NT, it took three floppy disks just to get to the point where you could begin to install Windows NT. After that, the setup program copied enough files off the CD-ROM so that you could reboot the system and continue with a Windows NT-based installation. There is, however, a way to start a machine that has corrupted or missing boot files. The Windows NT boot disk provides enough information to start a computer and point it at the existing Windows NT installation. It is not uncommon for a small configuration change made to your Windows NT environment, such as changing the partitions on a hard drive, to make your Windows NT system unbootable using the regular boot method. Luckily, there is a way that you can boot Windows NT from a floppy disk. This disk is known as the Windows NT boot disk.

Windows NT can also fail to boot if a file is missing or becomes corrupt on the system partition. A boot disk can be used in this situation as well.

Boot Disk Requirements

A couple of requirements must be met for a boot disk to be created successfully. The first and most important is how the floppy disk is formatted. Second, several files must be copied to the floppy disk to make it usable.

One thing you must remember when creating a Windows NT boot disk is that it *must* be formatted in Windows NT. A disk formatted in DOS, Windows 3.x, or Windows 9x will not work. This is because of the Partition Boot Sector. Remember that it is the Partition Boot Sector that finds the OS and passes control to it. A DOS, Windows 3.x, or Windows 9x boot disk will look for the files used by these operating systems to boot. When you format a floppy disk in Windows NT, it modifies the Partition Boot Sector so that it looks for NTLDR and passes control to it if it is found.

The second requirement has to do with files being copied to the boot disk. Which files are required depends on the configuration of the system (SCSI controllers, old OS, and so on). The required files for an x86-based system are listed here:

- NTLDR
- NTDETECT.COM
- BOOT.INI
- BOOTSECT.DOS (if you are booting a previously installed OS)
- NTBOOTDD.SYS (if you have a SCSI controller with the BIOS disabled in your system)

Creating the Boot Disk

Creating the boot disk is quite easy. Remember, all it does is replace the boot process as described in the beginning of this chapter. It does not place the Windows OS on the floppy. To create the boot floppy, you need to simply format the floppy disk using an existing Windows NT system. Copy the following files from the existing Windows NT installation to the newly formatted floppy disk:

- **NTLDR.**
- **NTDETECT.COM.**
- **BOOT.INI.** This file will have to be edited so it looks for the Windows NT Boot partition in the right location.
- **BOOTSECT.DOS.** You'll need this file if a previous OS was installed. The only pitfall is that the BOOTSECT.DOS that is created on a Windows 3.x system is not the same as one that is created on a Windows 9x system.
- **NTBOOTDD.SYS.** Although it's rare, if your system has a SCSI adapter with the BIOS disabled, you will need this file. It is the driver for the SCSI card and is specific to the SCSI card you have installed in the system. NTBOOTDD.SYS is actually the SCSI driver copied and renamed.

NT Boot Disk

Remember, for this disk to be of any use to you, you must already have Windows NT installed and configured. This is not a replacement to Windows NT. That is to say, this disk has just enough "smarts" to look for the Windows NT installation and pass control to the Windows NT Kernel.

Building Emergency Repair Disks

For fault tolerance, Microsoft has provided a way to store some of the information of a Windows NT installation that is crucial to the operation of the system. You can then use this information to restore some of the Registry settings prior to a Windows NT failure, including the Security Accounts Manager (SAM) database, security information, disk configuration information, software Registry entries, and other important system information. This information is stored on a disk called the Emergency Repair Disk (ERD). Table 5.2 lists the files stored on the ERD and their roles.

Table 5.2 **Files on the Emergency Repair Disk**

File	Description
SETUP.LOG	An information file created during the setup process that is used to verify that the files are installed on the system during the setup process. By default, this file is set with the Read-only, Hidden, and System attributes.
SYSTEM._	A copy of the SYSTEM hive from the Registry.
SAM._	A copy of the SAM from the Registry.
SECURITY._	A copy of the SECURITY hive from the Registry.
SOFTWARE._	A copy of the SOFTWARE hive from the Registry.
DEFAULT._	A copy of the DEFAULT hive from the Registry.
CONFIG.NT	A copy of the Windows NT version of the DOS CONFIG.SYS file. This file is used when running the Windows NT Virtual DOS Machine (NTVDM).
AUTOEXEC.NT	A copy of the Windows NT version of the DOS AUTOEXEC.BAT file. This file is used when running the Windows NT Virtual DOS Machine (NTVDM).
NTUSER.DA_	A copy of the default user profile. The original copy of this file is stored in the %systemroot%\profiles\default user\ntuser.dat.

The RDISK.EXE stores repair information in the %systemroot%\system32\repair folder that can be used to create the ERD using the Repair Disk utility (RDISK.EXE). The Repair Disk utility screen, shown in Figure 5.1, has two options:

- Update Repair Info
- Create Repair Disk

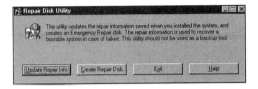

Figure 5.1   The Repair Disk utility.

Update Repair Info

It is a common misconception that the information stored in the %systemroot%\system32\repair folder is updated automatically. In truth, it is not, and you have to update it manually. You do so by using the Update Repair Info option in the Repair Disk utility.

After the information in the Repair folder is updated, the Repair Disk utility prompts you to decide if you want to create an ERD. If you choose to create the ERD, the utility will format the floppy disk and copy the necessary files to it.

Create Repair Disk

The Create Repair Disk option formats a floppy disk and copies the information from the Repair folder to the floppy disk. This option does not update the Repair folder with new information. What this means is that, if you have not updated the Repair information for a while and then you create an ERD, it will not have the most up-to-date information and may not recover the Windows NT installation properly.

Underscore in Filenames
The underscore (_) in the extension of the file denotes that the file is compressed. You can uncompress this file using the **EXPAND** command, which can be found in the \i386 directory on the Windows NT CD-ROM.

Remember When Changing Your System...
Remember to update your repair information and create a new ERD before and after every change you make to your system, including adding new applications, new users or groups, new hardware, and new drivers or making changes to the drives installed on your system. In addition, always date your ERD so you know whether it is the most recent version.

Multi-Boot Systems, the Microsoft Way

If you have Windows NT installed on your system, you know what the Microsoft multi-boot system looks like. We will now look at its strengths and limitations.

Simply stated, the Microsoft multi-boot system is written so that it works with Microsoft operating systems. This is both a strength and a weakness.

Its strength comes from its simplicity. To modify the boot menu, you can simply edit a text file in the root folder of the system partition. The next time you boot the system, the changes appear. In addition, because the multi-boot system is fully supported by Microsoft, literally hundreds of TechNet and Knowledge Base documents are available from Microsoft on the subject.

You have to remember that the Microsoft multi-boot system is very simple; this limitation is its weakness. It cannot handle more than one "non-Windows NT" OS (not directly from the boot menu, anyway). It is limited to only 10 entries on the boot menu. For example, create a Windows NT boot disk and modify the BOOT.INI file so that it has the following information:

```
[boot loader]
timeout=10
default=multi(0)disk(0)rdisk(0)partition(1)\WINNT
[operating systems]
multi(0)disk(0)rdisk(0)partition(1)\WINNT="Windows Installation # 1"
multi(0)disk(0)rdisk(0)partition(1)\WINNT="Windows Installation # 2"
multi(0)disk(0)rdisk(0)partition(1)\WINNT="Windows Installation # 3"
multi(0)disk(0)rdisk(0)partition(1)\WINNT="Windows Installation # 4"
multi(0)disk(0)rdisk(0)partition(1)\WINNT="Windows Installation # 5"
multi(0)disk(0)rdisk(0)partition(1)\WINNT="Windows Installation # 6"
multi(0)disk(0)rdisk(0)partition(1)\WINNT="Windows Installation # 7"
multi(0)disk(0)rdisk(0)partition(1)\WINNT="Windows Installation # 8"
multi(0)disk(0)rdisk(0)partition(1)\WINNT="Windows Installation # 9"
multi(0)disk(0)rdisk(0)partition(1)\WINNT="Windows Installation # 10"
multi(0)disk(0)rdisk(0)partition(1)\WINNT="Windows Installation # 11"
multi(0)disk(0)rdisk(0)partition(1)\WINNT="Windows Installation # 12"
multi(0)disk(0)rdisk(0)partition(1)\WINNT="Windows Installation # 13"
multi(0)disk(0)rdisk(0)partition(1)\WINNT="Windows Installation # 14"
multi(0)disk(0)rdisk(0)partition(1)\WINNT="Windows Installation # 15"
```

Now, boot your system using the Windows NT boot disk. Notice that it displays only the first 10 entries in the menu. Most users will never reach the 10-entry limit in the BOOT.INI file, but it is important to note it anyway.

Multi-Boot Systems, Other Ways

There are several third-party multi-boot systems out there. Many simply improve on the Microsoft version. The main player in the multi-boot market is BootMagic. BootMagic is a product that ships with PowerQuest's PartitionMagic and allows you to easily change between operating systems, regardless of the type of volume upon which it is located, the OS, or the type of hard drive. PartitionMagic can be purchased online directly from PowerQuest's Web page at **http://www.powerquest.com**.

Troubleshooting Boot Problems

Some of the most common error messages you might see when booting Windows NT are presented in this section. They usually appear when files are either missing or corrupt. Possible solutions for these problems will be suggested in the following sections.

NTLDR Boot Errors

A common error with the NTLDR file is this:

```
BOOT:  Couldn't find NTLDR.
Please insert another Disk.
```

If the NTLDR file is missing, you will see this error message. The message will appear before the boot loader menu is displayed because it is the role of NTLDR to display the menu. Simply replace the file using the emergency repair process.

NTDETECT.COM Boot Errors

A common error with the NTDETECT.COM file is this:

```
NTDETECT V4.01 Checking Hardware...
NTDETECT failed
```

Or you may get the following error message:

```
Error Opening NTDETECT
Press any key to continue
```

These errors usually mean that the NTDETECT.COM file is either missing or corrupt and must be replaced using the emergency recovery process. Another possible cause of these error messages is an incorrect ARC path in the BOOT.INI file.

NTOSKRNL.EXE Boot Errors

A common error with the NTOSKRNL.EXE file is this:

```
Windows NT could not start because the following file is missing or corrupt:
\winnt\system32\NTOSKRNL.EXE
Please reinstall a copy of the above file.
```

The Windows NT Kernel file is either missing or is corrupt. The best way to recover this file is to run the Windows NT emergency repair process.

BOOTSECT.DOS Boot Errors

A common error with the BOOTSECT.DOS file is this:

```
I/O Error accessing boot sector file
Multi(0)disk(0)rdisk(0)partition(1)\\bootss
```

You may also get the following error message:

```
Couldn't open boot sector file
Multi(0)disk(0)rdisk(0)partition(1)\BOOTSECT.DOS
```

These two error messages usually mean that the BOOTSECT.DOS file is either missing or corrupt. Use the emergency repair process to reinstall the files.

BOOT.INI Errors

One of the most common errors in the BOOT.INI files is an incorrect ARC statement. If the statement is incorrect, or if NTLDR cannot find the partition and folder defined in the ARC statement, you may see an error message similar to the following:

```
OS Loader V4.01
The system did not load because of a computer disk hardware configuration problem.
Could not read from the selected boot disk. Check the boot path and disk hardware.
Please check the Windows NT documentation about hardware disk configuration and
your hardware reference manuals for additional information. Boot failed.
```

The Emergency Repair Process

Should your Windows NT installation become corrupt, you will need the information stored either in the \repair folder or on the ERD you created. If the system is corrupt and you cannot repair it using the Emergency Repair Disk, you can try some of the third-party tools or reinstall Windows NT.

To restore Windows NT on an x86-based system using the ERD, follow these steps:

1. Boot Windows NT using the three setup floppy disks or the CD-ROM, or by running the WINNT.EXE program.

2. The Windows NT Setup screen appears, asking you if you would like to install Windows NT or repair a Windows NT installation. Press the R key to choose the repair option.

3. You will be asked what tasks you would like the setup program to complete. The tasks include inspection of the Registry files and the startup environment, verification of the Windows NT system files, and inspection of the boot sector. Choose the tasks you want performed (using the arrow keys to navigate and the Enter key to select or deselect). When you are ready to continue, press the Enter key when the Continue (Perform Selected Tasks) option is highlighted.

4. Press the Enter key to allow the Windows NT Setup program to find the floppy and hard disk controllers.

5. The Setup program asks if you have the ERD available. If you do have the ERD, press the Enter key. You will then be prompted to insert the ERD into the floppy drive. If you do not have the ERD, press the Esc key, and the Setup program will attempt to detect the Windows NT installations that are on the hard drives. It then prompts you to select which Windows NT installation to repair.

Copying Missing or Corrupt Files

It is not recommended that you simply copy the missing or corrupt files from another system running Windows NT. This is because many of the Windows NT Service Packs replace these files with updated versions. Some of the files will not work properly if they do not match the rest of the files in the system. For example, a copy of the NTOSKRNL.EXE file from a system running Windows NT Service Pack 4 may not be compatible in a Windows NT system running Service Pack 3.

6. Follow the instructions presented to you, inserting the ERD (if one is available) when requested.

7. When the emergency repair process is complete, remove the ERD and press Ctrl+Alt+Delete to reboot the system.

Third-Party Troubleshooting Tools

Sometimes, you will need to simply boot enough of Windows NT to allow you to rename or replace files in your installation. Although the emergency repair process will solve many of these problems, it will not help in some cases. For example, many Microsoft TechNet documents tell you to delete a file or a combination of files to clear the user database or reset security. The ERD process may not always allow you to complete these tasks. When a situation such as this occurs, Microsoft suggests that you install a new copy of Windows NT and use it to repair the damaged installation. This can be a tedious and time-consuming process.

Luckily, some third-party tools are available that both speed up and simplify this process. Two of these applications are available on the CD-ROM that accompanies this book (in their read-only versions). These two applications are NTFSDOS and ERD Commander.

NTFSDOS

NTFSDOS is a great utility that allows you to boot from a regular MS-DOS, Windows 3.x, or Windows 9x boot disk and mount NTFS volumes so that they are available to you. The NTFS volumes appear the same as the FAT volumes and allow you to view, navigate, and execute files and applications stored on these volumes.

The version that is available on the CD-ROM is the read-only version of the program. The fully functional program, called NTFSDOS Tools, gives you some limited write capabilities. It adds two commands to the read-only version of NTFSDOS, NTFSCopy, and NTFSRen.

NTFSCopy allows you to copy files to an NTFS volume as long as the following conditions are met:

- The destination file must exist for the copy to take place.
- The source and destination files must be the same size.

The NTFSRen utility allows you to "delete" a file by renaming it. This powerful feature does come with a price:

- The user cannot choose the new name of the file. The program changes the last character in the name of the file.
- The new filename cannot already exist in the directory.

Both of these small, yet extremely powerful, utilities can easily save you hours of repairing and installing Windows NT to fix a BSOD or a corrupted system file.

ERD Commander

If you have ever attempted to recover an MS-DOS or Windows system, you know that you can easily create a boot disk that allows you to access the information stored on your hard drives and to repair any necessary files or configurations. Unfortunately, Microsoft has not given us this option with Windows NT. ERD Commander provides Windows NT boot disk functionality.

It's important to note here that only disks formatted with NTFS have this problem. If you have Windows NT installed on a FAT partition, you can simply boot with a DOS/WIN95 boot disk and make a repair.

ERD Commander either takes an existing copy of the Windows NT Setup disks or creates a new set using the Windows NT Setup program, and then modifies them so that the three disks can be used to boot Windows NT. When you use the ERD Commander-modified Setup floppy disks, you will be given a command prompt similar to the one you might be familiar with from MS-DOS.

The upgraded version of ERD Commander comes in two flavors: the full function ERD Commander and the more powerful ERD Commander Professional. The ERD Commander not only gives you the ability to read information on all the Windows NT volumes, it also allows you to copy, rename, delete, move, and xcopy files on the volumes. ERD Commander Professional adds to the functionality and gives you the following features:

- Fault tolerance support for stripe set.

- The ability to replace lost Administrator passwords.

- The ability to run CHKDSK to repair corrupt drives.

- Built-in support for FAT32 volumes, meaning that you will be able to access volumes created by Windows 98.

- Built-in support for the Expand command so that you can uncompress files from the Windows NT setup CD-ROM.

- The ability to control device and service startup options in the Registry.

Obtaining Programs

The read-only versions of the programs are written by Systems Internals and are available on the CD-ROM that accompanies this book or from their Web page at `http://www.sysinternals.com`. The fully functional versions of the programs are available (with full support) from Winternals Software at `http://www.winternals.com`.

For More Information

For more information about the boot process for Windows NT, please consult the following references:

- TechNet (the technical subscription service from Microsoft): `http://technet.microsoft.com/`
- Microsoft Knowledge Base: `http://support.microsoft.com/`

6

Windows NT Control Panel Utilities

I N MICROSOFT WINDOWS NT WORKSTATION, a multitude of Control Panel applets
are installed by default. An untold number of applications and devices install their own
Control Panel applets to simplify management and configuration tasks specific to those
devices or applications. Many of the built-in applets are so straightforward that they do
not warrant coverage in this chapter. These applets include Fonts, Keyboard, Ports,
and Printers. This chapter reviews those Control Panel applets that need additional
documentation.

The History of the Registry

Although we will discuss the Windows NT Registry in great detail in Chapter 7,
"Introducing the Windows NT Registry," we provide a definition of the Registry here
so that you understand what the Control Panel applets are and how to use them. The
Registry is one of the most powerful features of Windows NT. In fact, the Registry
replaces the different .INI (initialization) files, as well as CONFIG.SYS,
AUTOEXEC.BAT, WIN.INI, SYSTEM.INI and several other configuration files used
by different versions of Windows. Remember that Microsoft Windows 95 and
Microsoft Windows 98 also contain a Registry, but those versions are not compatible
with the one found in Windows NT.

Anyone who has used Microsoft Windows 3.x will remember that, anytime you installed a new application, it would modify two internal initialization files, namely WIN.INI and SYSTEM.INI, to add functionality to Windows. Usually, it would also add its own .INI file that was used specifically by the application. There were three major problems with this approach. First, there was no real "standard" as to how to name these files or the structure of the files. Second, these files could exist anywhere on the hard drive. They were not limited to the default Windows installation directory (Winroot). This second item made it difficult at times to track down the correct file and to make modifications to it. Third, the .INI files are flat, whereas the Registry can contain subfolders.

The Windows NT Registry ended all that. Although more complex than the .INI files, it provided a standard way to make modifications to Windows NT systems. The main problem with the Registry is its complexity. Novice and intermediate users are warned to keep away from the Registry; one wrong move and a reinstallation of Windows NT and all your applications and settings is required. To simplify configuration issues, Microsoft created several Control Panel applets.

Looking back at Windows 3.x, you will notice that it too had Control Panel applets. The main difference between Windows 3.x and Windows NT Control Panel applets is that the former communicates with the .INI files and the latter communicates with the Registry. In essence, the Windows NT Control Panel applets are utilities that allow us to make modification to a very specific part of the Registry, without effecting any other components.

A Safer Way to Edit the Registry

For simplicity, in this chapter, we look at the Control Panel applets in alphabetical order. You may find that some of the Control Panel applets we discuss do not exist in your current installation. Some of these applets are added when you install applications or components to Windows NT. When this is the case, the application or component will be mentioned, and the process of adding it will be covered.

The Control Panel Applets

You can access the Control Panel applets within Windows NT in several ways, as illustrated in the next paragraph. One method of accessing the Control Panel applets is not any simpler or better than another, its it is really just a matter of preference.

You can access the Control Panel applets by doing any of the following:

- Click the Start button, select Settings, and choose Control Panel.
- Double-click My Computer, and then double-click Control Panel.
- Start Windows NT Explorer and click Control Panel in the left pane.

- From the Start menu, select Run or a command prompt, and then type **CONTROL**. You can specify an applet by passing it with CONTROL. For instance, to launch the Add New Programs applet, you would type **CONTROL APPWIZ.CPL**.

- Drag and drop the applet onto the desktop and double-click it.

Add/Remove Programs Applet

The Add/Remove Programs applet has two major components. It allows you to install and remove applications from your system, as well as to add and remove Windows NT components.

Installing and Uninstalling Programs

Figure 6.1 illustrates the installation and removal of applications. One of the problems with installing applications in previous versions of Windows was that when you attempted to remove the application, several program and initialization files were left behind. This would cause Windows to load unnecessary drivers and information, slowing system performance.

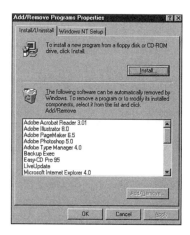

Figure 6.1   The Install/Uninstall component of the Add/Remove Programs applet.

In Windows 3.x, an application named Uninstaller was available to combat this problem. In essence, this application watched the installation process and kept track of what files were installed on the system and where they were placed. When you uninstalled an application, Uninstaller would backtrack and remove any files that were installed during the installation process that were no longer needed.

With Windows 95, Microsoft added this functionality as a Control Panel applet. Applications written to the Microsoft Windows 95/98 or Windows NT logo specification automatically appear in the *installed software* windows. Applications that are not written to Microsoft specifications can be installed by clicking the Install button.

When you click the Install button, a wizard runs that searches for a SETUP.EXE file on either the floppy drive or a CD-ROM drive. If the file is located, it is launched automatically, and the applet "watches" the installation process, noting all files that are added and Registry entries that are added or modified. If the file cannot be located, you will be prompted to browse for the setup application. When this file is located, the setup commences and is monitored by the applet. As stated previously, many of today's applications automatically add their entries into the program list window. If an application is listed in that window, you can simply click the Add/Remove button to run its setup program.

One of the issues you may run into when attempting to remove an application is that the setup files have been deleted or that the application itself has been erased. Windows NT will not dynamically change the Add/Remove list when an application is deleted manually. If you delete several applications manually, you will notice that there are several applications listed that cannot be removed. It's possible to get rid of these via the Registry. The key is HKEY_LOCAL_MACHINE/Software/Microsoft/Windows/CurrentVersion/Uninstall. Just delete the subfolder that corresponds to the deleted program. In addition, certain software applications can help you clean this list. These are three of the most popular:

- **Tweaki.** By JerMar Software
- **Tweak UI.** By Microsoft
- **WinHacker 95.** By Wedge Software

We briefly examine each of these tools as they relate to the Add/Remove Programs applet.

Tweaki

Tweaki is a shareware program by JerMar software. You can download it from **www.jermar.com** and evaluate it; if you decide to use it, you can register it for $15. Tweaki works with Windows NT, Windows 95, Windows 98, and even Windows 2000. Be aware, however, that some functionality is not available with some operating systems. For obvious reasons, we will explore the Windows NT components.

To modify the Add/Remove Program list with Tweaki, follow these steps:

1. Run TWEAKI.EXE.
2. Select the Win Tweaks tab.
3. Click the Select for More WinTweaks button.
4. Click the Remove entry from Control Panel's Add/Remove Applet button (see Figure 6.2).

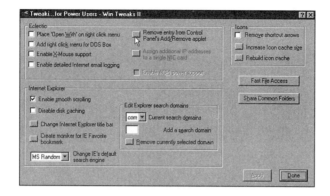

Figure 6.2   The Tweaki application Add/Remove list.

5. Select an entry, and then either delete it (click the Delete button) or modify its uninstall commands (by clicking the Edit button).

This second button is handy if you add or repartition a hard drive and the drive letters have changed, leaving the uninstall program unavailable.

Tweak UI

Tweak UI is available from Microsoft in a bundle with several other tools that is classified as a freeware program. To download it, go to the Windows NT Workstation download area at **http://www.microsoft.com/windows/downloads/winntw.asp**.

Installing Tweak UI can be a little tricky because it does not have an install program bundled with it. To install it, double-click the W95TWEAKUI.EXE file. This decompresses the executable zip file into its components. Find the TWEAKUI.INF file, right-click it, and choose Install from the drop-down menu. Whereas the other two programs discussed here are installed as applications, Tweak UI is actually installed as a Control Panel applet.

To modify the Add/Remove programs list with Tweak UI, follow these steps:

1. Launch the Control Panel and double-click the Tweak UI icon.

2. Click the Add/Remove tab, as shown in Figure 6.3.

3. You can remove an entry, edit one, or create a new one.

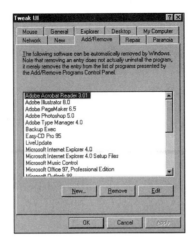

Figure 6.3   The Tweak UI Add/Remove list.

WinHacker 95

The third application we explore is WinHacker 95 from Wedge Software. This share-ware application can be downloaded and evaluated from **www.wedgesoftware.com** and registered for $17.95.

To access this feature in WinHacker 95, select the Add/Remove Programs option from the System folder (see Figure 6.4). You can now create a new entry, delete an old one, or modify it. Also note that WinHacker 95 installs itself as a Control Panel applet and an application.

Windows NT Setup

The second part of the Add/Remove Programs Control Panel applet allows you to add or remove Windows NT components that may have been installed during the installation process or are now required in your system. To accomplish this, follow these steps:

1. Click the Windows NT Setup tab.

2. Select the desired components.

3. Click OK.

If you are installing extra components, you may be prompted for your original Windows NT Workstation CD.

WinHacker 95 with Windows NT

Don't let the name fool you; WinHacker 95 works with Windows NT, but only if you download version 2.0. The previous versions of WinHacker 95 don't work with Windows NT.

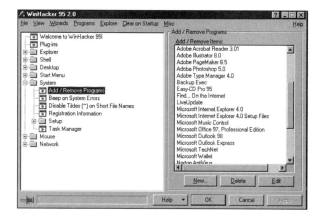

Figure 6.4   The WinHacker 95 Add/Remove list.

MS-DOS Console

Most power users will tell you that they still use Microsoft MS-DOS. When you run the MS-DOS window in Windows NT, you're not really running MS-DOS. Although it looks and acts like MS-DOS, it is truly Windows NT. Microsoft has redesigned Windows NT from the ground up and placed MS-DOS support in it for backward compatibility.

This Control Panel applet allows you to control how the MS-DOS Console window looks and feels when you run an MS-DOS application.

The MS-DOS Console applet is made up of four sections, each of which is contained in its own tab. These sections are Options, Font, Layout, and Colors. Of these four sections, Font and Colors are simple enough that we will not go into much detail on them. The other two sections, Options and Layout, deserve more attention.

Options

You will probably use this tab most often because it provides the most configuration options. You can control cursor size, display options, command history, and the different editing modes.

The Cursor Size and Display Options settings allow you to choose the size of the displayed cursor and the screen format. You can choose from three cursor sizes:

- **Small.** Shows a single flashing line as the cursor.
- **Medium.** Shows a flashing cursor that is about half the size of a character.
- **Large.** Shows a flashing cursor that is the full size of a character.

The Display Options setting allows you to choose between displaying your MS-DOS screen in a window or as a full text screen.

You use the next configuration option to control the command buffer that is initiated automatically when you launch the command prompt. If you used MS-DOS in the past, you may remember a command called DOSKEY. This command simply "remembered" the commands that you entered, allowing you to navigate them using the up and down arrow keys. The Windows NT version takes this to the next level. You can control the number of commands and buffers that the command prompt window will remember and whether it will automatically delete duplicated commands. When you are in the command prompt, you can scroll through the commands using the up and down arrow keys or press the F7 key to get a menu of all the available commands. From this menu, scroll to the command that you would like to execute and press the Enter key.

The last two settings deal with how editing is performed in the command prompt window. By default, you can cut and paste into the command prompt window by using the Edit option from the menu, which you access by right-clicking the window's title bar. You can configure your command prompt windows to allow you to use the mouse to cut and paste information by enabling the QuickEdit Mode check box. With this feature turned on, click the mouse button and highlight the text you would like to copy. Then, when you are ready to paste it, just click the right mouse button to paste your selection at the cursor location. If you enable the Insert mode, any copied text will be inserted at the cursor location; otherwise, it will overwrite text from the cursor location.

In addition, highlighting text and clicking the right mouse button copies the text to the Windows Clipboard. If no text is selected, right-clicking pastes the current contents of the Windows Clipboard to the cursor's current location. It is important to note that this causes problems with mouse-aware programs, such as EDIT.COM. If you have this selected, the program can't use the mouse inputs because the mouse is available only for copying and pasting.

Layout

The Layout tab allows you to control the size of the text buffer, the size of the screen, and the location of the window when it is executed. It also allows you to dynamically change the size of the command prompt window, up to the size of the height buffer. It is a good idea for you to create a command prompt window with a buffer of 50 characters or more in height. This allows you to scroll back and look at information that would normally scroll off the screen.

Command Prompt Screen
You can easily toggle between the window mode and the full screen mode by pressing the Alt and Enter keys simultaneously.

Devices

The Devices applet can be misleading. If you have used Windows 95 or 98, you know that you can easily add devices using Control Panel applets; you cannot do this, however, with the Devices applet. Instead, this applet allows you to control which devices are running, how they are started, and which hardware profile is used (if multiple profiles exist).

The Devices applet displays each device that Windows NT is aware of, its status, and its startup configuration. You can start or stop a device by highlighting it and clicking the appropriate button on the right of the screen. The startup configuration controls how the device is initiated (if it is at all). The following list compares the five different startup options. It is important to note that making changes here—especially changes that deal with boot and system options—could make the system unstable. Therefore, you should always update your emergency repair disk by running *RDISK /s* before changing these settings.

These are the startup options:

- **Boot.** Starts the device when the system is started. This occurs before any other device is started and is usually used for critical devices that the system relies on to function properly.

- **System.** Starts the device when the system is started but after the boot devices are started. You use this option to start a device that cannot be started unless another particular device is started first. For example, you cannot start the TCP/IP service unless the network card has started.

- **Automatic.** Starts the device during startup after the boot and system devices have started. This is used for devices that are not crucial to the operation of the system. That is, if the device fails to start, the system can continue to function.

- **Manual.** Requires that the device be started manually by a dependent service or device.

- **Disabled.** Prevents the device from being started by a user; however, the system can start it if necessary.

Windows NT has the ability to handle multiple hardware configurations. Although this is not normally activated for a desktop system, it can be very useful for running Windows NT Workstation on a laptop. Although the actual configuration of these hardware profiles is covered in the System applet section, we define them here for clarification.

Assume you have a laptop with Windows NT Workstation installed. In the office, the laptop is connected to a docking station. The docking station gives you access to a network card, a SCSI controller, and a DVD drive. At home, it is simply a standalone laptop using a modem to connect to the Internet. If you did not have the ability to disable and enable devices based on the hardware configuration, Windows NT would report errors that the network card, the SCSI controller, and the DVD drive were not starting up properly when the laptop was used anywhere but at the docking station.

When you configure hardware profiles, a menu appears at startup from which you can choose the desired profile. This prevents Windows NT from reporting error messages just because the devices are not started.

If you have two or more hardware profiles, you can control which devices will be enabled in which profiles. If you have two profiles, for example, one for connecting to the network and the other as a standalone system, the network card driver is disabled when the Disconnected from the Network profile is selected, and it is enabled when the Connected to the Network profile is active.

Dial-Up Monitor

The Dial-Up Monitor applet is one of the applets that might not appear on your configuration. To install this applet, you must have the Dial-Up Networking component of Windows NT. There are several ways to install Dial-Up Networking on your system. The simplest method is the following:

1. Double-click My Computer.

2. Double-click Dial-Up Networking.

3. An informational screen informing you what Dial-Up Networking is appears, prompting you to install the software. To install it, click the Install button. At this point, you may be asked to provide the Windows NT Workstation CD.

4. If you do not have any devices installed that can be used by Dial-Up Networking, you will be prompted to add a modem. Do so now.

5. When a device is available for Dial-Up Networking to use, you will be prompted to select it and continue. The Dial-Up Networking installation then continues, and you will be asked to restart the system to put the changes into effect.

6. When you restart the system, the Dial-Up Monitor applet appears in the Control Panel.

7. You may need to reinstall any service packs you had installed.

In this applet, you can add, remove, configure, and clone (copy) dial-up devices. These devices can be Integrated Services Digital Network (ISDN) adapters, modems, or X.25 pads (X.25 is an older networking technology). Once the devices exist, you can choose which protocols can be used over them and their dialing properties. For dial-in properties, you can choose Dial-in, Dial-out, or Both Dial-in and Dial-out.

Display

The Display applet is fairly simple to understand and control. You can access this applet either through the Control Panel or by right-clicking the desktop and selecting Properties from the pop-up menu. The Display applet gives you full control over how your screen appears. You can customize it to your preference, including the background pattern and color, the screen saver that is to be initialized and when, the appearance of the desktop, and the physical settings of your display. It is the last item we will concentrate on in this section.

You can use the Settings tab to control the number of colors displayed, the resolution to be used, and the refresh frequency of your display. You can also change the video driver through this tab. What options are available to you in the drop-down menus depend on your video card and the Video RAM (VRAM) installed on it. As a rule, the more VRAM you have, the higher the resolution and the higher the number of colors available.

The *refresh frequency* is a measure of your monitor and video card. It is defined as the frequency at which the complete screen is updated or redrawn. The refresh rate set in this applet must be within the range of frequencies the monitor can support. Notice the Test button on this screen. Using this button ensures that the settings you selected are compatible with the video card and the monitor. When you click this button, a dialog box appears, informing you that a test pattern will be displayed. If you see this pattern correctly, you can be sure that the setting you selected will work. If you don't, no harm is done; the settings will be reversed to those that were in effect when you started the test.

You can choose settings and apply them to the system without testing them first by clicking the Apply button. You should do this only if you are completely sure the settings are correct (or if you are extremely brave). Windows NT still warns you before allowing you to continue. If you choose to ignore all warnings and use the settings without testing them first and they happen to be incorrect, you will see either a blank screen or an illegible screen. If this occurs, your only real solution is to reboot the system and select either the Last Known Good option or the VGA Mode boot up option.

The Display Applet

The Display applet may look different in your particular installation of Windows NT Workstation. Many of today's more advanced video cards add functionality to this applet..

The last setting you can control on this screen is which video card driver is installed on your system. Each video card, even cards from the same manufacturer with the same name but different revision numbers, has its own driver. If you install the incorrect driver, you will have to reboot the system with one of the two methods mentioned previously to recover your system. In the past, when everyone used VGA, life was simple. VGA was an industry standard, which meant that every VGA video card could use a generic driver. (This is why you can always reboot the system in VGA mode.) SuperVGA, on the other hand, is a different story. Although technically an industry standard, it really is not. It is more a name given to video cards that can display resolutions and color depths that are higher than VGA. It is up to the manufacturer how that is achieved; therefore, each card must have its own driver.

Find Fast

The Find Fast applet is another that you may not have on your system. This is because this applet is installed when you install Microsoft Office. You will rarely use the Find Fast applet unless you are in a network environment using Windows NT Servers.

Find Fast indexes your permanent hard drives for Office documents. It does not index removable media (such as Zip disks and LS-120 disks) nor does it index read-only media (such as CD-ROM drives). While this applet is running, it automatically indexes documents with the following extensions: .DOC, .HT★, .DOT, .XL★, .PPT, .POT, .PPS, .OBD, .OBT, .TXT, .RTF, .MPP, .MPT, .MPX, .MPD, and .MDB. This index will be queried whenever an Office application attempts to open a file. If you have a Windows NT Server on the network, you can configure master indexes on it and allow the entire network to be indexed for Office documents.

Internet

Windows NT Workstation comes bundled with the Microsoft Internet Explorer Web browser. You use the Internet Control Panel applet to change how Internet Explorer looks and feels, as well as how it interacts with the Internet. The Internet applet contains six tabs: General, Connection, Navigation, Programs, Security, and Advanced. These are discussed in detail in the following sections.

Internet Applet

The Internet applet discussed here is the one that is installed with Internet Explorer version 3.x. The applet will be slightly different depending on which version you have installed on your system.

General Tab

You use the General tab to configure the multimedia, colors, links, and toolbar options. You use the Multimedia section to control whether to display pictures, play sounds, or play videos. You can use the Colors and Links section to customize those features in relation to Internet Explorer, or you can stick with the default settings. You can also control which toolbars will be displayed when Internet Explorer is started. Finally, you can select what fonts are used to display text in the Internet Explorer windows.

Connection Tab

You use the Connection tab to configure how Internet Explorer connects to the Internet. Internet Explorer can connect to the Internet in one of two ways: directly or through a proxy server. The direct connection is easy to configure: You simply do nothing. As long as your computer has access to the Internet, Internet Explorer will work. A proxy server is a server with specialized software that acts as a go-between for connecting the Internet and the internal network. All requests for Internet information are forwarded to the proxy server, which then forwards the request to the real server on the Internet. The Internet server then sends the response to the proxy server, which forwards it to the originating system. A proxy server offers a network both protection from the Internet (hiding the originator of the request) and a repository of often-accessed Web pages, storing them locally. To configure this option, enter either the name of the server or its TCP/IP address and the IP port upon which the request will be made.

Navigation Tab

You use the Navigation tab to configure the settings for the Start page, the Search page, and several quick link pages. You can also control the number of pages stored in the history, and you can view the pages and clear the history.

Program Tab

You use the Programs tab to set up the applications that will be used to read and send email and browse the newsgroups. You can also add, delete, or modify file associations in Internet Explorer.

Security and Advanced Tabs

You use the Security and Advanced tabs to control how certificates are used, to control the cryptography settings, to provide warnings if certain thresholds are reached, and how to manage temporary Internet file information.

Modems

The modem is one of the standard components in today's computer system. It is probably as rare to see a system without a modem as it is to see a system without a sound card or CD-ROM drive.

You use the Modems applet to add or remove modems, modify their properties, and change your dialing properties. When you add a modem, a wizard executes and attempts to detect your modem (unless you indicate otherwise). If you have a newer modem, there is a good chance it will not be detected properly because most newer modems are Plug and Play compatible, which is not fully supported in Windows NT. With newer modems, it is usually easier to configure the modem manually (but, hey, if you let the wizards do all the work, you wouldn't be a power user, would you?).

If you install a modem and it does not respond when you attempt to access it, it is time to begin troubleshooting. You should first run the wizard; this shows you whether Windows NT is even detecting a modem on the available COM port. When the wizard finds a modem, it notifies you that it is querying the modem, which tells you that Windows NT can see the modem. If the wizard does not query any modems, you must make sure the modem is configured on a port that exists on Windows NT. If it does not, either the modem must be configured or a new port must be added.

Monitoring Agent

Windows NT Server has a tool called the Network Monitor Tools. You use these tools to capture packets of information that are sent to and from the server. To enable the full functionality of these tools, a second component, called the Network Monitoring Agent, is installed. When this tool is installed, the Monitoring Agent applet appears.

The Network Monitoring Agent is installed as a service. To install it, follow these steps:

1. Double-click the Network Control Panel applet.
2. Click the Services tab.
3. Click the Add button.
4. Select the Network Monitoring Agent from the list that appears, and then click OK.
5. You may be prompted to provide the Windows NT installation CD. The installation process copies files to the system and prompts you to reboot the system. When the computer is rebooted, the Monitoring Agent applet appears.
6. Reapply the service pack.

Microsoft Systems Management Server

Microsoft Systems Management Server (SMS) has a more advanced version of the Network Monitor Tools that allows for the capturing of packets sent from any computer to any computer on the network. The version that comes with Windows NT Server allows you to capture only information that originates from or is sent to the Windows NT Server.

Three buttons are available to you in the Monitoring Agent applet. The third button will be accessible only if you have modified the configuration, because this button resets the system's default values. You use the other two buttons to change the passwords associated with the Network Monitoring Agent and to give descriptions to the network cards installed in your system.

Note that there are two passwords: the display and the capture passwords. The display password allows a user to view captured information that has been saved to disk, whereas the capture password allows the user to initiate a new information capture. Remember that if you give a user the capture password, he will automatically be given the display password because it is the least restrictive of the two.

If you have multiple network cards in your computer and another computer is connecting to capture data, you can distinguish between them using a custom description. In many cases, the multiple network cards will be of the same make and model, and you will be able to tell them apart quickly and easily by giving each a different description (for example, RedNet and BlueNet).

Multimedia

The Multimedia applet deals with all things multimedia, mainly the multimedia devices, how videos are displayed, and so on. When you first install Windows NT Workstation, many of your multimedia devices, such as your sound card, will not be installed. You will have to complete this process manually. If this is the case, you will notice that the options in several of the tabs (namely Audio and MIDI) will be grayed out. The process for installing your multimedia devices is simple:

1. Double-click the Multimedia applet.
2. Select the Devices tab.
3. Click the Add button and select the desired device from the list. If your device is not present but you have the driver that comes with the component, select the Unlisted or Updated Driver option, insert the media that contains the driver, and then click OK. The Multimedia applet will install the drivers. As a rule, you should reboot the system anytime you add or remove a device in this applet, even if you are not prompted to do so.

After the installation is complete and the system is rebooted, you will notice that the options that where grayed out before can now be accessed. In addition, a speaker icon appears in the system tray if you've just installed a sound card and the sound card driver is functioning. The five tabs available for configuration are Audio, Video, MIDI, CD Music, and Device. Because we already explored the Devices tab, we will skip it here and cover the other four tabs.

The Audio tab has two sections associated with it: Playback and Recording. You use this tab to control which devices should be used when playing sounds or music and which should be used to record sounds. This can be handy if you have multiple outputs or inputs for sound. Some high-end video cards, such as the ATI All-In-Wonder Pro, have both audio input and output capabilities. You can also control the default volume for each of these options.

You use the Video tab to control the default size of all video movies when they are played. You use the MIDI tab to control the instruments used by your system. And finally, you use the CD Music tab to control which CD-ROM drive (if multiples exist) will act like a music CD player and the associated headphone volume.

Network

Even if you don't have a network card installed in your system, you will use the Network applet a great deal, so it's a good idea to familiarize yourself with it. To access this applet, open the Control Panel, right-click the Network Neighborhood icon, and select Properties from the pop-up menu. If you connect to the Internet using a modem, you need this applet. Five tabs are available to you in this applet: Identification, Services, Protocols, Adapters, and Bindings.

The only configuration changes you can make on the Identification tab are to change the name of the computer and change its workgroup or domain. Windows NT requires you to define either a domain name or a workgroup name in order for it to function properly. If you choose to join a domain, you have two options: Either you can create an account for your computer on the domain ahead of time, or you can use an administrator account to create one while you're connecting.

When you install Windows NT Workstation, five services are installed by default (unless you install using the Custom method). The five services are Computer Browser, NetBIOS Interface, RPC Configuration, Server, and Workstation. Do not remove any of these services—doing so can render your system nonfunctional.

If you need to add a service, click the Add button and either select the service from the list or browse to a different location and install from there. You can also remove services, look at their properties (if available), and update the service information.

You can use the Protocol tab to install different "languages" that your computer can use to communicate with other computers, assuming that they are speaking the same network language. Networking protocols are discussed in Chapters 12, 13, 14, and 15.

Server Service in Windows NT

You might find it strange that there is a Server service in Windows NT Workstation and, if so, you would be right. The reason for it is fairly straightforward. Your workstation has a dual role. It can share information to others, therefore assuming the role of a server. It can also connect to shared information on another system, thus assuming the role of a workstation. When two computers are sharing information, the Workstation service of one system connects to the Server service of the other.

In the Adapter tab, you can add, remove, view properties of, and update different network adapters. It might seem strange to you, but ISDN "modems" are installed through this section of the applet and not through the Modems applet. This is because an ISDN device is more like a network adapter than a modem. Here is a helpful tip: Sometimes you will need to have a network card in your system, but you may not have the physical device. Microsoft was aware that this may occur and created what is called a Loopback Adapter. When you install an MS Loopback Adapter, it simulates a real network card and performs exactly like one (except that it does not allow computers to communicate). You can now install protocols and test different configurations and applications.

You use the Bindings tab to control the order in which protocols are bound to network cards—that is, the order in which the protocols are accessed when communicating over the network.

SCSI Adapters

You may think that you will never use the SCSI Adapters applet (because you have no SCSI adapters or devices installed in your system). But Windows NT sees an IDE controller as a SCSI adapter. Also, if you've ever installed an Iomega Zip drive, you will remember that this is where you perform the installation.

You use the Device tab of the SCSI Adapters to see the devices that are installed and to view their configuration. You use the Drivers tab to add or remove drivers for devices that you may have installed or removed from the system.

Services

The Services applet in Figure 6.5 is very similar to the Devices applet in its layout and functionality. In Windows NT, a service is a process that does not require that a user be logged on to run. Basically, a service acts as part of the operating system. The Services applet is generally a good place to go when troubleshooting system information. Many times, stopping and restarting a service, such as the Spooler service in particular, will bring the system back to working order.

Disappearing Changes

If you make changes to any portion of the Network applet, you will sometimes find that the changes do not appear in the other tabs. To get around this problem, you can either close the applet and reopen it, or you can click the Bindings tab. Doing so recalculates the bindings, and the changes will be reflected in all the tabs.

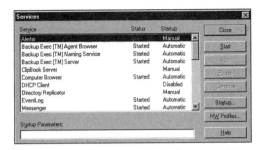

Figure 6.5   The Services Control Panel applet.

If you click the Startup button on the Services applet, you will notice that you have only three options (Automatic, Manual, and Disable) instead of the five in the Devices applet. You now also have the option to choose whether the service will log into the network as a local system account or will use a specific account. Except for these differences, the two Control Panel applets are effectively the same. In addition, the Services applet provides the same functionality as the **NET START** and **NET STOP** commands that are issued from a command prompt. The NET commands and their syntax are covered in detail in Chapter 11.

Sounds

The Sounds applet is one of the simplest of all the Control Panel applets. From this applet, you can assign sounds to system events, such as maximizing and minimizing windows, critical stops, and so on. In addition, you can also test your sound card from within this applet.

System

You can configure several important options in the System applet. The different configuration tabs for this applet include the following: General, Performance, Environment, Startup/Shutdown, Hardware Profiles, and User Profiles. The three important tabs are these:

- Performance
- Startup/Shutdown
- Hardware profiles

Performance

You can access this tab either through the Control Panel or by right-clicking My Computer and selecting Properties from the pop-up menu. You use the Performance tab to control how your Windows NT Workstation system treats background applications. If you move the slider to the left, background applications receive the same amount of CPU cycles as the foreground applications. On the other hand, if you move the slider to the right, more cycles are dedicated to the foreground applications than the background ones. You can also modify the virtual memory by clicking the Change button. If you have multiple physical hard drives (not partitions) in your system, you may want to create smaller paging files on the different drives, which improves overall performance. Performance tuning is discussed in detail in Chapter 20.

Startup/Shutdown

The Startup/Shutdown tab modifies which option on the boot menu is executed by default and the amount of time before it is selected. In Chapter 5, we looked at the BOOT.INI file. The Startup/Shutdown tab offers a quick and easy way to make minor modifications to that file. The bottom half of the applet defines how Windows NT deals with STOP errors (known as the Blue Screen Of Death, or BSOD).

On this screen, it's usually a good idea to select the Write An Event To The System Log option; this allows you to track frequent BSODs and possibly find a trend. The Send An Administrative Alert is good only if you have the Alerter service started and you want to be notified every time a machine BSODs. It's not a good idea to select the Write Debugging Information To option. In general, it only eats up drive space; plus, it slows down a reboot. You will need a core file only because you're having a reoccurring problem; check it just long enough to get a sample memory dump. It's nice to set the Automatically Reboot option, because it gets you up and going quicker. It also makes non-power users less frightened. The BSOD can be a scary screen to someone who does not understand it.

Hardware Profiles

You use the Hardware Profiles tab to create multiple profiles to use if the need occurs. If you need to create a new profile, simply select an existing one and click the Copy button. This prompts you to rename it, at which point you can change its properties to select whether it is connected to the network and is on a portable system. Hardware profiles are configured in the Devices applet.

Tape Devices

The Tape Devices applet is similar to the SCSI Adapters applet. The main difference is that, instead of just being able to look at which devices are installed and modify drivers, you can actually allow Windows NT to attempt to detect the installed tape drive and install the driver for it automatically. You do this by clicking the Detect button.

Tape Drivers and Third-Party Back Up

If you are installing a tape device to use with a third-party backup system, verify that you should install the Windows NT driver for the tape device here. Some backup software, such as Cheyenne's ARCserve, uses its own driver. Installing one here keeps the software from functioning properly.

For More Information

For more information about performance monitoring and network monitoring of Windows NT, please consult the following references:

- TechNet: The technical subscription service from Microsoft at `http://technet.microsoft.com/`
- Microsoft Knowledge Base: `http://support.microsoft.com/`

7

Introducing the Windows NT Registry

THE MICROSOFT WINDOWS NT REGISTRY is a 32-bit database that stores hardware, software, and user system configuration information. Older versions of Microsoft Windows stored system configuration information in the SYSTEM.INI and WIN.INI files. The .INI files have a maximum file size of 64KB; therefore, Microsoft developed the Registry database to overcome the size limitations of managing the system configuration data using .INI files.

Because the Windows NT Registry is 32-bit, 16-bit device drivers will not work correctly in Windows NT. However, 16-bit applications do run within Windows NT using the Windows NT Virtual DOS Machine (NTVDM) and the Windows On Windows (WOW) executive service. The NTVDM and WOW executive allow Win16 applications to run within a Win32 subsystem using a protected memory space. In Windows NT, 16-bit applications continue to reference the SYSTEM.INI and WIN.INI files for configuration information.

You launch the Registry Editor by selecting Start, Run and typing REGEDIT. Figure 7.1 peers into the Windows NT Registry with Registry Editor. Registry Editor is one of the many tools you can use to examine and manipulate the Registry. The Registry hierarchy and Registry keys are shown in the left pane of Registry Editor. The right pane lists the value labels and values associated with each key or sub-key. The first level keys are named *root keys*, *root handles*, or *hives*. The name HKEY is a combination of the words *handle* and *key*—hence, HKEY. By that definition,

HKEY_CLASSES_ROOT is considered a hive, or root key. Subkey values contain information in different formats; these formats include binary, hexadecimal, decimal, text, and other value types.

As previously mentioned, the right pane contains values. Each value has an associated data type. Each value may also contain data. It is important to understand that if the value appears blank, the value is actually a null value rather than a blank. Table 7.1 lists the most commonly used Windows NT data types.

Table 7.1   **The Windows NT Registry Data Types**

Data Type	Data Type Description
REG_BINARY	Binary data with no size limitation, expressed in hexadecimal format.
REG_DWORD	32-bit binary data in hexadecimal format.
REG_EXPAND_SZ	Expandable string data such as %username%. This value will expand to accept data length based on the user name.
REG_MULTI_SZ	Multiple string data such as combo box values.
REG_SZ	Text data type.

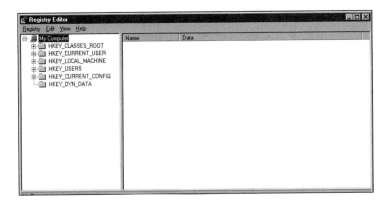

Figure 7.1   The Registry as seen through the Registry Editor.

Key and Subkey

The terms *key* and *subkey* are often interchangeable in meaning. A subkey may also be referred to as a key. Thus, when someone is referring to a key or subkey, they are generally indicating something about its location within the hierarchy rather than implying a fixed naming convention.

Registry Differences

The Registries of Microsoft Windows 95 and Microsoft Windows 98 are not compatible with those of Windows NT Server and Windows NT Workstation. The chapters in this book that discuss the Registry are specific to Windows NT Server and Windows NT Workstation. It is important, however, to discuss the Registry differences that exist between Windows NT and Windows 95 and 98 and also to elaborate on why an upgrade is not really an upgrade when migrating a Windows 95 or 98 system to Windows NT.

Windows 95 and 98 use an additional Registry key: HKEY_DYN_DATA. This key holds the Plug and Play configuration information for both Windows 95 and Windows 98. Windows NT 4.0 provides only limited support for Plug and Play, and therefore does not utilize this key, although it does show up in the Registry Editor. The Registries of Windows NT and Windows 95 and 98 look similar, but do not contain the same information. Therefore, when installing Windows NT on a computer running Windows 95 or 98, you must reinstall all 32-bit applications, you must create user accounts, you will almost always manually configure Plug and Play hardware (unless PCI auto-configuration support is enabled), and you must configure the environment to match the original settings.

In this book, we'll refer to the files comprising the Registry as *hives*. Each hive is discussed in a later section. The hive files and their locations are shown in Table 7.2. (See also Figure 7.2.)

Table 7.2   **Registry Hive Files and Their Locations**

Registry Hive File	Location
Default	HKEY_USERS\DEFAULT
SAM	HKEY_LOCAL_MACHINE\SAM
Security	HKEY_LOCAL_MACHINE\SECURITY
Software	HKEY LOCAL_MACHINE\SOFTWARE
System	HKEY_LOCAL_MACHINE\SYSTEM
NTUSER.DAT	HKEY_USER*SID of currently logged in user*

A listing of these files is located in HKEY_LOCAL_MACHINE\SYSTEM\ CurrentControlSet\Control\hivelist.

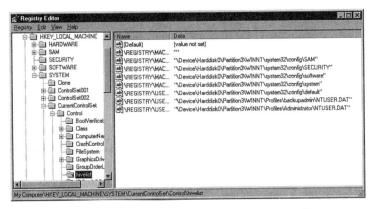

Figure 7.2 The location of the Windows NT hive files.

Windows NT Registry Hives

The Registry is subdivided into hierarchically organized hives. The five hives that make up the Registry are as follows:

- HKEY_LOCAL_MACHINE
- HKEY_USERS
- HKEY_CURRENT_CONFIG
- HKEY_CLASSES_ROOT
- HKEY_CURRENT_USER

The classification of five Registry hives is, in reality, incorrect. When a Registry editor is opened, such as RegEdt32, the editor does present five hives. All five Registry hives are actually part of two major hive groupings: HKEY_LOCAL_MACHINE and HKEY_USERS. The remaining hives are subhives, if you will, of the two major ones. Microsoft aliases the subhives and presents the five hives just listed for ease of editing and locating information within the hives.

HKEY_LOCAL_MACHINE

HKEY_LOCAL_MACHINE maintains hardware configuration and corresponding software driver data. This hive manages configuration data for the processors, video adapters, disks and controllers, network cards, and all other system hardware. HKEY_LOCAL_MACHINE also stores software-related information such as product keys and configuration information. This information is specific to the local computer.

HKEY_LOCAL_MACHINE contains all of HKEY_CURRENT_CONFIG and HKEY_CLASSES_ROOT. HKEY_CLASSES_ROOT is a copy of HKEY_LOCAL_MACHINE\SOFTWARE\Classes.

HKEY_USERS

HKEY_USERS manages database information specific to the user's profile, such as screen color, desktop preferences, backgrounds, and icon appearance order in the Start menu. Each time a new user is created, an additional HKEY_USER hive is created in %systemroot%\Profiles\%username%, where *%username%* is the Windows NT ID for that particular user. Files with .SAV, .LOG, and .ALT extensions reside within the user's profile subdirectory. The .SAV files maintain a copy of the hive file after the text-mode portion of setup is completed. The .LOG files hold logging of all changes to the hive. The .ALT files hold a backup of a hive. If the system fails during a load process, the .ALT files are automatically used as a backup.

HKEY_CURRENT_CONFIG

HKEY_CURRENT_CONFIG is an alias that points to HKEY_LOCAL_MACHINE\SYSTEM\CurrentControlSet\Hardware Profiles\Current and was added to Windows 4.0 for compatibility with Windows 95. When a Windows NT machine boots, configuration information about the system's hardware is gathered and stored. This is the same hive that maintains the Last Known Good Configuration data. Also, if multiple hardware profiles are configured for a computer, each of the profiles is stored within HKEY_CURRENT_CONFIG.

You might employ hardware profiles for a variety of reasons. In a hardware profile, specific devices may be included in one profile and excluded from another (for example, a LAN card for use on a laptop computer while attached to an office LAN, and a modem card to be used when out of the office). During the Windows NT boot process, a menu is presented listing the available hardware profiles. Choosing a profile invokes the settings configured for that particular profile and the system would be started accordingly. Suppose that you have a laptop that runs Windows NT Workstation. The laptop has three hardware profiles: docked, undocked with PCMCIA NIC, and undocked without network. Specific hardware is configured to start each profile when that profile is selected.

HKEY_CLASSES_ROOT

HKEY_CLASSES_ROOT manages the file extension to application reference data. For example, the .DOC extension relates to Microsoft Word for Windows. The extension and the application associated with the extension are included within this hive. It also keeps track of context menu information when an item is right-clicked.

HKEY_CURRENT_USER

HKEY_CURRENT_USER (HKCU) is a subkey of HKEY_USERS. HKU is the user currently logged into the system. Any changes to HKCU are written within HKEY_USERS. The user is not identified by name, but rather by a unique serial number called the *security identifier (SID)*. S-1-5-21-1882598320-951935002-1660491571-500 is the current user logged into the server. This key lists each of the attributes assigned to the current user. The DEFAULT key immediately above this serial number lists the default system attributes for all users

Windows NT Registry Files and Structures

The following sections discuss the Windows NT Registry files and structures. It is important to have a complete understanding of these files and their organization to fully understand how the Windows Registry works.

HKEY_LOCAL_MACHINE

HKEY_LOCAL_MACHINE contains five keys: HARDWARE, Security Accounts Manager (SAM), SECURITY, SOFTWARE, and SYSTEM. These keys are discussed in the following sections.

HARDWARE

HKEY_LOCAL_MACHINE\HARDWARE (shown in Figure 7.3) amasses the keys and values that make up the hardware inventory of a Windows NT system. It also contains information about devices and specific device drivers and settings associated with each piece of hardware. Windows NT does not allow an application to directly control or access a hardware device; therefore, when Windows NT boots, all system hardware is queried and the resulting data is stored within this key.

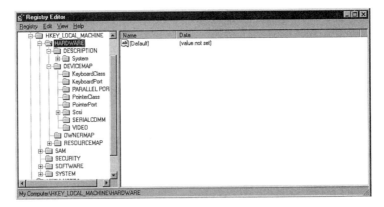

Figure 7.3   HKEY_LOCAL_MACHINE\HARDWARE.

It is not possible to make permanent changes to this key because it is generated dynamically. The information in this key is gathered every time a Windows NT system is booted. On an x86-based system, NTDETECT.COM extracts the system's hardware information and populates the HKEY_LOCAL_MACHINE\HARDWARE subkey's values. The Hardware Abstraction Layer (HAL.DLL) then calls these values to access system hardware. On an ARC-compliant system, this data is queried from the system's firmware. ARC stands for Advanced RISC (Reduced Instruction Set Computer) Computing, which is a type of computer architecture based on CPUs that are capable of executing a limited set of instructions which speed up processing. Use Windows NT Diagnostics to view the HARDWARE key information. To launch the Windows Diagnostics, select Run from the Start menu and type **WINMSD** at the prompt.

HARDWARE\DESCRIPTION

The HKEY_LOCAL_MACHINE\HARDWARE\DESCRIPTION key holds the descriptions for all system devices. Figure 7.4 illustrates values from the CentralProcessor key used in the Control Panel's System Properties applet. This key indicates the processor is a type Pentium II (Family 5, model 4, stepping 4) and is a 200MHz processor; shown by converting the ~MHz:REG_DWORD:0×c8 value to decimal. The Description key holds the descriptions of hardware devices referenced either by device or driver name throughout other parts of the Registry.

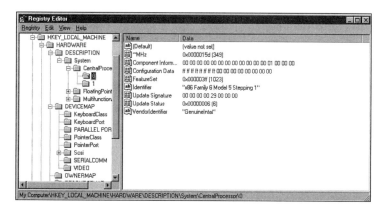

Figure 7.4   HKEY_LOCAL_MACHINE\HARDWARE\DESCRIPTION.

HARDWARE\DESCRIPTION\System

The System key houses information about the BIOS, system board, daughter boards, and the video BIOS.

HARDWARE\DESCRIPTION\System\CentralProcessor

The CentralProcessor key has one subkey of 0. This indicates the system has a single processor. Additional keys indicate multiple processors, as in 0 (for the first) 1, 2, 3, and so on.

HARDWARE\DESCRIPTION\System\FloatingPointProcessor

This key holds information about the floating-point processor.

HARDWARE\DESCRIPTION\System\MultifunctionAdapter

The name assigned to the MultifunctionAdapter key is chosen based on the computer's architecture. If the bus type is ISA or Multichannel (MCA), the subkey name is MultifunctionAdapter. If the bus type is EISA, the subkey name is EisaAdaptor. Finally, if the bus type is TurboChannel, the subkey name is TcAdapter.

The MultifunctionAdapter key lists three subkeys: 0, 1, and 2. The 0 key is for the PCI bus. BIOS-supported PCI devices are listed under this key. The 1 key is PNP BIOS (Plug and Play). The 2 key holds the information for one of the following:

- **DiskController.** Hard disk and floppy disk controller information
- **KeyboardController.** Keyboard controller information
- **ParallelController.** Configured parallel ports and controllers
- **PointerController.** Configured input/mouse devices
- **SerialController.** Configured COM ports and controllers

Each key under The MultifunctionAdapter key can contain the following values:

- **ComponentInformation Default: 0.** Stores the version number of the component and other information.
- **ConfigurationData.** Stores information about the hardware component as a resource, such as I/O port addresses and IRQ number. If data about the component is not available, this entry does not appear in the Registry, or the entry has no value.
- **Identifier.** Stores the name of a component. If the component name is not available, this entry does not appear in the Registry, or the entry has no value.

HARDWARE\DEVICEMAP

The DEVICEMAP subkey contains device drivers and the corresponding created names. When a device is called, a related, bound device driver is loaded. The DEVICEMAP subkey manages the relationships between the device names and the device drivers bound to them.

HARDWARE\DEVICEMAP\AtDISK

The AtDISK subkey stores information for AtDisk, the driver for non-SCSI hard disk controllers on Intel-based computers. This subkey appears in the Registry only if non-SCSI disk controllers are installed on the computer.

HARDWARE\DEVICEMAP\KeyboardClass

The KeyboardClass subkey maps to \REGISTRY\Machine\System\ControlSet001\Services\Kbdclass.

HARDWARE\DEVICEMAP\KeyboardPort

The KeyboardPort subkey maps to \REGISTRY\Machine\System\ControlSet001\Services\i8042prt. The i8042prt subkey stores data for the i8042prt driver. The i8042prt driver handles the keyboard and mouse port (also known as a PS/2-compatible mouse) for the Intel 8042 controller.

HARDWARE\DEVICEMAP\PARALLEL PORTS

The PARALLEL PORTS subkey maps to \DosDevices\LPT1. Additional mappings appear for each additional parallel port.

HARDWARE\DEVICEMAP\PointerClass

The PointerClass subkey maps to \REGISTRY\Machine\System\ControlSet001\Services\Mouclass.

HARDWARE\DEVICEMAP\PointerPort

The PointerPort subkey maps to \REGISTRY\Machine\System\ControlSet001\Services\i8042prt. The i8042prt subkey stores data for the i8042prt driver. The i8042prt driver handles the keyboard and mouse port (also known as a PS/2-compatible mouse) for the Intel 8042 controller.

HARDWARE\DEVICEMAP\SCSI

The Scsi subkey holds information about SCSI host adapters and devices. Figure 7.5 shows two SCSI ports, each with its own SCSI bus. SCSI (0) is the first SCSI device the system identifies. SCSI (1) is the second SCSI device the system identifies. The Logical Unit ID 0 subkey holds the identifier name and the type of device. The SCSI Port (0) subkey holds the DMAEnabled status, the current driver, the current interrupt used by the system, and the I/O address of the device. This subkey is very useful when you attempt to isolate interrupt conflicts with SCSI devices.

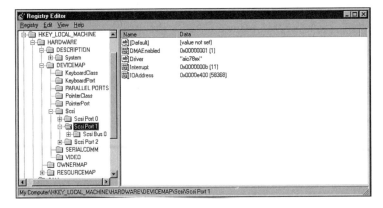

Figure 7.5 The SCSI subkey.

Security Accounts Manager (SAM)

The Security Accounts Manager (SAM) database, also known as the directory services database, is managed using User Manager For Domains or User Manager. The HKEY_LOCAL_MACHINE\SAM key is an alias of HKEY_LOCAL_MACHINE\Security\SAM. This key contains the security information about each user and group and is found on a Primary Domain Controller (PDC).

SECURITY

The HKEY_LOCAL_MACHINE\SECURITY key holds information about user rights, system and user policies, and group memberships. By default, the system account is granted Full Control. Administrators are granted only Special Access and cannot view the contents of the Security key without modifying Registry permissions. The data in the Security subkey are unique to Windows NT Server.

SOFTWARE

The HKEY_LOCAL_MACHINE\SOFTWARE key holds software settings unique to a specific computer. It's here that many of your software applications store their configuration data. The Classes subkey is under the Software key. The Classes subkey is aliased to HKEY_CLASSES_ROOT and keeps track of programs and file extension associations. This key also contains a Microsoft subkey that records settings specific to the Windows NT installation and configuration.

SYSTEM

The HKEY_LOCAL_MACHINE\SYSTEM key holds the Control Sets. (See Figure 7.6.) A Control Set is a database of hardware settings, device drivers, and service configuration information that Windows NT uses on startup.

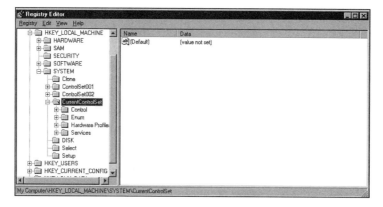

Figure 7.6   The SYSTEM\ControlSets subkey.

The SYSTEM key has many important subkeys that directly affect the boot process. In essence, a Control Set is like a hardware profile with each Control Set configured with potentially different settings.

SYSTEM\Clone

The Clone subkey is the Last Known Good Configuration. Discussed in Chapter 8, "Editing the Windows NT Registry," at length, the Last Known Good Configuration is the Control Set of the last successful Windows NT boot. This should not imply that boot process verification occurs, but rather that the machine was booted and the boot process seemed successful. Basically, it booted and didn't "blue screen." This key initializes during the Kernel Initialization phase.

SYSTEM\ControlSet and SYSTEM\CurrentControlSet

The ControlSet00# subkeys, numbered 0 through 3, are more likely numbered ControlSet001 and ControlSet002. The numbering sequence may vary. ControlSet001 and CurrentControlSet are the same. CurrentControlSet is mapped to ControlSet001 and contains duplicate information. These are the primary Control Sets used to boot Windows NT. ControlSet002 or ControlSet003 would be used if Windows NT fails to boot.

SYSTEM\CurrentControlSet\Control

This subkey holds a vast amount of information such as system layout, computer name, boot verification program, session manager, time zone information, product options, WOW settings, and the hive list.

SYSTEM\Select

The Select key holds values indicating which Control Set should be loaded when Windows NT boots, including which Control Set holds the Last Known Good Configuration. The values of this key are Current, Default, LastKnownGood, and Failed. Current is the value of the ControlSet Windows NT is using, Default is the Control Set used by NTOSKRNL.EXE by default, LastKnownGood is the value of the Last Known Good Configuration ControlSet, and Failed values indicate the last ControlSet that failed to boot. A 0 value indicates that no boot failures have occurred during any Windows NT boot process.

HKEY_USERS

The HKEY_USERS hive contains all actively loaded user profiles on the system. The HKEY_USERS hive contains two subkeys: DEFAULT, which stores the profile used when no users are logged on to the computer (such as when the Ctrl+Alt+Delete login prompt is displayed), and a subkey named for the *security identifier (SID)* of the current local user. This subkey contains the current user's profile. If the user is logged on remotely, the data for his or her profile is stored in the Registry of their local computer. The data in HKEY_USERS\SID# also appears in HKEY_CURRENT_USER. In Windows NT 4.0, the default user profile is not stored in the Registry—it is stored in %systemroot%\Profiles\Default User\NTUSER.DAT file.

HKEY_USERS\DEFAULT\AppEvents

The AppEvents (Application Events) key holds associations between Windows NT events and their associated program sound files.

HKEY_USERS\Console

The Console key holds settings for character-based programs. The command window is an excellent example of these settings in action. To open the dialog box, right-click the program icon in the upper-left corner of a command window, and then select Properties. This dialog box allows you to set window size, color, fonts, and other options.

HKEY_USERS\Control Panel

The Control Panel key holds setting data from many of the Control Panel applets. It is highly recommended that you use Control Panel applets to indirectly modify this data rather than direct manipulation through the Registry.

HKEY_USERS\Environment

The Environment key holds some of the data displayed in the Control Panel System applet's Environment tab. These items include environment variables, system path, user profile information, and startup/shutdown options.

HKEY_USERS\Keyboard Layout

The Keyboard Layout key holds language values and key preload information if, for example, you want to preload function settings or change the keyboard layout.

HKEY_USERS\Software

The Software subkey holds software settings that are unique to each named user. It holds such information as Microsoft software settings as well as system security certificates.

HKEY_USERS\Windows 3.1 Migration Status

The Migration Status key hold values indicate whether Windows NT has converted any .INI files to the Windows NT Server format. You may not have this key if a migration from Windows 3.1 to Windows NT 4.0 has not been performed.

HKEY_USERS\UNICODE Program Groups

The UNICODE Program Groups key holds values associated with Program Manager. Windows Explorer does not use this key.

Exploring the Registry

To examine the Registry in detail with descriptions for each of the Registry keys, the *Microsoft Windows NT Server 4.0 Resource Kit* CD includes a valuable tool. REGEN-TRY.HLP is your guide to the Registry values. This tool explores and explains many of the numerous Registry entries along with possible settings for each of the values. Many of the Registry settings are addressed in Chapter 8 and Chapter 9, "Important Registry Keys and Values," but REGENTRY.HLP is an invaluable reference for navigating and working with the Registry.

Security Information in the Registry

How long would it take to break every password in your PDC's security accounts database? More importantly, how long would it take to break a single Domain Admin password? Answer: too little time. If your Registry is like most, today's password-cracking programs can connect anonymously or as a service to your Registry, copy it, close the connection, and begin a dictionary, and brute-force password crack in the hope of obtaining one or more passwords. Using a shareware cracking program, for example, we were able to completely (that's right, completely) break every password on a 75-user network in 26 minutes. Although the Registry is complex and seemingly secure, it is not. You must take additional measures to successfully thwart this level of attack. This section focuses on ways to secure the Registry and programs to aid in that quest.

C2 Security

The United States Government, through the National Computer Security Center (NCSC), performs software security evaluations and maintains the standards for C2 security. *C2* is an evaluation criterion for determining security compliance. Microsoft provides a C2 Configuration Manager that examines a target computer system and tests that system for C2 compliance. The C2 Configuration Manager evaluates the system for several required compliance items. The Manager offers to fix each of the deficient items in order to bring the system into compliance. Configuration Manager is a useful tool in determining possible system deficiencies, but one of the requirements of C2 compliance is that the computer have no network services installed. Although that's great for security, it would certainly present problems if the server were an FTP server on the Internet. The C2 Configuration Manager can be found on the *Microsoft Windows NT Server 4.0 Resource Kit*.

Securing the Computer

Microsoft recommends the following strategies to secure your computer and Registry from hackers. (These recommendations can also be found at **http://technet.microsoft.com/cdonline/content/complete/analpln/intsecur.htm**.)

- Rename the Administrator account. Make sure that it has a strong password. This will make gaining administrative rights and Registry information more difficult for a potential hacker.

- Create a fake Administrator account that has no rights. This will give a potential hacker a bogus account to try to hack.

- Limit the membership of the local Administrators group. The more members there are in this group, the more targets a hacker has to gain administrative privileges.

- Disable the Guest account. The Guest account is disabled by default on Windows NT Server, but Guest is enabled by default on Windows NT Workstation. As an added safety measure, give the Guest account a strong password if it is enabled.

- Set your local account policy to ensure that strong passwords with a minimum length of six characters are used.

- Enable account lockout for local accounts.

- Secure the system's SAM. The SAM file contains encrypted copies of users' passwords. If it is not secured, hackers could get it and use it to crack the passwords. You can secure the SAM only by using the NTFS file permissions, so you must be using NTFS instead of FAT/FAT32.

- Secure the main copy of the SAM by securing the Winnt\System32\config directory.

- Remove the Everyone group from the list of users and groups that have permission to access the directory and files.

- Add the Users group to the list of users and groups that have permission to access the directory and files.

- Secure the backup copy in the Winnt\Repair directory. (This directory exists only if you have created a Repair Disk.)

- Allow only the System account and the local Administrators group to have access to the directory and files.

- Secure the system Registry, which requires these three steps:

  - Restrict Anonymous Access to the Registry by creating the RestrictAnonymous value under the LSA key. This action requires Service Pack 3 or greater. (See Knowledge Base article Q143474.)

  - Restrict Network Access to the Registry with the Winreg key. This action requires Service Pack 3 or greater. (See Knowledge Base article Q155363.)

  - Change the file association for the .REG extension to something like Notepad. This prevents a malicious Web site from inserting new keys into your Registry while you are browsing the Web. Also, double-clicking on any file with a .REG extension will attempt to overwrite current information with information contained in the .REG file.

Anonymous Logons

Knowledge Base Article Q143474 discusses a potential Windows NT security hole. It states the following:

> "Windows NT has a feature where anonymous logon users can list domain user names and enumerate share names. Customers who want enhanced security have requested the ability to optionally restrict this functionality. Windows NT 4.0 Service Pack 3 and a hotfix for Windows NT 3.51 provide a mechanism for administrators to restrict the ability for anonymous logon users (also known as NULL session connections) to list account names and enumerate share names. The Windows NT ACL editor requires listing account names from domain controllers; for example, to obtain the list of users and groups to select whom a user wants to grant access rights. Listing account names is also used by Windows NT Explorer to select from lists of users and groups to grant access to a share."

This article and its findings are important for two reasons. If a hacker knows a valid Windows NT user ID, she is one step closer to hacking your system. Second, this article reinforces the fact that newly created shares give the Everyone group Full Control by default. This is something that can be easily overlooked if you are in a hurry.

The shares, either administrative shares or regular shares, would then give "Everyone" "Full Control" to wreak havoc.

Windows NT System Key

Knowledge Base Article Q143475 discusses the System Key (SYSKEY) hotfix. It states the following:

> "The Windows NT Server 4.0 System Key hotfix provides the capability to use strong encryption techniques to increase protection of account password information stored in the Registry by the Security Account Manager (SAM). Windows NT Server stores user account information, including a derivative of the user account password, in a secure portion of the Registry protected by access control and an obfuscation function. The account information in the Registry is only accessible to members of the Administrators group. Windows NT Server, like other operating systems, allows privileged users who are administrators access to all resources in the system. For installations that want enhanced security, strong encryption of account password derivative information provides an additional level of security to prevent Administrators from intentionally or unintentionally accessing password derivatives using Registry programming interfaces."

The hotfix to correct this security weak spot can be obtained from ftp://ftp.microsoft.com/bussys/winnt/winnt-public/fixes/usa/nt40/hotfixes-postSP2/sec-fix/.

SMB Packets

Knowledge Base Article Q161372 reviews the fix for unsigned SMB packets. It states the following:

> "Windows NT 4.0 Service Pack 3 provides an updated version of the Server Message Block (SMB) authentication protocol, also known as the Common Internet File System (CIFS) file sharing protocol. For more information on SMB signing, please see the Windows NT 4.0 Service Pack 3 Readme.txt file."

Remote Registry Access

Knowledge Base Article Q155363 explains actions to prevent remote Registry access. This fix restricts Registry changes to the local console only. The article states the following:

> "Windows NT supports accessing a remote Registry via the Registry Editor and also through the RegConnectRegistry() Win32 API call. The default security on the Registry allows for easy use and configuration by users in a network. In some cases, it may be useful to regulate who has remote access to the Registry, in order to prevent potential security problems."

The security on the following Registry key dictates which users and groups can access the Registry remotely: HKEY_LOCAL_MACHINE\SYSTEM\ CurrentControlSet\Control\SecurePipeServers\Winreg.

If this key does not exist, remote access is not restricted, and only the underlying security on the individual keys control access.

In a default Windows NT Workstation installation, this key does not exist. In a default Windows NT Server installation, this key exists and grants Administrators Full Control for remote Registry operations.

The following optional subkey defines specific paths into the Registry that are allowed access, regardless of the security on the winreg Registry key: KEY_LOCAL_MACHINE\ SYSTEM\CurrentControlSet\Control\SecurePipeServers\Winreg\AllowedPaths\Machine (entry of type REG_MULTI_SZ)

The AllowedPaths Registry key contains multiple strings, which represent Registry entries that can be read by Everyone. This allows specific system functions, such as checking printer status, to work correctly regardless of how access is restricted via the winreg Registry key. The default security on the AllowedPaths Registry key grants only Administrators the ability to manage these paths.

Alternate Ways to Secure the Registry

The real threat to a Registry is a user. In general terms, administrators are not users and are certainly no threat to the Registry. However, for the sake of argument, we include administrators in this discussion as well.

Every user does not need Full Control, but users will argue this. Users with political power will win this argument, but in general, locking down Full Control is a start to securing the Registry and settings that relate to the Registry. Keep overzealous users out of harm's way by deleting REGEDIT.EXE and REGEDT32.EXE, plus any other tools discussed in Chapters 8 and 9 that permit Registry manipulation. If users must have one of these tools, take actions to restrict remote Registry access. This limits their Registry spelunking to their own machines.

Use REGEDT32.EXE to change the security settings on the different hives within the Registry. Note that the default permission for HKEY_LOCAL_MACHINE is that the Everyone group has READ permission.

Understanding out-of-the-box Registry permissions, access points to the Registry, and potential ways to secure the Registry will help protect your assets.

Remember to Reboot
Any changes to the Registry entries require a reboot to take effect.

For More Information

For more information about the Windows NT Registry, please consult the following references:

- Microsoft TechNet contains useful information about the Registry. Topics discussed in this chapter can be found by searching on keywords related to these topics.

- Johnson, Clayton. *Troubleshooting and Configuring the Windows NT/95 Registry*. SAMS Publishing, Indianapolis, IN, 1997. ISBN: 067231066X.

- Thomas, Steven B. *Windows NT 4.0 Registry: A Professional Reference*. McGraw-Hill, New York, NY. 1997 ISBN: 0079136559.

- Additional information about anonymous user lockdown can be obtained from **http://support.microsoft.com/support/kb/articles/q143/4/74.asp**.

- Additional information regarding SYSKEY.EXE can be obtained from the Microsoft Knowledge Base from **http://support.microsoft.com/support/kb/articles/q143/4/75.asp**.

- Additional information regarding SMB signing can be obtained from the Microsoft Knowledge Base at **http://support.microsoft.com/support/kb/articles/q161/3/72.asp**.

- Additional information about restricting anonymous Registry access can be obtained from the Microsoft Knowledge Base at **http://support.microsoft.com/support/kb/articles/q155/3/63.asp**.

8

Editing the Windows NT Registry

I**N THIS CHAPTER, WE BEGIN WORKING** with the Registry, which is a data file that includes configuration information about all 32-bit hardware and driver combinations as well as 32-bit applications within Microsoft Windows NT. In addition to providing general information about the Registry, we review a few tools that empower you during your work with the Registry. This chapter assumes that you are accustomed to poking around under the hood and that you are interested in the neat and useful things that can be achieved only by directly manipulating the Registry.

Editing the Registry is akin to tinkering with the brain—you should know what you're doing or suffer dire consequences. When you edit the Registry, you're manipulating Windows NT's configuration information; in doing so, one wrong change and your Windows NT configuration is dead.

You can edit the Registry directly and indirectly. Indirect editing is performed using the applets in the Control Panel, making user or group membership changes using User Manager for Domains, changing disk configurations in Disk Administrator, or changing the operating environment. Indirectly editing the Registry is safest because such changes are accomplished programmatically.

Direct editing of the Registry is done using tools such as REGEDIT, REGEDT32, or REGKEY. Several third-party tools are available for Registry manipulation as well. Direct editing is the most dangerous—making a minor mistake in a binary number or deleting the wrong value can have dramatic effects on your system.

Before you change the Registry, make a set of Windows NT boot disks and run `rdisk /s` to create or update an Emergency Repair Disk (ERD). This gives you the ability to get back where you started before you changed the Registry. Always be prepared for a change to cause your system to go south. If you're prepared for disaster, you can usually find a way to get the system up and running again.

Backing Up the Registry

Several tools and utilities for backing up the Registry are built into Windows NT, including the Backup utility. The Backup utility allows you to back up a computer's local Registry. Backing up a Registry is not enabled by default. In the Backup utility, the Backup Local Registry checkbox must be selected to perform this task. (See Figure 8.1.) The requirement for running Backup is that you have a tape drive installed in the computer you're attempting to back up.

The *Microsoft Windows NT Server 4.0 Resource Kit* provides additional tools for working with the Registry, including REGBACK, REGINI, and REGREST. You can use REGBACK to back up all or part of the Registry, REGINI to automate the rollout of changes to one or several Registries, and REGREST to assist in the restoration of Registry backups. Syntax and usage for REGBACK, REGINI, and REGREST are covered later in this chapter.

Figure 8.1   Backing up the Registry in Windows NT's native Backup utility.

REGBACK is a command-line utility and therefore can be scheduled using WIN AT (Windows Automated Task) jobs. You can use REGBACK to backup Registry hives while the system is still running. In addition, hives can be open while using REG-BACK; however, REGBACK will not back up hives that are not in use—you must use XCOPY or SCOPY for that. Members of the Administrators and Backup Operators group must have the SetBackupPrivilege right to use REGBACK. REG-BACK will fail if insufficient room is available to hold the backup; therefore, it's imperative to specify a target device with sufficient space. REGBACK supports backup of only HKEY_USERS and HKEY_LOCAL_MACHINE hives.

REGREST is a command-line utility for restoring Registry backups made with REGBACK. Both REGBACK and REGREST back up and restore the Registry hive-by-hive. As with REGBACK, members of the Administrators and Backup Operators groups must have the SetRestorePrivilege right to use REGREST. When REGREST replaces a hive, the old hive is saved into the \%systemroot%\system32\ config directory with a .SAV extension. Changes to a hive will not take effect until the system is rebooted. REGREST supports restoration of only the HKEY_USERS and HKEY_LOCAL_MACHINE hives.

Microsoft also provides a utility for making Emergency Repair Disks (ERDs), aptly named *RDISK.EXE*. During Windows NT installation, you're asked if you want to create an ERD. Creation of an ERD at this point really is a waste of time because most administrators make significant configuration changes to the system after installing Windows NT. We recommend that you wait until your system has been configured with appropriate system and device drivers, and then use the `RDISK` command to make an ERD. At this point, you will have the Registry information required to restore the Registry for a configured system rather than a shell installation of Windows NT. The ERD is discussed in more detail in the section "Emergency Repair Disk" later in this chapter.

The ERD contains the following components:

- AUTOEXEC.NT
- CONFIG.NT
- DEFAULT._
- REPAIR.INF
- SAM._
- SECURITY._
- SOFTWARE._
- SYSTEM._

Editing the Registry

Windows NT includes two utilities for editing and adding Registry data: REGEDIT
and REGEDT32. *REGEDT32* has been part of Windows NT since version 3.1
Advanced Server. Similar to File Manager, REGEDT32 displays the Registry in a tree
structure. Conversely, *REGEDIT* displays the Registry in a Windows NT Explorer-
type view.

REGEDT32

REGEDT32 (shown in Figure 8.2), the older Registry-editing sibling, provides functionality that REGEDIT does not. REGEDT32 permits setting security on the
Registry. Using REGEDT32, Registry permissions can be set to Read-only to prevent damage during Registry exploration. The downside of REGEDT32 is that it
only allows searching based on keys, whereas REGEDIT allows searching based on
keys, values, and data in the Registry. The following sections explore some of the commands available in REGEDT32.

Open Local

The Open Local menu option opens the machine's local Registry keys if they have
been closed.

Close

The Close menu option closes the selected instance of the Registry hives.

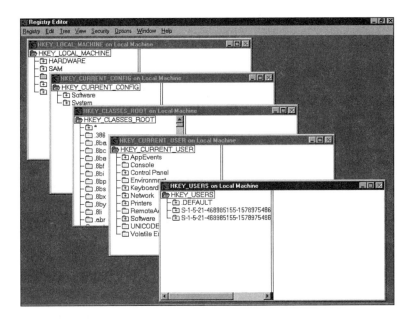

Figure 8.2   Microsoft Windows NT's REGEDT32.

Load Hive and Unload Hive

You can load a hive into the Registry that has been saved as a text file or remove a loaded hive from your system. Load Hive and Unload Hive affect only the HKEY_USERS and HKEY_LOCAL_MACHINE predefined keys, and are active only when these predefined keys are selected. When you load a hive into the Registry, the hive becomes a subkey of one of these predefined keys.

To load a hive into the Registry, follow these steps:

1. Select HKEY_USERS or HKEY_LOCAL_MACHINE.
2. From the Registry menu, select Load Hive.
3. Select the desired hive file and click the Open button.
4. In the Load Hive dialog box, enter the key name to assign the hive and click OK.
5. The selected hives now appear as subkeys of either HKEY_USERS or HKEY_LOCAL_MACHINE.

To unload a hive, the hive must have been previously loaded. You cannot unload the default hives. When a hive is loaded into the Registry, it becomes a subkey of either HKEY_USERS or HKEY_LOCAL_MACHINE.

To unload a hive from the Registry, follow these steps:

1. Select a hive that was previously loaded into the Registry.
2. From the Registry menu, select Unload Hive.

The unloaded hive no longer exists in the Registry.

Restore

The Restore menu option allows you to restore a Registry key from an exported binary Registry file. This overwrites existing key information. (Existing key information will be deleted.)

Save Key

The Save Key menu option allows you to save a selected key from the Registry. You must have either the Administrator or Backup Operator permission to save keys.

Select Computer

The Select Computer menu option opens a named pipe to a remote Registry for viewing. After a connection is established, you can load the HKEY_USERS and HKEY_LOCAL_MACHINE hives into the remote connected computer's Registry.

Add Key

The Add Key menu option allows you to add a new Registry key and class to the Registry. The entered class does not, however, show up in the Registry editor.

Add Value

The Add Value menu option allows you to add a Registry value. Adding to the Registry is discussed in detail later in this chapter in the "REG ADD" section; this option adds the value name, the data type, and the data associated with the type.

Permissions

The Permissions menu option in the Security menu presents the Security dialog box to add or change permissions for all or parts of the Registry. Unless you're specifically making Registry changes, you should assign Read permission. This prevents accidental changes from occurring and is a recommended strategy when editing the Registry.

Auditing

The Auditing menu option under the Security menu provides a trail for determining changes and access to the Registry. Registry auditing provides notification for success and failure event-logging of several important Registry items. Figure 8.3 depicts events that can be enabled for Registry auditing.

Owner

The Owner menu item is very similar to the file and folder Take Ownership right. The Owner item allows you to take ownership of an entire hive or certain keys within the hive.

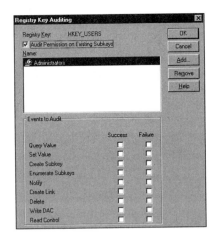

Figure 8.3   The Registry Key Auditing dialog box.

REGEDIT

This section examines the REGEDIT utility commands. As mentioned, REGEDIT allows you to search the Registry based on keys, values, and data in the Registry. REGEDIT was originally written to modify the Registration Database, the precursor to the Registry that was found in non-NT versions of Windows. Therefore, it doesn't support NT-only features such as security or auditing.

Connect Network Registry

From the Registry menu, select the Connect Network Registry command to connect to a remote computer to import and export entire Registries and keys.

Disconnect Network Registry

Disconnect Network Registry breaks the connection to a mounted remote network Registry.

New

You can add new Registry Keys, Strings, Binaries, and DWORD values by selecting New from the Edit menu.

Comparing REGEDIT to REGEDT32

In summary, you can use REGEDIT to perform any of the following tasks:

- Edit Microsoft Windows 95 or Microsoft Windows 98 Registries.
- Perform advanced searches that REGEDT32 doesn't offer.
- Import or export an entire Registry or certain hives.

You can use REGEDT32 if you need to do any of the following:

- Change the Registry's security settings.
- Take ownership of portions of the Registry.
- Add new keys, String values, Binary values, or DWORD values.

Working with Existing Keys and Values

There are five Registry hives: HKEY_CLASSES_ROOT, HKEY_CURRENT_CONFIG, HKEY_USERS, HKEY_CURRENT_USER, and HKEY_LOCAL_MACHINE. We cover these in more detail in the following sections.

The HKEY_CLASSES_ROOT Key

HKEY_CLASSES_ROOT is really a subkey of HKEY_LOCAL_MACHINE\ Software. It's used for Object Linking and Embedding (OLE) functions and it ensures that an application's associations are correctly invoked when a file type is selected and opened. HKEY_CLASSES_ROOT also includes the names of all drivers, strings that are used as pointing devices to the actual application text they represent, Class ID numbers, Dynamic Data Exchange (DDE) and OLE information, and the icons used for the applications and related documents.

HKEY_CURRENT_CONFIG Key

HKEY_CURRENT_CONFIG contains hardware profile information used during system startup. HKEY_CURRENT_CONFIG was added to Windows NT 4.0 to assure compatibility with Windows 95. This enables applications that support HKEY_CURRENT_CONFIG to run on Windows 95, Windows 98, and Windows NT. This is actually a subtree aliased to HKEY_LOCAL_MACHINE\ SYSTEM\CurrentControlSet\Hardware\Profiles\Current; therefore, the discussion of HKEY_LOCAL_MACHINE includes the HKEY_CURRENT_CONFIG key.

HKEY_USERS Key

HKEY_USERS is the root for all HKEY_CURRENT_USER profiles on the computer. It contains information related to the logged on user and the default user settings. The HKEY_USERS key contains the configuration information for all users, but makes it available only to the specific user when he or she logs in. This key is located in %systemroot%\Profiles\%username%, where %username% is the user that is currently logged on.

HKEY_CURRENT_USER Key

HKEY_CURRENT_USER contains information related to the currently logged on user. HKEY_CURRENT_USER is actually a subkey of HKEY_USERS. Table 8.1 describes the default subkeys for HKEY_CURRENT_USER.

Table 8.1 **Registry Subkeys and Their Functions**

Subkey	Function
Console	Stores window options and command prompt configuration.
Control Panel	Specifies Control Panel applet configuration information.
Environment	Stores environment variable information for the current user session.
Keyboard Layout	Holds information regarding user keyboard preferences.
Printers	Houses printer information for all mapped printers.
Program Groups	Stores settings for the current user's defined program groups.
Software	Houses settings for user installed software or preference settings for globally available software.

HKEY_LOCAL_MACHINE Key

The HKEY_LOCAL_MACHINE key manages the information related to the hardware and device drivers for the local computer. There are several subkeys of importance, which are discussed in the following sections.

HKEY_LOCAL_MACHINE\Software

This subkey contains configuration information for all the software installed on the local machine. The convention for storing this information, according to Microsoft, is \Software\Company Name\Product Name\Version Number. If you use this convention, you can query Registry information on all the computers on the network to check for installed software and version information.

HKEY_LOCAL_MACHINE\Software\Classes

This subkey contains file type to application association information as well as information related to COM objects.

HKEY_LOCAL_MACHINE\Software\Microsoft

This subkey contains information related specifically to Microsoft software installed on the local machine.

HKEY_LOCAL_MACHINE\Hardware

This subkey maintains a database of the hardware-specific information on the local machine. You can use it to get a clear picture of the physical configuration of the computer, including information about the processor, network interface card (NIC), memory, bus type, and so on.

HKEY_LOCAL_MACHINE\Hardware\Description

On an ARC-compliant machine, when the system boots, the firmware is queried and the result is copied to this subkey. On x86-based systems, NTDETECT.COM gathers the system hardware information that it recognizes and populates this subkey. Binary component identification information, the component ID, and configuration information, such as CPU type and speed, interrupt request (IRQ) settings, Direct Memory Access (DMA) channels, and input/output (I/O) ports, is gathered during this phase if the data is available.

HKEY_LOCAL_MACHINE\Hardware\DeviceMap

This subkey keeps a record of created device driver names and their associated device objects. It cross-references the drivers to the objects organized by device class. Therefore, when a disk array calls the underlying Windows NT subsystem, the appropriate device driver is called to perform the task.

HKEY_LOCAL_MACHINE\Hardware\ResourceMap

The ResourceMap subkey is dynamically created each time the machine is booted. It maintains a mapping of hardware devices to software drivers. This key detects and reports conflicts from the device drivers' memory addresses, interrupts, DMA channels, and I/O ports.

HKEY_LOCAL_MACHINE\SAM

This subkey, of course, contains the security accounts database for the local system. SAM is the abbreviation for Security Accounts Manager.

You can't actually see or manipulate the SAM from this key. It's here pretty much just for show.

HKEY_LOCAL_MACHINE\SYSTEM

This subkey maintains information regarding the Windows NT boot process. Table 8.2 shows the four control sets under HKEY_LOCAL_MACHINE\SYSTEM.

Table 8.2   **Control Sets under HKEY_LOCAL_MACHINE\SYSTEM**

Control Set subkey	Description
Clone	Created during the Kernel initialization phase of bootup. This subkey is a volatile copy of the ControlSet created from CurrentControlSet.
ControlSet001	Used to boot Windows NT.
ControlSet002	Is a backup to ControlSet001 if it fails to load.
CurrentControlSet	Mapped to ControlSet001 and is used to boot Windows NT.
CurrentControlSet\Control	Contains information such as computer name, file system, session manager, and memory manager settings.

Value Types

The Registry manages five main value types: Binary, String, DWORD, Multi-String, and Expandable String. Separate editing tools are invoked depending on the value type selected. The tools are, of course, provided with Windows NT.

Binary or REG_BINARY

The Binary type houses data in a binary format generally used to store hardware component information. Examples include entries under HKEY_LOCAL_MACHINE\SAM, although these entries in the Registry are relatively rare.

Simple String or REG_SZ

The String type is a sequence of characters that represent a Unicode user readable string. Entries might be names, titles, numbers, paths, or other text items. The SZ in REG_SZ stands for String Zero terminated. An example would be an entry under HKEY_LOCAL_MACHINE\HARDWARE\DESCRIPTION\System.

DWORD or REG_DWORD

This value is edited using the DWORD editor and represents a 32-bit, 4-byte number used in error control functions.

Multi-String or REG_MULTI_SZ

This value allows you to input multiple strings of data, such as items in a list box.

Expandable String or REG_EXPAND_SZ

This value uses the same editor as REG_MULTI_SZ, but indicates that the data has the ability to expand or have information added to it.

The other entries that appear in the Registry are listed in Table 8.3, along with their acceptable content formats.

Table 8.3 **Registry Value Types and Their Intended Uses**

Value Type	Description
REG_NONE	The value type does not exist or it is unknown due to encryption of the type.
REG_BINARY	Binary data in bit or binary form.
REG_DWORD	A 32-bit number expressed in hexadecimal, octal, or decimal.
REG_DWORD_BIG_ENDIAN	A 32-bit number with the high byte expressed first.
REG_EXPAND_SZ	An expandable string that can include embedded variables such as %systemroot%.
REG_FULL_RESOURCE_DESCRIPTOR	Hardware Resource Description in the \Hardware subkey of HKEY_LOCAL_MACHINE.
REG_LINK	A Unicode formatted symbolic link.
REG_MULTI_SZ	An array containing strings.
REG_RESOURCE_LIST	Hardware Resource Lists found in the \Hardware subkey of HKEY_LOCAL_MACHINE.
REG+RESOURCE_REQUIREMENTS_LIST	Resource requirements.

Importing and Exporting Registry Data

Backing up the local Registry is an essential part of system backups. The Backup utility, discussed in detail in Chapter 18, "Windows NT Backup and More," allows you to back up the Registry of the local server. (Refer to Figure 8.1.) If you don't have a tape drive available, other options are available to administrators to perform Registry backups. These options are discussed in Chapter 18.

Importing Registry Files

If you don't have access to a tape drive and need to back up a Registry, REGEDIT fills the need. You have two options when importing into the Registry. One of these options is to double-click the exported .REG file, which launches an import action and overwrites existing Registry keys. Because there's a potential to overwrite important Registry information, you should perform this action with great caution. In fact, it's a good idea to rename your old .REG files to .RE so that you don't import them mistakenly. This is one of those times when having a current ERD is imperative.

Another option is to import the .REG file using REGEDIT. From the Registry menu, select Import Registry File and then select a .REG file. This process imports an exported Registry or hive. Again, this overwrites any existing Registry information with no warning. Import Registries with caution, and only if you have a current Registry backup and ERD.

Exporting Registry Files

You can use REGEDIT to edit the Windows NT Registry and Windows 95 and Windows 98 Registries, whereas REGEDT32 is specific to Windows NT. To back up the Registry using REGEDIT, select the Export Registry File option from the Registry menu. This displays the dialog box shown in Figure 8.4. Select the location for the exported Registry. Using this method, you can export either the entire Registry or a selected portion of the Registry. The exported file is saved with a .REG extension. Double-clicking a Registry file that has a .REG extension runs the Import Registry command and overwrites existing Registry keys with the contents of the .REG exported file. Again, we cannot overstress the importance of having a current backup and ERD when performing these operations.

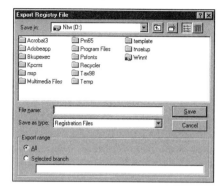

Figure 8.4   Exporting a Registry file in REGEDIT.

Avoiding Registry Problems

You can avoid Registry problems with careful planning and prevention. Avoiding Registry problems is better than the alternative every time. It's not really the Registry problem you should be worried about—it's that call at 2:00 Sunday morning to tell you about the server outage event that you should be worried about. This section discusses a strategy to follow to minimize the impact and downtime associated with Registry-related incidents.

Last Known Good Configuration

If you're unable to boot your system after making a change to the Registry, the best escape pod that Microsoft provides is the Last Known Good Configuration. When you boot Windows NT, you're presented with an option to press the spacebar to utilize the Last Known Good Configuration. After you press the spacebar, you're presented with a menu from which you may choose saved configurations. The Last Known Good Configuration means that, based on the last configuration, your system was able to get to the initial logon screen. It does not mean that your Registry was evaluated against some criteria for goodness—rather, that your boot appeared to be successful as far as Windows NT was concerned. Take this for what it's worth. With Last Known Good Configuration, you should be able to log in to the system to repair potential damage done.

Emergency Repair Disk

We covered RDISK and its use in Chapter 4, "Windows NT and Hardware," but we'll discuss it again here, along with some preventative strategies, for good measure. Creating the ERD is the equivalent of getting a flu shot. It's not the most entertaining thing in the world, but it may come in handy when you least expect it. We recommend creating an ERD on floppy. If your hard drives are inaccessible, an ERD stored an inaccessible drive is useless. Get a floppy mailer and tape it somewhere on your system. Run `rdisk /s` and create or update an ERD. Put that disk in the mailer. Any time you make configuration changes to Windows NT, create a new ERD to keep it up to date.

Maintaining the ERD is absolutely imperative to a successful prevention strategy. If you add a new controller, update the ERD. If you add five new groups, update the ERD. Update the ERD every time you make a significant change to your system. We also recommend keeping a few versions of the ERD handy, not just the latest one. Registry flaws often don't immediately manifest themselves. Continually overwriting a single ERD session might record the problem over an ERD instance that was fine. You can use the RDISK utility to create a new ERD, but you can also use it to update an existing one.

Updating repair information during the RDISK process creates an image of the ERD in the %systemroot%\Repair directory. It also overwrites any existing image in that directory. The Repair directory houses the image that gets invoked when using the Last Known Good Configuration option during Windows NT boot.

By default, the RDISK utility in Windows NT Server and Windows NT Workstation does not back up all of the Registry. RDISK is intended to be a last resort for making a system bootable, but not necessarily as it was. If you want RDISK to back up the entire Registry, including the DEFAULT, SAM, and SECURITY files, you must use the `/s` switch by running `rdisk /s`. For more information, see "Preparing for and Performing Recovery" in the *Windows NT Server Resource Guide* from the *Microsoft Windows NT 4.0 Resource Kit*.

Registry Security

Like NTFS, the Registry also has security controlled by Access Control Lists (ACLs). Registry Security must be set using REGEDT32.EXE. Setting Registry security correctly prevents unauthorized personnel from making direct or indirect changes to your system. The Registry security is broken down as follows:

- **Read.** Assigns Query Value, Create Value, Notify, and Read Control.
- **Full Control.** Assigns full control access.
- **Query Value.** Assigns the user or group to read the settings of a value entry.
- **Create Value.** Assigns the user or group the ability to set the value of an entry.
- **Create Subkey.** Assigns the user or group the ability to create a subkey.

- **Enumerate Subkeys.** Assigns the user or group the ability to identify all the subkeys of the selected key.

- **Notify.** Allows the user or group to receive subkey audit notifications.

- **Create Link.** Allows a user or group to create a symbolic link to the key.

- **Delete.** Allows a user or group to delete a subkey.

- **Write DAC.** Allows a user or group to read the Discretionary Access Control list for the selected subkey.

- **Write Owner.** Allows a user or group to take subkey ownership.

- **Read Control.** Allows a user or group to read the security information associated with a subkey.

Additional Registry Security

When it comes to Registry security, the Everyone group is a dangerous thing. By default, the Everyone group gets Full Control on a new share, Full Control when NTFS is applied, and unnecessary permissions to the Registry. The Everyone group should be restricted from the Registry by changing the default permissions to Special Access and setting permissions to include only Query Value, Enumerate Subkeys, Notify, and Read Control. By default, some sections of the Registry give Full Control to the Everyone group. This is a security risk and highly unnecessary—remember to change this setting any time you create a new share.

Troubleshooting the Registry

Let there be no doubt: Troubleshooting the Registry can be rocket science. Methodical investigation, however, generally gets past the symptoms to the root of the problem. Registry problems manifest themselves in several ways. Foremost, you know you have a problem when you receive a BSOD, lovingly known as the Blue Screen of Death.

A BSOD, or a STOP message, indicates the cause of the failure. Understanding this hieroglyphic screen in its entirety is not necessary. There are some key indicators that will greatly aid the investigation. The second line of the STOP message lists the type of error encountered. The error will read *Unhandled User exception* or *Unhandled Kernel exception* followed by some address information. This information focuses the troubleshooting search. Unhandled User exceptions involve user-mode operating system software, whereas Unhandled Kernel exceptions relate to the operating system, third-party software drivers, or hardware. The third and fourth lines of the STOP message indicate what caused the failure and the associated address or addresses. After the STOP information is evaluated, checking the Event Viewer's System and Application logs may narrow the problem search. In addition, you can search TechNet or `www.microsoft.com\kb` for the 8-digit stop code for further information.

Generally speaking, the following events are the most likely causes of problems with the Registry:

- **Installing and uninstalling software.** Software does not always install and uninstall as intended on every system. Always check with the software vendor to make sure it's compatible with Windows NT.

- **Hardware-specific changes to the Registry.** Events such as adding a new NIC might trigger downstream symptoms such as failure to authenticate to the domain, although the protocol seems to be working and bound properly. One issue that arises occasionally is having no protocols listed in the Network applet, although TCP/IP is functioning properly.

- **Direct changes to the Registry.** Everyone makes mistakes. Incorrect manipulations of the Registry are, unfortunately, common.

Uninstalling Applications

Sometimes, there is no Add/Remove Program item, the Add/Remove operation doesn't function correctly, or no uninstall utility was provided with an application. Simply deleting the installation directory doesn't remove all of a program's code. Here is one way to ensure the removal of a program:

1. In HKEY_LOCAL_MACHINE\Software and HKEY_CURRENT_USER\Software, locate the entry for the application you intend to remove and delete the program's entries.

   Remove any entries for the program from the Start menu under %systemroot%\Profile\All Users\Start Menu\Programs and %systemroot%\Profiles\%username%Start Menu\Programs. The program could exist in one or both, so always check both places.

   If the program had a component listed as a service, edit HKEY_LOCAL_MACHINE\System\CurrentControlSet\Services and delete the associated entry.

   If the program had an entry in the Add/Remove Programs list, edit HKEY_LOCAL_MACHINE\Software\Microsoft\Windows\CurrentVersion\Uninstall, locate the entry, and remove it.

2. If no entry existed in the Startup folders, but the program starts automatically, edit HKEY_CURRENT_USER\Software\Microsoft\Windows NT\CurrentVersion\Windows. Check load REG_SZ and run REG_SZ to see if they contain related program information and delete it.

3. There are several places in which an application can be placed to have it autostart. Here are the places that **www.ntfaq.com** recommends looking in the following locations:

HKEY_LOCAL_MACHINE\Software\Microsoft\Windows\CurrentVersion\Run

HKEY_LOCAL_MACHINE\Software\Microsoft\Windows\CurrentVersion\
RunOnce

HKEY_LOCAL_MACHINE\Software\Microsoft\Windows\CurrentVersion\
RunServices

HKEY_LOCAL_MACHINE\Software\Microsoft\Windows\CurrentVersion\
RunServicesOnce

HKEY_LOCAL_MACHINE\Software\Microsoft\Windows NT\
CurrentVersion\Winlogon\Userinit

HKEY_CURRENT_USER\Software\Microsoft\Windows\CurrentVersion\Run

HKEY_CURRENT_USER\Software\Microsoft\Windows\CurrentVersion\
RunOnce

HKEY_CURRENT_USER\Software\Microsoft\Windows\CurrentVersion\
RunServices

HKEY_CURRENT_USER\Software\Microsoft\Windows\CurrentVersion\
RunServicesOnce

HKEY_CURRENT_USER\Software\Microsoft\Windows NT\
CurrentVersion\Windows\run

HKEY_CURRENT_USER\Software\Microsoft\Windows NT\
CurrentVersion\Windows\load

%systemroot%\win.ini

4. Reboot.

Third-Party Registry Editing and Management Utilities

Several third-party editing and management utilities are available for maintaining the Registry. (*Third-party* refers to anything that doesn't ship on the Windows NT distribution CD.) This section discusses tools from the *Microsoft Windows NT Server 4.0 Resource Kit* CD as well as tools found on the Internet.

REGKEY

REGKEY.EXE is located on the *Microsoft Windows NT 4.0 Resource Kit* CD. REGKEY is one of those tools that allows indirect manipulation of Registry information. Using REGKEY's GUI, you can change the following settings:

- **Display Shutdown Button in Logon Dialog Box.** This setting activates the Shutdown button from the logon screen. This one is a beauty because you don't have to log in just to shut the server down in a controlled manner. (This setting is enabled by default on Windows NT Workstation and disabled by default on Windows NT Server.)

- **Display Last User in Logon Dialog Box.** For security-conscious users, this setting blanks the User Name from the Logon Information dialog box. Making this setting active requires that a user provide both a valid user name and a valid password to log on to the system.

- **Parse AUTOEXEC.BAT for SET/PATH Commands.** This setting tells Windows NT to parse an AUTOEXEC.BAT file, if it exists, to look for PATH statements or environment variable SET statements and merge them into the Registry. This is handy if you want to set environment variables without editing the Registry directly.

- **Set Number of User Profiles to Cache.** This one seems self explanatory, but has the benefit of caching roaming profiles and handling them as local profiles. If your network is slow or the profile file is large and times out, this enables the user to log in with the cached profile.

- **Change the Default Background Wallpaper.** This provides a quick way to set the background wallpaper for your computer.

- **Allow Long File Names in FAT.** This setting, if unchecked, forces users to utilize 8.3 filenames on a FAT partition for MS-DOS compatibility rather than deal with truncated filenames, such as micros~1.doc, micros~2.doc, and so on.

COMPREG

COMPREG, or the Compare Registry tool, is a command-line utility from the *Microsoft Windows NT 4.0 Resource Kit* CD you can use to compare Registries or keys between local and remote computers. Abbreviations for the keys are permissible in the command argument. For example, HKEY_LOCAL_MACHINE can be abbreviated as LM. The following example runs COMPREG on the local machine's session manager and compares it to the Registry on the server \\MOON:

```
COMPREG "\lm\system\currentcontrolset\control\session manager" \\MOON
```

If the second argument is only a computer name, the keyname specified with the first argument will be appended to the second argument automatically. The more valuable switches are as follows:

- **-v (verbose).** Prints both differences and matches.
- **-r (recurse).** Recurses into "dead" trees—that is, subkeys that exist only in one key.

REG

REG is a command-line manipulation utility provided by Microsoft on the *Microsoft Windows NT Server 4.0 Resource Kit* CD. The REG program contains the following subprograms: REG QUERY, REG ADD, REG UPDATE, REG DELETE, REG COPY, REG SAVE, REG BACKUP, REG RESTORE, REG LOAD, and REG UNLOAD. These replace the Registry commands REGCHG.EXE, REGDEL.EXE, REGDIR.EXE, REGREAD.EXE, REGSEC.EXE, RESTKEY.EXE, RREGCHG.EXE, and SAVEKEY.EXE. Each of these allows manipulation of local and remote Registries. When omitted as a syntactical argument, HKEY_LOCAL_MACHINE is assumed.

REG QUERY

Use the `REG QUERY` command for local or remote queries of a Registry. The syntax for `REG QUERY` is as follows:

```
REG QUERY RegistyPath [\\Machine] [/S]
RegistryPath  [ROOTKEY\]Key[\ValueName]
ROOTKEY       [ HKLM ¦ HKCU ¦ HKCR ¦ HKU ¦ HKCC ]
```

        Key is the full name of a Registry key under the selected ROOTKEY.
        ValueName is the value, under the selected Key, to query. When omitted, all keys and values under the Key are listed.
        Machine is the name of remote machine-omitting defaults to the current machine. Only HKLM and HKU are available on remote machines.
        /S, /s queries all subkeys.

```
Examples:
REG QUERY HKLM\Software\Microsoft\ResKit\Setup\InstallDir
Displays the value of the InstallDir Registry entry.
REG QUERY HKLM\Software\Microsoft\ResKit\Setup /S
Displays all keys and values under the Setup subkey.
```

Take It from the Source!

All of the information in the following sections is taken directly from the online documentation for the REG utility. That is, at any time, you can type one of the REG commands followed by a slash and question mark—REG QUERY /?, for example—and you'll be able to view the information that follows on-screen.

REG ADD

Use the `REG ADD` command to make additions into a local or remote Registry. The
syntax for `REG ADD` is as follows:

```
REG ADD RegistryPath=Value [DataType] [\\Machine]
RegistryPath  [ROOTKEY\]Key\ValueName=Value
ROOTKEY         [ HKLM ¦ HKCU ¦ HKCR ¦ HKU ¦ HKCC ]Optional.
When ROOTKEY is omitted, HKLM is assumed.
```

> **Key** is the Registry key's full name under the selected ROOTKEY.
> **ValueName** is the value, under the selected Key, to add.
> **Value** is the value to assign to the Registry entry being added.
> **DataType** can be one of the following: REG_SZ, REG_DWORD, REG_EXPAND_SZ, or
> REG_MULTI_SZ. (If omitted, REG_SZ is assumed.)
> **Machine** is the name of the remote machine. Omitting **Machine** defaults to
> current machine. Only HKLM and HKU are available on remote machines.

```
Examples:
REG ADD HKLM\Software\MyCo\MyApp\Version=1.00
Adds the Registry entry version=1.00 of type REG_SZ.
REG ADD HKLM\Software\MyCo\MyApp\Timeout=5 REG_DWORD \\ZODIAC
Adds the Registry entry Timeout=5 of type REG_DWORD on machine ZODIAC.
```

REG UPDATE

Use the `REG UPDATE` command specifically to make changes to existing Registry information on local or remote machines. The syntax for `REG UPDATE` is as follows:

```
REG UPDATE RegistryPath=Value [\\Machine]
RegistryPath  [ROOTKEY\]Key\ValueName
ROOTKEY         [ HKLM ¦ HKCU ¦ HKCR ¦ HKU ¦ HKCC ] Optional.
When ROOTKEY is omitted, HKLM is assumed.
```

> **Key** is the full name of the Registry key under the selected ROOTKEY.
> **ValueName** is the value, under the selected key, to update.
> **Value** is the value assigned to the Registry variable being updated.
> **Machine** is the name of the remote machine. Omitting **Machine** defaults to the
> current machine. Only HKLM and HKU are available on remote machines.

```
Examples:
REG UPDATE Software\MyCo\MyApp\Timeout=10
Replaces the existing value for Timeout with 10. This setting defaults to HKLM.
REG UPDATE HKLM\Software\MyCo\MyApp\Version=2.01 \\ZODIAC
Replaces the existing value for Version with 2.01 on machine ZODIAC.
```

REG DELETE

Use the REG DELETE command to locally or remotely delete Registry keys. The syntax
for REG DELETE is as follows:

```
REG DELETE RegistryPath [\\Machine]
RegistryPath  [ROOTKEY\]Key[\ValueName]
ROOTKEY       [ HKLM ¦ HKCU ¦ HKCR ¦ HKU ¦ HKCC ]OPTIONAL
```

When ROOTKEY is omitted, HKLM is assumed.

Key is the full name of a Registry key under the selected ROOTKEY.
ValueName is the value, under the selected Key, to delete. The **ValueName** is
optional. When omitted, ALL keys and values under the Key are DELETED.
Machine is the name of the remote machine. Omitting **Machine** defaults to
current machine. Only HKLM and HKU are available on remote machines.
/F, /f forces the deletion(s) without questions. Be careful with this one!

```
Examples:
REG DELETE HKLM\Software\MyCo\MyApp\Timeout
Deletes the Timeout Registry entry.
REG DELETE HKLM\Software\MyCo \\ZODIAC /F
Deletes the ENTIRE hive MyCo on ZODIAC without asking for confirmation.
```

REG COPY

Use the REG COPY command to locally or remotely copy Registry keys. The syntax for
REG COPY is as follows:

```
REG COPY Source [\\Machine] Destination [\\Machine]
Where Source and Destination are in the RegistryPath format are as follows:
RegistryPath  [ROOTKEY\]Key[\ValueName]
ROOTKEY       [ HKLM ¦ HKCU ¦ HKCR ¦ HKU ¦ HKCC ] Optional.
When ROOTKEY is omitted, HKLM is assumed.
```

Key is the full name of a Registry key under the selected ROOTKEY.
ValueName is the value, under the selected Key, to copy. This setting is
optional. When omitted, ALL keys and values under the Key are copied.
Machine is the name of the remote machine. Omitting **Machine** defaults to the
current machine. Only HKLM and HKU are available on remote machines.

```
Examples:
REG COPY HKLM\Software\MyCo\MyApp HKLM\Software\MyCo\SaveMyApp
Copies the key MyApp and all of its entries to SaveMyApp under MyCo.
REG COPY Software\MyCo \\SAFARI Software\MyCo \\ZODIAC /F
Copies the ENTIRE hive MyCo on SAFARI to MyCo on ZODIAC.
```

Differences Between Windows NT and 95

Windows NT: On remote machines, the file is written to the System32 directory. Windows 95: On remote
machines, the file is written to the Windows directory.

REG SAVE **or** REG BACKUP

REG SAVE and REG BACKUP are identical in function. Each is used to save or backup a local or remote Registry. For brevity, only the syntax for the REG SAVE command is detailed here.

```
REG SAVE RegistryPath FileName [\\Machine]
RegistryPath   [ROOTKEY\]Key
ROOTKEY        [ HKLM ¦ HKCU ¦ HKCR ¦ HKU ¦ HKCC ]Optional.
When ROOTKEY is omitted, HKLM is assumed.
```

> **Key** is the full name of a Registry key under the selected ROOTKEY.
> **FileName** is the name of the disk file to save to without an extension.
> **Machine** is the name of the remote machine. Omitting **Machine** defaults to the current machine. Only HKLM and HKU are available on remote machines.

```
Examples:
REG SAVE HKLM\Software\MyCo\MyApp AppBkUp
Saves the hive MyApp to the file AppBkUp.
REG SAVE HKLM\Software\MyCo MyCoBkUp \\ZODIAC
Saves the hive MyCo on ZODIAC to the file MyCoBkUp also on ZODIAC.
```

REG RESTORE

Use the REG RESTORE command to restore Registry information. The source of the Registry information must be created using the REG BACKUP or REG SAVE command. The syntax for REG RESTORE is as follows:

```
REG RESTORE FileName KeyName [\\Machine]
ROOTKEY        [ HKLM ¦ HKCU ¦ HKCR ¦ HKU ¦ HKCC ]Optional.
When ROOTKEY is omitted, HKLM is assumed.
```

> **FileName** is the name of the hive file without an extension. You must use Save or Backup to create this file.
> **KeyName** is equal to [ROOTKEY\]Key.
> **Key** is the key name in which to restore the hive file. this setting overwrites the existing key's values and subkeys.
> **Machine** is the name of the remote machine. Omitting **Machine** defaults to the current machine. Only HKLM and HKU are available on remote machines.

```
Examples:
REG RESTORE NTRKBkUp HKLM\Software\Microsoft\ResKit
Restores the hive file NTRKBkUp overwriting the subkey ResKit.
REG RESTORE NTRKBkUp HKLM\Sofware\Microsoft\ResKit \\ZODIAC
Restores NTRKBkUp, overwriting the subkey ResKit on ZODIAC.
```

REG LOAD

Use the REG LOAD command to load Registry information. The syntax for REG LOAD is as follows:

```
REG LOAD FileName KeyName [\\Machine]
ROOTKEY        [ HKLM ¦ HKU ]Optional.
When ROOTKEY is omitted, HKLM is assumed.
```

       FileName is the name of the hive file without an extension.
       KeyName is equal to [ROOTKEY\]Key.
       Key is the key name in which to load the hive file. This setting is able to create a new key.
       Machine is the name of the remote machine. Omitting **Machine** defaults to the current machine. Only HKLM and HKU are available on remote machines.

```
Examples:
REG LOAD TempHive HKLM\TempHive
Loads the hive file TempHive to the Key TempHive under HKLM.
REG LOAD TempHive HKLM\TempHive \\ZODIAC
Loads the hive file TempHive to the key HKLM\TempHive on ZODIAC.
```

REG UNLOAD

Use the REG UNLOAD command to load Registry information. The syntax for REG UNLOAD is as follows:

```
REG UNLOAD KeyName [\\Machine]
ROOTKEY        [ HKLM ¦ HKU ]Optional.
When ROOTKEY is omitted, HKLM is assumed.
```

       KeyName is equal to [ROOTKEY\]Key.
       Key is the key name of the hive to unload.
       Machine is the name of the remote machine. Omitting **Machine** defaults to the current machine. Only HKLM and HKU are available on remote machines.

```
Examples:
REG UNLOAD HKLM\TempHive
Unloads the hive TempHive from HKLM.
REG UNLOAD HKLM\TempHive \\ZODIAC
Unloads the hive TempHive from the machine ZODIAC.
```

REGINI.EXE

The REGINI.EXE utility is provided by Microsoft on the *Microsoft Windows NT Server 4.0 Resource Kit* CD. This utility uses character-based batch files to add keys to the Windows NT Registry by specifying a Registry script. You can review detailed help information with the `REGINI /?` command. You can use a Registry editor (REGEDIT or REGEDT32) to perform similar tasks as an interactive process, but REGINI supports a wider range of data types than Windows NT's built-in Registry editors. REGINI also provides a quick way to add or modify drivers in the Registry:

```
usage: REGINI [-m \\machinename ¦ -h hivefile hiveroot
                    ¦ -w Win95 Directory]
              [-i n] [-o outputWidth]
              [-b] textFiles...
where:

        -m specifies a remote Windows NT machine whose Registry is to be manipulated.
        -h specifies a specify local hive to manipulate.
        -w specifies the paths to a Windows 95 SYSTEM.DAT and USER.DAT files
        -i n specifies the display indentation multiple. The default is 4.
        -o outputWidth specifies how wide the output is to be. By default, the
outputWidth is set to the width of the console window if standard output has not
been redirected to a file. In the latter case, an outputWidth of 240 is used.
        -b specifies that REGINI should be backward compatible with older versions of
REGINI that did not strictly enforce line continuations and quoted strings
Specifically, REG_BINARY, REG_RESOURCE_LIST, and REG_RESOURCE_REQUIREMENTS_LIST
data types did not need line continuations after the first number that gave the
size of the data.
        TextFiles is one or more ANSI or Unicode text files with Registry data. The
easiest way to understand the format of the input textFile is to use the REGDMP
command with no arguments to dump the current contents of your Windows NT Registry
to standard out. Redirect standard out to a file and this file is acceptable as
input to REGINI.
```

Some general rules are as follows:

- The semicolon character (;) is an end-of-line comment character, provided it is the first non-blank character on a line.

- The backslash character (\) is a line continuation character.

- All characters from the backslash up to, but not including, the first non-blank character of the next line are ignored. If there's more than one space before the line continuation character, it's replaced by a single space.

- Indentation is used to indicate the tree structure of Registry keys. The REGDMP program uses indentation in multiples of four. You may use hard tab characters for indentation, but embedded hard tab characters are converted to a single space regardless of their position.

- Values should come before child keys because they are associated with the previous key at or above the value's indentation level.

- For key names, leading and trailing space characters are ignored and not included in the key name, unless the key name is surrounded by quotes. Embedded spaces are part of a key name.

- Key names can be followed by an ACL, which is a series of decimal numbers, separated by spaces, set apart by square brackets (that is, [8 4 17]). The valid numbers and their meanings are defined in Table 8.4.

Table 8.4 **Valid ACL Numbers and Their Meanings**

ACL Number	Meaning
1	Administrators Full Access
2	Administrators Read Access
3	Administrators Read and Write Access
4	Administrators Read, Write, and Delete Access
5	Creator Full Access
6	Creator Read and Write Access
7	World Full Access
8	World Read Access
9	World Read and Write Access
10	World Read, Write, and Delete Access
11	Power Users Full Access
12	Power Users Read and Write Access
13	Power Users Read, Write, and Delete Access
14	System Operators Full Access
15	System Operators Read and Write Access
16	System Operators Read, Write, and Delete Access
17	System Full Access
18	System Read and Write Access
19	System Read Access
20	Administrators Read, Write, and Execute Access
21	Interactive User Full Access
22	Interactive User Read and Write Access
23	Interactive User Read, Write, and Delete Access

If there is an equal sign on the same line as a left square bracket, the equal sign takes precedence, and the line is treated as a Registry value. If the text between the square brackets is the string DELETE with no spaces, REGINI will delete the key and any values and keys under it.

For Registry values, the syntax is as follows:

```
value Name = type data
```

Leading spaces, spaces on either side of the equal sign, and spaces between the type keyword and data are ignored, unless the value name is surrounded by quotes. If the text to the right of the equal sign is the string DELETE, then REGINI deletes the value.

The value name can be left off or be specified by an at sign character (@), which means the same thing, namely the empty value name. Therefore, the following two lines have identical result:

```
= type data
@ = type data
```

This syntax means that you can't create a value with leading or trailing spaces, an equal sign, or an at sign in the value name, unless you put the name in quotes. Valid value types and format of data are as follows:

```
REG_SZ text
REG_EXPAND_SZ text
REG_MULTI_SZ "string1" "str""ing2" ...
REG_DATE mm/dd/yyyy HH:MM DayOfWeek
REG_DWORD numberDWORD
REG_BINARY numberOfBytes numberDWORD(s)...
REG_NONE (same format as REG_BINARY)
REG_RESOURCE_LIST (same format as REG_BINARY)
REG_RESOURCE_REQUIREMENTS (same format as REG_BINARY)
REG_RESOURCE_REQUIREMENTS_LIST (same format as REG_BINARY)
REG_FULL_RESOURCE_DESCRIPTOR (same format as REG_BINARY)
REG_MULTISZ_FILE fileName
REG_BINARYFILE fileName
```

If no value type is specified, the default is REG_SZ. For REG_SZ and REG_EXPAND_SZ, if you want leading or trailing spaces in the value text, surround the text with quotes. The value text can contain any number of embedded quotes, and REGINI will ignore them, because it looks for quote characters only at the first and last character of the text string.

For REG_MULTI_SZ, each component string is surrounded by quotes. If you want an embedded quote character, double quote it, as in string2 in the preceding code.

For REG_BINARY, the value data consists of one or more numbers. The default base for numbers is decimal. Hexadecimal may be specified by using the 0x prefix. The first number is the number of data bytes, excluding the first number. After the first number, there must be enough numbers to fill the value. Each number represents one DWORD or four bytes. Therefore, if the first number is 0x5, you need two more numbers after that to fill the five bytes. The high order three bytes of the second DWORD would be ignored.

Whenever specifying a Registry path, either on the command line or in an input file, the following prefix strings can be used:

- HKEY_LOCAL_MACHINE
- HKEY_USERS
- HKEY_CURRENT_USER
- USER

Each of these strings can stand alone as the key name or be followed by a backslash and a subkey path.

REGFIND.EXE

REGFIND is a command-line utility provided by Microsoft on the *Microsoft Windows NT Server 4.0 Resource Kit* CD that you can use to search the Windows NT Registry for arbitrary data, key names, or value names, and optionally replace any of these with new values. REGFIND has a special flag for finding malformed `REG_SZ` strings in the Registry. To access parts of the Registry, you must be a member of the Administrators group.

The usage is as follows:

```
REGFIND [-h hivefile hiveroot ¦ -w Win95 Directory ¦ -m \\machinename]
            [-i n] [-o outputWidth]
            [-p RegistryKeyPath] [-z ¦ -t DataType] [-b ¦ -B]
            [-y] [-n]
            [searchString [-r ReplacementString]]
where:
```

> **-h** specifies a specify local hive to manipulate.
> **-w** specifies the paths to a Windows 95 SYSTEM.DAT and USER.DAT files.
> **-m** specifies a remote Windows NT machine whose Registry is to be manipulated.
> **-i n** specifies the display indentation multiple. The default is 4.
> **-o outputWidth** specifies how wide the output is to be. By default, the outputWidth is set to the width of the console window if standard output has not been redirected to a file. In the latter case, an outputWidth of 240 is used.
> **-p RegistryPath** specifies where to start searching

Valid prefix names for easy access to well known parts of the Registry are as follows:

```
HKEY_LOCAL_MACHINE -> \Registry\Machine
            HKEY_USERS -> \Registry\Users
            HKEY_CURRENT_USER -> \Registry\Users\...
            USER:    -> HKEY_CURRENT_USER
where:
```

> **-t** specifies which Registry types to look at: REG_SZ, REG_MULTI_SZ, REG_EXPAND_SZ, REG_DWORD, REG_BINARY, and REG_NONE. The default is any of the _SZ types.
> **-b** is valid only with _SZ searches, and specifies that REGFIND should look for occurrences of the searchString inside of REG_BINARY data. This search cannot be specified with a replacementString that is not the same length as the searchString.

> **-B** is the same as -b but also looks for ANSI version of string within REG_BINARY values.
>
> **-y** is only valid with _SZ searches, and specifies that REGFIND should ignore case when searching.
>
> **-n** specifies to include key and value names in the search. May not specify -n with -t.
>
> **-z** specifies to search for REG_SZ and REG_EXPAND_SZ values that are missing a trailing null character and/or have a length that is not a multiple of the size of a Unicode character. If -r is also specified, any replacement string is ignored, and REGFIND will add the missing null character and/or adjust the length up to an even multiple of the size of a Unicode character.
>
> **searchString** is the value to search for. Use quotes if it contains any spaces. If searchString is not specified, just searches based on type.
>
> **-r replacementString** is an optional replacement string to replace any matches with.

The searchString and replacementString values must be of the same type as specified to the -t switch. For any of the _SZ types, it is just a string. For REG_DWORD, it is a single number (that is, 0x1000 or 4096). For REG_BINARY, it is a number specifying number of bytes, optionally followed by the actual bytes, with a separate number for each DWORD (for example, 0x06 0x12345678 0x1234).

If just the byte count is specified, then REGFIND will search for all REG_BINARY values that have that length. You cannot search for length and specify -r.

When performing replacements, REGFIND displays the value after the replacement has been made. It's usually best to run REGFIND once without the -r switch to see what values will be change before it the replacement takes place.

REGBACK.EXE

REGBACK is a command-line Registry backup utility provided by Microsoft on the *Microsoft Windows NT Server 4.0 Resource Kit* CD. It must be used with REGREST to restore its backup. The following describes the key points of REGBACK. Microsoft recommends that if you have a tape drive installed, it should be used rather than REGBACK and REGREST. (You can start the Backup utility by double-clicking its icon in the Administrative Tools program group.) The following rules apply to the REGBACK and REGREST utilities:

- REGBACK and REGREST save and reload the entire hive, including access control lists. So, it's possible to restore a hive and find that you have different ACLs than before.

- REGBACK does not back up hives that aren't loaded. You can just copy these files, because they are not loaded in the Registry.

- REGBACK does not automatically back up hives that don't reside in the CONFIG folder (specifically, some user profiles), but it will do so manually. This avoids name conflicts.

- REGBACK stops at the first bug, except when backing up manual hives.
- REGBACK will not overwrite existing files; instead, it reports an error.
- REGBACK fails if the hive files don't all fit on the target, so often it's best to use REGBACK to back up hives to a hard disk folder and then use BACKUP.EXE, or use XCOPY.EXE or SCOPY.EXE to save the backed up hives on floppy disks.
- REGBACK does not copy the files in the CONFIG folder that are not currently kept open by the Registry. Use XCOPY.EXE or SCOPY.EXE to save inactive hives.

The syntax for REGBACK is as follows:

```
regback <directory argument>
```

This code backs up all of the Registry hives whose files reside in the config directory to the named directory. (This is normally all hives.) It also warns of hives that must be backed up manually or of those with errors. Use the following format for a "manual" backup:

```
regback c:\monday.bku
if ERRORLEVEL 1 echo Error!
```

```
regback <filename> <hivetype> <hivename>
```

This backs up the named hive to the named file. The backup will fail if *hivetype* isn't "machine" or "users," or if *hivename* isn't a hive root.

hivetype is either "machine" or "users." *hivename* is the name of an immediate subtree of HKEY_LOCAL_MACHINE or HKEY_LOCAL_USERS.

```
regback c:\special.sav\system machine system
regback c:\savedir\prof users s-1-0000-0000-1234
if ERRORLEVEL 1 echo Error!
```

REGDMP.EXE

REGDMP is a command-line utility on the *Microsoft Windows NT Server 4.0 Resource Kit* CD that writes all or part of the Windows NT Registry to the standard output (STDOUT). The output format is suitable for input to REGINI. The syntax for REGDMP is as follows:

```
usage: REGDMP [-m \\machinename ¦ -h hivefile hiveroot
               ¦ -w Win95 Directory]
              [-i n] [-o outputWidth]
              [-s] [-o outputWidth] RegistryPath
       where:

          -m specifies a remote Windows NT machine whose Registry is to be manipulated.
          -h specifies a local hive to manipulate.
          -w specifies the paths to Windows 95 SYSTEM.DAT and USER.DAT files.
```

```
     -i n specifies the display indentation multiple. The default is 4.
     -o outputWidth specifies how wide the output is to be. By default, the
outputWidth is set to the width of the console window if standard output has not
been redirected to a file. In the latter case, an outputWidth of 240 is used.
        -s specifies summary output. Summary information includes value names, type,
and first line of data.
```

RegistryPath specifies where to start dumping.

COMPREG.EXE

Use the COMPREG utility from the *Microsoft Windows NT Server 4.0 Resource Kit* CD to compare Registries on two machines. This utility is useful in detecting that a component on one computer fails to function and the other computer works perfectly on two machines thought to be configured identically. If REGDMP detects any REG_SZ or REG_EXPAND_SZ value string that is missing the trailing null character, it will prefix the value string with the following text:

```
(*** MISSING TRAILING NULL CHARACTER ***)
```

The REGFIND tool can be used to clean these up; this is a common programming error.

Whenever specifying a Registry path, either on the command line or in an input file, the following prefix strings can be used:

- HKEY_LOCAL_MACHINE

- HKEY_USERS

- HKEY_CURRENT_USER

- USER

Each of these strings can stand alone as the key name or be followed by a backslash and a subkey path. The syntax for COMPREG is as follows:

```
- - - - - - - - - - - - - -usage: COMPREG <1> <2> [-v] [-r] [-e] [-d] [-q] [-n] [-h] [-?]

<1> <2>  local or remote keys to compare (default root ==
  HKEY_CURRENT_USER)
        (e.g., \\HOTDOG\HKEY_LOCAL_MACHINE\Software)
The rootkeys can be abbreviated as follows:

        HKEY_LOCAL_MACHINE--lm
        HKEY_CURRENT_USER--cu
        HKEY_CLASSES_ROOT--cr
        HKEY_USERS--us

If the second argument is only a computer name, the keyname specified with the first
argument will automatically be appended.
The subkey path syntax for COMPREG is as follows:

     -v (verbose)--Prints both differences and matches.
```

```
            -r (recurse)--Recurses into "dead" trees; that is, subkeys that exist in
only one key.
            -e--Sets errorlevel to the last errorcode. By default, errorlevel is set.
            -d--Doesn't print the value data (just the keys).
            -q--Prints only the number of differences.
            -n--Specifies that no color is to be used in the output (default : use
color).
            -h--Displays additional help.
            -?--Displays the basic usage screen.


Examples:
COMPREG "\lm\system\currentcontrolset\control\session manager" \\MOON

COMPREG HKEY_CURRENT_USER\Cheech HKEY_CURRENT_USER\Chong
```

REGREST.EXE

The REGREST utility from the *Microsoft Windows NT Server 4.0 Resource Kit* CD
allows you to recover the Registry from a backup. The recovery is done one hive at a
time. The changes will take effect only after the system is rebooted.
SetRestorePrivilege is required to make use of this program and is enabled for Backup
Operators and Administrators by default. REGREST requires that REGBACK was
used to perform the original backup.

REGREST works by doing RegReplaceKey calls. The original hive will be stored
into a .SAV file. You must have sufficient space for this or the restore will fail. A reboot
is required for the changes to take effect. All files must be on the same volume—they
are renamed, not copied. The syntax for REGREST is as follows:

```
regrest <new files> <save files>
```

For each active Registry hive whose file resides in the config dir, this setting will
attempt to replace its current file with a like named file in the new file's directory, and
move the old file to the save files directory. It also warns of hives that must be restored
manually, or of errors. Use the following form for "manual" restoration:

```
regrest c:\monday.bku  c:\install.sav
if ERRORLEVEL 1 echo Error!
```

```
regrest <newfilename> <savefilename> <hivetype> <hivename>
```

The hivetype is either "machine" or "users." Hivename is the name of an immediate
subtree of HKEY_LOCAL_MACHINE or HKEY_LOCAL_USERS.

This setting renames the specified hive's file to <savefilename>, and then moves the
file specified by <newfilename> to be the backing for the specified hive. (No changes
take effect until the next boot.)

```
regrest c:\special.sav\system c:\oldsystem.sav machine system
    if ERRORLEVEL 1 echo Error!
```

SCANREG.EXE

The SCANREG utility, also from the *Microsoft Windows NT Server 4.0 Resource Kit* CD, is another variant for searching in the Registry. SCANREG allows case-sensitive searches as an option. The syntax for SCANREG is as follows:

```
scanreg 1.05 <[-s] string> < [-k] [-v] [-d]> [[-r] key] [-c] [-e] [-n]
The root key can be abbreviated as follows:

        HKEY_LOCAL_MACHINE--lm
        HKEY_CURRENT_USER--cu
        HKEY_CLASSES_ROOT--cr
        HKEY_USERS--us

The SCANREG switch syntax is as follows:

        -s specifies the string to search for.
        -r is the root key to start search from (default = HKEY_CURRENT_USER).
        -k specifies a search by keyname.
        -v searches by valuename.
        -d searches data.
        -c specifies that the search is case sensitive. (The default is case
INsensitive.)
        -e returns only an exact match. (The default is to return all matches.)
        -n specifies no color in the output. (The default is that keys are red,
values are green, and data are yellow.)

Examples:
SCANREG -s Windows -k -v -d
SCANREG -s Windows -kvd
SCANREG /s Windows /r \lm\software /kvde
SCANREG Windows \lm -kd -n
SCANREG Windows \\MOON\HKEY_LOCAL_MACHINE -d
SCANREG Windows HKEY_CURRENT_USER\software –kvd
```

Windows NT Registry Monitor

The Windows NT Registry Monitor utility, which can be found at **www.sysinternals.com**, was written by Bryce Cogswell and Mark Russinovich. This very handy utility allows you to track events that don't show up in Event Viewer. You should use this utility for its advanced filtering options. It allows you to filter Registry events based on process, path include, path exclude, and log reads. It displays events based on process, request, path, and result as success or failure. The process is the image file of the process that triggered the Registry event, the request is the Registry Application Programming Interface (API) requested by the specific key, the path is the path to the key selected, and the result is the success or failure of the event.

For More Information

The following resources will provide you with valuable information regarding the Windows Registry:

- *Microsoft Windows NT Workstation 4.0 Resource Kit*. Microsoft Press, 1996. ISBN: 1572313439.

- Microsoft TechNet: `http://www.microsoft.com/technet/`

- *Windows NT Registry*. Osborne, Sandra. Macmillan, 1998. ISBN: 1562059416.

- *Expert Guide to Windows NT 4 Registry*. Hipson, Peter D. Sybex, 1998. ISBN: 0782119832.

9

Important Registry Keys and Values

THIS CHAPTER EXAMINES REGISTRY SETTINGS and configurations, as well as shareware and freeware software that add value to Microsoft Windows NT. Since the release of Windows NT 4.0, administrators have tweaked and modified the operating system beyond what originally was offered out of the box. This chapter explores Registry entries that save time, add functionality, improve security, and enhance the look and feel of Windows NT. It also examines the differences between Windows NT Workstation and Windows NT Server.

Comparing Windows NT Workstation and Windows NT Server

Are there any real differences between Windows NT Server and Windows NT Workstation? This question has been hotly debated among different groups. Table 9.1 lists the key differences between these two operating systems.

Table 9.1 **Differences Between Windows NT Server and Windows NT Workstation**

Difference	Windows NT Server Workstation	Windows NT
Minimum RAM	16MB	12MB
Required disk space	160MB	110MB
Number of supported CPUs	32	2
Maximum inbound RAS connections	256	1
Web services Information Server (IIS)	Microsoft Internet Server (PWS)	Peer Web
Microsoft BackOffice support	Yes	No
Fault tolerance	Mirroring, RAID 5	No
DNS server	Yes	No
DHCP server	Yes	No
WINS server	Yes	No

Judging by the differences in Table 9.1, one would assume that Windows NT Workstation and Windows NT Server are completely different products. In reality, they are very similar. If you compare the files from a Windows NT Workstation installation to a Windows NT Server installation, you will immediately notice similarities. According to Microsoft, Windows NT Server is optimized to benefit networking performance, whereas Windows NT Workstation is optimized with the single user in mind.

The differences between the two are evident in Windows NT Server's support for the following services, which are not supported by Workstation:

- Dynamic Host Configuration Protocol (DHCP)
- Domain name service (DNS)
- Windows Internet Naming Service (WINS)
- Remote Access Service (RAS)
- Wizards
- Network Client Administrator
- IIS
- NetWare tools
- Network monitor
- Remote Boot Manager
- License Manager

- Services for Macintosh
- User Manager (Workstation) and User Manager For Domains (Server)

Cosmetically, however, the user interface is consistent between the two operating systems.

Basic Console Operations

You can make most of the changes to the Windows NT console through the Control Panel. Use the Registry to make these changes directly if you want to change the settings for all domain desktops programmatically. To configure the Console using the Registry for the logged-in user, edit HKEY_CURRENT_USER\Console; for all users, edit HKEY_USERS\.DEFAULT\Console. Table 9.2 describes console settings for the Windows NT Registry.

Table 9.2   **Console Settings for the Windows NT Registry**

Value	Type	Default	Description
CursorSize	REG_DWORD	25 percent	The percentage of the character cell occupied by the cursor. Valid entries are 25 percent (small), 50 percent (medium), and 100 percent (large).
FullScreen	REG_DWORD	0	Valid entries are 0 (Windowed) and 1 (Full Screen).
FaceName	REG_SZ	none	Alternate command window font name. If blank, a raster font is used.
FontFamily	REG_DWORD	0	Font type. 0 = raster, 48 = TrueType.
FontSize	REG_DWORD	0x00000000	This is an eight-character hex number representing pixel height and pixel width. The default (0x00000000) is 8x12, and an entry of 0x000C0005 is 12x5.
FontWeight	REG_DWORD	0	0 is the default weight of the chosen font.
HistoryBufferSize	REG_DWORD	50	The number of commands that can be stored in each command buffer.

continues

Table 9.2 **Continued**

Value	Type	Default	Description
InsertMode	REG_DWORD	0	0=overtype, 1=insert.
NumberOf HistoryBuffers	REG_DWORD	4	The number of command buffers.
PopupColors	REG_DWORD	0x000000F5	This eight-character hex represents background color and text color.
QuickEdit	REG_DWORD	0	0 means the user must use commands to cut and paste; 1 means the user can use the mouse to cut and paste.
ScreenBufferSize	REG_DWORD	0x00190050	This eight-character hex represents lines of text and character per line. The default is 25 lines of 80 characters.
ScreenColors	REG_DWORD	0x000000007	This eight-character hex represents background color and text color.
WindowSize	REG_DWORD	0x00190050	This eight-character hex represents lines of text and character per line. The default is 25 lines of 80 characters.
WindowPosition	REG_DWORD	none	If not present, the system selects a position. This eight-character hex represents y/x.

For each console configuration you save, a subkey is created with the name of the window. This subkey has the same value entries as the console key. You can create the subkey by right-clicking the title bar of the command window and choosing Properties.

Windows NT Logon and Logoff Controls

The following sections explore editing the Registry to change logon and logoff controls for Windows NT.

Shut Down Windows NT with a Power Off

This Registry edit powers off a Windows NT computer while bypassing the It Is Now Safe To Turn Off Your Computer message that follows a Shutdown command. To make this change, select the HKEY_LOCAL_MACHINE\Software\ Microsoft\Windows NT\CurrentVersion\Winlogon Registry entry and double-click PowerDownAfterShutdown or add it as REG_SZ. Set it to 1. This works only if your Hardware Abstraction Layer (HAL) supports it.

Logon Without Prompting

This Registry edit enables a user to log on to Windows NT without going through the logon process. TweakUI and the *Microsoft Windows NT Server 4.0 Resource Kit* utility AUTOLOG.EXE can accomplish this change as well. To configure this using the Registry, edit HKEY_LOCAL_MACHINE\Software\Microsoft\Windows NT\ Current Version\Winlogon. Set the DefaultDomainName, DefaultPassword (cannot be blank), and DefaultUserName. Set AutoAdminLogon to 1. If you ever want to log on as a different user, hold down the Shift key as you log off.

Automatically Run Check Disk at Startup

To configure Windows NT to automatically run Check Disk at startup, select the HKEY_LOCAL_MACHINE\SYSTEM\CurrentControlSet\Control\Session Manager key. Change the BootExecute entry from `autocheck autochk * /........` to `autocheck autochk *`.

If you have scheduled CHKDSK for multiple volumes, there will be an autocheck entry for each volume. Delete the string from the BootExecute Registry value for each volume you do not want checked. If you have Windows NT 4.0 with Service Pack 2 or later applied, a new command-line utility (CHKNTFS) assists in preventing repeated CHKDSKs during reboots if the "dirty" bit is set. Type **CHKNTFS /?** and see Knowledge Base article Q160963 for more details.

Build an NTFS Boot Disk

If your installation of Windows NT on an NTFS partition ever fails to boot, you can jump start it with an NTFS boot disk. Perform the following steps to create an NTFS boot disk:

1. Format a disk in Windows NT Explorer.
2. Copy the following files to the disk: NTDETECT.COM, BOOT.INI, and NTLDR.
3. If you want to boot to a non–Windows NT operating system, you will need the appropriate BOOTSECT file. (Normally, this is BOOTSECT.DOS.)
4. If Windows NT is on a SCSI device being controlled by a SCSI card that does not have an on-board BIOS, copy the NTBOOTDD.SYS file as well. If you don't need it, it won't be on your C drive.

Password Viewing

Your password is stored in plain text in the Registry and can be seen by anyone with the authority to view a remote Registry.

Add the Shutdown Button to the Welcome Dialog Box

To display a shutdown button at logon, select the HKEY_LOCAL_MACHINE\
SOFTWARE\Microsoft\Windows NT\CurrentVersion\Winlogon key and then edit
the value ShutdownWithoutLogon REG_SZ to 0.

When this value is set to 1, you can select Shutdown from the Welcome dialog box.
If the value is 0, the Shutdown button does not appear. This setting is particularly useful in a multiboot situation when Windows NT is booted by mistake.

Add a Logon Welcome or Legal Notice

The Registry value entries that control the logon sequence for starting Windows NT
are found under the HKEY_LOCAL_MACHINE\SOFTWARE\Microsoft\
Windows NT\CurrentVersion\Winlogon Registry key.

The LegalNoticeCaption REG_SZ value specifies a caption for the message that
appears in the warning dialog box. Add this value entry if you want a warning to be
displayed when a user attempts to log on to a Windows NT system. The user cannot
proceed without acknowledgment of this message. To specify text for the message, you
also must specify a value for LegalNoticeText. You can use the System Policy Editor to
change this value.

The LegalNoticeText REG_SZ key specifies the message that appears when the
user presses Ctrl+Alt+Delete during logon. Add this value entry if you want a warning to be displayed when a user attempts to log on to a Windows NT system. The user
cannot proceed without acknowledging this message. To include a caption for the
logon notice, you also must specify a value for LegalNoticeCaption. You can use the
System Policy Editor to change this value.

The LogonPrompt REG_SZ key's default is Enter A User Name And Password
That Is Valid For This System. The text entered appears in the Logon Information dialog box. This is designed for additional legal warnings to users before they log on. This
value entry does not appear in the Registry unless you add it.

The Welcome REG_SZ key sets welcome message text. The text entered appears in
the caption bar beside the title of the Begin Logon, Logon Information, Workstation
Locked, and Unlock Workstation dialog boxes. This value entry does not appear in the
Registry unless you add it. Note that the text you enter here goes immediately next
to the text in the title bar, so you'll probably want to add a space at the beginning of
the value.

Blank Username in Logon Dialog Box

To help deter hackers, you can blank the Username field from the logon dialog box.
This forces a hacker to gather one more piece of information to break into the system. You also can rename the Administrator account to something else. When you
know a username, all you need is a password. To blank out the username in the logon
dialog box, edit the DontDisplayLastUserName REG_SZ value in the
HKEY_LOCAL_MACHINE\SOFTWARE\Microsoft\Windows NT\
CurrentVersion\Winlogon key. By default, Windows NT displays the name of the last

person to log on in the Username field of the Logon Information dialog box. If you add this value entry and set it to 1, the Username field always is blank when the Logon Information dialog box appears.

Activate Screen Saver If Nobody Logs On

To activate the screen saver if no one logs on, edit the HKEY_USERS\.DEFAULT\ Control Panel\Desktop key and change the value for ScreenSaveActive to 1. Edit SCRNSAVE.EXE and enter the full path to the screen saver you want to use such as SCRNSAVE.SCR or SSTARS.SCR. Double-click ScreenSaveTimeOut and enter the number of seconds of inactivity before activation. You must reboot for this to become effective.

Display Your Company Logo During Logon

To display your company logo during logon, save a bitmap in the 8.3 file format with a .BMP extension in the %systemroot% directory on your machine. To display the bitmap at logon, edit the HKEY_USERS\.DEFAULT\Control Panel\Desktop key, edit or add the value REG_SZ: Wallpaper, and set it to the full path of your bitmap. In this example, the path would be `%systemroot%\BITMAPNAME.BMP`. Edit or add the value REG_SZ: TileWallpaper. A setting of 0 means don't tile; 1 means tile. Edit or add the value REG_SZ: WallpaperStyle. A setting of 0 is normal; 2 means stretch to fill the screen. (This is mutually exclusive with TileWallpaper = 1.)

If you use a normal (not tiled) logo, you can position it by adding the following REG_SZ values:

- **WallpaperOriginX.** Sets the wallpaper to the number of pixels from the left side of the screen.
- **WallpaperOriginY.** Sets the wallpaper to the number of pixels from the top of the screen.

Speed Start Menu Navigation

To speed up Windows NT's response time for presentation of fly-out menus from the Start button, edit the HKEY_CURRENT_USER/Control Panel/Desktop key's MenuShowDelay value to `100`. You must reboot for this to take effect.

Configure Service Startup Dependencies

If you have a service (such as a Document Management System) that is dependent on a database to be running first, you should try this tip. You can configure the startup of a service based on the completion of one or more services.

In the HKEY_LOCAL_MACHINE\System\CurrentControlSet\Services entry, scroll to the first service you want to control and highlight it. If the right pane contains a DependOnService, double-click it and add a service. If DependOnService is not present, add the value DependOnService with type REG_MULTI_SZ. If you want to add multiple values, each one should be on a separate line.

Run a Job the First Time a User Logs On

RunOnce entries, as the name implies, are run one time and then deleted from the Registry. This might be helpful in welcoming a new employee or in displaying a special message. To create a RunOnce entry, edit the HKEY_LOCAL_MACHINE\ Softwate\Microsoft\Windows\CurrentVersion\RunOnce entry and add a value with any name of type REG_SZ. Set the value to the full path of the executable or batch file. A simple example might be to add value Welcome REG_SZ set to `\\ServerName\%username%\WELCOME.CMD` where WELCOME.CMD might contain:

```
@echo off
pause The Microsoft Corporation is pleased
to welcome %UserName% to your first logon to
%ComputerName%.

Exit
```

Upon completion, the value Welcome is deleted from the RunOnce subkey.

Establish Default Logoff and Shutdown Settings

To establish logoff and shutdown settings, edit the HKEY_CURRENT_USER\ Software\Microsoft\WindowsNT\CurrentVersion\Shutdown key and add the value LogoffSetting as a REG_DWORD. Its values are as follows:

- **0:** Log off
- **1:** Shut down
- **2:** Shut down and restart
- **3:** Shut down and power off (when supported)

Add the Value ShutdownSetting as a REG_DWORD

Its values are the same as those shown in the "Establish Default Logoff and Shutdown Settings" section.

Keep RAS Connections Alive After Windows NT Logoff

To keep RAS connections alive after a Windows NT logoff, edit the HKEY_LOCAL_MACHINE\Software\Microsoft\Windows NT\CurrentVersion\ Winlogon entry. Add the value KeepRasConnections as a type REG_SZ and then set it to 1.

Speed Up Windows Shutdown

To speed the Windows NT shutdown process, edit the HKEY_LOCAL_MACHINE\
SYSTEM\CurrentControlSet\Control\WaitToKillServiceTimeout entry or add it as a
REG_SZ. This key tells the Service Control Manager how long to wait for services to
complete the shutdown request. The default is 20000 milliseconds. You must wait long
enough for the services to complete an orderly shutdown. This varies depending on
what services you have loaded. Check the documentation for your services before
making this change.

Allow Logon Script to Finish Prior to Loading Desktop

To allow a logon script to finish before loading desktop settings, edit or add the value
REG_DWORD to the HKEY_CURRENT_USER\SOFTWARE\Microsoft\
Windows NT\CurrentVersion\Winlogon entry and set the value to
RunLogonScriptSync. Settings for this entry are as follows:

- **0:** Don't wait for the logon script to complete before loading the desktop.
- **1:** Wait for the logon script to complete before loading the desktop.

You also can add the value REG_WORD to the HKEY_LOCAL_MACHINE\
SOFTWARE\Microsoft\Windows NT\CurrentVersion\Winlogon entry.

Reduce Disk Usage for Roaming Profiles

When a user with a roaming profile logs off a workstation, a copy of the profile is
cached on the local hard drive. If other users with roaming profiles use that workstation, disk space is being consumed to keep these cached profiles. To configure a system
so that roaming profiles are not cached, edit the HKEY_LOCAL_MACHINE\
SOFTWARE\Microsoft\Windows NT\CurrentVersion\Winlogon entry and edit or
add the value DeleteRoamingCache as type REG_DWORD. Set it to 1.

Change Logon Background Color

You can change the logon background color by altering the RGB values in the
HKEY_USERS\.DEFAULT\Control Panel\Colors\Background entry. If you set it to
0 0 0, you will have a black background. If you set the RGB value to 255 255 255,
you will have a white background.

Clear the Page File at System Shutdown

Because the PAGEFILE.SYS holds cached information about the system, you might
want to clear it for security reasons when you shut down the system. To do so, edit
the HKEY_LOCAL_MACHINE\System\CurrentControlSet\Control\Session
Manager\Memory Management entry and add a value named
ClearPageFileAtShutdown as type REG_DWORD. The default is 0. When you set it

to 1, inactive pages in the PAGEFILE.SYS will be filled with zeros. Some pages cannot be cleared because they are active during shutdown.

Set Logon Hours from the Command Prompt

You can use the NET USER command to allow username to log on to the server between 08:00 and 17:00 on weekdays:

```
net user username /time:M-F,08:00-17:00 /Domain
```

The format of the /times parameter is /times:{times ¦ all}.

This specifies the times during which the user is allowed to use the computer. The times value is expressed as day[-day][,day[-day]] ,time[-time][,time[-time]].

The value is limited to one-hour time increments. Days can be spelled out or can be abbreviated (M, T, W, Th, F, Sa, Su). Hours can be in 12-hour or 24-hour notation. For 12-hour notation, use AM and PM or A.M. and P.M. Using the value All means a user can always log on. A null value (blank) means a user can never log on. Separate day and time with commas and separate units of day and time with semicolons (for example, M,4AM-5PM;T,1PM-3PM). Do not use spaces when designating /times.

The /domain setting performs the operation on the PDC of the computer's primary domain. This parameter applies only to Windows NT Workstation computers that are members of a Windows NT Server domain. By default, Windows NT Server computers perform operations on the PDC. This setting also can be made from the User Manager (see Chapter 2, "Common Windows NT Administrative Utilities," for details).

Windows NT Shell

Changes to the Windows NT shell are discussed in the following sections.

Remove Entries from the Start Button Content Menu

To remove entries from the Start button content menu, use REGEDT32.EXE to edit the HKEY_LOCAL_MACHINE\Software\Classes\Directory\Shell or HKEY_CLASSES_ROOT\Directory\Shell. Edit Shell and delete any of these subkeys such as DOS Here and Find. Navigate to the HKEY_LOCAL_MACHINE\ Software\Classes\Folder\Shell or HKEY_CLASSES_ROOT\Folder\shell entry and then double-click Shell to delete any of these subkeys such as Root Explore, Open, or Explore.

Add Entries to the Right-Click Content Menu

When you right-click a file in Windows NT Explorer, the valid choices for that extension are presented. To add a new choice, perform the following steps:

1. Select Options from the View menu and then select File Types.
2. Select the file type you want to add and click the Edit button.

3. Click the New button.

4. Type the action (**Edit**, **Print**, **View**, and so on), the full path to the application, and any command-line switches or parameters required to perform the action. If you want to change an action, click Edit instead of New.

Restrict System Features in Windows NT

Some restrictions to system features are easier to change with the System Policy Editor. To restrict the use of system features using the Registry, edit the HKEY_CURRENT_USER\Software\Microsoft\Windows\CurrentVersion\Policies\ entry and add the System subkey. All the following entries are type REG_DWORD and have a default of **0**. If these entries are set to **1**, the restriction is enabled.

- **DisableTaskManager.** Prevents TASKMGR.EXE from running. This entry is supported only from Windows NT 4.0 with Service Pack 2 or later.

- **NoDispAppearancePage.** Removes the capability to change the colors or color scheme on the desktop from the Control Panel.

- **NoDispBackgroundPage.** Removes the capability to change wallpaper and background patterns from the Control Panel.

- **NoDispCPL.** Disables the Display applet in the Control Panel.

- **NoDispScrSavPage.** Prevents the Screen Saver tab from appearing in the Display applet in the Control Panel.

- **NoDispSettingsPage.** Prevents the Settings tab from appearing in the Display Properties applet in the Control Panel.

Remove Shortcut Arrow from Desktop Shortcuts

To remove the Shortcut Arrow from your desktop shortcuts, browse to HKEY_CLASSES_ROOT\Lnkfile. Select the IsShortcut value name in the right pane and delete it. You must reboot to see the change.

Open Explorer and My Computer in Detail View

To open Windows NT Explorer and My Computer in detail view, perform the following steps:

1. Open HKEY_LOCAL_MACHINE\Software\Classes\Folder\Shell\Open and set the REG_BINARY value name of EditFlags to `01000000`.

2. Open HKEY_LOCAL_MACHINE\Software\Classes\ Folder\Shell\Open\Command and set the unnamed type REG_EXPAND_SZ value to `C:\WINNT\EXPLORER.EXE /idlist,%I,%L %1`.

3. Edit HKEY_LOCAL_MACHINE\Software\Classes\Folder\Shell\Open\ ddeexec and set the unnamed type REG_SZ value to `[ExploreFolder("%l", %I, %S)]`.

4. Reboot the system.

5. Double-click My Computer and then click Details.

6. On the View menu, click Options.

7. On the File Types tab, scroll to Folder and select it.

8. Click the Edit button.

9. Click Open in the Actions box and press Set Default.

10. Click Close.

Lock Down the Desktop

You can implement desktop restrictions by editing Windows NT Explorer values in the Registry (all values default to 0). Open the HKEY_CURRENT_USER\ Software\Microsoft\Windows\CurrentVersion\Policies\Explorer NoCommonGroups REG_DWORD and set it to 1 so that common program groups do not appear on the Start menu. Set NoDesktop REG_DWORD to 1 to hide all desktop icons.

   To hide a drive, select the NoDrives REG_DWORD. The lowest order (right-most) bit is drive A; the 26th bit is drive Z. To hide a drive, turn on its bit. These drives will still appear in File Manager. To remove File Manager, delete WINFILE.EXE. If you're not happy working in hex, add the decimal number shown in Table 8.3 to hide the drives.

Table 8.3 **Drive Decimal Numbers**

A: 1	B: 2	C: 4	D: 8
E: 16	F: 32	G: 64	H: 128
I: 256	J: 512	K: 1024	L: 2048
M: 4096	N: 8192	O: 16384	P: 32768
Q: 65536	R: 131072	S: 262144	T: 524288
U: 1048576	V: 2097152	W: 4194304	X: 8388608
Y: 16777216	Z: 33554432	ALL: 67108863	

The following are some additional settings for hiding other Windows NT elements:

- **NoFileMenu REG_DWORD.** A value of 1 removes the File menu in Windows NT Explorer.
- **NoFind REG_DWORD.** A value of 1 removes the Find command from the Start Menu.
- **NoNetConnectDisconnect REG_DWORD.** A value of 1 removes the Map Network Drive, Disconnect Network Drive, and right-click options.

- **NoNetHood REG_DWORD.** A value of 1 removes the Network Neighborhood icon and prevents network access from Windows NT Explorer. (It will still work from a command prompt.)

- **NoRun REG_DWORD.** A value of 1 removes the Run command from the Start menu.

- **NoSetFolders REG_DWORD.** A value of 1 hides Control Panel, Printers, and My Computer in Windows NT Explorer and on the Start Menu.

- **NoSetTaskbar REG_DWORD.** A value of 1 indicates that only drag and drop can be used to alter the Start menu and desktop. The taskbar does not appear on the Start menu.

- **NoTrayContextMenu REG_DWORD.** A value of 1 prevents menus from displaying upon right-click of the taskbar, Start button, clock, or taskbar application icons. This entry is available only for Windows NT 4.0 with Service Pack 2 or later.

- **NoViewContextMenu REG_DWORD.** A value of 1 prevents menus from displaying upon right-click of the desktop or Windows NT Explorer's results pane. This entry is available only for Windows NT 4.0 with Service Pack 2 or later.

- **RestrictRun REG_DWORD.** A value of 1 enables only the programs you define in HKEY_CURRENT_USER\Software\Microsoft\Windows\CurrentVersion\Policies\Explorer\RestrictRun to be run on the computer.

- **NoClose REG_DWORD.** A value of 1 removes the Shut Down option from the Start menu. This does not disable shutdown from Ctrl+Alt+Delete. To totally disable a user's capability to shut down, remove the advanced right to Shutdown The System from Policies and User Rights in User Manager for Domains.

To really lock down the desktop, replace the Windows NT Explorer or Program Manager shell with your own launcher. Edit HKEY_LOCAL_MACHINE\Software\Microsoft\WindowsNT\CurrentVersion\Winlogon\Shell and replace the current .EXE with your shell (with a .EXE extension). See the "For More Information" section at the end of this chapter for more details.

Remove Icons from the Desktop

To remove the Microsoft Internet Explorer, Inbox, and Recycle Bin icons from the desktop, edit HKEY_LOCAL_MACHINE\Software\Microsoft\Windows\CurrentVersion\Explorer\Desktop\NameSpace. The NameSpace entry reveals the keys for these three desktop icons. Clicking each one shows you the icon name in the right pane. To remove an icon, select the key and delete it.

Per-User Properties

The following sections detail additional user settings in Windows NT.

Move a Profile from a Workgroup Model into a Domain Model

You've been using a workgroup model and decide to move to a domain model. If you'd like to keep your users' desktop settings that they use to log on as a domain user, do the following:

1. Log on with the local username on the computer and launch REGEDIT.
2. Select the HKEY_CURRENT_USER hive.
3. Select Export Registry from the Registry menu.

Users can use the exported Registry file after they log on to their domain account by double-clicking it. You must verify that the user has appropriate permissions for the Registry key he or she is modifying.

Point a Mail Client to the User's Directory

Windows NT provides a Personal directory as the default location for saving mail and user files. Even though it makes the profile bigger and takes it longer to load, it is better to centralize user files. To point the mail client to the user's directory, edit HKEY_USER\<User_SID>\Software\Microsoft\Windows\Current Version\Explorer\User Shell Folders\Personal while the user is not logged on and change the path to the user's home directory (`%HOMEDRIVE%\%HOMEPATH%`).

To modify the directory for new (not yet created) users, select the HKEY_USERS hive and Load Hive. Navigate to the %SYSTEMROOT%\Profiles\Default User\ NTUSER.DAT directory and enter a unique name when prompted for a key name. Select the Storage key and edit the Storage\Software\Microsoft\Windows\Current Version\Explorer\User Shell Folders\Personal entry and change the value to `%HOMEDRIVE%\%HOMEPATH%`. Select the HKEY_USERS\Storage key and then select Unload Hive from the Registry menu.

Mouse and Keyboard Settings

The following sections discuss how to edit mouse and keyboard settings in Windows NT.

Configure the Snap To Button Function in the Registry

You can configure the Snap To button in the Control Panel's Mouse applet, and you also can configure it in the Registry. To configure it in the Registry, select HKEY_CURRENT_USER\Control Panel\Mouse, edit SnapToDefaultButton or Add Value of type REG_SZ, and set it to `1`.

Force Serial Mouse Detection at Startup

If you have a serial mouse on the COM1 or COM2 serial port and it fails detection at startup, you can force a connection without rebooting. You can do this by adding the value entry OverrideHardwareBitstring as a type REG_DWORD to the HKEY_LOCAL_MACHINE\System\CurrentControlSet\Services\Sermouse\ Parameters entry. A data value of 1 indicates that the mouse is installed on COM1, and a data value of 2 specifies COM2. This entry causes the driver to load even if the mouse is not detected.

Microsoft Natural Keyboard Support in Windows NT

The following are the key combinations supported for the Natural Keyboard under NT 4.0:

- **Menu+Win.** Displays the Start menu.
- **Win+R.** Displays the Run dialog box.
- **Win+M.** Minimizes all open windows.
- **Win+Shift+M.** Undoes the minimizing of all windows.
- **Win+F1.** Displays Help.
- **Win+E.** Displays Windows NT Explorer.
- **Win+F.** Displays Find Files/Folders.
- **Ctrl+Win+F.** Displays Find Computer.
- **Win+Tab.** Cycles the minimized taskbar icons.
- **Win+Break.** Displays system properties.

Force Mouse Wheel Detection

If you have a PS/2 Wheel Mouse without a special driver and the wheel is not functional, it probably is not being detected. To force detection, select the HKEY_LOCAL_MACHINE\SYSTEM\CurrentControlSet\Services\i8042prt\ Parameters entry and edit or add the value EnableWheelDetection with a type REG_DWORD. Set the data to 2 and then restart your computer. The wheel detection settings are as follows:

- **0:** Don't use the wheel.
- **1:** Autodetect the wheel.
- **2:** Always enable the wheel.

Force Windows NT to Use Custom Keyboard Layout During Logon

To force Windows NT to use a custom keyboard layout (for international keyboards) during logon, edit the HKEY_USERS\.DEFAULT\Keyboard Layout\Preload entry. Change the value to 1 and change the number to your local layout, which is located in the HKEY_CURRENT_USER\Keyboard Layout\Preload\1 key. You also can change the HKEY_USERS\.DEFAULT\Control Panel\International\Locale entry to this value, but it is not mandatory. Reboot the computer for the settings to take effect.

Toggle Num Lock Key at Startup

To toggle the Num Lock key at startup, edit the HKEY_Current_User\ControlPanel\Keyboard\InitialKeyboardIndicators entry, which is of type REG_SZ. If this value is set to 0, Num Lock is disabled for the current user after logging on. If the value is 2, Num Lock is enabled and will retain the settings from the last shutdown.

Enable X-Mouse Functionality in Windows NT

To enable X-Mouse functionality in Windows NT 4.0, edit the HKEY_CURRENT_USER\Control Panel\Mouse\ ActiveWindowTracking key and set the REG_DWORD to 1.

Device Keys and Controls

The following sections explore how to edit Registry settings for device keys and controls in Windows NT.

Turn Off CD AutoRun

Some users prefer to turn off the AutoRun feature for a CD-ROM. You can make a Registry change if you prefer to browse when you double-click instead of activating the AutoRun feature. Set the HKEY_LOCAL_MACHINE\SYSTEM\CurrentControlSet\Services\Cdrom\Autorun key, a type REG_DWORD, to 0. Setting the value to 1 turns on the AutoRun feature.

Delete a Device Driver or Service

If you want to remove a service or a device driver, open the Control Panel, launch either the Services or Devices applet (depending on what you are editing), locate the object, and stop it (if it is started). If it won't stop, configure StartUp as Disabled and reboot. Otherwise, you can edit the HKEY_LOCAL_MACHINE\SYSTEM\CurrentControlSet\Services entry, locate the object, highlight it, and delete it.

Plug and Play Devices

If you begin to install a Plug and Play device but subsequently respond "No" when prompted to install a device, you will never be prompted to install that device again. To enable this prompt, you must delete any occurrences of the device from the HKEY_LOCAL_MACHINE\SYSTEM\CurrentControlSet\Services\pnpisa and HKEY_LOCAL_MACHINE\SYSTEM\CurrentControlSet\Enum\ISAPNP keys. Note that you might not have adequate permissions to change the keys. Use REGEDT32 to set proper security.

Locate the device subkey by inspecting the Description value in each subkey. When you locate the device, delete its subkey. When you are finished, locate the device driver (mentioned in the subkey) and delete its filename. Reboot the computer for the settings to take effect.

Change a Service or Driver Startup

To change the startup parameters of a service or driver when it can't be accessed through the Control Panel, edit the HKEY_LOCAL_MACHINE\SYSTEM\CurrentControlSet\Services entry, navigate to the service or driver, and select it. In the right pane, edit the Start value and change this REG_DWORD to one of the following settings:

- **Boot.** Loaded by kernel loader. Components of the driver stack for the boot (startup) volume must be loaded by the kernel loader.
- **System.** Loaded by I/O subsystem. Specifies that the driver is loaded at kernel initialization.
- **Automatic.** Loaded by Service Control Manager. Specifies that the service is loaded or started automatically.
- **Manual.** The service does not start until the user starts it manually, such as by using Services or Devices in Control Panel.
- **Disabled.** Specifies that the service should not be started.

Important Registry Miscellany

The following sections explore some miscellaneous Registry settings that you can configure in Windows NT.

Windows NT 4 Filename Completion

This Registry change enables filename completion at the command prompt when you hit the Tab key. Select the HKEY_CURRENT_USER/Software/Microsoft/Command Processor key and edit CompletionChar or add the value of REG_DWORD and set it to **9**. Reboot the computer for the changes to take effect.

Rename a Domain Controller

The methods for renaming a primary domain controller differ from the methods for renaming a backup domain controller. To rename a PDC, do the following:

1. Open the Control Panel.
2. Launch the Network applet.
3. Select the Identification tab.

4. Click the Change button and enter the new computer name.

5. Reboot the computer for the changes to take effect.

6. Launch the Server Manager.

7. Select Add To Domain.

8. Add the new name as a BDC. (It actually will be added as a PDC.)

9. Select Remove From Domain.

10. Remove the old name and any duplicate new name entry as a BDC.

To rename a BDC, do the following:

1. Launch Server Manager.

2. Select Add To Domain.

3. Add the new name as a BDC.

4. Open the Control Panel.

5. Launch the Network applet.

6. Select the Identification tab.

7. Click the Change button and enter the new computer name.

8. Close the Control Panel and reboot the computer for the changes to take effect.

9. From the PDC, launch the Server Manager.

10. Select the new BDC and synchronize it with the PDC.

11. Select the old BDC and remove it from the domain.

Disable Dr. Watson

Dr. Watson is a handy utility. There are times when it must be disabled, however, such as when you install certain virus protection programs. To disable Dr. Watson, open the HKEY_LOCAL_MACHINE\Software\Microsoft\WindowsNT\CurrentVersion\Ae Debug\Auto entry. A data value of 0 in this type REG_SZ causes the system to display a message box notifying the user when an application error occurs. A data value of 1 (the default) causes the debugger to start automatically.

You can disable Dr. Watson by deleting the AeDebug subkey. If you want to re-enable it, type **drwtsn32 -i** from a command prompt.

Restore Explorer-Like Task List

To enable a Ctrl+Esc Task List, go to HKEY_LOCAL_MACHINE\ SOFTWARE\Microsoft\WindowsNT\CurrentVersion\WinLogon. Select Add Value from the Edit menu. Type **TASKMAN** for the Value Name and click OK. Then, type **TASKMAN.EXE** in the String Editor.

Hide a Computer from the Browse List

To hide a computer from the browse list, open HKEY_LOCAL_MACHINE\
SYSTEM\CurrentControlSet\Services\LanmanServer\Parameters. Select Add Value
from the Edit menu and add the type `Hidden with the value set to REG_DWORD =
1`. Setting the value to 0 makes the computer visible.

Remove Nag Prompt for File Location

If Windows NT was installed from a CD but the distribution files live on a share,
Windows NT will prompt for the location of the files each time it needs them.
To remove this prompt, edit HKEY_LOCAL_MACHINE\SOFTWARE\
Microsoft\Windows NT\Current Versions and set the SourcePath to the desired path.
This points Windows NT to the share where the distribution files reside.

Disable Source Routing

Source routing permits the originator of a datagram to designate specific gateways for
a packet to follow during routing from source to destination. This is analogous to way-
points on a hiking trip where each hiker must pass through specific checkpoints from
the trip's beginning to end as defined prior to the beginning of the trip. This causes
additional overhead on the computers. To disable source routing, open the
HKEY_LOCAL_MACHINE/SYSTEM/CurrentControlSet/Services/Nwlnkipx/Net
Config/*XXXXX* entry (where *XXXXX* is the name of the NIC device for which you
want to disable source routing). Change the Source Routing value from 1 to 0.

Disable 8.3 Name Creation in NTFS

You can increase NTFS performance if you disable 8.3 name creation. If you make
this change, however, some 16-bit programs might have trouble finding long filenames. Don't set this option if you want to install Norton NT Utilities. Open the
HKEY_LOCAL_MACHINE\SYSTEM\CurrentControlSet\Control\FileSystem key.
The value is NtfsDisable8dot3NameCreation REG_DWORD. The default is 0. Set it
to 1 to disable 8.3 name creation. The change won't take effect until you reboot the
computer.

Ghosted Connections

Ghosted connections are resource connections, such as network drives, that appear to
be constantly connected but are really connected only when an access attempt is
made. Unghosted connections are permanent connections. If you want to ghost or
unghost persistent connections, edit the HKEY_LOCAL_MACHINE\
SYSTEM\CurrentControlSet \Control\NetworkProvider entry with a value of
RestoreConnection REG_DWORD. Change the value to 0 for ghost connections or
to 1 for persistent (not ghosted) connections.

Manage the Mapped Network Drive Drop-Down List

If you want to remove some of the connections in the Mapped Network Drive drop-down list, edit the HKEY_CURRENT_USER\Software\Microsoft \WindowsNT\ CurrentVersion\Network\PersistentConnections key and then highlight and delete unwanted entries. Double-click Order and remove the letters that have been deleted. You can rearrange the letters to change the display order.

Move Shares from One Windows NT Server to Another

To move shares from one server to another, navigate to the HKEY_LOCAL_ MACHE\SYSTEM\CurrentControlSet \Services\LanmanServer\Shares key and then save the key to a filename on a floppy. On the new server, navigate to the same key and save its empty Shares key to a floppy before restoring it from the first server. This destroys any existing shares on the new server. Next restore the empty Shares key you saved from the new server to the first server or delete the values manually (also from the Security subkey). Create at least one new share on each server. This is required so that Windows NT Explorer can refresh its shares. In the Services applet in the Control Panel, stop and restart the Server Service. If you don't want that new share, unshare it normally.

Change the Default Spool Directory

You can change the default printer spool directory for all printers or the default printer spool directory for specific printers. To change the default printer spool directory for all printers, open the HKEY_LOCAL_MACHINE \SYSTEM\ CurrentControlSet\Control\Print\Printers entry and add a value named DefaultSpoolDirectory with a data type of REG_SZ. Add a full path string to the printer spool directory. To change the default printer spool directory for specific printers, open the HKEY_LOCAL_MACHINE\SYSTEM\CurrentControlSet\ Control\Print\Printers\ key and add a value named SpoolDirectory with a data type of REG_SZ. Add the full path string to the printer spool directory. You must make sure the path specified actually exists. If it does not exist, Windows NT uses the default spool directory.

Prevent Printer PopUps and Event Logging

To prevent PopUp messages from appearing upon print job completion, open the HKEY_LOCAL_MACHINE\SYSTEM\CurrentControlSet\Control\Print\Providers entry. To prevent pop-up notification, add a value name of NetPopup and set REG_DWORD to 0. To prevent logging, add the value EventLog and set REG_DWORD to 0. You will have to stop and restart the spooler from the Services applet in the Control Panel, but you might want to reboot to make sure the changes take effect.

Activate a Screen Saver from an Icon

To activate a screen saver from an icon, perform the following steps:

1. Open HKEY_CURRENT_USER\SOFTWARE\Microsoft\ Windows NT\CurrentVersion\Windows.

2. Select the Programs value and then choose String from the Edit menu.

3. Add the *SCR* extension to the string as follows: `Programs: REG_SZ: EXE COM BAT PIF CMD SCR`.

4. Click OK, close the Registry editor, and log off.

5. Log back on and, from Windows NT Explorer, highlight the screen saver you want and right-click to define a shortcut. For example, `\WINNT\SYSTEM32\SSBEZIER.SCR /s`.

6. The `/s` switch forces the screen saver to start immediately. Remove `/s` to display a setup screen. Screen savers that use passwords can be used, but the password security is not used.

Control Which Errors Pop Up in Windows NT

You can control which errors pop up to interrupt you. (Errors are still recorded in the event logs.) To do so, open the HKEY_CURRENT_USER\SOFTWARE\ Microsoft\Windows NT\CurrentVersion\Windows entry and add the value NoPopUpsOnBoot as a REG_DWORD. When set to 1, boot pop-up messages are suppressed. The default is 0. Add a value named ErrorMode as a REG_DWORD. The following settings can be configured for this value:

- **0:** All system and application errors pop up. (This is the default.)
- **1:** Errors from system processes are suppressed.
- **2:** All system and application errors are suppressed.

Create Separate Processes for the Desktop, the Taskbar, and Windows NT Explorer

By default, the shell creates one process with the taskbar and desktop as one thread and each instance of Windows NT Explorer as an additional thread. A failure in any thread affects the entire process. If you have at least 24MB of RAM and a fast Pentium, you can create a separate process for the desktop and taskbar and one for each instance of Windows NT Explorer by editing the HKEY_CURRENT_USER\ Software\Microsoft\Windows\CurrentVersion \Explorer entry and adding value DesktopProcess (REG_DWORD). Set it to 1 and reboot. On a dual processor, this provides increased desktop performance.

Prevent Windows NT from Running an Unknown Job at Logon

One indication that Windows NT is running an unknown job at logon is that the %systemroot%\system32 box pops up when you log on. This is caused by a reference to a file that does not exist in one of the Registry entries that follow. If you can't find it in the startup group, check the HKEY_CURRENT_USER\Software\Microsoft\ Windows NT\CurrentVersion \Windows, load REG_SZ and run REG_SZ. Remove the offending value.

Other places where a program can be loaded at startup in Windows NT include the Startup folder for the current user (and all users) and in one of the following Registry entries:

- HKEY_LOCAL_MACHINE\Software\Microsoft\Windows\ CurrentVersion\Run
- HKEY_LOCAL_MACHINE\Software\Microsoft\Windows\ CurrentVersion\RunOnce
- HKEY_LOCAL_MACHINE\Software\Microsoft\Windows\ CurrentVersion\RunServices
- HKEY_LOCAL_MACHINE\Software\Microsoft\Windows\ CurrentVersion\RunServicesOnce
- HKEY_CURRENT_USER\Software\Microsoft\Windows\ CurrentVersion\RunOnce
- HKEY_CURRENT_USER\Software\Microsoft\Windows\ CurrentVersion\RunServices
- HKEY_CURRENT_USER\Software\Microsoft\Windows\ CurrentVersion \RunServicesOnce

Connect to Microsoft's FTP Site as a Drive

To connect to the Microsoft FTP site as a network drive, you must have Windows NT Server or Windows NT Workstation with the TCP/IP and NetBEUI protocols installed as well as a functional Internet connection. To connect to the FTP site as a drive, perform the following steps:

1. Edit your LMHOSTS file (in \%systemroot%\system32\drivers\etc) using your choice of text editors and add **198.105.232.1 FTP #PRE** at the bottom.
2. Save the file. (Make sure the name is LMHOSTS with no extension.)
3. Open an MS-DOS window.
4. Issue the command **nbtstat -R**. (The R must be uppercase.)
5. Type **net view \\ftp**. You should see what the Microsoft FTP site has to offer.
6. To create the FTP drive (the share is called DATA), go to Windows NT Explorer and choose Map Network Drive from the Tools menu.
7. For the share name, enter **\\ftp\data**. For the username, enter **anonymous**.
8. When the dialog box asks for the password, leave it blank.

Shareware and Freeware Tools

The following sections explore some useful shareware and freeware tools to help you configure additional areas in Windows NT.

Baptize

This command-line tool sets the computer name to a specified value without having to reboot the machine. The syntax at the command prompt is `BAPTIZE` *new_name*. After the program finishes, your computer is visible to others on the network under its new name. BAPTIZE is tested to work with NetBEUI and TCP/IP.

Hyena

The built-in utilities for managing Windows NT networks generally are adequate for administering relatively simple networks with a limited number of users. As larger organizations begin to implement Windows NT networks, however, management and administration of users, groups, shared resources, printers, and the various local versus centralized elements of Windows NT can quickly maximize all available support resources. Hyena, from Adkins Resource, Inc., brings together many of the features of User Manager, Server Manager, File Manager, and Windows NT Explorer into one centralized program. In Hyena, all Windows NT domain objects, such as users, servers, and groups, are hierarchically arranged for easy and logical administration. Here's a sample of what Hyena can do:

- Create, modify, delete, and view users, groups, and group members
- Export files of users, groups, printers, computers, and group members
- Browse server shares and copy and delete files without drive mappings
- Create new network drives and printer connections
- View events, sessions, shares, and open files for any server
- View and control services and drivers for one or more computers
- Manage share and file permissions
- Remotely schedule jobs for multiple computers at the same time
- Remotely shut down and reboot any server
- View remaining disk space for multiple computers at the same time

For more information, visit `http://www.adkins-resource.com/`.

BAPTIZE

Depending your computer's configuration, this program might run for up to one minute. During some of this time, your computer might not be visible on the network—don't panic!

HideIT!

HideIT!, from German Salvador, is freeware. HIDE-IT! is a small applet that enables you to hide windows, taking them off the screen, off the taskbar, and off the Alt+Tab chain. This enables you to hide windows that you want to keep open but that you don't need to monitor very often such as an FTP application, Microsoft Exchange, and so on.

WinInfo

WinInfo, from SavillTech, Ltd., is a simple, handy pop-up dialog box that lists the Windows NT version, build, service pack, Plus! version number, processor type, product type, installation type, registered organization, registered owner, install data, source path, and system root. This is a great tool if you need to verify whether your systems are running full copies or evaluation copies of Windows NT as well as applied service packs. You can get WinInfo from **http://www.savilltech.com**.

Windows NT User Wizard

The Windows NT User Wizard automates and simplifies some of the tasks associated with managing user, group, and share security on a Windows NT Server. The wizard does not, however, replace the administrative tools provided with Windows NT. Administrative tasks you can accomplish using the wizard include the following:

- Create and delete single user accounts
- Create and delete multiple user accounts by importing a file
- Create new groups
- Assign group access permissions to a print or directory share
- View a log of the actions performed by the wizard

If Microsoft Exchange 4.0 or higher is installed on your Windows NT Server, you also can do the following:

- Create and delete single user mailboxes in conjunction with creating or deleting a single Windows NT logon account
- Create and delete multiple user mailboxes in conjunction with creating or deleting multiple Windows NT logon accounts by importing a file
- Create mailboxes for all the existing Windows NT logon accounts on your server

Administrative tasks you cannot perform using the wizard include the following:

- Delete a group
- Alter file or directory permissions
- Share (or discontinue sharing) a printer or directory

- Alter the Account, User Rights, or Auditing policies
- Alter any aspect of Microsoft Exchange site security or configuration
- Create template accounts

DumpReg

Somarsoft's DumpReg is a program for Windows NT and Microsoft Windows 95 that dumps the Registry, making it easy to find keys and values containing a string. For Windows NT, the Registry entries can be sorted by reverse order of last time modified. This makes it easy to see changes made by recently installed software, for example. This is a must-have product for Windows NT power users and administrators alike. You can download shareware by Somarsoft at `http://www.somarsoft.com`.

For More Information

If the information about Windows NT Registry settings presented in this chapter has piqued your interest, you can use several resources to obtain additional knowledge.

- Microsoft TechNet has several Registry and system-setting resources available at `http://www.microsoft.com/syspro`.
- You can search Microsoft's knowledge database at `http://www.microsoft.com/kb/` or check out the FAQs at `http://www.microsoft.com/support/default-faq.htm`.

Some helpful Web sites include:

- The ultimate site for Windows NT information is `http://www.ntfaq.com`.
- Jerold Schulman operates JSI, Inc., at `http://www.jsiinc.com`. This is a definitive source for Windows NT information, hacks, tips, and tricks.
- Mark Russonivich and Bryce Cogswell run `http://www.sysinternals.com`. This is a really good site for must-have Windows NT utilities.
- A great site for Windows NT utilities is `http://winfiles.com`. It includes a replacement for the Windows NT Explorer or Program Manager shell and shell enhancements.

III

Networking Windows NT

10

Windows NT Networking Explored and Explained

I N ITS MOST BASIC FORM, a network is nothing more than two or more computers attached for the purpose of sharing information and resources. This principle seems basic enough, but as many of us know, theory and application are not always one in the same.

Networks require specialized software and hardware, and each piece of the network must function properly or the rest of the network will go down. In this chapter, we cover advanced Microsoft Windows NT networking and other networking elements that are often misunderstood or poorly implemented in today's networks.

The Redirector

The Windows NT *Redirector* enables computers to gain entry to other computers for file access. The Redirector connects to other Windows NT computers, Microsoft LAN Manager, Microsoft LAN Server, Microsoft Windows 95, and Microsoft Windows 98 computers. The Redirector is a file system driver that interacts with the lower-level network drivers through the Transport Driver Interface (TDI). This computer-to-computer connection is illustrated in Figure 10.1.

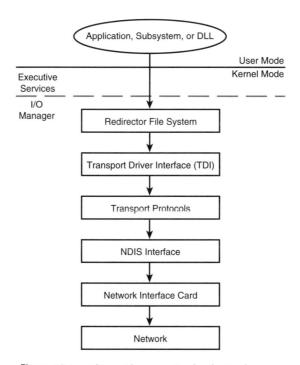

Figure 10.1 Client-side processing by the Redirector.

Microsoft implemented the Redirector as a Windows NT file system driver, which means that applications call a single application programming interface (API) to access files on local and on remote computers. The Redirector runs in Kernel mode, which allows it to call other drivers and Kernel mode components while improving its own performance. The Redirector is loaded and unloaded dynamically just like other system drivers and can coexist with other redirectors.

Windows NT goes through the following steps when connecting to a remote computer:

1. The user-mode request calls the I/O Manager to open a remote file.

2. The I/O Manager identifies the request as a file access request and passes it to the Redirector file system.

3. The Redirector forwards the request to the Network layer for remote server processing.

The Redirector has several Registry values that you can modify directly. The subkey for the Redirector service (RDR.SYS) is located under HKEY_LOCAL_MACHINE\SYSTEM\CurrentControlSet\Services\Rdr\Parameters.

The Redirector Registry values and their default settings are illustrated in Table 10.1:

Table 10.1   **Redirector Registry Values and Settings**

Registry Value	Default setting
ConnectTimeout	Defaults to 300 seconds.
LowerSearchBufferSize	The default is 16KB.
LowerSearchThreshold	The default is 16KB.
UpperSearchBufferSize	The default is 32KB.
UseAsyncWriteBehind	The default is true (1).
UseWriteBehind	The default is true (1).

As mentioned previously, the Redirector interacts with the lower-level network drivers through the Transport Driver Interface (TDI). The TDI allows you to write new drivers that are independent of the network card. Also, it is possible to write applications to use the TDI rather than relying on a protocol, such as Transmission Control Protocol/internet Protocol (TCP/IP).

Windows NT Workstation Service

The Windows NT Workstation service processes all requests originated by users and consists of two components: the user-mode interface and the Redirector. The Workstation service accepts user requests and passes them to the Kernel mode Redirector. The Workstation service is dependent on both the Multiple Universal Naming Convention Provider (MUP) and an exposed protocol that enables the Workstation service to start.

The Workstation service has several Registry values that you can directly modify. The Registry path to the Workstation service entries is HKEY_LOCAL_MACHINE\ SYSTEM\CurrentControlSet\Services\LanmanWorkstation\Parameters.

The Workstation service Registry values and their default settings are shown in Table 10.2.

For More Information about Registry Values

For complete definitions of each Registry value discussed in this chapter, consult the either the TechNet CD or its online version at **http://technet.microsoft.com** and search by the value's name. In addition, see the "For More Information" section at the end of this chapter for more references.

Table 10.2 **Workstation Registry Values and Defaults**

Registry Value	Default Setting
BufFilesDenyWrite	The default value is true (1).
BufNamedPipes	The default value is true (1).
BufReadOnlyFiles	The default value is true (1).
CacheFileTimeout	The default value is 10 seconds.
CharWait	The default value is 3600ms with a range of 0 to 65,535ms.
CollectionTime	The default value is 250ms with a range of 0 to 65,535,000.
LockIncrement	The default value is 10ms.
LockMaximum	Default value is 500ms.
LockQuota	The default value is 4,096 bytes.
LogElectionPackets	The default value is false (0).
MailslotBuffers	The default value is 5 buffers.
MaxCmds	The default value is 15 with a range of 0 to 255.
MaxCollectionCount	The default value is 16 bytes with a range of 0 to 65,535 bytes.
NumIllegalDatagramEvents	The default value is 5datagrams.
PipeIncrement	The default value is 10ms.
PipeMaximum	The default value is 500ms.
ReadAheadThroughput	The default value is 0xffffffffKB.
ServerAnnounceBuffers	The default value for this key is 20.
SessTimeout	The default value is 45 seconds with a range of 10 to 65,535 seconds.
SizCharBuf	The default value is 512 bytes with a range of 64 to 4,096 bytes.
Use512ByteMaxTransfer	The default value is false (0).
UseLockReadUnlock	The default value is true (1).
UseOpportunisticLocking	The default value is true (1).
UseRawRead	The default value is true (1).
UseRawWrite	The default value is true (1).
UseUnlockBehind	The default value is true (1).
UseWriteRawData	The default value is true (1).
UtilizeNtCaching	The default value is true (1).

Windows NT Server Service

The Windows NT Server service processes connections from the client-side Redirectors and grants access to requested resources. Similar to the Redirector, the Server service resides above the TDI and is implemented as a file system driver. It directly interacts with various file system drivers to serve I/O requests such as file reads and writes. The Server service is made up of two components: the actual Server service, which is not dependent on the MUP services because it does not provide Universal Naming Convention (UNC) connections, and SRV.SYS, which is a file system driver that communicates with the lower protocol layers to satisfy command requests.

The following activities take place when a Server service receives a client request:

1. The network drivers receive and forward the request to the server driver.

2. The server forwards the file required to the local file system driver.

3. The file system driver calls low-level disk drivers to access the file.

4. The requested data is returned to the file system driver.

5. The file system driver returns the requested information to the server.

6. The server forwards the data to the network drivers for relay to the requesting client.

The Server service has several Registry values that you can directly modify. The keys associated with the Server service are located in HKEY_LOCAL_MACHINE\ SYSTEM\CurrentControlSet\Services\LanmanServer\Parameters. The Server service Registry values and their default settings are illustrated in Table 10.3.

Table 10.3   **Server Registry Values and Settings**

Registry Value	Default Setting
AlertSched	The default value is 5 minutes with a range of 1 to 65,535 minutes.
BlockingThreads	The default depends on configuration, with a maximum of 4 for Windows NT Workstation.
ConnectionlessAutoDisc	The default value is 15 minutes with a range of 15 minutes to infinity.
CriticalThreads	The default value is 1 with a range of 1 to 9,999.
DiskSpaceThreshold	The default value is 10 percent with a range of 0 to 100 percent.
EnableFCBopens	The default value is true (1).
EnableOplocks	The default value is true (1).
EnableRaw	The default value is true (1).

continues

Table 10.3   **Continued**

Registry Value	Default Setting
ErrorThreshold	The default value is 10 with a range of 1 to 65,535.
Hidden	The default value is false (0).
InitConnTable	The default value is 8 with a range of 1 to 128.
InitFileTable	The default value is 16 with a range of 1 to 256.
InitSearchTable	The default value is 8 with a range of 1 to 2048.
InitSessTable	The default value is 4 with a range of 1 to 64.
InitWorkItems	The default depends on configuration, with a range of 1 to 512.
IRPstackSize	The default value is 5 with a range of 1 to 12.
LinkInfoValidTime	The default value is 60 seconds with a range of 0 to 100,000 seconds.
MaxFreeConnections	The default depends upon configuration, with a range of 2 to 8 items.
MaxGlobalOpenSearch	The default value is 4,096.
MaxLinkDelay	The default is 60 seconds with a range of 0 to 100,000 seconds.
MaxKeepSearch	The default value is 1,800 seconds with a range of 10 to 10,000 seconds.
MaxMpxCt	The default value is 50 with a range of 1 to 100 requests.
MaxNonpagedMemoryUsage	The default value depends on server configuration, with a range of 1MB to infinite bytes.
MaxPagedMemoryUsage	The default value depends on system configuration, with a range of 1MB to infinite bytes.
MaxRawWorkItems	The default depends on configuration, with a range of 1 to 512 items.
MaxWorkItems	The default value depends on configuration, with a range of 1 to 512 items.
MinFreeConnections	The default value depends on system configuration, with a range of 2 items to 5 items.
MinFreeWorkItems	The default value is 2 items with a range of 0 to 10 items.
MinLinkThroughput	The default is 0 bytes per second with a range of 0 to infinite bytes per second.
MinRcvQueue	The default value is 2 items with a range of 0 to 10 items.

Registry Value	Default Setting
NetworkErrorThreshold	The default value is 5 percent with a range of 1 to 100 percent.
NonBlockingThreads	The default value depends on configuration, with a maximum of 8 for Windows NT Workstation, and a range of 1 to 9,999 for Windows NT Server.
OpenSearch	The default value is 2,048 searches with a range of 1 to 2,048 searches.
OplockBreakWait	The default value is 35 seconds with a range of 10 to 180 seconds.
RawWorkItems	The default value depends on system configuration, with a range of 1 to 512 items.
RemoveDuplicateSearches	The default value is true (1).
ScavTimeout	The default value is 30 seconds with a range of 1 to 300 seconds.
ScavQosInfoUpdateTime	The default value is 300 seconds with a range of 0 to 100,000 seconds.
SessConns	The default value is 2,048 connections with a range of 1 to 2,048 connections.
SessOpens	The default value is 2048 files with a range of 1 to 2,048 files.
SessUsers	The default value is 32 users with a range of 1 to 64 users.
SharingViolationRetries	The default value is 5 with a range of 0 to 1,000.
SharingViolationDelay	The default is 200ms with a range of 0 to 1,000ms.
SizReqBuf	The default is 4,356 bytes with a range of 512 to 65,536 bytes.
ThreadPriority	The default value is 1 with possible values of 0, 1, 2, or 15.
Users	The default is 0xffffffff (infinite), with a maximum of 10 for Windows NT Workstation.
XactMemSize	The default is 1MB with a range of 64KB to 16MB.

Protocol Stacks

Computers on the Internet are able to communicate because of the TCP/IP protocol stack. The TCP/IP stacks reside on each computer attached to the Internet. The Open Systems Interconnection (OSI) reference model presents a model for creating such a protocol stack. Common protocol stacks are TCP/IP, Internetwork Packet Exchange/Sequenced Packet Exchange (IPX/SPX), NetBIOS Enhanced User Interface (NetBEUI), AppleTalk, and Systems Network Architecture (SNA).

The OSI model is a seven-layer representation of how networked computers communicate. The layers are as follows: Physical, Data Link, Network, Transport, Session, Presentation, and Application. Each layer performs a certain function to a data packet before passing it to the next layer.

Protocol stacks are combined with drivers for installed network adapters to permit communication with a network. Each layer, or level, of a protocol performs a different function and communicates with the layer directly above or directly below itself. The exception to this rule is the Physical layer. At this layer of the stack, a packet is transmitted on the physical network media. The Physical layer is the lowest layer of a stack.

Figure 10.2 illustrates a basic protocol stack. As data moves from layer to layer, header information is added to or stripped from each packet. Each layer concerns itself with a certain aspect of the data and, in effect, insulates the packet from the other layers. This is analogous to placing a letter in an envelope, the envelope in a small box, the small box in a larger box, the box in a shipping container, and the shipping container in a truck. Each layer provides services for the adjacent layer, but hides information from the remainder of the layers. When the letter arrives at the destination, each container must be opened in sequence. It would therefore be impossible to open the envelope without first opening the small box, and so on. With actual data transmission, when the letter is ready to be sent, it is broken down into packets. Individually, each packet follows the preceding process.

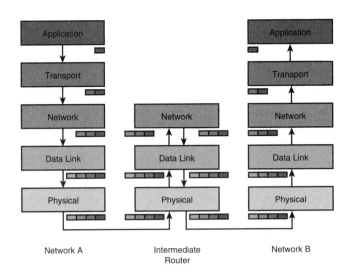

Figure 10.2 Protocol stack packet processing.

Suppose a request is sent from an application on network A to an application on network B; each layer adds some information to the packet as it passes down layer by layer. Likewise, when the packet reaches the receiving network, information is stripped from the packet as it passes up the protocol stack.

The Internet is a network with connections between adjacent networks made through routers. Your packet passes through routers as it moves across the Internet toward the destination computer. A router operates at the Network layer. A received packet arrives at the Physical layer, passes through the Data Link layer, and arrives at the Network layer. The router determines the correct destination for the packet, repackages (encapsulates) it, and passes it to the Physical layer components.

For review, the OSI model contains seven layers. In the broadest sense, layers 1 and 2 (Physical and Data Link) define a network's physical media and those signaling characteristics necessary to request access to the medium for transmission and to send and receive information across the network medium. Layers 3 and 4 (Network and Transport) move information from sender to receiver and handle the data to be sent or received. Layers 5 through 7 (Session, Presentation, and Application) manage ongoing communications across a network and deal with how data is to be represented and interpreted for use in specific applications or for delivery across the network.

The Network Driver Interface Specification (NDIS) provides hardware and protocol independence for network drivers; in addition, it enables a host to contain multiple protocol stacks. NDIS 5.0 extends the functionality of NDIS 3.x and 4.0, so the basic requirements, services, terminology, and architecture of the earlier versions also apply to NDIS 5.0. The NDIS 5.0 architecture is included with Windows 98 and will be included in the Microsoft Windows 2000 operating system. Windows NT Server 4.0 and Windows NT Workstation do not support NDIS 5.0.

Multiple Universal Naming Convention Provider

When a user or application calls a UNC-compliant path, the request is sent to the Multiple Universal Naming Convention Provider (MUP) (see Figure 10.3). The syntax of a UNC path starts with a pair of backslashes, followed by the computer name, IP address, or fully qualified domain name, then followed by a single backslash and a share name. Examples of valid UNC paths are as follows:

- `\\server_name\share_name`
- `\\199.221.84.12\share_name`
- `\\microsoft.com\share_name\file_name_in_share`

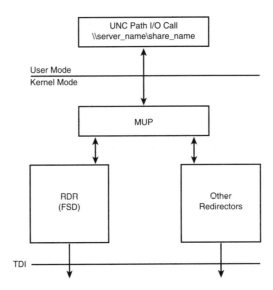

Figure 10.3   Multiple Universal Naming Convention Provider.

The required component in a UNC name is the server name. For example, in Windows NT, Windows 95, or Windows 98, select Run from the Start menu and type **server_name** where server_name is another computer on your network. The result is three shares, one of which is for shared printers.

One of the design goals of networking with Windows NT is to provide a platform that vendors can use to build networking services. MUP permits multiple Redirectors to exist on the same computer and does not require applications to maintain UNC provider listings. The MUP is a driver with paths defined to the existing Redirectors. I/O requests containing UNC names are sent to the MUP. If the MUP has not seen the name within the past 15 minutes, it begins negotiations with each Redirector to determine which Redirector can process the request. The selection criteria are based on the highest registered response time for the UNC that each Redirector reports. The connection to the Redirector is open as long as there is activity and times out after 15 minutes.

Multi-Protocol Router

Not all requests are UNC-based, so the Multi-Protocol Router (MPR) exists to process other I/O requests. The MPR works with the MUP to process application requests. Applications also request access to network resources by using the Win32 network API. The actions MPR takes are similar to the MUP. The application generates the request for resources based on the Win32 API; the MPR determines which

Redirector can fulfill the request, and then sends the request to the appropriate Redirector. Different vendors supply their own Redirectors and provide the appropriate .DLLs for MPR to Redirector communication.

Administrative Shares

A *shared* resource is any resource that is made available over a network. An *administrative* share is a share created automatically when Windows NT is installed on a computer system. Using Server Manager, select Shares to show all shares on a particular computer. There are four shares under the Sharename label. Three of the four shares contain the $ character as the tailing character. When the $ character is appended to a share name, the share becomes a *hidden* share, adding a level of security known as "out of sight, out of mind." Hidden shares do not show up in a browse list; however, a user can connect to the share if he or she is aware of its existence.

Logical drives, such as the C$ drive, are referred to as *administrative* shares although the shares are appended with a $ like a hidden share because they are created as part of the Windows NT installation process. These shares are enabled for administrative access to information. Table 10.4 lists the default permissions assigned to administrative shares. These administrative shares created during a Windows NT installation are well known and a target for unwanted resource intrusion; therefore, you might consider disabling these shares if security is a big concern in your organization.

Table 10.4 **Default Administrative Share Permissions for a Logical Drive**

Group	Share Permission
Creator Owner	Full Control
Domain Admins	Full Control
Domain Users	Read
System	Full Control

You can take several measures to protect a share from unauthorized access. Most power users generally leave defaults alone. Because the administrative shares are well known, hackers attack them. To eliminate this potential security hole, rename the administrative shares. In Microsoft Windows Explorer, right-click a logical drive administrative share. From the Context menu, select Sharing. In the Properties dialog box, select the Sharing tab. Change the share name from C$, or whatever the drive letter happens to be, and rename as another hidden share, such as system$. Back in Windows Explorer, create a folder and several subfolders to mimic your actual C drive. Create a new hidden share using the same method described above. Right-click the new share, select Sharing from the context menu, and select Security from the Properties dialog box. Click the Auditing button and select Success and Failure Auditing for the new hidden share. Because there is nothing of value contained within the share, you risk nothing while providing an inviting target for unsuspecting hackers.

It is also possible to set permission limits on the shares by reducing or removing share level permissions. To permanently delete the shares, you must use the Registry. If the share is deleted manually and Windows is subsequently rebooted, the shares will return. They will, however, be gone for that session. To remove the shares completely, perform one of the following actions:

- For Windows NT Server, edit HKEY_LOCAL_MACHINE\SYSTEM\CurrentControlSet\Services\ LanmanServer\Parameters\AutoShareServer and change the key value to 0. It will be necessary to add the REG_DWORD value for AutoShareServer and assign a value of 0 to disable (1 to enable), then reboot.

- For Windows NT Workstation, edit HKEY_LOCAL_MACHINE\SYSTEM\CurrentControlSet\Services\ LanmanServer\Parameters\AutoShareWks and change the key value to 0. It will be necessary to add the REG_DWORD value for AutoShareWks and assign a value of 0 to disable (1 to enable), then reboot.

Network Bindings

Binding is the process of linking services and protocols to the lower-layer adapter drivers on a computer. Protocols bound to a network card permit the card to communicate using those protocols. This multi-protocol capability is a major benefit of Windows NT. The binding interface for Windows NT is NetBIOS. NetBIOS can be bound to several protocols such as TCP/IP, NWLink, and NetBEUI. Binding several protocols to a network card adds potentially unnecessary overhead to each network communications request. If the most frequently used protocol is listed first in the binding list, average connection time decreases. When a connection request is processed, the local Redirector sends a TDI connection request to each transport simultaneously. The Redirector waits for a response from the higher priority transports. Additional traffic is also generated because of multiple protocol bindings.

For example, a network card has NetBEUI and TCP/IP bound to it. NetBEUI is first in the binding order. The host then makes a request for a network resource. Because NetBEUI is more efficient, it binds first. TCP/IP, which is the second bound protocol, makes the connection to the resource, and the NetBEUI connection is dropped. This is all in addition to the NetBEUI broadcast initially made to establish the connection to begin with. In small, single-subnet networks, NetBEUI is a fast and efficient protocol. Because it is not routable, it is not usable on large, enterprise-wide networks. IPX/SPX is not as fast as NetBEUI, but it is easier to configure and maintain than is TCP/IP. TCP/IP is the "Internet" protocol and the most widely used. There are instances in which multiple protocols might exist within a network. For heightened network security, some companies will deploy IPX/SPX within a network and use proxy agents for Internet access because IPX/SPX is more secure than TCP/IP. The proxy computers will have TCP/IP and IPX/SPX bound to one network card acting as an interpreter between the protocols. TCP/IP-based tools would be useless to a hacker on an IPX/SPX-based network. For the proxy server, both protocols are bound to the internal network interface and only TCP/IP is bound to the external network interface.

Binding Optimization

The first step in binding optimization is to understand the required features of the network. Is Internet connectivity required? Is high security an issue? How large is the network? How is the network laid out? Do I need tools that are a function of a protocol (PING, TRACERT, and so on)? Because networks are often subnetted, it is also important to evaluate the functions within a subnet. (A *subnet* is a separate portion of a network that shares a network address with the other parts of the network and is distinguishable by its subnet number.)

The easiest method for optimizing bindings is to eliminate unnecessary bindings. How do you know which protocols are unnecessary in a network? If the path from a computer to a resource must pass through a router, NetBEUI is out. Unless the network is small and removed from the Internet, NetBEUI is not a good choice. Large-scale NetBEUI networks use available bandwidth with broadcasts, which make effective network communication difficult.

To remove an unnecessary binding, open the Network applet from the Control Panel. Select the Protocol tab. Highlight the name of the protocol you want to remove and then click the Remove button. The Registry information is updated and you are prompted to reboot to effect the change.

Changing the Binding Order

Another equally simple optimization is to move the most frequently used bindings to the top of the binding order. Again, it is important to understand the mission of the network. Assume that your binding order has NetBEUI first and TCP/IP last. Also assume that you need both protocols; however, TCP/IP is the most frequently used.

To modify the binding order, follow these steps:

1. Open the Network applet in Control Panel.
2. Select the Bindings tab.
3. Click the Move Up or Move Down button to reorder the protocol sequence.

To add a new binding to a network adapter, follow these steps:

1. Open the Control Panel.
2. Select the Protocols tab.
3. Click the Add button and select the desired protocol.

After the protocol has been added, you can manage protocol bindings for each interface device. Select the Bindings tab in Control Panel. Using the Show Bindings As combo box, select All Adapters. Bindings are viewed by service, adapter, or protocol. The Adapter view shows each adapter and associated bound protocol. To unbind a protocol, simply disable it. Expand the adapter's entry by clicking the + symbol preceding the adapter's value, highlight the desired protocol, then click the Disable button. This effectively unbinds the protocol from the adapter.

If you have concerns about bindings in your networking environment and about exactly what is going on behind the scenes, running Network Monitor from a Windows TN Server is a good starting point for investigation and troubleshooting. Fewer protocols means less traffic, less exposure to hacks, and less administration.

For More Information

- **Microsoft TechNet.** Useful information about networking and binding topics discussed in this chapter can be found by searching on keywords related to these topics.

- Osborne, Sandra. *Windows NT Registry*. Macmillan Publishing Company, Indianapolis, IN, 1998. ISBN: 1562059416.

- Suhy, Scott B. *Optimization and Tuning of Windows NT*. This is an extremely well written guide to tuning and optimizing Windows NT that can be found at `http://technet.microsoft.com/cdonline/content/complete/boes/bo/winntas/tips/nt301.htm`.

- Thomas, Steven B. *Windows NT 4.0 Registry: A Professional Reference*. McGraw-Hill, New York, NY, 1998. ISBN: 0079136559.

11

Windows NT Networking Models

Y OU MUST MAKE SOME BASIC INFRASTRUCTURE decisions when planning for a network installation. As part of that process, you need to consider items such as security, information sharing, connectivity, user and resource location, and network administrative skills in your enterprise. You also need to determine the available skill set of your employees when deciding what type of networking model to employ.

This chapter focuses on the key elements in choosing and maintaining the network model that's most appropriate for your organization. Because the technology environment remains a moving target, this chapter also focuses on the long-term viability of your decision. It addresses often overlooked issues such as moving from a workgroup to a domain model or from one domain model to another. It also reviews the domain models that Microsoft recommends for most situations. Finally, this chapter reviews some third-party software tools related to network and domain management tasks.

Workgroup Networks

Workgroup networks, or peer-to-peer networks, are network models that offer ease of setup, noncentralized security, and low costs as their key benefits. The workgroup networking model can contain a mixture of operating systems and hardware spread across a large geographic area. Typically, though, workgroups are smaller network installations used when employees have minimal network administrative skills, when money is an issue, when there are few networked computers or users, or when security is not a major concern.

The definition of a *workgroup* is a group of computers on a common network that are linked by a workgroup name. You can view the computers that are part of your workgroup in Network Neighborhood in Windows NT Workstation. You can easily move a particular computer from one workgroup to another.

To move a computer from one workgroup to another, do the following:

1. Open Settings from the Start menu.
2. Select the Control Panel.
3. Double-click the Network icon.
4. Select the Identification tab.
5. Click the Change button.
6. Specify the new workgroup name and then exit.

If the workgroup name you enter doesn't already exist, a new workgroup is created.

You can join a domain from this same dialog box if one exists. Instead of entering a different workgroup name, select the domain radio button and enter the name of the domain you want to join. For Windows NT machines, you must create a computer account in the domain by supplying a domain administrator ID and password. Assuming the account and password information is valid, you will be welcomed into the domain.

Security in a workgroup model is based on share-level security. In Windows NT Workstation, a local Security Accounts Manager (SAM) database contains local account information for user validation on that workstation. Resources can be password-protected. Users are not granted explicit access because there is no central authority for user validation as in a domain model; rather, resources are shared and, when required, protected with passwords. Workgroup models do not provide a robust security model; therefore, if security is of even moderate concern, you're better off using a domain model.

As previously mentioned, typical workgroups are small and are used for logical organization of a small group of computers. A network can consist of multiple workgroups. Assuming that your network is organized into workgroups, you can browse the network within Network Neighborhood. The view shows several workgroups rather than many individual computers, but those computers can be found within their specific workgroups at a lower level in the browser hierarchy. Workgroups do not, however, offer much in the way of centralized administration or user-level security. Domain-based networks were created to address these issues.

Domain-Based Networks

A domain-based network differs from a workgroup-based network in that it contains users and computers that share a centralized security model and user account information. In a Windows NT network, a domain is like a medieval kingdom with a central authority or monarch (the PDC), members that participate in the monarchy as potential rulers (the BDCs), members that provide services to the kingdom but cannot participate in ruling the kingdom (member servers), and ordinary users as the commoners in that kingdom. A domain consists of users and resources just like a kingdom is made up of people and property.

Domain members do not necessarily need to be in the same geographical area; however, members all belong to the same domain. In fact, the purpose of a domain is to provide a more secure relationship among its members and better, more centralized control over its resources.

Domains, like kingdoms, do not trust one another without some negotiation. Advanced domain models use trust relationships to define trusts. Windows NT trusts are one-way, intransitive relationships. Using the kingdom metaphor, King George trusting Queen Alice does not imply that Alice trusts George. In addition, Alice trusting King Henry does not imply that George trusts Henry or that Henry trusts George. According to Microsoft documentation, Microsoft Windows 2000 will offer transitive trust relationships that will make such relationships possible.

When a computer running Windows NT Workstation or Windows NT Server logs on to a network, the NetLogon service on the client computer creates a secure communications channel with the NetLogon service on a domain controller. A secure communications channel exists when computers at each end of a connection are satisfied that the computer on the other end has correctly identified itself. Computers identify themselves using their computer accounts. When the secure channel is established, secure communications can take place between the two computers.

To maintain security during a communications session, internal trust accounts are set up between a workstation and a server, between the primary domain controllers (PDCs) and the backup domain controllers (BDCs), and between domain controllers in both domains when a trust relationship exists between the two domains.

Trust relationships and the secure channels they provide enable administrators to remotely manage workstations and member servers. Trusts also affect the relationships between workstations and domain servers and between PDCs and BDCs.

Primary and Backup Domain Controllers

The first Windows NT Server domain controller installed in a network automatically is designated a PDC. A PDC maintains the master copy of the security accounts (SAM) database. When a domain user password is changed, it is changed on the PDC, not the BDC. The BDC authenticates user logons. The BDC's copy of the SAM is exactly that, a copy. Changes to account and group information occur on the PDC. These changes are then replicated to the BDCs in the domain.

The NetLogon service provides users with a single access point to a domain's PDC and BDCs. NetLogon also synchronizes changes to the directory database stored on the PDC. The size of the directory database is limited only by the number of Registry entries permitted and by the performance limits of the computers and network connections involved.

The Windows NT Server NetLogon service automatically synchronizes the directory databases from the PDC to all BDCs. Based on settings in the Registry, the PDC sends timed notices that signal the BDCs to request directory changes from the PDC. These notices are staggered so that not all BDCs request changes at the same time. When a BDC requests changes, it informs the PDC of the last change it received so that the PDC always is aware of which BDC needs changes. If a BDC is up-to-date, the NetLogon service on the BDC does not request changes.

PDC and BDC Deployment

To successfully implement domains, you must clearly understand the roles of the PDC and BDC. The PDC is the first Windows NT Server created in a domain. Each domain can have only one PDC. The PDC contains the master SAM database. The SAM database is used to validate NetLogon requests; in fact, the primary role of the PDC is to manage this database.

The SAM houses all domain account information including user accounts, groups, and computer accounts. The primary identifier for each object in a domain is its security identifier, known as a SID. The SID uniquely identifies each component in a domain. When a PDC is renamed, its SID still identifies it uniquely. In fact, some Windows NT experts state this succinctly as "Users care about names; Windows NT cares about SIDs."

A BDC is responsible for authenticating user logon requests. BDCs maintain a replica of the master SAM that resides on the PDC. Therefore, the secondary responsibility for any PDC is to replicate its master SAM to all BDCs within the domain of the PDC. Should the PDC become unavailable, BDCs within a domain can authenticate user logon requests. This property makes BDCs a networking necessity. You should add an additional BDC to a domain for approximately every 2,000 users. For a domain in which users are located centrally, an additional BDC for every 4,000 to 5,000 users might be appropriate. Performance monitoring is essential when planning for and deploying BDCs.

The physical distribution of BDCs is determined by several factors, including line speed, link reliability, administrative access, protocols used, user authentication requirements, the number of users to be supported at a site, and locally available resources. For a domain model in which users are geographically dispersed, Microsoft recommends that you place a BDC in close proximity to each group of users.

Installing a BDC also is recommended for fault tolerance. You might, for example, have users in Houston, San Francisco, and New York who are upset that network logon requests take an extraordinary amount of time. If your PDC is located in Houston, place a BDC in San Francisco and another in New York. User logon requests will be validated through the local BDCs instead of traversing the WAN links back to Houston for authentication. If both the New York and Houston domain controllers go down, San Francisco still can handle user authentication requests.

As BDCs are added to a domain, the PDC keeps each of them updated periodically. Therein lies a potential problem. If there are too many BDCs in a domain, unnecessary network traffic might be transmitted from the PDC to the BDCs as it works to keep their SAM replicas updated. We recommend that, on slow WAN links, you place a BDC on the remote subnet to handle local user authentication. The PDC will replicate on a periodic basis to the remote BDCs.

Also consider how much traffic the periodic account synchronization will cause on the WAN or Remote Access Service (RAS) dial-up lines. Avoid full synchronization across WAN links. Full synchronization is required when first setting up a new BDC or when bringing a new location online. Full synchronization also is initiated by default when more than 2,000 changes happen to users or groups in less than one hour. If you anticipate a large volume of change activity, increase the value for the size of the change log. If the preceding conditions do not exist, the synchronization process includes only those changes made to the directory database since the last time synchronization occurred.

Ask the following questions when considering placement of BDCs:

- **Where will users log on?** Make sure there is adequate access to an authenticating BDC.

- **Do users need to be able to log on from more than one location?** If so, their accounts cannot be tied to any single location. Consider using a single master domain model or multiple master domain models, both of which are covered later in this chapter.

- **What resource availability is required?** Does a user need to be able to log on even when the WAN to the central location is down? Or is all data centralized so that no local processing can be done without the WAN?

- **How fast are the WAN links?** The speed of the links between locations should be determined by resource usage across the links and by frequency of changes to settings for users and groups.

Configuring Replication

The following Registry entries relate to PDC and BDC replication. If a large number of BDCs are required or if replication is not completing because of overloaded WAN connections, the following settings can be added or changed to better manage replication. Note that Windows NT does not add any of these value entries to the Registry. You must add them by editing the Registry.

- **PulseConcurrency REG_DWORD 1 to 500 pulses. Default: 20.** This defines the maximum number of simultaneous pulses the PDC sends to BDCs. This value is designed to limit the workload placed on the PDC by sending and processing responses to pulses. The PDC must be powerful enough to support the number of concurrent replication RPC calls in this value. Increasing the value of PulseConcurrency increases the load on the PDC. Decreasing the value of PulseConcurrency increases the time it takes for a domain with a large number of BDCs to replicate a SAM change to all the BDCs.

- **PulseMaximum REG_DWORD 60–172,800 seconds (Up to 48 hours). Default: 7200 (2 hours).** This defines the maximum time between pulses. If the time specified in this value expires, the PDC sends at least one pulse even if all BDC databases are current.

- **PulseTimeout1 REG_DWORD 1–120 seconds. Default: 5.** This defines how long the PDC waits for a response from a BDC before it considers the BDC to be unresponsive. An unresponsive BDC is not counted against the limit specified by PulseConcurrency. This enables the PDC to send a pulse to another BDC in the domain. If this value is too high, a domain with a large number of unresponsive BDCs takes a long time to complete a partial replication. If this number is too low, a slow BDC might mistakenly be treated as unresponsive. When the BDC finally does respond, it will partially replicate from the PDC, increasing the load on the PDC.

- **PulseTimeout2 PulseTimeout2 REG_DWORD 60–3600 seconds. Default: 300 (five minutes).** This defines how long a PDC waits for a BDC to complete each step in the replication process. If the value of this entry is exceeded, the PDC regards the BDC as unresponsive and can send a pulse to another BDC in the domain. PulseTimeout2 applies only to PDCs and is used only when a BDC cannot retrieve all the changes to the SAM database in a single Remote Procedure Call (RPC).

To be considered responsive, a BDC must respond to a pulse and must continue reporting its progress on the replication. If the interval between progress reports exceeds the value of PulseTimeout2, the BDC is considered to be unresponsive. An unresponsive BDC is not counted against the limit specified by PulseConcurrency. This enables the PDC to send a pulse to another BDC in the domain.

If the value of this entry is set too high, a slow BDC or one whose replication rate is too slow consumes one of the PulseConcurrency slots. If the value of this entry is too low, the PDC workload increases because of the large number of BDCs doing a partial replication.

- **PulseTimeout1. Randomize REG_DWORD 0–120 seconds. Default: 1.**
  This specifies how long a BDC waits after receiving a pulse before it responds to the PDC. The value of Randomize must be smaller than the value of PulseTimeout1; otherwise, the PDC will consider the BDC to be unresponsive. When calculating an optimum value for Randomize, remember that the time required to replicate a SAM change to all the BDCs in a domain will be greater than the following:

  [(Randomize/2) × NumberOfBDCsInDomain]   PulseConcurrency

  If this value entry does not appear in the Registry, NetLogon determines optimum values for the server depending on the domain controller's workload.

- **ReplicationGovernor REG_DWORD 0–100 percent. Default: 100.** This defines the proportion of data transferred in each call to the PDC and the frequency of the calls. If the value of ReplicationGovernor is 50, for example, a 64KB buffer is transferred rather than a 128KB buffer, and a replication call can be outstanding on the network for no more than 50 percent of the time. If the value of ReplicationGovernor is 0, NetLogon never replicates and the SAM database will not be synchronized. If the value of ReplicationGovernor is too low, replication might never be completed.

You can configure different replication rates at different times of the day by using REGINI.EXE, a tool on the *Microsoft Windows NT Server 4.0 Resource Kit* CD, and the AT utility, which is included in Windows NT. Write REGINI scripts that set and change the value of ReplicationGovernor and then use AT to execute the REGINI scripts when you want to change these values.

Choosing a Domain Model

A domain model defines the relationships between domains in a networked environment. Choosing a domain model depends on several factors. This section reviews Microsoft's recommendations including factors you should consider when choosing a domain model.

The size of a domain is restricted to the maximum size of a Windows NT security accounts (SAM) database. Microsoft's recommendation for maximum SAM size is 40MB. Unless you are part of an enormous organization, such as IBM or General Electric, a 40MB SAM satisfies the requirements for a very large domain. Every user account consumes about 1KB of SAM space. Every computer account uses 0.5KB of SAM space. Depending on the number of users in a group, groups consume between 3KB and 4KB of space on average.

The size limitation on the SAM database rarely comes into play. For larger networks that choose to maintain a single domain model, however, you might reach this limit. In any domain model, four types of computers can exist: PDCs, BDCs, member servers (Windows NT Servers that do not perform domain controller duties such as servers, print servers, and so on), and workstations (Microsoft Windows 95, Microsoft

Windows 98, Windows NT Workstations, Microsoft Windows 3.11). When installed as
domain controllers, Windows NT Servers are either PDCs or BDCs. The first one
installed in a domain always is the PDC. The remaining domain controllers installed
within the same domain are BDCs.

Table 11.1   **Domain Model Recommendations by Domain Attribute**

Domain Attribute	Single Domain	Single Master	Multiple Master	Independent Single with Trust Relationships
< 40,000 users per domain	X	X	X	
> 40,000 users per domain			X	
Centralized account management	X	X		
Centralized resource management	X		X	X
Decentralized account management			X	X
Decentralized resource management		X	X	
Central MIS	X	X		
No central MIS				X

Single Domain Model

The single domain model consists of exactly one domain. It is like one castle with one
lord, so to speak. According to Microsoft, "For ease of administration, the preferred
domain model is the single domain model. If the single domain model cannot be
used, the second choice should be the single master domain model. If neither of these
is available, an administrator can use trust relationships to centralize all user administration into a single domain, eliminating the need to administer each domain separately."
Further, "In a single domain network, network administrators can always administer all
network servers because the ability to administer servers is at the domain level. The
single domain model is an appropriate choice for organizations that require both centralized management of user accounts and the simplest domain model for ease of
administration."

In the single domain model, the domain Administrators group can oversee all servers within the domain. This simplifies administration tremendously. A single administrator can manage the domain as long as the number of elements in it remains relatively small.

The single domain model allows expansion using multiple domains that have their own administrator or administrators. You can establish trust relationships to expand a single domain model. Each single domain is a separate entity, and trusts allow one domain's users to use another domain's resources. Trusts are discussed in greater detail in the "Single Master Domain Model" section that follows. A trust relationship involves users and resources. The domain with the resources trusts users to use the resources properly. The domain containing the resources is the one that must trust the other domain and therefore is called a *trusting domain*. The domain with the users is trusted with some resource and is known as the *trusted domain*.

A trust does not, however, ease administrative burdens. Each domain is separate and has its own users and administrator. With large enterprise networks that include numerous domains and trust relationships, tracking and managing trusts can be a time-consuming endeavor. As networks increase in size or scope, the single master domain model often is a more efficient option.

Single Master Domain Model

The single master domain model consists of a number of domains, one of which—the single master domain—acts as a centralized administrative domain for user accounts named.

All user and machine accounts are defined in the master domain, and all user accounts belong to the master domain. Resources such as printers and file servers are located in the resource domains. Each resource domain establishes a one-way trust with the master domain that enables users with accounts in the master domain to access resources in all the resource domains. A system administrator can manage the entire multidomain network, users, and resources. This model balances the requirements for account security with the need for readily available resources on a network because users obtain permission to access resources based on their master domain logon identity.

The single master domain model offers numerous benefits including the following:

- **Centralized account management.** You can centrally manage user accounts in the master domain.

- **Decentralized resource management or local system administration capability.** Department domains can have their own administrators that manage department-specific resources such as printers, file shares, and databases.

- **You can group resources logically, corresponding to local domains.** You might have a Sales domain, an Engineering domain, and an Accounting domain. Resources can be grouped within these domains for easy management at the department level, while users are managed in a single master domain.

To construct a single master domain:

1. Create a domain.

2. Install Windows NT Server as a domain controller. As the first controller in the domain, it becomes the PDC and maintains the master SAM database. Designate this domain as the master.

3. Add all user accounts to this domain.

4. Install a BDC for logon fault tolerance and load balancing.

5. Create one or more resource domains.

6. Install Windows NT Server as a domain controller for each resource domain. As the first server in the resource domain, it becomes a PDC and contains the master SAM database for this domain.

7. This domain and any others will function as resource domains.

8. Even in resource domains, it makes sense to install BDCs for the master domain, especially if users log on locally in those parts of the network. Larger departments also should consider installing BDCs for resource domains.

9. Establish a trust relationship. The master domain contains the domain users, and the resource domains contain their respective resources such as files and printers. Remember that the domain with the resources always is the trusting domain, and the people domain always is the trusted domain. In Microsoft documentation, the trust arrow always points to the users.

10. Using User Manager for Domains, select Trust Relationships from the Policies menu.

11. Next to Trusted Domains, click the Add button. Enter the name of the master domain in the dialog box along with a password. The password is for the trust relationship, not a Windows NT account.

12. From the User menu, choose Select Domain.

13. Select the resource domain with which you want to establish the trust relationship.

14. Next to the Trusting Domains field, click the Add button. Enter the name of the resource domain with a password for the trust relationship. Remember that trusting domains trust domains containing users (in this case, the master domain).

If either the trusted or trusting domain cancels its trust relationship, the trust is over. In User Manager for Domains, perform the following steps to completely remove a trust:

1. Choose Select Domain from the User menu and choose the Trusted domain.

2. From the Policies menu, select Trust Relationships.

3. Select the domain name from the Trusted Domains window and click Remove.

4. Choose Select Domain from the User menu and choose the Trusting domain.

5. From the Policies menu, select Trust Relationships.

6. Select the domain name from the Trusting Domains windows and click Remove.

The single master domain model is a two-tiered model in which every resource domain must have a trust set up with the master domain because these trust relationships are nontransitive. Microsoft's recommended 15,000 object limit now applies to user IDs and groups only because the file, print, and application server objects exist in the resource domains.

Multiple Master Domain Model

Use the multiple master domain model when you reach the recommended 15,000 user ID and group object limit within a master domain. To implement the multiple master domain model, set up a one-way trust between each resource domain and every master domain. In addition, two one-way trusts must be established between each pair of master domains.

In addition to object counts, other factors must be considered in an enterprise Windows NT domain design. Among these factors are organization, geography, administration, security, and scalability for future growth.

Organizational issues might include budget issues. Keep in mind that the fewer domains there are, the lower the cost of associated equipment will be to implement the multiple master domain model. If resources are separated for each organizational unit, however, it might be in the best interest of the organization to use separate domains. If these domains are dispersed geographically, political factors can influence the location and control of the master domains involved.

Several geographical issues can influence whether you decide to use the multiple master domain model. For example, how robust is your wide area network (WAN)? The more robust the WAN, the more flexibility your domain design can tolerate. Because domains can be separated geographically, additional local resources might be required to manage this model, especially when 24-7 operation might be required.

You can use the following equation to calculate the number of trusts needed in the multiple master domain model (where n is the number of domains and m is the number of master domains):

```
(n-m)*m + m / (m-2)
```

Complete Trust Domain Model

The complete trust model is basically a multiple master domain model in which every pair of domains has two one-way trusts. Every domain effectively becomes a peer to every other domain. Each domain can contain users and resources. The key administrative overhead item with this model is maintaining the trusts. This is the best model for large, decentralized organizations in which providing access for any user to any resource is the most important factor.

To calculate the number of trust relationships required, use the following formula (where *n* is a domain):

Number of domains equals $n \times (n-1)$

For 10 domains, 10×9=90 trusts must be established to fulfill the requirements for a complete trust domain model. For 100 domains, this number grows to a staggering 9900 (100×99)!

Understanding Groups

Groups are the most frequently mismanaged element in Windows NT or any other network operating system. Understanding group creation and management is essential to minimizing administrative overhead, managing security, and assuring maintainability of Windows NT Servers and domains. Windows NT supports two types of groups: global and local.

Microsoft has an acronym for user management in Windows NT: AGLP. AGLP stands for domain **A**ccounts go in **G**lobal groups, global groups go in **L**ocal groups, and local groups are assigned **P**ermissions. Although this might seem simple, Windows NT includes built-in local groups and default permissions that can complicate group management if you are unaware of them. Without knowledge of default groups and permissions related to domain controllers, member servers, Windows NT Workstations, shares, and the Registry, you can open your network to security risks. This section reviews default groups, built-in groups, default permissions for those groups, and how to apply proper security.

Global groups are essentially domain groups and are created on the PDC. A global group can contain only user accounts from the domain in which they were created. Global groups cannot contain local groups. On the other hand, *local groups* can contain user accounts and global groups from any trusted domain. A local group cannot contain other local groups. Given an appropriate strategy for managing users and groups, this makes perfect sense.

When defining a domain strategy for groups, the key is to minimize local group creation. As with database normalization, find the least common denominator—the most common thread—that links users and place those user accounts into a common group. The benefit of this strategy is that you can assign common user rights without the need to create superfluous groups. Default groups predefined in Windows NT can aid this process.

A computer will have different built-in groups depending on the role it plays in a network. Windows NT domain controllers include the following default local groups:

- Account Operators
- Administrators
- Backup Operators
- Guests

- Print Operators
- Replicator
- Server Operators
- Users

In addition to the preceding groups, Windows NT domain controllers have the following global groups:

- Domain Admins
- Domain Guests
- Domain Users

Windows NT member servers and Windows NT Workstations include the following built-in groups:

- Administrators
- Backup Operators
- Guests
- Power Users
- Replicator
- Users

Windows NT provides more than we ask for. Some of these built-in groups contain other groups by default. Being aware of these groups is essential to managing security properly and to minimizing administrative overhead (see Table 11.2).

Table 11.2 **Default Group Members in Windows NT**

Group	Default Members
Administrators (local)	Domain Admins (global)
Domain Admins (global)	Administrator (default user)
Domain Guests (global)	Guest (default user)
Domain Users (global)	Administrator (default user)
Guests (local)	Domain Guests (global)
Users (local)	Domain Users (global)

In addition to default global groups within default local groups, Windows NT specifies another relationship that exists inherently within the system. The Everyone group is an intrinsic group whose membership consists of all local and network domain users logged in at any time. Known security issues that exist with Everyone include shares, New Technology File System (NTFS) drives, and the Registry. By default, when a

new share is created, Everyone is granted Full Control. When a new NTFS partition is
created, Everyone is granted Full Control. In the Registry, the HKEY_LOCAL_
MACHINE root gives Everyone Read permissions. Some Registry keys also give
Everyone Full Control. You must be aware of what the Everyone group is given by
default so you can close up such breaches in security.

Assigning users to the proper group simplifies user and group management. The
following sections explore the groups built into Windows NT by default.

Administrators

The Administrators group has complete control over the domain as well as servers,
workstations, groups, and resources within the domain. Administrators are superusers
in the domain and therefore have rights and permissions to manage all aspects of the
domain. Administrators, by default, have Take Ownership permissions. Although you
might think NTFS permissions forbid the Administrator to access your files, the
Administrator can take ownership of those files and change the NTFS permissions.

Account Operators

The Account Operators group does not contain any users or other groups by default.
Account Operators can create and manage user account information in the domain to
which they belong. It is interesting to note that Account Operators cannot manage
user and group accounts created by Administrators; rather, Account Operators create
accounts and add those accounts into groups that have been previously set up by an
Administrator. Account Operators cannot assign user rights.

Backup Operators

By default, Administrators, Backup Operators, and Server Operators have the rights to
back up and restore Windows NT volumes, directories, and files. Backup Operators
can specifically back up and restore files even when Read and Write permissions have
not been explicitly given to the group's members.

The Backup Operators group is empty by default. It is common practice in an
enterprise environment to define a global group named Backup Operators into which
the personnel responsible for backups are added. On each domain controller and
member server, the global Backup Operators group is added to the local Backup
Operators group. This promotes simplified group management. Backup Operators can
shut down servers, but they cannot change security settings on the files they are permitted to back up.

Domain Admins

Each local Administrators group contains a global group called Domain Admins. This group is added by default to the local Administrators group to give domain administrators access to newly created Windows NT computers. This implies that all Domain Admins are domain administrators. Depending on your networking model and your definition of administration, new administrators can be added either into the global Domain Admins, effectively granting permissions to all servers in the domain, or into the local Administrators group on specific machines, thereby granting permissions only to the specified computers.

Guests

The Guest account is disabled by default. Guests are exactly that—guests. Just like someone visiting your home, you don't have complete knowledge of or confidence in a Guest. Guests must log into resources over a network and cannot log on locally. Typical installations never use the Guest account, and it is recommended that you leave the Guest account disabled.

Domain Guests

The Guest account is included by default in the Domain Guests group, and the Domain Guests group is a default member of local Guests. This group is specifically used to grant Guests permissions across multiple domains.

Domain Users

When an account is created in a domain, it automatically becomes a member of the Domain Users group. Because the Domain Users group is a default group within the local group Users, each member of Domain Users can connect to the network from any machine on the network unless specific policies prevent this practice.

Power Users

The Power Users group is commonly misunderstood. A Power User has rights and privileges much like a Server Operator except that the Power User group appears by default on only Windows NT Workstation machines. Power Users have default administrative-like rights that permit user management for the users they create. Power users also can add users to the Guests, Power Users, and Users groups. Power Users have local machine permissions to share and remove file and printer shares.

Print Operators

In addition to complete management of printer-related duties, Print Operators have the capability to log on locally to a server and to shut down a server.

Replicator

Replicator is a system-level group used only for Windows NT's built-in directory replication service. This group has no default members. If you make a Windows NT Server or Windows NT Workstation computer a replication partner, however, the account associated with the replication service on that machine must be inserted into this group.

Server Operators

Server Operators exist only on domain controllers and exist specifically for the purpose of managing servers. Server Operators can do everything an Administrator can do except manage security. The Server Operators group can perform all duties related to the file system, can perform backups and restores, can manage shares, can manage disks, and can shut down the server.

Users

Who are Users? Unlike the Everyone group, the Users group is permitted to use the Log on Locally right on all Windows NT machines except domain controllers. On a Windows NT Workstation, members of the Users group can create and delete local groups, can shut down and lock the local workstation, and can maintain a local profile.

Integrating Workgroups into Domains

This section addresses some of the preparatory issues in domain planning. Let's assume you have a hypothetical network that contains 25 Windows NT Workstations and 10 Windows NT Servers configured as member servers. You now want to add another workgroup containing Windows 95 and Windows 98 clients and combine these into a domain. Centralized user management is an issue because of limited administrative resources. How might you go about planning this migration?

Domain models require domain controllers so that users can obtain logon authentication services and can pass domain security checks when requesting access to domain resources. With the limited number of computers described for this environment, a single domain model makes sense.

Based on the roles that the member servers play in their current network, take two of these member servers that match the requirements for a domain controller and move any applications or services to other Windows NT member servers. On one of these servers, reinstall Windows NT Server. This machine will become the domain's PDC. After this machine is installed and up on the network, you can start on the second server.

On the second server, move all applications and services to one of the other member servers and then reinstall Windows NT Server. This machine will become a BDC. In this example, we'll format the drives and start from scratch. The BDC joins the domain during the installation process. This requires an administrative account and a password for the PDC. After the BDC is running, master SAM replication occurs automatically. As soon as all service packs and hotfixes are applied, make an Emergency Repair Disk (ERD) for each domain controller. (The rdisk /s command creates an ERD.) Make one for the PDC as well as the BDC. Keep them handy because you'll be working with them again shortly.

At this point, you are ready to begin creating computer accounts in the domain for the member servers and workstations. You can do this from within Server Manager or separately on each Windows NT computer. From within Server Manager, select the Computer menu and then select the Add to Domain menu item.

After all the Windows NT member servers and workstations are added to the domain, it's time to add the Windows 95 and Windows 98 machines. You must add each of these clients individually. On each machine, choose the Network applet in the Control Panel, double-click Client For Microsoft Networks, select the General Properties page, select the Log On To Windows NT Domain check box, and click OK. Restart the Windows 95 and Windows 98 clients. To enable a user to log into the domain, you must use User Manager for Domains to add a domain user account. The user will be able to log in from any client, assuming no logon restrictions exist.

To move a slightly larger number of clients (say, several hundred) into a domain, this change is better accomplished by remotely manipulating the Registry on each Windows 95 and Windows 98 client. Chapters 8, "Editing the Windows NT Registry," and 9, "Important Registry Keys and Values," discuss just such procedures. Using REGINI or some of the other remote Registry tools, you can perform an upgrade of several thousand clients. Managing domain controllers, however, can be a little more difficult.

Managing domain controllers is not quite a black art, but it does require an understanding of what a PDC can do, how BDCs function in a domain, and how PDCs and BDCs communicate. Other interesting issues crop up as well, as you'll learn in the following sections.

Understanding the Security ID

SIDs are part of Windows NT's security system. A *SID* is a unique key that identifies objects in a Windows NT domain. Each user, group, and computer has a unique key. A username or computer name can change, and Windows NT needs some a to track what's going on in the system.

▌ **Upgrading a Member Server**
  There is no way to upgrade a member server to a domain controller without reinstalling Windows NT.

Enter the SID. Let's say you have a BDC named Matthew, and for whatever reason, you decide to rebuild Matthew from the ground up. Even if you name the new BDC Matthew, it really isn't Matthew—just as a clone isn't the original but a close copy. Because the system SID changes based on a new installation of Windows NT—even though the machine name is the same and it is built to be identical to the original—Windows NT won't be fooled into letting this machine enter the domain and assume Matthew's responsibilities. If a PDC is damaged, it is imperative not to rebuild Windows NT on that machine. It can cause harmful effects on your domain that will require additional work to repair.

The topics of moving a server and domain controller promotion and demotion are discussed shortly. For now, suffice it to say that individuals are handled nearly the same way as computers so that each user account has a unique SID matched to an account name. If any account, group, or computer is deleted, its SID cannot be reused nor can that account, group, or computer be restored to its original condition. Two instances of an object with the same name will always have different SIDs and, therefore, do not represent the same object!

Moving a Domain Controller to a New Domain

You can relocate a domain controller into a new domain in two ways: create a new domain or rename an existing domain. Each of these methods has the same net effect. BDCs cannot be moved from one domain to another. Windows NT must be re-installed, and these newly minted BDCs must join the new domain.

When you want to create a new domain, it is possible (but not advisable) to change a PDC's domain designation. You can change the domain for the PDC within the Network applet in the Control Panel. This moves all user and group accounts into the new domain; however, all Windows NT member server and workstation accounts must be re-created in that new domain. You must also re-establish trust relationships with the newly named domain. You must modify existing Windows clients (Windows 3.11, Windows 95, or Windows 98) to change their logon domains in Control Panel and then reboot.

Creating a New Domain

When you create a new domain, you can move the PDC alone and change the domain name, but it usually is simpler to start from scratch.

Promotion and Demotion

BDCs maintain a copy of the PDC's master SAM database to perform user logon authentication. When a user attempts to log on, a broadcast is sent out to contact a BDC. The first BDC to respond—not necessarily the closest—authenticates the user. BDCs are particularly handy when the PDC needs to be taken offline for scheduled maintenance or when the PDC fails. In this scenario, the BDCs continue to authenticate user logon requests. When a PDC fails or is scheduled to be taken down for maintenance, one BDC should be promoted to assume the PDC's responsibilities in the interim.

Promoting a BDC to PDC Status

When you modify a user's account, the change is written to the master SAM on the PDC and then is replicated to the BDCs within the domain. If the PDC is rebooted during the time that password is being changed, the change does not take place. Only a PDC can accept changes to the SAM database. If no PDC is available, changes are not accepted. This is why it's important to promote a BDC to take over for the PDC when the PDC fails or is unavailable; otherwise, the SAM database becomes static and no changes are possible.

Use Server Manager to promote and demote domain controllers. Member servers cannot become domain controllers, just as domain controllers cannot become member servers. To switch from member server to domain controller or vice versa, you must reinstall Windows NT.

You can perform the following steps to promote a BDC to a PDC:

1. Notify users that the PDC will be shut down.
2. On the PDC, open the Control Panel and then the Services applet.
3. Stop the Server service. This prevents new user logons while the change is taking place.
4. On a domain controller, open Server Manager.
5. Select Properties from the Users menu and click the Computer button.
6. Click the Disconnect All button to disconnect all users.
7. Select the BDC to be promoted.
8. Select Promote To Primary Domain Controller from the Computer menu.
9. Restart the Server service on the PDC.

Promoting a BDC

A PDC that is online when a BDC gets promoted will automatically be demoted to a BDC.

Demoting a PDC to BDC Status

If you need to demote a PDC manually and the preceding procedure won't work (possibly due to hardware or Registry-related failure), try the following approach to perform a PDC demotion:

1. Notify the users that the PDC will be shut down.
2. On the PDC, open the Control Panel and then the Services applet.
3. Stop the Server service. This prevents new user logons while the change is underway.
4. Open Server Manager.
5. Select Properties from the Users menu and click the Computer button.
6. Click the Disconnect All button to disconnect all users.
7. Select the PDC.
8. Select Demote To Backup Domain Controller from the Computer menu.
9. Restart the Server service on the former PDC.

Synchronizing Domains

There are times when a user's password gets changed, and it is unable to authenticate against some network resource or application even after several hours. This condition seems to occur when the copy of the SAM on a BDC becomes corrupted or when one BDC's information differs from the another domain controller's SAM, making the two systems out of sync. Here is how to ensure that the PDC's and all BDCs' SAMs stay properly synchronized:

1. Open Server Manager.
2. Select the PDC.
3. Select Synchronize Entire Domain from the Computer menu.

Domain Management Tools

The following sections cover some important utilities from the *Microsoft Windows NT Server 4.0 Resource Kit* CD. These utilities make it easier and more convenient to manage Windows NT domains than ever before.

Domain Monitor

The Domain Monitor utility monitors the status of servers in a specified domain and its secure channel status to the local domain controller and to domain controllers in trusted domains. If any status shows errors, Domain Monitor displays various status icons along with the domain controller name and a list of trusted domains. You can find the cause of errors by checking the error numbers reported in the Windows NT Messages database.

Domain Monitor connects to servers to retrieve status information using the current user's username and password. If the current user account doesn't exist in a domain or in the database of a trusted domain, the status query can fail. Any user who is logged on can query the status information, but only administrators can use the Disconnect button to disconnect and restore connections.

NetWatch

NetWatch enables you to view all connections to a particular machine on the network. This is a useful tool for finding out whether a user is attempting to access information to which he or she shouldn't have access.

QuickSlice

QuickSlice enables you to view which process ID is consuming the most CPU utilization including its Process ID, PagedPool and NonPagedPool memory consumption, and its percentage of process CPU utilization statistics.

GroupCopy

GroupCopy performs the sometimes cumbersome task of moving a whole group from one domain to another without being forced to re-create it. Using GroupCopy, you can specify the source and target domains and the specified groups to copy. You also can take a global or local group and use it to create a new global or local group in the new domain. GroupCopy is a very handy utility.

Troubleshooting Techniques for Networks

There are many ways in which domain controllers can become the focus for networking problems. The symptoms and fixes described in the following sections cover the most common problems and their related workarounds.

BDC Fails to Authenticate a User's Password

If the computer that provides authentication for a logon is a BDC for the domain in which the user account is defined and that BDC fails to authenticate a valid user password, this usually indicates that the password has changed but the BDC is not synchronized with the PDC when the user attempts to log on. When this happens, the BDC should pass that logon request to its PDC.

As a precaution, users who change their passwords should log on to all computers to which they have access within 15 minutes of making the change. This ensures that cached credentials are up-to-date on each machine and that the user can log on using these credentials even if the PDC is unavailable during a later logon.

IP Address Connection Works but Name Resolution Fails

If you encounter a situation in which the IP address connection works but name resolution fails, try the following:

1. Make sure the appropriate HOSTS file and DNS setup are configured for the computer. First, check the host name resolution configuration using the Network applet in the Control Panel. Then choose the DNS tab in the Microsoft TCP/IP Properties dialog box and make sure the settings are correct.

2. If you are using a HOSTS file, make sure the name of the remote computer is correct and is capitalized exactly as it appears in Network Neighborhood, in the file and in the application that uses the file.

3. If you are using DNS, make sure the IP addresses for all DNS servers are correct and are entered in the proper order. Use PING with the remote computer by typing both the host name and its IP address to determine whether the host name is being resolved properly.

TCP/IP Connection to Remote Host Hangs

If a TCP/IP connection to a remote host hangs, you can use the Windows NT NET-STAT command to display protocol statistics and current TCP/IP network connections that can be helpful in diagnosing problems. The NBTSTAT command displays statistics and connections related to NetBIOS connections that run over TCP/IP.

Here is the syntax involved in using the NETSTAT command:

```
NETSTAT [-a] [-e] [-n] [-s] [-p proto] [-r] [interval]
```

The following list details the switches used with NETSTAT:

- **-a.** Displays all connections and listening ports. (Server-side connections usually are not shown).
- **-e.** Displays ethernet statistics. This can be combined with the -s option.
- **-n.** Displays addresses and port numbers in numerical form.
- **-p proto.** Shows connections for the protocol specified by proto; proto might be tcp or udp. If used with the -s option to display per-protocol statistics, proto might be tcp, udp, or ip.
- **-r.** Displays the contents of the routing table.
- **-s.** Displays per-protocol statistics. By default, statistics are shown for TCP, UDP and IP; the -p option can be used to specify a subset of the default.
- **interval.** Redisplays selected statistics, pausing interval seconds between each display. Press Ctrl+C to stop redisplaying statistics. If omitted, NETSTAT will print the current configuration information once.

NETSTAT **Details**

You can obtain a listing of all NETSTAT commands at any time by typing **NETSTAT /?** at the command prompt.

Use the `netstat -a` command to show the status of all activity on TCP and UDP ports on the local computer. The state of a good TCP connection usually is established with 0 bytes in the send and receive queues. If data is blocked in either queue or if the state is irregular, it is likely that there is a problem with the connection. If not, you are probably experiencing network or application delay.

Unable to Resolve a NetBIOS Name

NBTSTAT displays protocol statistics and current TCP/IP connections using NetBIOS over TCP, which also is known as NBT. NBTSTAT is one of the primary tools to use whenever you fail to connect to a specific Windows NT Server where TCP/IP is the primary (or only) networking protocol in use. To determine the cause of connection problems, use the `nbtstat -n` command to determine what name the server registered when it came up on the network. The output of this command lists several names that the computer registers. A name that resembles or matches the computer's name should appear. If not, try one of the other unique names that NBTSTAT displays.

The following is a syntax description for the NBTSTAT command:

```
NBTSTAT [-a RemoteName] [-A IP address]
[-c] [-n] [-r] [-R] [-s] [-S] [interval] ]
```

- **-a (adapter status)**. Lists the remote machine's name table when given its name.
- **-A (Adapter status).** Lists the remote machine's name table when given its IP address.
- **-c (cache).** Lists the remote name cache including the IP addresses.
- **-n (names).** Lists local NetBIOS names.
- **-r (resolved).** Lists names resolved by broadcast and via WINS.
- **-R (Reload).** Purges and reloads the remote cache name table.
- **-S (Sessions).** Lists the sessions table with the destination IP addresses.
- **-s (sessions).** Lists the sessions table converting destination IP addresses to host names via the hosts file.
- **RemoteName.** Provides the remote host's machine name.
- **IP address.** A dotted decimal representation of the IP address.
- **interval.** Redisplays selected statistics, pausing interval seconds between each display. Press Ctrl+C to stop redisplaying statistics.

You also can use the NBTSTAT utility to display cached entries for remote computers from either #PRE entries in LMHOSTS or recently resolved names. If the name remote computers use for the server is the same, and other computers are on a remote subnet, make sure they have a name-to-address mapping for that computer in their LMHOSTS files. To troubleshoot a problematic connection or an apparent name-resolution problem, try the following commands:

- **nbtstat -n.** Displays the names registered locally on the system by applications such as the server and Redirector.

- **nbtstat -c.** Shows the NetBIOS name cache, which contains name-to-address mappings for other computers.

- **nbtstat -R.** Purges the name cache and reloads it from the LMHOSTS file.

- **nbtstat -a** *<name>*. Performs a NetBIOS adapter status command against the computer specified by name. The adapter status command returns the local NetBIOS name table for that computer plus the Media Access Control (MAC) address of the adapter card.

Host on the Same Network Fails to Resolve

The Address Resolution Protocol (ARP) enables a host to find the MAC address of a destination host on the same physical network when given the destination host's IP address. To make ARP efficient, each computer caches IP-to-MAC address mappings to eliminate repetitive ARP broadcast requests.

The arp command enables a user to view and modify ARP table entries on the local computer. The arp command is useful for viewing the ARP cache and for resolving address-resolution problems. The arp command displays and modifies the IP-to-physical address translation tables used by the built-in TCP/IP ARP.

The following is the syntax for the arp command:

```
ARP -s inet_addr eth_addr [if_addr]
ARP -d inet_addr [if_addr]
ARP -a [inet_addr] [-N if_addr]
```

- **-a.** Displays current ARP entries by interrogating the current protocol data. If inet_addr is specified, the IP and physical addresses for only the specified computer are displayed. If more than one network interface uses ARP, entries for each ARP table are displayed.

- **-g.** Provides the same as -a.

- **inet_addr.** Specifies an Internet address.

- **-N if_addr.** Displays the ARP entries for the network interface specified by if_addr.

- **-d.** Deletes the host specified by inet_addr.

- **-s**. Adds the host and associates the Internet address `inet_addr` with the physical address `eth_addr`. The physical address is given as six hexadecimal bytes separated by hyphens. The entry is permanent.

- **eth_addr**. Specifies a physical address.

- **if_addr**. If present, this specifies the Internet address of the interface whose address translation table should be modified. If not present, the first applicable interface is used.

NET **Commands**

The NET commands comprise a NetBIOS-based set of networking commands that cover the full range of network capabilities on a Microsoft network. Several useful domain-related commands and utilities are covered in the following sections.

NET COMPUTER

Use the NET COMPUTER command to add or remove a computer from a Windows NT domain. The following is the syntax for the NET COMPUTER command:

```
NET COMPUTER \\computername {/ADD ¦ /DEL}
```

In the preceding, \\computername is the name of the computer, and /ADD or /DEL specify whether the computer is to be added or deleted from a domain.

NET START

Use the NET START command to manage your installed Windows NT services from the command line. The following is the syntax for the NET START command:

```
NET START ServiceName
```

The following Windows NT services can be started by NET START:

- Alerter
- COM+ Event System
- Computer Browser
- Event Log
- FTP Publishing Service
- License Logging Service
- Messenger
- Microsoft Dynamic Host Configuration Protocol (DHCP) Server
- Microsoft Domain Name Service (DNS) Server
- Microsoft Exchange Directory
- Microsoft Exchange Information Store

- Microsoft Exchange Message Transfer Agent
- Microsoft Exchange System Attendant
- Microsoft Proxy Server Administration
- Microsoft WinSock Proxy Service
- Modem Sharing Service
- NetLogon Service
- Windows NT LM Security Support Provider
- Plug and Play
- Protected Storage
- Proxy Alert Notification Service
- Remote Access Autodial Manager
- Remote Access Connection Manager
- Remote Procedure Call (RPC) Locator
- Remote Procedure Call (RPC) Service
- Seattle Lab Remote Administration
- Server Service
- Spooler Service
- System Event Notification Service (SENS)
- Task Scheduler
- TCP/IP NetBIOS Helper
- Telephony Service
- Windows Internet Name Service (WINS)
- Workstation Service
- World Wide Web Publishing Service

For More Information

To find out more information about domain models and troubleshooting network problems, access one of the following resources:

- Microsoft TechNet contains useful information about networking models. The troubleshooting topics discussed in this chapter can be found by searching on keywords related to these topics.
- *Microsoft Windows NT Server 4.0 Resource Kit*. Microsoft Press, 1996. ISBN: 1572313447.

12

Windows NT and TCP/IP

THE TRANSMISSION CONTROL PROTOCOL/INTERNET PROTOCOL (TCP/IP) suite is
the most widely used networking protocol suite in the world, largely because it is the
primary protocol of the Internet. Windows NT supports TCP/IP and is an excellent
platform for hosting Internet information services.

This chapter provides an overview of TCP/IP, investigates the details of Windows NT
support for TCP/IP, and discusses built-in TCP/IP tools and utilities. It also covers
hosting information services, troubleshooting TCP/IP problems, and a few third-party
TCP/IP applications and utilities.

The TCP/IP Suite

TCP/IP is a suite of protocols rather than a single networking protocol. If you are
developing applications and/or service protocols, the complex underpinnings of
TCP/IP are important. If you are a system administrator or a power user, knowing
how TCP/IP is constructed won't help you configure clients, use name resolution services, connect to other systems, or troubleshoot problems. If you'd like more information about protocol development, see one of the excellent TCP/IP references listed in
the "For More Information" section at the end of this chapter.

TCP/IP is a bulky protocol stack, but its size is required to support its wide range
of capabilities. TCP/IP requires more system resources than other protocols, mainly

due to its size and its supported features, which are used to sustain enhanced network communications. The resource footprint of TCP/IP is really no longer a significant issue because most modern home and office systems rarely include less than 32MB of RAM per computer.

Any discussion of TCP/IP covers a number of issues, including:

- Providing unique client identification
- Supporting communications
- Dynamic addressing capabilities
- Name and IP address translation
- Phone line connections and secure Internet communications
- Hosting information services

TCP/IP is a reliable, robust networking protocol; however, compared to other protocols, it is difficult to configure and uses more than its share of system resources. These facts notwithstanding, under Windows NT, TCP/IP is the best protocol choice for networking environments of almost any size or purpose.

The protocol's packet switching capability is a principal reason for the deployment of TCP/IP on the Internet. TCP/IP does not rely upon a single logical communication pathway between the source and destination. In fact, the packets of a single communication can each take a unique path. When they are received at their destination, they are automatically sorted into the proper order. Packet switching reduces the importance of any single network segment. Using TCP/IP, communications are more likely to reach their destination in spite of physical damage to some links. With the addition of error checking and retransmission of corrupt or missing packets, TCP/IP is a reliable communications vehicle.

Another benefit of TCP/IP is its interoperability. Nearly every computer in use today supports TCP/IP. This means that this protocol virtually guarantees communications between computers. If you find a system that can't support TCP/IP, it can't communicate with the Internet, and you've discovered a legacy system that's ready for the junk pile.

Microsoft has added some custom features, capabilities, and application programming interfaces (APIs) to TCP/IP. For example, the graphical user interfaces (GUIs) and simplified configuration requirements for client addressing—Dynamic Host Configuration Protocol (DHCP), Windows Internet Name Service (WINS), Domain Name Service (DNS), and other TCP/IP services—have greatly simplified setup.

When you install Windows NT Workstation, you can select TCP/IP as the protocol of choice. There are a few specific configuration details you need to know before starting the installation. Let's look at the overall addressing environment of TCP/IP before looking at the details of the installation and configuration process.

Addressing, Subnet Masks, and Domain Names

In a TCP/IP network, a unique identifier known as an *IP address* is assigned to each networked device. Every device on a network must have a unique IP address to communicate with other network devices. A network device is called a *host*. A host is simply any computer or other type of networking device that has a communication interface, such as a network interface card (NIC), that is assigned an IP address. A single host can have multiple IP addresses assigned to the same interface or multiple interfaces, depending on the operating system used.

An IP address is composed of two pieces of information: a network ID followed by a host ID. The network ID defines the network segment with which the host is allowed to communicate. The host ID defines the identity of the device within the network segment. Routers use the network ID to determine whether communication packets should be kept within the current network segment or sent on to other segments. When the correct network segment receives a packet, the host ID from its destination address is used to pinpoint delivery.

The Internet is actually made up of thousands of networks connected by routers. Each of these networks, or network segments, is assigned its own unique network ID. Every device within that segment uses the network ID to form the first part of its IP address.

An IP address is a 32-bit binary number that's usually written in dotted-decimal notation to make it easier to read. For example, the IP address 11001111 00101110 10000011 10001001 has the dotted-decimal equivalent 207.46.131.137. The decimal version is created by converting octets (eight binary digits) into decimal equivalents (0 to 255) separated by periods. The binary version is what computers and routers use to direct network communications; TCP/IP tools and utilities display the dotted-decimal equivalents. However, even the decimal version of an IP address is difficult to remember, so there are further equivalencies. These include domain names (such as **www.microsoft.com**) and NetBIOS names (such as NTS-02-BDC). We will discuss these names later in this chapter in the section "DNS, WINS, and Other IP Matters."

Address Classes

The current TCP/IP addressing scheme allows for nearly 4.3 billion hosts. Instead of allowing people to pick and choose their addresses, the distribution of IP addresses is handled by the Internet Network Information Center (InterNIC). Using a class scheme, the InterNIC assigns blocks of addresses to networks based on their size and purpose.

There are five classes of IP addresses labeled A through E. Classes A, B, and C are those that concern us here; Classes D and E are reserved for special use and don't follow the same rules. Class D addresses are used for multicasting, and Class E addresses are used for experimentation. The first three classes differ in the number of octets used by the network ID. Class A addresses use a single octet network ID, Class B uses two, and Class C uses three. The number of octets in the network ID determines the construction of the base subnet mask (see Table 12.1).

You can recognize the class of an address by viewing either its binary or its decimal form. In binary form, Class A addresses have a zero in the first bit place, Class B addresses have 10 as the first two bit places, and Class C addresses have 110 as the first three bit places. In decimal form, this results in the first number being between 1 and 126 for Class A, between 128 and 191 for Class B, and between 192 and 223 for Class C. See Table 12.2 for more details.

Table 12.1   **Address Classes and Corresponding Network and Host IDs**

Address Class	IP Address	Network ID Component	Host ID Component
A	w.x.y.z	w	x.y.z
B	w.x.y.z	w.x	y.z
C	w.x.y.z	w.x.y	z

Table 12.2   **Division of IP Address Component Octets According to Class**

Address Class	High-Order Bits	First Octet Decimal Range	Networks Available	Hosts Available
A	0xxxxxxx	1-126.x.y.z	126	16,777,214
B	10xxxxxx	128-191.x.y.z	16,384	65,534
C	110xxxxx	192-223.x.y.z	2,097,152	254

Two further limitations for IP addresses restrict the host ID from being all 1s or all 0s (that is, 1.1.1.1 or 0.0.0.0 in decimal). A host ID of all 1s is a broadcast address that is used to send traffic to all hosts within the segment. A host ID of all 0s is a network address that is used to send traffic to a segment without designating a host.

Subnets and Masks

A *subnet* is a logical division of a TCP/IP network. All hosts within a subnet can communicate directly with one another but cannot communicate directly with hosts outside the subnet. Subnets reduce traffic congestion by limiting communications to only local hosts. To send data to remote systems, a router must be used to move the communication from one subnet to another.

Note on Table 12.2
Notice that the network ID of 127 is missing from Table 12.2. This is because 127 acts as a loopback address (that is, it transmits to itself). PINGing the IP address 127.1.1.1 is a good way to see whether your network interface card is receiving communication.

Dividing a network ID into smaller segments is known as *subnetting*. Subnetting is used to divide the large blocks of class addresses into smaller networks. A *subnet mask* performs the division process. A subnet takes bits of the host ID and uses them as a network ID extension. This effectively creates multiple smaller networks. This is analogous to the way a telephone number consists of local and remote information. If you call someone with the same area code (network ID), the call is local. If he or she has a different area code, the call is remote or long distance.

A subnet mask is a 32-bit address that defines which bits are used as the network ID for a given IP address. This is accomplished by using 1's and 0's. Ones are used to mark off the area of an address to be used as the network ID. For example, the default subnet mask for a Class A address is 11111111 00000000 00000000 00000000 or 255.0.0.0. Table 12.3 lists the default subnet masks for the major address classes.

Table 12.3 **Default Subnet Masks for Classes A, B, and C**

Address Class	Mask Decimal Value	Mask Binary Value
A	255.0.0.0	11111111 00000000 00000000 00000000
B	255.255.0.0	11111111 11111111 00000000 00000000
C	255.255.255.0	11111111 11111111 11111111 00000000

Subnet masks used to divide class address spaces extend the network ID mask into the next octet. For example, dividing a Class B network can create a subnet of 11111111 11111111 11110000 00000000 or 255.255.240.0. This creates 14 new sub-networks with 4,094 hosts in each. You can determine the number of new subnets that will be added and the hosts in subnets by using the 2^n-2 formula. For the number of subnets created, count the number of 1s after the base network ID octets. The base network ID for Class A is the ninth digit; for Class B, it's the seventeenth digit; and for Class C, it's the twenty-fifth digit. The resulting number equals n. For the number of hosts in the subnet, count all the 0s. Table 12.4 shows the possible subnet masks and the results for each class type.

Table 12.4 **Subnet Masks and Results**

Binary Mask	Decimal Equivalent	Number of New Subnets	Number of Hosts
00000000	A: 255.0.0.0 B: 255.255.0.0 C: 255.255.255.0	1	A: 16,777,214 B: 65,534 C: 254
10000000	A: 255.128.0.0 B: 255.255.128.0 C: 255.255.255.128	not valid	A: not valid B: not valid C: not valid

continues

Table 12.4 **Continued**

Binary Mask	Decimal Equivalent	Number of New Subnets	Number of Hosts
11000000	A: 255.192.0.0	2	A: 4,194,302
	B: 255.255.192.0		B: 16,382
	C: 255.255.255.192		C: 62
11100000	A: 255.224.0.0	6	A: 2,097,150
	B: 255.255.224.0		B: 8,190
	C: 255.255.255.224		C: 30
11110000	A: 255.240.0.0	14	A: 1,048,574
	B: 255.255.240.0		B: 4,094
	C: 255.255.255.240		C: 14
11111000	A: 255.248.0.0	30	A: 524,286
	B: 255.255.248.0		B: 2,046
	C: 255.255.255.248		C: 6
11111100	A: 255.252.0.0	62	A: 262,142
	B: 255.255.252.0		B: 1022
	C: 255.255.255.252		C: 2
11111110	A: 255.254.0.0	126	A: 131,070
	B: 255.255.254.0		B: 510
	C: 255.255.255.254		C: not valid

Default Gateway

A gateway must be used to send information from one subnet to another. A *gateway* is simply another term for the router interface that directs data when it is destined for an alternate subnet. The default gateway is defined as the IP address used by the host where all non-subnet packets are directed. If a default gateway is not defined, the host cannot communicate outside of its subnet.

Obtaining IP Addresses

When you create a network, you have a choice as to how you obtain the IP addresses for your hosts. You must first determine whether or not the network will ever be connected to the Internet. If the network will be connected to the Internet, you can select to lease an IP address block from an Internet service provider (ISP) or use the addresses allocated for private intranets. RFC (Request For Comments) 1918 (`http://www.faqs.org/rfcs/rfcs1918.html`) describes the Class A, B, and C addresses that private networks can use. These addresses are specifically set aside by the Internet Assigned Numbers Authority (IANA) and are not forwarded by routers. If you use ISP-assigned addresses, your network hosts can communicate directly with the Internet. To use addresses from RFC 1918, you must have a proxy server to gain Internet access. In most cases, using a proxy server and RFC 1918 addresses is less expensive, more secure, and easier to maintain. Even if your network will never connect to the Internet, using the reserved addresses allows you to side-step possible problems in the future.

Routers, Proxies, and Firewalls

Routing is the simple activity of transmitting network packets from one subnet to another. *Routers* are devices (or computers) that have two or more network interfaces, each of which is a member of a different subnet. A router examines each packet that traverses its interfaces to determine if delivering the packet to its destination requires the packet to be moved to a different subnet. Because routers provide a pathway from one subnet to another, they are often called *gateways*.

Windows NT can act as a router with the support of multiple NICs and the Multi-Protocol Router (MPR) service. MPR includes the Routing Information Protocol (RIP) for TCP/IP. You can view and manage the routes supported by Windows NT by using the ROUTE command from a command prompt. Check the Windows NT Help for syntax and use of the ROUTE command.

Proxies and firewalls are basically routers with special capabilities. A *firewall* is a software or hardware solution that restricts communications over a link. Firewalls can block inbound or outbound traffic based on its source, destination, protocol, port, or content. A *proxy* is a software solution that is basically an enhanced firewall. Proxies mediate external access for internal hosts. The mediation hides the address and identity of the internal host. Proxies are also capable of storing a cache of often-accessed external information so internal hosts experience shorter retrieval times.

Working from Microsoft Windows NT Workstation, you might not be dealing with routers, firewalls, and proxies except as a client for their services. As a client, you are assigned a gateway address for your TCP/IP stack and a proxy address for your information service utilities (email, Web browser, FTP, and so on). Most of the software products that offer routing, firewall, and proxy services do not operate on Windows NT Workstation due to the simultaneous connection limitation imposed by the Microsoft user license. If you need to deploy these products, you will have to install Windows NT Server.

Proxy Recommendation

Microsoft's Proxy Server 2.0 is an excellent product that offers a wide range of filtering, access control, logging, and caching capabilities.

As a proxy client, you should check the documentation or ask a network administrator about the configuration process required to gain Internet access over the installed proxy server. If you are using Microsoft Proxy Server 2.0, client configuration is automated. Just launch your Web browser and point it to the URL at which the client software installation page is located. This location is typically `http://`
`<servername>/MSProxy/` (where *<servername>* is the NetBIOS name or IP address of the proxy server host). This loads a welcome page with a link to the client configuration software. After the software is installed, all your Internet utilities should automatically use the proxy server to access the Internet. However, this is assuming that the proxy server is configured to allow traffic other than just Web traffic; if it is not, contact whoever is responsible for proxy server configuration.

DNS, WINS, and Other IP Matters

As we mentioned earlier in this chapter, because the IP address dotted-decimal notation is too complex for most people to remember, there are other, more people-friendly naming conventions. Two popular schemes are used by Windows NT: Network Basic Input/Output System (NetBIOS) names and Fully Qualified Domain Names (FQDNs). Windows NT uses NetBIOS names no matter what protocol is used for network communication. A NetBIOS name is a name (of up to 15 characters) that you assign to objects, such as NTS-01-PDC. NetBIOS names apply to computers, shares, users, Windows NT domains, and so on. TCP/IP networks use FQDNs to assign people-friendly names, such as `www.microsoft.com`, to hosts.

When you first install Windows NT Workstation, one of the setup dialog boxes prompts you for a computer name. The name you provide becomes the NetBIOS name for that system. If you don't remember what name you assigned, you can either view the Identification tab of the Network applet or issue the **HOSTNAME** command from a command prompt.

FQDNs

FQDNs are more complex and structured than NetBIOS names are. The FQDN name scheme is designed to apply a unique name to every host on the Internet. The same scheme can, however, be employed on private intranets. FQDNs are names comprised of many parts separated by periods. The right-most element is the top-level domain. There are six top-level domains in use in the United States, each of which is used for a specific purpose, as shown in the following list:

- **.com.** Designates commercial sites.
- **.edu.** Designates educational sites.
- **.gov.** Designates government sites.
- **.net.** Designates network service companies or ISPs.
- **.mil.** Designates United States military sites.
- **.org.** Designates non-profit organization sites.

Sites located outside of the United States have a country code to the right of their top-level domain, such as .uk for the United Kingdom or .at for Austria. See **http://www.rtw.com.au/internet/suffixes.html** for a list of countries and their codes.

The element immediately to the left of the top-level domain is called the domain name. This is a unique name owned by a single company or organization. Microsoft's domain name is **http://www.internic.com**. Domain names are assigned by the InterNIC located at **http//www.internic.net/**. You can sign up for your own domain name at that Web site.

When you have an assigned domain name, you have complete control over additional labeling of your FQDNs. Common additions to the domain name include www, ftp, secure, mail, and so on. These additions give information about the services the host offers. Most FQDNs are comprised of three elements, but longer names are possible.

FQDNs are not defined on the system with which they are associated. Instead, they are defined through the services hosted by the system and in the DNS service of the attached ISP. Remember that FQDNs are not actually used by the computers to guide communications. The computer system requires a binary IP address to transmit information over a TCP/IP network. This requires resolving the FQDN into an IP address. This function is performed by DNS.

DNS is a TCP/IP service hosted by Windows NT Server or any number of UNIX computers either within your own network or on the Internet (such as your ISP). For an FQDN to work, it must be added to a DNS system's listing table and associated with an IP address. The information in an ISP's local DNS system is distributed to other DNS systems on the Internet. When someone uses your FQDN to access resources, the FQDN is resolved into an IP address that directs the communication packets across the Internet to your host.

NetBIOS

NetBIOS names (also called *local intranet names*) have a NetBIOS-to-IP name resolution server called WINS. WINS is used in a Microsoft client-server intranet environment in which NetBIOS names are used instead of FQDNs to reference hosts . A Windows NT Workstation system cannot host WINS, which is a Microsoft Windows NT Server service.

Changing FQDN Naming Schemes

The FQDN naming scheme, top-level domains, and other aspects of Internet naming, as well as the controlling bodies of the scheme, might change. Keep an eye on this issue by watching **http://www.cnet.com/**, **http://www.infoworld.com/**, and **http://www.internetnews.com/** for up-to-date information.

WINS is a dynamic service that automatically updates itself as hosts (even those running DHCP) come online and go offline. You must configure DNS manually; however, it is possible to use WINS to update DNS. To do this, check the Enable WINS Lookup check box in the DNS Administrator tool. By checking this box, you allow DNS to query the WINS database for names it cannot resolve. If you are not running Windows NT Server or don't have a network large enough to warrant deploying a DNS or WINS server, you can still take advantage of FQDN and NetBIOS name resolution.

HOSTS and LMHOSTS are text files that contain static name resolution lists and are stored on client or server machines. A HOSTS file resolves FQDNs to IP addresses, and LMHOSTS resolves NetBIOS names to IP addresses. Sample versions of these files can be found in the \Winnt\System32\Drivers\Etc folder in Windows NT. You can use a text editor, such as Notepad, to view their contents and modify the resolution lists. The sample files contain brief instructions, but we highly recommend that you view the *Microsoft Windows NT 4.0 Resource Kit* or TechNet documentation before modifying them.

You must maintain the HOSTS and LMHOSTS files manually and copy them to each client computer on your network. A few tools are available that offer graphical interfaces for configuring your HOSTS and LMHOTS files. The "For More Information" section at the end of this chapter contains a list of these tools.

Working with DHCP

DHCP is a service hosted by a Windows NT Server or a UNIX system that provides automated configuration each time your NT Workstation computer boots. DHCP assigns TCP/IP address settings to computers as the computers come online. DHCP serves two purposes. First, it simplifies client setup because configuration information is not required during installation. Second, it allows a smaller pool of IP addresses to support a larger number of transient clients because IP addresses are not used when clients don't need them, freeing them for other clients.

DHCP assigns an IP address, subnet mask, default gateway, and DNS and WINS server address to a client each time it boots onto the network. ISPs also use DHCP to assign an IP address, subnet mask, default gateway, and DNS server to systems connecting to the Internet over nondedicated dial-up connections.

DHCP uses a leasing process to manage address distribution. When a client requests IP configuration details, DHCP issues a lease of an IP address to that client for a specified amount of time (typically one hour). When the lease duration is half over, the client automatically requests a lease extension. If it's granted, the lease continues for another hour. If it's denied or no response is received, the lease renewal request is issued again when 87.5 percent of the lease duration has expired.

If no response or a denial is received again, the client makes a final renewal request when the lease has expired. If a lease terminates without renewal, the client can no longer communicate with the network. However, a new IP address lease can be initiated by using the `ipconfig /renew` command from a command prompt.

You can use the `ipconfig /release` parameter to terminate the current lease. This parameter is often used to terminate an IP address that is suspect before issuing another `/renew` command to obtain a new lease. The IPCONFIG utility has one other parameter: `/all`, which displays all the IP configuration information for the system. In most cases, you should use the command line `ipconfig /all ¦more` so only a single page is displayed at a time. Here is a sample of the output from this command:

```
Windows NT IP Configuration
        Host Name . . . . . . . . . : ntw01
        DNS Servers . . . . . . . . :
        Node Type . . . . . . . . . : Broadcast
        NetBIOS Scope ID. . . . . . :
        IP Routing Enabled. . . . . : Yes
        WINS Proxy Enabled. . . . . : No
        NetBIOS Resolution Uses DNS : No
Ethernet adapter El90x1:
        Description . . . . . . . . : 3Com 3C90x Ethernet Adapter
        Physical Address. . . . . . : 00-60-08-A7-E1-C5
        DHCP Enabled. . . . . . . . : No
        IP Address. . . . . . . . . : 172.16.1.9
        Subnet Mask . . . . . . . . : 255.255.255.0
        Default Gateway . . . . . . : 172.16.1.7
Ethernet adapter NdisWan5:
        Description . . . . . . . . : NdisWan Adapter
        Physical Address. . . . . . : 00-00-00-0000-00
        DHCP Enabled. . . . . . . . : No
        IP Address. . . . . . . . . : 0.0.0.0
        Subnet Mask . . . . . . . . : 0.0.0.0
        Default Gateway . . . . . . :
```

Installing and Configuring TCP/IP

If TCP/IP is not installed when you first install the operating system, you can add it through the Control Panel via the Protocols tab in the Network applet. If your computer is a standalone system, you don't need to install any protocols. However, if your Windows NT Workstation is a client to a network or intranet or will be connected to the Internet, you need to install several items.

To network a Windows NT Workstation, you must physically install a NIC in the machine, install and configure the drivers, and add the protocol. Windows NT Workstation already includes the Microsoft Client for Microsoft Networks as a central core component of its networking architecture.

You install the protocol by selecting it from the list in the Network Applet's Protocols tab and pointing the installation dialog box to the proper distribution file path. (This is usually the Windows NT Workstation CD.) Before setup is complete, you'll be prompted for several items of information in the main Microsoft TCP/IP Properties dialog box.

You define the client's IP address on the IP Address tab of the Microsoft TCP/IP Properties dialog box. Use the Adapter drop-down list to select the NIC to which all the settings will apply. A computer hosting multiple NICs can have a unique TCP/IP configuration for each card. If you select an adapter, all the settings in this dialog box apply to that adapter. On the IP Address tab, you also indicate whether you are using DHCP or defining the IP address information manually. A manual definition should include an IP address, subnet mask, and default gateway.

Define FQDN-to-IP address resolution configuration items on the DNS tab. These items include the host name, the domain name, a list of DNS server IP addresses, and a list of domain suffixes to search first.

You define NetBIOS name-to-IP address resolution configuration items on the WINS tab. These items include options for defining which adapter to attempt WINS resolution over, specifying the primary and secondary WINS server addresses, enabling DNS resolution if WINS fails, indicating whether to import and use the LMHOSTS file, and defining the scope ID (if required).

On the DHCP Relay tab, you can define details about interacting with a DHCP Relay agent. The DHCP Relay agent transmits DHCP messages across a router. This tab allows you to define the threshold period, the maximum router hops, and the DHCP server(s) to which messages should be directed. By default, a DHCP client initially broadcasts a DHCP Request packet. Because most routers do not pass broadcasts, the DHCP Relay option allows you to specify a host to which your machine can unicast a DHCP request packet to request an IP address.

The Routing tab applies only to systems with two or more network interfaces. Remember that a LAN connection and an Internet connection both count as network interfaces. The check box on this tab enables or disables IP forwarding. In other words, it allows data packets from one network to be transmitted over this computer onto another network as if it were a router.

The IP Address tab has an Advanced button that reveals the Advanced IP Addressing dialog box. In this dialog box, you can define additional IP addresses and subnet masks for the installed NICs and backup gateways. If this interface is connected to the Internet, you can set it to receive only Point-to-Point Tunneling Protocol (PPTP) traffic by selecting Enable PPTP Filtering. Selecting the Enable Security check box opens the Configure button, which, when selected, reveals the TCP/IP Security dialog box. On the TCP/IP Security dialog box, you can configure TCP/IP security settings by TCP Ports, UDP Ports, or IP Protocols to either allow all traffic or restrict all but the defined exceptions. In general, it is better to use a firewall or a proxy server because this configuration scheme is too restrictive.

Remember to Reboot

Each time you make a change to TCP/IP, be sure to reboot the system even if you are not prompted to do so.

Connecting to the Internet

You usually do not have to manually configure TCP/IP to connect a standalone Windows NT Workstation to the Internet via a modem. Instead, you define the Dial-Up Networking (DUN) phonebook entry to request the TCP/IP configuration details upon connection. You access DUN through the Start menu or My Computer. The first time it is launched, the New Phonebook Entry Wizard is started. After you create a phonebook entry, you'll see the main DUN dialog box.

To configure the TCP/IP settings for a phonebook entry, select Edit Entry and Modem Properties from the More menu, and then select the Server tab. Make sure the TCP/IP check box is selected and click the TCP/IP Settings button. This displays the PPP TCP/IP Settings dialog box. In most cases, you want to leave the defaults of Server Assigned IP Address and Name Servers selected. Only if your ISP tells you otherwise should you alter these settings. Chapter 16 provides additional information about DUN.

Information Services over IP

TCP/IP allows your network to interact with Internet information services, such as email, Web, and FTP. If you don't need access to these services, you should switch to the IPX/SPX protocol (referred to as Microsoft NWLink in Windows NT). Let's look at the services typically accessed by a TCP/IP network in a little more detail.

Email and IP

Email is the oldest and still the most often used information service on computer networks. Windows NT Workstation does not support email directly, but through support of TCP/IP, it offers a platform for email applications to operate. Microsoft Internet Explorer 4 includes a side product called Microsoft Outlook Express. Outlook Express is a slimmed-down version of Microsoft Outlook 2000, which is part of the Microsoft Office suite. You can use both Outlook Express and Outlook 2000 to send and receive Internet email.

Outlook Express is installed with Internet Explorer. Simply select the Install option to include Outlook Express. You can get information on Outlook 2000 at `http://www.microsoft.com/office/outlook/default.htm`.

Internet email is based on one of two systems. The most common is the POP3/SMTP system. The Post Office Protocol (POP) is used to transfer email messages from an email server to the email utility on a client. The Simple Mail Transfer Protocol (SMTP) is used to send email from an email utility to an email server and from one email server to another. The other system uses the Internet Message Access Protocol (IMAP) as an alternative method of transferring messages from an email server to an email utility on a client. In each case, email utilities manipulate messages in the same manner from the user's perspective.

Most email servers are secured so that only the specific user to whom the mail belongs can receive it. Also, most ISPs do not accept outbound mail except from their own customers. You'll need to check with your ISP about how to configure your email clients.

Your Web Browser and IP

The Windows NT Workstation distribution CD includes an old version of Internet Explorer (version 2.0). We highly recommend that you install the latest full release. You can find the downloadable files from the Internet Explorer Web site at `http://www.microsoft.com/ie/`. You can obtain information about additional Web browsers at `http://browserwatch.internet.com/` or `http://browsers.com/`.

Accessing FTP Sites

Windows NT Workstation includes a command-line FTP program that you access from the command prompt with the `ftp` command. The command-line FTP tool uses the same commands as the UNIX-based tool used with shell accounts. You can get information about the commands for FTP by typing `help` at the FTP prompt or through the Windows Help system.

You can access FTP sites through Internet Explorer. However, its FTP capabilities are a bit more limited. Anonymous sites are simple to access. Sites that require user-name and password authentication sometimes display a pop-up dialog box, but most often they require you to assemble a special URL to gain entry: `http://username:password@www.domain.com/`. Internet Explorer 4 does not support file uploads to FTP sites. If you want full GUI interaction with FTP sites, we highly recommend Ipswitch's WS_FTP program. This tool is available from `http://www.ipswitch.com/` and, in our opinion, is the best available Windows FTP application.

Hosts Internet Services

From a Windows NT Workstation client, you can host Web services by installing Microsoft's Peer Web Services (PWS). PWS adds Web and FTP service hosting to Windows NT Workstation. It is intended to be used as a personal Web server for distributing Web content to a network. It has a license limitation of 10 simultaneous connections, so it's not a legal alternative for hosting an Internet-accessible Web site.

Network Monitor
Network Monitor is available only on Windows NT Server.

PWS is part of the Microsoft Windows NT Option Pack, which requires that Service Pack 3 or greater and Internet Explorer 4 or greater be installed on the system. You can order a copy of the Option Pack CD or download a copy from the Microsoft Web site at `http://www.microsoft.com/windows/downloads/`. After you install these, you can host your own Web sites to the intranet or Internet. PWS also includes FTP service support, which means you can offer file download and upload sites as well as Web sites. The Server Watch Web site at `http://serverwatch.`
`internet.com` reviews other Web servers that are viable options for Windows NT Workstation.

Troubleshooting IP

TCP/IP problems are most often associated with improper configuration. Always check your settings as the first step in troubleshooting. If your network is connected to an ISP, you might need to contact them for further troubleshooting steps.

You can choose from several tools and utilities to get insight into network communication problems. In Chapter 20, we discuss two of these: Performance Monitor and Network Monitor. We discussed NET commands in Chapter 10.

Microsoft's implementation of TCP/IP includes several utilities that you can be use to troubleshoot problems. We've already mentioned IPCONFIG; let's look at the other tools.

PING is a utility that tests whether a remote system is online or if there is a viable communication pathway between your host and the remote system. You issue a PING command from a command prompt using a NetBIOS name, domain name, or an IP address of the remote system. PING will send four test packets to the remote system and display the results, listing a reply with its transfer times. If packets are not returned, you will see a `Request Timed Out` message. If you see a reply, you know that communication between your host and the remote server is possible. If you see the timed out message, the pathway might be interrupted, traffic might be high, or the remote server might be offline.

Use TRACERT (Trace Route) to examine the path taken by communications between your host and a remote system. Issue a TRACERT command from a command prompt using a NetBIOS name, a domain name, or an IP address of the remote system. A test packet is sent to the remote system, and the results are displayed. Each computer or router encountered on the journey is listed; these are known as *hops*. Each hop lists three response times or an asterisk when no response data is received. The data from TRACERT can tell you whether a router between your host and the remote system is overloaded or if a route is too long.

TELNET is a terminal emulator that you can use to interact with remote systems via a command-line interface. Windows NT does not include a native Telnet server, so you will need a third-party product. TELNET can be used to connect to any remote TELNET server. Some ISPs offer subscribers shell accounts that the TELNET utility can access. Telnetting to a shell account transforms your client into a remote interface for a distant system. Every character you type is sent to the remote system. Applications or utilities executed in a TELNET session are on the remote system, not on your local client.

LanExplorer is a product from Sunbelt Software that adds a wide range of protocol analysis and monitoring capabilities to Windows NT. LanExplorer translates the binary information used by protocols into human readable form. For more information and to download a trial version, visit the Sunbelt Web site at `http://www.sunbelt-software.com/lantrace/lantrace.htm`.

NetTools from Orion offers a set of TCP/IP diagnostic tools in an easy-to-use GUI interface. For more information and a demo, visit `http://cs.wheatonma.edu/nbuggia/NetOrion/`.

The WS_FTP tool from Ipswitch includes in its install routine a collection of diagnostic tools (FINGER, WHOIS, PING, TRACERT, and so on).

For More Information

If you need further information about TCP/IP in regard to Windows NT Workstation, you can reference one of the following resources:

- Bisaillon, Teresa and Brad Werner. *TCP/IP with Windows NT Illustrated.* McGraw-Hill, 1998. ISBN: 0079136486.

- Carl-Mitchell, Smoot and John S. Quarterman. *Practical Internetworking With TCP/IP and UNIX.* Addison-Wesley, 1993. ISBN: 0079136486.

- Comer, Douglas E. *Internetworking with TCP/IP, Vol. I-III.* Prentice Hall ESM, 1995, 1996, 1997. ISBN: 0132169878, 0139738436, 0138487146.

- Microsoft TechNet: `http://www.microsoft.com/technet/`

- *Microsoft Windows NT Workstation 4.0 Resource Kit.* Microsoft Press, 1996. ISBN: 1572313439.

- Stevens, W. Richard. *TCP/IP Illustrated Volumes 1, 2, & 3.* Addison-Wesley, 1994. ISBN: 0201633469, 020163354X, 0201634953.

- Wilensky, Marshall and Candace Leiden. *TCP/IP For Dummies, 2nd Edition.* IDG Books Worldwide, Inc., 1997. ISBN: 0764500635.

Here is a list of firewall information sites that have links to product sites and a few proxy product sites:

- 4 Firewalls: `http://www.4firewalls.com/`

- Aventail VPN: `http://www.aventail.com/`

- Deerfield Communication's WinGate Pro: `http://www.deerfield.com/`

- Firewall Overview: `http://www.access.digex.net/~bdboyle/firewall.vendor.html`

- Great Circle Associates: `http://www.greatcircles.com/`

- Microsoft's Proxy Server 2.0: `http://www.microsoft.com/proxy/`
- Netscape's Proxy Server: `http://www.netscape.com/`
- Ositis Software's WinProxy: `http://www.ositis.com/`
- Zeuros Firewall Resource: `http://www.zeuros.co.uk/`

The following list provides information about applications you can use to configure HOSTS and LMHOSTS files:

- CIP is a HOSTS file update system. It is located at `http://www.radsoft.net/Gallery/CIP/`.
- Essential NetTools' NBScan provides a GUI management tool for LMHOSTS. It is located at `http://www.tamos.com/soft/`.
- NetLightning 2.1 offers a HOSTS editor in addition to several other functions. It is located at `http://www.netlightning.mknight.wl.net`.
- TweakDUN 2.2 enables you to edit the HOSTS file in addition to many other functions. It is located at `http://www.pattersondesigns.com/TweakDUN/`.

If you want to check out other tools, you can find them on any of the following shareware/software distribution sites by searching by the type of tool you're looking for (such as *FTP, browser, TCP/IP, IP tools, Internet utilities, Windows NT tools,* and so on).

- `http://www.shareware.com/`
- `http://www.tucows.com/`
- `http://www.slaughterhouse.com/`
- `http://www.32bit.com/`
- `http://www.winfiles.com/`

Firewalls and Proxies

You can find plenty of information about firewalls, but the data on proxy servers is often limited to the documentation for a specific product.

13

NetBEUI and Windows NT

AS ONE OF THE THREE NATIVE PROTOCOLS OF WINDOWS NT (along with TCP/IP and IPX/SPX), NetBEUI offers small networks an elegant alternative when routing and Internet access are not required. In this chapter, we look at NetBEUI and how it is deployed on Windows NT.

When to Use NetBEUI

NetBEUI is a small, fast, and efficient protocol. It is included with Windows NT as a small non-routing protocol solution as well as for communication over an SNA gateway. NetBEUI is self tuning, requires no configuration, and has a small system resource footprint.

As implemented by Windows NT, NetBEUI is actually a NetBIOS Frame (NBF) implementation. Microsoft documentation and applications consider the terms NBF and NetBEUI to be equivalent. There is a slight difference in how each protocol interacts with NetBIOS, but this difference is negligible because operation and packet construction are exactly the same in both. With the use of NBF, Windows NT is not limited to 254 simultaneous NetBEUI sessions.

NetBIOS Frame (NBF) is different from NetBIOS, however. NBF is a protocol; NetBIOS is a programming interface. NBF/NetBEUI is used to provide communications between computers on a non-routing network. NetBIOS is a naming scheme and programming interface used by Windows operating systems for system communications both internally and with other networked systems. For more information, see the "NetBIOS" section later in this chapter.

You should use NetBEUI on networks with 10 or fewer users in which routing and Internet access are not required. If you plan ever to create subnets, add gateways, or connect to the Internet, you should use TCP/IP. NetBEUI is a great protocol for temporary network connections, such as transferring data between two computers.

Managing the Stack

NetBEUI is self-tuning, so there is really little you need to do to manage the protocol. However, if you must fine-tune NetBEUI, there are several Registry entries you can adjust. Changing the default values of the NetBEUI Registry entries can cause unexpected problems. Microsoft highly recommends that you do not alter the default settings.

For those brave enough to venture into the Registry despite this warning, the NetBIOS parameters are located in the HKEY_LOCAL_MACHINE\System\CurrentControlSet\Services\NBF\Parameters key. An exhaustive detailed list of the value entries, their effects, and valid values are contained in the REGENTRY.HLP file from the *Windows NT Server 4.0 Resource Kit Supplement 3*. The following list contains a few settings you can change to fine-tune NetBIOS:

- **LLCMaxWindowSize.** This value has a default of 10. It determines the window size (how many packets are transmitted before an acknowledgement is required). By increasing this value, you can improve performance, but you also increase the chance of retransmissions.

- **DefaultT1Timeout.** This value has a default of 600ms. It determines how long to wait for an LLC poll packet acknowledgment before resending it. The default value is used only upon link establishment; from there it is dynamically adjusted based on performance. Increasing the default value may improve performance over slow links.

- **LLCRetries.** This value has a default of 8. It determines how many times the LLC poll packet will be sent without receiving a response before the NBF link is closed. On high traffic networks, this value can be increased to improve performance.

Be Safe: Back Up

Before making any changes to the Registry, be sure to back it up and take note of the default values.

Mixing and Matching Protocols

NetBEUI can be installed on a network where NWLink (IPX/SPX) and/or TCP/IP are installed. This type of configuration offers improved performance on internal network communications. Binding NetBEUI with priority over other network protocols allows internal traffic to be completed quickly, although external traffic (that is, over routers or to the Internet) is delayed slightly.

However, you should test the response times and network traffic load for your particular network. In some cases, using only TCP/IP (for Internet connected networks) or NWLink (for routed networks not using the Internet) provides faster performance than a hybrid protocol network. Keep in mind that maintaining multiple protocols increases administration, installation, and troubleshooting time.

Troubleshooting NetBEUI

NetBEUI problems typically occur only in either of two situations. The first situation occurs if the drivers for the protocol are corrupted due to virus, read/write I/O error, or hardware failure. In this case, removing and reinstalling NetBEUI will resolve the problem. A second situation involves the Registry control values, which can be changed by an administrator to a non-viable configuration. Such a situation requires resetting the Registry entries to their default values, or removing and reinstalling the protocol. In both cases, the system (or systems) involved must be rebooted.

Performance Monitoring and NetBEUI

Installing NetBEUI adds two new objects to Performance Monitor. These objects— NetBEUI and NetBEUI Resource—offer insight into NetBEUI activity. Exhaustive details of the counters from both of these objects are contained in the COUN-TERS.HLP file from the *Windows NT Server 4.0 Resource Kit Supplement 3*. We discuss Performance Monitor details in Chapter 20, "Tuning and Optimizing Windows NT."

The NetBEUI object can be used to track various facets of traffic levels. Here are several counters worth watching:

- **Bytes Total/sec.** This counter measures the total amount of actual data transmitted over the network.
- **Connection Session Timeouts.** This counter keeps a running total of the number of sessions terminated due to timeout expiration. A quickly increasing value for this counter can indicate a clogged network or an unresponsive system.
- **Failures Adapter.** This counter keeps a running total of the number of sessions terminated due to hardware failures. A quickly increasing value for this counter can indicate a faulty NIC.
- **Window Send Average.** This counter tracks the average number of data bytes sent before waiting for an acknowledgement.

The NetBEUI object also includes several datagram, frame, and packet counters that can be used to obtain detailed information about inbound and outbound traffic patterns.

The NetBEUI Resource object tracks the use of NetBEUI buffers. Information about how often all buffers are exhausted, the average use, and the maximum use of system resources (buffers) can be monitored for numerous parameters of the protocol/adapter combo.

NetBIOS

Network Basic Input/Output System (NetBIOS) is not a protocol, but an application interface and naming convention. Windows NT employs NetBIOS as its primary means of communicating with internal core services and other networked systems. NetBIOS is attached to every protocol used by Windows NT. NBT is NetBIOS over TCP/IP, NWLink is NetBIOS over IPX/SPX, and NBF is NetBIOS Frame or NetBIOS over NetBEUI. The Workstation, Server, Browser, Messenger, and Netlogon services are all NetBIOS clients.

NetBIOS governs the naming of objects within the Windows NT environment. The NetBIOS is flat, so all names within each domain and on each system must be unique. NetBIOS names can be up to 16 characters in length, but because the 16th character is reserved for special use, only 15 characters can actually be used in an object's name.

Each time a computer boots, its NetBIOS names are registered into the local NetBIOS cache. When attempting to access resources using a NetBIOS name whether locally or remotely, the following resolution resources may be used:

- NetBIOS name cache
- NetBIOS name server (WINS)
- IP subnet broadcasts
- Static LMHOSTS files
- Static HOSTS files
- DNS servers

The order in which these resolution methods are used depends on the computer's configuration and the node type. For more information on NetBIOS registration and resolution, consult the Resource Kit and TechNet materials.

For More Information

For more information about NetBEUI, NBF, and NetBIOS, please consult the following resources:

- *Windows NT Workstation 4.0 Resource Kit.* Microsoft Press, 1996. ISBN: 1572313439.

- Microsoft TechNet: `http://www.microsoft.com/technet/`

14

NWLink (IPX/SPX) and Windows NT

Aの LTHOUGH MICROSOFT WINDOWS NT has taken the network operating system market by storm, Novell's NetWare is still a definite presence. Recent estimates indicate that NetWare still has a market share of nearly 60% for PC-based servers. Numerous versions of NetWare are on the market, including NetWare 2.2, NetWare 3.12, NetWare 4.11/IntranetWare, and NetWare 5.0. On many networks, you will find yourself dealing with both Windows NT and Novell NetWare and will need to ensure that the two network operating systems work well together.

This chapter covers the information you need to successfully integrate Windows NT and NetWare networks. There are several tools available to make this integration as painless as possible.

Integrating with NetWare

Integrating Windows NT and NetWare is fairly straightforward, thanks to some tools that Microsoft includes with Windows NT. Before we can look at these tools, however, it is important that you understand the different integration options. The three primary methods you can use to access a Novell NetWare server from Windows NT are:

- Microsoft's NWLink IPX/SPX compatible protocol
- Microsoft's Windows NT Client Services for NetWare
- Microsoft's Windows NT Gateway Services for NetWare

The last two items on the list are covered in detail later in this chapter. We discuss the NWLink protocol and when to use it in the section that follows.

What Is the NWLink IPX/SPX Compatible Protocol?

Until NetWare 5, IPX/SPX was NetWare's primary networking protocol suite. IPX and SPX stand for the Internetwork Packet Exchange protocol and the Sequenced Packet Exchange protocol, respectively. These two separate protocols are grouped into a single set of capabilities, not unlike the many protocols and services included under the TCP/IP umbrella.

The IPX protocol is a connectionless protocol that resides at the Network layer of the OSI model. This means that IPX information is simply sent out on the wire in the hopes that it will get to its destination. This is also known as a "best-effort" delivery mechanism.

Think of it this way: You have a letter you would like to deliver to your Aunt Bessy. She lives in a different state or country than the one in which you live. The easiest, cheapest, and hopefully fastest way to get the letter delivered is to write Aunt Bessy's address on the envelope, paste on the appropriate postage, and drop it in the nearest mailbox. You don't care how it gets there (the path the letter takes); you only care that it does get there in a reasonable amount of time. The only way you might be informed that the letter did not arrive is if Aunt Bessy calls you and complains that you never write. This protocol can be compared to the User Datagram Protocol (UDP) or Internet Protocol (IP), both of which offer little in the way of error correction, detection, or recovery services.

SPX is connection-oriented and resides at the Transport layer of the OSI model. With SPX, a connection (or session) is created and authenticated, and only then is any information sent.

Using the same analogy we used for IPX, SPX goes something like this: Once you have prepared Aunt Bessy's letter, you call her and let her know that you are sending her a letter. She informs you that she is home to receive it and when she might be going out. You then take the letter, get into your car, and drive the letter to Aunt Bessy's house. When you get there, you walk up to the front door and ring the bell. If everything works out properly, Aunt Bessy answers the door. You can now deliver the letter and go home. You are certain that she got the letter, and you know there will be no nasty messages on your answering machine when you get home. The SPX protocol can be likened to TCP, both of which offer excellent error detection, correction, and recovery services.

The SPX protocol sits atop IPX, and the two protocols work together. Together, SPX and IPX offer a fast and efficient protocol suite that is able to access NetWare systems and other Windows NT workstations or servers using this protocol suite as well. In fact, IPX/SPX is faster and easier to configure than the TCP/IP protocol suite used on the Internet today.

Novell invented the IPX and SPX protocols for use with its Novell NetWare operating system. Microsoft provides the ability to communicate with these protocols so its operating systems can coexist with the huge installed base of NetWare networks. Microsoft developed NWLink, its own implementation of IPX/SPX in a so-called "clean room" environment. Essentially, Microsoft reverse-engineered the IPX/SPX protocols. NWLink is a protocol suite that is completely compatible with Novell's IPX/SPX.

Installing NWLink

NWLink is available on the CD-ROM that ships with Microsoft Windows NT Workstation and Microsoft Windows Server. To install NWLink, follow these steps:

1. Open the Network applet in the Control Panel.

2. Choose the Protocols tab.

3. From the list, choose NWLink IPX/SPX Compatible Transport and click OK. You will probably be asked to insert the Windows NT Workstation CD-ROM. When you reboot the system, the NWLink protocol will be installed.

NWLink, by itself, is not a connectivity tool that integrates Windows NT and Novell NetWare functionality. Using only NWLink, you will not be able to access file or printer information on a NetWare server from a Windows NT Workstation. However, using only NWLink, you will be able to access socket-based applications that use IPX protocols. For example, if you have access to a Novell NetWare server that supports a structured query language (SQL) database, you can access that application using only NWLink. Microsoft provides other services that work with NWLink to integrate NetWare and Windows NT systems.

CSNW Versus GSNW

Two other services included with Windows NT that help to integrate Windows NT and NetWare are the Client Services for NetWare (CSNW) and the Gateway Services for NetWare (GSNW). CSNW is a component of GSNW.

Client Services for NetWare

Client Services for NetWare connects Windows NT Workstations to NetWare file servers and allows them to operate in that environment. With CSNW installed, a NetWare server can validate a Windows NT Workstation to access files and printers on that server. Remember that these services rely on the NWLink protocol.

When you install CSNW, it checks to see if NWLink is installed. If NWLink is not installed, the installation process automatically installs the NWLink protocol and proceeds with the installation. Figure 14.1 illustrates how a Windows NT Workstation with CSNW installed can communicate with a Novell NetWare server.

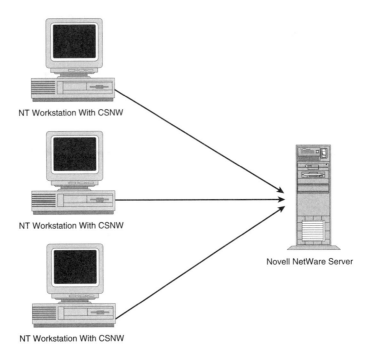

NT Workstation With CSNW

NT Workstation With CSNW

NT Workstation With CSNW

Novell NetWare Server

Figure 14.1 Client Services for NetWare.

Gateway Services for NetWare

CSNW is a component of GSNW. When you install CSNW, you might notice that the GSNW option is not available. This is because GSNW is available only on Windows NT Server, whereas CSNW is available only on Windows NT Workstation. However, when you install GSNW on a Windows NT Server, you should notice that the formal name for this service is actually the Gateway (and Client) Service for NetWare. So as you can see, CSNW is a subset of GSNW.

GSNW includes the features of CSNW and takes things to the next level. GSNW connects Windows NT Servers to NetWare servers. This service provides a gateway for Microsoft workstations that require access to NetWare servers but do not have NetWare client software (or IPX/SPX protocols) installed. GSNW also allows workstations that connect using RAS to access resources on a NetWare server.

Administering NetWare 4.x

A Windows NT computer with NWLink and CSNW installed can administer a NetWare server running version Microsoft Windows 3.x or earlier, using utilities such as SYSCON, RCONSOLE, or PCONSOLE. At present, however, you cannot administer a NetWare 4.x or higher-numbered server version unless you install Novell's Client32 for Windows NT.

The actual process a Windows NT Server follows when it acts as a gateway is fairly complex. However, this entire process is completely transparent to the workstations that use the gateway. After the gateway service is installed and configured, all workstations are able to see whatever file and printer resources the Windows NT administrator sees fit to share, as if the resources were ordinary file and printer shares on a Microsoft network.

Two features make GSNW a powerful and useful network service. First, no extra software is required on workstations that already participate in a Microsoft network environment. This includes not only Windows NT Workstation, but also Microsoft Windows 95, Microsoft Windows 98, and Microsoft Windows for Workgroups. Second, only a single user license on the NetWare server is required for the gateway to operate. To understand why this so, let's discuss how Windows NT creates a NetWare gateway using GSNW.

After installing GSNW, you must create a special user account on the Windows NT Server where it resides. This account is used to log into the NetWare server on the far side of the gateway. Likewise, the NetWare server must include a valid user account whose name and password match the special user account for the gateway on the Windows NT Server.

Next, you must create a group on the NetWare server. The group must be named NTGATEWAY for GSNW to function properly. After this group is created, you can assign it permissions to file and printer resources on the NetWare server. Microsoft Network clients can then access these NetWare resources in the form of shared folders on the Windows NT Server. To set this up, you must decide which resource to share and then assign appropriate permissions to the NTGATEWAY group, so the account in that group can access those resources.

When a workstation attempts to access information stored on the NetWare server, it sends a request for that information to the Windows NT Server in which GSNW resides. The GSNW software logs into the NetWare server (using the special gateway access user account) and grabs the requested information. Finally, GSNW sends the requested information back to the client workstation. To the workstation, it appears as if the requested information resides on the Windows NT server itself; the workstation remains unaware of the gateway's background activity (except, perhaps, for slower-than-normal response times, which are typical when using GSNW or any other gateway software in fact). Figure 14.2 illustrates how GSNW works.

Using GSNW

You should use GSNW for only occasional access to a NetWare server because the speed of the gateway depends on the number of clients that connect through it. Increasing the number of clients for the gateway results in slower access speed for all clients. Windows NT Servers with GSNW installed can administer a NetWare server using the same utilities that work with CSNW. Client computers accessing a NetWare server through the gateway cannot administer the NetWare server. Here again, a gateway connection works only for the administration of NetWare 3.x or lower-numbered versions; administration of 4.x or higher-numbered versions requires that you use the Novell Client32 for Windows NT software.

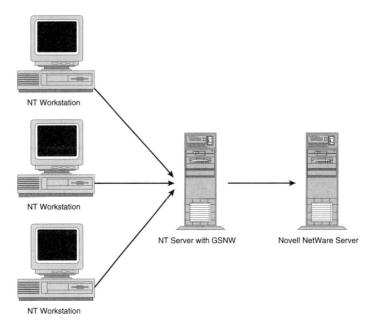

NT Workstation

NT Workstation

NT Server with GSNW

Novell NetWare Server

NT Workstation

Figure 14.2 The Gateway Services for NetWare.

Installing GSNW

Installing GSNW is similar to installing CSNW. To install GSNW, complete the following steps:

1. Launch the Network applet in the Control Panel.

2. Select the Services tab, and then click the Add button. Select Gateway (and Client) Services for NetWare and click the Continue button. You will be prompted to insert the Windows NT CD-ROM but can point at a source directory (for example, a copy of the /I386 directory on a local hard disk or a network server) where the necessary files reside.

   The system will reboot. When it resumes operation, GSNW will be available.

RAS Support

If you have RAS installed, you will receive the following message: Setup has discovered that you have Remote Access Services installed. Do you want to configure RAS to support NWLink protocol? If you do want RAS to support NWLink, click OK; otherwise, click Cancel.

Creating the Gateway User Account

You must now create the user account and the Gateway group on the NetWare server. Here's how to go about completing these tasks:

1. Using your favorite NetWare Administration utility (SYSCON, NWADMIN, NETADMIN, and so on), create a user whose name matches that of the user account that will be logging into the Windows NT Machine. For example, you might use NWUSER as the account name.

2. Create a group on the NetWare server (using the same administration tools) called NTGATEWAY. Remember that the group name *must* be NTGATEWAY.

3. Place the newly created user, NWUSER, into the newly created group, NTGATEWAY.

4. Make sure the password of the user matches that of the Windows NT account with the same name.

5. Assign any necessary permissions (called *rights* in the NetWare world) to whatever file and printer resources you want users to be able to access through the gateway.

When you have completed these steps, the NetWare server will be ready to accept service requests from the gateway software on the Windows NT Server where GSNW resides.

Configuring the Gateway Service

After the Windows NT server reboots, you will notice that it attempts to log into a NetWare server. You must choose one of two methods for logging in, based on the type of NetWare server to which the gateway connects:

- *If GSNW logs in to a NetWare 3.x server,* or one with a lower version number, you must select the Preferred Server method. GSNW then attempts to log in to whichever NetWare server you designated as the preferred server.

- *If GSNW logs in to a NetWare 4.x server,* or one with a higher version number, you must select a Default Tree and Context for GSNW to log in to the proper part of the NetWare Directory Services (NDS) directory tree. If you use only the Client component of GSNW on a Windows NT Server machine, you can choose that option right away. However, if you are configuring a system to act as a gateway for others to use, cancel this screen and proceed to configure the gateway itself instead.

When you install GSNW, it does not appear on the Start menu. Instead, GSNW creates a Control Panel applet called GSNW where you must choose the type of NetWare server to which the gateway will connect. This is also where you must designate either a Preferred Server (for 3.x and lower-numbered versions of NetWare) or the Default Tree and Context (for 4.x and higher-numbered versions of NetWare that use NDS).

Now that you have selected which server to log in to, you can enable the gateway. To accomplish this, click on the Gateway button. The Configure Gateway window appears. To enable the gateway, follow these steps:

1. Enable the gateway by checking the Enable Gateway check box.

2. In the Gateway Account field, enter the name of the user account you created on the NetWare server.

3. Enter the password in the Password field and confirm it.

The gateway is now configured, but you have not yet made any NetWare resources available to your clients. To do this, click the Add button. When the New Share window appears, follow these steps:

1. In the Share Name field, enter the name of the share you want to create. This is the name clients will see when they browse for resources available on the Windows NT Server. Remember, too, that MS-DOS and Windows 3.x clients can access only shares whose names are eight characters or fewer in length.

2. In the Network Path field, enter the Universal Naming Convention (UNC) path for the NetWare server and share.

3. Enter a comment that will appear when the clients browse for this resource. This field is optional, but can be helpful when you're searching for resources because it is not subject to the same length restrictions as UNC names.

4. Select the drive letter that should be used when attaching this share to the server.

5. Choose the User Limit to apply to the gateway. You can either choose Unlimited or select some limit for the number of users that can access the share simultaneously. Be careful when setting this to Unlimited (the default). You might find that your gateway runs unacceptably slowly if too many users try to access it at the same time.

6. Click OK. Immediately thereafter, the Gateway applet attempts to connect to this share and authenticate the user account. If the Gateway applet connects successfully, the open windows disappear, and the newly created share appears in both the Configure Gateway dialog box and in Network Neighborhood information obtained from the local browser service (subject to update propagation to local browse masters).

Checking the Username

The first line of the GSNW applet in the Control Panel reads Username: NWUSER. This confirms the name of the user account that GSNW will use to log in to the NetWare server. Confirm that GSNW logs in as that user by going to the Services applet in Control Panel and double-clicking Gateway Services for NetWare. In the Service window that appears, check the entries in the Log On As: pane.

UNC Name

A UNC name takes the form: \\servername\sharename. For a server named NWAcctg and a share named Monthly, the resulting UNC name is \\NWAcctg\Monthly. UNC names are not case sensitive.

Microsoft Clients Versus Novell Clients

Novell also offers software tools that make it easier to integrate Windows NT and NetWare. Some of them perform as well, if not better in certain circumstances, than do their Microsoft counterparts.

Novell's NetWare is a fairly closed network operating system. To develop applications that are truly compatible with NetWare, you need to follow specific development and deployment guidelines from Novell. Obtaining access to some of Novell's code has been difficult and expensive, so only a small number of companies have done so.

On the other hand, Microsoft has positioned Windows NT as a relatively open operating system, especially for development of client/server applications and server-based services. This strategy is the result of Microsoft's belief that if developers can find out how to write applications and services for Windows NT easily and cheaply, they will choose to do so. Further, the more applications that become available for Windows NT, the more widely the operating system will be used. History appears to have vindicated this position. Today, many more applications are available for Windows NT than for NetWare.

Microsoft has done a good job of creating client software, services, and applications that interoperate with Novell's more closed operating system. For this reason, some of Novell's newest and most proprietary offerings work better than their Microsoft counterparts, especially where advanced client capabilities and NetWare Directory Services are concerned. Novell has an edge where providing advanced client capabilities for their own network operating system is concerned, even when the client involved is Windows NT.

Several networking clients are available for use in a mixed Windows NT and NetWare environment. These include the following:

- The Microsoft Client for NetWare Networks (protected-mode client)
- The Novell Client32 for Windows NT (protected-mode client)
- NETX (real-mode Novell network client)
- VLM (real-mode Novell network client)

Although Windows NT Workstation will support networking clients that operate in real mode, this practice is not recommended. In real mode, all the CPU's protection options are disabled, as are memory paging and multitasking features. Protected mode is recommended because it is more advanced than real mode and offers support for multitasking, virtual memory, and data security. Using a protected-mode client instead of a real-mode client provides greater stability and faster data transfers across the network.

To help you decide which protected-mode networking client best fits your needs, we look at some reasons *not* to use a particular networking client.

Known Issues with Microsoft NetWare Clients

Microsoft has had to build and design its NetWare utilities and tools blindly because they do not have access to proprietary Novell NetWare applications and components. In fact, Microsoft itself recommends against using the Microsoft NetWare client if any of the following conditions apply:

- *If you need to use some of the proprietary NetWare utilities, including the Novell Application Launcher (NAL), Novell IP Gateway, Remove Access Dialer, and NetWare Distributed Printer Services (NDPS).* NAL allows an administrator to configure applications so they appear as icons to the users. To run the application, the user simply double-clicks the corresponding icon. The Novell IP Gateway allows dissimilar networks to communicate using TCP/IP externally, but IPX/SPX internally. Remote Access Dialer is a utility for connecting clients using Windows, Mac OS, and MS-DOS operating systems to the network so they can access network resources. Finally, NDPS eases the task of creating printers for users by installing print drivers and configuration on client computers automatically. None of these utilities work with the native Microsoft Client for NetWare Networks.

- *If NetWare NCP packet signature is required.* NetWare NCP packet signature is an enhanced security feature that allows packets to be digitally signed to protect their recipients from spoofing or forgeries. Only NetWare Client32 for Windows NT and VLM support this capability.

- *If your network requires NetWare IP for NetWare 4.x.* Microsoft TCP/IP will not communicate with NetWare IP for NetWare 4.x. To use this functionality, you must use Novell's NetWare Client32 for Windows NT, its VLM client, or its NETX client software.

- *If 3270 emulators are required.* If you use 3270 emulators that need MS-DOS TSR (Terminate and Stay Resident) programs or need to run applications in MS-DOS using a 3270 emulator, you need to use either the VLM client or the NETX client.

- *If you use custom VLM components.* Because custom VLM components do not work with the Microsoft NetWare Client, you should use the Novell VLM client instead.

- *If even one program does.* You should use one of the Novell clients.

NetWare Client32

You can download the NetWare Client32 for Windows NT by linking to **http://www.novell.com/download/index.html** and selecting the appropriate link. For more information about limitations of the Microsoft Client for NetWare Networks, consult the *Resource Kits* from Microsoft Press for Windows NT Workstation, Windows NT Server, or Windows 98. Even though Windows 98 information is not directly applicable to Windows NT, this is the newest of the resource kits mentioned, and it includes the most current NetWare information.

Known Issues with Novell NetWare Clients

You should use the Microsoft Client for NetWare Networks if you encounter any problems running Setup using the Microsoft unattended installation facilities. Microsoft Client for NetWare Networks is available on the Microsoft Windows NT Workstation CD-ROM. Several other tools and utilities are also available for Windows NT Server that support integration of NetWare and Windows NT and permit information to migrate from Novell NetWare to Windows NT, including File and Print Services for NetWare and the NetWare migration tool. These and others will be discussed in the next sections.

FPNW

Until now, you have learned about only those NetWare-related client and server tools that are bundled with Windows NT Workstation and Server. All of those tools offer certain abilities to connect Windows NT clients to Novell NetWare servers. You will find that most networks in the real world require connections in reverse as well. Thus, there will be the need for NetWare clients to connect to resources on an NT system.

To solve this problem, Microsoft developed File and Print Services for NetWare (FPNW). This tool is not built into Windows NT; it must be purchased as an add-on component for Windows NT Server. Like GSNW, FPNW is available only for Microsoft Windows NT Server and does not work on Windows NT Workstation. FPNW retails at an estimated $149. You can find out how and where to purchase FPNW (and an accompanying product called Directory Services Manager for NetWare) at **http://www.microsoft.com/ntserver/nts/exec/feature/ addonservices.asp**. FPNW works the same as CSNW except in reverse. Essentially, FPNW makes a Windows NT Server computer appear to NetWare clients as a NetWare 3.x server. FPNW clients can access any information about file and print shares and services that the system administrator chooses to share with them.

FPNW and NetWare

FPNW emulates a NetWare 3.x server or lower. FPNW cannot emulate a NetWare 4.x server or any higher-numbered version of NetWare.

NetWare Migration Tool

Both Microsoft and Novell offer tools to help administrators migrate their servers from one network operating system to another. In real life, however, system migration does not occur often.

The Windows NT Server migration tool (NWCONV.EXE) helps you migrate a variety of data from NetWare servers to Windows NT servers. This tool allows you to transfer user and group accounts, as well as files and directories from one or more NetWare servers to at least one Windows NT domain controller. With a special proviso, this also includes transferring file and directory permissions.

You must choose what information you wish to migrate before you can migrate any NetWare-based information or resources to Windows NT. The NetWare Migration tool supports three object types:

- User accounts
- Group accounts
- Files

We mentioned previously that permissions are transferred only under a special case. For permissions to transfer from NetWare to Windows NT, you must meet all of the following conditions:

- You must have both administrator rights in Windows NT and supervisor rights on the Novell server (or admin rights in NetWare 4.x or higher).
- The destination drive must be formatted with NTFS.
- Both NWLink and GSNW must be installed and running.
- You must be migrating from a NetWare 2.x or 3.x server. You can migrate from a NetWare 4.x or 5.0 server, but only if it is running in bindery emulation mode.

Because Windows NT and NetWare are so different, you must make some choices and decisions before you start any migration process. These are covered in the sections that follow.

Object Types for Migration

When using the NetWare Migration tool, you can choose to migrate any or all instances of user accounts, group accounts, and files.

Dealing with Duplicate Names

When you run two distinct and very different network operating systems, there are often duplicate account or group names on the two networks. This is normal because a user might need access to both systems before a migration occurs, and often the only way to accomplish this is to create two separate accounts, one for each of the two networks. When you plan a migration, you must be aware of such duplicate names and what you can do with them. Here are some possible solutions to duplicate name problems:

- Overwrite the existing account (replace the current Windows NT account with a NetWare-derived alternative).

- Log the duplicate name. Simply note the presence of a duplicate name in the NetWare space, but make no changes to the Windows NT environment.

- Ignore the duplicate name. Do nothing at all for NetWare account information if a NetWare account name duplicates an existing Windows NT account.

- Migrate the name from NetWare to Windows NT, but add a prefix to any duplicate usernames. For example, add the prefix *nw* to all duplicate accounts. This creates multiple accounts whenever duplicates are encountered, so information can be transferred from the NetWare-derived account to the existing account, or both accounts can be maintained in parallel.

Dealing with Supervisor Rights

Both of these network operating systems have their own administration accounts. The migration tool does not, by default, transfer users with supervisory rights into the Domain Administrators group in the receiving domain. This means that a user who is a supervisor on the NetWare network does not automatically become an administrator on the Windows NT Server. To automate this process, you must select the Supervisors check box in the User Options dialog box in the Migration tool setup.

Dealing with File Migration

When migrating files from NetWare to a Windows NT domain, you can choose from a variety of File Options, as outlined here:

- You can select which files are to be copied from NetWare to Windows NT. If you are transferring the selected NetWare files to an NTFS partition, all copied directories and files retain their effective permissions.

- You can choose what resource share names to use.

- You can choose whether hidden and system files are transferred. By default, they are not.

By default, all the files with the proper settings are migrated except for the files stored in the NetWare Administrative directories, including \ETC, \LOGIN, \MAIL, and \SYSTEM. This is because these are files and directories that are specific to NetWare and cannot be used on a Windows NT system.

The differences between Windows NT and NetWare mean that certain file and directory properties might not translate perfectly from NetWare to Windows NT. We have constructed three tables to illustrate how file and folder properties migrate. Table 14.1 illustrates how NetWare file rights map to NT file permissions; Table 14.2 illustrates how file attributes migrate; Table 14.3 illustrates the relationship between NetWare folder rights and Windows NT folder permissions.

Table 14.1 **NetWare File Rights and Windows NT File Permissions Compared**

NetWare File Rights	Windows NT File Permissions
Access Control (A)	Change Permissions (P)
Create (C)	Ignored and not transferred
Erase (E)	Change (RWXD)
File Scan (F)	Ignored and not transferred
Modify (M)	Change (RWXD)
Read (R)	Read (RX)
Supervisory (S)	Full Control (ALL)
Write (W)	Change (RWXD)

Table 14.2 **NetWare and Windows NT File Attributes Compared**

NetWare File Attributes	Windows NT File Attributes
Archive Needed (A)	Archive (A)
Copy Inhibit (C)	Ignored and not transferred
Delete Inhibit (D)	Ignored and not transferred
Execute only (X)	Ignored and not transferred
Hidden (H)	Hidden (H)
Indexed (I)	Ignored and not transferred
Purge (P)	Ignored and not transferred
Read Audit (Ra)	Ignored and not transferred
Rename Inhibit (R)	Ignored and not transferred
Read Only (Ro)	Read Only (R)
Read Write (RW)	None; files without the Read attribute can be read and written to

NetWare File Attributes	Windows NT File Attributes
System (SY)	System (S)
Shareable (Sh)	Ignored and not transferred
Transactional (T)	Ignored and not transferred
Write Audit (Wa)	Ignored and not transferred

Table 14.3 **Comparison of NetWare Folder Rights and Windows NT Folder Permissions**

NetWare Folder Rights	Windows NT Folder Permissions
Access Control (A)	Change Permissions (P)
Create (C)	Add (WX) (not specified)
Erase (E)	Change (RWXD) (RWXD)
File Scan (F)	List (RX) (not specified)
Modify (M)	Change (RWXD) (RWXD)
Read (R)	Read (RX) (RX)
Supervisory (S)	Full Control (All) (All)
Write (W)	Change (RWXD) (RWXD)

To Migrate or Not to Migrate?

After you start the migration process, it is important to know what information will migrate from NetWare to Windows NT and what information will not make this transition. The following items can migrate from NetWare to Windows NT:

- User accounts
- Group accounts
- Account permissions
- Files
- Directory structures

The following will not migrate from NetWare to Windows NT:

- Login scripts (However, Windows NT can execute NetWare login scripts, so if you copy the files that contain these scripts to an appropriate Windows NT Server and invoke those scripts as part of each user's account setup, you can continue to use such scripts in the Windows NT environment.)

- Print server and queue information

- Passwords

- Workgroup and user account managers

The Migration Tool for NetWare

When you install Windows NT Server, the installation process automatically installs the Migration tool for NetWare. The actual program is called NWCONV.EXE, but the installation process places a shortcut on the Start, Programs menu, under Administration Tools (Common).

Before you perform any actual migration from NetWare to Windows NT, it is best to select the list of servers and related migration options and perform a trial migration. When the trial migration starts, the server goes through the motions of performing the specified migration but does not commit any of the changes. Instead, three log files are generated as the trial migration proceeds:

- **LOGFILE.LOG.** Contains information on users, groups, and files.

- **SUMMARY.LOG.** Presents an overview of the migration that includes the server names and the number of users, groups, and files that were transferred.

- **ERROR.LOG.** Contains a list of errors that occurred during the migration.

A trial migration lets you observe any changes that the migration tool will make and take corrective action to deal with any problems or conflicts that it might encounter when it's underway for real. You can perform as many trial migrations as you want, making minor or major configuration changes for each one, until the results match your needs and your expectations.

Preserving Information

There are third-party utilities that can capture and preserve some of the information the Microsoft Migration Tool for NetWare cannot handle. If you're considering any large-scale or wholesale migrations, you might want to investigate products and services from companies such as Softnet Systems (`http://www.softnetsys.com/migrate.asp`), Now Technologies (`http://www.nowtechs.com/`), or BindView Development Corporation (`http://www.bindview.com/`).

Troubleshooting NetWare-to-Windows NT Connections (and Vice-Versa)

Some of the toughest tasks you will ever be required to handle will involve troubleshooting computer systems. Even when problems appear to be the same from one instance to the next, the same solution almost never works more than once.

One of the most common problems you will run into with Windows NT-to-NetWare integration involves IPX frame types. Ethernet uses what are called frame types to send information across a network. You can configure Ethernet to use one of several IPX frame types; the most common of these frame types are the IEEE 802.2 and IEEE 803.3 frame formats. Although their names appear similar, these two frame formats are not at all the same.

As an analogy, take the coins you deal with every day. Some vending machines take only certain coins; others will take nearly all denominations. Frame types work the same way. A protocol usually accepts only one frame format, although you can configure it to accept multiple types. If you are communicating with a NetWare 3.x or earlier server, that frame format usually uses 802.3. However, NetWare 4.x and higher numbered versions usually use 802.2. If a client attempts to communicate with a NetWare server using an unrecognized frame format, it won't be able to communicate with that server.

For More Information

For more information about the available Windows NT and NetWare utilities, consult the following references:

- TechNet: The technical subscription service from Microsoft. Check out the documents under MS BackOffice, MS Windows NT Server, MS Windows NT Server Manuals, Networking Supplement at **http://technet.microsoft.com/**.

- Microsoft Knowledge Base: **http://support.microsoft.com/**. Check out the following articles: Q187789, Q177601, Q104024, and Q121394.

- Search the Web using the following keywords: IPX/SPX, NWLink, CSNW, GSNW, and FPNW. You will find Windows NT FAQs like the one found at **http://www.stats.ox.ac.uk/~clifford/ntfaq.html#NetWare** to be quite useful as well.

15

Windows NT Meets UNIX

I T IS A FACT OF CORPORATE LIFE THAT MANY business networks are hybrid or multi-platform environments. This might be the result of natural evolution or of a business decision. One of the more common hybrid networks is one running both Microsoft Windows NT and UNIX. Each of these operating systems has its respective strengths and weaknesses. This chapter discusses how to integrate these two systems on the same network. When discussing UNIX, we are generalizing about the many available UNIX flavors—including Solaris, AIX, and Linux—that are divided into two broad categories or families: System V and BSD.

Windows NT

This section examines the strengths and weaknesses of the Windows NT operating system.

Windows NT has a number of strengths including the following:

- Windows NT is not a patch or an upgrade; it is a complete rewrite of the earlier Windows DOS-based operating systems·such as Windows 95 and Windows 98.

- Windows NT runs DOS-based, Win16, POSIX, and Win32 applications and retains some backward compatibility with earlier software. Windows NT runs DOS-based and Win16 applications so that application failure has no impact on the server, protecting Windows NT from subsystem failure.

- Microsoft designed Windows NT with security in mind, both to prevent attacks from the outside and to make the system user-proof. Windows NT uses both New Technology File System (NTFS) and share-level security.

- Windows NT has a simple user interface. Windows NT and earlier versions of Windows have a similar graphical user interface (GUI), which eases the learning curve for previous Windows users. There also is less maintenance overhead because the operating system provides administration wizards and GUI tools. The Microsoft Management Console (MMC), for example, is a single administration tool that manages a Windows NT installation. The MMC enables administrators to snap in components and to manage the network via a single interface.

- One main benefit Windows NT has going for it is the Microsoft BackOffice product line. BackOffice is a collection of products you would have to purchase from third-party companies if you ran UNIX. SQL Server, Exchange Server, Proxy Server, SMS Server, SNA Sever, and Site Server all are BackOffice components. With UNIX solutions, you must manage vendor relationships with multiple companies. A comparison between Microsoft BackOffice, Netscape SuiteSpot Professional Edition, and IBM's IBM Suite for Windows NT is viewable at `http://www.microsoft.com/backofficeserver/prodinfo/competitive.htm`.

- Windows NT Server includes a free, scaleable Web server called Internet Information Server (IIS). IIS is managed via Internet Services Manager for IIS 2.0 or 3.0, Internet Services Manager (HTML) using a Web browser, or the Microsoft Management Console (MMC) for IIS 4.0. For smaller networks with no more than 10 clients, Windows NT Workstation offers Peer Web Services (PWS). Both IIS and PWS include Web, FTP, and Gopher servers, although IIS 4.0 dropped Gopher support because of the declining popularity of the protocol.

Levels of Security

The most secure system is one with no users and with C2-level security; the least secure system is one whose users have Full Control and the file system provides no security. Your network probably falls somewhere between these two extremes. Versions of Windows prior to Windows NT provided no real security. Although UNIX also has a number of security features, Windows NT arguably provides better tools to manage and monitor security.

Five years ago, Linux was the poor man's operating system. College students used it because it was free. Everybody and his brother (or sister) could code to it. The source is still free. Now large IT organizations are embracing Linux. Compaq developed RAID software drivers for it, IBM provides service agreements for it, Oracle has a database for it, and Caldera and Red Hat have books and Linux certification programs. Major companies are looking at Linux because of its large and still growing installed user base and because it is a free operating system. Microsoft has an even larger installed base and support systems, which implies safety for corporate users and developers alike. As with Linux, everybody wants to write software for Windows NT because of its large installed customer base.

Just as there is no silver lining without a cloud, Windows NT has some weaknesses in addition to its strengths. Compared to UNIX, Windows NT is less reliable. It is not uncommon practice on Windows NT networks to reboot Windows NT Servers on a scheduled basis to stave off an attack of blue screens. UNIX, on the other hand, tends to run for months or years without O/S failure. Scalability is a common requirement in large-scale companies and on e-commerce Web sites. Until recently, Windows NT was not very scaleable; UNIX has always done this better. Currently, Windows NT scalability is achieved through a technology called clustering.

A *cluster* is a group of computers that the end user sees as a single machine, even when computers are added to it. Clusters provide fault tolerance and distributed processing. A failure of a single server in a cluster will be noticed only by an administrator without any performance degradation or service outage from the end standpoint. Microsoft has a cluster technology in Microsoft Cluster Server (MSCS), beta code-named "Wolfpack," that provides the following benefits:

- **Availability.** MSCS automatically can detect application or server failure and can quickly restart services on a surviving server. Users experience only a momentary pause in service.

- **Manageability.** MSCS lets administrators quickly inspect the status of all cluster resources and easily move the workload around onto different servers within the cluster. This is useful for manual load balancing and to perform "rolling updates" on the servers without taking important data and applications offline.

- **Scalability.** Cluster-aware applications can use the MSCS services through the MSCS Application Programming Interface (API) to perform dynamic load balancing and to scale across multiple servers within a cluster.

Third-party vendors also provide applications that improve the scalability of Windows NT. BrightTiger Technologies, for example, offers server-clustering solutions that provide scalability and fault tolerance for Windows NT in one package—ClusterCATS Enterprise. ClusterCATS Enterprise has nine critical capabilities that provide important benefits in the areas of Web site performance, availability, manageability, and scalability. The application improves user response time, server load management, and network trip time location selection capabilities.

The bottom line is that Windows NT scalability means buying another product. This is unlike UNIX, which offers scalability inherently.

UNIX

Remote administration is another area in which UNIX provides better capabilities than Windows NT. Programs such as Symantec's pcAnywhere and Compaq's Carbon Copy exist to enable remote administration of Windows NT and Windows 95/98 computers. On the other hand, Telnet enables a UNIX administrator to connect to every other UNIX box in the world—or to any system running a Telnet Server— and administer it. For UNIX implementation, remote administration comes with the package; for Windows NT, it does not.

UNIX is stable. System crashes are possible with any computer, but on the whole, UNIX runs longer without a crash. Historically, companies with large, mission-critical enterprise applications have run on UNIX. If you were to ask the CEOs of Fortune 500 companies about which operating system their companies use, you will get more UNIX answers than Windows NT. Compaq, for example, advertises that the "Integrity SA-series will provide continued improvements in fault-tolerant system availability, with availability in the range of 99.999 to 99.9999 percent." This statistic screams stability.

As previously mentioned, UNIX provides better scalability than Windows NT. By nature, Windows NT has limits. Windows NT scales to several hundred users but does not scale well for several thousand. UNIX servers have higher limits on maximum processors, maximum memory, and maximum drive space. Windows NT places more restrictive limits on each of these.

It is common in the UNIX world to code a great tool and release the source code into the public domain. This is not a Windows NT practice. UNIX has been around a lot longer than Windows NT and has more administration tools and utilities. There also are an extraordinary number of available news servers, email servers, FTP, and Web servers for UNIX, many of which are freeware or shareware and therefore are more cost-effective than Windows NT.

With all this free stuff and years of public release, what could possibly be wrong with UNIX? If you have never stared down the throat of the UNIX monster, you are missing the intimidation factor. The proliferation of command prompts is a bit unnerving at least in the beginning. A # sign or a $ sign as your only point of contact with the UNIX OS scares people. UNIX is harder to administer. Take a seasoned UNIX administrator and throw him or her into a Windows NT environment while tossing a Windows NT admin over to UNIX. Guess who quits and goes home? It does not take a lot of expertise to poke around and find User Manager for Domains, to play with the menus, and to figure out how to add a group. The difference between local and global groups also is relatively obvious. Now imagine doing the same thing on UNIX. Unless you know the keyboard commands and what the prompts mean, you'll become hopelessly lost in no time.

The other big UNIX negative is the diversity of the operating system. Even with small differences among the UNIX flavors, a developer has to code his or her UNIX application for each version of UNIX. This contrasts with coding for a single platform on Windows NT. It is difficult for a vendor to support a lot of varying platforms. For this reason, corporate decision makers consider vendor support for UNIX weak or incomplete.

Hybrid Environments

Few companies operate in a single computing environment. As companies and networks expand, the networks tend toward heterogeneity rather than homogeneity. Compaq Computer Corporation is a good example of this. Historically, Compaq was a WinTel (Windows on Intel) computer manufacturer. In 1998, however, Compaq acquired Digital Equipment Corporation and got Digital UNIX in the deal. Compaq now markets and uses both UNIX and Windows NT.

How do you manage a hybrid network? Both UNIX and Windows NT have strengths and weaknesses, so exploit their respective strengths and avoid their weaknesses. The key to this is integration. Networks grow out of necessity and are difficult to redesign after they are constructed. UNIX and Windows NT can live companionably together. Your long-term integration strategy should include avoiding excessive costs through standardization. Minimize differences in hardware and software wherever possible. Windows NT can run on Intel and Alpha, so consider running everything on a single-processor platform. If this is not cost-effective for you, at least consider minimizing the diversity of the operating systems.

The OSI Model

The concept of networking is nearly as important as the reality of networking. Over the years, different networking models have been introduced to illustrate the theory of physical networking. Of the proposed standards, the most widely used is the Open System Interconnection (OSI) reference model. The OSI model characterizes how data flows between the network connection and an application. Several other models closely resemble the OSI model, but few match its openness.

The OSI model intentionally excludes proprietary vendor information or requirements and proposes an open systems approach to physical and theoretical networking. To see the benefits of the OSI model, envision it as a template. The OSI model provides clues and guidance about how a network is supposed to function. As with other templates, the OSI model lacks detail and substance; it provides the framework, and you supply the details.

The OSI reference model is divided into seven layers: Physical, Data Link, Network, Transmission, Session, Presentation, and Application. Each layer has certain explicit responsibilities (see Table 15.1). With the exception of the Physical layer, each layer communicates only with the layer directly above or below it. In the Physical layer, transmissions pass from the stack to the physical transmission media. When a packet of information passes from layer to layer, each layer adds or removes information. The OSI model provides routing and addressing functions for transmitted data. Each of the layers are discussed in the following sections.

Table 15.1   **OSI Layers and Functions**

OSI Layer	Function
Application	Transfers information from program to program
Presentation	Handles text formatting and displays code conversion
Session	Establishes, maintains, and coordinates communication
Transport	Ensures accurate delivery of data
Network	Determines transport routes and handles the transfer of information
Data Link	Codes, addresses, and transmits information
Physical	Manages hardware connections

The Physical Layer

The Physical layer is the lowest or "bottom" layer in the model. It encodes and decodes digital bits over a physical connection. The Physical layer manages the computer's connection to the network and coordinates the network adapter driver software in sending data bits. This interaction typically is a function of the network interface card (NIC). Both the Physical layer and the Data Link layer define the necessary components for sending and receiving information across a network. This layer handles the transmission and reception of data bits between two network components. It specifies the timing of the transmissions, the data encoding, and the form the transmission signal takes.

The Data Link Layer

The Data Link layer is concerned with data transmission between computers by means of the Physical layer or NICs. The NICs enable Data Link protocols such as Token Ring and Ethernet protocols. This layer sends data frames (or packets) between the Physical layer and the Network layer. The Data Link layer packages the frames by including sender and receiver information, similar to the way an envelope is addressed with a recipient address and a sender's address. Control information is added to the frame containing frame type information as well as routing and segmentation data. The frame also includes verification using Cyclical Redundancy Check (CRC), in which a checksum is calculated and attached to the frame. Upon frame receipt, the checksum is verified. If the checksum is invalid, the frame is resent; otherwise, the data is assumed intact. The Data Link layer listens not only for failed packets but for unacknowledged packets. Packets not acknowledged are re-sent. Bridges operate at the Data Link layer.

The Network Layer

The Network layer is responsible for message addressing by translating network addressing into its physical equivalent. Network layer protocols include the IPX portion of Internetwork Packet Exchange/Sequenced Packet Exchange (IPX/SPX) and the IP portion of Transmission Control Protocol/Internet Protocol (TCP/IP). Routers operate at the Network layer. The Network layer decides how a packet travels from source to destination including the path the packet takes. The Network layer also is responsible for packet switching, data routing, and congestion handling.

The Network layer manages packet sizing during transmission. If the packet size is changed based on different media or protocols, the Network layer segments or fragments the packets for delivery. When a packet arrives at its destination, the Network layer restructures the packet data units (PDU) into their original size.

The Transport Layer

The Transport layer is responsible for the successful arrival of messages. The Transport layer is similar to a fax transmission. It makes sure the receiver is aware that a message is being sent, it verifies that the message was received correctly, and it negotiates speed so that the data is sent as fast as possible but not too fast to be understood. Transport layer protocols include the TCP portion of TCP/IP and the SPX portion of IPX/SPX. The Transport layer specifically handles flow control and error handling. It also resequences packets as they arrive at their destination.

The Session Layer

The Session layer is the stack manager for all the layers underneath it. It establishes a session, or connection, for as long as communications last. Take, for example, a conference call. The Session layer organizes the phones for the call, the call itself, the exchanges between participants, and the security during the call. It also monitors the duration of the call and tears everything down when the call is complete. The Session layer provides checkpoint information during the connection. As information is sent, the Session layer adds markers (checkpoints) to the data stream. If the connection is broken or lost and must be restarted, only the lost information is re-sent. It acts as an intelligent traffic cop letting each side know when it is acceptable to send information, and it keeps the connection open even if communication is silent for short periods of time.

The Presentation Layer

The Presentation layer is the interpreter that translates data into a format understood by the network media and translates it back to the original format from the Application layer upon receipt. It might, for example, translate data from ASCII to EBCDIC. The Presentation layer also handles protocol conversion and data encryption/decryption. The Redirector, which was discussed in Chapter 10, "Windows NT Networking Explored and Explained," operates at the Presentation layer.

The Application Layer

As the "top" layer, the Application layer provides the user's interface to network services and supports networked applications directly. The Application layer supports file transfer, message handling, database queries, and general network access.

IEEE 802 Networking Specifications

In the late 1970s, the Institute of Electrical and Electronic Engineers (IEEE) proposed defining standards for local area networks (LANs) to ensure that networking components, specifically NICs and cabling, would be compatible. This endeavor, called Project 802, is the basis of that effort. The number 802 stands for the year and month (February 1980) of its origin. This specification has formed a basis in modern networking environments.

The IEEE 802 model predates the OSI model. The OSI model was not widely used until 1984, although both OSI and IEEE collaborated. The key difference between the two is that the IEEE 802 specification focuses on the physical network components, specifically NICs, cables, connections, media access controls, and signaling methods. All these elements reside within the two lowest layers of the OSI model, the Physical and Data Link layers. These layers are further divided into 12 standard categories. Additional information is available at **http://www.ieee.org**.

Table 15.2 **IEEE 802 Categories**

Standard Number	Name	Description
802.1	Internetworking	Routing, bridging, and internetwork communications
802.2	Logical link control	Error control and flow control over data frames
802.3	Ethernet local area networks	Ethernet media and interfaces
802.4	Token bus local area networks	Token bus media and interfaces
802.5	Token ring local area networks	Token ring media and interfaces
802.6	Municipal area networks (MANs)	MAN technologies, addressing, and services

Standard Number	Name	Description
802.7	Broadband	Broadband networking media, interfaces, and equipment
802.8	Fiber-optic	Fiber-optic media, interfaces, and equipment
802.9	Integrated voice/data networks	Integration of voice and data over a single network medium
802.10	Network security	Network access controls, encryption, and certification
802.11	Wireless networks	Standards and components for wireless networks
801.12	High-speed networks	100+Mbps technologies

The IEEE 802 specification expands the OSI model's Physical and Data Link layers by dividing the Data Link layer into two sublayers, the Logical Link Control (LLC) layer and Media Access Control (MAC) layer. The LLC layer is for error correction and flow control, and the MAC layer addresses access control.

The LLC sublayer defines Service Access Points (SAPs), giving other computers an access point for direct upper-layer communication. The MAC sublayer enables multihomed (multiple NICs) access to the Physical layer within a single computer. It also is responsible for error avoidance and correction in computer-to-computer transmissions. The MAC sublayer supports CSMA/CD, Token bus, Token ring, and 802.12's Demand Priority.

TCP/IP Protocol Stack

The TCP/IP stack, or suite, originally was a U.S. Department of Defense Advanced Research Projects Agency (originally ARPA, later DARPA) development. Internet development began in 1969, predating the OSI model by several years. TCP/IP was the protocol chosen for UNIX system connectivity because of the protocol's scalability and wide area networking functionality. It since has become the standard protocol suite for Internet connectivity.

The TCP/IP protocol has two parts: the Transmission Control Protocol (TCP) and the Internet Protocol (IP). Although several protocol stacks are available for Internet use, TCP/IP is the protocol of choice. The other common protocol stacks, such as IPX/SPX and NetBEUI, either are not routable or are proprietary. TCP/IP offers several benefits that the other protocols do not. TCP/IP is hardware-independent, and it works over wireless, ethernet, token ring, dial-up, and satellite connections. Unlike NetBEUI, TCP/IP is a routable protocol and can specify and control data routes. TCP/IP is an efficient protocol with low overhead. Because no one owns it, it is free from corporate monopoly over its use and development. The real benefit of TCP/IP is that any computer that can run TCP/IP can communicate over a network. This means a mainframe can communicate with a UNIX server, and the UNIX server can communicate with a Windows NT server.

If you were to relate the TCP/IP protocol to the OSI model, you would see that there are three generic relational supercategories, or layers. There are the Application protocols made up of the Application, Presentation, and Sessions layers; the Transport protocols made up of the Transport layer; and the Network protocols made up of the Network, Data Link, and Physical layers. Each of these layers maps to elements within the TCP/IP suite.

The Application protocols for TCP/IP are tools such as File Transfer Protocol (FTP), Simple Mail Transfer Protocol (SMTP), and Telnet. TCP/IP Transport protocols are made up of Domain Name Service (DNS), Transmission Control Protocol (TCP), and User Datagram Protocol (UDP). The Network protocols are more closely linked to the OSI model with the Network layer housing Internet Protocol (IP), Internet Control Messaging Protocol (ICMP), Address Resolution Protocol (ARP), Open Shortest Path First (OSPF), and Routing Information Protocol (RIP). The Data Link layer contains the Open Data Interface (ODI), which is similar to NDIS. The Physical layer is used for the physical connection to the network media.

TCP

TCP is a connection-oriented protocol and is the primary Internet transport protocol. Connection-oriented protocols such as TCP are more reliable because they ensure transmission success and verification. TCP is more reliable than IP connections because IP is connectionless.

TCP accepts messages of any length from upper-layer protocols and provides a transport mechanism to another TCP peer on a remote node. TCP establishes a connection to a certain TCP port with up to 1,024 well-known ports. FTP, for example, is commonly connected on TCP port 23; the Hypertext Transfer Protocol (HTTP) commonly is on TCP port 80.

IP

IP is a connectionless protocol. It is not as reliable as TCP, but it is faster. The IP protocol provides source and destination addressing and routing for the TCP/IP protocol stack.

ICMP

The Internet Control Messaging Protocol (ICMP) is a Network layer protocol used to send confirmations and errors. The PING utility uses ICMP to return responses such as timeouts or time response data from a remote host.

ARP

The Address Resolution Protocol (ARP) is a Network layer protocol responsible for relating IP addressing to MAC layer addressing. ARP resolves the IP-to-MAC address so the Data Link protocol can manage the conversation between two hosts.

OSPF

Open Shortest Path First (OSPF) is a distance vector-based routing protocol used to determine the best path, point-to-point, on a network.

DNS

The Domain Name Service (DNS) provides a fully qualified domain name (FQDN) for IP address resolution. DNS operates at the Transport layer. This protocol permits the use of friendly names such as **www.microsoft.com** rather than 207.46.130.14, Microsoft's IP address.

UDP

The User Datagram Protocol (UDP) is a connectionless Transport layer protocol used primarily for speed rather than the reliability offered by TCP. A function that uses UDP usually uses the return of the call to verify whether the packet arrived. The Network File System (NFS), for example, uses UDP. When an NFS client makes a request, there is no need for packet verification. If the client doesn't get a response from the NFS server, it can be assumed that the packet didn't make it. The overhead of a TCP packet would be redundant.

RIP

The Routing Information Protocol (RIP) is another distance vector-based routing protocol functionally identical to RIP for NetWare.

Name Resolution

Name resolution was devised to make network communications a little easier for human beings. People don't do as well with numbers as they do with recognized patterns and names. Name resolution is a computing system's attempt to make network identification easier for users to manage. In the early days of networking, when the number of hosts was manageable, host-to-IP name resolution tables were managed on each host in a static file, the HOSTS. This file contained static mappings of names to IP addresses. Although this works well with a small number of hosts, it becomes a maintenance nightmare as new hosts are added.

In a strict UNIX environment, the Domain Name Service (DNS) is the standard for name resolution, although you also might see the anachronistic Berkley Internet Name Domain (BIND) pop up. BIND is an RFC-compliant implementation of DNS.

In a strict Windows NT environment, there is Microsoft's implementation of DNS, which is BIND-compliant, and the Windows Internet Naming Service (WINS). There also can be two static files, HOSTS and LMHOSTS. The HOSTS file is similar to a static, local DNS file. It provides FQDN-to-IP address resolution. The LMHOSTS file is a static WINS database. WINS services NetBIOS (host) name-to-IP address resolution in a Windows NT environment. In a hybrid environment, you usually use DNS and WINS and possibly HOSTS and LMHOSTS.

In a Windows NT environment, NetBT (also NBT or NetBIOS over TCP/IP) binds to the TCP/IP protocol, allowing host name resolution over TCP/IP. When a computer attempts to join a network, it broadcasts a request either on the local subnet using a UDP protocol or, if available, to a NetBIOS server. The purpose of the broadcast is to make sure the host name is not currently in use and to register the host. If the host name is not in use, the host registers with a name server such as a WINS server. The name server dynamically manages the host-to-IP resolution information for the host machine.

Suppose you want to resolve an IP address of a computer on your network with a NetBIOS name of MAGNACARTA. Table 15.3 lists the resolution order of precedence.

Table 15.3 **Name Resolution by Type**

Resolving NetBIOS Name (LAN Manager, Windows, Windows NT)	Resolving Host Name (UNIX)
Cache	HOSTS
WINS	DNS
Broadcast	Cache
LMHOSTS	WINS
HOSTS	Broadcast
DNS	LMHOSTS

Because you are trying to resolve a NetBIOS name, use the left column in Table 15.3. First, NetBIOS cache is checked. Issuing the `nbtstat -c` command shows what names are in cache.

```
D:\>nbtstat -c
No names in cache
```

The result of this command indicates that no names are currently in cache. WINS is queried following examination of the cache. NetBIOS names can be automatically registered with a WINS server (if the client is a Windows machine), or you can manually enter names for non-WINS computers using the Add Static Mappings option. If WINS fails to respond or is not aware of the name, a broadcast is issued to the local network in an attempt to locate the host. If the host acknowledges the broadcast, a connection is made; otherwise, the static LMHOSTS file is examined. The LMHOSTS file is similar to a static WINS database and is located in the %systemroot%\system32\drivers\etc subdirectory. You might recall that the LMHOSTS file is similar to a static WINS database. If there is a failure, the HOSTS file is examined. This file also is located in the %systemroot%\system32\drivers\etc directory. If the host still cannot be located, DNS is queried and the NetBIOS name is potentially matched against a DNS entry. Assuming that the host still cannot be found, the message `Bad IP Address MAGNACARTA` is returned.

If at any time during this process the NetBIOS name is resolved, the following is returned by the `nbtstat -c` command.

```
D:\>nbtstat -c
Node IpAddress: [0.0.0.0] Scope Id: []
NetBIOS Remote Cache Name Table
Name              Type      Host Address    Life [sec]
----------------------------------------------------------
MAGNACARTA     <00>  UNIQUE     10.0.0.12          660
```

This indicates that MAGNACARTA was found at IP address 10.0.0.12. The Life column indicates the length of time in seconds that the entry will remain in cache. If another attempt to locate the host MAGNACARTA is made within the 660 seconds (11 minutes), it will be returned from NetBIOS name cache instead of repeating this process. Remember that, although NetBIOS names are not case sensitive in Windows, UNIX host names are. Magnacarta and MAGNACARTA are considered the same in Windows, but they are different in UNIX.

If the host MAGNACARTA is frequently accessed, a WINS server is not available, and the time it takes to find MAGNACARTA is excessive, MAGNACARTA can be preloaded into the NetBIOS name cache. The LMHOSTS file uses associated tags to perform cache and name resolution management. Table 15.4 lists the tags associated with the LMHOSTS file.

Table 15.4 **LMHOSTS Tags**

Tag Name	Description
#PRE	Preloads the name into cache.
#DOM:domain_name	Specifies a domain master browser in another domain. Must be preceded by the #PRE tag.
#INCLUDE:\\servername\sharename\lmhosts	Permits parsing an LMHOSTS file on another computer as if it were local.
#BEGIN_ALTERNATE	Must precede multiple #INCLUDE statements.
#END_ALTERNATE	Servers to delineate the end of multiple #INCLUDE statements.

IP Subnetting

Subnetting is a means of dividing a network into segments or sections. Administrators subnet networks for a number of reasons such as network organization and reducing network traffic. An administrator might want to create subnets based on floors in a building or by department. This greatly aids in troubleshooting a network connectivity problem. Another reason to subnet is because network segments are unaware of one another. This means that a broadcast storm on one subnet won't affect the systems on another subnet. It generally is acceptable practice to group similar users within a subnet. It is unlikely that a failure caused by a computer in one subnet will disrupt another.

Two components are required to subnet a network: an IP address and a subnet mask. Subnet masking is a difficult concept, and incorrectly implemented subnet masking causes headaches when troubleshooting is required. A Class A subnet mask is 255.0.0.0, a Class B mask is 255.255.0.0, and a Class C subnet mask is 255.255.255.0. Because the Class A and B network addresses already are allocated by the InterNIC, we'll focus on subnetting a Class C address. Although it's a bit simpler, subnetting a Class C address is very similar to subnetting Class A and B networks.

A subnet mask divides the network portion of the IP address and the host portion of an IP address, as shown in Table 15.5.

Table 15.5 **Subnet Mask Information**

IP Mask	Subnets	Class C Hosts	Class B Hosts	Class A Hosts
.192	2	62	16,382	4,194,302
.224	6	30	8,190	2,097,150
.240	14	14	4,094	1,048,574
.248	30	6	2,046	524,286
.252	62	2	1,022	262,142
.254	126	NA	510	131,070
.255	244	NA	254	65,534

Suppose you've obtained a new Class C address. The IP address is 199.199.199.0, and you want to subnet it into three subnets. You believe the number of subnets will grow to five in the near future. You have 110 client computers in your company. What is the appropriate subnet mask, and how many clients can you have in each subnet?

Look again at Table 15.5. If more than two subnets are required, .192 won't work. The .192 mask, meaning 255.255.255.192, would result in two subnets with a maximum of 62 hosts per subnet. Because you need more than that, move up to the .224 subnet. The .224 value yields up to six subnets with up to 30 hosts per subnet. This further yields 180 host IP addresses available for use. Notice the number of IP addresses remaining from the original 254. If you want to subnet and have at least 15 hosts per subnet with room for growth, use the .224 mask. The .224 subnet mask yields up to 30 hosts and six subnets for a Class C address.

The disadvantage of subnetting is that the more subnets you have, the less efficient the network is and the fewer usable IP addresses you have. Try remembering that the hosts-to-networks relationship within a Class C address is an inverse. Memorizing the decimal value and either the network portion or the hosts portion will enable you to subnet in your head.

DHCP

As you might recall, one of the key benefits of Windows NT is easy administration, and the Dynamic Host Configuration Protocol (DHCP) is one of the administrative tools Windows NT provides. If you have ever manually configured a network client for TCP/IP access, you will learn to love DHCP Manager.

The following are some benefits of DHCP:

- The administrator can specify global and subnet-specific TCP/IP parameters for the entire internetwork centrally.

- Client computers do not require manual TCP/IP configuration. The clients must only be DHCP-client capable to reap the benefits of DHCP.

- When a client computer moves between subnets, the old IP address is freed for reuse, and the client is reconfigured for TCP/IP automatically when the computer is started.

- Most routers can forward DHCP configuration requests, so DHCP servers are not required on every subnet on the network. (This is true only if BOOTP forwarding is enabled on the routers.)

The following are some drawbacks of DHCP:

- There is no guarantee of a specific IP address. DHCP is arbitrary in assigning IP addresses—what you get is what you get.

- DHCP does not autodetect IP addresses in use. If a DHCP scope overlaps existing static IP addresses, you might have duplicate IP addresses on your network. Service Pack 3 added a feature to DHCP Manager, however, that enables to you select whether you want the DHCP service to ping the address it was trying to assign, alleviating this very problem.

- DHCP servers do not communicate with other DHCP servers. This makes it possible to have duplicate or overlapping scopes on two servers. It also makes administration more difficult.

- If the client has manually entered IP address information, DHCP will not overwrite it. The manually assigned address information is used.

- In a hybrid TCP/IP environment, you must exclude non-DHCP clients from the scope to prevent assigning an existing address.

In a homogenous Windows NT environment with DHCP clients, DHCP saves time in the client network configuration process. In a hybrid UNIX/Windows NT environment, the benefit of DHCP should be weighed carefully against the administrative issues previously covered. Generally speaking, DHCP is a good choice if you have to manage 100+ clients that are DHCP-capable.

Windows NT and UNIX Integration

UNIX and Windows NT share the problem of providing access to local resources to a client with a different operating system. Although not impossible, hybrid environments present complex issues for administrators. A common problem is password synchronization. Do you require users to have a different logon ID and password for every operating system to which they connect? This section examines some of the available tools for easing UNIX and Windows NT integration.

Microsoft Windows NT Services for UNIX

On the Microsoft Web site in the Windows NT Services for UNIX section, you will find the following statement: "Microsoft is broadening its interoperability product offering to include Microsoft Windows NT Services for UNIX Add-On Pack, an integrated suite of utilities designed to ease integration of existing UNIX environments with Windows NT Server and Windows NT Workstation. Windows NT Services for UNIX provides the core interoperability components that customers have most frequently requested including resource sharing, administration, and security features. Customers are expected to benefit from lower deployment costs, improved supportability of mixed environments, and the most complete integration with current and future Windows NT-based technologies and initiatives." In a nutshell, Windows NT Services for UNIX offers a suite of tools to make system interoperability easier.

The following are the key benefits of Windows NT Services for UNIX:

- **Resource sharing.** Windows NT Workstation users are now able to access files on UNIX systems, and UNIX workstation users are now able to access resources on Windows NT Server. To provide resource-sharing capabilities, Microsoft is licensing Network File System client/server software from Intergraph Corp., a leading vendor of Windows NT and UNIX interoperability solutions.

- **Remote administration.** Remote administration through Telnet client and server gives remote users the capability to remotely log into and execute commands on Windows NT- or UNIX-based systems.

- **Password synchronization.** One-way password synchronization enables customers to maintain a common password between their Windows NT- and UNIX-based machines. Password changes made on Windows NT Workstation or Windows NT Server will automatically synchronize on UNIX systems. This reduces the burden of maintaining separate passwords for multiple systems.

- **UNIX shell and commands.** Windows NT Services for UNIX enables users to use common UNIX commands and utilities in a Windows NT environment. As part of these scripting capabilities, Microsoft has licensed from Mortice Kern Systems Inc. (MKS) more than 25 UNIX scripting commands and its leading KornShell, which gives users the capability to automate common processes and

administrative tasks across both Windows NT and UNIX platforms. MKS is a
leading provider of Windows NT scripting and migration tools and software
configuration management (SCM) products. For more information, visit the
Mortice Kern Systems Web site at `http://www.mks.com/`.

SMB

Server Message Block (SMB) is a protocol for sharing files, printers, serial ports, and
server communications such as named pipes and mail slots. SMB is a client server,
request-response protocol that makes file systems and other resources available to
clients on the network. SMB first was defined in the Microsoft/Intel document
"Microsoft Networks/OpenNET-FILE SHARING PROTOCOL" in 1987 and was
subsequently developed further by Microsoft and others.

Clients connect to servers using TCP/IP, NetBEUI, or IPX/SPX. After they have
established a connection, clients can send commands using the SMB protocol to the
server that enables them to access shares, open files, read and write files, and perform
file system operations over the network.

Common Internet File System (CIFS)

The Common Internet File System (CIFS) is the generation beyond SMB. CIFS provides a way for platform-independent collaboration over the Internet. CIFS is a
remote file system access protocol that enables clients to collaborate over a network
using native file-sharing protocols built into operating systems such as Windows NT
and UNIX. CIFS is unique in that no additional client-side software is necessary to
utilize CIFS.

CIFS is comparable to the Hypertext Transfer Protocol. HTTP enables cross-platform independence for serving up HTML content regardless of what OS the
client is running. A Web server can run on UNIX, Windows NT, MacOS, or NetWare
and service clients using any Web browser. In much the same way, file system content
can be handled independently of any platform using CIFS. Applications from any
operating system can now share data that was previously unavailable to them.

CIFS incorporates multiuser read and write operations, file record locking, and file
sharing. Other CIFS features include the following:

- Global file name support
- Unicode-compatible file naming conventions
- Scalability
- Performance
- Optimization for slow network links
- Fault-tolerant connections
- File integrity checking and concurrency checking

SAMBA

SAMBA is a program suite developed by Andrew Tridgell from Australia that permits a UNIX server to offer Windows NT-native file and print sharing support. SAMBA enables a PC client to access remote UNIX file system and printer resources. The SAMBA service handles client connections and NetBIOS name server requests. It can run either on demand in inetd mode or as a daemon (service). SAMBA uses the Server Messaging Block protocol, enabling clients to communicate without additional software. The only restriction is that each user who accesses resources via SAMBA must be a registered UNIX user granted appropriate SAMBA permissions. SAMBA is freeware available under public license from `http://www.samba.org`.

Other SMB/CIFS Implementations

FacetWIN from Facet*Corp* offers Transparent File Services, Bidirectional Print Services, Terminal Emulation, Graphical Administration, POP3 Email Server, and Simple Sign-On™ (SSO). For more information, go to `http://www.facetcorp.com/`.

Sharity from Objective Development is a client for the CIFS protocol currently used by Windows NT, Windows 95, Windows for Workgroups, OS/2, SAMBA, and others. Sharity enables you to mount directories exported by these systems as if they were Network File System (NFS) directories. For more information, go to `http://www.obdev.at/Products/Sharity.html`.

TotalNET Advanced Server (TAS) software from Syntax, Inc. is the only network solution that is ready to tackle any client-to-server connection right out of the box. TAS enables UNIX computers to operate as powerful file, print, and application servers, sharing resources among Windows (3.x, NT, 95, 98), DOS, OS/2, NetWare, Macintosh, and other UNIX computers. No client changes are required. For additional information, go to `http://www.syntax.com`.

UNIX File Services Running on Windows NT

The Network File System (NFS) mounts remote file systems across both homogenous and heterogeneous systems. NFS consists of both client and server systems. An NFS server can export local directories for remote NFS clients to use. NFS most commonly runs over IP using UDP. There are NFS implementations that will work using TCP as the network transport service. NFS originally was developed by Sun Microsystems Computer Corporation, and it is now part of their Open Network Computing (ONC) initiative. NFS has been accepted by the IETF in certain RFCs as a standard for file services on TCP/IP networks on the Internet.

NFS is based on the Remote Procedure Call (RPC) protocol, is client/server-based, and is fast. An NFS server has mount points to one or more file systems and makes those file systems available to clients through the NFS server. Windows NT can act as an NFS server or client, and NFS enables UNIX clients to access Windows NT file systems and vice-versa as if the file systems were native to the client. NFS server software maps Windows NT to UNIX security. Although Windows NT NTFS security is stronger than UNIX security, a typical NFS server maps the permissions relative to UNIX security, enabling a similar permission structure to Windows NT.

NFS Security

Access to a file or directory is determined by examining three pieces of information: user and group information, file and directory ownership, and file and directory permissions. If a client does not meet these standards, it is not given access to the file or directory.

Users and Groups

Each user account on a UNIX host computer has a unique username and primary group name. To identify your username and primary group name, connect to a UNIX host using Telnet and type **id** at the prompt. UNIX uses User Identifications (UIDs) and Group Identifications (GIDs) to track individuals and group members. User and group names are provided by the operating system to simplify administration. UIDs and GIDs and their corresponding names are maintained in the /etc/passwd file on the UNIX host.

Files and Directories

File and directory security in UNIX is not as robust as in Windows NT. Permissions are granted based on the OGW model: Owner, Group, and World (sometimes referred to as Other). The following is an example of a file listing from a Telnet session:

```
$ -rwxrwxrwx 1 gary admin 763 Feb 22 22:08  INDEX.TXT
```

Following the prompt will be either a d, an l, or a - character (a dash). The d indicates a directory, the l indicates a link, and the - indicates a file. The following nine letters really are three groups of three letters. These three sets represent the Owner, Group, World (Other) permissions. The individual letters designate the permissions assigned to the object. The owner of the file is gary, and gary's primary group is the admin group. Based on the letters in each three-letter set, the Owner, Group, and World all have Read, Write, and Execute permissions to the file INDEX.TXT. Each letter is assigned a value where Read=1, Write=2, and Execute=4 for a total of 7. The numeric equivalent for rwx, therefore, equals 7. The numeric value for the INDEX.TXT permissions is 777.

Exporting File Systems

Exporting a UNIX file system makes that file system available to others. To export a file system, it must be added to the host's /etc/exports file. The exports file controls which file systems are available to users, which users have access to which file system, and the user access limitations to the exported file system. The reference to the /etc/exports file is generic because not all UNIX systems use the exports file for NFS exports.

Windows NT uses share-level and NTFS security combinations, whereas UNIX uses NFS permissions and /etc/exports permission combinations. In Windows NT, share-level permissions and NTFS permissions first are evaluated separately and then evaluated against each other. The most restrictive combination then applies. UNIX is no different. By evaluating NFS and /etc/exports, UNIX applies the most restrictive permission to the user accessing the resource. This is not unlike the Windows NT NTFS approach to security.

The Domain Name System

The Domain Name System (DNS) is implemented differently in Windows NT and UNIX. This section explains what DNS is. Subsequent sections explore both UNIX and Windows NT implementations of DNS.

The primary use of DNS is to translate, or resolve, the IP address from the FQDN. This is important because an IP address is required to initiate a connection to a remote system. DNS defines a hierarchical namespace for hosts, provides a host table that is implemented as a distributed database, and delivers a protocol for exchanging naming information.

The DNS namespace is a tree of domains with ascending authority. Each domain represents a distinct part of the namespace and is maintained by a single administrative body. The root of the tree is recognized by "." (referred to as "dot"). Beneath it are top-level domains that are relatively fixed. There are two types of top-level domain names. In the United States, top-level domains describe organizational and political structure. They usually are identified by three-letter words. Domains outside the United States have two-letter International Standardization Organization (ISO) country codes. Both conventions coexist within the same global space.

Each host using DNS is either a client of the system or a client and a server simultaneously. Programs use the gethostbyname method to map host names to IP addresses. When a host is configured to use DNS gethostbyname, it uses the DNS resolver to query a name server for the address. Name servers are either recursive or nonrecursive. *Recursive servers* use answers from a previous query that resides in cache, or they return a referral to authoritative servers of another domain that are more likely to know the answer. The client must be the one to accept and act on the given referrals.

A *nonrecursive server* returns only real answers and error messages for queries. It follows up on referrals by itself. The procedure for resolving a query is still the same except the name server handles the referrals rather than the client. Low-level name servers usually are recursive, whereas high-level servers (top-level and some second-level) are not. Why does caching increase efficiency? Caching increases the efficiency of lookups; a cached answer is almost free and usually is correct because mappings do not frequently change. Most queries are for local hosts and can be answered quickly. Users also inadvertently help with efficiency because many queries are repeated.

Caching usually is applied to positive answers. If a host name or address cannot be found, that information is not saved.

Each organization with a network maintains at least one Domain Name Server that contains a list of all the IP addresses within the organization. Each computer on a network only needs know the location of one Domain Name Server. When a request is made for an IP address outside that particular organization, one of three things happens:

- If the system is registered locally, the local DNS server responds with an IP address.

- If the system is not registered locally but someone within your local organization recently requested the IP address, the DNS server retrieves the information you need from its cache.

- If the system you are asking about is not local and you are the first person to request information about this system in a certain period of time (meaning the address is not in cache), the local DNS server performs a search on behalf of your workstation. This search might involve contacting two or more other DNS servers at potentially remote locations. These queries can take anywhere from a second or two to up to a minute, depending on how well-connected you are to the remote network and how many intermediate servers must be contacted. Sometimes, because of the lightweight protocol used for DNS, you might not receive a response. In these cases, your workstation or client software might continue to repeat the query until a response is received, or you might receive an error.

UNIX DNS

This section discusses DNS running under UNIX. The discussions here do not map directly to all versions of UNIX. Rather, this section should be used as a guide to understanding the differences between UNIX DNS and Windows NT DNS.

Under UNIX, DNS runs from the named daemon. Configuration information is gathered at boot time from the named.boot file or the named.conf file in the /etc directory. After the named server is running, it responds to system DNS requests. The named.boot file can contain a listing of the primary, secondary, and cache DNS servers. It also lists the storage directory for DNS zone filters and specifies whether the DNS server should forward failed DNS requests to another server or act merely as a slave, only redirecting requests to forwarders.

Primary name servers get host configuration information from zone files. *Zone files* specify information related to the Primary name server's zone of authority. A typical zone file might contain resource record information. Table 15.6 lists the resource record types found in a zone file.

Table 15.6 **Resource Record Types**

Record Type	Description
A (address)	Maps a host (computer or other network device) name to an IP address in a DNS zone.
AAAA (address)	Maps a host (computer or other network device) name to an IPv6 address.
AFSDB	Gives the location of either an Andrew File System (AFS) cell database server or a Distributed Computing Environment (DCE) cell's authenticated name server.
CNAME (canonical name)	Creates an alias (synonymous name) for the specified host (computer or other network device) name.
HINFO (host information)	Identifies a host's (computer or other network device) hardware type and operating system.
ISDN (Integrated Services Digital Network)	Is a variation of the A (address) resource record.
MB (mailbox)	Is an experimental record that specifies a DNS host (computer or other network device) with the specified mailbox.
MG (mail group)	Is an experimental record that specifies a mailbox that is a member of the mail group (mailing list) specified by the DNS domain name.
MINFO (mailbox information)	Is an experimental record that specifies a mailbox that is responsible for the specified mailing list or mailbox.
MR (mailbox rename)	Is an experimental record that specifies a mailbox that is the proper rename of the other specified mailbox.
MX (mail exchanger)	Specifies a mail exchange server for a DNS domain name.
NS (name server)	Identifies the DNS name server(s) for the DNS domain.
PTR (pointer)	Maps an IP address to a host (computer or other network device) name in a DNS reverse zone (those in the In-addr.arpa DNS domain).

Record Type	Description
RP (responsible person)	Indicates who is responsible for the specified DNS domain or host (computer or other network device).
RT (route through)	Specifies an intermediate host (computer or other network device) that routes packets to a destination host.
SOA (start of authority)	Indicates that this DNS name server is the best source of information for the data within this DNS domain.
TXT (text)	Associates general textual information with an item in the DNS database.
WKS (well-known service)	Describes the services provided by a particular protocol on a particular interface. The protocol usually is UDP or TCP.
X25	Is a variation of the A (address) resource record.

Secondary DNS servers receive updates from Primary DNS servers. Secondary DNS servers do not control IP address information; the Primary DNS servers do that instead. Earlier in this chapter, the strengths and weaknesses of UNIX and Windows NT were discussed. These apply to DNS and UNIX too.

If UNIX expertise is available and DNS currently is running on a UNIX platform, by all means keep DNS on UNIX. UNIX is more reliable and scalable. If only Windows NT expertise exists, however, consider Windows NT DNS. Windows NT DNS offers GUI-based administration. This is not trivial because the majority of DNS errors are a result of the text file manipulation.

It is not the purpose of this book to teach DNS. Rather, it attempts to explain the basic files and processes DNS takes running under UNIX. For more information about UNIX DNS and Bind, refer to Paul Albitz, Cricket Liu, and Mike Loukides's book, *BIND and DNS*, from O'Reilly & Associates (September 1998, ISBN: 1565925122).

Windows NT DNS

Why choose Microsoft? As previously mentioned, DNS on Windows NT is GUI-based. Windows NT DNS maintains the same file format as UNIX to remain RFC compliant.

On Windows NT, DNS runs as a service. If DNS is not installed on your server, it can be installed from the Network applet in the Control Panel. Windows DNS also offers benefits that UNIX DNS does not. For Windows clients, DNS offers the capability to link to the Windows Internet Name Service (WINS) for IP address resolution. Thus, DHCP-capable clients using DHCP can be located using DNS. This is set for each zone in the Zone Properties window.

Microsoft's DNS implementation supports integration of DNS and WINS within the same architecture. In a hybrid environment, a method exists for UNIX computers to resolve NetBIOS names. Assuming you are using Microsoft DNS integrated with WINS, the process from a UNIX client would be similar to the following:

1. A UNIX client pings a NetBIOS name such as COMPUTER1.

2. Microsoft DNS attempts to resolve COMPUTER1 from its zone file.

3. If name resolution fails, the DNS server looks to see whether it has a WINS resource record. If a record is found, the DNS server queries the WINS server for resolution.

4. If found, WINS passes the information back to the DNS server, where it is cached, then returned to the UNIX client.

The Realities of Integrating UNIX and Windows NT

Integrating two or more network operating systems is never trivial. Most hybrid environments simply become that way instead of being planned that way. Both Windows NT and UNIX have significant strengths and weaknesses as illustrated in this chapter. So what are the realities of integrating the two?

Instead of really attempting to answer this question (the chapter is long enough already), here's a training outline from a major training corporation. A quick Internet search will reveal that UNIX/Windows NT integration is a big business, and many resources exist to train you and to answer important questions.

The following are key elements covered in a Windows NT and UNIX integration course:

- Integrate Windows NT and UNIX networks to access enterprise-wide resources.

- Identify appropriate platforms for common network services.

- Build a heterogeneous network architecture using DNS, DHCP, and WINS.

- Administer an integrated environment.

- Configure platform-independent access to UNIX and Windows NT applications.

- Establish cross-platform file and print connectivity using Windows NT Services for UNIX.

- Enable uniform Web and email access.

Choose your operating systems with careful consideration of their strengths and the ongoing maintenance requirements to maintain your choices.

Troubleshooting Windows NT-to-UNIX Connections (and Vice-Versa)

In any computing environment, there are two ways to resolve network-related issues: preemptive troubleshooting (trouble avoidance) or troubleshooting (trouble already found you). This section covers issues to consider that are independent of the computing environment plus some UNIX and Windows NT tools that will help along the way.

DNS

One of the most common trouble areas of Windows NT-to-UNIX connections is DNS. Human error is the most likely candidate for problems in name resolution. The following are some guidelines for implementing DNS successfully:

- **SOA, CNAME, and A records with misspelled names.** These records contain both computer names and IP addresses. Spelling errors and errors in numeric data entry are the most likely cause of failure. Keep backup copies of changed zone files just in case.

- **SOA serial numbers not incremented on zone file change.** When zone files are modified, the SOA serial number must be changed so the secondary DNS servers properly reload the files.

- **Absolute host names lack training period.** Absolute host names require a trailing period. That pesky little dot is very simple to miss and can cause quite a migraine until discovered.

- **Reverse resolution entry doesn't match primary zone file information.** Make sure reverse entries in the reverse resolution zone file match the primary zone file's entry. Again, this error is caused by lack of attention to detail during data entry.

To troubleshoot DNS use nslookup. Nslookup is both a Windows NT tool and a UNIX tool. The following are the commonly used options of nslookup:

- **[no]recurse.** Sets the query type to recursive. When toggled to norecurse, nslookup performs iterative queries.

- **Querytype=type.** Sets the query type to the DNS data type specified. Common types include a (address), any (any data type), mx (mail exchanger), and ns (name server).

- **Retry=n.** Resends the query n times before giving up.

- **root=root server.** Sets the root server to the server you enter.

- **timeout=n.** The period of time nslookup waits for a response after the query is sent. This period doubles between each retry.

Printing

Troubleshooting printing problems from either operating system requires similar knowledge and techniques. The following are key points to monitor:

- **Remember the basics.** Make sure the cable is plugged in, the paper isn't jammed, the printer is on, and paper is available. If a user cannot print to a specific printer, try printing to another. Also have another user print to the suspect printer.

- **Wrong printer driver.** Windows and UNIX handle printer drivers differently. Make sure the correct driver is available and loaded.

- **TCP/IP printing services not running or not installed.** This is on the Windows NT side. It grants the capability to use networked printing devices and enables TCP/IP applications to directly communicate to a network-attached printer.

- **Incorrect printer privileges.** In Windows NT, a printer is shared and permissions apply to the share. Make sure the user has sufficient permissions to use the print device. In Windows NT, verify that a policy is not restricting printer availability. Users and groups can be locked out of a printer during certain hours.

- **Use LPQ to investigate the print queue.** In UNIX, the LPQ command displays the jobs in the print queue. A very large job could be pending or hung. Also remember to check printer status with the LPC command.

- **Verify LPSCHED is running.** The LPSCHED daemon manages print jobs and controls where a print job is sent.

For More Information

- Gunter, David, Steven Burnett, and Lolo Gunter. *Windows NT & UNIX Integration Guide.* Orborne McGraw-Hill, 1997. ISBN: 0078823951.

- Crawford, Sharon and Charlie Russel. *NT and UNIX Intranet SECRETS.* IDG Books Worldwide, 1997. ISBN: 0764530976.

- Albitz, Paul, Cricket Liu, and Mike Loukides. *Bind and DNS.* O'Reilly & Associates, September 1998. ISBN: 1565925122. This is the current authoritative resource on DNS and BIND.

- Visit UnixINTEGRATION.COM at `http://www.performancecomputing.com/unixintegration/artchive.shtml` for some excellent articles about everything Windows NT and UNIX including some excellent articles about DNS and integrated system security.

16

Dial-Up Networking and Remote Access

WINDOWS NT WAS DESIGNED to provide access to file, print, and application services for a variety of clients in various environments. Now that networks are so indispensable to most businesses and organizations, access to network-based resources no longer can be limited by geography or network bandwidth. As sales of laptop and notebook computers rapidly approach those of desktops—and with the explosive growth of telecommuting—reliable, efficient, remote LAN access not only is a necessity, it is in many organizations regarded as mission-critical.

This chapter examines the remote access components built into Windows NT 4.0, and it covers their installation, setup, and fine-tuning as well as diagnosing some common problems with remote access. This chapter also discusses other software utilities from Microsoft and third parties that can be used to improve Windows NT's remote access capabilities.

Remote Access Versus Remote Control

Remote access and remote control represent two basic types of remote LAN access. Both types have strong points, and both types provide access to network resources. The main differences between these two methods relate to the type of traffic that passes over the connection between a remote computer and a computer on the network and where application processing occurs.

Programs such as PC Anywhere, Reach Out, and NetOp provide remote control over network computers. These programs require two pieces of software to work. The first is a client piece on the remote workstation that enables users to reach across the connection to operate the network-attached computer. The second is a server piece on the network-attached computer that responds to user input from the remote client, and then sends screen updates and data from the network-attached computer to the remote machine.

These programs connect from a remote location, usually through a dial-up connection to a computer on the LAN that permits the remote computer to take control of a LAN-attached computer. The remote user takes over the keyboard, screen, and mouse of the local computer so that whatever keys are typed on the remote computer are processed on the local machine. When the screen is updated on the local computer, the screen also is updated on the remote computer. Remote users have the same access to programs and resources as they would if they were sitting at a LAN-attached computer. The LAN applications that the remote user runs actually run on the locally attached computer with only screen images and mouse and keyboard commands passing across the communications link back to the remote computer.

Remote control generally works pretty well, especially over slow communication links, as long as the applications running remotely do not require constant updates to high-resolution displays. Remote control also is subject to several limitations; the most serious limitation is the requirement for a dedicated computer on the LAN for each concurrent remote connection. When a local computer is servicing a remote user, it can't be used for anything else. For a smaller LAN, in which only a couple of concurrent remote sessions might be needed, it should not be a problem to dedicate a computer for each remote session. On larger LANs that require a large number of concurrent remote sessions, however, remote control that requires a network-attached computer for each remote user is neither cost-effective nor manageable.

There are other derivatives of remote control software. The most popular are Microsoft's own Windows NT Terminal Server, which is a modified version of Windows NT Server 4.0, and Citrix WinFrame (originally built only for Windows NT Server 3.51). These two alternatives are server products that support multiple concurrent remote control sessions on one server. This reduces the need for dedicated computers, and it also is far more manageable because all remote sessions run on the same machine.

These products, however, require high-end servers to deliver the processing power necessary to support numerous remote concurrent sessions. When organizations must support applications such as legacy database applications that need access to numerous files or voluminous data across slow communication links, such server-based remote control products can be quite effective.

The other type of software that provides remote access to LAN resources is *remote access software*. Windows NT's Remote Access Service (RAS) enables a remote computer to access a network from a remote location. The remote computer has the same access to network resources as it would have if it were locally connected. In effect, RAS makes a modem act like a network interface card. Because modems generally provide much lower bandwidth than direct network attachments, remote access runs more slowly. When applications are built to conform to a client/server-computing model, however, such applications operate on remote computers in a way that minimizes network traffic and maximizes data delivery. In fact, perceived performance often can exceed the kind of performance that remote control software delivers for similar applications.

RAS also is more scalable and provides remote access at a lower cost per remote workstation than remote control software running on dedicated machines. Instead of adding additional computers to a LAN, you merely need to add additional communication ports, and possibly more memory, or take advantage of RAS's capability to provide remote access across the Internet. The current version of RAS bundled with Windows NT Workstation can handle only a single dial-in or dial-out connection, but the version included with Windows NT Server 4.0 is capable of handling as many as 256 concurrent remote sessions on a single machine.

RAS and TAPI

Although remote access has been included in Windows NT since its initial 3.1 release, Windows NT 4.0 includes support for the 32-bit Telephony Application Programming Interface (TAPI) version 2.0 (2.1 after installing the service packs) and the Unimodem driver that previously was supported only in Windows 9x. The 32-bit TAPI is a framework that provides a standard way for communication applications and drivers to control various hardware functions for applications such as data, fax, voice, video, and even full-blown PBX-like call centers. TAPI also can manage quality of service (QoS) negotiation.

The TAPI layer manages all signaling between the computer and the associated hardware. TAPI 2.0 supports 32-bit applications, and it also supports older 16-bit applications through a thunking layer that converts 16-bit addresses to the 32-bit APS required to access Windows NT system services. TAPI is scheduled to be updated to version 3.0 for Windows 2000 with features that will allow complete PBX systems to be based on Windows NT along with more sophisticated video functions.

Dial-Up Networking

By including TAPI, Microsoft has greatly improved its implementation of RAS and Dial-Up Networking (DUN), both of which are now TAPI-aware. RAS represents the server side that handles incoming calls. Incoming calls are not limited to Microsoft clients; they can originate from any Point-to-Point Protocol (PPP) compatible client. DUN is the client side (dial-out telephony) that can be configured to connect either to a RAS Server or to an Internet service provider (ISP) that supports either PPP or the Serial Line Internet Protocol (SLIP).

The version of RAS included in Windows NT version 4.0 is so well integrated into the operating system that a computer that accesses a network remotely uses essentially the same network client as a LAN-connected machine. It simply substitutes a modem, an Integrated Services Digital Network (ISDN) link, or an X.25 PAD for a network interface card. The RAS Server functions as a gateway between the remote client and the network.

After a DUN client has connected to the network, which might even involve the same Windows NT logon information that a local user might supply, the user interface functions no differently than it would if the user was logging in locally. This single, consistent interface permits remote users to access files and printers, and it also enables them to operate client/server applications.

Two of the best TAPI features that have been added to Windows NT 4.0 are the Phonebook and Locations. Any TAPI-compliant application can use the information in these two shared databases.

The Phonebook is a listing of telephone numbers and other information needed to connect the client to remote networks. To add new numbers to the Phonebook, select New from the DUN dialog box. DUN provides a wizard that makes entering Phonebook entries very simple, so it doesn't need to be covered here.

Locations are used to modify telephone numbers selected from the Phonebook so you can include special numbers needed to dial out from unique locations. An example of this would be the extra digits needed to reach an outside line in a hotel or office environment. There also is a feature that enables you to enter your calling card numbers. After the calling card numbers are entered, they are encrypted and are not displayed. Locations can be entered from the Telephony applet in the Control Panel.

Working with Communication Hardware

The introduction of the TAPI and associated Unimodem standards to Windows NT 4.0 puts it on common ground with Windows 9x so that, in most cases, hardware designed for use with Windows 9x also works with Windows NT. Windows NT now supports a wide variety of modems and connection types including ISDN, X.25, and even cable modems. A warning is in order, however. It usually is best to check either your modem's packaging or its manufacturer's Web site to see whether Windows NT drivers are available. You also can check Microsoft's current version of the Hardware Compatibility List (HCL) at **http://www.microsoft.com/ntworkstation/ info/hcl.htm**.

Multiport Serial Boards

Although Windows NT Server 4.0 RAS supports 256 concurrent connections, you've probably never seen a server with 256 bus slots. If your server includes a built-in PS/2-type mouse port, you theoretically can install up to four internal modems. Unfortunately, COM1 and COM3 share IRQ4, and COM2 and COM4 share IRQ3.

Sometimes this actually works, but the reliability of interrupt sharing is dependent on your server's system BIOS and motherboard design. It usually is best to use no more than two internal modems in a server.

Multiport serial boards are the best way to support multiple modems. You can purchase these boards with 4, 8, or 16 ports per board, along with additional features. Some boards use IRQs; others do not. Some of the higher-end boards are equipped with an on-board microprocessor that minimizes the overhead on your server's CPU caused by handling multiple connections.

It is important for you to select multiport serial boards that support the highest possible port speeds. Because most newer boards support both analog modems and ISDN, this automatically offers an upgrade path if you start with analog modems and decide to upgrade to ISDN or some other technology later on. Higher port speeds also improve communications efficiency. Make sure that any multiport serial board you attempt to install on your machine appears on the Windows NT HCL or that the manufacturer supplies Windows NT 4.0 drivers.

Working with Analog Modems

The ubiquitous analog modem has been with us for a while and comes in a variety of models, the latest and greatest being the 56K v.90. Most modems manufactured within the past couple years will connect with each other with few problems. If you have control over modem purchasing at all the sites to which you plan to connect, however, it is best to buy similar modems. This ensures that you'll have fewer connection problems, and some modems are more efficient in terms of speed, hardware compression, and errors when connecting to a similar model. If you do not have purchasing control over all your connection sites, purchase a mainstream model to minimize problems.

The highest-speed analog modem currently available is the 56K v.90. These modems do not actually reach the full 56K because of the poor quality of most telephone lines and because of an obscure FCC regulation that limits the top speed of analog telephone lines to 53K. Technically, the FCC limits the voltage of the phone line to prevent crosstalk. 56K speeds are attainable with the designed voltage, but with the voltage that the FCC mandates, they are limited to 53K. In addition, these modems attain high-speed mode only in the downstream direction. This means you can receive at high speed, but you send back at a lower speed, usually 28K.

If you are setting up a client to communicate with an ISP that supports 56K, this isn't a bad deal. If you are setting up a communications server, however, you can't just buy a stack of 56K modems off the shelf and expect to give your users fast access. The reason is that, to support 56K, the link between your server and the telephone switching office has to be digital. This line can be a T-1, T-3, or ISDN line. This digital line is then fed into a commercial-grade, rack mount modem chassis configured for digital support. Some of the better ones manufactured by 3Com/US Robotics and Ascend allow incoming calls from either ISDN or 56K on the same line.

If you are setting up a communication server to support just a few users, this probably is not cost-effective. For a smaller configuration, it is best to buy a stack of quality 33.6K modems. You gain nothing by using 56K modems. In actuality, you lose speed because most fall back to 28K if they fail to get a high-speed connection.

There are two types of analog modems that you should avoid trying to use with Windows NT. The first is the so-called WinModem, which you will see advertised at a lower cost than the average modem. The cost of these modems is reduced by using your PC's CPU to do the call processing and by moving all the modem protocols, error correction, and data compression into software.

This architecture lets modem makers develop a much cheaper model that does not need the RAM or processing chips of traditional modems. This saves a significant amount of money per unit, but it also puts a strain on the resources of your PC. WinModems can use anywhere from 8 to 20 percent of your CPU, depending on your machine, and a significant amount of RAM. In addition, they require a driver to be installed on your PC that is usually *not* compatible with Windows NT because it needs direct control of the hardware, which Windows NT does not allow. Supposedly, some of the newer ones will be Windows NT-compatible, but the ones we have tested so far are not.

The second type of analog modem to avoid is the Plug and Play (PnP) modem designed for the Plug and Play capabilities of Windows 9x. Windows NT 4.0 does not officially support Plug and Play, so these modems usually do not work with Windows NT.

Using Unsupported Modems with Windows NT

If the modem you want to use is not on the HCL or is a Plug and Play modem, you might be able to use it with Windows NT anyway. In most cases, however, some of the more exotic features will not be supported.

To make a Plug and Play modem work with Windows NT, you must first understand how PnP works. When installing legacy devices, you have to manually set switches or jumpers to assign IRQs, ports, and Dams. You also have to keep track of what is in use so that you don't try to assign the same resource to multiple devices. The purpose of PnP is to do all of this for you. When a new device is installed on the machine, it automatically is sensed. It is assigned resources that are not in use, and the drivers automatically are installed. PnP requires that both the operating system and the system BIOS be PnP aware.

If your motherboard hardware supports PnP, you can configure Windows NT to use PnP by turning on the service in the Devices applet in the Control Panel. Microsoft doesn't currently support PnP in Windows NT 4.0, however, so you are on your own as far as support. The best thing to do if you insist on buying a PnP modem is to make sure it comes with support for DOS. The better modems come with software that enables them to be used in older machines or with DOS. With this software, you can manually configure the IRQ, I/O, and COM ports used by the card. Just boot from a DOS disk, run the utility, and then install the modem under Windows NT.

To make a non-HCL–supported modem work with Windows NT, you first need to verify that the COM port to which the modem is connected has been detected. Start the Ports applet in the Control Panel to see whether the COM port to which the modem is connected is listed. If it is listed, Windows NT recognizes the COM port. If the COM port is not listed, there could be a configuration problem. Use the following steps to troubleshoot the problem:

1. Check the System Log in the Event Viewer for I/O or IRQ conflict errors.

2. Power down and remove the new modem from the system.

3. Restart Windows NT, go to the Ports icon in Control Panel, and verify that the IRQ settings and the I/O addresses are correct. If possible, always use the standard settings for COM ports:

- SERIAL 1 COM1: I/O Address = 3F8h IRQ = 4
- SERIAL 2 COM2: I/O Address = 2F8h IRQ = 3
- SERIAL 3 COM3: I/O Address = 3E8h, IRQ = 4
- SERIAL 4 COM4: I/O Address = 2E8h, IRQ = 3

4. If you are using an external modem, make sure the COM port you want to use is not disabled in the BIOS.

5. Verify that no other devices are configured to use the I/O address or IRQ you want to use. You can check this in Windows NT Diagnostics (Start, Programs, Administrative Tools, Windows NT Diagnostics, Resources).

6. If you are installing an internal modem and it is configured for a port assigned to the motherboard, you can set the modem to use a different COM port not in use, or you can disable the COM port on the motherboard using the system BIOS.

7. After all conflicts are resolved, open the Control Panel and select the Modems applet to start the Install New Modem Wizard. Make sure to select the Don't Detect My Modem, I Will Select It From a List option.

Installing Modems

It generally is a good idea to run through the steps described in this section before installing modems even if they are listed on the HCL.

Adding an Internal Modem

If you are adding an internal modem, do not add a new port manually. NTDETECT automatically detects the internal modem and assigns it to the port the board is configured to use. If NTDETECT does not assign the modem a port, there probably is a conflict with an existing device.

Letting Windows NT Detect Your Modem

Even if the modem is on the HCL list, it sometimes is better not to allow Windows NT to detect your modem. In the current release, a lot of modems on the HCL are not being identified properly.

In the Install New Modem dialog box, you have the option to select a listed modem or to load drivers from a disk. If your modem has drivers for Windows 9x, you might be able to use those drivers with Windows NT. Just select the Have Disk option and insert the disk containing the Windows 9x drivers. Remember, however, that not all Windows 9x drivers will work properly with Windows NT 4.0. You're running the risk of installing a device that could end up being inoperable if the driver doesn't work.

If you do not have the correct drivers for your modem, other options are available. You can select the Standard Modem Types option and select a generic driver. The downside of this is that any extra functionality the modem has will not be used. You also can select a modem that is similar in features to the one you are trying to install. This usually works fairly well, but it still is not a perfect solution.

The best way to circumnavigate an incorrect driver for your modem is to edit the MODEM.INF file to support your modem. The MODEM.INF file is the configuration file that contains all the initialization commands your modem processes whenever it is reset. This file is located in the C:\WINNT\SYSTEM32\RAS directory. You can add a custom section to this file with the necessary initialization commands for your modem. The easiest way is to copy one of the existing sections to use as a template and rename it for your modem. It probably would be best to use one of the generic sections or one from the same manufacturer with similar features to get started. Consult your modem documentation as a reference to add or remove commands to customize the file for your modem. The following is an example of a section in the MODEM.INF file:

```
[US Robotics Courier V.32bis]
CALLBACKTIME=10
DEFAULTOFF=compression
MAXCARRIERBPS=19200
MAXCONNECTBPS=38400

<speaker_on>=M1
<speaker_off>=M0
<hwflowcontrol_on>=&R2&H1
<hwflowcontrol_off>=&R1&H0
<compression_on>=&K1
<compression_off>=&K0
<protocol_on>=&M4
<protocol_off>=&M0
<autodial_on>=ATDT
<autodial_off>=ATD

DETECT_STRING=ATI4<cr>
DETECT_RESPONSE=USRobotics Courier V.32

COMMAND_INIT=ATE1&F&C1 &D2 &A1 &B1 V1 Q0 S0=0 S2=128 S7=55<cr>
COMMAND_INIT=AT<hwflowcontrol><compression><protocol><speaker><cr>
```

```
COMMAND_DIAL=<autodial><phonenumber><cr>
CONNECT=<cr><lf>CONNECT <carrierbps><cr><lf>
CONNECT_EC=<cr><lf>CONNECT <carrierbps>/ARQ<cr><lf>

COMMAND_LISTEN=ATS0=1<cr>
CONNECT=<cr><lf>CONNECT <carrierbps><cr><lf>

CONNECT_EC=<cr><lf>CONNECT <carrierbps>/ARQ<cr><lf>
```

Because the MODEM.INF file is read every time the modem is initialized, you can make changes anytime you want, and they can be applied without a reboot. Because modems are not a critical part of Windows NT, feel free to experiment. Nothing you can do to this file will crash Windows NT. Of course, before you start tweaking, you should save a copy of the file somewhere handy. Even if you trash it, the original file is on the Windows NT CD-ROM.

Working With ISDN

Integrated Services Digital Network (ISDN) is a switched telephone service that first was introduced in 1984. It was widely predicted at that time that ISDN eventually would replace all the existing analog telephone lines. Even though ISDN provides digital connections that are faster, more reliable, and more flexible than existing analog lines, it just recently has become commonly available in most areas.

ISDN is available in two forms, Basic Rate Interface (BRI) and Primary Rate Interface (PRI), with BRI being the most common. Each ISDN line consists of three separate digital channels, a 16K D-channel (data channel) used for signaling information such as ring signals, caller ID data, dialing instructions, and two 64K B-channels (bearer channels) that each provide 64Kbps of dial-up bandwidth. This usually is referred to as 2B+D. Most telephone companies also offer what is referred to as a 1B+D, which is the signaling channel with only one bearer channel.

The BRI installation, monthly charge, and usage charges vary widely among the different Regional Bell Operating Companies (RBOCs). Some RBOCs bill for ISDN by the call, some by the minute, and some use both methods. Other providers charge a flat rate for unlimited usage.

PRI is a bundle of 24 BRI lines (23B+D) that can handle up to 1.544Mbps, the same as a T1 line. Like BRI, PRI pricing varies widely. Generally, if there is a need for the capacity of a PRI line, it usually is cheaper and less complicated to use a T1 line.

Always Save a Copy

After everything is configured properly, save a copy of the customized MODEM.INF file somewhere other than in the RAS directory. Several of the service packs, some hotfixes, and some modem-installation procedures will overwrite this file.

With the proper equipment, the B-channels can be used for voice calls or for data. Each B-channel has a separate phone number, enabling you to place voice calls on one channel while sending or receiving data over the other. They also can be bonded together using Multilink Point-to-Point Protocol (MPPP) to provide a full 128Kbps of data flow. Unlike 56K modems, ISDN channels deliver that bandwidth in both directions.

With the channels bonded together, ISDN provides roughly two and a half times the throughput of a typical 56K modem. ISDN calls also have an extremely fast call setup time—typically under half a second—compared to the 30 seconds or more for high-speed modems. Most users do not notice a delay when they try to access a remote resource. This last point is especially important because most ISDN devices are configured to dial and disconnect on an as-needed basis, and they incur per-minute charges when connected. ISDN devices also support the Bandwidth Allocation Control Protocol (BACP), a protocol that lets ISDN devices add the second channel to a connection or drop it, depending on the data traffic. BACP also can be configured to drop the second channel to answer an incoming call. This is transparent to the user.

A new ISDN technology that is not yet widely available is the Always On/Dynamic ISDN (AO/DI), which enables the modem to maintain a data connection without tying up costly B-channels. This is done by using the D-channel, which usually is used only for signaling (to send and receive data at 9,600Kbps). This means the connection to the ISP or the company network can be continuously maintained without being charged for using B-channels. This usually is enough capacity for email or some low-usage client/server applications. When more throughput is needed, the connection kicks up to a higher one and uses one or two B-channels. Some RBOCs are pricing this at only $10 more than the standard rate, but there potentially can be large financial savings if billing is based on usage.

There are three common types of ISDN interfaces: terminal adapters, Ethernet/Token Ring terminal adapters, and ISDN routers. Note that using the term "modems" is not really accurate because modems are analog devices, whereas ISDN is purely digital. A lot of ISDN products, however, are advertised as modems.

Supporting 128K ISDN

Not all ISPs or organizations can support full 128K ISDN. For the two channels to be bonded, both connections must be to the same server or to the same rack mount modem chassis. Some ISPs will guarantee a full connection, but most will not.

ISDN Terminal Adapters

ISDN terminal adapters are available in both external and internal models. The external adapters emulate modems and plug into the serial port just like an analog modem. Terminal adapters usually are the easiest ISDN devices to install and configure because they look just like another modem to RAS and DUN. Unfortunately, the external terminal adapters provide slower connections because they have to use the asynchronous serial protocol, which adds the overhead of start and stop bits.

In addition, a high-speed serial port should be added to support an external ISDN adapter because ISDN's 128Kbps throughput is so fast that it overruns the 115Kbps speed of standard serial ports. If compression is being used, the bottleneck will be even more pronounced. Internal ISDN terminal adapters can provide connections at the maximum ISDN data rate because they interface directly with the PC's bus.

ISDN Ethernet/Token Ring Terminal Adapter

ISDN Ethernet/Token Ring terminal adapters connect to the PC through a network card, usually Ethernet. The adapter can be connected via a crossover cable to one machine or to a hub in a small network. Multiple users, usually fewer than 10, can share a terminal adapter for connection to an ISP or a remote server. Most terminal adapters also come equipped with analog telephone jacks so that one or both sides of the ISDN line can be used with a standard telephone or fax machine.

ISDN Router

The third type of device is the ISDN router. Like the ISDN Ethernet terminal adapters, ISDN routers can be connected via a crossover cable to one machine or to a hub in a small network. ISDN routers usually are overkill for a single user. Most ISDN routers can handle an unlimited number of users and are used when a large volume of ISDN traffic is expected. Most models also can handle IP or IPX routing, DHCP, and many other options. There are, however, some new models being advertised as "personal" ISDN routers that are available for less than $500. They are very economical for small- to medium-size networks.

Many choices are available for ISDN connection devices. Apart from type, there are plenty of differences to help you choose the right one. Always select a device listed on the Windows NT HCL.

A new type of ISDN terminal adapter stands out for its unique capability to accept incoming 56Kbps analog connections as well as regular ISDN connections. This feature enables one line to support both types of connections, providing flexibility for power users or small companies that need to receive a lot of calls from different sources. It enables the power user to dial out to an ISP or remote server with an ISDN connection or to receive either ISDN or 56Kbps incoming calls. Incoming 56Kbps is possible because the incoming line is digital. This previously was available only to organizations that could afford a commercial-grade rack mount modem chassis configured for digital support.

Setting Up ISDN

A lot of horror stories are floating around about the problems of getting an ISDN connection working. Unfortunately, most of them are true. Installing an ISDN line in your home or office is a complicated process that requires cooperation between the ISP, the router vendor, and the local telephone company. The following are the major steps:

1. Set up an ISDN account with an ISP.
2. Order ISDN from the telephone company.
3. Select the desired ISDN device.
4. Configure the ISDN device.
5. Configure Windows NT to support the device.
6. Test the installation.

This seems easy, but there are a lot of potential problems. In addition, several shortcuts are available.

Before you purchase anything, check with your ISDN device vendor; some companies offer a line provisioning service. This service makes the arrangements with your local phone company to set up and configure the ISDN line for you.

Some ISPs will sell you an ISDN device preconfigured for their service. This can save a lot of time and frustration, especially with ISDN routers. If you have never configured a router before, this probably is not the time to start. Too many variables have to be set correctly for proper operation. If you insist on configuring your own router, make sure it is one the ISP supports. They usually will fax or mail you instructions for how to configure it.

If your ISDN device vendor doesn't provide line provisioning, you'll need to order ISDN service directly from your phone company. When the telephone company installs your line, make sure you record your two ISDN phone numbers, the Service Profile Identifiers (SPIDs), and the switch type. You will need this information to configure your ISDN device. Here's a word of warning: The telephone company business office is supposed to give you this information, but they usually forget. The installer that comes out to set up your line will have it if you just ask. Without these three pieces of information, it can be difficult to configure your ISDN device.

Now that you have been forewarned, there are ways to guess this information. The telephone installer usually writes down the telephone number on the punchdown block at the demarcation point. This is the point at which the telephone company line ends and yours begins. Even if the installer wrote down just one number, the two numbers usually are sequential. The SPIDs usually are just the telephone numbers with the area codes + 0101 (for example, 88855512120101 and 88855512130101). The switch type usually is NI-1, the most common type in North America right now. Some of the newer ISDN devices can sense the SPIDs and the switch type automatically.

This should get the line set up. The configuration of the device will vary by manufacturer and device type. Most ISDN devices have installation wizards, so you'll only have to enter the line configuration information and configure Transmission Control Protocol/Internet Protocol (TCP/IP) support. Remember, Windows NT has the **IPCONFIG** command that shows you your IP configuration to assist you in troubleshooting.

After you have installed the ISDN device, try to connect to your ISP. If you don't seem to have a connection, go back to the DOS prompt and try PINGing the ISP's IP address. If you get a successful PING reply, the problem most likely is with the ISP's ISDN support, and you should call its technical support line. If the PING reply fails, double-check your network connections and configuration and try again.

After you have connected, the ISDN device should give you a way to check whether it is using both B-channels, either through lights on the case or through a software-monitoring window. Because the second B-channel might only kick in when traffic is high, try downloading a large file from the Internet. If the second B-channel doesn't kick in, you are getting only half the speed for which you are paying. Recheck your configuration. If you cannot find any problems, call your router company's technical support.

Working with Cable Modems

One of the latest technologies available for remote access is a cable modem. Although the cable "modem" technically still qualifies as a modem because it modulates and demodulates signals like its dial-up predecessors, all similarities end there. A cable modem is far more complicated than the typical analog modem. In fact, it has more in common with the technology used in network routers and hubs. The cable modem utilizes a digital signal brought in through RF coaxial cable to a box similar to a router. In fact, it is installed and configured in a similar fashion as a router, and it doesn't utilize RAS or DUN at all. The connection to the network is full-time, so no call setup is required. Your cable modem is assigned an IP address, and it is treated like a node on the cable system's network. The cable modem is connected to your PC or network through a 10-BaseT connection, and 10-Base100, Asynchronous Transfer Mode (ATM), and Fiber Distributed Data Interface (FDDI) will be available in the future.

Cable Modems

Although symmetrical cable modems (with the same data rate in both directions) are available in some areas, they are not as common as the asymmetrical type.

There currently are two major types of cable modems: the standard cable modem and the telco-return cable modem. Both types are asymmetrical, in that the downstream channel has a much higher data rate than the upstream (similar to 56K modems). The telco-return cable modem uses cable lines for fast downstream transmission, and a telephone modem handles upstream communication over the public telephone network. This type most commonly is used where the cable operator has not yet upgraded the cable infrastructure to the full digital, fiber-optic–based backbone needed to support two-way operation. The telco-return cable modem is fine for home use and might be adequate for a very small business network of fewer than 10 users. Because the upstream link usually is limited to about 28.8K, however, it should be avoided for serious business use or for any situation in which there will be a significant amount of upstream traffic.

The standard cable modem uses cable lines for data transfer in both directions. The maximum downstream rate generally is 28 to 36Mbps with the upstream rate being about 10Mbps. This is the aggregate rate for the ring to which you will be assigned, so you will be sharing this capacity with other users.

Tips and Tricks for Cable Modem Users

The first thing to remember is that using cable modems for remote access is a recent phenomenon. This is not a mature technology! Most of the major cable systems are starting to offer access, but the December 1998 issue of *Cable Datacomm News* estimated the number of North American subscribers at less than 400,000 but growing rapidly. Some cable systems are offering access to small businesses; others are concentrating strictly on home users. Some of the business offerings are attractive price-wise, and some providers are offering to set up a virtual private network (VPN) for small companies. The monthly cost for cable modem rental with unlimited access ranges from $35 to $60, which is comparable to the monthly cost for a telephone line and Internet access from an ISP (but at a higher access speed). This is a good deal for home users and an ever better deal for a business with telecommuters.

Because the ISP business is new to most cable companies, there can be some advantages for early adopters. Because each ring, which is the number of potential connections to be fed by the aggregate 27 to 36Mbps, is based on potential subscribers and not actual subscribers, the early adopters can get phenomenal speed for a very low price. Most cable companies are planning to regulate the speed to the individual user according to pricing tiers in the future, but this business model has not been implemented yet in most places.

DSL and ADSL

Digital Subscriber Line (DSL) is the latest high-speed technology being offered for remote access. DSL is known generically as xDSL because it is a collection of various technologies. Of the various flavors of xDSL, Asymmetric Digital Subscriber Line (ADSL) seems to be more advantageous than many other upcoming bandwidth solutions because it doesn't require a whole new infrastructure.

ADSL promises superfast Internet access, up to 8Mbps downstream. Because ADSL works with existing copper telephone wires, it requires less upgrading of telephone companies' networks than some other broadband solutions. ADSL-based services will always be connected, just like a LAN or a cable modem. The ADSL modem operates simultaneously with the phone so that regular telephone service can continue unaffected by the modem. Because each ADSL customer has his own dedicated copper line, throughput is unaffected by neighboring users. It does not suffer the disadvantage of a cable modem, which has multiple users sharing a common coaxial cable network, reducing the speed available to each user.

The telephone company will have to come to your location and install a splitter that separates the voice line from the ADSL line. This ADSL line will plug into a box that is similar to a cable modem or an ISDN router, and it can be connected to your PC or your network using an Ethernet cable.

Like cable modems, the service is asymmetrical, meaning that the upstream speed is less than the downstream. The consumer ADSL service is rapidly becoming available in most areas, averaging around $30 to $60 per month for an upstream rate between 64 and 384Kbps and a downstream rate between 384 and 768Kbps.

Security Is an Issue

A common characteristic of xDSL and cable modems is the full-time connection to the Internet. Any machine that is permanently connected to the Internet needs to be secured against unauthorized access. Be sure to review the material in other chapters about securing your machine.

DUN Is RAS from the Client's Side

With the explosive growth of the Internet and the emergence of telecommuting, RAS and DUN have become more complicated and more commonly used. The version of RAS included in previous versions of Windows NT was only designed to dial in to a computer and to access the resources on that computer or on a corporate network. The version included with Windows NT 4.0 is designed to be far more flexible, supporting a variety of LAN access and remote access protocols.

In previous versions of Windows NT, the term Remote Access Service applied to both the server and the client applications. The client side of RAS is now known as DUN and is used to connect to dial-up servers. The Dial-Up Networking applet is located in the My Computer dialog box and in the Accessories folder on the Start menu.

New Features in Windows NT 4.0 DUN

DUN adds several new features, most of which were brought over from the Windows 95 implementation to improve remote computing's ease of use. These features include

- Restartable file copy
- Idle disconnect
- AutoDial and Logon Dial
- Multilink PPP (MPPP)
- Point-to-Point Tunneling Protocol (PPTP)

Restartable File Copy

Restartable file copy is a new feature that remembers the status of a file transfer. If a file transfer is in progress when a DUN connection is lost, DUN will resume the file transfer instead of having to start over when the connection is restored.

Idle Disconnect

Idle disconnect automatically disconnects a DUN connection after the specified period of no data transfer activity. Inactivity is measured by lack of NetBIOS session data transfer such as copying files, accessing network resources, and sending and receiving electronic mail. This can be configured from the User Preferences dialog box of DUN. This feature, however, seems to operate more reliably if it is set in the Registry. The Registry key is HKEY_LOCAL_MACHINE\SYSTEM\CurrentControlSet\ Services\RemoteAccess\Parameters\AutoDisconnect. The allowed range is 0-1000 minutes, 20 minutes is the default, and 0 disables the feature.

AutoDial

AutoDial is a dial-on-demand feature that enables Windows NT to automatically dial a remote network connection via DUN when there's an attempt to access data on that network. If you have a program on your machine, for example, that needs to access data on a remote computer to which you are not connected, a dialog box will pop up and ask whether you want DUN to connect to the remote network. If you answer Yes, AutoDial will connect to the remote server. If you don't answer within 15 seconds, AutoDial will default to No, Do Not Dial.

AutoDial maintains network addresses and maps them to DUN Phonebook entries. This enables them to be automatically dialed when referenced from an application or from the command line. A network address can be an Internet host name, an IP address, or a NetBIOS server name. This process is transparent to the application that requests the data.

AutoDial learns about every connection made over a RAS link for possible automatic reconnection later. When a user connects to a network address, an entry is created in the AutoDial database. This entry maps the Phonebook entry for the current DUN session to the network address.

There are several configuration options for AutoDial. AutoDial can be disabled, or you can have it automatically dial the remote connection without asking. It also can be disabled from specific dialing locations, and it can be configured to automatically redial on a link failure. Most of the AutoDial options can be selected from Dial-Up Networking, User Preferences, but you have to select the Appearance tab to turn AutoDial completely off.

When you log on to Windows NT, if you have any desktop shortcuts or persistent network connections that reference network addresses, AutoDial tries to create a connection. To correct this, you can turn AutoDial off, delete the remote paths from your desktop shortcut icons, or change them to reference a local file.

Sometimes there will be a remote path that cannot be deleted. Unfortunately, you cannot selectively delete items in the AutoDial database. You can, however, delete the entire database by removing the HKCU\Software\Microsoft\Windows\CurrentVersion\Explorer\RunMRU key in the Registry and then restarting your machine. AutoDial then relearns your addresses.

To look at the AutoDial database, you can run the following command from the command prompt:

```
C:> rasautou -s
```

AutoDial Support

AutoDial does not work over IPX; only TCP/IP and NetBEUI are supported.

The status output has two parts: network adapter card bindings and a list of learned
AutoDial addresses. The following example lists network adapter card bindings and
contains a list of learned addresses:

```
Checking netcard bindings...
NetworkConnected: ignoring \Device\NetBT_NdisWan4
NetworkConnected: ignoring \Device\NetBT_NdisWan6
NetworkConnected: network (\Device\NetBT_Proteon7, 2) is up

Enumerating AutoDial addresses...

There are 20 Autodial addresses:
128.185.22.12
146.115.28.11
151.196.212.46
165.87.194.212
165.87.194.229
as400.halldata.com
ftp.proteon.com
home.microsoft.com
JCL_MASTER
netshow.microsoft.com
pop03.ca.us.ibm.net
pop03.ny.us.ibm.net
RIC_02
search.yahoo.com
smtp-gw01.ca.us.ibm.net
smtp-gw01.ny.us.ibm.net
www.compaq.com
SERVER1
www.greetingsonline.com
www.hightechcareers.com
www.hotmail.com
www.jcl.lib.ks.us
www.microsoft.com
www.ntsystems.com
www.nwfusion.com
www.proteon.com

www.windowsmedia.com
```

For AutoDial to work properly for mobile users, you might have to set up multiple
dialing locations in the Phonebook. You might always dial the same number to reach a
remote resource, for example, but there might be a need to dial a sequence of numbers
before or after this telephone number depending on where you currently are located.
Instead of having to manually edit the telephone number according to where you
happen to be at the time, you can set up or choose a predefined location.

You can add the prefixes to disable call waiting and name this location Home. If
you travel a lot, you can select a different dialing location with a different area code,
outside line-access number, or calling card number.

Multilink PPP (MPPP)

Windows NT 4.0 now supports Multilink PPP connections. The multilink protocol enables you to combine the bandwidth of two or more physical communications links to increase your remote access bandwidth and throughput. DUN with the multilink protocol can be used to combine analog modem paths, ISDN paths, and even mixed analog and digital communications links on both client and server PCs.

When used with two or more modems or ISDN B-channels, Multilink PPP supports simultaneous data transfer across multiple connections. This speeds up your access to the Internet or to your remote server and reduces the amount of time you have to be remotely connected. It can potentially reduce your costs for remote access and can effectively improve transfer rates by two, three, or even four times.

A Windows NT client with two 33.6Kbps modems, for example, can connect to a Windows NT Server with multiple modems and maintain a sustained transfer rate of 67,200Kbps. The speeds of the modems and ISDN lines can vary, but multilink coordinates traffic across the various links to achieve performance equal to the combined speed of the devices.

A few limitations apply to MPPP. You can use MPPP to dial out with Windows NT Workstation 4.0, but you cannot accept incoming MPPP calls due to Windows NT Workstation's limitation of only allowing one dial-in connection. In addition, MPPP cannot be used with the callback security feature because only one telephone number can be specified for callback.

Both the DUN client and the server must support multilink RAS or MPPP. If you use RAS to connect to your Internet service provider (ISP) but it doesn't support multilink connections, multilink RAS will not work. This usually is not a problem for ISDN users because MPPP originally was developed for ISDN, and most ISP and corporate routers are MPPP capable.

Most ISPs already offer dual-channel ISDN service, but not many support multilink service via analog lines. Those that do typically are pricing multilink analog service at approximately 50 percent more than the price of standard modem access.

Even with the minor difficulties, MPPP is a good solution for users that need a faster dial-up connection to a remote server, as long as two phone lines are available and a Windows NT Server is at the data center. MPPP does not require special hardware or software, is cheaper than ISDN, and competes well with ISDN speeds, especially if the modems at both ends are 56Kbps models.

MPPP or MP?

When inquiring about this service from your ISP, you might need to specify it as MP instead of MPPP. Microsoft seems to be the only organization that refers to it as MPPP.

Implementing multilink DUN in Windows NT 4.0 is not very difficult. To use multiple RAS devices to dial a Phonebook entry, edit the Phonebook entry and go to the Basic tab. In the Dial Using section, choose Multiple Lines. When you click the Configure button, you can choose which of your installed RAS devices to use for this connection. Select the devices you want and the phone numbers the devices will dial. When you make a multilink RAS connection, Windows NT automatically bundles the lines into one logical connection.

Point-to-Point Tunneling Protocol (PPTP)

Windows NT 4.0 includes a new network protocol, the Point-to-Point Tunneling Protocol (PPTP). PPTP is a WAN protocol that enables a RAS client and server to establish a secure point-to-point connection over a TCP/IP connection, such as the Internet. PPTP enables you to set up virtual private networks (VPNs) economically. A VPN is a wide area network link that uses the Internet rather than a dedicated phone line or a dial-up connection as its transport medium.

PPTP is aptly named because it can set up a point-to-point secure connection over an unsecured network. It is referred to as *tunneling* because PPTP works by encapsulating network packets, which can be IP, IPX, or NetBEUI, within IP packets routed directly from one point to another over a public medium, the Internet. As an added precaution, the packets also can be encrypted. Because the packets are encapsulated and encrypted, the communication is very secure. Encapsulation also enables the transport of packets, such as IPX and NetBEUI, that otherwise would not be routable over the Internet.

PPTP is installed like any other protocol in Windows NT. The only configuration option is to tell Windows NT how many virtual private networks (VPN) to install. As you will see in the next paragraph, when configuring an entry in the Phonebook, the VPN is the PPTP equivalent of a modem.

To use PPTP, you can use an existing network connection, or you can dial an ISP to get to the Internet. Once connected to the Internet, you use DUN to connect to a remote PPTP server. Connecting to the remote server is just like using DUN to make a telephone connection except that you specify an IP address instead of a telephone number and a VPN adapter instead of a modem.

With PPTP, power users or small organizations can use the Internet as an economical WAN backbone for secure remote network connections. The only downside to the current version of PPTP is that Windows NT Workstation 4.0 users can only dial-out to a Windows NT 4.0 Server. Accepting PPTP calls is an option only on a Windows NT 4.0 Server.

RAS and NetBOIS

When using a RAS connection to access NetBIOS resources, the maximum number of simultaneous connections to a NetBIOS resource is 250.

Windows NT Workstation and Server Differences

The DUN clients in Windows NT Workstation and Windows NT Server are virtually identical. The RAS component of Windows NT Workstation, however, is limited to one concurrent connection, while the RAS service included with Windows NT Server enables up to 256 simultaneous connections, either inbound or outbound. This enables Windows NT Server to be used as a reasonably priced communications server, especially since RAS is more I/O than CPU intensive. This enables it to be implemented on a moderately priced server.

RAS Server Explained and Explored

A RAS server is the host machine through which you connect to network resources. Any computer running Windows NT 4.0 can act as a RAS server. A Windows NT Workstation computer can be used as a RAS server, but it can support only one inbound connection. In contrast, a Windows NT Server computer can be used as a true communications server, supporting up to 256 incoming connections simultaneously.

The RAS server component of Windows NT acts as a gateway to the resources on your network. RAS enables remote users using a variety of remote client software to connect to the network using NetBEUI, TCP/IP, or IPX/SPX. The only limitation is that the client dial-up software must support PPP.

Security is provided through the standard Windows NT security model, and passwords can be encrypted when transmitted over dial-up lines. In addition, dial-up clients can be restricted to the RAS machine only or can be given access to the network.

RAS installation is not difficult, but it is far more involved than installing DUN. The Microsoft installation documentation is fairly good, but some things are not covered that you should know. The following are some examples:

- To install and configure RAS, you must be logged on as a member of the Administrators group.

- RAS installation varies slightly depending on which network protocols are installed. If you will be using TCP/IP or IPX with RAS, make sure they are properly installed and configured *before* you install RAS.

- If your remote clients need to reach a resource other than your RAS server, install the protocols supported by your LAN.

- Install and test communication devices, modems, and ISDN before you install RAS. This is especially true if you are using multiport serial cards, many of which use nonstandard ports.

- If you are supporting remote TCP/IP clients and they need to browse parts of your network outside of the RAS machine, it is advisable to set up a DHCP and a WINS server to provide IP addresses and name resolution for them. (These services don't have to be installed on the RAS machine.)

- Windows NT 4.0 RAS only supports PPP dial-in clients; no SLIP support is available.

- Install at least Service Pack 3; it contains a lot of fixes for RAS.

RAS starts answering calls as soon as it is installed. If you are in test mode and don't want to be interrupted, disable call-in on the Configure Port Usage dialog box.

There are a lot of advantages to having your remote users dial-up using NetBEUI. With NetBEUI, virtually no configuration is involved, and it will run faster over a RAS connection than IP or IPX with less overhead on the client. RAS utilizes a NetBEUI gateway that translates the network traffic to IPX or TCP/IP. This enables the remote client to connect to another computer system on the network even though that computer does not have NetBEUI installed.

The disadvantage is that, although this works fine for access to file and print resources, client applications that depend on having TCP/IP or IPX on the client computer will not work. If your applications have this requirement, you still need to install the appropriate protocols on the client.

RAS Server Security

Windows NT RAS server uses Windows NT's integrated security system so that RAS does not have to maintain a separate user account database. A valid user account and password, however, are still not enough to let just anyone dial in. Every user must be granted dial-in permission either from the User Manager's User Properties dialog box or from the Remote Access Admin program in the Administrative Tools folder.

To provide an additional level of security, there also is an option set for each user for callback. When the server receives a call, it identifies the user. It then hangs up and calls the user back at a preset telephone number. This prevents remote users from connecting from sites other than trusted sites.

There also are three types of encryption that can be selected. The default is Require Microsoft Encrypted Authorization. This is Microsoft's version of the Challenge Handshake Authentication Protocol (CHAP). Currently, only Microsoft products support this method.

The second choice is Require Encrypted Authentication, a generic authentication method that works with most non-Microsoft clients. The third choice is Allow Any Authentication Including Clear Text. This is not recommended because it offers little security. Anyone with a network sniffer can see the passwords coming into the RAS server if clear text is used.

NetBEUI and RAS

A lot of network-browsing problems have been reported in situations where remote clients are running TCP/IP only. Installing NetBEUI on the RAS server seems to correct the problem.

If you are using Microsoft CHAP, you have the option of selecting the Require Data Encryption box. This secures your data using the RSA Data Security RC4 encryption algorithm. This is a very difficult algorithm to break so your data will be very secure; however, it does slow your RAS connection noticeably.

Routing and Remote Access Service

No discussion of RAS Server would be complete without mentioning the new Routing and Remote Access Service (RRAS) offered as a free add-on to Windows NT 4.0. RRAS adds many new features to Windows NT, most of which enable Windows NT to be a more efficient router. A few additional RAS features also are included. The following are the most significant:

- **Remote Authentication Dial-In User Service (RADIUS) client support.** This enables remote authentication against a RADIUS Server, which creates a single, central location for user authentication data.

- **Unified administrative tool.** A new unified administrative tool that enables all RAS configuration to be performed in one place.

- **Remoteable tools.** Both the new administrative tool and the command-line utilities can be run from a remote machine.

- **PPTP Server-to-Server.** This enables a server to place a call to another server, allowing more sophisticated VPNs to be constructed.

- **Extensible Authentication Protocol.** This addition enables third parties to design plug-in security modules for RRAS authentication.

This update is available from Microsoft's Web site at **http://www.microsoft.com/ ntserver/nts/downloads/winfeatures/RouteRASNT.asp**.

RRAS on Workstation
RRAS is only supported on Windows NT Server 4.0. It does not run on Windows NT Workstation.

Troubleshooting Dial-Up Networking and Remote Access

Troubleshooting RAS problems is not rocket science; mostly, it just means applying common sense. For Remote Access problems, start with the following simple things:

- Is the modem turned on?
- Is the telephone line connected?

There have been a lot of little problems with RAS in Windows NT 4.0. Always make sure you are using the latest service pack (Service Pack 3 at the very least). Also remember to reapply the service pack after any major reconfigurations and after installing new programs or hardware.

Using HyperTerminal to Test Modem Connections

A quick way to test the telephone line and to verify that Windows NT recognizes your modem is to use the HyperTerminal program to make a test call. To do so, follow these steps:

1. Make sure that DUN and RAS are not running.
2. Click Start, Programs, Accessories, HyperTerminal.
3. When the New Connection Wizard is displayed, click Cancel.
4. Select File, Properties and then select the modem you want to test in the Connect Using list.
5. Select Configure and verify that the correct port is selected. Adjust the speaker volume, and then click OK.
6. Type **AT** in the HyperTerminal window and press Enter.
7. If **OK** is displayed after you press Enter, HyperTerminal recognizes the modem properly. If **OK** is not displayed after you press Enter, review the "Working With Analog Modems" section of this chapter to verify that your modem is installed properly in Windows NT.
8. To verify that your modem can dial out, type **ATDTxxxxxxx** and press Enter (xxxxxxx represents any telephone number). You should hear a dial tone and the sound of the modem dialing the phone number. If it does not seem to dial, see the following section, "Connection Problems."
9. To test whether your modem can connect with a remote system, click File, Open and select one of the preconfigured HyperTerminal profiles.
10. Click Dial and listen to make sure the number is dialed. Watch the screen to see whether you get the login screen for that service.

If this works, you can be sure the modem and telephone line are working and are properly configured.

Connection Problems

Failure to connect to a remote host is the most common problem you will experience with DUN and RAS. Connection problems can be caused by a variety of things such as improper hardware configuration, incorrect modem initialization strings, or poor-quality telephone lines. Most problems in new installations are the result of improper hardware or software configuration, whereas telephone lines or authentication issues are the most likely problems in existing configurations.

To check an analog line, plug an analog telephone into the line and see if you have a dial tone. Consider the following questions:

- Can you dial out?
- Can you receive calls on this line?
- Is the line noisy?

If you hear static or crosstalk, or if the dial tone is weak, chances are it is your problem. If you have trouble hearing, the modem will have trouble getting a clean signal.

Many problems can be detected by listening to the call progress, the sounds the modem makes while dialing, and the screeches you hear when it is trying to connect. After a little experience, most people can tell the connect speed by listening to the tones. The default for most modems is to turn the volume of the speaker down. To increase the volume, go to the Control Panel and select the Modems applet. From the General Properties dialog box, you should be able to adjust the speaker volume.

Some modem drivers do not support changing the speaker volume from the General Properties dialog box. Generic modem drivers are a good example of this. It can still be done, however; just go to the Modems applet in the Control Panel and select Properties, Connections, Advanced. In the Extra Settings field, you can insert a modem command. For most modems, you can turn the speaker on using M1, and you can adjust the volume using L1 for low, L2 for medium, and L3 for high.

Still Having RAS Problems?

If RAS still does not work properly after checking and rechecking your configuration, uninstall it, reboot, and then install it again. Sometimes RAS does not install properly, and it can be repaired only by a complete delete and reinstall.

ISDN Terminal Adapter

Because ISDN lines are digital, there is no dial tone. If you have an ISDN terminal adapter that has an analog telephone jack, however, you still can try to dial in or out using an analog telephone plugged into the terminal adapter.

Windows NT includes several applications that can assist you in diagnosing RAS and DUN problems. The first thing you should check is the Event Viewer.

The Windows NT Event Viewer tracks the success and failure of just about all system functions including RAS and DUN. The red stop sign indicates an error, yellow indicates a warning, and blue is an informational message. Select an event in the Event Viewer and double-click for more information. The Event Viewer is especially good for diagnosing connection problems because it frequently indicates the type of failure.

In Windows NT 4.0, you can view the modem log file to see the commands and result strings sent to the modem. This file is not created by default; it has to be turned on. Start the Modems applet in the Control Panel, click the Properties button, select the Connection tab, and then select Advanced. Next click the check box next to Record A Log File. You don't have to restart your computer for this change to take effect. The output will be recorded in the %systemroot% directory in a file called MODEMLOG_ModemName.txt. You can view this file with any text editor. Some of the things you will find in the file include the following:

- The command string sent to the device
- The echo of the command string
- The response from the device

This file is a great troubleshooting aid for bad connections. It should give you plenty of information with which to work. When the problem is fixed, remember to disable logging. The log file will fill your hard drive pretty quickly.

The Dial-Up Networking Monitor is another good tool for diagnosing problems. It can be accessed from the Control Panel by selecting the Dial-Up Monitor applet. The DUN monitor provides a wealth of details and statistics about each RAS connection including bytes sent and received, device errors, compression efficiency, and connection speed.

The DUN Monitor also enables you to disconnect RAS connections and view a summary of active and inactive lines. You can run the DUN Monitor from the Control Panel, or it also can be configured to start automatically when connections are made.

If your modem does not have status lights, select the Preferences tab on the Dial-Up Monitor dialog box. You can select the option to show the modem status lights on your desktop or on your taskbar so you can track the progress of your call.

Extra Settings Field

This field can be used to insert extra modem initialization commands without having to edit the MODEM.INF file.

If you've checked your telephone line and modem configuration using these tools and utilities with no success, it is time to dig a little deeper into Windows NT. There are two additional log files you can use to diagnose problems. As a word of caution, to enable these files you have to add or change some Registry keys. Always have a current backup of the Registry before you perform any edits—unless you enjoy rebuilding your system from scratch.

The first log file is DEVICE.LOG. This file can be used to diagnose basic connection issues. Although the MODEMLOG_ModemName.txt file shows the result of the modem initialization string, the DEVICE.LOG file shows the actual communication between your modem and the remote modem. This file is created in \systemroot\SYSTEM32\RAS.

To turn on logging to the DEVICE.LOG file, use REGEDT32 to change the value of HKEY_LOCAL_MACHINE\SYSTEM\CurrentControlSet\Services\RasMan\Parameters\Logging to 1.

You can start logging by restarting Remote Access or the Remote Access Server service from the Services applet in the Control Panel. You are not required to shutdown and restart Windows NT.

Trace information is recorded in the DEVICE.LOG file only while a connection is being attempted. Logging is suspended after successful connection to the remote device and the initial transmission of data. Logging resumes when a new connection is attempted, and the data will be appended to the DEVICE.LOG until the file size exceeds approximately 100K. At that time, the DEVICE.LOG will be cleared and logging will resume. DEVICE.LOG also will be cleared whenever any RAS component is started or after all RAS components have been stopped. If you need to save a DEVICE.LOG file, make sure you copy it to a different location before restarting or stopping any RAS component.

The next log file is PPP.LOG. This file is used only for PPP connections. It records the complete PPP handshaking process between your machine and the remote machine. This can assist you in determining whether you have a protocol issue or an authentication problem. This file is created in WINNT\SYSTEM32\RAS.

To turn on logging to the PPP.LOG file, use REGEDT32 to change the value of HKEY_LOCAL_MACHINE\SYSTEM\CurrentControlSet\Services\RasMan\PPP\Logging to 1.

Turn Logging Off

When you successfully have diagnosed the problem, remember to turn logging off. These files grow quickly and consume a lot of hard drive space.

Special Information for Business Users

If you are working in an office, your telephone system most likely is digital. You cannot connect an analog modem to a digital telephone line and expect it to work. There are two ways around this. The first is to have the telephone company install an analog line to use for your modem connection. The other option is to have the vendor of your telephone system install a digital-to-analog converter for every line you need. Either option works fine; just pick the one that is most economical for your situation.

Make sure your telephone system vendor knows that you need the converter to support a modem. There usually are several different converters available, and the older models support modem call speeds only up to about 9,600Kbps.

Third-Party DUN and RAS Utilities

Due to the popularity of Windows NT, quite a few add-on products are available for DUN and RAS. Our favorites are detailed in the following sections.

RasTracker

Argent Software's RasTracker is a RAS management tool that enables administrators to generate site reports detailing who is using ports, when they are being used, and for how long. RasTracker can prevent multiple logins, can set limits on connection time, and can reserve ports for important users. Another feature is QuickMonitor, which automatically alerts the administrator when RAS changes occur. RasTracker also lets administrators customize greeting messages to inform users of their allowed RAS connection time, the total RAS usage for a period of time, or daily company updates. For more information, see Argent Software's Web site at `www.argent-nt.com`.

Point B Remote Net-Accelerator

Traveling Software's Remote Net-Accelerator is a client/server solution that speeds up remote access to an office network. It reduces transfer times by caching network files locally, by sending only changes to a file rather than the whole file, and by compressing data to send it more efficiently. It can be used with RAS connections and virtual private networks (VPNs) to reduce the amount of information transmitted through the network and it can improve network performance on slow WAN links. For more information, visit Traveling Software's Web site at `http://www.travsoft.com`.

RAS Manager for Windows NT 4.0

NTP Software's RAS Manager enables you to impose limits on users and to monitor remote access to a greater degree than you can with Windows NT's standard RAS support. RAS Manager is most useful for limiting users' remote access during peak hours. It can be configured to send warning messages at predetermined intervals before the end of a session and then when time expires, automatically disconnect the session. For more information, visit NTP Software's Web site at `http://www.ntpsoftware.com`.

SmartDUN

NetcPlus Internet Solutions' SmartDUN is a RAS/DUN handler system that helps Windows 95/98 and Windows NT 4.0 users access and control their dial-up RAS/DUN system. SmartDUN enables you to rapidly select different DUNs to be used, to create new DUNs, to edit DUNs, to optionally save passwords, and to connect and disconnect at any time quickly and easily. For more information, visit NetcPlus Internet Solutions' Web site at `http://netcplus.co.uk`.

RAS-Costs

Ras-Costs is a small freeware program that automatically tracks your online time. For more information, visit Timo Engelke's site at `http://people.frankfurt.netsurf.de/Timo.Engelke/rcosts/`.

For More Information

- For more information or to download the Routing and Remote Access Service Update, see `http://www.microsoft.com/ntserver/nts/downloads/winfeatures/rras/rrasdown.asp`.

- For information about Microsoft's communications and telephony offerings, visit `http://www.microsoft.com/communications/telephony.htm?RLD=40`.

- For a directory of ISDN services and ISPs in your area and for more ISDN information, check out `www.microsoft.com/windows/getisdn/` or `www.isdnzone.com`.

- To check Microsoft's current version of the Hardware Compatibility List (HCL), see `http://www.microsoft.com/ntworkstation/info/hcl.htm`.

- Iseminger, David. *Inside RRAS: Remote Access Solutions for Windows NT*. John Wiley & Sons, 1998. ISBN: 0471251593.

- Dhawan, Chander. *Remote Access Networks: PSTN, ISDN, ADSL, Internet, and Wireless Computing*. McGraw-Hill, 1998. ISBN: 0070167745.

IV

Managing Your NT System

17

Windows NT and Storage

THE WINDOWS NT STORAGE SUBSYSTEM IS AN ESSENTIAL element of the secure, reliable computing environment required by both personal and professional users. The storage subsystem's capabilities and features are focused on maintaining a working environment in which data and system files are protected and available for authorized use. This chapter examines the Windows NT Workstation storage subsystem, with a focus on issues such as file systems, adding more storage, and configuring the storage subsystem.

File Systems

The Windows NT storage subsystem supports two primary file systems: File Allocation Table (FAT) and the New Technology File System (NTFS). NT Workstation actually supports an enhanced version of Virtual FAT (VFAT). However, even enhanced FAT doesn't offer the feature set most serious system administrators and power users want. The NTFS file system, developed by Microsoft for the Windows NT platform, offers more features and flexibility.

The FAT File System

The version of FAT supported by Windows NT is an enhanced and amended version of the file system originally used by DOS. The FAT name structure is a linear structure that must be searched from beginning to end, one entry at a time, to locate a file. FAT has been implemented on many different platforms with several modifications of its central features and capabilities. In general, FAT has a filename limitation of an eight-character filename and three-character file extension (called an 8.3 filename).

Fortunately, Windows NT supports an enhanced version of FAT that is compatible with all other versions of FAT included with other Microsoft operating systems—with the exception of FAT32. The FAT32 system was developed after Windows NT 4.0 was released and is available in Windows 95 OSR2 and Windows 98. FAT32 is a 32-bit enhanced version of FAT (or VFAT). A Windows NT driver for FAT32 partitions is available from the System Internals Web site (`http://www.sysinternals.com/`). However, we don't recommend using FAT32 (Windows 95/2 or 98) and Windows NT in a dual-boot configuration on a production system. BIOS-level system changes must be made for FAT32 to function, so it is not the best choice for dual- or multi-boot systems. According to Microsoft, FAT32 support will be included in Windows 2000.

The version of FAT supported by Windows NT 4.0 is compatible with other file systems and is cross-platform compatible. Linux and OS/2 both have FAT drivers that can read data from FAT drives originally created and managed by Windows NT. Windows NT's FAT operates in protected mode (as opposed to real mode for DOS FAT) to provide faster and more reliable data management. In addition, it includes long filename (LFN) support, which was first introduced in Windows 95. The LFN support includes a system-level auto-equivalency mechanism that maps all 255-character names to their 8.3 equivalents. Under Windows NT, FAT can be hosted on volumes up to 4GB; non-Windows NT FAT is limited to 2GB. The enhanced version of FAT still has a limit of 512 file entries in the root directory, but it has no limit in subdirectories. When LFNs are used, fewer than 512 files are allowed in the root because multiple 11-character entries are needed to construct LFNs. The major characteristics of Windows NT's FAT are listed in Table 17.1.

Table 17.1 **Windows NT FAT Characteristics**

Characteristic	Maximum/Support
Volume size limit	4GB
File size limit	16MB
Files in root	512
Files in non-root directory	No limit
Long filenames	255 characters
8.3 compatible	Yes
File-level security	No
File-level compression	No

The NTFS File System

The New Technology File System (NTFS) is Windows NT's native file system that was designed to support larger, more efficient drives and offers several security, reliability, and fault tolerance features. To the user, an NTFS volume and a FAT volume look and operate alike, but NTFS is significantly different. NTFS treats root directories and non-root directories in the same way and does not use a linear FAT table to store filenames. Table 17.2 lists the major characteristics of NTFS.

Table 17.2 **Windows NT NTFS Characteristics**

Characteristic	Maximum/Support
Volume size limit	16EB
File size limit	16EB
Files in root	No limit
Files in non-root directory	No limit
Long filenames	255 characters
8.3 compatible	Yes
File-level security	Yes
File-level compression	Yes

NTFS is self-repairing (through the use of transaction logs), supports POSIX file naming conventions, and uses a B-tree data structure to store filenames. These features make NTFS the preferred file system for Windows NT installations.

File Systems and Hard Drives

Hard drives are divided into clusters when they are formatted with a file system. A *cluster* is the smallest unit of drive space that can be allocated to a file and is a defined unit consisting of one or more disk sectors. A disk sector is a division of the physical hard disk platter, which can hold 512 bytes of data. If only the first byte of a cluster is used, all remaining bytes in that cluster remain empty. When larger cluster sizes exist, more space is wasted due to clusters being under-utilized. Maximum file storage is achieved when stored files are all multiples of the cluster size.

The number of sectors per cluster and cluster size vary between FAT and NTFS partitions. As you can see in Table 17.3, NTFS is much more efficient in terms of cluster size. FAT should be used only on drives smaller than 512MB or when access is required on a dual-boot system by operating systems other than Windows NT. Again, we do not recommend using FAT32 for dual-boot systems.

Table 17.3   **Vital Statistics of Cluster Size Based on Logical Volume Size**

Drive Size	Sectors per Cluster (FAT)	FAT Cluster Size (KB)	Sectors per Cluster (NTFS)	NTFS Cluster Size (KB)
0MB–15MB*	8	4	1	512 bytes
16MB–127MB	4	2	1	512 bytes
128MB–255MB	8	4	1	512 bytes
256MB–511MB	16	8	1	512 bytes
512MB–1,023MB	32	16	2	1
1,024MB–2,047MB	64	32	4	2
2,048MB–4,095MB	128	64	8	4
4,096MB–8,191MB	256	128	16	8
8,192MB–16MG	512	256	32	16
16GB–32GB	not supported	not supported	64	32
>32GB	not supported	not supported	128	64

*Volumes less than 15MB use 12-bit FAT; all others use 16-bit FAT.

The High Performance File System (HPFS) is an OS/2 file system that is not supported by Windows NT 4.0. Before installing Windows NT 4.0, you must convert any HPFS drives to FAT or NTFS to be able to access them from Windows NT. You can use the CONVERT.EXE utility from Windows NT 3.51 or tools from OS/2 to make this conversion. The CONVERT.EXE utility included in Windows NT 4.0 supports only FAT to NTFS conversions.

Installing Disks

You can install additional storage either before or after you install an operating system. Doing this before you install the system causes the fewest potential problems. When possible, install all the drive space you think you'll ever need before you install the operating system.

Problems caused when adding new physical hard drives to an existing system include shifting drive letters and breaking the boot process. In Windows NT, the first drive letters are added to the primary partitions of each installed drive. Shifting drive letters occur on single- and multiple-drive technology systems when a new drive is logically added between drives or before another drive. By "logically added," we mean that the logical drive ID (such as the SCSI ID) is logically earlier than an existing drive letter. For example, drive D is earlier than drive E. Logically adding a new drive between or before existing drives often causes the system to recognize the new drive before the old drive, and it then assigns the old drive's letter to the new device. Fortunately, Windows NT can compensate for this through the Disk Administrator, which allows you to redefine drive letters for drives. The drive letter shuffle problem can be serious if it causes a change in the boot partition.

The *boot partition* is where the main system files (the main \Winnt directory) for Windows NT reside. The location of this partition is defined in the BOOT.INI file on the system partition. This definition is in the form of an Advanced RISC Computing (ARC) name. If the order of recognition alters the logical position of the boot partition, the BOOT.INI file must be edited to correct the ARC name. Figure 17.1 shows a sample BOOT.INI file.

Figure 17.1 A BOOT.INI file viewed through Notepad.

An ARC name is a special syntax used to indicate the path to the Windows NT system files stored on the boot partition. To define this path, you indicate the drive controller, physical drive, partition, and folder path. The following are two possible ARC names in the BOOT.INI:

```
multi(1)disk(0)rdisk(1)partition(2)\WINNT="Windows NT Workstation Version 4.00"

scsi(0)disk(0)rdisk(0)partition(1)\WINNT="Windows NT Workstation Version 4.00"
```

ARC name construction can change, and these changes can cause a boot failure if the order, number, or configuration of your storage devices change (including if you modify, create, or delete partitions). If you make changes to your drives while running Windows NT, the Disk Administrator tells you what to edit to correct the BOOT.INI file. If you perform changes outside of Windows NT (such as when the power is off or you're in another OS on a multi-boot system), you have to figure out the new ARC name on your own.

ARC Names

Fortunately, ARC names are fairly logical and easy to understand. Here are the important points to remember:

- The ARC name appearing in the `default=` line must exactly match one of the names listed under `[operating systems]`.
- The first four elements of an ARC name (those items followed by a number in parentheses) are always lowercase.
- The first element is either `multi(#)` or `scsi(#)`. This is the drive controller type. The `scsi(#)` designation is used only for SCSI controllers that do not have onboard BIOS translation enabled; in all other cases, `multi(#)` is used.
- The number appearing in the parentheses following `multi(#)` or `scsi(#)` is the ordinal number of the controller. The first controller is zero (0), the second controller is one (1), and so on.
- The second element in an ARC name is `disk(#)`. This element is used only when the first element is `scsi(#)`, and it represents the number of the drive on the indicated controller. You can remember this because both "disk" and "scsi" have four letters in their names.
- The number appearing in the parentheses following `disk(#)` is the ordinal number of the drive. The first device is zero (0), the second device is one (1), and so on. If `disk(#)` is not used (that is, `multi(#)` is the first element), it will have a default value of zero (0).
- The third element is `rdisk(#)`. This element is used only when the first element is `multi(#)`, and it represents the number of the drive on the indicated controller. You can remember this because both "rdisk" and "multi" have five letters in their names.

- The number appearing in the parentheses following `rdisk(#)` is the ordinal number of the drive. The first device is zero (0), the second device is one (1), and so on. If `rdisk(#)` is not used (that is, `scsi(#)` is the first element), it will have a default value of zero (0).

- The fourth element is `partition(#)` and is the number of the partition on the designated drive. This is the only element of the ARC name that is numbered cardinally. The first partition is one (1), the second partition is two (2), and so on.

- The fifth element is the name of the folder hosting the system files. The default value for this is \WINNT. This element must be the exact name of the main Windows NT directory.

- The data following the ARC name are not technically part of the ARC name. They are used in the BOOT.INI file to provide a meaningful label for the ARC name in the boot menu. After the fifth element, an equals sign points to a phrase in quotation marks.

- Following the ARC name label, there can be a boot switch to change how the selected operating system starts. Consult the book *Windows NT Workstation 4.0 Resource Kit* or TechNet for descriptions and details of the various boot parameters.

Drive Letter Shuffling

Drive letter shuffling can cause problems with more than BOOT.INI. Applications and utilities use drive letters in their path variables to locate data and configuration files. If a drive letter changes, you might find that some applications no longer function. The Start menu and all shortcuts created in your Windows NT environment also rely on drive letters. When drive letters change, these items fail to operate.

Most commonly, problems with changing drive letters occur with SCSI drives. Because up to seven or 14 devices can be attached to a single SCSI chain, it's easy to add a new drive between existing drives. This happens when SCSI ID numbers are not used in sequence and a new device is added with a low SCSI ID. The computer recognizes SCSI devices in the order of the ID. You should always set SCSI device IDs in sequential order. SCSI adapters take ID 7 by default, so you should use 0 through 6 to number your devices.

The drive letter shuffle can occur on ATA (Advanced Technology Attachment) drive systems (such as IDE, EIDE, and UDMA), but it's not quite as common on those as it is with SCSI. ATA drive cables can typically host only two to four drives; one drive is labeled as the master and all other drives are set to act as slaves. Having multiple slave drives on a single cable might cause the letter-shuffling problem. ATA drive systems often have two cable connectors. These are labeled as the primary and secondary IDE ports. The system recognizes drives in the following order:

1. Primary master
2. Primary slaves
3. Secondary master
4. Secondary slaves

If you add new partitions on a primary slave drive to a system with a secondary master, drive letters will shift.

Drive letter shifting can also occur on multiple-drive technology systems. When you employ both ATA and SCSI drives, adding new ATA drives can cause the SCSI drives to increment in drive letters.

In general, problems related to breaking the boot process occur when an ATA drive is added to a computer system that employs only SCSI drives. The x86 architecture generally attempts to boot from the ATA drive, even if the active partition is on a SCSI drive (although some BIOSs have a switch that allows you to boot to IDE or SCSI). If you need extra drive space on a SCSI-only system, stick with SCSI drives. You can always add another SCSI drive controller if you populate the existing chain.

Configuring and Partitioning Disks

After a hard drive is physically installed, you need to configure the device so it can store data. This involves creating partitions and formatting the partitions with file systems. The Disk Administrator (which you access by choosing Start, Programs, Administrative Tools) is the primary tool used to create partitions within Windows NT. You also can use FDISK from DOS or other third-party partition tools, but Disk Administrator is the best choice.

A *partition* is a logical division of the available space on a physical hard drive. A hard drive can host a partition that encompasses all available space, or it can host multiple partitions that take up portions of the available space. You do not need to partition all the space on a hard drive. It is possible to have a partition using only 25 percent of the available space. Each partition can be formatted with its own file system type. You must format a partition with a file system before you can store data on it.

There are two types of partitions: primary and extended. A *primary partition* is typically used to host an operating system, but it can also be used to host data. Only primary partitions can be marked as active, so they are the only type of partition capable of hosting operating systems. *Extended partitions* are not formatted, but they act as containers in which logical drives are defined. A logical drive is just another name for a subpartition within an extended partition. A logical drive is formatted with a file system before it is used to hold data.

A hard drive can host a maximum of either four primary partitions or three primary partitions and an extended partition. An extended partition can be used to bypass the four-partition limit on drives. A single hard drive can host up to 32 formatted partitions—three primary and 29 logical drives within an extended partition.

Individual partitions can be created and deleted without destroying other partitions; however, deleting an extended partition destroys the logical drives it contains. Deleting logical drives or partitions can affect drive letter assignment and destroys the data hosted by the deleted object.

A *volume* is a drive organizational structure that consists of one or more partitions or logical drives formatted with a single file system. A volume can consist of partitions and logical drives from more than one physical drive. Windows NT supports volume sets with up to 32 members. After it's created, a volume acts as a single drive even when it is the aggregation of space from several different locations on the same or different drives. Adding new partitions can expand a volume set; however, shrinking a volume means destroying and re-creating it, which destroys any data it contains. A volume set is destroyed if any of its partitions are destroyed or removed.

Volumes are assigned drive letters when they are created. Windows NT supports the use of 24 drive letters (C–Z) and can access a volume only if it has a drive letter. If 25 volumes exist on a system, only the first 24 can be accessed. Drive letters are assigned automatically to new partitions before they are formatted, using the first unassigned letter closest to the beginning of the alphabet. If you use Disk Administrator to assign a drive letter, that drive will retain its drive letter no matter what changes are made to other physical drives, partitions, or volumes. We highly recommend assigning drive letters to each drive as you assign it to your system.

We also recommend that you decide on a drive-lettering scheme to help you to keep track of storage-device types. Be sure to use the same drive-lettering scheme on every system. Here is one possible scheme:

- Floppy drives: A, B
- Local hard drives: C–K
- CD-ROM and optical drives: L, M, N
- Other removable media drives: O, P, Q, R
- Network mapped shares: S–Z

Disk Administrator, Windows NT Explorer, and My Computer can all be used to format a partition with the FAT or NTFS file systems. We recommend using Disk Administrator because formatting immediately follows partitioning. Don't select the Quick Format option the first time you format a drive; allow the whole formatting process to run its course. This can take 15 minutes or more on 1GB and larger drives because the long format process inspects every sector on the drive and marks any defects to help you avoid problems.

File Management Utilities

The Windows NT native file management utilities (included with the operating system) are Disk Administrator, Windows NT Explorer, and My Computer. You could include the command prompt in this list because you can issue file manipulation commands from this command-line interface. However, in addition to these direct file management utilities, you should not forget that NT Backup and Performance Monitor are also important to managing a disk subsystem.

The operation and use of all these tools are detailed in their respective Help systems, the Windows NT Resource Kit (both Server and Workstation versions), and TechNet. Let's review the major functions of each.

Disk Administrator

Disk Administrator allows you to perform the following tasks:

- Create, modify, and delete partitions
- Format partitions with FAT or NTFS
- Create, extend, and delete volume sets
- Create and delete stripe sets
- Assign drive letters
- Mark a primary partition active

The Windows NT Server version of Disk Administrator is capable of several other functions, most of which focus on fault-tolerant volume constructs. These additional functions include disk striping with parity, disk mirroring, and disk duplexing.

Windows NT Explorer

Windows NT Explorer is a hierarchy detail tree view of formatted partitions (now called drives) contents. My Computer is an object-oriented view of drives. They both perform the same kinds of operations, including these:

- Formatting drives
- Creating, moving, copying, renaming, and deleting folders, files, and shortcuts
- Viewing the properties of drives, folders, files, shortcuts, and shares

- Sharing folders
- Setting security on folders, files, and shares
- Setting auditing on folders, files, and shares
- Mapping network shares to local drive letters
- Launching, viewing, and opening folders, files, and shortcuts

Command Prompt, NT Backup, and Performance Monitor

The command prompt can be used to issue most file or drive manipulation commands used under DOS, such as `format`, `move`, `copy`, `rename`, `del`, `mkdir`, and `xcopy`.

The Windows NT Backup application stores data from hard drives onto tape devices. Although this tool lacks some features found in third-party backup applications, it can function as a source of data protection. As discussed in Chapter 18, you may want to consider a third-party backup application that is capable of performing backups across the network.

Performance Monitor is used to keep an eye on the quality of activity on disk subsystems. Although enabling the disk performance counters can cause some performance digression, the counters can alert you to developing problems before they cause downtime. See Chapter 20 for more information about this utility.

Maintenance

Perform disk maintenance on a regular basis. Hard drives store your data, and you should make an effort to protect those resources from loss or destruction. Disk management is mostly a preventive action with few effective recovery solutions.

Actions you need to perform regularly include disk defragmentation and system-wide backups. Backing up the system is discussed in Chapter 18. Defragmentation is discussed in the next sections.

Fragmentation

The organizational layout of files becomes increasingly complex as they are saved, changed, and deleted. This complexity arises out of the need to split a file into smaller chunks for storage when contiguous space is unavailable on the storage device. When a file is saved to a drive that does not have enough contiguous space available to store it in a single location, the storage subsystem divides the file into segments to match the size of the available spaces. As files are written, changed, and deleted, the size of contiguous space quickly diminishes. The level of fragmentation is the percentage of files that are not stored in contiguous sections. A high fragmentation level results in significantly slower access times and can result in lost or corrupted data.

The DOS FAT file system is notorious for becoming fragmented very quickly. The NTFS file system is much more reliable and robust, but it still succumbs to fragmentation—it just takes a little longer.

Most drive systems are affected by fragmentation only after 30 percent or more of the files stored on the drive are fragmented. The real measure of performance loss is not overall fragmentation, but the percentage of often-accessed files that are fragmented. It doesn't matter if 90 percent of a drive is fragmented if the unfragmented 10 percent is the only part of the drive being accessed regularly. However, in most cases, 30 percent or more fragmentation causes some performance degradation. A drive that is more than 60 percent fragmented may start corrupting files, misreading data, or causing system timeouts.

Defragmentation

The only solution for fragmentation is *defragmentation*, the process of rearranging the data stored on a drive so all data files are stored contiguously and all free space is also in a contiguous block. Defragmenting a hard drive often results in immediate performance improvements; however, a defragmented drive often starts to become fragmented again quickly. You need to make defragmenting your drives a regular habit. Once a week is good for personal systems; defragmenting once a day or at least every two days may be required for high-traffic production systems.

No defragmentation software existed for NTFS when Windows NT 4.0 was released. Fortunately, two third-party companies have since released excellent defragmentation software for NTFS:

- Symantec's Norton Windows NT Tools Speed Disk: **http://www.symantec.com/**
- Executive Software's Diskeeper: **http://www.execsoft.com/**

If you want to defragment only a single file, such as the pagefile, you can use the Contig tool from System Internals. This is a great utility for defragmenting files that are either skipped by the professional products or that become fragmented too often to be fixed by scheduled defragmentation. You can find Contig at **http://www. sysinternals.com/**.

Removable Media and Windows NT

Windows NT does not readily accept removable media devices due to their hot-swappable nature. Windows NT includes some native support for removable media devices, such as Zip and Jazz drives from Iomega, optical drives from Toray, and cartridge drives from SyQuest. However, getting these devices to operate as expected can be a challenge. We highly recommend that you obtain updated drivers from the vendor's Web site before attempting the installation. Windows NT has no trouble supporting floppy drives and CD-ROM drives.

Because hardware is isolated from the user environment, removable media drivers have to work their way around system restrictions. This can cause your system to operate in strange ways when media is being ejected, when a new or different media is inserted, or when a drive is empty.

Since the release of Windows NT, most of the removable media vendors have modified their products and drivers to provide some kind of support. However, the support varies widely. Some devices work exactly as expected with full capabilities for inserting, removing, and changing media without adversely affecting the operating system. Other devices require that media switches occur only across reboots. This limits the benefits and use of some devices, especially when you use them as backup storage or to transfer large amounts of data.

You need to remember a few important factors when working with removable media under Windows NT:

- Always use a software-based eject. Initiating a manual hardware eject of the media can result in lost data due to unwritten cache contents. The software eject command instigates a cache flush before the media is ejected.

- When offered, use the utilities from the device's vendor to format and otherwise manage the media. Some devices do not format correctly when Windows NT Explorer or My Computer is used.

- Don't perform spanning operations such as WinZip's disk spanning option to store data across multiple media. If data will not fit on a single media, employ a splint tool before storing the data on more than one media.

- Do not power cycle external removable media devices while Windows NT is booted. The power cycle process may reset the drive, but Windows NT is not designed to handle this type of hot-action. Windows 95 and 98 can often detect and manage power cycling of external peripherals due to their Plug and Play support.

- As a general rule, keep media in the drive during the Windows NT boot process. In some cases, Windows NT will not boot properly if the media is not present. In other cases, the drivers for the device will not be loaded.

Third-Party Storage Management Utilities

The built-in or native Windows NT management utilities (with the exception of Backup) are generally adequate for managing the disk subsystems and storage devices on any network. However, several quality tools are available from other vendors that may be of interest. The following sections outline some of the more popular and feature-rich options available to you.

QuotaAdvisor for Windows NT

W Quinn's QuotaAdvisor is a disk quota manager that sets limits on storage space on a user-by-user basis. QuotaAdvisor uses hard quotas to stop a user from writing, or soft quotas that report, but take no immediate action. Without this sort of limitation, users can store any amount of data in their home directories up to the drive's capacity, rendering systems nearly inoperative due to the lack of free drive space for system operations and temporary files. QuotaAdvisor is the first second-generation quota tool. It uses a filter driver as opposed to first-generation quota utilities that use NT's security to lock out users. For more information and a demo, see the Sunbelt Web site at `http://www.sunbelt-software.com`.

Storage Resource Manager

High Ground Systems' Storage Resource Manager is a storage system monitor utility that automatically watches over your disk subsystems. By managing disk use, tracking system alerts, monitoring users, and analyzing disks, Storage Resource Manager offers a proactive solution to disk problems. In most cases, this utility can detect when problems are about to occur, so you can resolve the issue before downtime is required. Information about this tool is available from the High Ground Systems Web site at `http://www.highground.com/`.

Norton Utilities for Windows NT

Symantec's Norton Utilities for Windows NT is a suite of multi-function disk system tools. Norton Utilities has been the *de facto* disk maintenance application for years. In the latest release for Windows NT, Norton Utilities offers defragmentation, deleted file recovery, system resource monitoring, in-depth system information, and online product updates. For more information, see the Symantec Web site at `http://www.symantec.com/`.

Troubleshooting Disk Drives and Storage Subsystems

Disk drive and storage subsystem troubleshooting can be broken down into two key areas. The first is actual data recovery and the second deals with problem devices.

Recovering Your Data

Data recovery is required when files are lost, damaged, or corrupted. Files stored on disk drives are susceptible to several forms of damage, including user deletion, management utility corruption, virus infection, disk platter defects, and read-head bounces.

No matter what form of damage you are dealing with, there is only one guaranteed method of protecting your data: regular backups. Chapter 18 discusses the need for backups and methods that can be used to provide duplicate copies of your important data. If you don't have a backup, your options for recovery are limited, to say the least. Data recovery measures to use when a backup is unavailable include the following:

- Restoration from the Recycle Bin

- Recovery from the .CHK files created by CHKDSK (discussed later in this section)

- Recovery from an application's .TMP file (with Word or Excel, for example)

- Drive repair performed by Symantec's Norton Utilities or a similar product

None of these solutions guarantee that you will actually recover lost or damaged data. Regular backups are the best solution.

Device Failure

Either problems with devices are resolved or the device is replaced. You may be able to resolve this kind of problem by performing one of the following tasks:

- Replace the driver.

- Switch the controller card.

- Run a virus-cleaning program.

- Verify that adequate power is being given to the devices (the problem may be your power supply). Be sure to consult with a professional computer repair center to test the power supply; don't attempt it yourself.

- Run CHKDSK on the suspect drive. This utility can sometimes extract data from damaged sectors.

- Use NTFS4DOS from System Internals to attempt to read the data if you cannot access the drive from Windows NT (see Chapter 23).

- Use NTRecover from System Internals to read data from drives over a serial port when the drive's host system fails to boot (see Chapter 4).

CHKDSK

CHKDSK is a drive error detection and data recovery tool for MS-DOS. This simple tool inspects the file structure, directory structure, and actual surface of an entire physical drive. When it finds errors, it can attempt a repair, or if a repair is not possible, it can extract found data into text files and mark the disk sector as bad. The Windows NT disk subsystem does not use bad sectors; in fact, it keeps track of them and uses the disk space around them. Thus, it is possible to continue to successfully use a drive that has a few physical defects. However, because drive prices are so cheap these days, it may be better to buy a new drive for peace of mind.

You access CHKDSK by opening a drive's Properties dialog box from Windows NT Explorer or My Computer. The Tools tab lists three drive tools. Click the Check Now button to open the Check Disk dialog box. This is a simple dialog box with two check boxes: Automatically Fix File System Errors and Scan for and Attempt Recovery of Bad Sectors. We recommend that you select both check boxes before clicking Start. In most cases, Windows NT will indicate that it cannot gain exclusive access to the drive and will perform the drive exam upon the next reboot. When this message is displayed, you should restart Windows NT to allow CHKDSK to perform its magic. Any data recovered from bad sectors will be stored in the root directory of that drive with a filename of file*XXXX*.chk (where *XXXX* is a number equal to or greater than 0001). Most text editors, such as Programmer's File Editor, can read these files.

Professional Help

If these options fail to restore your system or recover your lost data, your last resort is to take the drive to a professional recovery service. These businesses dissect the drive and reassemble the data in an attempt to read the data from the original platters (metal disks inside a hard drive, where data is actually recorded). Usually, they will provide you with a backup tape or another hard drive with the recovered data. This type of service is quite expensive, so we recommend that you use this solution only when in dire need.

If a hard drive or a drive controller proves to be defective, replace the device. Attempting to operate any system using defective devices is asking for trouble. In most cases, the replacement device will be of higher quality and will store more data than the defective device; it might even cost less.

For More Information

- *Windows NT Workstation Resource Kit.* Microsoft Press, Redmond, WA, 1996. ISBN: 1572313439.
- Microsoft TechNet: `http://www.microsoft.com/technet/`

To search for additional third-party utilities for use with Windows NT, check out the following sites:

- `http://www.serverxtras.com/`
- `http://www.bhs.com/`
- `http://www.winntmag.com/`

Visit one of the following online hardware distributors for information and price comparisons:

- `http://www.shopper.com/`
- `http://www.outpost.com/`
- `http://www.hardwarestreet.com/`

18

Windows NT Backup and More

Y OU DON'T NEED A REMINDER ABOUT JUST HOW important an up-to-date backup is. It is probable that every power user has lost information at some point. Placing a backup system on a computer was once too cost-intensive for most users. Today, however, backup systems come in many shapes, sizes, and prices.

This chapter examines that are some of the backup features installed and ready to go when you first install Windows NT Workstation. It also looks into other available backup systems. It offers some rules and guidelines for a successful backup and disaster recovery plan. Finally, this chapter looks at some of the most common third-party backup software packages available for Window NT.

Windows NT's Built-In NTBACKUP.EXE

All versions of Windows NT ship with a backup program called Windows NT Backup (NTBACKUP.EXE). The application can be found in the Winnt\system32 directory by default (your root directory may be something other than Winnt, but this is the default directory name).

The Windows NT Backup application is a simple, solid backup program that is only Windows NT-aware. However, installing applications such as Microsoft Exchange Server and Microsoft SQL Server adds functionality to the backup program. Functionality is also added when you install a service pack on your system. Table 18.1 lists the most common versions of NTBACKUP.EXE. If you have a version newer than the ones listed in the table, you have all the functionality you need.

Table 18.1 **The Versions of Windows NT's Native Backup Application**

File Name	Size and Version	File Description
NTBACKUP.EXE	675 504 09/23/95 10:57a	Exchange-aware; ships with Exchange Server version 4.0 or higher.
NTBACKUP.EXE	329 777 08/02/96 11:00p	Exchange-aware; ships with Exchange Server 4.0a (Service Pack 2).
NTBACKUP.EXE	375 488 03/08/96 4:00a	Not Exchange-aware; ships with Windows NT 3.51 Service Pack 4.
NTBACKUP.EXE	716 560 07/15/96 3:30a	Not Exchange-aware; ships with Windows NT 4.0.
NTBACKUP.EXE	716 560 03/08/96 4:00a	Not Exchange-aware; ships with Windows NT 3.51.

Running a Backup Using NT Backup

To execute a backup using the Windows NT Backup program, log on as a user with backup permissions and complete the following steps:

1. From the Start menu, choose Programs, Administrative Tools (Common), Backup. A window similar to the one shown in Figure 18.1 appears.

2. Select the drive(s) you want to back up by clicking on the square to the left of the drive letter. In our example, drives E and F are selected. If the check box has an X in it and a white background, the entire drive will be backed up. However, if the check box has an X in it and a gray background, only selected files and/or folders are selected. To select which files and directories are to be backed up, double-click on the name of the volume and choose the desired files by checking the check boxes to the left of the names.

3. After the drive is selected and the tape is inserted and ready in the drive, start the backup by clicking the Backup button. A window like the one shown in Figure 18.2 appears to allow you to select the backup options.

Service Pack 5

Service Pack 5 is now available and can be downloaded from
`http://www.microsoft.com/ntserver/nts/downloads/recommended/sp5/`.

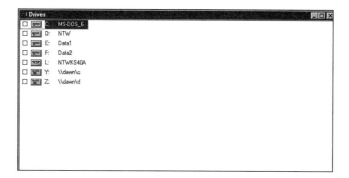

Figure 18.1   The Windows NT Backup application.

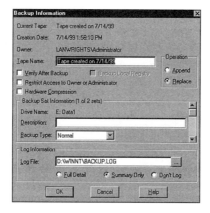

Figure 18.2   The Backup Information dialog box.

It is important to understand all the available options in the Backup information windows; we look at each of the options in detail in the following list:

- **Current Tape.** This is the name of the tape in the drive. The name takes the form *Tape created on dd/mm/yy*, where *dd* is the day, *mm* is the month, and *yy* is the year. If the tape in the drive is blank, you will be notified in this section.

- **Creation Date.** If you use a different name from that of the date the tape was created, this informs you of the tape's creation date.

- **Owner.** This lists the user name of the person who created this backup and the domain to which the user belongs.

- **Tape Name.** This is where you specify the name of this particular tape. By default, the name will take the format *Tape created on dd/mm/yy*. You can, however, specify any other name that you want.

- **Verify After Backup.** When you select this option, the backup program checks to make sure that the files on the backup media match those on the drives. Note that although turning on this feature means the backup process will take longer, it is still a good feature to enable. This process double-checks to make sure that the data is not corrupted as it is saved to the tape.

- **Backup Local Registry.** Check this box if you want the backup program to create a copy of the local Registry files in the backup set. The Registry stores information such as user, group and computer accounts, and the server's disk configuration information. If you choose not to back up the Registry, you will have to re-create all the Registry entries if your system ever fails.

- **Operation.** This option allows you to specify what is to be done with any data that already exists on the tape. If you select Append, the new data will be added to the existing information. You must ensure that you have enough space to store both backup sets on the tape if you choose this option. If you select Replace, the new backup information overwrites any existing data. If the tape in the drive is blank, the Append option is grayed out.

- **Restrict Access to Owner or Administrator.** It is usually a good practice to restrict access to any backed up files to only the owner or the administrator. If a user requires a file on the backup set, either the administrator or the owner of the file (preferably both) should authorize user access.

- **Drive Name.** This is the name of the drive (or drives) you selected for backup; after you select it, you cannot change it without exiting and starting over.

- **Description.** This field allows you to enter additional information about the backup set that can be used for easy identification when you restore information from the backup.

- **Backup Type.** Windows NT assigns each file and directory an archive attribute, which is checked when the file or directory has been modified. Backup applications use this to decide which files need to be copied. The five available backup options from the Backup Type drop-down menu are as follows:

  - *Normal.* With a normal (also known as full) backup, all the selected files get backed up, regardless of whether the archive bit is set. By default, after the files are backed up, the archive bit is cleared. You should perform a full backup on a fairly regular basis to ensure that all the data on your hard drives is backed up to tape.

  - *Copy.* A copy backup is identical to a normal backup except that the archive bit is not cleared. With a copy backup, you will not notice that any of the files have been backed up.

- *Differential.* A differential backup backs up only those files that have changed (have had the archive bit set) since the last full backup. The archive bit is not cleared after a differential backup. To restore data from a differential backup, restore the last full backup followed by the last differential backup.

- *Incremental.* This backup option is like the differential except it resets the archive bit. To restore from an incremental backup, you must restore the last full backup and then every incremental backup performed since the full backup.

- *Daily.* A daily backup backs up only those files that have been modified that day. The archive bit is not set.

- **Log Information.** This is where a log file is created that tracks how many files were backed up, how many files were skipped and why, how many errors were encountered, and how long the backup took to complete.

After you start the backup, a status window similar to the one shown in Figure 18.3 appears and informs you which files are being backed up, the elapsed time, and the amount of information backed up.

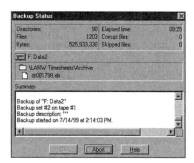

Figure 18.3   The NTBackup Status window.

Restoring A Backup

Restoring a backup is simple. When you run the NTBackup program and insert the required tape, the program automatically detects the backup set(s) stored on the tape (see Figure 18.4). When you double-click on the catalog in the Tapes window, the program lists the files stored on the tape and allows you to select the ones that you want restored. Click the Restore button, select the restoration options, and the data will be restored.

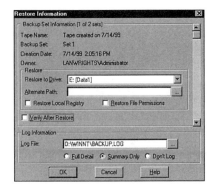

Figure 18.4 Restoring files from a backup.

Less Expensive Backup Alternatives

In this section, we look at some of the less expensive alternatives to backup tape drives, including the following:

- Zip drives and their equivalents
- Jaz drives and their equivalents
- Recordable CD-ROMs
- Rewritable CD-ROMs
- Recordable DVD drives
- Duplicate hard drives
- Enterprise backup devices

Zip Drives and Their Equivalents

The Zip drive from Iomega (**http://www.iomega.com/product/zip/**) changed the high-capacity, removable media market, allowing users access to inexpensive and relatively fast media with 100MB of storage space. The parallel port version of Zip drive allows you to simply attach the drive to your printer port, install the software, and be up and running. Iomega recently announced a 250MB version of the Zip disk that is backward compatible with the 100MB disks. Visit the documentation at **http://www.iomega.com/product/zip/zip250.html** for more information.

Some of the Zip Drive's major competitors include the following:

- **Imation SuperDisk.** A 120MB drive that can read and write not only the LS-120 disks, but also the regular 3.5-inch floppy disks. Information on the Imation SuperDisk can be found at `http://www.superdisk.com`.

- **Sony HiFD.** A 200MB floppy drive replacement. (`http://www.ita.sel.sony.com/jump/hifd/`).

- **Olympus SYS.230.** A 230MB drive available in both SCSI and a parallel port flavors. More information can be found at `http://www.olympusamerica.com/cgi-bin/section.cgi?name=storage&product=SYS_230`.

- **O.R. Technology A:Drive.** A 120MB drive that uses the LS-120 disk format. (`http://www.ortechnology.com/adrive.html`).

Jaz Drives and Their Equivalents

If the 100MB to 200MB drives do not have enough storage for you, move to the next level, made popular by the Iomega Jaz Drive. The Jaz Drive is a SCSI drive that boasts 1GB (also available in a 2GB model) removable cartridges. (`http://www.iomega.com/jaz/`).

The Jaz Drive's major competitor is the SyQuest SyJet 1.5, which is a 1.5GB SCSI drive (`http://www.syquest.com/products/m_syjet.html`).

Recordable CD-ROMs

A recordable 4x CD-ROM (CD-R) can be burned in under 20 minutes, store up to 650MB, and is not susceptible to magnetic interference. After the CD-ROM has been burned, it can be read by almost all CD-ROM drives. However, the recording is permanent and the CD cannot be erased.

Re-Writeable CD-ROMs

The CD re-writeable (CD-RW) allows you to erase information on the CD and re-write to it many times over. The media used in the CD-RW is different from that used in a CD-R and is not backward compatible with CD-R media. CD-R disks can be read (and on newer models, written to) by the CD-RW drive, but unless your CD-ROM documentation explicitly says so, it probably can't read CD-RW disks.

Recordable DVD Drives

DVD stands for digital versatile disc or digital video disc. DVD disks are double-sided and store information on both sides. A CD drive cannot read DVD disks, but DVD drives can read the CD format. DVD currently has two incompatible formats: DVD-RAM and DVD+RW.

The DVD-RAM is put out by a group called the DVD Consortium and boasts storage capacity of 5.2GB, 2.6GB. Hewlett-Packard, Philips, and Sony support DVD+RW. The DVD+RW technology allows for around 3GB of storage per side, for a total of roughly 6GB.

Duplicate Hard Drives

A duplicate hard drive can also be used for backups. Usually, you duplicate the boot and system drives after you complete a clean or new installation of Windows NT. The duplicate drive allows you to restore the operating system in a matter of minutes. Normally, if your system fails, you must reinstall the drive partitions, the operating system, and all necessary drivers before restoring the system. With a copy of the operating system on a secondary drive, you simply install the drive, reboot the system, and restore from tape.

Inexpensive removable drive cases (*caddies*) are available for use with such a system. The caddies range in price from $20 for the basic plastic model to hundreds of dollars for metal models with built-in fans. Caddies allow you to replace a failed drive without having to open the computer, which is especially convenient if the system is difficult to access. There are different versions of caddies, including IDE or SCSI controllers, cooling fans, heat sensors, and built-in RAID controllers. For more information about removable drive cases, search for the phrase "removable hard drive bay" with your favorite Internet search engine.

Enterprise Backup Devices

We could easily dedicate an entire chapter to this subject, but we will look at only a few available options here. Remember that most of these devices are not just expensive, but very, very expensive.

Three of the more popular tape backup systems are the DLT, the DAT, and the AIT formats. *Digital Linear Tape (DLT)* can currently support up to 35GB on a single uncompressed tape (up to a whopping 70GB of storage on a tape with compression enabled). The DLT tapes can sustain transfer rates of up to 18GB per hour. This means that a completely full 4.3GB drive will be backed up in approximately 14minutes. *Digital Audio Tape (DAT)* can store up to 24GB (compressed) on a single tape in less than three hours.

Choosing a Backup Device

The size and speed of the backup device you use is extremely important. If the device is too slow, your backup may still be running when the system is required for other tasks. Open files may be skipped and incorrect file versions stored on tape. Open files copied to tape may be corrupt when restored or may not restore at all. The time during which a workstation is not being used and is available for a backup is known as the backup "window." You always want your backup to fit (easily if possible) into this backup window.

If the media size is too small, you will have to swap media during the backup. Because most backups take place at night, this is not a convenient or efficient solution. You also need to keep in mind how fast a backup can be restored. If the system being backed up is not mission-critical, a slower backup device will work just fine. However, for a mission-critical system, you want to be able to restore as quickly and efficiently as possible.

Rules for Backing Up

What should you back up? As a rule, we suggest that you back up data and operating system information (such as users, groups, and security), but not application files. You may want to back up your application files, however, if a fast, full recovery of the system is required.

There are some files that should never be backed up because they do not contain anything that would matter if they were lost to a disk failure. These types of files are as follows:

- **Swap files.** A swap file is a large file used by the operating system for virtual memory. When the system requires more memory than is installed in the computer, it creates a virtual memory space and applications share the real space by swapping pieces of memory (called *pages*) to the hard disk. With Windows NT Server, the swap file should be at least the same size as the amount of physical memory, plus 12MB. If, for example, your server has 256MB of memory installed, the size of the swap file should be 268MB. Because this file contains no real data, it would be a waste of backup and restore time to back it up.

- **Temporary files.** Windows and applications use temporary files to store information on the hard drive. For example, when you download a large file from the Internet, it is first saved in the temporary directory before being copied to its final destination. Such files generally end in the .TMP file extension, or are stored in the Temp directory.

Choosing a Backup Process

As a rule, if the backup process is not as efficient, or as painless, as possible, you will find that it will not take place.

Managing Backup Media

The process of managing the tapes used during a backup can range from simple to extremely complex. By far, the most commonly used media rotation scheme is known as the *Grandfather-Father-Son* schedule. This scheme uses daily (Son), weekly (Father), and monthly (Grandfather) backup sets. There are really three different backup schemes under the Grandfather-Father-Son umbrella: Son, Father-Son, and Grandfather-Father-Son, as discussed in the following sections.

Son

With the Son method, only a single tape is required to complete the backup and the same tape is used everyday to complete the backup. With this method, the storage life of the backup data is limited to the last backup.

The Son scheme is simple to manage, but it is not an effective backup strategy because the magnetic media used to backup eventually wears out and must be replaced. Also, the data is only as complete as your last backup. Table 18.2 shows a typical Son backup rotation.

Table 18.2 **The Son Backup Rotation Scheme**

	Monday	Tuesday	Wednesday	Thursday	Friday
Week # 1	Tape 1	Tape 1	Tape 1	Tape 1	Tape 1
	Normal	Normal	Normal	Normal	Normal

Father-Son

With the Father-Son method, six backup tapes are required to complete the backup. Using this method increases the storage life of the backup media to two weeks. In this rotation scheme, four tapes are used Monday through Thursday for a differential or incremental backup. The other two tapes are used to complete a Normal backup on Friday. They are rotated each week and stored off-site. Table 18.3 shows the Father-Son backup rotation scheme.

Table 18.3 **The Father-Son Backup Rotation Scheme**

	Monday	Tuesday	Wednesday	Thursday	Friday
Week # 1	Tape 1	Tape 2	Tape 3	Tape 4	Tape 5
	D/I	D/I	D/I	D/I	Normal
Week # 1	Tape 1	Tape 2	Tape 3	Tape 4	Tape 6
	D/I	D/I	D/I	D/I	Normal

*D/I = differential or incremental

The Father-Son scheme is easy to manage and allows you to keep data longer than the Son scheme. To implement the Father-Son scheme, perform the following steps:

1. Label four of your tapes as differential or incremental backups. For example, tape1, tape2, and so on, or Monday, Tuesday, and so on.

2. Label two of your tapes as Normal backups. For example, tape5 and tape 6, or Friday1 and Friday2.

3. Follow the schedule shown in Table 18.3 for performing backups Monday through Thursday.

4. Rotate tapes 5 and 6 off-site for maximum protection.

Grandfather-Father-Son

The Grandfather-Father-Son (GFS) scheme is the most complex and most secure of the three schemes discussed here. It is also easy to manage and comprehensive enough to find files easily when they need to be restored.

Label four backup media tapes for the day of the week that each tape will contain—for example, Monday through Thursday. Although differential backups can be performed on the Son group of tapes, an incremental backup is more common. The Son media is reused each week on the day matching its label. You use a set of up to five weekly backup media tapes that are labeled Week1, Week2, and so on. Normal backups are used on these tapes, on the days that a Son tape is not used—Friday in our example. The Father tapes are reused monthly. The last three media tapes are labeled Month1, Month2, and Month3. These Grandfather tapes are used to complete a Normal backup on the last business day of the month and are reused quarterly.

Each of the media can include either a single tape or a set of tapes, depending on the amount of data that needs to be backed up. A total of twelve sets are required for this basic rotation scheme, which allows you to store two to three months of information. To increase the amount of time information is available, simply pull tapes to be archived from the rotation periodically and replace with new tapes. Table 18.4 shows the Grandfather-Father-Son backup rotation scheme.

Table 18.4 The Grandfather-Father-Son Backup Rotation Scheme

	Monday	Tuesday	Wednesday	Thursday	Friday
Week # 1	Tape 1	Tape 2	Tape 3	Tape 4	Tape 5
	D/I	D/I	D/I	D/I	Normal
Week # 2	Tape 1	Tape 2	Tape 3	Tape 4	Tape 6
	D/I	D/I	D/I	D/I	Normal
Week # 3	Tape 1	Tape 2	Tape 3	Tape 4	Tape 7
	D/I	D/I	D/I	D/I	Normal

continues

Table 18.4 **Continued**

	Monday	Tuesday	Wednesday	Thursday	Friday
Week # 4	Tape 1 D/I	Tape 2 D/I	Tape 3 D/I	Tape 4 D/I	Tape 8 Normal
Week # 5	Tape 1 D/I	Tape 2 D/I	Monthly Normal		

★D/I = differential or incremental

Benefits of Offsite Storage

It is estimated that fifty percent of businesses that rely on information stored in computer systems and do not back up that information will never reopen their doors after a major failure. Of the remaining fifty percent, an estimated ninety percent will close their doors within one calendar year of having the failure. With numbers like that, backups suddenly become extremely important.

Completing regular backups is only half the battle. Suppose you complete backups on a regular basis without missing a single one and fully test the backups regularly. What happens if the building in which the servers are located burns down?

Offsite storage of backups is an expensive option. The company that stores your data has a lot of money invested in their storage facilities. The facilities have to be secure, protected from the elements (such as floods, earthquakes, and fire), and climate controlled. Some storage companies go so far as making their buildings bombproof. Although these features do not come cheap, in the long run, they are well worth the expense. Offsite storage companies will pick up new media to be stored and return old ones on a regular schedule that you set up.

You do not have to pay an offsite storage company to store your tapes. The idea of offsite storage is simply that the backup media is not onsite. You can just take the media home with you. It is now offsite and protected should a fire occur at the office.

Some companies forego the expense or inconvenience of storing information offsite and purchase a fireproof safe; however, these safes are designed to protect paper. If you store your tapes in one of these safes and a fire breaks out, you will find that they do not protect backup media from one of its main enemies: heat.

Third-Party Backup Tools and Utilities

If the Windows NT Backup program does not suit your needs, you may want to consider a third-party backup option. Perhaps you need to copy a system across the network. If you require such a feature, you will need a third-party backup application. Several of these applications exist on the market today. The three most popular programs available for Windows NT are as follows:

- ARCServeIT
- Backup Exec
- NetWorker for Windows NT

ARCServeIT

One of the top players in the Windows NT backup market is ARCServeIT from Computer Associates (**http://www.cai.com/**). ARCServeIt delivers backup, restore, and disaster recovery for single Windows NT Workstations, small- and enterprise-level backup. You can find more information on this program and download a trial version at **http://www.cai.com/arcserveit/**.

Backup Exec

Backup Exec by Seagate Software (**http://www.seagatesoftware.com/**) includes tools to backup Microsoft Exchange, SQL and SMS severs. It is a fully functional backup, restore, and disaster-recovery backup system that can handle anything from the smallest to the largest networks. The current shipping version is 7.0. More information and a free evaluation copy can be found at **http://www.seagatesoftware.com/bewinnt/demod/**.

Double-Take Copy

High availability and disaster recovery are combined in this utility that recently won the *NTools* E-News Target Award. It allows you to replicate mission-critical data in real time to another server (that might be hundreds of miles away) and fail over to this server in case of downtime. More information and a 30-day evaluation can be downloaded from **http://www.sunbelt-softtware.com**.

NetWorker for Windows NT

Like its two counterparts, NetWorker by Legato Systems (**http://www.legato.com/**) is a full backup, restore, archive, and disaster-recovery application that can handle any size of network, from single node to enterprise. To find more information, you can visit **http://www.legato.com/Products/html/legato_networker.html** and download a trial version.

For More Information

For more information about the Windows backup utilities available to you, please consult the following references:

- TechNet (the technical subscription service from Microsoft): **http://technet.microsoft.com/**
- Microsoft Knowledge Base: **http://support.microsoft.com/**
- Search **http://www.pcwebopedia.com/** for extra information on the backup components.

19

Scripting and Automation

FACED WITH NETWORKS MADE UP OF A NUMBER of systems and workstations, most users want to handle the task of running and maintaining these systems with as little hands-on intervention as possible. This chapter looks at the Windows Scripting Host for Windows NT, command line–based and Windows-based scripting hosts, and scheduling utilities from Microsoft and third-party vendors.

The Windows Scripting Host

The Windows Scripting Host (WSH) provides a scripting host for Microsoft 32-bit operating systems (Windows 95/98/NT) that is both language-independent and extremely flexible. The following sections explore both the DOS and Windows portions of WSH.

DOS Portion

The DOS-based portion of WSH, CSCRIPT.EXE, is found in the %systemroot%\
system32 folder. The CSCRIPT.EXE application can be executed using the following
syntax:

```
CScript scriptname.extension [option...] [arguments...]
```

The switches listed behave as follows:

- **scriptname.extension.** This refers to the name of the script to be executed. It
  can be a Visual Basic script, a Java Script, or a third-party add-on script.
- **option.** This switch lets you enable and disable the various WSH options that
  always are preceded by two forward slashes (//). Script options also are known as
  host parameters.
- **arguments.** CSCRIPT.EXE can pass information (arguments) to the script for
  processing. WSH arguments always are preceded by a single slash (/).

If, for example, you want to execute the Visual Basic script named REBOOT.VBS and
have it time out in 60 seconds, enter the following command:

```
CSCRIPT reboot.vbs //t:60
```

Table 19.1 lists all the options available in WSH version 5.0.

Table 19.1 **CSCRIPT.EXE Switches and Options**

Option	Description
//B	This option executes WSH in batch mode, in which all error messages and script prompts are suppressed and are not displayed on the screen.
//H:CSCRIPT	This changes the default scripting host to CSCRIPT.EXE.
//H:WSCRIPT	This changes the default scripting host to WSCRIPT.EXE. This is the default setting.
//I	This option executes WSH in interactive mode. All error messages and script prompts are displayed on the screen. Interactive Mode is the opposite of the //B option and is the default.
//logo	Enabling this option displays an execution banner when the script is executed. This is the default setting.
//nologo	The opposite of //logo, this option prevents any banners from being executed when the script is run.
//S	This option saves the current command-line options for the user currently logged in to the system. This can be done on a per-user basis.

Option	Description
//T:nn	This enables you to control the amount of time (in seconds) that a script can execute. It prevents a script from hogging system resources for an extended period of time. The default for this option is no time limit.
//?	Invoking this option displays the available options and their usage. It is the same as executing CSCRIPT.EXE without any options.

You must specify a script name to enter script options. Typing **CSCRIPT.EXE** brings up a list of all the available options. The next section looks at a sample script.

WSCRIPT

The Windows portion of WSH is WSCRIPT.EXE. The options and command prompts are the same as for CSCRIPT.EXE. If you run WSCRIPT without specifying options, a graphical script properties window appears. This also is true when you enter the **WSCRIPT.EXE** //? command.

There are three ways to execute a registered script using WSCRIPT.EXE. Note that the second option works only if a scripting engine for the scripting language you are using is registered with WSH. The easiest way to determine whether your scripting engine is registered is to inspect the icon Windows assigns to the script file. If the icon is a default Windows icon (usually a note with the Windows logo in it), the scripting engine is not registered. If the icon looks like a note in the shape of the letter S, the scripting engine is registered. You also can check whether your scripting engine is registered by simply running the script. If the scripting engine is registered, the script will execute properly. An error dialog box appears if the scripting engine is not registered with WSH. (In CSCRIPT, the same error appears as a DOS error.)

1. Run WSCRIPT.EXE from the DOS command prompt with the desired options.
2. Double-click the script you want to execute.
3. Run the script from the Run command on the Start menu.

Sample Script

If the Windows version of WSH is installed on your system, you have a directory called wsamples in your %windir% (your Windows folder) that contains sample scripts. One of the sample scripts is called SHORTCUT.VBS. Its role is to simply create a shortcut for NOTEPAD.EXE on your desktop. The script listing (for the Visual Basic version) is as follows:

```
' Windows Script Host Sample Script
'
' ----------------------------------------------------------------------
'                 Copyright (C) 1996-1997 Microsoft Corporation
'
' You have a royalty-free right to use, modify, reproduce and distribute
' the Sample Application Files (and/or any modified version) in any way
' you find useful, provided that you agree that Microsoft has no warranty,
' obligations or liability for any Sample Application Files.
' ----------------------------------------------------------------------

' This sample demonstrates how to use the WSHShell object to create a shortcut
' on the desktop.

L_Welcome_MsgBox_Message_Text   =
"This script will create a shortcut to Notepad on your desktop."
L_Welcome_MsgBox_Title_Text     = "Windows Scripting Host Sample"
Call Welcome()

Dim WSHShell
Set WSHShell = WScript.CreateObject("WScript.Shell")

Dim MyShortcut, MyDesktop, DesktopPath
DesktopPath = WSHShell.SpecialFolders("Desktop")
Set MyShortcut = WSHShell.CreateShortcut(DesktopPath & "\Shortcut to notepad.lnk")
MyShortcut.TargetPath = WSHShell.ExpandEnvironmentStrings("%windir%\notepad.exe")
MyShortcut.WorkingDirectory = WSHShell.ExpandEnvironmentStrings("%windir%")
MyShortcut.WindowStyle = 4
MyShortcut.IconLocation = WSHShell.ExpandEnvironmentStrings
➡("%windir%\notepad.exe, 0")
MyShortcut.Save
WScript.Echo "A shortcut to Notepad now exists on your Desktop."

Sub Welcome()
    Dim intDoIt
    intDoIt = MsgBox(L_Welcome_MsgBox_Message_Text,   _
                     vbOKCancel + vbInformation,      _
                     L_Welcome_MsgBox_Title_Text )
    If intDoIt = vbCancel Then
        WScript.Quit
    End If
End Sub
```

Sample Windows Scripting Host files

Sample Windows Scripting Host files can be found on the Web at
http://msdn.microsoft.com/developer/default.htm.

The preceding script is divided into two sections. The first section is the actual script including all the variable declarations. The second section is the Welcome screen. The Welcome screen subroutine contains information used to create the dialog box displayed when you issue the `//logo` option.

WSH Files

Properties you define in the WSCRIPT.EXE property page are set for all scripts executed on that machine. When Microsoft developed WSH, it built in the capability to set script properties on a script-by-script basis. To accomplish this, you create a WSH file (a file that has a WSH extension associated with it).

You can create a WSH file manually, or you can have the Windows Scripting Host create it for you. To have the file created automatically, simply right-click the script file, set the desired properties, and click OK. Notice that the new file with the .WSH extension has the same name as the original script. The .WSH file is simply a text file. You can edit it with Windows Notepad or MS-DOS's Edit applications. The following is a sample listing of a .WSH file:

```
[ScriptFile]
Path=D:\WINNT\Profiles\Administrator\Desktop\WSH\test.vbs

[Options]
Timeout=10
DisplayLogo=1
BatchMode=0
```

After the .WSH file has been created, you can execute it either by double-clicking the new .WSH file or by using the following command:

```
CSCRIPT.EXE SomeScript.wsh
```

The .WSH file is divided into two sections: [ScriptFile] and [Options]. The [ScriptFile] section specifies the path to the location of the script file itself. The [Options] section specifies some of the options you can configure with a particular script. These options include Timeout (the amount of time for which the script is allowed to run), DisplayLogo (whether the logo is to be displayed when the script execute), and BatchMode (runs the script in either Batch or Interactive Mode).

DisplayLogo and BatchMode

A value of either zero (0) or one (1) is assigned to the DisplayLogo and BatchMode options. With the DisplayLogo option, 0 indicates that the logo will not be displayed, and 1 forces the logo to be displayed when the script is executed. With the BatchMode option, 0 enables the Batch Mode, and 1 enables the Interactive Mode.

AT and WinAT

Now that you've seen a few scripts, you might be thinking "That's great, but now what?" You can use scripting to make your computer independent. You can configure the system to run the scripts according to a specific schedule. Windows NT has a built-in tool called AT.EXE (found in the %systemroot%\system32 folder). AT.EXE is a command line–based application that enables you to configure the system to automatically execute scripts. WINAT.EXE is a graphical version of the AT.EXE program. Although it is not included with the Windows NT operating system, it is available free from the Windows NT Resource Kit.

The Schedule Service

Before AT.EXE or WINAT.EXE can execute properly, Windows NT must be able to monitor and control them. This is done through the Schedule service, which both the AT.EXE and WINAT.EXE rely on to function properly. By default, this service is set to Manual startup. If you are setting up an event to take place on a regular basis, you need to change the startup of this service to Automatic. To start the Schedule service, follow these steps:

1. Click Start, Settings and choose the Control Panels option.
2. Double-click the Services control applet.
3. Scroll down and highlight the Schedule service. (Its status should be blank and startup should be set to Manual.)
4. Click the Start button.
5. Click the Startup button.
6. Choose the Automatic radio button and click OK.
7. Click the Close button to close the Services applet in the Control Panel. You can find information about this utility and can download a copy of it at `http://www.windowsnt.digital.com/products/software/entsw/dvb.asp`.

You also can use Window NT's NET command to start the service. To start the service, enter the command **Net start schedule**. To stop the service, enter **Net stop schedule**.

The AT.EXE and WINAT.EXE applications issue an error message if you attempt to execute either AT.EXE or WINAT.EXE with the Schedule service stopped. The AT.EXE application simply does not execute. The WINAT.EXE, on the other hand, informs you that the Schedule service is not running and asks whether you want it started for you.

Scripting

It is important for you to realize that AT.EXE and WINAT.EXE are simplified applications. If you require advanced applications to schedule your scripts and events, you need a third-party application. Some of these applications are discussed later in this chapter.

AT

AT.EXE is a simple, DOS-based application for scheduling events. Although the commands are simple, they can become frustrating because the application does not always cooperate.

The AT.EXE command syntax is as follows:

```
AT [\\computername] [ [id] [/DELETE] ¦ /DELETE [/YES]]
```

The following are the switches and options:

- **\\computername.** This switch specifies the system on which this event is to be scheduled. If the switch is omitted, the commands will be scheduled to execute on the local computer. Remember that, if you are scheduling events on remote systems, you must make sure that the Schedule service is started on the remote system and that you have the proper rights to run this service on the remote machine. You can start this service (and even control its startup method) through Windows NT's Server Manager application.

- **id.** This is a value assigned to each scheduled command. The value is assigned automatically when you configure a scheduled event, and you cannot set it yourself. You can use this value to delete and modify scheduled events that already are in the queue.

- **/DELETE.** By issuing this command, you can delete specific or all scheduled events. If you include an Id, only that scheduled event will be deleted. If you omit the Id value, all the scheduled events will be deleted.

- **/YES.** When deleting scheduled events, the system informs you that you are about to delete scheduled events and asks whether you agree to do so. By issuing the /yes switch, the system automatically answers any of these questions with Yes.

- **time.** The time value specifies the time at which this scheduled event is to take place. It is expressed in *hours:minutes* in the 24-hour notation (00:00 through 23:59). For example, 5:26 p.m. would be entered as 17:26.

- **/Interactive.** This switch enables the scheduled job to interact with the desktop of the user that is logged in to the system when the event executes.

- **/Every:date[].** This enables you to control the day on which the event runs. You can specify either the day(s) of the week or the day(s) of the month (either every Wednesday or the 15th of every month). You can specify the dates as either one or more days of the week (M, T, W, Th, F, S, Su) or one or more days of the month (1 through 31). To enter multiple days, simply separate the days with a comma. If you omit the day, the system assumes you want to execute the event on the current day.

- **/next:date[].** Entering this switch executes the commands on the next occurrence of the day (for example, next Monday). You can specify the numbers the same way you did before (as one or more days of the week or month). Again, if you omit this switch, the current day of the month is assumed.

- **"*Command*".** This is the actual command to be executed according to the set schedule. You must enter the command in quotation marks. If you are running a command that resides on a remote system, specify the server and sharename rather than the remote drive letter. If the command you want executed is not an executable file (.EXE), you must precede the command with cmd /c.

WinAT

If you have a choice, use the WinAT application over the AT application. Both applications are basically the same, but the WinAT application is much easier to troubleshoot than its DOS-based counterpart. The WinAT application can be found in the Windows NT Resource Kit. You can either install the entire resource kit or copy the file (WINAT.EXE) from the i386\config folder into your %systemroot%\system32 folder.

After you execute the WINAT.EXE application, you will see a WINAT.EXE scheduled jobs window listing the jobs that are scheduled.

You automatically are connected to the local computer. If you want to connect to a remote computer and add scheduled events to it, follow these steps:

1. Choose the New option from the File menu. The Select Computer dialog box appears.

2. Browse to the desired system, highlight it, and click OK.

After you are connected, you can configure the events you want to take place. To accomplish this, follow these steps:

1. Choose the Add option from the Edit menu. The Add Command On %computername% dialog box appears.

2. Enter the command you want executed in the command field.

3. Choose a schedule (Today, Tomorrow, Every, or Next) by selecting the corresponding radio button.

4. If you select either the Every or the Next option, you can choose either the day(s) of the week or the day(s) of the month.

5. If you select either the Today or the Tomorrow option, the day(s) of the week or month will be grayed out.

6. Select the time at which you want the event to execute.

7. If you want the event to interact with the desktop of a user logged in when the event executes, select the Interactive option.

8. When you have completed the configuration, click OK. The event will be listed in the WinAT application window.

To edit an existing event, you can either highlight it and select the Change option from the Edit menu or simply double-click the event.

Windows Batch Files and Commands

You also can create script files by creating DOS-like batch files. This section discusses how some of the batch files are executed. It also covers some of the commands available to you.

Batch files and script files are executed in Windows NT through the Windows NT command shell. You can start a Windows NT command shell in several ways:

- Select Run from the Start menu and enter **CMD** in the Open box. Click OK.
- Choose Start, Programs, Command Prompt.
- If you are in a command prompt (that is, a DOS prompt), type **CMD**.
- Double-click a .BAT or .CMD file, either in the Windows Explorer application or from the drives on the desktop.

The command shell is executed using the following syntax:

```
cmd [/x ¦ /y] [/a ¦ /u] [/q] [/t:fg] [ [/c ¦ /k] [string]
```

Table 19.2 covers the different switches available to you with the CMD command shell.

Table 19.2 **The CMD.EXE Parameters**

Parameter	Description
/c	Executes the command as specified by *string* and then exits.
/k	Executes the command as specified by *string* and then continues.
/q	Turns echo off.
/a	Configures output as ANSI.
/u	Configures output as Unicode.
/t:fg	Enables you to control the foreground and background colors for the command shell.
/x	Enables the extra extensions that exist in the Windows NT version of CMD.EXE.
/y	Disables the extra extensions that exist in the Windows NT version of CMD.EXE. This usually is used for backward compatibility

Configuring an event

All that WINAT.EXE and AT.EXE do is interface with the Schedule service. After you configure an event, the information is passed to the Schedule service, which writes the job to the HKEY_LOCAL_MACHINE\SYSTEM\CurrentControlSet\Services\Schedule Registry key. Neither WINAT.EXE nor AT.EXE need to be running for the event to be scheduled nor does anyone need to be logged into the machine where the event is scheduled to execute. Rebooting the system does not lose the configuration information.

Third-Party Scripting and Automation Alternatives

This section looks at some of the available third-party scripting and automation solutions. There are a number of alternatives to AT and WinAT. This section looks at the Batch Scheduler, a scripting and automation solution from Compaq, and OpalisRobot from Opalis Software, Inc.

Batch Scheduler

The Batch Scheduler from Compaq is a solution that covers both scripting and automation. The Batch Scheduler is a visual tool that enables you to create scripts without having to hash out code. A person who has never written scripts can very quickly and easily create complex scripts using this tool. You can find information about this utility and can download a copy of it at `http://www.windowsnt.digital.com/products/software/entsw/dvb.asp`.

OpalisRobot

Another third-party application for scheduling jobs is OpalisRobot by Opalis Software Inc. OpalisRobot is a powerful scheduler application that you can use to automate different tasks under Windows NT. OpalisRobot is an event-driven program that is powerful and easy to configure. It can monitor different Windows NT services and events and can react to them according to a set of rules you configure. A trial version of this utility can be downloaded from `http://www.optimus.co.uk/opalis/robot/download.html`.

Visual Batch

This product was known as Visual Batch when it was marketed by Digital Equipment Corporation and became Batch Scheduler when Compaq acquired Digital. You can find information about this utility and can download a copy of it at `http://www.windowsnt.digital.com/products/software/entsw/dvb.asp`.

Scripting and Automation Scenarios

A whole book could be dedicated the creation of scripts. Although that is not the focus of this book, some of the most common scripts in everyday use on networks are mentioned here. See the "For More Information" section at the end of this chapter for useful sources.

Modifying the Registry

You will encounter situations in which you have to modify the Registry on more than one system on your network at the same time. The following script listing illustrates how you can create several Registry entries and then remove them. The script listing for REGISTRY.VBS is as follows:

```
' Windows Script Host Sample Script
'
' ----------------------------------------------------------------
'                 Copyright (C) 1996-1997 Microsoft Corporation
'
' You have a royalty-free right to use, modify, reproduce and distribute
' the Sample Application Files (and/or any modified version) in any way
' you find useful, provided that you agree that Microsoft has no warranty,
' obligations or liability for any Sample Application Files.
' ----------------------------------------------------------------
'
' This sample demonstrates how to write/delete entries in the registry.


L_Welcome_MsgBox_Message_Text   = "This script demonstrates how to create and
delete registry keys."
L_Welcome_MsgBox_Title_Text     = "Windows Scripting Host Sample"
Call Welcome()


' *************************************************************************
' *
' * Registry related methods.
' *

Dim WSHShell
Set WSHShell = WScript.CreateObject("WScript.Shell")

WSHShell.Popup "Create key HKCU\MyRegKey with value 'Top level key'"
WSHShell.RegWrite "HKCU\MyRegKey\", "Top level key"

WSHShell.Popup "Create key HKCU\MyRegKey\Entry with value 'Second level key'"
WSHShell.RegWrite "HKCU\MyRegKey\Entry\", "Second level key"

WSHShell.Popup "Set value HKCU\MyRegKey\Value to REG_SZ 1"
WSHShell.RegWrite "HKCU\MyRegKey\Value", 1
```

```
WSHShell.Popup "Set value HKCU\MyRegKey\Entry to REG_DWORD 2"
WSHShell.RegWrite "HKCU\MyRegKey\Entry", 2, "REG_DWORD"

WSHShell.Popup "Set value HKCU\MyRegKey\Entry\Value1 to REG_BINARY 3"
WSHShell.RegWrite "HKCU\MyRegKey\Entry\Value1", 3, "REG_BINARY"

WSHShell.Popup "Delete value HKCU\MyRegKey\Entry\Value1"
WSHShell.RegDelete "HKCU\MyRegKey\Entry\Value1"

WSHShell.Popup "Delete key HKCU\MyRegKey\Entry"
WSHShell.RegDelete "HKCU\MyRegKey\Entry\"

WSHShell.Popup "Delete key HKCU\MyRegKey"
WSHShell.RegDelete "HKCU\MyRegKey\"

' *******************************************************************************
' *
' * Welcome
' *
Sub Welcome()
    Dim intDoIt

    intDoIt =  MsgBox(L_Welcome_MsgBox_Message_Text,   _
                    vbOKCancel + vbInformation,   _
                    L_Welcome_MsgBox_Title_Text )
    If intDoIt = vbCancel Then
        WScript.Quit
    End If

End Sub
```

Viewing System Variables

This script enables you to view all the values assigned to variables on a Windows NT system. This is useful in troubleshooting systems that are acting irregularly.

The script listing for SHOWVAR.VBS is as follows:

```
' Windows Script Host Sample Script
'
' ----------------------------------------------------------------
'              Copyright (C) 1996 Microsoft Corporation
'
' You have a royalty-free right to use, modify, reproduce and distribute
' the Sample Application Files (and/or any modified version) in any way
' you find useful, provided that you agree that Microsoft has no warranty,
' obligations or liability for any Sample Application Files.
' ----------------------------------------------------------------
'
' This sample demonstrates how to use the WSHNetwork object.
' It reads network properties (username and computername),
' connects, disconnects, and enumerates network drives.
```

```
L_Welcome_MsgBox_Message_Text   = "This script demonstrates how to use the
➥WSHNetwork object."
L_Welcome_MsgBox_Title_Text     = "Windows Scripting Host Sample"
Call Welcome()

' *********************************************************************************
' *
' * WSH Network Object.
' *

Dim WSHNetwork
Dim colDrives, SharePoint
Dim CRLF

CRLF = Chr(13) & Chr(10)
Set WSHNetwork = WScript.CreateObject("WScript.Network")


Function Ask(strAction)

   ' This function asks the user whether to perform a specific "Action"
   ' and sets a return code or quits script execution depending on the
   ' button that the user presses.  This function is called at various
   ' points in the script below.

   Dim intButton
   intButton = MsgBox(strAction,                    _
                      vbQuestion + vbYesNo,         _
                      L_Welcome_MsgBox_Title_Text )
   Ask = intButton = vbYes
End Function

' **************************************************
' *
' * WSHNetwork.AddNetworkDrive
' *
' *

Function TryMapDrive(intDrive, strShare)
   Dim strDrive
   strDrive = Chr(intDrive + 64) & ":"
   On Error Resume Next
   WSHNetwork.MapNetworkDrive strDrive, strShare
   TryMapDrive = Err.Number = 0
End Function

If Ask("Do you want to connect a network drive?") Then
   strShare = InputBox("Enter network share you want to connect to ")
   For intDrive = 26 To 5 Step -1
       If TryMapDrive(intDrive, strShare) Then Exit For
   Next
```

```
    If intDrive <= 5 Then
        MsgBox "Unable to connect to network share. "              & _
               "There are currently no drive letters available for use. "  & _
               CRLF                                                & _
               "Please disconnect one of your existing network connections " & _
               "and try this script again. ",                     _
               vbExclamation + vbOkOnly,            _
               L_Welcome_MsgBox_Title_Text
    Else
        strDrive = Chr(intDrive + 64) & ":"
        MsgBox "Connected " & strShare & " to drive " & strDrive,  _
               vbInformation + vbOkOnly,                           _
               L_Welcome_MsgBox_Title_Text

        If Ask("Do you want to disconnect the network drive you just created?")
➥Then
            WSHNetwork.RemoveNetworkDrive strDrive

            MsgBox "Disconnected drive " & strDrive,        _
                   vbInformation + vbOkOnly,                _
                   L_Welcome_MsgBox_Title_Text
        End If
    End If
End If


' ********************************************************************************
' *
' * Welcome
' *
Sub Welcome()
    Dim intDoIt

    intDoIt = MsgBox(L_Welcome_MsgBox_Message_Text, _
                     vbOKCancel + vbInformation,    _
                     L_Welcome_MsgBox_Title_Text )
    If intDoIt = vbCancel Then
        WScript.Quit
    End If
End Sub
```

Connecting and Deleting Network Drives

It is common for users to require access to shares on the network to run specific applications. One of the problems with mapping network drives is that they are still connected after the user has closed the application. The script in this section enables you to map a drive letter to a network share and then disconnect that drive after the application quits.

The script listing for NETWORK.VBS is as follows:

```vbnet
' Windows Script Host Sample Script
'
' -------------------------------------------------------------------
'                 Copyright (C) 1996 Microsoft Corporation
'
' You have a royalty-free right to use, modify, reproduce and distribute
' the Sample Application Files (and/or any modified version) in any way
' you find useful, provided that you agree that Microsoft has no warranty,
' obligations or liability for any Sample Application Files.
' -------------------------------------------------------------------
'
' This sample demonstrates how to use the WSHNetwork object.
' It reads network properties (username and computername),
' connects, disconnects, and enumerates network drives.


L_Welcome_MsgBox_Message_Text   = "This script demonstrates how to use the
➥WSHNetwork object."
L_Welcome_MsgBox_Title_Text     = "Windows Scripting Host Sample"
Call Welcome()

' *********************************************************************************
' *
' * WSH Network Object.
' *

Dim WSHNetwork
Dim colDrives, SharePoint
Dim CRLF

CRLF = Chr(13) & Chr(10)
Set WSHNetwork = WScript.CreateObject("WScript.Network")


Function Ask(strAction)

    ' This function asks the user whether to perform a specific "Action"
    ' and sets a return code or quits script execution depending on the
    ' button that the user presses.  This function is called at various
    ' points in the script below.

    Dim intButton
    intButton = MsgBox(strAction,                   _
                    vbQuestion + vbYesNo,           _
                    L_Welcome_MsgBox_Title_Text )
    Ask = intButton = vbYes
End Function

' **************************************************
' *
```

```
' * WSHNetwork.AddNetworkDrive
' *
' *

Function TryMapDrive(intDrive, strShare)
    Dim strDrive
    strDrive = Chr(intDrive + 64) & ":"
    On Error Resume Next
    WSHNetwork.MapNetworkDrive strDrive, strShare
    TryMapDrive = Err.Number = 0
End Function

If Ask("Do you want to connect a network drive?") Then
    strShare = InputBox("Enter network share you want to connect to ")
    For intDrive = 26 To 5 Step -1
        If TryMapDrive(intDrive, strShare) Then Exit For
    Next

    If intDrive <= 5 Then
        MsgBox "Unable to connect to network share. "                  & _
               "There are currently no drive letters available for use. "  & _
               CRLF                                                    & _
               "Please disconnect one of your existing network connections " & _
               "and try this script again. ",                         _
               vbExclamation + vbOkOnly,                _
               L_Welcome_MsgBox_Title_Text
    Else
        strDrive = Chr(intDrive + 64) & ":"
        MsgBox "Connected " & strShare & " to drive " & strDrive,      _
               vbInformation + vbOkOnly,                _
               L_Welcome_MsgBox_Title_Text

        If Ask("Do you want to disconnect the network drive you just created?")
Then
            WSHNetwork.RemoveNetworkDrive strDrive

            MsgBox "Disconnected drive " & strDrive,          _
                   vbInformation + vbOkOnly,                  _
                   L_Welcome_MsgBox_Title_Text
        End If
    End If
End If


' ********************************************************************************
' *
' * Welcome
' *
Sub Welcome()
    Dim intDoIt
```

```
        intDoIt =  MsgBox(L_Welcome_MsgBox_Message_Text, _
                          vbOKCancel + vbInformation,     _
                          L_Welcome_MsgBox_Title_Text )
    If intDoIt = vbCancel Then
        WScript.Quit
    End If
End Sub
```

For More Information

- TechNet (the technical subscription service from Microsoft):
  `http://technet.microsoft.com/`

- Microsoft Knowledge Base: `http://support.microsoft.com/`

- Microsoft's Scripting Web page:
  `http://msdn.microsoft.com/scripting/default.htm`

- To request an evaluation copy of Compaq's Batch Scheduler, you can either call 800-344-4825 or visit the company's Web site at
  `http://www.windows.digital.com/products/Software/visual_batch_abstract.asp`.

- Information about OpalisRobot3 can be found at Opalis Software's Web page at
  `http://www.opalis.com`.

- Hill, Tim. *Windows NT Shell Scripting*. Macmillan Technical Publishing, 1998. ISBN 1578700477.

20

Tuning and Optimizing Windows NT

Windows NT 4.0 IS A POWERFUL NETWORK operating system. Straight out of the box, however, it might not live up to your expectations or requirements. Taking the time to fine-tune a deployment of Windows NT can greatly improve performance and reliability. Windows NT includes several utilities that offer you direct or indirect control over performance settings, plus there are several backdoors to squeeze out even more efficiency.

This chapter takes a look at Performance Monitor, Network Monitor, and a handful of other tools included with Windows NT. There's also some discussion about *Windows NT Workstation 4.0 Resource Kit* utilities. After you have a grasp of the tools and an understanding for the basics of performance tuning, you'll learn about some specific actions you can take to improve your system's efficiency and speed.

Establishing a Baseline

The art and science of performance tuning requires a general understanding of the normal operational parameters of the system being tuned. In other words, if you don't know how a system typically operates, you won't know how to improve it. Establishing a measurement of common operation levels offers you direct insight as to what components can be improved, how much improvement can be gained, and how much improvement you've obtained. This measurement standard is called a *baseline*.

Establishing a baseline is simple but often tedious. It involves recording performance information for each aspect or component of a system over a reasonable length of time. From this data set, you can derive the average performance levels for each component. After you have an understanding of the normal operating parameters, you can use this to evaluate future levels and to calibrate system changes.

The primary tool used to establish a baseline (excluding third-party utilities) is Performance Monitor. With Performance Monitor, you'll need to record from days' to weeks' worth of performance data for each major object within your system (CPU, memory, disk, network, and so on). Then, using all four views from Performance Monitor (Chart, Alert, Log, and Report), you can extract the median performance levels for each significant counter or object and even its standard deviations.

Windows NT is a modular, object-oriented network operating system. Each subsystem within Windows NT is an object. The CPU is an object, for example, the memory is an object, the storage subsystem is an object, and so on. Each object has several performance-measuring functions called *counters*. Each counter offers insight into a different aspect or function of the object. The CPU object (called Processor in Performance Monitor), for example, has counters that measure % Active Time, % Time Used By User Applications, number of interrupts per second, and more. Performance utilities take advantage of this design by reading the counters and then presenting the information to you in a human-readable format (numbers or graphs).

The logging feature of Performance Monitor operates on an object basis rather than a counter basis. This means that you configure a log to record all the data for an object instead of using individual counters. Therefore, after a log file is recorded, you can select any counter from an object to examine. After you've determined what to record, you need to determine two time-related issues—the measurement interval and the length of time to record the log file.

The measurement interval determines how often a performance reading is taken. Too short an interval can produce spurious results and can cause additional workload on your system. Too long an interval might hide performance changes. Although most readings are insignificant, frequent readings can cause significant performance degradations.

The length of time over which a log file is recorded should be long enough to capture all the normal operational activities. This typically means recording a log file for at least a week. A shorter time period might not offer you a complete picture of your system's normal weekly performance.

Counter

A *counter* is a unit measured by Performance Monitor to establish whether the component to which the counter is related is performing optimally.

It also is important to balance the number of objects recorded in a log file at one time against the load placed on the system. It typically is not recommended to record more than three or four objects at any one time. This means that, when 16 objects are required to establish a complete baseline, you are better off recording a week's worth of data for four objects over four weeks.

Let's look at Performance Monitor to see how both real-time and historical measurements operate.

Working with Performance Monitor

Performance Monitor is Windows NT's built-in investigation tool. Although it has some limitations and has few automated capabilities, it is a useful tool in a system administrator's arsenal. Performance Monitor can measure the operations of a stand-alone system or an attached network, or it can manage measurements from multiple remote systems. Performance Monitor has four views that offer different interfaces and functionality. These views are real-time charting, threshold alerts, logging, and report generation.

Chart View

When Performance Monitor is launched (using Start, Programs, Administrative Tools [Common]), Performance Monitor), it defaults to the Chart view. The Chart view is used to view real-time measurements (see Figure 20.1) or to review data stored in a log file. Each counter is displayed as a colored line. Multiple counters from the same system or from remote systems can be viewed simultaneously. The Chart view is used mostly to inspect data from log files. Real-time counter measurements are used to quickly check the effect of a recent system adjustment.

You can add counters to the Chart view through the Add To Chart dialog box (see Figure 20.2). This dialog box can be accessed by clicking the Add Counter button (the plus sign on the toolbar) or by issuing the Add To Chart command from the Edit menu. From this dialog box, you can select counters based on the host computer (local or remote), the object, the object's instance (when multiple instances of the same object are present on the computer, such as three disk drives or two network interface cards), and the actual counter itself. There are options to modify the appearance of the counter such as color, line width, and line style. The scale setting is used to tune the measurements either to fit better on the display screen or to more closely match the magnitude of other counters. To obtain information about the selected counter, click the Explain button.

> **Menu Commands**
>
> The menu commands of Performance Monitor are mostly self-explanatory. If you don't understand the function of a menu command, use the online Help interface.

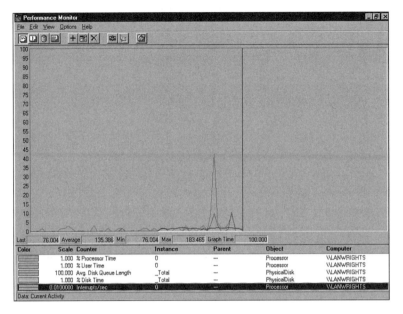

Figure 20.1   Performance Monitor's Chart view showing current activity measurements.

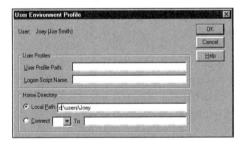

Figure 20.2   The Add to Chart dialog box with the Explain button selected.

You can use the Chart Options dialog box (accessed through Options, Chart on the menu bar or by clicking the Options toolbar button) to control the display area as follows:

- Display the legend and value bar
- Display vertical or horizontal grid lines or both
- Display the vertical scale labels
- Display as a graph (like an EKG) or as a histogram (like a thermometer bar)
- Set the vertical maximum
- Set the measurement interval for automatic updates or specify when manual updates should occur

The main area of the Chart view is the display area where the measurements are plotted. From the left border to the right border, the display is divided into 100 intervals. No matter how small or large the Performance Monitor window, it will display only 100 measurements. When displaying real-time measurements, the values wrap around from the right to the left, overwriting the older values. When displaying historical measurements, the total number of values is reduced to 100 points by using evenly spaced values throughout the log file.

At the bottom of the Chart view is a selected counter detail line (a value bar) and a list of all displayed counters (a legend) with their selected properties. When a counter is selected in the legend, its details (Last, Average, Min, and Max) are displayed in the value bar. Pressing Backspace when a counter is selected toggles the highlight for the selected graph line.

In the Chart view, and every other view, you can save a configuration file for each view or for all views together (called a workspace) so that your settings and counter/object selections are retained. A stored configuration file can be reloaded during future sessions of Performance Monitor on the same or a different system. All locally referenced counters will become local to the new machine, but all remotely referenced counters will retain their original designations.

Alert View

The Alert view (see Figure 20.3) is used to define threshold alerts. These can be used with real-time measurements or with historical log files. An alert is issued when a specific counter crosses a defined threshold value. When this occurs, a trigger event is initiated. The following are the trigger events:

- Switching to Alert view
- Logging the alert in the Application Log of the Event Viewer
- Sending a network message to a user or group
- Launching a program or batch file

Alerts are created in much the same way as counters are added to the Chart view. The Add to Alert dialog box (accessed by clicking the Add Counter button or by selecting the Add To Alert command from the Edit menu) is used to select the counter to monitor by computer, object, instance, and counter. The Alert If area is used to define the threshold of a specific value and to specify whether the alert should occur when the measurements are above or below that value. The only trigger event defined on a counter level is the launching of a program or batch file. This event can execute only the first time or every time the alert occurs.

The Alert Options dialog box is where you can switch to Alert view, log in the Application log, and send a network message. The test interval also is set in this dialog box (the default is five seconds).

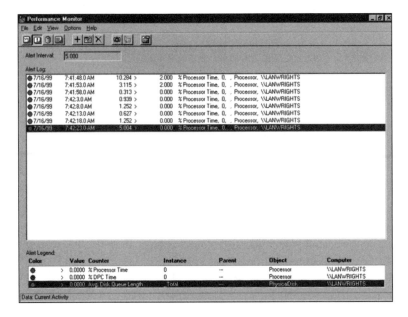

Figure 20.3 Performance Monitor's Alert view.

The Send Network Message alert from the Alert Options dialog box is limited to a single name. If you need to send an alert to more than just one user or the members of just one group, you must use a batch file to launch a command-line messaging tool. To send network pop-up messages, you can use the **NET SEND** command in a batch file. If you want to send SMTP email messages, you'll need a third-party tool to use in a batch file.

Alerts are more often used to locate highs and lows in a log file than to monitor systems in real time. Important alerts to watch for when viewing a log file are low disk space, swap file usage, and task queues for network cards and CPUs. Any of these items can point to a current or potential system problem.

Alerts

Defined alerts are listed at the bottom of the Alert view in the Alert Legend section. All instances of an alert's occurrence are displayed in the Alert Log.

Log View

The Log view (see Figure 20.4) is the recording device of Performance Monitor. Logging records the activities of an entire object (that is, all counters of the selected object) into a file, which can be viewed later. The logging capabilities of Performance Monitor are by far its most valuable asset. The operation of the logging is quite simple. First, add objects to the log using the Add To Log dialog box. The added objects are listed in the main window. Second, define a path and filename for the log file in the Log Options dialog box, set the interval (the default is 15 seconds), and then click Start Log. When you want to stop logging, return to the Log Options dialog box and click Stop Log. The only limitation to log file recording is the free disk space on the destination drive.

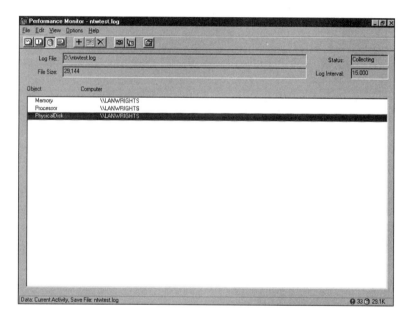

Figure 20.4 Performance Monitor's Log view.

You should always name your log files with as much description as possible within the 255-character filename limitation. Try to include the name of the system, the start and end date/time, and the object names recorded. A properly labeled log file is easy to use and locate.

After a log file is recorded, it can be loaded into Performance Monitor using the Data From command from the Options menu. Just specify the path and filename of the log file and click OK. You can return to viewing current activity (real time) through this dialog box as well.

As activity is being recorded in a log file, you can employ bookmarks to highlight important happenings, events, or issues in the log file. From any view, select the Bookmark command from the Options menu. You'll be prompted for a name for the bookmark. A *bookmark* is nothing more than a point in time named in the log file. You can use bookmarks later when selecting time windows. You'll want to create bookmarks for significant events that affect performance such as system shutdowns, the starting of new services, network backup software execution, large data transfers, and so on.

A *time window* is a selected block of time from a log file. When a log file is used as the source of data, Performance Monitor automatically sets every data point within the log file as active. (That is, it views the data from the start to the end of the log file.) Through the use of a time window, you can shorten or otherwise alter the data in use. The Time Window command from the Edit menu reveals the Input Log File Timeframe dialog box. From this dialog box, you can slide the start and end points manually, or you can select a bookmark as a start or stop point. Only the data in the selected time frame (between the start and stop points and shaded gray) will be used by Performance Monitor.

While it is being recorded, don't try to view a log file from the same instance of Performance Monitor that is performing the logging. If you need to view the contents of the open log file, use another instance of Performance Monitor. You'll be able to view all data points up to the point when you opened the log file, and new data will continue to be recorded into the file by the first instance of Performance Monitor.

After a log file is recorded, you can append and resample the file to combine multiple files or to remove spurious readings. To record new data into an existing log file, just specify the path to the existing file in the Log Options dialog box. Resampling or removing bad data can be accomplished with the following steps:

1. Use the Data From command to select the existing log file.

2. Define a time window from the start to just before the spurious data.

3. Add objects to the Log view and then record the log to a new file name (such as log2.log).

4. Define another time window, this time from after the spurious data to the end.

5. Add the same objects to the Log view and then record the log to the same file (log2.log).

This process creates a new file (log2.log) that doesn't contain the bad data. You also can change the sampling interval. Performance Monitor averages surrounding data points to extract missing data. The only restriction to this process is that log files must be combined in chronological order. Performance Monitor is not able to sort out-of-order log files and will be unable to read the data.

When recording a log file for the PhyiscalDisk and LogicalDisk objects, don't record the file to the same drive being measured. You will not be recording accurate values because the act of reading the object and writing to the drive adds a significant amount of additional workload.

If a process is not active from the moment a log file is recorded, it initially will not appear in the instance list when viewing data from that log file. Instead, you must alter the time window to a point at which or after the process is active. The process then will appear in the instance window.

Report View

The Report view (see Figure 20.5) is a snapshot tool that generates an organized report of counter values. The Report view is almost useless when working with real-time activity. When working with recorded data, however, the Report view is a great tool to extract averaged information quickly. Real-time data is displayed on an instantaneous basis, meaning the data collected from the current measurement interval is displayed. Logged data is shown as an average over the selected time window. Therefore, with the Report view, you can see the average levels of counters over a five-minute or five-day period or whatever time frame you specified. The Report view often is used to create quick baselines simply by viewing various time windows from log files. Adding counters to the Report view is just like adding counters to the Chart view. Just select the computer, object, instance, and counter from the Add To Report dialog box. Selected counters are displayed in order of computer, object instance, and counter in an easy-to-read format suitable for printing. The only control in the Report Options dialog box is the measurement interval.

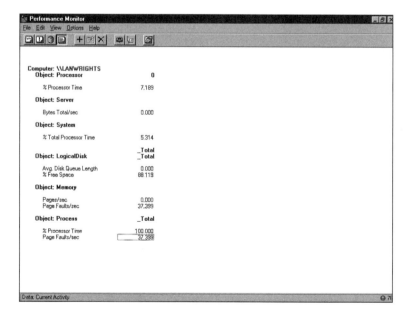

Figure 20.5 Performance Monitor's Report view.

Baselining Revisited

Performance Monitor is your primary tool for recording performance data from which to extract a baseline. Extracting a baseline can be accomplished manually by viewing the log file data in the Chart view. You also can use the Report view to generate averaged values over various time windows. Create a report that includes all the counters that interest you. (Several important counters you might want to include in your reports are examined later in this chapter.) Then define various time intervals to obtain a multiperspective picture of your system's performance. Some suggested time intervals are as follows:

- 5-minute blocks every 30 to 60 minutes
- 30-minute blocks every 1 to 2 hours
- 1-hour blocks every 2 to 4 hours
- 6-hour blocks
- 24-hours blocks
- full-week blocks

Viewing your report for each of these intervals gives you plenty of information about the average or normal activity of your system. This information is the baseline. All future measurements should be compared to this to determine whether performance has improved or degraded.

You should update your baseline regularly. If your system changes frequently, your update time frame can be short (such as every month). If your system changes very little over time, your update time frame can be longer (such as every quarter or six months). As your network grows and evolves, its performance will change. You need to be aware of these changes and their magnitude. Each time you create a new baseline, take the time to compare it to your last baseline. This helps identify the areas of a system where performance problems are most likely to occur. The areas with the most change (toward higher loads or slower performance) often are candidates for future problems.

If you don't know where to start in creating a baseline, start with recording log files for the following objects: Memory, Processor, System, Network Segment, Network Interface, LogicalDisk, and PhysicalDisk. Using these object-level log files and the counter-specific information later in this chapter, you'll have a solid basis from which to design your own system-specific baseline.

Bottlenecks

A *bottleneck* is a component in a computer system that is preventing some other part of the system from operating at its optimum performance level. A bottleneck does not necessarily refer to components operating at 100 percent of their capability. It is possible for components operating at only 60 percent to slow down other components. Bottlenecks can never be fully eliminated; there always is a slowest or limiting component. The goal of removing bottlenecks is to attempt to make the user the most significant bottleneck rather than having a computer component be the bottleneck. This way, the system will be faster than its user.

Bottleneck discovery and elimination is not an exact science. In fact, it's not even an automated process. Through a comparison between a baseline and current or recorded activity, you'll need to decipher the clues that might indicate a bottleneck. The "Key Objects and Counters" section later in this chapter discusses several counters and common values that can indicate a bottleneck.

Every system is different. You'll need to use the methods discussed in this chapter and learn to apply them to your own unique situation. A measurement value that indicates a bottleneck on one system might not be a bottleneck on another. Typically, you want to look for areas of your computer that are operating outside of your normal baseline measurements or that are affecting other components adversely. After you've identified a trouble spot, you'll need to take action in software configuration or hardware replacement to improve the performance of the suspect area.

Don't just look for low-throughput measurements. Other common tell-tale signs of bottlenecks include long task queues, resource request patterns, task frequency, task duration, task failures, retransmissions or re-requests, and system interrupts. With a little practice and by using some of our suggestions, you are sure to get a feel for bottleneck discovery.

Special Issues

Performance Monitor is able to extract performance data from most objects by default. There are three specific objects native to Windows NT that are not enabled or present by default. They are the Disk, Network Segment, and Network Interface objects.

The disk objects—PhysicalDisk and LogicalDisk—are present but are disabled by default. When these objects are enabled, they add additional workload to the disk subsystem, even when measurements are not being taken by Performance Monitor. Although the effect typically is negligible, we recommend turning these objects on only when recording measurements—then turn them back off. The **diskperf -y** command issued from a command prompt enables the disk objects after a reboot. Similarly, the **diskperf -n** command disables the disk objects after a reboot. When the disk objects are disabled, they only return a value of zero.

 RAID
If you are using RAID, you need to use **diskperf -ye** to accurately monitor the disks in an array.

The Network Segment object is present in Performance Monitor only when the Network Monitor Agent is installed. You can install this software component from the Services tab of the Network applet. It is used by both Performance Monitor and Network Monitor. On Windows NT Server systems, be sure to install the Network Monitor Tools and Agent rather than the Network Monitor Agent. Otherwise, the Network Monitor tool itself will not be installed. When Performance Monitor obtains measurements from the Network Segment object, it places the NIC into promiscuous mode. Therefore, you should avoid reading from the Network Segment object (except when necessary) because this causes a significant performance degradation.

The Network Interface object is added to a system using the TCP/IP protocol when the SNMP Service is installed. The SNMP Service is installed from the Services tab of the Network applet. This object is used to obtain data about the network communications over NICs.

Key Objects and Counters

Here are some subsystem-specific objects and counters with typical measurements of which you should be aware. Keep in mind that this list does not contain all possible bottleneck identifiers, nor do the discussed values necessarily indicate a bottleneck on your system. If you are unsure of what is normal on your system, the details in these sections will be of little use to you. You cannot properly evaluate your system without a baseline.

Memory Object

The Windows NT memory system is based on the concept of virtual memory. The physical RAM is combined with space from a swap file stored on the hard disk to provide plenty of accessible memory. The Virtual Memory Manager (VMM) from Executive Services manages the swapping of pages in and out of RAM. Because disk systems often are 10,000 times slower than physical RAM, the goal of memory management is to reduce the occurrence of paging as much as possible. This most often is accomplished by installing enough RAM so that the foreground application does not cause paging.

You need to watch your memory performance for two situations. First, watch for when memory is a bottleneck (meaning when the CPU and other components wait on memory before they can accomplish a task). Second, watch for abnormal virtual memory performance. This means watching out for a constant high level of page faults.

> **Measuring Objects**
> When measuring an object, try to record or obtain the measurements by a pathway other than over the object being measured. Don't record a log file to the same drive being measured, for example, and don't obtain network performance information remotely over the same interface transmitting the data.

Memory bottlenecks can easily be discovered by watching counters for the following objects:

- **Memory: Pages Input/sec.** When this counter remains at a low value (2 or less), it indicates that all operations are occurring within physical RAM. This means that paging is not occurring and therefore is not the cause of the performance degradation.
- **LogicalDisk: % Disk Time and Processor: % Processor Time.** These and other percent-active or utilization measurements will remain low even during high-work operations and tasks.

When both of these conditions are met, the physical RAM of your system is suspect. Most likely, it is too slow for your system and the services hosted by your system.

Virtual memory–related bottlenecks also are easily revealed. They involve watching for hard page faults. A *hard page fault* is when a requested memory page must be moved from the swap file to physical RAM. A high level of hard page faults degrades system performance. *Soft page faults* occur when the requested memory page already is in physical RAM. The three counters used to determine the level of hard page faults are as follows:

- **Memory: Page Faults/sec.** Measures the number of page faults (hard and soft) per second.
- **Memory: Pages Input/sec.** Measures the number of pages read from the disk every second (hard page faults). This counter measures pages read, not disk accesses.
- **Memory: Page Reads/sec.** Measures the number of disk reads per second involved in hard paging. This counter measures disk accesses, not individual pages read.

Add all these counters to the Chart view (either from the current activity or a log file). Look at the lines for Page Faults and Pages Input. Where these two lines intersect, the VMM is reading a page from the swap file (a hard page). Compare the values of Pages Input and Page Reads. Where these two lines intersect, one page is read per disk access. When there is space between the two lines, there are multiple page reads per disk access.

Excessive hard paging occurs when more than 20 percent of the total number of page faults result in a disk access (Pages Input/Page Faults). A consistent level of Page Reads above 5 also indicates excessive hard paging.

Another method to determine whether virtual memory is a bottleneck is through examining the amount of disk time consumed by page faults. When more than 10 percent of disk activity is due to page faults, you need to adjust your system (such as adding more physical RAM). Use the following counters to determine the portion of disk activity used by paging:

- **LogicalDisk: Avg. Disk Read Queue Length: _Total.** Measures the average number of disk tasks waiting to be processed. A consistent value of 2 or greater indicates a bottleneck.

- **LogicalDisk: Disk Reads/sec: _Total.** Measures the number of disk reads per second.

Too little physical RAM causes excessive paging. This is evident by a lengthy disk queue and by the amount of disk time used by paging (Memory: Page Reads/sec and LogicalDisk: Disk Reads/sec). If more than 10 percent of active disk time is caused by paging, your system needs more physical RAM.

A third method to detect virtual memory problems is to monitor the usage of the paging file (swap file). As more memory space is needed, Windows NT uses more disk space to store memory pages. The paging file can grow until the limit defined in the System applet is reached or until all available disk space is used. You can monitor the size of the paging file by viewing the Process: Page File Bytes counter. If the paging file is reaching its maximum size, your system needs either more physical RAM or a larger swap file.

To eliminate virtual memory bottlenecks, you can take several actions. The following list of suggestions is in recommended trial order:

1. Define a larger maximum swap file size.
2. Use multiple fast drives to host the swap file.
3. Use only required applications and services to reduce memory usage.
4. Install faster RAM.
5. Install more RAM.
6. Install a faster drive subsystem (controller card and drives) to host the swap file.

Processor Object

The processor, or CPU, is the core of a computer. Every transaction of data and every calculation is made by or through the processor. It is important to maintain a system in which the CPU is not a bottleneck. Before you can determine that the CPU is not a bottleneck, you need to check memory, applications, and disk subsystems.

You can identify processor bottlenecks using the following counters:

- **Processor: % Processor Time.** Measures the time the CPU is actively processing nonidle work. Although this counter often peaks around 100 percent, it should not remain above 90 percent on a consistent basis.

- **Processor: % Total Processor Time.** Provides the same type of information as the preceding counter but for multiprocessor systems.

- **System: Processor Queue Length.** Measures the number of threads waiting for CPU execution time. A consistent value of 2 or greater indicates the CPU cannot keep up with tasks.

CPU bottleneck removal often is an expensive task. You can try several actions, however, before replacing the CPU. The following is a list of suggestions:

- Remove all screen savers that are graphics intensive.

- Reduce the number of large applications (that is, move heavy apps to other systems).

- Reduce the execution priority of unimportant processes.

- Add an L2 or secondary cache.

- Upgrade older motherboards.

- Install a faster CPU. (This might require replacing the motherboard and memory.)

- Install a second (or third or fourth) CPU.

Disk Objects

Disk bottlenecks center around the speed at which data is written to and read from storage devices. When the disk subsystem is operating slowly, the entire computer's performance suffers. Because Windows NT relies on hard drive space for virtual memory management, a fast disk subsystem often is a significant speed improvement throughout a system.

The two disk objects in Performance Monitor are PhysicalDisk and LogicalDisk. PhysicalDisk focuses on a hard drive as a whole device; LogicalDisk focuses on volumes by drive letter. To obtain readings from either disk object in Performance Monitor, you must use the **diskperf** command to enable them.

Disk bottlenecks are sustained levels of activity for significant periods of time. A % Disk Time value at a consistent level of 85 percent or more might indicate a problem, but this factor should not be considered in isolation. You need to combine it with other symptoms such as an Avg. Disk Queue Length of 2 or more.

Disk bottlenecks most often are eliminated by device replacement, but there are actions you can try to see whether they remedy your disk bottlenecks. The following is a list of suggestions:

- Defragment the drive. Windows NT 4.0 does not include a defragmentation tool, so download a trial version of Symantec's Norton NT Tools Speed Disk (**http://symantec.com/**) or Executive Software's Diskeeper (**http://www.execsoft.com/**).
- Verify that diskperf is turned off when you have completed your performance monitoring.
- Avoid using compression on files and folders that the system, applications, and users often access.
- Install faster drives and drive controllers. This means a new disk subsystem with seek times and transfer rates better than the currently installed set.
- Buy 32-bit or 64-bit bus-mastering drive controller cards.
- Buy drives that employ faster drive technologies (such as UltraDMA or Wide Ultra SCSI).
- Use drive controllers that support asynchronous I/O.
- Install drives on separate controller cards.
- Use RAID to distribute workloads across multiple devices.
- Use hardware-based RAID rather than Windows NT's built-in software RAID.

Network Objects

Network bottlenecks often center around the capability of a computer to send and transmit data—that is, the network interface. Network bottlenecks, however, are not limited to local NIC problems. They also can include server overload (when a system is not responding to requests properly), network overload (when the medium is supporting too much traffic), and data loss (when a physical or configuration problem causes data to be lost or corrupted).

Some general networking problems can be discovered by watching the following counters:

- **Network Interface: Bytes Total /sec.** Measures the traffic load on the NIC. During active use, if this value remains below 75 percent of the device's rated capacity, communication is not occurring as freely as it should.
- **Network Interface: Current Bandwidth.** Measures the current level of available bandwidth. This value will change only on variable bandwidth devices such as modems or other bandwidth-on-demand devices.

- **Network Interface: Output Queue Length.** Measures the number of packets waiting to be processed by the NIC. If this value remains at 2 or higher, your NIC is too slow.

- **Network Segment: % Network utilization.** Measures the amount of bandwidth actually being used for data transmission. If this value remains at 85 percent or greater, your network technology might not be suitable for your level of network activity.

- **Redirector: Server Sessions Hung.** Measures the number of active sessions that have timed out due to failures in communications. This is a cumulative counter. A value of 5 or more within a short time frame (about 4 hours) might indicate a network problem.

- **Redirector: Current Commands.** Measures the number of queued service requests. When this value is more than two times the number of NICs plus two, a network bottleneck exists.

- **Server: Sessions Errored Out.** Measures terminated sessions caused by error conditions or dropped communications. This is a cumulative counter. A value of 5 or more within a few hours might indicate a network problem.

- **Server: Work Item Shortages.** Measures the number of requests that fail because the system is unable to provide resources to handle the task. A value of more than 3 indicates a problem.

Network bottlenecks can be resolved or eliminated in several ways, from modifying your workload to exchanging devices. The following are some suggestions to improve network performance:

- Install only required protocols and services.

- Remove or disable all NICs, protocols, and services not in use.

- Bind the most often used protocols and services in priority on NICs.

- Install more RAM on servers.

- Use the same speed NICs on all network members. The network operates at the speed of the slowest device.

- Use NICs from the same vendor and, if possible, of the same type to maintain a high level of consistency, compatibility, and similarity of performance.

- Use multiple NICs where possible. This requires the installation of a routing protocol such as RIP for IP, RIP for IPX, or even the Routing and Remote Access Service (RRAS) Update.

- Use 32-bit or 64-bit PCI bus-mastering NICs.
- Divide your network into multiple logical segments. Use multihomed servers or routers to enable communication between segments.

Troubleshooting and Tips

Performance Monitor is a good tool, but it does have limitations. You need to be aware of several issues and workarounds to extract the most out of this bundled tool. This section looks at a few troubleshooting issues and some tips for using Performance Monitor.

Process Time Starvation

Performance Monitor, or any other process, can experience process time starvation on active systems. *Process time starvation* is when the process does not receive enough execution time to perform its tasks adequately. For Performance Monitor, this can mean missing data points or providing skewed measurements. You can attempt to track this problem by viewing the Process: % Processor Time, Process: % User Time, and Process: % Privileged Time counters for the starving process. (In the case of Performance Monitor, this is PERFMON.) If these counters do not indicate a level of activity above 1% for an extended period of time, the process is being starved.

If a process is being starved, you must either move that process to a different system or reduce the workload on the current system to enable more CPU time to be obtained. In some cases, just increasing the execution priority of the starved process can help. Because Microsoft built in only four levels of user priority settings out of the 32 possible, however, this offers little hope.

Process and Thread IDs

Performance Monitor reads counters based on their object name. This can cause problems when an object (such as an application or a service) is terminated and another object is launched with the same name. To identify when this problem occurs, add the Process or Thread ID counters. These values are unique between process launches. If the value changes during a monitoring session, you know Performance Monitor is reading data from two (or more) different processes with the same name.

Zero Measurements and Logging

Performance Monitor displays readings of zero for several reasons, including the following:

- Negative differential values
- Disabled counters
- Invalid measurements
- Process or object terminations during measurement
- Measurement read errors

Although Performance Monitor itself cannot display negative or invalid values, these values can be recorded in the Application log. Just edit the Registry and create or change the ReportEventsToEventLog value to 1 in the HKEY_CURRENT_USER\ Software\Microsoft\PerfMon key. You must restart Performance Monitor for this to take effect. Setting the value back to 0 turns off this logging feature.

Performance Monitor errors also can be recorded in the Application log. Just change or add the EventLogLevel value to the HKEY_LOCAL_MACHINE\ Software\Microsoft\WindowsNT\CurrentVersion\Performance Library key. Record such errors with one of the following settings:

- **0:** No logging
- **1:** Errors only (the default value)
- **2:** Errors and warnings
- **3:** Errors, warnings, information, and success and failure conditions

You must restart Performance Monitor for this to take effect.

Multiple Alerts

The Alert view of Performance Monitor is unable to set more than one alert for a given counter. To set multiple alerts, you need to launch multiple instances of Performance Monitor. Each instance of Performance Monitor can have a unique alert defined for the counter or for different instances of that counter. If multiple alerts are set for a counter, only the readings from the first instance are used to test the alert.

Monitoring Remote Machines

If you are monitoring remote machines, you must make this change to the remote machine and then either restart the remote or restart your session with the remote machine.

Windows NT Workstation 4.0 Resource Kit Performance Tools

The Windows NT Resource Kit includes a handful of performance tools that can be used to expand your performance-monitoring capabilities. Most of these tools are for developers or for load-testing a system. You should read the complete documentation included in the Resource Kit for instructions about installation and use of these tools. This brief discussion is included to give you some insight into their existence and to help determine whether these tools can be of use to you.

The Resource Kit performance tools are installed by default into a directory called PERFTOOL off the main Resource Kit installation directory. Within PERFTOOL are seven subdirectories that contain the tools and Help files.

CNTRTOOL is a directory containing counter-related tools including:

- A command-line tool for listing all objects and counters on a system (CTRLIST)

- A Help file that lists and describes most of the objects and counters from Windows NT and many commonly installed Microsoft applications (COUNTERS.HLP)

- A set of configuration files used to quickly monitor IIS performance (WORKSPC)

LOGS is a directory containing sample log files of RAID systems. These log files can be used as a benchmark (or baseline) to compare your own RAID performance.

LOGTOOLS is a directory containing tools focused on logging. The primary utility in this directory is the Performance Data Log Service. This installable service can be used to record performance data from objects and counters directly into a tab-delimited or comma-delimited text file instead of the proprietary Performance Monitor log file format. If you want a quick and simple way to import performance data into a custom application, the Performance Data Log Service is a good tool to use.

MEASTOOL is a directory containing several tools for testing and stressing specific areas of your system. These tools are designed for a development environment (when applications and processes are being constructed) and have only limited use in general performance monitoring. With a little ingenuity, however, you might be able to apply these tools in unique ways. Table 20.1 lists the utilities in this directory.

P5CTRS is a directory containing installable objects that extract special performance information from Pentium CPUs.

PROBE is a directory that contains a system stress tool known as the Response Probe. This tool can be configured to simulate workloads for stress-testing a process or a development environment.

TOTLPROC is a directory containing an add-in counter used to obtain Total Processor Usage statistics from a multi-CPU system as an aggregate measurement.

Table 20.1   **Utilities in the MEASTOOL Directory**

Utility	Explanation
CLEARMEM	A command to force all pages out of memory
CPUSTRES	A tool to push processor usage to 100 percent
DRIVERS	A command to list all loaded device drivers
EMPTY	A command to purge the resource set of a process or task
HEAPMON	A utility to display heap information
KILL	A command to terminate an active process
LEAKYAPP	A tool that consumes memory like a leaky application
PFMON	A tool to monitor page faults
PMON	A tool to display memory statistics
PROFILE	A tool to expose the code segments most often executed from an application
PVIEWER	A tool to view process statistics
TLIST	A tool to list all active processes
VADUMP	A command to list the address space configuration of a process

Other Windows NT Performance Tools

In addition to Performance Monitor itself, you should be aware of a few other performance-related tools and settings within Windows NT. This section discusses these tuning utilities and interfaces.

Task Manager

Almost a mini-Performance Monitor, this tool provides a quick glance into a system's well-being. Task Manager can be accessed by pressing Ctrl+Alt+Delete and selecting Task Manager or by right-clicking the taskbar and selecting Task Manager. There are three tabs: Applications, Processes, and Performance.

The Applications tab lists all active applications, displays status (running/not responding), and enables application termination and new task launching. The Processes tab lists all active processes and their activity metric details. From this tab, you can make process execution priority changes from or to low, normal, high, and real time. You also can make these changes by selecting View, Update Speed. The Performance tab displays CPU and memory usage graphs along with memory, page file, and kernel usage statistics.

Windows NT Diagnostics

The Windows NT Diagnostics tool contains a multitabbed dialog box that lists the configuration specifics for many areas of Windows NT. This interface offers an easy-to-locate storehouse of information about the OS version, system hardware, video, drives, memory, services, system resources, environment, and the network. This tool most often is used to determine whether IRQs or I/O address space is available for new devices before they are installed. This utility can be used on remote machines and can print a detailed report about your system. This is very helpful when you want a cursory view of a system's configuration.

Virtual Memory Management

You can access the virtual memory settings for Windows NT by clicking the Virtual Memory button in the Performance tab of the System applet. This interface controls the size and placement of the swap file. The swap file is placed by default on the same volume that hosts the main Windows directory and is created as 12MB larger than the amount of physical RAM.

To set the paging file to 0 on the main Windows directory host drive, you must deselect all the Recovery settings (except for Reboot) from the Startup/Shutdown tab of the System applet. Even if the page file is never used, Windows NT requires that a 2MB minimum page file exist somewhere.

At the bottom of the Virtual Memory dialog box is the setting for maximum size of the Registry. This defines how much of the Registry can be loaded into memory at any given time, not how large the Registry is as whole. The default value of 13MB is sufficient for most systems except Windows NT Server PDC and BDCs. This is because the SAM must always be loaded into RAM on a domain controller, and it is pulled from the machine's Registry.

Network Monitor

Network Monitor is a Windows NT Server tool used to capture network communication packets. This tool cannot be installed on Windows NT Workstation. Network Monitor is a simple packet capture and examination utility. The version of Network Monitor that ships with Windows NT Server has a significant limitation in that it only can capture packets that are either inbound or outbound of the local network interface. If you have SMS, however, it includes a full version of Network Monitor that enables you to put agents on other subnets and to monitor them as well as any local NICs.

In Windows NT Server, Network Monitor is installed through the Services tab of the Network applet as Network Monitor Tools and Agent. Once installed, it can be launched from the Start menu (Start, Programs, Administrative Tools [Common], Network Monitor). The main display window of Network Monitor is divided into four panes: graph, session stats, station stats, and total stats. Within each pane, real-time statistics and other information about the current capture session are recorded and displayed.

The basic functions and menu commands of Network Monitor are self-explanatory. If you need help deciphering a window or a command, the online Help system is more than adequate. To start a capture, for example, issue the Start command from the Capture menu or click the Start Capture button on the toolbar. (This button looks like the play button on a VCR.)

You can view data packets captured by Network Monitor. This means you can inspect the contents of the packets—down to individual bytes—by using the Display Captured Data command. Every packet is listed in order of capture. Each packet can be inspected to reveal its complete header and content information.

The use of filters can reduce the amount of data captured. Capture filters select packets to capture based on protocol, address, or data pattern match. Using capture filters can simplify the task of locating information in a sea of network traffic. A capture filter is a multibranched logical decision tree. Any packet that meets all the requirements of the filter is captured in the buffer. All others are discarded. Capture filters are created using the design interface accessed with the Capture, Filter command.

Network Monitor captures packets into physical RAM only. This requires that a section of physical RAM be designated for the capture buffer. By default, only 1MB is designated for the capture buffer. Using the Buffer command in the Capture menu, you can increase this to 8MB less than the total amount of RAM installed in the system. In this same dialog box, you can limit the size of each packet stored in memory from 64 bytes to the entire packet to further improve the amount of useful data captured in the buffer.

You must always start capture sessions manually, but they can be terminated automatically. Such an event is called a capture trigger. A *capture trigger* is a defined set of circumstances for which Network Monitor watches. When they occur, the defined action is taken. The trigger event can be the percentage of buffer-storing captured packets, the existence of a matched pattern in a captured packet, or both. After the trigger event occurs, Network Monitor can stop the capture and can execute a command line (to launch an application or run a script).

When viewing captured packets, you can use a display filter to reduce data further. A *display filter* acts much like a capture filter except it simply prevents unqualified packets from being displayed. They are retained in the capture buffer. Using a decision tree interface once again, a display filter is built to sort captured packets by address, protocol type, and protocol property.

The benefits of Network Monitor are only as significant as your knowledge of protocols and network technologies. In other words, Network Monitor gives you direct insight into the communications on your network. Without knowledge about what that communication means and how to look for problems, however, the capability is

worthless. Detailed protocol examination is beyond the scope of this book, but there
are plenty of great resources upon which you can draw. In addition to the Microsoft
material available from the online Knowledge Base and Support Web site
(`http://support.microsoft.com/`) and TechNet (`http://technet.microsoft.com/`), a
few great books on this subject are listed in the "For More Information" section at the
end of this chapter.

Using Network Monitor in more general endeavors is possible without too much in-
depth protocol knowledge. The following are several uses for Network Monitor:

- Detecting and locating broadcast/multicast storms.

- Detecting NIC bottlenecks through a steady increase in # Frames Dropped statistics in the Stats pane.

- Creating a list of active IP addresses. Capturing TCP packets and manually
  extracting the IP destination and source addresses from the headers. Comparing
  this list with the known active list to locate spoofs, unauthorized systems, and
  misconfigured devices.

- Tracking Internet application protocols by capturing TCP packets. Manually creating a list of the application/service protocols from the Source Port field from
  each packet.

- Detecting traffic bypassing your firewall and proxy servers by capturing traffic
  and examining the source and destination addresses. Every packet should have a
  firewall/proxy server interface address for its source or destination address.

Network Monitor is a Windows NT Server-based tool that can often prove itself
invaluable when locating packet-level information or problems.

Monitoring Tools

The Windows NT Resource Kit does not include any add-ons or other utilities that
can be used directly with Network Monitor. There are, however, a handful of other
useful tools that fall into a similar category as Network Monitor.

The first tool is Browser Monitor (BROWMON), which gives you a GUI insight
into the world of the browser service. With BROWMON, you can see the current status of master, backup, and potential browsers. To improve the performance of the
browser service, try the following:

- Disable PDC and BDC from being a master browser (that is, set
  MaintainServerList to No).

- Disable all nonpermanent servers and clients from being a master browser (that
  is, set MaintainServerList to No).

- Designate the least active permanent server as the master browser (that is, set
  MaintainServerList to Yes).

Another tool is the Domain Monitor (DOMMON). This tool displays the status of servers within a domain and in trust relationships with other domains. This is a great tool for determining whether a trust is active.

Network Watcher (NETWATCH) is similar to Server Monitor. It displays a list of shared folders by computer and the users connected to those shares.

The last tool worth mentioning in this area is Server Info (SRVINFO). This command-line tool reveals status information such as active services, storage drives, up time, active protocols, and more.

Third-Party Performance and Network Monitoring Tools

Most of the third-party commercial utilities aimed at monitoring and tuning general and network performance have two common problems. First, they focus on Windows NT Server as a network host instead of Windows NT Workstation as a client or stand-alone system. Second, they often are very expensive. When it comes to commercial software, little is offered that Performance Monitor does not already include. You might want to explore the shareware and freeware utilities, however, that might offer capabilities not even the commercial products include.

There is a wide variety of performance and monitoring software. Determining which product is best for you is often more difficult than locating them in the first place. When possible, take the time to read as much documentation about the product as possible. Next, download available demos and trial versions before making a decision and laying out the cash. You also should solicit advise from other users. This can be done over the public newsgroups, the Microsoft-hosted NNTP news server (**msnews.microsoft.com**), or one of several software distribution sites. The following are several Web sites that should be included in your search for software of any type:

- **SERVERxtras.** As a quarterly publication and a Web site, SERVERxtras provides reviews of software and an online store. It has a great search engine to help you locate software of any type quickly. All the software reviews are written by industry professionals. You can find more information at `http://www.serverxtras.com/`.

- **Beverly Hills Software (BHS).** This is a clearinghouse of Windows NT information and software. It is a great place to read peer reviews of software and to obtain technical recommendations from experts. You can find more information at `http://www.bhs.com/`.

- *Windows NT Magazine.* This solid technical magazine offers as much value online as it does on the newsstand. If you are looking for product reviews and information about new technology, this is your source. You can find more information at `http://www.winntmag.com/`.

- *Windows NT Systems.* This is another solid reference magazine to find resources for Windows NT professionals. You can find more information at `http://www.ntsystems.com/`.

Here is a list of performance-related software. Each of these Web sites includes detailed information about the product, and most offer a downloadable trial version.

- PerfMan from The Information Systems Manager, Inc.: `http://www.infosysman.com/`
- PerformanceWorks from Landmark Systems Corporation: `http://www.landmark.com/`
- NetTUNE PRO from BMC Software: `http://www.bmc.com/`
- TME 10 NetFinity from Tivoli (an IBM company): `http://www.tivoli.com/`
- Capacity Planner for Windows NT from Digital Equipment Corp.: `http://www.digital.com/capacity/`
- Observer from Network Instruments, LLC: `http://www.networkinstruments.com/`
- LanExplorer by IntelliMax: `http://www.intellimax.com`
- EtherPeek from The AG Group, Inc.: `http://www.aggroup.com/`
- NTManage from LANWARE, Inc.: `http://www.lanware.net/`
- NetMetrix/Win from Hewlett-Packard Co.: `http://www.hp.com/`
- ForeView from FORE Systems, Inc.: `http://www.fore.com/`
- ClearStats from GulfBay Network Systems, Inc.: `http://www.clearstats.com/`
- AlertPage Enterprise from Geneva Software/Denmac Systems: `http://www.genevasoft.com/`
- EventMon from First Chair Technologies: `http://www.first-chair.com/`
- TrendTrak from Intrak Inc.: `http://www.intrack.com/`
- AutoPilot from Sunbelt Software: `http://www.sunbelt-software.com/`
- Alert! and Uptime Monitor for Windows NT from MiraLink: `http://www.miralink.com/`

Performance tools are not just available as typical commercial products. Many shareware and freeware tools offer amazingly useful features and functions. Many of these tools can be found by using your favorite shareware search engine (such as **www.shareware.com**). To give you a head start in locating some of the better options, however, take a look at the System Internals Web site and the book *Optimizing Windows NT* (see the reference at the end of the chapter).

System Internals is a Windows NT resource center maintained by Mark Russinovich and Bryce Cogswell. These two men designed and created all the software on this site. If you've not visited the System Internals Web site (`http://www.sysinternals.com/`) it's about time you did. These descriptions are pulled directly from the System Internals Web site for accuracy. All copyrights are maintained by System Internals.

Some of the utilities available include:

- **ListDLLs.** Lists all the DLLs that are currently loaded including where they are loaded and their version numbers. Version 2.0 prints the full path names of loaded modules.

- **Handle.** This handy command-line utility shows you what files are open by which processes and much more.

- **Regmon for Windows NT.** This is a GUI/device driver combo that uses a technique developed by Russinovich and Cogswell, kernel-mode system call hooking, to watch all Registry-related activity.

- **Filemon for Windows NT.** This is a Windows NT GUI/device driver program that layers itself above all the file systems on a system in order to watch all file system activity.

- **Diskmon.** This is a GUI/device driver program that watches all hard disk activity.

- **Pmon.** This is a Windows NT GUI/device driver program that watches process and thread creation and deletion as well as context swaps if running on a multi-processing or checked kernel.

- **CPUMon.** Use this advanced tool to read the performance counters of Pentium, Pentium Pro, and Pentium II processors. Not for the faint of heart, CPUMon is intended for those with a good familiarity of processor architecture.

- **Contig.** Wish you could quickly defragment your frequently used files? Use Contig to optimize individual files or to create new files that are contiguous.

- **CacheSet.** CacheSet is a program that allows you to control the Cache Manager's working set size using functions provided by Windows NT. It's compatible with all versions of Windows NT and full source code is provided.

- **NTFSDOS Tools.** This NTFSDOS add-on provides NTFSDOS with limited rename and file overwrite capability aimed at disaster recovery.

- **NTFSDOS 2.0R+.** This is the long-awaited release of NTFSDOS V2.0. It contains significant enhancements and bug fixes over the previous release, V1.3. Plus, NTFSDOS Tools, an add-on kit that provides limited write capability for disaster recovery, is available.

- **Undelete for Windows NT.** It works just like Recycle Bin but tracks files deleted from the command prompt or from inside of programs in case you need to recover them. Download a free trial version!

- **Sync.** Forces Windows NT to flush all modified file system data to disk, ensuring that it will be safe in the face of a crash.

For More Information

- The TechNet technical subscription service from Microsoft: `http://technet.microsoft.com/`

- Microsoft Knowledge Base: `http://support.microsoft.com/`

- Edmead, Mark T. and Paul Hinsberg. *Windows NT Performance: Monitoring, Benchmarking, and Tuning*. New Riders, 1998. ISBN 1562059424.

- Gardiner, Kenton. *Windows NT Performance Tuning & Optimization*. Osborne/McGraw-Hill, 1998. ISBN 0078824966.

- Daily, Sean. *Optimizing Windows NT*. IDG Books, 1998. ISBN 0764531107.

- Bisaillon, Teresa and Brad Werner. *TCP/IP with Windows NT Illustrated*. Osborne/McGraw-Hill, 1998. ISBN: 0079136486.

- Chappell, Laura. *Novell's Guide to LAN/WAN Analysis: IPX/SPX*. IDG Books Worldwide, 1998. ISBN: 0764545086.

- Dickie, Mark. *Routing in Today's Internetworks: The Routing Protocols of IP, Decnet, NetWare, and AppleTalk*. John Wiley & Sons, 1997. ISBN: 0471286206.

21

Managing Applications

WINDOWS NT VERSION 4.0 IS A 32-bit operating system that provides a fast, reliable, multitasking environment. Windows NT supports preemptive multitasking and the execution of applications in separate address spaces. Windows 3.x used cooperative multitasking that allowed applications to control how long they had access to the CPU. In preemptive multitasking, the operating system controls which application has access to the CPU, and for how long. The operating system is free to switch resources at any time to an application with a higher priority. This also allows the operating system to revoke resources from a defective or a poorly designed program that tries to hog resources.

Windows NT also uses multithreading, the operating system's capability to support multiple units of execution for a single process. In a multithreaded environment, a process can be broken up into subtasks, called *threads*, which can execute independently of the main process. This allows a program to perform multiple tasks simultaneously instead of sequentially. For example, when you are using Microsoft Outlook 98, you can read messages or create a new message while downloading new messages or sending messages. Multithreading means one process does not have to wait for another to finish.

Windows NT also allows users to run their favorite applications written for MS-DOS, Windows, and other operating systems. In this chapter, we briefly discuss how Windows NT handles different types of applications and provide tips on how to run your applications more efficiently.

Windows Environment Subsystems

One of the principal features of Windows NT is its capability to execute applications written for other operating systems by means of its built-in environment subsystems. The environment subsystems can run applications written for several operating systems by emulating those operating systems. Windows NT accomplishes this by translating the applications' native instructions into instructions that the Windows NT Executive can understand. Windows NT 4.0 ships with the following environment subsystems:

- Win32
- VDMs
- Win16
- WOW
- POSIX
- OS/2

POSIX and OS/2 applications are scarce, so we concentrate on the Win32 subsystem.

Win32

The primary application environment for Windows NT is Win32, which supports 32-bit Windows applications. In this environment, each Win32 application runs in its own 2GB virtual address space. This provides protection from other applications, so that a bad application does not affect other applications. The Win32 environment is not only responsible for handling Win32 applications, it is also the host, or interface, which manages the keyboard, mouse, and display for the entire system. All other environments, including MS-DOS and Win16, send their operating system tasks and messages through Win32 for processing by the kernel (see Figure 21.1). We discuss two of the environments, Win16 (WOW) and VDM, in this chapter.

VDMs

Windows NT provides support for MS-DOS applications in an environment called an NT Virtual MS-DOS Machine (NTVDM), a Win32 application that looks like MS-DOS. Because it is a Win32 application, NTVDM can be preemptively multitasked just like any other Win32 application. NTVDM provides a simulated MS-DOS 5.0 environment for MS-DOS applications. Each MS-DOS program has its own VDM, a necessity because MS-DOS programs expect to have full and exclusive use of all system resources.

> **Windows NT Executive**
>
> For more information about the Windows NT Executive, refer to the "Windows NT Architecture" section in Chapter 1, "Introducing Windows NT."

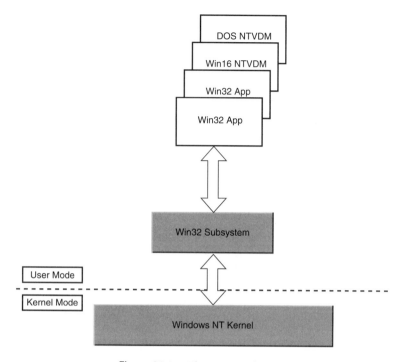

Figure 21.1 The Win32 subsystem.

NTVDM acts as a wrapper around the MS-DOS application and simulates PC hardware by providing Virtual Device Drivers (VDDs). Because Windows NT does not allow programs to access the hardware directly, the VDDs intercept the hardware calls from the MS-DOS applications and pass the equivalent 32-bit instruction to the Windows NT device drivers. The VDDs allow most, but not all, MS-DOS applications to run on Windows NT. The exceptions are applications that directly communicate with hardware (such as scanners or fax cards), applications that directly communicate with disk drivers (such as disk maintenance software), and applications that use their own graphics device drivers to communicate with the hardware.

PIFs

To configure MS-DOS applications to run more efficiently (or to run at all) you configure the settings of the VDM using the application's Program Information File (PIF). To create and modify PIFs from Windows Explorer or My Computer, right-click the application filename and select Properties (see Figure 21.2). Change the Run properties on the Program tab to specify whether an MS-DOS program starts in a full screen or in a window. (Note that some MS-DOS programs cannot run in a window.) Windows NT also supports terminate-and-stay-resident (TSR) programs running in an MS-DOS session. You can create a custom batch file that starts the TSR without adding the memory-resident program to the AUTOEXEC.NT or CONFIG.NT files. If the memory-resident program is added to one of the configuration files, additional copies of the program start every time you open the command-prompt window.

Figure 21.2 MS-DOS PIF Program tab.

Windows NT PIFs are similar to the PIF used with Windows 3.x, except that the Windows NT PIF allows you to specify a custom AUTOEXEC or CONFIG file. Doing this allows you to add parameters or device drivers that apply only to a particular program. Windows NT supports the following commands from MS-DOS 5.0:

- CALL
- ECHO
- ENDLOCAL
- FOR
- GOTO
- IF
- PAUSE
- REM
- SETLOCAL
- SHIFT

Any unsupported commands are ignored.

Checking the Compatible Timer Hardware checkbox reduces the rate at which the computer's timer sends timer signals. This is used mostly for games because a lot of them use timing loops instead of interrupts to control timing. Unfortunately, running an application when this box is checked could hurt performance because Windows NT must spend additional time processing the application's needs.

The PIF file has a number of memory configuration options. You can configure your MS-DOS application to use conventional; EM; XMS, with or without HM; and DPMI (see Figure 21.3).

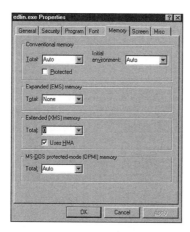

Figure 21.3 MS-DOS PIF Memory tab.

- **Conventional Memory.** Usually, setting this option to Auto is fine. Selecting the Protected checkbox, on the other hand, allows some applications to run, but it also prevents Windows NT from moving applications around in memory. Some applications that access memory directly need this kind of protection. The downside of checking this box is that a fixed session in memory always increases memory fragmentation and the chance that you will artificially run out of memory.

- **Initial Environment.** This option specifies the number of bytes of memory reserved for the command interpreter and is equivalent to the /p switch in MS-DOS. If this configuration is set to Auto, the initial size of the environment is determined by the SHELL= line in your CONFIG.NT file. Some applications need a specified amount of time.

- **Expanded (EMS) Memory.** This option specifies the maximum amount of expanded memory (in kilobytes) to be allocated to the program. Usually, setting this to Auto is fine.

- **Extended (XMS) Memory.** This option specifies the maximum amount of extended memory (in kilobytes) to allocate to the program. Usually, setting this to Auto is fine.

- **MS-DOS Protected-Mode (DPMI) Memory.** This option specifies the maximum amount of MS-DOS protected-mode (DPMI) memory (in kilobytes) to allocate to the program. Usually, setting this to Auto is fine.

If there is no PIF file set up for an application, Windows NT always uses the settings in the DEFAULT.PIF file by default. In most cases, this is fine. However, if you create an application-specific PIF file and set any memory entries you do not need to None, this conserves system memory and allows Windows NT to provide better services to the rest of the applications on your machine.

There are several options for displaying your MS-DOS application. You can configure the application to display in a window or full-screen and configure the number of lines displayed (see Figure 21.4). When the application is displayed in a window, you have the further options of having the MS-DOS toolbar displayed and of restoring any changes that you make to the window size, position, and fonts when the application is restarted.

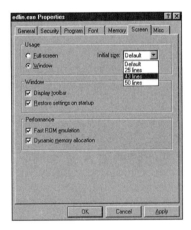

Figure 21.4   MS-DOS PIF: Screen tab.

Setting No Limit

If you set Expanded (EMS), Extended (XMS), or DPMI to Auto, no limit is imposed. If your program has difficulty coping with no limit, set the value to 8192.

Native Performance

In full-screen mode, most applications can run with native performance because they do not have to be virtualized to run within a window.

Two settings control display performance. Selecting the Fast ROM Emulation check-box usually causes applications to write to the screen faster. Disable this setting if you experience problems with the application writing text to the screen. The Dynamic memory allocation setting maximizes the amount of memory available to other applications when you are running an application that switches between text and graphic modes. When the application switches to text mode, which generally requires less memory, more memory becomes available to other applications. Disable this setting for most games. Both settings are enabled by default.

The Misc tab contains the settings that do not fit anywhere else, including options for shortcut keys, the mouse, and screen savers. The two most important are the Background and Idle Sensitivity settings. The Background option prevents any system resources from being used by the application when it is not in the foreground. The Background option is the default, but should not be used with any time-sensitive applications, such as a communications program.

Many MS-DOS applications use keyboard loops. The application runs in a loop while waiting for keyboard input. Looping requires system resources, but was not a problem in the MS-DOS environment with only one application running; however, this can be an extreme drain on system resources in a multitasking environment. The Idle Sensitivity setting determines how long the application can remain idle before Windows NT reduces the CPU resources allotted to the application. Setting Idle Sensitivity to Low lets the application run longer before the CPU resources allotted to it are reduced. The default of Medium is fine in most cases, but sometimes under the default, Windows does not give the application sufficient resources to complete a task. This is especially true with communications applications and certain games. If this happens, lowering the Idle Sensitivity setting causes the application to run better (see Figure 21.5).

Figure 21.5   MS-DOS PIF Misc tab.

The Warn If Still Active checkbox in the Termination group displays a message if you try to close the MS-DOS application window or do a system shutdown without first ending the program. This should remain selected for any program that can potentially lose data if not ended properly.

Note on BIOS Shadowing

Many machines have the option to shadow the system or other BIOS to memory. *Shadowing* is the process of copying the BIOS from slow ROM into fast RAM and remapping the address space. Although this provides a noticeable speed increase with MS-DOS, it is not necessary with Windows NT. Windows NT uses the BIOS only during startup. Therefore, it is advisable to turn off BIOS shadowing with Windows NT because it results in slightly more memory being available to the operating system.

Win16 (WOW)

A Win32 application referred to as Win16 on Win32, or Windows on Windows (WOW) provides support for Windows 3.x applications. Like MS-DOS applications, Windows 3.x applications are supported by Windows NT in an environment called an NT Virtual MS-DOS Machine (NTVDM). Because the NTVDM is a Win32 application, it is preemptively multitasked just as with any other Win32 application. The Windows emulator, WOWEXEC.EXE, runs in an NTVDM and simulates the Windows 3.x environment. All Windows 3.x applications run in this environment by default, and Windows 3.x applications are cooperatively multitasked within this environment and share the same address space.

Running all Windows 3.x applications in the same VDM provides maximum compatibility with the native Windows 3.x environment. Unfortunately, just as with Windows 3.x, if an application fails or behaves improperly, it can affect all of the other applications running in the same NTVDM. The WOW VDM has the same weaknesses as Windows 3.x. It allows Windows 3.x applications to access memory that belongs to other Windows 3.x applications or to WOW, with potentially disastrous effects. It also allows a single Windows 3.x application that does not yield control of the processor to effectively crash all other Windows 3.x applications. A crashed Windows 3.x application does not affect the other VDMs, nor does it affect applications running under other subsystems.

Default Settings
The settings you specify are used each time you start the application by double-clicking its icon. If you start the application from a Command Prompt window, the settings from _DEFAULT.PIF will be used.

Windows 3.x and WOW
In some cases under Windows NT, a Windows 3.x application that fails will crash the WOW session and not permit any Windows 3.x applications to run until the entire Windows NT system is shut down and restarted.

Fortunately, Windows NT provides a way for you to run a Windows 3.x application in its own WOW session, allowing Windows NT to run the application as a separate process without affecting other Windows 3.x applications. To run a Windows 3.x application in its own WOW session, modify the application's shortcut. From the Shortcut tab, enable the Run In Separate Memory Space checkbox. You can also use the Run command to run a Windows 3.x application in its own WOW session (see the section "Using the Run Command to the Max" later in this chapter).

Running Windows 3.x applications in their own VDMs keeps faulty applications from affecting other Windows 3.x applications, allowing the Windows 3.x applications to be preemptively multitasked. Each application is treated as a separate Win32 application. On a multiprocessor machine, this allows multiple Windows 3.x applications to run on separate processors. This is not possible when they are running in a shared session because that session is confined to one processor. The disadvantage is the additional overhead due to starting an additional NTVDM. This is a minimum of approximately 2MB of page file space and 1MB of system memory per session.

The Windows NT default is for all Windows 3.x applications to share the same address space and run in one WOW session. You can change this default behavior so that each Windows 3.x application runs in a separate address space. To do this, change the Registry key HKEY_LOCAL_MACHINE\SYSTEM\CurrentControlSet\Control\WOW\DefaultSeparateVDM to Yes.

Because the MS-DOS and WOW VDMs are essentially just Win32 applications running in their own address space, Windows NT allows MS-DOS and Windows 3.x applications to be isolated from other Win32 applications. This isolation provides a high degree of reliability, ensuring that an errant MS-DOS or Windows 3.x application has no effect on other Win32 applications.

VxDs

Windows NT does not support Windows 3.x virtual device drivers (VxDs) running in a VDM. Therefore, any applications that require VxDs, some multimedia applications and games, do not run under Windows NT.

Understanding Foreground Priority

In a preemptive multitasking system, individual tasks cannot dictate how long they use the system resources. This means that some type of priority system is necessary to ensure that critical tasks get a larger share of the processor's time. The priority system is part of the operating system, but the individual tasks can tell the OS what priority they need. This works well in theory, but there are always situations in which a system might get loaded with high-priority tasks and keep the low-priority tasks from getting any system resources at all. This is one of the problems that can happen in a *static* priority system.

Windows NT 4.0 uses a *dynamic* priority system that allows it to adjust the priority of tasks to reflect constantly changing system conditions. For example, if a low-priority task is passed over in favor of a high-priority task, Windows NT increases the priority of the low-priority task until it gets some system resources. After a high-priority task runs, Windows NT lowers that task's priority. The dynamic priority system ensures that some tasks get more system resources than others and that every task gets at least some system resources.

A *foreground* application is one that is made active by selecting it on the Windows NT desktop, thus bringing it to the foreground. All other applications running are then termed *background* applications with respect to the foreground application. By default, Windows NT runs a foreground application with a longer timeslice than any background applications in the same priority class.

To change the default behavior, open the System applet in the Control Panel (see Figure 21.6). From the Performance tab, you can change the responsiveness of applications that are running simultaneously. The default is Maximum, in which the foreground priority is two points higher than the background priority. The Intermediate selection runs foreground applications at one point higher and the None selection runs all applications at the same priority.

Performance Tab

When some database applications are installed on Windows NT Server, they reset the Performance setting to None, so that these applications are not CPU starved by foreground processes.

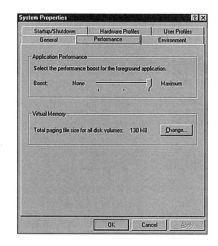

Figure 21.6   System applet Performance tab.

Managing Application Priority

As explained in the previous section, Windows NT can distribute processing time by
prioritizing applications. Priority levels are assigned numbers from 0 to 31; applications
and non-critical operating system functions are assigned levels of 0 to 15. Real-time
applications such as the kernel, which cannot be written to the page file, are assigned
levels of 16 to 31. The normal base priority is level 8.

The 32 priority levels that Windows NT supports are divided into two classes: a
real-time class and a dynamic-priority class. *Real-time* classes use priority levels from 16
to 31 and generally are time-critical processes. Only the NT kernel can use these priority levels. The levels 0 to 15 that are used by applications are called *dynamic-priority*
classes. The system can dynamically alter the priority by as many as two levels while it
is waiting for user interaction. The interactive processes always run at a higher priority—usually 10 to 15—whereas compute processes generally run at a much lower priority level, such as 1 to 5.

The priority level is very important. If a low priority thread is running when a
higher priority thread starts to run, the low priority thread is halted so that the higher
priority thread can execute. The priority of a process increases when it returns from a
voluntary wait condition. All processes receive a priority boost at regular intervals to
prevent lower priority processes from having to wait too long for execution.

You can manually change the priorities of running processes from the Task Manager applet (see Figure 21.7). To start Task Manager, follow these steps:

1. Start Task Manager (right-click the Start button and select Task Manager).
2. Click the Processes tab.
3. Right-click the required process and select Set Priority.
4. Select a different priority.

Figure 21.7 Task Manager Processes tab.

Task Manager does not allow you to set a process to a specific number; it only allows you to set base priorities. The priorities are as follows:

- Realtime = priority 24
- High = priority 13
- Normal = priority 8
- Low = priority 4

Using Task Manager to tune an application in this manner is a temporary fix because after you reboot your system or stop and start the application, you lose the priority properties.

`/realtime`

To use the `/realtime` option, you have to be logged on as a user with Administrator rights.

Normally, there should be no need to change the priority of processes. However, suppose you have a database query process that cannot complete because the process is not getting enough CPU time. In this case, you can temporarily change the priority of the process to High to enable the task to complete successfully. Be warned that if you run applications at high priority, this may in some cases slow overall performance because other applications get less I/O time. Also, changing the base priority of an application to Realtime makes the priority of this application higher than the process that monitors and responds to keyboard input. If the process you set to Realtime completes successfully—fine. However, if it requires any input for processing or recovery, your only option is to reboot the system.

To get a better idea of the current priority settings of running processes, configure Task Manager to display priorities (this is not the default). From the Task Manager Processes tab, select View, Select Columns.

Using the Run Command to the Max

The Run command on the Start menu allows you to browse for and quickly access folders, network shares, and documents and to run programs with a variety of custom command line switches.

The Run command can use the Start command to do a variety of different things. The syntax of the Start command is as follows:

```
START ["title"] [/Dpath] [/I] [/Min] [/MAX] [/SEPARATE¦/SHARED][/LOW ¦ /NORMAL ¦
/HIGH ¦ /REALTIME] [/WAIT] [/B] [command/program][parameters]
```

- **title** is the title displayed in the window-title bar.
- **path** is the program directory.
- **I** is the new environment passed to the CMD.EXE command processor.
- **Min** starts the window minimized.
- **MAX** starts the window maximized.
- **SEPARATE** starts the program in a separate memory space.
- **SHARED** starts the program in a shared memory space.
- **LOW** starts the process with a priority value of 4.
- **NORMAL** starts the process with a priority value of 8.
- **HIGH** starts the process with a priority value of 13.
- **REALTIME** starts the process with a priority value of 24.
- **WAIT** starts the process and waits for it to terminate.

- **B** starts the process, but doesn't create a window. The process also ignores Ctrl + C signals. Ctrl + Break is the only way to terminate a process started in this manner.

- **command** is the name of the program to run.

- **parameters** are a list of the parameters that the program needs.

For the Start command to work properly, it is essential that all the command-line switches, application switches, and filenames are in the correct order. If you change this order, the application usually starts, but it reports some type of error in opening your file. Sometimes it even insists that it cannot find the program.

The Start command offers a lot of control for running programs. You can start it minimized or maximized using the appropriate switches. When running a Windows 3.x application, you have the option of starting a separate NTVDM in which to run the program or running it in a shared NTVDM. You can also use the Start command to change the priority of a program as it starts. If you use the Start command in a batch file to start your application, it ensures that the application always starts at a higher priority level with the appropriate settings.

When you use the Run command on the Start menu to start an MS-DOS application, Windows NT searches for a PIF to use with the application. If it finds one, Windows NT starts the application using the PIF. If no PIF is available, Windows NT uses _DEFAULT.PIF.

Use the Run command to access network shares or type in the appropriate path or sharename. The Run command can browse folders for files or shares.

Processor-Bound Apps

Never start processor-bound applications at real-time priority.

Windows NT 4 Bug

When you use the Start command with one of the priority class arguments other than Normal to start a 16-bit Windows application, you will find that the priority is still Normal. This is a known bug in Windows NT 4.0.

Making the Most of Virtual Memory

Windows NT's design utilizes a 32-bit flat memory model that allows it to address up to 4GB of memory. Memory in the top 2GB is available only to the operating system, whereas the operating system and applications must share memory in the bottom 2GB. The exception is Windows NT Enterprise Edition, which has the option of providing 3GB of address space to applications and only 1GB to the operating system.

The Virtual Memory Manager

To keep track of this relatively large address space, Windows NT uses a component called the *Virtual Memory Manager (VMM)*. The VMM provides applications with a virtual address instead of a physical memory address. When an application attempts to accesses memory, the VMM translates the virtual address into the physical address where the associated code or data actually resides in physical memory. Because the VMM performs the translation of virtual addresses to physical addresses, applications do not need to know where their code and data actually reside or how much memory is available. The VMM can move code and data in physical memory whenever and wherever necessary and can also store the code and data outside of physical memory.

Because computer memory continues to be relatively expensive, most machines are not equipped with the full 4GB of physical memory that Windows NT can use. A concept that has been used for years in the mainframe world, where memory is far more expensive, is called demand paging. *Demand paging* is a process by which the VMM moves data from fixed-length 4KB units (pages) in physical memory to a temporary file on the hard disk. When they are not needed for processing, code and data are saved to the hard disk, freeing physical memory for use by other code and data. When an application needs the data, the data moves back into physical memory. The algorithm that Windows NT uses for paging is optimized to perform per-process paging as opposed to system-wide paging. Pages are stored in files called page files and can be copied between page files and physical memory efficiently because all pages are the same size. Any available space in physical memory or the page file can accommodate a page transferred from either.

Paging is used to increase the amount of memory available to applications. The Windows NT VMM performs paging to make it seem to applications that the computer has more physical memory than is actually installed. The amount of virtual memory available on a computer is equal to its physical memory plus whatever hard disk space is configured for VMM to use as paging files.

The most efficient way to use virtual memory is not to use any at all. Accessing the hard drive is always a lot slower than reading directly from physical memory. Unlike Windows 3.x, which allowed you to turn off paging if you had enough system memory, Microsoft designed Windows NT to use paging for virtual memory independently of how much physical memory is available. To help optimize your system's use of virtual memory, add more physical memory. Adding additional memory reduces the amount of paging, but does not eliminate it completely. Because NT uses the page file regardless of the amount of available memory, it is essential to optimize the use of the page file.

Optimizing the Page File

The best way to optimize the use of the page file is by monitoring your system's memory requirements and properly configuring the paging file for maximum paging performance. The most important factors to consider are page file location, disk access speed, and size.

Page File Location

When Windows NT is installed, it creates the paging file PAGEFILE.SYS, using contiguous disk space in the boot partition's root directory. Unfortunately, this creates problems because Windows NT generally performs simultaneous disk I/O on the system directory and the page file. We recommend moving the page file to a different physical hard disk so Windows NT can handle multiple I/O requests more efficiently. It is also a good idea to put the page file on the fastest disk. If your system has only one hard disk, consider adding a second hard disk. Windows NT supports as many as 16 paging files that it can distribute across multiple drives. Configuring the system to have multiple paging files allows the system to make multiple simultaneous I/O requests to the various hard disks, which increases the speed of I/O requests to the paging file. However, using multiple paging files spread across multiple partitions on the same drive reduces system performance because the hard disk must move constantly between partitions when handling paging requests. Spreading multiple paging files across multiple partitions should be used only when you only have one physical disk and you do not have a partition large enough to store an entire paging file. If possible, locate the page file on its own separate hard drive or partition. This prevents the file from becoming fragmented.

To add multiple page files, follow these steps:

1. Open the System applet in the Control Panel.
2. Select the Performance tab.
3. Click Change to display the Virtual Memory Configuration window.
4. Set the initial size and the maximum size for a drive.

5. Click Set to store the new values.

6. Repeat steps 1 through 5 on the next drive.

7. Click OK twice to exit.

8. Reboot the machine.

Removing the page file from the boot partition prevents Windows NT from creating the crash dump file MEMORY.DMP if a kernel mode STOP error occurs. On a critical system, this can be a problem if the STOP requires a debug. The workaround is to create one page file on the boot partition using the default settings and create your main page file on a less frequently used partition. The paging algorithm in Windows NT uses the page file on the less frequently used partition before it uses the page file on the heavily used boot partition. In most situations, you can disable the crash dump without any problems. To disable crash dump, follow these steps:

1. Open the System applet in the Control Panel.

2. Select the Startup/Shutdown tab.

3. Deselect Write Debugging Information To.

4. Click OK to exit.

5. Reboot the machine.

The Registry keys for crash dump reside at HKLM\SYSTEM\CurrentControlSet\Control\CrashControl. You can make a .REG file for a script or remotely enable or disable crash dump, if you want.

Disk Access Speed

Hard disk type makes a big difference in access speed. Generally, SCSI drives are faster than IDE or EIDE, and a single host or bus mastering SCSI controller can simultaneously access multiple hard drives. Two drives on the same IDE or EIDE controller are accessed sequentially. If you are limited to IDE or EIDE, it is best to have your boot partition on a hard drive that is connected to a different controller from the hard drive on which the page file is located. Always make sure that you put the page file on the fastest, least used hard drive.

Page File Performance

The page file performs better on a FAT drive than on an NTFS drive. This works especially well if you dedicate a drive to paging that is less than 500MB.

Sizing the Page File

The size of the paging file is critical; proper sizing gives you the best system performance. The Windows NT default for the initial size is the amount of physical RAM plus 12MB (example: 64MB installed + 12MB = 76MB page file). The default is rarely acceptable, except in large memory machines, because it usually results in an initial page file that is too small. When the system needs to enlarge the file due to increased paging activity, it must create new space for the paging file while handling paging requests, which increases system overhead. Expanding the paging file on the fly also causes fragmentation. The system can scatter the paging file throughout the disk rather than maintaining it in contiguous space. This fragmentation increases additional system overhead and severely degrades performance.

Setting the page file to a fixed size can increase performance. For best results, run a hard drive defrag utility before setting the page file size. This ensures that your new page file is created in contiguous disk space. To change the size of the page file, follow these steps:

1. Open the System applet in the Control Panel.

2. Select the Performance tab.

3. Click Change to display the Virtual Memory Configuration window.

4. Set the initial size and the maximum size to the same value.

5. Click Set to store the new values.

6. Click OK twice to exit.

7. Reboot the machine.

If you set the minimum and the maximum size to the same value, you will experience less disk fragmentation and get a slight speed boost. Matching these sizes reduces the file fragmentation that occurs to a dynamically resizable paging file as the system grows and shrinks the file. It also eliminates the processing overhead required to manipulate the size of the file. The page file size needs to be large enough to easily accommodate the maximum virtual memory usage on your system.

There are several ways to discover the appropriate size for the paging file. The first is to start all the applications that you usually run. Then start Task Manager. To start Task Manager, follow these steps:

1. Press Ctrl+Alt+Delete.

2. Select Task Manager.

3. Click the Performance tab.

The Commit Charge section indicates whether the Commit Peak, which is the highest amount of virtual memory that has been allocated so far, approaches or exceeds the Commit Limit. The Commit Limit is equal to physical memory + initial page file size and represents the amount of virtual memory available without expanding the paging file. You should set the size of your page file to the value of (Commit Peak) ÷ 2 + 15 to 20%.

Another way to track page file size and usage is by using the NT Diagnostics program, which can be started from Programs, Administrative Tools, NT Diagnostics. Select the Memory tab. NT Diagnostics gives you more information than Task Manager, but it is not in realtime. Hit the Refresh button for updates. Check the Page File Space section to see the peak page file usage.

Either of these methods for estimating page file size is adequate in most situations. However, for the most accurate view of page file usage, you should use Performance Monitor.

Using Performance Monitor gives you several options for monitoring page file usage. Use it just as you used Task Manager and Windows NT Diagnostics—by starting all typical programs to get a typical page file size. You get the most accurate page file size figure by using Performance Monitor to track page file usage over a period of time and saving it to a log file. This allows you to closely examine your page file use over an extended period and to see how the size is affected by daily tasks.

Whichever method you decide to use, the two counters you want to watch are % Usage and Usage Peak (Bytes) under the Paging File object type. If you have multiple paging files, the counter path name of each file appears as an instance of the Paging File object type. You can either add a counter for each paging file or select the total instance to look at combined usage data for all your paging files. To determine your optimal paging file size, multiply the initial file size by the Usage Peak % value. It is best to add an additional 10 to 15% to this value, for "insurance."

Another way to improve paging performance is by not paging operating system code. Windows NT pages portions of itself to disk during system operation. By default, it does this even on systems with a large amount of free physical memory. On systems with a lot of memory, you can disable the paging of the operating system to improve performance. To turn off OS paging, change the value of the Registry key HKEY_LOCAL_MACHINE\SYSTEM\CurrentControlSet\Control\ Session Manager\Memory Management\DisablePagingExecutive. This forces all drivers and the Windows NT kernel to remain in memory at all times. If you make this change, be sure your system has plenty of available memory after you load the system and user applications, or performance will suffer. On systems with plenty of physical memory, this reduces paging and improves performance.

Third-Party Application Management Tools

Most of the third-party commercial utilities aimed at application management on the Windows NT platform focus on Windows NT Server as an enterprise host rather than on Windows NT Workstation as a client or standalone system. These utilities are too expensive for the average user. Among the third-party utilities with application management capabilities are PerfMan, Serverbench, Netbench, and BAPCO.

Performance Management (PerfMan) for Windows NT is a commercial product that provides extensive performance and application management with reporting capabilities. An evaluation copy is available on the Web site **http://www.infosysman.com/perfman/**.

Both Serverbench and Netbench are very good benchmarking tools. They can be very useful in tuning applications on your system. They are available as free downloads from **http://www.zdnet.com**.

BAPCO is benchmarking software for both workstations and servers. See the Web site for more information at **http://www.bapco.com**.

Troubleshooting Application Difficulties

Windows NT can run most MS-DOS and Windows applications, even when they are not designed for Windows NT. However, sometimes a device driver designed to run with Windows NT is required. If you have an application that does not include the device driver for Windows NT, contact the manufacturer of the application for a version of the software that is compatible with Windows NT.

MS-DOS Applications

If you are not satisfied with the performance of your MS-DOS applications, try one of the following solutions:

- If the application is in a window and the video display performance is slow, try full-screen mode.
- Disable the Compatible Timer Hardware feature in the _DEFAULT.PIF or in the application's program information file (PIF).
- If the application is in a window and seems to pause periodically, try disabling Idle Sensitivity.
- If the MS-DOS application can be configured for printing, choose LPT1 or LPT2 rather than parallel port. Most MS-DOS applications use Int 17 to print when configured for LPT<x>. If you select parallel port mode, these applications print directly to printer ports. Parallel port mode is significantly slower in Windows NT compared to Windows 3.1.

Windows Applications

Applications that attempt to directly access hardware such as private device drivers (VxD) are not supported.

Windows NT uses CONFIG.NT and AUTOEXEC.NT files for running MS-DOS applications, rather than the CONFIG.SYS and AUTOEXEC.BAT files used in real MS-DOS. This means that when you run the MS-DOS-based install program in Windows NT, any changes that are made in the CONFIG.SYS and AUTOEXEC.BAT files has to be copied over to the *.NT files.

General Applications

When Windows NT shuts down, it sends a shutdown request to all processes. Most 32-bit applications will shut down, but applications running in the Virtual MS-DOS Machine usually will not. The operating system will prompt you with a dialog box asking if you want to kill the task, wait for the task to die on its own, or cancel the shutdown. You can force NT to kill all running processes on shutdown by changing HKEY_USERS\.DEFAULT\ControlPanel\Desktop\AutoEndTasks to 1.

If an unwanted application starts every time you start Windows NT, you need to determine how it is starting. Applications can be started from a number of places:

- In the Startup Folder for the current user, all users, or default users
- HKEY_LOCAL_MACHINE\Software\Microsoft\Windows\ CurrentVersion\Run
- HKEY_LOCAL_MACHINE\Software\Microsoft\Windows\ CurrentVersion\Runonce
- HKEY_LOCAL_MACHINE\Software\Microsoft\Windows\ CurrentVersion\RunServices
- HKEY_LOCAL_MACHINE\Software\Microsoft\Windows\ CurrentVersion\RunServicesOnce
- HKEY_LOCAL_MACHINE\Software\Microsoft\WindowsNT\ CurrentVersion\Winlogon\Userinit
- HKEY_CURRENT_USER\Software\Microsoft\Windows\ CurrentVersion\Run
- HKEY_CURRENT_USER\Software\Microsoft\Windows\ CurrentVersion\RunOnce
- HKEY_CURRENT_USER\Software\Microsoft\Windows\ CurrentVersion\RunServices
- HKEY_CURRENT_USER\Software\Microsoft\Windows\ CurrentVersion\RunServicesOnce
- HKEY_CURRENT_USER\Software\Microsoft\WindowsNT\ CurrentVersion\Windows, run and Load keys %systemroot%\win.ini

Finding an Entry

The easiest way to find an entry in the Registry is to search the Registry using REGEDIT on the application name, if you know it.

If you receive a message from NTVDM that there is no disk in drive A or a CD-ROM drive letter, it may be that the path statement contains a reference to this drive. To find it, check the following:

- The System applet, Environment tab in Control Panel
- AUTOEXEC.BAT
- A reference in an application shortcut
- HKEY_LOCAL_MACHINE\SYSTEM\SETUP\WinntPath

For More Information

- TechNet (the technical subscription service from Microsoft):
  http://technet.microsoft.com/
- Microsoft Knowledge Base: **http://support.microsoft.com/**
- Edmead, Mark T. and Paul Hinsberg. *Windows NT Performance: Monitoring, Benchmarking, and Tuning.* New Riders, Indianapolis, Indiana, 1998. ISBN: 1562059424.
- Gardiner, Kenton. *Windows NT Performance Tuning and Optimization.* Osborne/McGraw–Hill, New York, NY, 1998. ISBN: 0078824966.
- Daily, Sean. *Optimizing Windows NT.* IDG Books, Foster City, CA, 1998. ISBN: 0764531107.
- Cowart, Robert and Kenneth Gregg. *Windows NT 4.0 Administrator's Bible.* IDG Books, Foster City, CA, 1998. ISBN: 0764580094.

22

Printing with Windows NT

P RINTING IS ONE OF THE KEY CAPABILITIES around which networks and computers are designed. Most computer operators cannot function without being able to transfer displayed images onto paper. Accessing a shared printer is one of the most frequently used network capabilities. The Windows NT printing subsystem is an advanced architecture capable of supporting a large user base, managing a wide variety of printer types and capabilities, and offering several layouts and access controls. As long as the printer host is a member of a network, any type of network client(s) can use printers hosted by a Windows NT system including Windows NT Server and Windows NT Workstation, Windows 95/98, Windows for Workgroups, Windows 3.x, DOS, NetWare servers, Macintosh, UNIX, and other TCP/IP clients. This chapter examines the Windows NT printing system and covers printer installation, management, configuration, and troubleshooting.

The Windows NT Print Architecture

The Windows NT print architecture design is comprehensible, but many of the terms and concepts it uses must be defined because they are used in ways contrary to common sense or common usage. The following list explains most of Microsoft's printing-related terms. You should become familiar with these terms before working with the Windows NT printing system.

- **Logical printer.** This term is used by Microsoft to refer to the software construct that redirects print jobs from a client to the print server. Logical printers appear in the Printers folder, and you can create them using the Add Printer Wizard from that folder. The logical printer is where you define configuration settings for the physical print devices. Logical printers also are used to control and manage access to physical printers. The term "logical printer" often is synonymous with "printer" in Microsoft documentation.

- **Print device.** This is the actual physical device that creates the printed document. In some cases, this term is synonymous with physical printer.

- **Client.** A client is either a computer hosting a specific operating system or an application submitting a print job. The terms "client," "client system," "client computer," and "client application" are used interchangeably in most cases. The client can be a true network client that submits a print job to a print server on the network, or the client can be the same computer system that serves as the print server. The term "client" refers to the relationship between the object submitting the print job and the object hosting the printer spool.

- **Connecting to a printer.** This action creates a logical printer that redirects print jobs to a network printer share. Use the Add Printer Wizard in the Printers folder to create a logical printer.

- **Creating a printer.** This term is similar to connecting to a printer, but it is used in reference to a locally attached physical printer (that is, a printer connected directly to the computer via a parallel cable). In creating a printer, you also use the Add Printer Wizard from the Printers folder. Creating a printer involves installing the device-specific driver, setting any configuration options, and possibly sharing the printer with the network.

- **Dynamic print clients.** Dynamic print clients do not have printer drivers installed locally for network printer shares. Each time a print job is sent to a logical printer, the print server sends a printer driver for the appropriate client operating system to the client. The client uses the driver to format and submit the print job. This system enables printer drivers to be stored in a single location, simplifying maintenance and upgrades.

- **Network attached printer.** A network attached printer is a print device that has a built-in or specially attached network interface connected to the network media instead of to a computer. Such printers still require that you define a computer as the print server where the spool file(s) resides, but they are independent network devices. Network-attached printers typically employ TCP/IP or DLC for communications.

- **Print client.** This term is used interchangeably with client, client system, client computer, and client application. A print client is any object that submits a print job to a printer.

- **Print job.** The object transmitted from a client to a printer server that contains not only the document or content to be printed but also control and processing instructions. The client creates print jobs and sends them to a print server via a logical printer redirector. The print server stores the print job to a spool, and when the printer is available, the print job is pulled from the spool and sent to the physical print device.

- **Print server.** This is the actual computer that controls and manages a printer. It accepts print jobs from clients, stores them in a spool, supervises the physical printer, and sends print jobs from the spool to the physical printer when it is available. A print server can manage either a locally attached or a network-attached printer. The print server also is the storage location for printer drivers used by dynamic print clients. On Windows NT networks, print servers can be Windows NT Server, Windows NT Workstation, or Windows 95/98 systems. Print drivers are stored on these servers in the \\printserver\print$ directory.

- **Print resolution.** Print resolution is a measurement of pixel density in dots per inch (dpi). It determines how sharp and clear the printed document appears. In most cases, a higher dpi results in a better printed document. The base dpi for most laser and ink-jet printers is around 300 dpi; however, several printer models can print up to 2,400 dpi. Higher-DPI resolutions are obtainable on professional printing systems.

- **Print server services.** You can expand the Windows NT print system's printing capabilities through the use of print server services. These add-on modules are used to broaden the client base from which print jobs can be submitted. Print server services include Services for Macintosh, File and Print Services for NetWare, and TCP/IP Print Services. Print server services not only add support for additional client types, they also expand the range of protocols that can be used to submit print jobs.

- **Print spooler or spooler.** The spool is the temporary storage area hosted by the print server for submitted print jobs. The software component of the printer server that manages the spool is the spooler. The spooler is responsible for saving new print jobs to a file and for sending print jobs from the spool to the physical printer. In most cases, the print job is retained in the spool until it has successfully printed. The spooler can be bypassed with a change to the logical printer configuration, causing print jobs to be sent directly to the printer instead of being stored in the spool. Doing this suspends the client sending the print job; the print job is communicated only as fast as the printer can create the printed output.

- **Print users.** A print user is any user on the local system or network who has been granted the privilege of printing. Print users can be given Print, Manage Documents, or Full Control access privileges. Print access enables users to submit print jobs and to manage their own print jobs (pause, resume, restart, and delete). Manage Documents access enables a user to submit print jobs and to manage any print job in the queue (pause, resume, restart, delete). Full Control access enables a user to submit print jobs, to manage any print job in the queue (pause, resume, restart, delete), to make changes to the settings and configuration of the logical printer, and to alter the security settings and access privileges for the logical printer.

- **Printer.** Also called the logical printer, this refers to the logical printer software construct that redirects print jobs from a client to the printer server rather than to the physical print device. The type of device used as the physical printer does not affect the rest of the print model as long as the correct device driver is installed.

- **Printer driver.** A printer driver is a software element used to inform the printer server or print client about the capabilities and limitations of a printer. It informs the print server how to communicate with the physical printer, and it informs print clients how to format print jobs.

- **Queue or print queue.** The printer server maintains a queue (or list) of print jobs for each physical print device. These jobs are automatically managed by the printer server. Each logical printer has its own print queue. Each physical printer can have multiple logical printers defined for it, so it can have multiple print queues. Multiple queues allow for priority processing of print jobs. Print users can manipulate only those print jobs they have submitted. Print users with Manage Documents access can manipulate any print job in a queue. Print users with Full Control access can manipulate any print job in a queue and can change the settings and configuration of the queue and the logical printer. You can view a print queue by opening the logical printer from the Printers folder. Individual print queues operate in first in, first out (FIFO) mode.

- **Rendering.** Rendering is the process of transforming video display images from video system-specific instructions to printer model-specific language codes that reproduce the image on paper. The Windows NT print system renders images using the printer driver installed for a particular logical printer/physical printer.

From this list, you can see that the Microsoft print system is not focused on the physical print device but on the software redirecting mechanisms that direct print jobs from the client to the physical printer's connection point to the print system (a print server). After you attach the physical print device either directly to a computer or to the network and install the proper drivers, the Windows print system pays little further attention to the physical device. You'll interact with the physical printer only to retrieve documents, to add paper, and to troubleshoot hardware-specific problems.

The actual Windows NT print system architecture is fairly extensive. As a system manager or a print user, you do not need to know the architectural details. All that is required to adequately support printing under Windows NT is that you understand how to add, configure, and troubleshoot printing. Discussion of the architecture is included here so you will have a clearer understanding of what actually is going on under the hood when a print job is submitted by a client.

The print system design is modular like that of every other part of Windows NT. This enables you to interchange, tweak, control, and replace individual components of the overall system based on the needs of the system and the types of hardware present.

Each element of the print architecture is designed to manage or perform a single task. A print job traverses the system one step at a time, providing a seamless procession from print client to printed document. Each module of the system can communicate with its immediate neighbors but not with other components located elsewhere in the system. This smoothes processing. The following list presents the key elements of the print architecture in the order in which a print job encounters them:

- A Windows-based print client uses an application to create a document or other printable element and then initiates a print job.

- The print client application interacts with the graphics device interface (GDI) and printer driver to create a valid print job for the specified logical printer. GDI is a software element that interacts with both the video and printer systems to enable images to be rendered for display or print. GDI is what makes Windows' What You See Is What You Get (WYSIWYG) capability possible. The interaction of the GDI with the actual printer driver helps create a print job that accurately reproduces the displayed image.

- The print job is sent to the local print spooler. The print job is held there until it can be transmitted to the print server by the remote print provider.

- Non-Microsoft print clients perform similar functions that result in a formatted print job being sent to the appropriate print server service hosted by the print server.

- The spooler is a multipart element that consists of the router, the local print provider, the print processor, and the separator page processor. The spooler is responsible for accepting print jobs from clients and holding them until they are passed on to the print monitor.

- The router is responsible for directing print jobs to either local or remote printers. The router passes print jobs for a local printer to the local print provider. It passes print jobs for a remote printer to the remote network print server such as a NetWare print server.

- The local print provider writes the print job to a spool file (.SPL).

- The print processor despools print jobs and performs any additional processing before sending it on to the print monitor.

- The separator page processor adds any logical printer-specific separate pages to the beginning of each document as it is sent to the print monitor.

- The print monitor is the print system component that communicates directly with the printer. It manages the connection port and the language used by bidirectional print devices.
- The print device receives the print job and prints the data.

If you need more details or additional information about the structure, elements, and architecture of the Windows NT print system, consult the *Windows NT Resource Kits* and the TechNet CD.

Adding Local or Networked Printers

Whether you are installing a printer for local use only, configuring a network print server, or even defining a print server for a network attached printer, Windows NT makes adding new printers easy. The following sections discuss each of these printer installation issues.

Locally Attached Printers

Local printers are attached directly to the computer. The type of attachment you use doesn't matter as long as the OS recognizes the bus type and the printer driver corresponds. Printers usually are attached using parallel cables, but serial ports, USB, and other technologies also can be used.

Before beginning the installation of a local printer, you need to have a few key pieces of information on hand:

- The exact make and model of the printer
- The port to which the physical print device is connected
- The location of printer drivers if they are not included on the Windows NT distribution CD
- A name for the logical printer (if you are using a naming convention, be sure to comply with its rules)
- Whether you will be sharing the printer with the network
- Whether you want to print a test document

The following are the basic steps for adding a local printer:

1. Physically set up and attach the printer to the computer.
2. Power up the printer.
3. Open the Printers folder (Start, Settings, Printers).
4. Launch the Add Printer Wizard by double-clicking the Add Printer icon in the Printers folder. This brings up the Add Print Wizard's first page.
5. Select My Computer for a locally attached printer.
6. Click Next. This reveals the port selection page of the Add Printer Wizard.

7. Select the port to which the printer is connected.

8. Click Next. This brings up the Printer Model Selection page. This is a list of printer drivers included on the Windows NT distribution CD.

9. Select the manufacturer in the left column.

10. Select the printer model in the right column.

    If your printer is not listed, click the Have Disk button. You'll need to point the dialog box to the location of the manufacturer-supplied drivers.

11. Click Next. This brings up the Printer Name page. This is the name that will appear below the logical printer icon in the Printers folder on your local machine. Enter a name or accept the offered default name. Remember that, if you want MS-DOS applications to print to this printer, the printer name must be no more than eight characters long and must have no spaces.

12. Click Next. This brings up the Printer Sharing page.

13. By default, local printers are not shared. If this printer is to be used by the local system only, accept the default selection of Not Shared. (See "Network Shared Printers" for more information about this page of the Add Printer Wizard.)

14. Click Next. This brings up the Print A Test Page page. The default is to print a test document to the newly installed printer to verify that setup was successful. It is recommended that you print a test page. If you do not want to print a test page, select No.

15. Click Finish.

This final step of the Add Printer Wizard initiates the actual printer installation routine. The wizard might prompt you for the path to the printer driver and associated print system files. After the required drivers are installed, the newly installed printer icon will appear in the Printers folder. You might need to refresh the display (by selecting View, Refresh or F5) to see the new icon. If you selected to print a test page, a dialog box appears asking whether the page printed successfully. If the page printed, click Yes. If the page failed to print, click No. The hardware troubleshooter for printers will appear and will walk you through several options for remedying the printing problem. Most of these options are discussed in the "Troubleshooting Printing Problems" section later in this chapter.

If you've installed a printer on this system before, you will see an additional question on the Printer Name page asking whether to make the printer you currently are installing the default printer. The default selection is No. If you want the new printer to be the printer to which all applications print to by default, select Yes.

If you already have installed on this system a printer of the same type or a printer that uses the same printer driver, you will see an additional page (after the Printer Model Selection page) asking whether to keep the existing driver or to replace the existing driver. In most cases, you can accept the default and recommended option of retain the existing driver. If you want to reinstall the driver or install a new driver from a new source, select to replace the existing driver.

Network Shared Printers

You can create network shared printers through a simple procedure of installing a locally attached printer, sharing that logical printer, and connecting to that printer from each client. The simplest way to share a local printer is to select the Shared option during the Add Printer Wizard installation process. If you want to share an existing logical printer, however, you need only modify the Sharing tab of the printer's properties.

Creating a new printer to be shared with the network requires the same preparation and installation steps as a local-only printer with a few additions. You need to have the following additional pieces of information hand:

- The name of the printer share (if you are using a naming convention, be sure to comply with its rules)
- The operating system-specific printer drivers you want to host from the printer server

The installation process is the same as for a local-only printer with the following changes. Follow steps 1 through 12 for local-only printer installation and then follow the following steps to complete the installation:

1. Select Shared. This enables the Share Name and Print Driver list.
2. In the Share Name field, enter the name to be used on the network for this printer share. Remember that, if you want MS-DOS, Windows 3.x, Windows for Workgroups, and other non-LFN operating system clients to use this print share, the share name must be no more than eight characters long.
3. In the list of available printer drivers, highlight all the operating system types and versions present on your network. (See the discussion later this chapter about Point and Print.)
4. Click Next. This brings up the Print A Test Document page. The default is to print a test document to the newly installed printer to verify that the setup was successful. It is recommended that you print a test page. If you do not want to print a test page, select No.
5. Click Finish.

This final step of the Add Printer Wizard initiates the printer installation routine. The wizard might prompt you for the path to the printer driver and associated print system files. After the required drivers are installed, the newly installed printer icon will appear in the Printers folder. You might need to refresh the display (View, Refresh) to see the new icon. If you selected to print a test page, a dialog box appears asking whether the page printed successfully. If the page printed, click Yes. If the page failed to print, click No. The hardware troubleshooter for printers will appear and will walk you through several options for remedying the printing problem. Most of these options are discussed in the "Troubleshooting Printing Problems" section later in this chapter.

At this point, you have installed a local printer that is shared with the network. The next step is to connect the client to the network printer share. This is performed from each client. The actual process varies depending on the operating system, although it is the same on all Windows 95, Windows 98, Windows NT 4.0 Server, and Windows NT 4.0 Workstation systems. If you need additional information about connecting other clients to network printer shares, consult TechNet or the manufacturer of the client operating system.

On any Windows 95/98/NT system, follow these steps to connect to a network printer share:

1. Open the Printers folder (Start, Settings, Printers).

2. Launch the Add Printer Wizard by double-clicking the Add Printer icon in the Printers folder. This brings up the Add Print Wizard's first page.

3. Select Network Printer Server to connect to a network printer share.

4. Click Next. This brings up the Connect To Printer dialog box.

5. Traverse the network resource browser tree to locate the print server and the share name of the printer share. Select the desired printer share.

6. Click OK and then click Finish.

If the printer server hosts the printer drivers for the local operating system, the Add Printer Wizard requires no additional files. If printer drivers must be installed locally, you'll be prompted to provide the path to their location. After the required drivers are installed, the newly installed printer icon will appear in the Printers folder. You might need to refresh the display (View, Refresh) to see the new icon.

If you selected to print a test page, a dialog box will appear asking whether the page printed successfully. If the page printed, click Yes. If the page failed to print, click No. The hardware troubleshooter for printers will appear and will walk you through several options for remedying the printing problem. Most of these options will be discussed in the "Troubleshooting Printing Problems" section later in this chapter.

Network-Attached Printers

A network-attached printer is a printer equipped with its own network interface, making the printer a network device. Use network attached printers when communication speed is important (such as when printing large or complex documents) or when no suitable system has an available communication port. Network-attached printers require a print server. That is, a printer attached directly to the network relies on a computer to manage print jobs, to process the spool, and to control user access.

Windows NT includes the Data Link Control (DLC) protocol that can be used for IBM mainframe interaction or for communicating with network attached printers. DLC is not the only protocol that can be used to communicate print data from a print server to a network attached printer; both TCP/IP and IPX also can be employed. In addition, some printer vendors have proprietary protocols. Ultimately, the protocol used to support printing on network attached printers is not important as long as the printer and the supporting software function.

Configuring a network attached printer can involve a variety of steps, configurations, and driver installations. You need to read the installation instructions included with the printer to learn exactly what must be done for that particular device. In general, the steps are as follows:

1. If not already present, install the network interface into the printer.

2. Attach the printer to the network.

3. Perform any necessary hardware-specific routines to prepare the device for network communications. This might include switching print modes, defining protocol-specific parameters, or enabling the network interface. The printer/NIC manual should detail the required steps.

4. Install the communication protocol on the system destined to be the print server for the network attached printer: DLC, TCP/IP, IPX, or a vendor-supplied protocol.

5. Add a virtual port to the print server. This is a process in which a new port that is used to redirect print jobs from the print server to the actual print device is defined to the system. A port usually is created on the Port Selection Page of the Add Printer Wizard by clicking the Add Port button. Some vendors, however, have their own installation routine. The Windows NT distribution CD includes several ports that can be installed including the Hewlett-Packard and Digital network ports.

6. Using the Add Print Wizard, complete the printer installation by selecting the new port as the connection point for the network attached printer. Because the entire network often uses network attached printers, be sure to share the printer.

Following these steps results in a logical printer icon in your Printers folder. Network attached printers are managed and controlled in the same manner as locally attached printers. In some cases, vendors provide additional control or interface software that can enhance the foundational controls offered through the Windows NT print system.

Print Clients

Printing within the Windows NT environment is much easier than the complex architecture suggests. After a logical printer is defined on a client, any application can send print jobs to that printer. Logical printers are a design element of the Microsoft print system that most of the Microsoft operating systems support. The Windows NT print system, however, is not limited to Microsoft clients. In fact, support for non-Microsoft clients is included on the Windows NT distribution CD. To encourage Windows NT deployment, Microsoft includes print services for Macintosh and TCP/IP clients, thus broadening the range of networks to which Windows NT can bring new services and resources.

Services for Macintosh (SFM) is a Windows NT Server-only installable service. This service adds capabilities to the Windows NT network so that Macintosh clients can participate. Basically, this service enables Macintosh clients to share and access files and printers. Macintosh clients are able to submit print jobs to Windows NT Server-hosted printers by sending them to a print device redirector created by SFM within the AppleTalk network. Likewise, SFM is able to capture Macintosh shared printers and enable Windows NT to connect to them. For more details about installing and configuring SFM, see the Windows NT Server manuals, the *Windows NT Server Resource Kit*, and TechNet.

TCP/IP clients can host printers for Windows NT network clients, or they can print to Windows NT network print servers. The Microsoft TCP/IP Printing service adds Line Printer Daemon (LPD) and Line Printer Remote (LPR) functionality to the existing Windows NT print system. LPD is used to enable UNIX or other TCP/IP clients to print documents on Windows NT network-hosted print server printers. LPD accepts print jobs from LPR utilities hosted by TCP/IP clients. Likewise, Windows NT clients can use LPR to send print jobs out to LPDs hosted on TCP/IP clients, allowing Windows NT clients to print to UNIX or other print servers.

The Microsoft TCP/IP Printing service is installed from the Services tab of the Network applet. It requires that the TCP/IP protocol be present on the Windows NT host print server. After the service is installed, you can use the Add Printer Wizard to create logical printers that use the LPR port. The LPR port can be directed to either a Windows NT Print share or to a UNIX or other TCP/IP operating system LPD print queue. To make this link, you'll need to know the IP identifier of the print server or the print device itself (typically the DNS name or the IP address) and the name that the LPD print server uses to reference the print device. For more details about TCP/IP printing, see the Windows NT manuals, the *Windows NT Server Resource Kit*, and TechNet.

NetWare clients also can enjoy access to Windows NT resources; however, this requires an additional software component. The File and Print Service for NetWare (FPNW) grants NetWare clients access to printers and file shares hosted by Windows NT systems without requiring additional software on each client. FPNW makes Windows NT systems look and act like NetWare 3.11 servers to NetWare clients. For more information about FPNW, consult the Microsoft Web site (`http://www.microsoft.com/windows/`), the *Windows NT Resource Kit*, and TechNet.

Printer Settings and Configurations

After you've installed a printer using the Add Printer Wizard, you can modify and change its settings and configurations to meet your specific needs. You can change a printer's configuration either from the print server itself or from any logical printer on any client connected to a printer share. In both cases, you must have sufficient access (Full Control) to manipulate the configuration of a printer.

You can make configuration changes using the multitabbed printer Properties dialog box. You can access this dialog box by opening the Printers folder, selecting a printer, and then issuing the File, Properties command from the menu bar (or by right-clicking over the printer and selecting Properties from the pop-up menu). This brings up the Properties dialog box specific to this printer. Keep in mind that changing the settings on a client also changes the settings on the print server for that printer, so all clients using that printer share will have the same configuration settings applied to them.

The General tab of the printer Properties dialog box enables you to

- Provide comments about the printer.

- Describe the physical location of the printer.

- Select the installed printer driver to use or to install a new printer driver.

- Indicate a separator page to print before each print job.

- Select the print processor data type to use. Usually, this is changed only for Macintosh or UNIX print clients when the default settings do not produce the desired output. The default data type is EMF for PCL printers and RAW for PostScript printers.

- Print a test document to investigate the current printer settings.

The Ports tab of the printer Properties dialog box enables you to

- Define the communication port(s) used to send print jobs to the physical print device

- Add or remove specialty ports

- Configure ports

- Enable bidirectional communication support

- Enable printer pooling (See the "Printer Pooling" section later in this chapter.)

The Scheduling tab of the printer Properties dialog box enables you to

- Set printer availability to Always or to a specific time range. Print jobs sent to the printer while it is unavailable are stored by the spooler and are printed when the printer becomes available.

- Set the processing priority for this logical printer from 1 (lowest) to 99 (highest). This feature is useful only when multiple logical printers serve a single printer. Granting high priority to one logical printer instructs the print server to print its documents before those of the lower priority logical printers.

- Enable or disable spooling. When spooling is enabled, print jobs are stored to disk. This frees up the client quickly so it can perform other tasks while the print job is processing. When disabled, print jobs are sent directly to the printer. This situation suspends the client while it waits for the print job to complete.

- Set whether to begin printing only after the entire print job is spooled or as soon as possible.

- Hold mismatched documents. The print server can inspect each print job before it is sent to the print monitor to verify that the job has valid credentials, such as origin, printer destination, and data type. Invalid documents will not be printed. Mismatched documents can cause printer errors that take a printer offline, requiring human intervention at the physical print device.

- Instruct the print server to give print priority to spooled documents over direct-to-printer documents. This feature is useful only when multiple logical printers serve a single printer.

- Retain print jobs in the spool after they have successfully printed. If your organization needs to keep track of all printed materials, this provides an electronic means to maintain a paper trail of print jobs.

The Sharing tab of the printer Properties dialog box enables you to

- Enable sharing of this printer.

- Define the share name for the printer. Remember that, if you want MS-DOS, Windows 3.x, Windows for Workgroups, and other non–LFN operating system clients to use this print share, the share name must be no more than eight characters.

- Select the operating system type and version-specific printer drivers to maintain on the print server for Point and Print capabilities support.

The Security tab of the printer Properties dialog box enables you to access permission, auditing, and ownership controls. Clicking the appropriate button on this tab reveals a topic-specific dialog box.

Clicking the Permissions button reveals the Printer Permissions dialog box in which users and groups are granted access to use this logical printer. The types of access that can be assigned are as follows:

- **No Access.** Users are prevented from using the printer.

- **Print.** Users can send print jobs to the printer and can manage (pause, resume, restart, delete) their own print jobs in the print queue.

- **Manage Documents.** Users can send print jobs to the printer and can manage (pause, resume, restart, delete) any print job in the print queue.

- **Full Control.** Users can send print jobs to the printer, can manage (pause, resume, restart, delete) any print job in the print queue, can change printer settings, and can alter access permissions.

When you first create a printer, it has the following default access permissions:

- Creator Owner (user): Manage Documents

- Everyone (group): Print

- Administrators (group): Full Control

- Power Users (group): Full Control

Clicking the Auditing button reveals the Printer Auditing dialog box. By default, the Name list is empty. We added the Everyone group to display the Events to Audit section. Through this dialog box, you can define the printer-related events to be audited on the basis of success or failure for all listed users and groups in the Name list. You need to enable auditing, however, before this information actually is recorded in the Security log of the Event Viewer. Basically, you need to enable auditing and select File and Object Access Success and/or Failure from the Audit policy of the User Manager.

Clicking the Ownership button reveals the Owner dialog box, which lists the name of the printer and the current owner's username. If you are not already the owner of this printer, you can click the Take Ownership button to obtain ownership. Administrators can always take ownership of an object to gain access to the access permissions of the object. Nonadministrators must have Full Control to use this feature.

Use the printer Properties dialog box Device Settings tab to configure device-specific settings, options, and features. This GUI interface grants you a Windows NT-based control mechanism to all the printer capabilities usually accessed through a clunky LCD/LED multibutton control interface on the physical print device itself. You'll see common features such as memory settings, paper sizes, tray capabilities, support for envelope feeders, hardware-based fonts, graphical controls, and print density. Consult the printer's documentation for specifics about how to properly configure your printer using this GUI interface.

Separator Pages

A separator page is a special document printed before each print job to indicate the end of a document and to provide other information such as the name of the sender. Separator pages are useful when multiple users print documents on the same printer or when a paper "receipt" is required for each document. Windows NT includes several separator pages, or you can create your own. The provided separator pages are found in the %systemroot%\System32 folder. The following settings are available for separator pages:

- **PCL.SEP.** This file is for PCL-compatible printers. It switches the printer into PCL mode and then prints the separator page.
- **PSCRIPT.SEP.** This file is for PostScript-compatible printers. It switches the printer into PostScript mode but does not print a separator page.
- **SYSPRINT.SEP.** This file is for PostScript-compatible printers. It switches the printer into PostScript mode and then prints a separator page.

You can create custom separator pages from scratch, or you can use one of the provided pages as a foundation. Either way, a separator page is nothing more than a scripted text file. You can use Notepad or any other basic text editor to create and modify a separator page. The first line of the separator page defines the escape character to be used throughout the document as the command delimiter. A common delimiter is the backslash (\) character. Table 22.1 lists the commands that can be used within a separator page.

Table 22.1 **Windows NT Separator Page Commands (with a Backslash Used as Command Delimiter)**

Command	Function
\N	Provides the name of the user who submitted the print job.
\I	Provides the document number as determined by the sequence of print jobs handled by this printer.
\D	Provides the date that the document was printed.
\T	Provides the time that the document was printed.
\L*xxxx*	All characters following *L*, represented by *xxxx,* are printed until another delimiter is reached or until the character count reaches the maximum width (see \W*nn*).
\F*pathname*	Includes the contents of the specified file in the separator page.
\H*nn*	Sends a printer-specific hexadecimal printer control code.
\W*nn*	Sets the width of the separator page in characters. The default is 80 with a maximum of 256.
\B\S	A monospace font is used for all characters until \U is encountered.
\E	Ejects the page from the printer. This code is used to start a new page or to eject a completed page. If extra blank pages are included in the printed output, remove this code.
n	Skip *n* number of lines (1 to 9) and then continue printing.
\B\M	A double-width font is used for all characters until \U is encountered.
\U	Returns print characters to normal.

If you need more information about separator pages, consult the *Windows NT Resource Kit* and TechNet.

Printer Pooling

Printer pooling is a Windows NT print system function that enables a single logical printer to serve multiple physical printers. Print pooling is often used in offices where many documents are printed on a continuous basis and a single printer is inadequate. As print jobs are sent to the logical printer, the print server sends each print job to the next available printer. This results in an overall faster and more efficient use of multiple printers.

All the printers in a print pool must be operated by the same printer driver. In most cases, it is best to use identical printers, but this is not strictly necessary. Working with printers from the same manufacturer within a generation or so of each other provides adequate similarity for printer pooling.

You can configure printer pooling just as you would any locally attached printer. Instead of working with a single port, however, you must select all the ports to which a printer is attached that should be a member of the pool.

As you know, the Windows NT print system allows for multiple logical printers to serve a single printer. Likewise, multiple logical printers can serve a printer pool. This enables you to create logical printers with different printing priorities, varied availability time frames, or different paper trays.

Updating Print Drivers and Who Needs Them

Point and Print is a term created by Microsoft to describe a collection of print features. Not all of these features require a printer driver to be installed on the client; some allow the print server to host the printer drivers. Windows 95, Windows 98, and Windows NT (3.1, 3.5, 3.51, and 4.0) all support Point and Print. When a printer is shared from a print server, you can select additional operating system version-specific[md]and platform-specific[md]printer drivers for local storage. When a client that supports Point and Print uses the printer, the print server sends the appropriate print driver to the client. This enables the client to properly process the print job before actually submitting it to the print server. The printer driver remains on the client system until it is rebooted or until a new user logs on.

This print driver management scheme allows for a single repository of print drivers so that upgrading is quick and easy. This also reduces the complexity of connecting to network printer shares from a client perspective.

Another benefit of this scheme is drag-and-drop printing. Even if a client does not have a logical printer defined for a printer share, a document can be dropped onto the printer share (as listed in a browse list from Network Neighborhood or Windows Explorer). This initiates the printer driver exchange, and the document is printed.

Printer drivers must be installed locally for any Microsoft operating system before Windows 95 and all non-Microsoft operating systems. Installing new or upgraded drivers for existing printers is a snap. The General tab of the printer's Properties dialog box contains a New Driver button. A warning will appear stating that changing the driver might change the layout and configuration options offered through the Properties dialog box for this printer. Click Yes to continue. This brings up the list of manufacturers and printers that can be used to select new drivers. In most cases, you'll be using the Have Disk button to indicate the path to the new drivers. As a rule of thumb, print a test page to verify that everything worked out the way you planned after you switch drivers.

Managing Printers

Printer management tasks range from changing print server configurations to manipulating active print jobs in a queue. This section looks at several print-related management functions.

Server Management

Server management focuses on the configuration options for a print server as a whole rather than for a specific logical printer. You can access the options for server management by issuing the File, Server Properties menu command from the Printers folder. This opens up the Print Server Properties dialog box.

In the Forms tab of the Print Server Properties dialog box

- You can delete available print forms on this print server. A form is a defined paper type. Form definitions are used rather than tray designations.

- You can create new forms. New form creation requires a name, the paper size, and margin area specifications.

In the Ports tab of the Print Server Properties dialog box

- Existing ports and their associated printers are listed.

- You can create or add new ports.

- You can delete existing ports.

- You can configure existing ports.

In the Advanced tab of the Print Server Properties dialog box, you can do the following

- Define an alternate location for the spool files. The default location is %systemroot%\System32\spool\PRINTERS\.

- Log spooler error events to the System log.

- Log spooler warning events to the System log.

- Log spooler information events to the System log.

- Request audio warning of remote document errors.

- Request notification of successfully printed documents.

The setting changes made to the printer server affect all printers served by this print server.

Print Job Management

You can manage print jobs through the Print Queue window. Each logical printer has its own print queue that can be accessed by double-clicking its icon in the Printers folder. You can manage documents by selecting one or more documents in the queue and then issuing one of the following commands from the Document menu:

- **Pause.** This command prevents the selected document(s) from being printed; the document(s) is retained in the queue.

- **Resume.** This command releases the selected document(s) so it prints normally. This could be called "unpause."

- **Restart.** This command stops the current print processing of the selected document(s) and starts the process over.

- **Cancel.** This command removes the selected document(s) from the print queue.
- **Properties.** This command displays the properties for the selected document(s).

In addition to these commands, you also can alter the order of print jobs in the queue. Any document that does not have a status of Printing can be dragged and dropped into a different position in the queue. The last document, for example, can be moved to the front of the queue to speed printing.

Keep in mind that the documents you can manage depend on your access level. If you have only Print access to the printer, you can manage only your own documents. If you have Manage Documents or Full Control access to the printer, you can manage any print job in the queue.

If you have Manage Documents or Full Control access to a printer, you also can use the commands from the Printer menu of the Print Queue window. These commands include:

- **Pause Printing.** This halts the printing process for all print jobs in the queue. Any data in the physical printer's buffer continues to print, but no new data will be sent from the print server.
- **Set As Default Printer.** This sets the current logical printer as the default printer for all print applications on this client.
- **Document Defaults.** This opens the Default Document Properties dialog box. The Page Setup tab of this dialog box is used to define the association of paper type to trays, the number of copies to print, and whether to print in portrait or landscape mode. The Advanced tab displays the same controls discussed previously for the Device Settings tab of printer Properties dialog box.
- **Sharing.** This accesses the Sharing tab of the printer Properties dialog box, as previously discussed.
- **Purge Print Documents.** This removes all documents in the print queue.
- **Properties.** This opens the printer Properties dialog box (previously discussed and accessed directly from the Printers folder).

Third-Party Print Management Tools

You'd be hard pressed to find an add-on or replacement utility that actually improves upon the Windows NT print system already in place, but here is a list of some tools that have promise:

- **Print Manager Plus from Software Shelf.** A quota and tracking system for printers that can record every activity associated with printing. This develops a usage pattern, which in turn can be used to justify print access, to reduce waste, and to delegate printing costs (paper, toner, repairs, and so on) by user, group, or department. As a quota controller, you can limit printer access to a specific page count per user or per printer. For more information, visit the Software Shelf Web site at **http://www.softwareshelf.com/**.

- **Printer Accounting Server from Software Metrics.** A straight-up usage tracking system. This tool helps you find out exactly how many pages are being printed on which printers and by which users. For more information, visit the Software Metrics Web site at `http://www.metrics.com/`.

- **Zenographics.** Offers several print-related utilities including SuperPrint, InterPrint, and Zj. SuperPrint is a Windows NT print system replacement package that transforms Windows NT into a true 32-bit printing system with better multitasking and background printing. In addition, SuperPrint enhances the printed graphic output. InterPrint is an add-on package that enables remote users to email print jobs to a print server. It transforms Windows NT into a true cross-platform Internet/intranet printing solution. For more information, visit the Zenographics Web site at `http://www.zeno.com/`.

- **FinePrint from Single Track Software.** A shareware utility used to print multiple pages (one, two, four, or eight) on a single sheet of paper. This is a great tool for previewing large documents or for providing amazingly legible small-print overviews of presentations. For more information, visit the Single Track Software Web site at `http://www.singletrack.com/`.

- **Beverly Hills Software.** The 32-bit download area has many other specialized utilities and single-function tools including font printers, directory list printers, CD-ROM label layout printers, print screens, and business card design and printing tools. Check out the latest additions by visiting `http://www.bhs.com/`.

Troubleshooting Printing Problems

Troubleshooting problems with the Windows NT print system is a fairly straight-forward endeavor. Problems can occur in one of the following six areas:

- **The physical print device.** The printer itself can experience problems including paper jams, paper feed problems, ink depletion, toner cartridge malfunction, power surges, or failed memory/control chips. In most cases, clearing out the paper, replacing print cartridges, and cycling the power will restore the printer to operation. If not, consult the printer's manual for additional troubleshooting steps before calling a repair technician. One of the most common problems is a simple oversight of making sure the printer is online. Some printers must be manually enabled to receive print jobs; others automatically switch into online mode after their power-on self-test. If you've changed or manipulated the default settings of the printer, you might want to issue a memory/setting reset to return the printer to its factory defaults.

- **The print driver.** The print driver, if installed properly to begin with, also can develop problems. The most common driver-failure problem occurs when a disk becomes highly fragmented or a virus infection causes a corruption in a driver file. In most cases, reinstalling or replacing the driver will resolve the issue. In rarer cases, updating Windows NT might change print driver-dependent DLL files. In these cases, you need to obtain from the manufacturer newer driver files that have been tested with the new service pack. In some cases, the problem can be found in the logical printer itself. If replacing the driver fails to resolve the problem, try deleting the logical printer and re-creating it from scratch. Keep in mind that, if the logical printer is shared with the network, you'll need to re-create the logical printers connecting to that share on every client. (The name might be the same, but to Windows NT, it is a completely different object with a new SID).

- **Access permissions.** Resolving print-related access permission problems involves the same steps as resolving them for any other type of security object. First, try accessing the object from another account with the same or similar privileges. Next, test the problem account from different clients. Then test a Manage Document, a Full Control, and an Administrator account from the original fault client. These tests should tell you whether the problem is specific to a user account, a computer, or the object. In any case, you should check the permission settings at the printer server to make sure you've set access correctly. You might want to review the group memberships through the User Manager.

- **Network shares.** Network share-related problems revolve around failed network connections, unshared printers, offline servers, or congested traffic pathways. To determine whether the problem is printing related, try accessing other shared objects from the suspect client and server. If these succeed, check to see that the printer is actually shared. If they fail, inspect the network for a point of failure and make sure the server is online.

- **Communications and connections.** Communications between the print server and the actual physical print device are essential to the printing process. If they are disrupted, printing will cease. Resolution of these problems often centers around disconnected cables. Release and reconnect all connections between the print server and the printer (whether locally attached or network attached). Next, verify that the protocol required by network attached printers is installed on the print server and is properly configured on both the print server and the print device.

- **Spooler.** The spooler is the final place to check for problems. It is possible for the spooler to be interrupted so that it hangs in the middle of an operation. This can happen when the Windows NT kernel grants more processing time to tasks other than the print system. Hung spoolers might continue to accept new print jobs or might reject them. (This means either the client receives an error or the print job is dropped with no error.) Usually, spooler problems can be corrected by stopping and restarting the Spooler service through the Services applet. If this fails to resolve the problem, check to make sure the spooler's host drive has at least 50MB of free space. If it doesn't, change the spool host drive and reboot the system. In some cases, a simple reboot will correct the spooler problem. In addition, sometimes it's necessary to delete the .SPL files from the spooler and restart.

If these suggestions fail to resolve your printer problems, you might want to contact the vendor or a licensed printer repair center for further help. In rare cases, reinstalling Windows NT might solve the problem. It is recommend, however, that you exhaust all other options before attempting this final solution.

For More Information

- Microsoft TechNet: `http://www.microsoft.com/technet/`
- Windows NT FAQ: `http://www.ntfaq.com`
- *Windows NT Workstation Resource Kit.* Microsoft Press, 1996. ISBN: 1572313439.

For more information about network attached printers, visit the manufacturers' Web sites, such as

- Digital Equipment Corp/Compaq: `http://www.dec.com/` or `http://www.compaq.com/`
- Hewlett Packard: `http://www.hp.com/`

23

Managing Windows NT System Security

SYSTEM SECURITY IS DEFINED AS THE CAPABILITY to restrict access to a computer system to only those individuals specifically authorized. Within the world of Windows NT, there are many security issues to think about and deal with. Right out of the box, Windows NT is not a secure environment, but with a few patches, configuration changes, and a little sly tweaking, you can deploy a secure system. This chapter looks at Windows NT from a security perspective, discusses how to configure and improve Windows NT's security, and examines a handful of security utilities.

NT Workstation

Most of the issues discussed in this chapter apply to both networked systems and standalone worksta-tions. Except where explicitly stated, all comments are directed to a Windows NT Workstation system. The networking issues apply only if your computer is a client on a network.

Managing Users and Groups

The key to gaining access to Windows NT is to employ a user account. A user account at its most basic level is an authorization entity with a name and password attached. If someone knows the name and password password combination, the person can enter your system and enjoy the privileges of that user account. For this reason, protecting your user account authentication information and properly dolling out privileges is critical to maintaining a secure environment.

Protecting user account authentication information does not mean simply telling everyone to use strong passwords; you must actually develop and enforce a security policy. A security policy is a set of security guidelines that all operations of an organization must follow. A security policy can include guidelines such as the following:

- Use strong passwords with mixed characters of eight letters or more.
- Do not walk away from your workstation while logged on without locking the workstation.
- Do not share your user account with anyone inside or outside the organization.
- Do not copy business data to removable media.
- Do not establish an unauthorized Internet connection by installing a modem or bypassing the firewall or proxy.
- Do not install unapproved software.

This is just the beginning. Additional security-policy items are discussed throughout this chapter. If you are interested in developing a security policy, you should consult some of the references listed at the end of this chapter.

External Intrusion Protection

Outsiders attempting to gain access to your network only need to obtain two pieces of information: a user account name and its password. Therefore, it is important to protect both of these items as much as possible. The following are some ways to protect user account names:

- Create user account names from first and last names; never use just the first name of an individual.
- Always rename common account names such as administrator, guest, and iusr_<servername>.
- Do not use the logon name as the first half of a user's email address.
- Encourage or require users not to use their logon name for systems outside the organization network.
- Track failed logon attempts and rename accounts with frequent logon failure issues (see the section "Auditing For Security Purposes" later in this chapter).

These conventions help protect user account names, but fully protecting them often is a difficult, if not impossible, task. Thus, more importance lies on protecting passwords. Strong password use is the only reliable method for protecting a system against unauthorized access. Windows NT Service Pack 4 (discussed in detail later) includes a DLL file that helps force stronger passwords. PASSFILT.DLL must be installed manually, but it requires that passwords meet the following criteria:

- There is a six-character minimum.
- Four types of characters should be used: uppercase, lowercase, numeric, and non-alphanumeric (symbols, punctuation).
- No part of the email address, account name, or real name is allowed.

In addition to the requirements of this DLL, you can employ the Account policy to enforce password strength. The Account policy can be defined through the User Manager. The following are some recommendations to improve passwords using the Account policy:

- **Set Maximum Password Age to 30, 45, or 60 days.** This forces users to change their passwords on a regular basis.
- **Set Minimum Password Age to 5, 10, or 15 days.** This prevents users from attempting to outwit the password history.
- **Set Minimum Password Length to 6, 8, or 10 characters.** This reduces the benefits of performing dictionary attacks on your security database.
- **Set Password Uniqueness to 6, 10, or 20.** This prevents old passwords from being reused quickly or ever.

Setting Account Lockout to lock out after three bad logon attempts and to reset the counter after 30 minutes for a duration of 120 minutes will also help improve password security. This prevents brute-force attacks on individual accounts during that time period without requiring administrative intervention to restore accounts to active status. If you want to require administrative intervention after any lockout, set the lockout duration to Forever.

Also make sure that you do not select the Users Must Log on in Order to Change Password check box. Doing so prevents users from changing their password if the maximum password age has passed.

Even with the Account policy, there still are several more ways to improve the strength of passwords. These items are not system enforceable, however; they must be part of your organization's general security policy and be enforced on a personnel level. They include the following:

- Avoid using common words, slang, dictionary terms, or other real words.
- Never write a password down, unless you plan to place it in a vault or safety deposit box.

- Avoid using words or names pertaining to your family, friends, hobbies, interests, favorite books or movies, or anything else someone could guess by looking at your workspace, car, or home.

- Create passwords that include numbers and nonalphanumeric characters in the middle of real words (such as Ban4&ana).

- Create passwords that are acronyms of easy-to-remember sentences. "There are 12 days until Xmas" would be Ta12duX.

By combining system-level enforcement of strong passwords, a solid Account policy, and a detailed organizational security policy, you are well-equipped to protect your computer system by maintaining strong passwords.

Simply protecting a user account from compromise is not the complete extent of distilling security on Windows NT. What about authorized users? Studies have shown that a significant number of security breaches occur from within an organization by the very people who were thought to be trustworthy. This means you need to protect your system from both external and internal attacks.

Internal Attack Prevention

The key to internal attack protection and prevention is the proper use of rights and privileges. The basic premise is to "deny all, grant only when necessary." Be a pessimist and not an optimist when granting access privileges. This boils down to micromanagement of NTFS and share permissions on all objects. As you recall, the permission levels on objects are granted by user and/or group and are stored in Access Control Lists (ACLs). These lists define who has access, what level of access is granted, who is denied access, and who does not have defined access for the object.

The Everyone Group

The biggest hole in Windows NT ACL-based security is use of the Everyone group. This default group does not display in the User Manager, but it is there nonetheless. The Everyone group includes everyone: null sessions, anonymous logons, and every defined user account. The application of Service Pack 3 or later adds a group named Authenticated Users, which should be used in place of the Everyone group in most instances.

This is not to say that you can remove the Everyone group from your system with one sweeping command. Doing so renders your NT system defunct, and you'll be forced to completely reinstall. Removing the Everyone group must be performed with caution. The "Securing Windows NT 4.0 Installation" document from the "Windows NT Server, Technical Notes" section of TechNet describes where the Everyone group must remain to sustain a functioning system. Table 23.1 shows the various system directories and files that require the Everyone group and the level of permissions groups should be assigned to maximize security while maintaining system functionality.

Table 23.1   **The Everyone Group's Required System Permissions**

Directory	Everyone Permissions
\WINNT and all subdirectories under it.	Everyone: Read
\WINNT\REPAIR	Everyone: Remove from permissions list
\WINNT\SYSTEM32\ CONFIG	Everyone: List
\WINNT\SYSTEM32\ SPOOL	Everyone: Read
\WINNT\COOKIES, \WINNT\FORMS, \WINNT\HISTORY, \WINNT\OCCACHE, \WINNT\PROFILES, \WINNT\SENDTO, \WINNT\Temporary Internet Files	Everyone: Special Directory Access "Read, Write and Execute, Special File Access" None
\PAGEFILE.SYS	Everyone: Full Control
\AUTOEXEC.BAT, \CONFIG.SYS	Everyone: Read
\TEMP directory	Everyone: Special Directory Access "Read, Write and Execute, Special File Access" None

Other than the items listed in Table 23.1, you can safely remove the Everyone group from the permissions list. Remember that you cannot set the Everyone group to No Access. Doing so prevents all access to that object rather than just not granting access to everyone. Also keep in mind that, when you create new partitions or shares, the Everyone group automatically has Full Control over the new objects.

Setting these permissions can be accomplished using the command line CACLS command. Be sure to use the /e switch so the ACLs are edited instead of replaced. If you prefer a GUI interface, you can either use NT Explorer or obtain the Security Explorer from Small Wonders of Orlando. (A demo is available for download at **http://www.smallwonders.com/**.) This handy tool gives you all the functionality of CACLS in a user-friendly graphical interface.

Managing User Rights

Another key to protection from internal attacks is proper management of user rights. A user right is a high-level system operation or privilege granted to users or groups of users. These privileges enable or restrict activities. The default user rights policy (as defined and controlled through the User Manager) is reasonably secure, but the following tweaks can seal the breach more effectively:

- Remove the Everyone and Guests groups from the Log on Locally right. This prevents nonauthenticated users from gaining unauthorized access.
- Remove the Everyone group from the Shut Down the System right. This prevents nonauthenticated users from powering down the computer.
- Remove the Everyone group from the Access This Computer from the Network right. This prevents nonauthenticated users from gaining access to hosted resources over the network.
- Remove the Everyone group from the Bypass Traverse Checking right. This prevents nonauthenticated users from jumping into subdirectories for which they do not have access to parent directories.
- Remove the Backup operators group from the Restore Files and Directories right. This prevents nonadministrators from restoring files from backup tapes. This is important because file restoration can be pointed to a FAT volume where file-level security restrictions are lost.

If you remove the Everyone group from these rights, you need to verify that the remaining groups with these rights are sufficient. In other words, if you want all users to access resources over the network, the Users group should be granted the Access This Computer from the Network right.

Restricting Permissions

Finally, be a pessimist. When granting users access to resources, always grant as little as possible so the required activities can take place. Don't give a group Change access when all they really need is Read access. Don't grant the Authenticated Users group access when only the Server Operators group needs access. This just makes sense. Start out with no defined access levels for anyone but the Administrators group and the Owner, which both should be set to Full Control. Then add in only those groups or users that need access, and only grant them the minimum level of access required to accomplish their tasks. In general, it's a good idea to permit as little access as possible, and then grant access to users or groups as needed. By doing this, you provide stricter access to resources.

Sticking with these recommendations—protecting usernames, forcing strong passwords, removing the Everyone group, micromanaging ACLs, and altering user rights—enables you to create and maintain a secure Windows NT environment.

Applying the Right Service Packs and Hotfixes

In 1996, Windows NT was released after much testing and refinement; however, many bugs remained in the code. In an attempt to deal with these problems after the product is deployed by customers, Microsoft releases service packs and hotfixes. A *hotfix* is a code-patching tool designed to correct a single problem. A *service pack* is a collection of many hotfixes in a single installable module.

The differences between service packs and hotfixes go beyond their size. Hotfixes are not supported by Microsoft. This means that, if you apply a hotfix, you are removing yourself from the umbrella of Microsoft support. Hotfixes are released to appease the masses without indemnifying Microsoft. Plus, hotfixes often cause other difficulties with their crude method of patching problems, and they cannot be uninstalled without tedious reconfiguration. It is therefore recommended that you only apply a hotfix if you are experiencing the specific problem it was designed to eliminate or if the hotfix offers a significant security improvement.

Service packs, on the other hand, are more thoroughly tested, are fully supported by Microsoft, provide an uninstall path, and don't cause as many problems as hotfixes. Microsoft recently promised to improve its testing of service packs and to release them on a quarterly basis. Information about current service packs is available on the Microsoft Web site. Typically, a link to service packs can be found on the product's page, but you'll have to look for yourself because the Microsoft Web site changes frequently.

Service packs are cumulative releases. Each service pack includes its immediate predecessor plus all hotfixes released since. Service Pack 5 (SP5), for example, includes SP4 and all post-SP4 hotfixes. Only the latest service pack needs to be installed along with any required post-SP hotfixes.

Service Pack 5

Applying the latest service pack is important because it resolves many issues. Service Pack 5 solves, fixes, and patches many problems including the following:

- Printer and print spooler problems
- Ever-present memory leaks
- User-mode (access violation) and kernel mode (stop code) failures
- RRAS problems
- Security vulnerabilities

If you are serious about maintaining a secure environment, you should deploy Service Pack 5 or the latest service pack release. Even with user account restrictions and service packs, however, Windows NT is not an impregnable fortress.

Applying Service Pack 5

Service Pack 5 should be installed immediately after installing Windows NT. Fixing more than 200 bugs and memory leaks and bringing NT into Y2K compliance, SP5 is indispensable in sustaining an operational and secure operating system. Before installing any service pack or hotfix, take the following precautions:

- Back up all important data and the Registry (if not your entire system).
- Update your ERD ("rdisk /s").
- Reboot the system.
- Terminate all applications and stop all unneeded services.
- Take the time to review the documentation and KnowledgeBase documents associated with the service pack and hotfix.

After you install a service pack or hotfix, many key system files will have been changed. Attempting to install additional services or components from the original distribution CD might cause system failures or other strange problems. You should install everything you need from the distribution CD before applying a service pack. The following is a general step-by-step procedure:

1. Install Windows NT.
2. Install all protocols, drivers, and services required.
3. Configure the network, RAS, and other connections.
4. Install the service pack.
5. Install any necessary hotfixes.
6. Install applications.
7. Reapply the service pack.
8. Reapply hotfixes.

If you add new applications in the future, it's a good idea to reapply the service pack and hotfixes. If you discover an application that does not work with the service pack-altered system files, you should contact the application's vendor for a workaround, a patch, or another solution.

You can determine which service pack (if any) has been applied to your system by doing the following:

- Issuing the `WINVER` command from a command prompt
- Issuing the Help, About command from any Windows NT native application (such as NT Explorer)
- Viewing the CSDVersion value in the HKEY_LOCAL_MACHINE\ SOFTWARE\Microsoft\WindowsNT\CurrentVersion Registry key

Obtaining Service Packs and Hotfixes

Service packs can be downloaded through the Microsoft Web site, or you can jump straight to Microsoft's FTP area using a Web browser (`ftp://ftp.microsoft.com/ bussys/winnt/winnt-public/fixes/usa/nt40/`). The service packs are in a subdirectory labeled "ussp5" for US Service Pack 4. The hotfixes can be found in the "hotfixes-postsp5" directories.

The Microsoft Web site contains cursory information about service packs and absolutely nothing about hotfixes. Several third parties maintain great knowledge sites that collect tons of useful information about hotfixes and service packs. We highly recommend that you keep an eye on these sites because Microsoft releases hotfixes without informing the general public.

- NT Bug Traq Web site: `http://www.ntbugtraq.com/`
- Paperbits Web site: `http://www.paperbits.com/`
- NT FAQ Web site: `http://www.ntfaq.com/`

The documentation associated with service packs and hotfixes typically is Knowledge Base documents. These are technical papers written by Microsoft technicians that are assigned a Q reference number. You can search for KnowledgeBase documents using this Q number (remember to always include the Q) at the following locations:

- Microsoft support and KnowledgeBase Web site: `http://support.microsoft.com/`
- TechNet CD
- Microsoft Network or CompuServe (**GO MICROSOFT**)

Closing Well-Known Backdoors to Windows NT

The hacker term "backdoor" is a holdover from the days of bulletin boards (BBS). Many authors of BBS systems included hidden user accounts or special passwords that could gain unrestricted access to resources hosted on the BBS. In most cases, the inclusion of backdoors backfired. When a backdoor was discovered, the BBS community distributed the information, produced patches, or stopped using the software. Windows NT does not include any traditional backdoors, but there are enough cracks in the walls of a Windows NT system that a conniving user can pry open a hole to gain unauthorized access.

The following sections discuss the various cracks in the walls of Windows NT.

Administrative Shares

Windows NT creates hidden shares of all local hard drives each time the system boots. These hidden shares are known as the *administrative shares* because only users with administrative privileges can access them. They are used to guarantee access to drives in the event that standard ACL permissions for the system prevent authorized access. A hidden share is just a normal share with a sharename ending in a dollar sign. Hidden shares can be viewed through the Server Manager tool (native to Windows NT Server or installed as an administrative tool onto Windows NT Workstation). Administrative shares can be deleted, but they automatically are recreated during the next bootup.

Administrators can take advantage of hidden shares by mapping drive letters across the network to gain access to files not available through the standard public shares created on the network. Anyone who can obtain an administrator password, however, can map these drives as well. Furthermore, they can be mapped over any network connection including RAS, VPN, and PPTP.

The administrative shares are not strictly required by the system to function properly. They can be disabled by adding AutoShareServer (Windows NT Server) or AutoShareWks (Windows NT Workstation) to the HKEY_LOCAL_MACHINE\System\CurrentControlSet\Services\LanManServer\Parameters Registry key. A value of 0 turns the administrative shares off; a value of 1 turns them back on.

Predefined Accounts

Because everyone knows that Windows NT automatically creates user accounts when it is installed, these accounts are potential security breaches. The Administrator, Guest, and IUSR_<servername> accounts should be renamed to prevent easy access. In addition, be sure to define a complicated password for each.

Additional protection for these accounts can be obtained by creating dummy accounts. A *dummy account* is a user account with a common name (administrator, guest, admin, and so on) that is not a member of any group and that enjoys no access privileges whatsoever. Such an account will draw the attention of any hackers attempting to break into your system. If they succeed in gaining entry, they will be unable to do anything but give you time to detect their presence and discover their identity.

NetBIOS Interface

NetBIOS is used by Windows NT for many system-level functions. Even though NT manipulates user activity based on SIDs, it still shuffles their associated username around. Unfortunately, this means intelligent snoopers can discover usernames simply by watching network traffic. The NetBIOS Interface service is used by Windows NT to maintain communications with other Windows systems. These communications can include usernames, computer names, domain names, and more. On internal systems, this is not necessarily a problem. For connections to external systems such as the Internet, however, this is effectively broadcasting security information to the world. The NetBIOS interface should be disabled (its binding should be removed) on all external devices and protocols using the Binding tab of the Network applet.

Just restricting the NetBIOS Interface service does not bring you into the clear. Microsoft has embedded NetBIOS communications into all of its three native network protocols: NBT (NetBIOS over TCP/IP), NWLink (NetBIOS over IPX/SPX), and NBF (NetBIOS Frame). Blocking these pathways of NetBIOS traffic requires a firewall or proxy server with port filtering capabilities. Microsoft Proxy Server 2.0 includes port filtering. TCP ports 135–139 must be blocked to prevent NetBIOS traffic from crossing network connections.

Obtaining System-Level Privileges Through the Debugger

When an application crashes, the Dr. Watson utility is launched automatically. The autolaunch of Dr. Watson is a debugging function that can record information about the status of the system when the application failed. The Registry setting in which the debugger is defined is not protected. The HKEY_LOCAL_MACHINE\Software\ Microsoft\Windows NT\CurrentVersion\AeDebug Registry key contains the value of Debugger. This value can be changed to launch any program such as Explorer, User Manager, or even Regedt32. The next time an application fails and the system launches the debugger, the alternate program defined in the Debugger value will be launched with the security context of the failed application. For most applications, this does not pose a security problem. If the user can force a system-level application to fail, however, the individual will be granted system-level access. This Registry key should be modified so that the Everyone group does not have editing capabilities. (You'll need to use Regedt32 to modify Registry permissions.)

Logon Window Displays Information

When a user presses Ctrl+Alt+Del to initiate the authentication process, the WinLogon process displays the logon dialog box in which the username and password are to be entered by the user. By default, this dialog box displays the username of the last user to successfully log in. To change this, edit the HKEY_LOCAL_MACHINE\Software\Microsoft\WindowsNT\CurrentVersion\WinLogon Registry key. Change the DontDisplayLastUserName value to 1 to prevent the display of the last logged-on user. This also can be changed using the TweakUI application from the Windows NT Server Resource Kit CD-ROM.

While you are manipulating this area of the Registry, you also might want to make a few other modifications. When Ctrl+Alt+Del is pressed, the WinLogon dialog box contains several action buttons, one of which is Shutdown. On Windows NT Workstation systems, users can shut down the system without logging on. On Windows NT Server systems, you must log on before you can gain access to the shutdown command. To disable the Shutdown button, change the ShutdownWithoutLogon value set to 0.

Another change in this Registry area is to display a notification message. A notification message is a pop-up dialog box that appears just after Ctrl+Alt+Del is pressed and before the WinLogon dialog box appears. This pop-up message warns unauthorized users that the system is monitored and that any attempt to gain access without permission will be prosecuted. To create a message, add the LegalNoticeCaption and LegalNoticeText values. The former value is the dialog box title; the latter is the body of the message.

NTFS Drivers

Microsoft claimed that NTFS volumes could be read only from Windows NT; however, programmers did not let this impossibility go on for too long. System Internals developed a DOS driver called NTFSDOS, and a German developer created a Linux NTFS driver. The DOS driver enables NTFS drives to be read when a DOS floppy is used to boot the system. The latest edition of this driver also enables you to rename files and to replace damaged files when the byte length remains constant. To download this driver or for more information, visit the System Internals Web site at `http://www.sysinternals.com/`. To download the Linux NTFS driver, visit `http://www.informatik.hu-berlin.de/~loewis/e_index.html`.

Password-Cracking

Password-cracking is the art of extracting passwords from an encrypted database. The hash code used by the SAM database is a widely known formula. Because the hash function is only a one-way function, a brute-force method of password extraction must be waged against the SAM database. A password-cracking tool basically picks a sequence of keyboard characters, hashes them, and then compares the result to the SAM database. If a match is found, a password is known. If no match is found, another string of characters is tried.

Cracking tools can either use a predefined list of text strings or sequentially attempt all combinations. (The former is called a dictionary attack.) Either way, the time required to decipher a strong password (as previously described) is too lengthy to be worthwhile. If any password fails the strong password test, however, the success of a password-cracking tool is greatly improved. In our tests, passwords with two common words of four letters each were extracted in only 8 minutes.

Most password-cracking tools require direct access to the SAM database. This means that, at some point, the security of your network has been breached. Unfortunately, you might have inadvertently handed out the SAM database without your knowledge. The SAM database can be obtained in the following ways:

- From an Emergency Boot Disk
- From the Winnt\Repair directory
- From backup tapes without password locking or physical security
- From any user with administrator-level access who has extracted the SAM from the Registry using REGEDT32

It's a good idea to tighten security using the same tools that hackers are using against you. In other words, download and execute password-cracking tools against your own SAM and force users to change weak passwords. There are probably dozens of password crackers on the Internet, but the following are three popular ones:

- L0phtCrack: `http://www.l0pht.com/` (Note that the second character is a zero.)
- ScanPro: `http://www.ntsecurity.com/Products/ScanPro/index.html/`
- NT Crack: `http://www.secnet.com/`

Complete details about how to use each of these tools is provided on their respective Web sites.

Auditing for Security Purposes

The auditing system built into Windows NT can be used for many ends, but it primarily is used to track security problems. With the proper configuration, the auditing system can pinpoint areas or individuals for which security is a threat.

Auditing is configured through the User Manager, and all audit events are recorded in the Event Viewer's Security log. If you are unfamiliar with auditing, consult the Resource Kit and TechNet.

Auditing just for the sake of auditing is a waste of system resources and time. In fact, too much auditing can cause performance degradation. Instead, decide exactly which areas are the most critical to monitor and audit activity only in those areas. Table 23.2 shows several types of security issues that can be tracked by employing only part of the auditing capabilities of NT.

Table 23.2 **Security Issues and Associated Auditing Elements**

Issue	Audit Elements
Brute-force password-cracking	Logon and Logoff: Failure.
Compromised user accounts	Logon and Logoff: Failure. (Note: Look for logons during odd hours or days when the user is not present.).
Abuse of admininistrative privileges	Use of User Rights: Success; User and Group Management: Success; Security Policy Changes: Success; and Restart, Shutdown, and System: Success.
Virus infections	File and Object Access: Success & Failure for write access on .EXE and .DLL files for the Everyone group.
Unauthorized access to critical files	File and Object Access: Success & Failure for read and write access on all critical files for all suspect groups/users.
Unauthorized use of printers	File and Object Access: Success & Failure for print access on each printer for all suspect groups/users.

The Windows NT auditing system automatically records each audited event in the Security log. To discover a security breach, you must review each recorded event manually. There are, however, several third-party products that can automatically perform pattern matching, trend extraction, and symptomatic reasoning against the event data. These tools highlight occurrences and trends that indicate security threats and actual breaches. Intrusion-detection software is expensive and typically is designed for high-traffic, large networks. Standalone systems typically do not benefit enough from such software to warrant the expense.

If you are interested in learning more about intrusion-detection software, visit the following Web sites and obtain their downloadable demos:

- Trusted Information Systems' (Network Associates) WebStalker Pro: `http://www.tis.com/`
- Internet Security Systems' Internet Scanner: `http:///www.iss.net/`
- Harris Corporation's STAT: `http://www.sunbelt-software.com/stat.htm`

System Policies

If user activity poses a threat to the security and stability of your network, you might consider imposing system policies. A system policy is an administration and control tool that restricts functions within the operating system on a user, group, or computer basis. You can, for example, restrict access to the Control Panel for all members of the Sales group. This restriction effectively prevents them from installing new hardware drivers.

System policies are created and managed through the System Policy Editor—Start, Programs, Administrative Tools (Common), System Policy Editor. This tool is basically a Registry-editing tool. It can be used on policies or on the Registry itself. System policies are Registry configuration files that overwrite the existing Registry when a user logs in. The default system policies have no restrictions defined, and all restrictions or changes must be implemented by an administrator. A policy can be created that addresses issues anywhere in the Registry.

Policies are created on a user, group, or computer basis. Two basic policies—Default Computer and Default User—apply to every computer and every user, respectively. Unless absolutely necessary, don't alter the default policies. Instead, create specific policies for users, groups, or computers as they are needed.

Policies can be used to erect barriers between users and any areas of the system to which you don't want them to gain access. This can include, but is not limited to, the following:

- **Display settings.** Prevent changing of drivers, color depth, resolution, wallpaper, screensavers, and color scheme.

- **Shell-based restrictions.** Prevent shutdown, restrict network neighborhood, and hide drives.

- **Registry editing.** Prevent Registry editing.

- **Applications.** Prevent access to and installation of unauthorized applications.

Using the System Policy Editor, new policies can be created from a template. Custom templates can be created to reach any part of the Registry. For details about creating custom templates, consult the Resource Kit. New policies must be assigned a name when created. For a policy to apply to a user, group, or computer, the policy name must match the user, group, or computer name. A policy's details (see Figure 23.1) can be managed by selecting various check boxes. Each check box can be selected, deselected, or grayed to enforce the restriction, to remove the restriction, or to maintain the current setting, respectively.

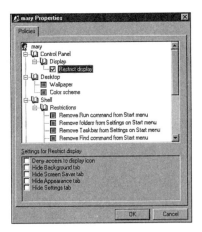

Figure 23.1   A specific user policy's Properties dialog box.

All the user, group, and computer policies are stored in a single policy file called NTCONFIG.POL. This file must be stored in the \%systemroot%\System32\ Repl\Export\Scripts directory on a PDC or BDC so that it can be accessed by every workstation on the network.

If multiple group policies are defined, you also must define the priority in which the group policies should be applied to users. The Options, Group Priority command opens a dialog box in which you can sort the group policies. The most important group policy should be applied last; the least important should be applied first. This ensures that the settings of the important policy will be applied regardless of the settings in the other applicable policies.

When multiple policies are in use, an application scheme is used to apply the policies to users. The order of application is as follows:

1. If a user has a specific user policy, it is applied. No group policies are applied.

2. If a user does not have a specific user policy, the group policies are applied based on membership using the defined priority order.

3. If a user does not have a specific user policy, the Default User policy is applied.

You should take care not to define a policy that completely restricts access to everything within a system, especially with a Default User or Default Computer policy. Such a policy renders a system unable to perform any operations and forces a complete reinstallation.

Security Is a Philosophy, Not Just a Procedure

A secure computer system entails more than just the software and configuration of the computer, it involves physical access control and user training. Think of security as a three-legged stool—operating system, physical access, and users. If any one leg is not sufficient, the stool will not support its intended purpose. Likewise, if you fail to address every area to sustain a secure environment, you might as well not even try at all.

Physical access control is the simple act of preventing all unauthorized persons from touching the computer, its peripherals, its communication links, and its power source. This can involve locked doors, security badges, and locked cases, but it doesn't stop there. You need to keep in mind that the building's structure and construction might not offer you a secure storage environment. Can ceiling tiles be moved and walls scaled? Can access be gained through ventilation shafts or windows? Are the temperature controls secure? Is electricity protected, and is a UPS attached to the computer?

Even this doesn't cover all the aspects of physical security. You need to shred and possibly incinerate all printouts and other hard-copy output from the computer system. This also should include handwritten materials that might contain passwords, usernames, or other system information. You'd be amazed at how much information can be gleaned by reading your trash.

Still not convinced? Think about the following issues as well:

- Is the after-hours cleaning crew bonded? Can they gain access to your computer room?
- Are floppy drives installed on your critical systems?
- Are extra ports open and ready to accept a new attachment?
- Where are your backup tapes stored?
- Who watches your systems after hours?

Theft

One of the more common methods of gaining access to an organization's network is to steal notebook computers. More often than not, traveling businessmen's notebooks are remote terminals for their networks. With a simple RAS connection, they can connect to the office. In addition, some users configure their notebooks to automatically authenticate them or use an operating system that stores passwords in an extractable format. Just think about how often you've gotten stuck behind someone getting searched at the airport metal detector just after you've placed your carry-on items into the X-ray machine, only to wonder if someone else might pick them up while you can't see them or get to them. If you aren't thinking about it, you can be assured that some criminal is.

User Education

Another aspect of security that must be addressed is user education. Without proper training that informs users of the necessity and operation of security on your network, they will make every effort to subvert the system to simplify their life regardless of the resulting security threats. User education requires that you explain (at least generally) what types of security are in place to protect both physical access and computer/network access. It also requires that you explain the consequences for violating security and enforce the punishment strictly.

The following items should be addressed during user education if they apply to your situation:

- Have users sign a nondisclosure agreement that details the importance and proprietary nature of your organization's internal data and information.
- Users should never share passwords, user accounts, or security badges.
- Users should never walk away from a workstation while they are still logged on without locking the workstation.
- Users should not install unapproved software.
- Users must not tamper, subvert, or bypass any security measure.

- Users must respect the privacy of the organization and the other users.
- The consequences of violating any element of the security policy needs to be detailed and enforced without reservation or exception.

Several companies have reported that, after developing, discussing, and deploying a security policy, they experienced an increase in security. Before a benefit was gained, however, they lost a few good employees who were too lazy to maintain vigilance within security boundaries. This termination of users sent a clear signal to the remaining employees that the security policy should not be tested. Compliance became self-enforced after the first martyr was slain. Most analysts agree that the loss of a few people during the early stages of security deployment is insignificant compared to the prevention of profit loss or market share due to security breaches.

Security and Viruses

Maintaining a secure environment entails more than just preventing unauthorized access from external sources and internal sources. It also means protecting the data from loss, corruption, or destruction. This means you need to protect your data from loss due to hardware destruction as well as virus destruction. Although it might not be possible to prevent natural disasters, you can protect your data by maintaining off-site, secure storage of backup tapes.

Preventing virus destruction of data requires vigilance. The only way to protect against viruses is to be proactive and have a defense mechanism in place before infection occurs. A good defense mechanism is a virus scanning tool that automatically scans inbound data and that downloads updates regularly. There are several great products from which to choose, but their effectiveness rests on your ability to install and configure them correctly.

Keep in mind that any communication pathway—a network, the Internet, email, floppy disks, and serial ports—can be a route traversed by a virus. You must deploy a reliable software solution instead of hoping that luck and user-activity management will protect the system. As with security in general, a policy should be constructed and enforced to guide the protection endeavor. A virus-protection policy needs to include the following elements:

- **100% virus-free servers.** No file should be saved to a server before it passes a virus scan.
- **Regular virus-free backups.** If you back up a virus, it returns when you restore your system.
- **Identification of users who take risks.** These users bring in external floppies, install unauthorized software, download lots of software from the Internet, and revoke their access privileges.
- **Updated software.** This includes automatic virus list updates and software patch/upgrade installation.

There are many solid virus-protection systems on the market today. We've worked with the following five that have received industry approval:

- Symantec's Norton Anti-Virus: **http://www.symantec.com/**
- Cheyenne's InocuLAN: **http://www.cheyenne.com/**
- Dr. Solomon's Anti-Virus Toolkit: **http://www.drsolomon.com/**
- Network Associates' Anti-Virus: **http://www.nai.com/products/antivirus/**
- McAfee's VirusScan: **http://store.mcafee.com/**
- IBM's Anti-Virus: **http://www.av.ibm.com/**

Just as you wouldn't survive without your natural immune system, neither can a computer system maintain reliable operations without virus protection.

Third-Party Security Tools

No chapter about power tools would be complete without a good dose of third-party utilities. The following sections take a look at several utilities you can employ to simplify security management and to improve your protection.

Managing ACLs, Events, and the Registry

The interfaces for managing Access Control Lists on objects; viewing the system, security, and application logs; and looking at the Registry are somewhat limited. If you've ever tried to get a general overview or even just extract sorted data from the built-in Windows NT tools, you've probably come away frustrated. Somarsoft has developed the following excellent tools that you'll soon be unable to live without:

- **DumpACL.** This tool builds a sorted list of all the permission settings for any object type within Windows NT. This makes it simple to create a detailed system-wide view of the ACLs of files, folders, printers, shares, and the Registry.
- **DumpEvt.** This tool extracts information from the Event Viewer log files into a format readable by other programs and applications. It most often is used to format the Event Viewer logs into a database file format for long-term trend analysis or historical tracking.
- **DumpReg.** This tool dumps the entire contents of the Registry into a text file, making searching for text strings easy. DumpReg also can sort the exported file by modification date so the last modification to the Registry appears first in the output file.

All three of these tools can be downloaded from the Somarsoft Web site absolutely free of charge. They are all GUI interfaces, are easy to use, and include help documentation. For more information and to obtain these tools, visit **http://www.somarsoft.com/**.

Resource Kit Jewels

The Windows NT Workstation 4.0 Resource Kit includes several security-related tools. Instead of delving into the details of how to use each of these tools, we will leave that to the extensive documentation already included in the Resource Kit. Here is a list of the tools to which you should pay close attention:

- REGENTRY.HLP contains extensive information about Registry values.
- C2CONFIG helps you configure your NT system to fully comply with C2 security standards.
- FIXACLS restores the default security permissions on all system files.
- FLOPLOCK locks floppy drives so that only Administrators and Power Users can access them.
- SCOPY can be used to copy files from one partition to another and to maintain the original security settings on the copied files and folders.
- PASSPROP can force password complexity and can enable the administrator account to be locked out.

These are just a few of the security-related tools from the Windows NT Resource Kit. We suggest you take the time to review the entire Resource Kit. You might find other useful tools that apply to your particular situation.

Application Password Recovery

If you suspect that someone is really out to get you, you've probably employed application-specific password encryption on your files. Tools from the Microsoft Office suite, databases, spreadsheets, and other productivity tools can protect data files by encrypting the files and locking them with a password. In the past, if you forgot the password, you had to forget the data in the file. With AccessData, however, password recovery is now possible.

The Password Recovery Toolkit includes modules capable of extracting passwords from data files created by Access, Word, WordPerfect, Excel, Lotus 1-2-3, Paradox, Q&A, Quattro Pro, Ami Pro, Approach, QuickBooks, Professional Write, DataPerfect, and ACT. For more information and to download a trial version, visit the AccessData Web site at **http://www.accessdata.com/**.

Security Scanners

Internet Security Systems has developed scanning software that evaluates the security of your system and reports to you any weaknesses or outright security holes. By examining ACLs, ownership, network services, user accounts, installed applications, OS configuration, and much more, the ISS System Scanner often can detect problems that might be overlooked by a human administrator.

ISS also offers a related product called RealSecure, an integrated intrusion-detection system that keeps watch over your network in search of security breaches. The automatic surveillance from RealSecure offers a 24/7 solution to the human watchdog.

To download trial versions of ISS software, visit `http://www.iss.net/`.

For More Information

- Microsoft Security Advisor & Notification Service:
  `http://www.microsoft.com/security/`

- Microsoft Security Partners: `http://www.microsoft.com/security/partners/`

- *Windows NT Magazine*: `http://www.winntmag.com/`

- *Windows NT Systems Magazine*: `http://www.ntsystems.com/`

- *Windows NT Enterprise Computing*: `http://www.entmag.com/`

- NTsecurity.com: `http://www.ntsecurity.com/`

- NT Shop, NT Security News: `http://www.ntshop.net/`

- Security Bugware: `http://oliver.efri.hr/~crv/security/bugs/NT/nt.html`

- Robert Malmgren's NT Security FAQ: `http://www.it.kth.se/~rom/ntsec.html`

- Bill Stout's Known NT Exploits:
  `http://www.emf.net/~ddonahue/NThacks/ntexploits.htm`

- TISC Security: `http://tisc.corecom.com/`

- Somarsoft: `http://www.somarsoft.com/`

- Security mailing lists: `http://oliver.efri.hr/~crv/security/mlist/mlist.html`

- l0pht: `http://www.10pht.com/`

- BHS Software: `http://www.bhs.com/`

- SERVERxtras, Inc.: `http://www.serverxtras.com/`

- Microsoft KnowledgeBase: `http://www.microsoft.com/kb/`

- MSNEWS.MICROSOFT.COM - NNTP server:
  microsoft.public.inetexplorer.ie4.security; microsoft.public.java.security;
  microsoft.public.windowsnt.★

- Microsoft Security reporting mailing list: `secure@microsoft.com`

- NTSecurity mailing list: `Majordomo@iss.net - subscribe ntsecurity`

- Chapman, D. Brent and Elizabeth D. Zwicky. *Building Internet Firewalls*. O'Reilly & Associates, Sebastopol, CA, 1995. ISBN: 1565921240.

- Cheswick, William R. and Steven M. Bellovin. *Firewalls and Internet Security: Repelling the Wily Hacker*. Addison-Wesley, Reading, MA, 1994. ISBN: 0201633574. New edition announced for 1999.

- Edwards, Mark Joseph. *Internet Security with Windows NT.* Duke Press, 1998. ISBN: 1882419626.

- *Maximum Security.* Sams.net, 1997. ISBN: 1575212684.

- Rutstein, Charles B. *Windows NT Security: A Practical Guide to Securing Windows NT Servers and Workstations.* Computing McGraw-Hill, 1997. ISBN: 0070578338.

- Sheldon, Tom. *Windows NT Security Handbook.* Osborne McGraw-Hill, 1997. ISBN: 0078822408.

- Sutton, Stephen A. *Windows NT Security Guide.* Addison-Wesley, 1996. ISBN: 0201419696.

- Chellis, James. *MCSE: Internet Explorer 4 Administration Kit Study Guide.* Sybex, 1998. ISBN: 0782123090.

V

Windows NT Goes Online:
Internet or Intranet Access

24

Windows NT as a Web Client

T HE INTERNET IS A VAST, expanding resource of information, entertainment, and community. To gain access to the Internet, you need three things: a computer system, a network connection to the Internet, and the proper client utility. This chapter discusses why Windows NT Workstation is a solid and versatile platform from which to access Internet and intranet resources.

Configuring Internet Access

To access resources on the Internet, you must have a network connection to the Internet. As you know from previous chapters, the Internet is a TCP/IP-based computer network. To communicate with resource hosts on the Internet, you must be a client of that network. There are several ways to obtain Internet access including dial-up connections, LAN access, and proxied service. Windows NT Workstation is amenable to any of these connection methods.

Dial-up connections are the most common method because they cost the least and often are the easiest to configure for home or nonprofessional users. A dial-up connection typically employs a standard analog modem, but other technologies, such as ISDN, cable modems, and ADSL, can and are being used as dial-up networking devices. Dial-up networking simply refers to any form of establishing a connection between your personal computer system and a remote network on demand. In most cases, you'll use a public communications network (such as a telephone system, digital communications systems, cable television network, and so on) to provide a communications pathway. Fortunately, you have little more to worry about than a phone number, a user account name, and a password when establishing your connection.

The first step in establishing a dial-up connection (or any type of connection) to the Internet is to have an access account with an ISP. The first step in purchasing service from an ISP it to locate ISPs that provide service to your area. This can be done in several ways:

- Check local newspapers and telephone books.
- Ask local technical retailers.
- Use the ISP Connection Web site hosted by Internet.com at **http://www. internet.com/**.

You should select two to six ISPs and compare services and prices. Make a decision about the best bang for your buck and sign a service contract. When making your selection, keep the following items in mind:

- Does the ISP supports Windows NT clients?
- Does it provide 24-hour customer support?
- Is there a range of connection technologies such as modem, ISDN, ADSL, cable, and so on?
- Are there extra charges for extra services?
- What does the basic package actually includes (email, Web, FTP, IRC, home directories, Telnet)?
- Are there time limits and time charges (if applicable)?

After you've jumped through all the hoops required by the ISP to start service, you must obtain a few key elements:

- A dial-up access number(s)
- A user account name or logon name
- A password

This is all that is strictly required to configure your Windows NT Workstation system to connect to most ISPs over a modem using a standard telephone line. Depending on the logon system used by the ISP and how its DHCP services are configured, however, you might need the following:

- A logon script to walk through logon menus
- A second name and password (one set for the dial-up server and another to connect to the ISP's network and ultimately the Internet)
- DNS primary and secondary server IP addresses
- The default gateway IP address

- An assigned IP address for your client
- Proxy configuration or usage settings and parameters
- Specialized software for encryption, compression, and proxy

No matter what is required by the ISP, it should provide you with a detailed, step-by-step guide about how to fully and accurately configure your Windows NT Workstation client to connect. If one is not provided, you should seriously consider whether to actually contract with that ISP.

Dial-Up Access

For most ISPs, configuring your system to connect to theirs is simple. Here are the required steps:

1. Verify that the modem is physically installed, that its driver is loaded through the Modems applet, and that it is defined as an outbound RAS port through the Remote Access Service (RAS) on the Services tab of the Networking applet.

2. Launch the Dial-Up Networking (DUN) utility (Start, Programs, Accessories, Dial-Up Networking).

3. If DUN is not already installed, you'll be prompted for the Windows NT Workstation distribution CD-ROM.

4. If DUN is installed and this is the first time you've used it, a message will appear stating that the phonebook is empty. Click OK to launch the New Phonebook Entry Wizard.

5. If DUN already has been used, you'll need to click New to launch the New Phonebook Entry Wizard.

6. The first page of the wizard asks for a name for the connection. Provide one and then click Next.

7. On the next page, define the server type to which you are connecting. Select the I Am Calling the Internet check box and then click Next.

8. The next page requests the phone number; provide it and then click Next.

9. Click Finish on the last page to create the DUN phonebook entry.

10. The Dial-Up Networking main dialog box appears with the newly created phonebook entry selected.

11. Before you use this newly created entry, you need to make one more modification. Click the More button and select Edit Entry And Modem Properties.

12. Select the Security tab. Select the Accept Any Authentication Including Clear Text radio button. Click OK. (This change removes authentication encryption, which typically is not used by most ISPs.)

If you click the Dial button, you'll be prompted for your username and password. Windows NT also provides a field for the domain; when connecting to an ISP, leave this blank. After you click OK, Windows NT will attempt to connect to the ISP using the provided phone number and authentication data. If a connection is established, a pop-up message stating the speed of the connection will display for a few seconds.

High-Speed Access

If you are connecting to an ISP using ISDN, a cable modem, or nearly any other type of connect-on-demand technology, the process of connecting to an ISP is almost identical to using an analog modem. Most ISPs support analog modem connections, but only some ISPs support alternative connection methods. When they do, they typically offer only one option not several.

The ISPs in our area treated ISDN and ADSL as simple, high-speed, dial-up access methods. This means that, as far as the customer is concerned, the configuration is no different than if the person was using an analog modem. ISDN users need to have their telephone company run an ISDN line into their homes, and they must purchase an ISDN modem or router. Likewise, ADSL customers must have their phone lines tested for the capability to support the high-speed signals, and they must purchase an ADSL modem. Both ISDN and ADSL devices can be installed through the Modems applet. The only real difference is speed.

Cable modems are slightly different (at least in our area). Cable modem service is offered by the cable company instead of an independent ISP. Furthermore, the cable company provides special connection establishment and management software. Therefore, you don't actually use DUN. You'll also need the cable company to drop a special data-only line from your external cable box to your home. (You typically can't just connect the cable modem to the outlet to which a television usually is attached.)

When you examine ISPs, you should take the time to discuss which alternative connection technologies currently are supported and which ones they plan to add in the near future. You might find that ADSL with one ISP is more cost effective than ISDN with another, or you might find that going with a cable modem is the smartest route. Therefore, remember to contact your local cable provider to inquire about Internet services; this type of company might not appear on lists of typical ISPs.

TCP/IP

Connecting to the Internet directly requires that TCP/IP be present on your client. Therefore, TCP/IP must already be present on your system, or you must manually install it before configuring DUN; otherwise, it will automatically be installed when you install RAS or DUN.

Connection Services

You've probably heard or seen many advertisements for obtaining Internet access through AOL, Microsoft Network, or other large connection services. These services often provide lots of value-added private network bonuses such as localized content, focused advertising, and moderated discussion forums. What they don't offer, however, is high-speed access or guaranteed technical support. In our opinion, AOL and the like are great starter services, but technically savvy people should work with a real ISP with real options. Internet access is no different than any other product or service. You get what you pay for, and the larger the organization from which you purchase, the less personal attention you'll get.

Network Access

If your Windows NT Workstation computer is not a standalone system and is attached to a network, there are other options for obtaining Internet access. As a network client, you still can use a dial-up connection if you have a modem (or another connection device) attached directly to your computer. This is not allowed in most organizations, however, to protect network security. On a network, the two methods of granting Internet access to clients are through a direct connection or proxied service.

Direct Connection

A direct connection is a network configuration in which the network itself is attached to the Internet via an ISP (in much the same way as a standalone system). The network is granted a block of IP addresses. These addresses are assigned to each device on the network. The connection between the LAN and the ISP often is an ISDN, T1, or greater connection to provide adequate bandwidth for the LAN users.

Every client on the network is connected to the Internet at all times, so they all have direct access to Internet resources. The drawbacks of a direct connection are the expense of a dedicated high-speed connection and the leasing of the IP address block. Furthermore, by connecting the network directly to the Internet, there is a much broader possibility for attacks from hostile external users.

Proxy Service

Internet access over proxy services is a much safer solution that usually also is much more cost effective. The network itself is not connected to the Internet; rather, a single server is connected. That server is the only device within the LAN that has direct Internet access. A proxy server is installed on that machine (such as Microsoft Proxy Server 2.0). A proxy server acts as a middleman between the Internet and internal network clients.

Clients gain Internet access by communicating with the proxy server to request Internet resources. The proxy server accesses the requested resource on the client's behalf and then sends the received data to the client. This provides a double-blind method of communication. The client never communicates directly with the Internet, and all information about the client is hidden from the Internet. A proxy server protects the internal network by completely preventing Internet-originating traffic from entering the network. In fact, the Internet network can use IP addresses that are not routable (see RFC 1918 at `http://www.faqs.org/rfcs/rfc1918.html`) or a network protocol other than TCP/IP (if supported by the proxy service such as NWLink [IPX/SPX] when Microsoft Proxy Server 2.0 is used). Proxied Internet access does not require the leasing of a block of IP addresses, nor does it require a dedicated connection.

If you need more information about connecting a network to the Internet either directly or using a proxy server, consult the Microsoft Web site (`http://www.microsoft.com/`), the Windows NT Resource Kits, and TechNet.

Internet Services and Tools

After Internet access is obtained for your Windows NT Workstation, you need the proper tools to access the abundant resources. The Internet is a collection of dozens of information services including Web, FTP, email, IRC, newsgroups, streaming audio/video, and more. This book is not about Internet information services, but it does discuss two of the most often used services: Web and email. The remainder of this chapter looks at Web access and the tools used to access the Web. Chapter 25, "Windows NT as an Email Client," examines email and its associated tools. You might notice that many Internet tools have overlapping capabilities. Just consider it a benefit that you might not need multiple individual utilities to access multiple information services.

Intranets

The Internet is not the only place where information service utilities might be required to access content. Many larger networks are deploying their own internal services that host and distribute private content to their clients. This information is not released onto the Internet. These networks, typically called intranets, are little more than a LAN using TCP/IP as a network protocol with at least one information server hosting content. Intranets offer private Web sites, file storage, and retrieval repositories via FTP; employ email for communication; and use newsgroups as discussion forums.

The technologies originally developed and deployed on the Internet are quickly making their way into private networks. Therefore, it is not uncommon for networks to host their own content (by design and purpose) completely isolated from the Internet. As a client, accessing intranet resources is no different than accessing Internet resources. The only possible difference is the actual URL or access locator employed to retrieve the resource. The Internet employs fully qualified domain names, whereas intranets can use Fully Qualified Domain Names (FQDNs) or NetBIOS host names. (Both can use just plain IP addresses.)

Internet Explorer

Internet Explorer is the Internet information service tool created and distributed by Microsoft for Windows platforms (versions also are available for Macintosh and UNIX). Internet Explorer primarily is a Web accessing tool (called a Web browser), but it includes many other capabilities for other information services. At the time this book was written, Internet Explorer was in version 5.0. You might find that Microsoft has updated this tool with either a microincrement or a full new release. In any case, most of the information discussed here should be applicable to Internet Explorer for several generations. Keep in mind that the best place to obtain new and updated information about any Microsoft or Internet product is not a published book (which often is two to three months behind when it is printed) but the Internet itself. Later in this chapter, many Internet URLs are provided that offer valuable and timely information.

Internet Explorer is a multifunctional Web browser. Its primary feature offers users the capability to access content hosted by Web sites on the Internet or on an intranet. Internet Explorer is not just a Web browser, however; it can be used to access many other types of Internet information, such as

- Email
- Subscriptions/channels (previously called push technology)
- Newsgroups (also called discussion groups)

As a Web browser, Internet Explorer is more than just a simple Web accessing tool. It fully supports HTML and other basic Web technologies such as HTTP, CGI, JavaScript, and more. It also includes support for Java, Dynamic HTML, XML, and VBScript. Microsoft has developed and deployed its own Web-based technologies, such as ActiveX and Active Server Pages, and has integrated them into Internet Explorer. This just scratches the surface, however, of the capabilities associated with Web interaction. IE boasts many other capabilities and features including the following:

- The capability to view remote and local resources through the same IE interface
- Consistent toolbars that are "common" throughout the latest releases of Microsoft products
- Support for offline browsing of local, cached, or subscribed content
- Security based on zones (Local Intranet, Trusted Sites, Internet, Restricted Sites)
- Subscriptions to channels and nonchanneled content
- Desktop integration (known as Active Desktop)
- Search, history, channel, and favorites hot lists
- Support for plug-ins and helper applications

It would take hundreds of pages to explain every detail of Internet Explorer, but you probably are already intimately aware of its capabilities and how it is used to access resources. If you need detailed information about IE, its features, its capabilities, and its use, consult the Internet Explorer Web site at **http://www.microsoft.com/ie/**. You might want to view documentation such as the Internet Explorer Administration Kit, Reviewer's Guide, Manuals, and Service Pack information as found on the IE Web site and TechNet.

Active Desktop: Customizing Your Desktop

If you are like most Internet users, you are a creature of habit. You'll visit the same Web site every day to get updates on the news, to check the weather, to get movie times, to find recipes, to start new searches for information, or even to access cartoons. Microsoft has taken the idea of visiting the same sites often and has expanded Internet Explorer from just storing the URL in a favorites list to enabling content to be placed onto your desktop. This feature, called Active Desktop, is a unique technology application that transforms your otherwise static desktop into a multiview, multisite, content-hosting area. You'll never be bored seeing the same old wallpaper day after day. You'll now enjoy your own personalized custom information space consisting of a collage of multiple content sources that are constantly updated directly from the Internet (or intranet).

Active Desktop was released as an optional feature of Internet Explorer 4.0, which introduced this wallpaper come dynamic Web document to Windows 95 and Windows NT. Active Desktop was integrated into Windows 98 and is slated for inclusion in Windows 2000.

Active Desktop is a more than just a special wallpaper enhancement. It also adds special Web browser-like features to many other interfaces found in Windows 95/98 and Windows NT. Enhancements from Active Desktop can be found in the Start menu, the taskbar, Control Panel, My Computer, Network Neighborhood, and Windows Explorer. Most of these interfaces benefit from drag-and-drop support, customizable menus, content/context-based displays, and additional pop-up/help/side displays of information.

Active Desktop does have a down side. The content added to your desktop consumes system resources and employs your Internet connection to maintain fresh content. The latter issue is not a problem for dedicated connections, but dial-up connections might find it a bit annoying when Active Desktop initiates a connection each time it wants to update its hosted content. You'll need to weigh the benefits of constantly updated desktop content against connection charges and use of the primary household telephone line.

When installing Internet Explorer 4.0 or later, you are offered an opportunity by the installation wizard to install and activate Active Desktop. If you elect to remove Active Desktop later, it can be done through the Add/Remove Software applet. Just select Microsoft Internet Explorer 4.0 from the list and click Add/Remove. This reveals the Internet Explorer 4.0 Active Setup dialog box. From this dialog box, select the Remove Active Desktop option. If you want to add Active Desktop later, select Add a Component from the same dialog box.

More information about Active Desktop, its use, and how you can take full advantage of its features for personal entertainment and improved productivity can be found on the Internet Explorer Web area (`http://www.microsoft.com/ie/`) and TechNet.

Working Outside the Web

Internet Explorer offers access to more than just Web resources. Natively, Internet Explorer can interact with FTP sites. With several add-on utilities from Microsoft, IE can be expanded to access email, newsgroups, interactive streaming multimedia, Web server administration, Web site publishing, and integrated real-time chat.

FTP

Accessing FTP through Internet Explorer is simply a function of creating the proper URL to gain initial access to the FTP site. After you are logged on to the FTP site, you can surf the content in much the same manner as a Web site. In general, an FTP URL is constructed in this manner: `ftp://doman_name:port/path`. This basic FTP URL can be used to access anonymous sites (sites that do not require authorized usernames and passwords to gain access). The *domain_name* portion can be either an FQDN for an FTP site such as `ftp.microsoft.com` or an IP address such as 207.46.133.140. The *port* is the TCP port used to access the FTP service. By default, this is 21. As long as the FTP server is using the default, you don't need to specify the port in the URL. Many FTP sites, however, are using alternate port addresses to limit unnecessary access and to prevent Web crawlers/robots/wanders from traversing the site. The logic is that, if you host an FTP site on a nondefault port address, users must visit your Web site or otherwise interact with you before they learn the proper method to gain access to your FTP site. A path statement can be added to jump immediately to a sublevel of the FTP site.

If the FTP site is requires a username and password to gain access, you can construct an URL to include this data, such as `ftp://username:password@domain_name:port/path/`. This URL provides the logon mechanism with the authentication information needed to authorize access. You need to remember, however, that an URL such as this does not protect the password in any way; it is transmitted as clear text.

After you have entered an FTP site using Internet Explorer, you can traverse the directory structure by clicking on the displayed links. Depending on the operating system hosting the FTP site, the display of file and directory information will vary. In most cases, directories are identified with a <DIR> located to the left of the linked name. All other links are files. Traversing down a directory tree is simple, just click on a <DIR> labeled link. Traversing up a directory tree can be tricky. Depending on the host system type and how it is configured, moving to a parent directory might require one of the following:

- Clicking on a <DIR> link of ".." (see `ftp.3com.com`)

- Clicking on a link labeled "up to parent directory" or just "Parent Directory" (see `wuarchive.wustl.edu`)
- Manually editing the current URL to remove the last element of the path (see `ftp.microsoft.com`)

Internet Explorer can be used to explore an FTP site and download files; however, you can only select to download one file at a time. After a file download is started, you can select another file to download, but you cannot select two or more files at one time. Furthermore, Internet Explorer does not have the capability to upload files to an FTP site.

Email and Newsgroups

As part of the full installation of Internet Explorer, the Outlook Express email and newsgroup client is installed. Outlook Express technically is not part of IE, but it ships with IE. Outlook Express offers two key features to your system: email and newsgroup interaction. Windows NT Workstation and email are discussed in the next chapter, but they are mentioned here in relation to Internet Explorer.

As an email client, Outlook Express offers all the standard functions you've come to expect from such utilities. When it comes to Internet email and address book management, Outlook Express has all the capabilities that its parent product, Outlook 98, boasts. If you are not a licensed user of Microsoft Office 97 or Exchange Server and are therefore unable to download the full Outlook 98 product, Outlook Express as bundled with Internet Explorer is a solid alternative. The next chapter discusses the benefits of the full product and compares and contrasts the capabilities of both.

As a newsreader, Outlook Express is functional. It offers an interface to the 20,000+ Internet newsgroups. This interface is similar to Windows Explorer. Outlook Express offers you the capability to employ multiple news servers, to subscribe to individual groups, to browse or search through message headers, to read messages and posting details, and to post messages of your own.

Additional Services

Interactive and streaming multimedia support is added to Internet Explorer via several means. These means include the following:

- **Microsoft NetShow.** A one-to-many communications platform that offers streaming multimedia as its primary method of content delivery. For more information, visit `http://www.microsoft.com/ntserver/mediaserv/`.
- **Microsoft Interactive Music Control with MS Synthesizer.** Employs a proprietary music format to add custom sounds and musical scores to Web sites. For more information, visit `http://www.microsoft.com/music/`.

- **Microsoft VRML 2.0 Viewer.** Adds support for the popular Virtual Reality Modeling Language to IE. It offers viewers the capability to explore virtual three-dimensional worlds. For more information, visit **http://www.microsoft.com/vrml/**.

- **DirectShow.** An ActiveX control that enhances playback of multimedia streams. This previously was known as ActiveMovie. For more information, visit **http://www.microsoft.com/directx/pavilion/default.asp/**.

- **VDOLive Player.** A client for on-demand streaming A/V multimedia in the VDO format. For more information, visit **http://www.vdo.net/**.

- **Microsoft Agent.** Brings animated characters with interactive personalities to the Windows environment. These characters can offer help or provide guidance regarding software. For more information, visit **http://www.microsoft.com/msagent/**.

- **Macromedia Shockwave Director and Flash.** These products add support for the popular multimedia formats. You must see these in action to believe them. For more information, visit **http://www.macromedia.com/**.

- **Progressive Network's RealPlayer.** Brings the most popular streaming audio and video tool to your desktop. Accesses prerecorded and live multimedia presentations from thousands of sites across the globe. For more information, visit **http://www.real.com/**.

All these add-ons, with the exception of the Real Networks offerings, are available for direct download and installation through the Internet Explorer online Windows Update service. Because these are multimedia enhancements, you really can't understand what they are or what they can do until you experience them for yourself. We highly recommend installing these multimedia add-ons (because they are free and are integrated into the update site anyway). Visit the sample galleries offered for each media type (using the URLs listed in the preceding bulleted list).

In addition to interacting with Web sites, Internet Explorer can be used to create and publish Web documents. The Microsoft FrontPage Express and Web Publishing Wizard authoring components included as part of the full installation of Internet Explorer bring the basics of Web publishing to your desktop. FrontPage Express is a What You See Is What You Get (WYSIWYG) Hypertext Markup Language (HTML) editor that offers most of the document creation features found in the full version of Microsoft FrontPage.

The Microsoft Web Publishing Wizard is a step-by-step tool used to transfer locally created content to a Web server for public consumption. By using FrontPage Express and the Web Publishing Wizard in tandem, beginning Web designers can get a taste of the professional development environment offered by Microsoft FrontPage. For more information about Microsoft FrontPage, visit **http://www.microsoft.com/frontpage/**.

The final add-on to Internet Explorer is Microsoft Chat. Previously called Comic Chat, this is a real-time, text-based chatting utility. With a unique application of graphical features, Microsoft Chat brings interactive communication to everyone. Using Microsoft Chat, you can communicate with thousands of people all across the world.

The components included in the Internet Explorer full installation bring additional information service interaction capabilities to the Microsoft Web browser. You have the option to add or remove these components as your needs and desire for these additional features change. Simply use the Add/Remove Programs applet or the Help, Product Updates command directly from Internet Explorer's menu bar.

Third-Party Add-Ons for IE

Internet Explorer, with or without its add-on components, is a versatile Internet information service client. It natively supports a wide range of standard, proprietary, and developing Internet technologies from HTML to ActiveX to XML. Programmers across the globe continue to develop new technologies and file formats designed to entertain, inform, or improve the quality of communication. As you explore the ever-growing universe of the Internet, you'll often encounter sites that showcase these new methods of content distribution. Fortunately, the same companies that create these new media formats create add-ons for your Web browser that enable you to interact with their content.

These add-ons fall into two major categories: plug-ins and helper applications. The real difference between them is that a *plug-in* adds support for alternate media types to the browser itself, whereas *helper applications* support the alternate media types as external applications. Plug-ins enable the new media to be viewed within the Web browser's own display area, just as if it was a GIF image or a Java applet; the new element is just another part of the viewed document. Helper applications handle the new media types in their own display windows. Internet Explorer hands off the media file (whether it's a complete file or a link to a streaming data source) to the helper application, which takes over management, control, and display of the media. Internet Explorer often is free to perform other activities or even view different content (on the same or a different site) without affecting the activity of the helper application.

In most cases, you don't have a choice whether a media-type support is a plug-in or a helper application. The developing vendors typically select one or the other according to what they think is best for their products, their intellectual property, and the consumer. Plug-ins are the most common form of browser enhancement, but many streaming media types seem to function best as independent helper applications.

Literally hundreds of plug-ins and helper applications are available on the Internet. It ultimately is up to you to decide whether to install them. Our recommendation is to install only those enhancements used by the majority of Web sites and to avoid single-site or single-purpose enhancements. This is our recommendation for two reasons. First, it keeps system resource allocation to a minimum by keeping the number of additional DLLs loaded by Internet Explorer as low as possible. Second, it prevents system problems caused by too complex a configuration for a single application. (Remember that most plug-ins are created by different vendors without any thought as to how their code will interact, good or bad, with another vendor's code.)

The following is a list of the plug-ins we typically install on our Web browsers:

- Microsoft NetShow: `http://www.microsoft.com/ie/`
- Microsoft VRML 2.0 Viewer: `http://www.microsoft.com/ie/`
- DirectShow: `http://www.microsoft.com/ie/`
- VDOLive Player: `http://www.vdo.net/`
- Macromedia Shockwave Director and Flash: `http://www.macromedia.com/`
- Progressive Network's RealPlayer: `http://www.real.com/`
- Adobe Acrobat Reader: `http://www.adobe.com/`
- Apple QuickTime: `http://quicktime.apple.com/`

You should notice that all but the last two already are included in the full distribution of Internet Explorer. Acrobat Reader is used to read PDF files, and QuickTime is used to view the QuickTime movie format. Both of these add-ons are from very reputable vendors, Adobe and Apple, whose media format types are among the most popular in the industry.

You are welcome to take our advice as you see fit, but don't forget that we warned you. If you decide to install other add-ons to Internet Explorer, keep the following in mind:

- Installing software from a third party might void your capability to obtain technical support from Microsoft. This is especially true for all beta or demo versions of add-ons and for vendors with whom Microsoft does not have a software agreement or partnership.

- Add-ons installed on one computer system might operate differently compared to the same add-ons installed on a different computer system. This is because of the complexity of the Registry and the order in which changes, updates, and modifications are made to a system. In every instance, always back up your system before deploying new software.

- An Internet Explorer enhancement can cause IE to fail completely. Although this occurrence rare, the installation procedure for some enhancements modifies the Registry in such a way as to render IE unable to properly launch. Your only protection against this is to back up your system before performing the installation.

- After an enhancement is installed, 95 percent of the time it cannot be easily removed. This is more true of plug-in enhancements than helper applications. Always review the documentation for the enhancement before installation to determine whether the vendor has provided for the removal of the product.

- Always test a new browser enhancement on a nonproduction system first. Although this is not a foolproof activity, it can reveal glaring incompatibilities before you cause irreversible problems on your production systems.

That said, there are a plethora of enhancements from which you can choose. We could easily devote dozens of pages to just listing the names and URLs. Instead, we've provided a collection of resource, archive, and list sites that contain current information and links to all the latest browser enhancements.

- Internet.Com's BrowserWatch: `http://www.browserwatch.com/`
- C|Net's Download.COM: `http://www.download.com/`
- TUCOWS: `http://www.tucows.com/`
- WinFiles.com Windows NT Shareware: `http://www.winfiles.com/apps/nt/`
- 32bit.com: `http://www.32bit.com/`

Internet Explorer Administration Kit (IEAK)

The Internet Explorer Administration Kit (IEAK) is an administration tool used to develop and deploy customized installations of Internet Explorer. IEAK was created to simplify the management headaches of a large network attempting to maintain software consistency. IEAK is able to centrally deploy, customize, and manage Internet Explorer on multiple platforms (Windows 3.1/95/98, Windows NT 3.51/4.0, Macintosh 68K/PPC, and UNIX Solaris 2.5.1/2.6). IEAK can be used to deploy upgrades, to synchronize versions, to deploy new enhancements, to customize profiles, to manage channels, and to migrate from other utilities. Basically, anything you can do to alter, customize, enhance, or modify Internet Explorer as a user can be programmed into IEAK so that all instances of IE on a network are synchronized.

For small networks, IEAK is too much work for too little benefit. For moderate to large networks with hundreds or thousands of users, however, you'll find IEAK to be a great time saver and a preventative troubleshooting measure. IEAK can be ordered on CD or downloaded from the Microsoft Web site. It generally is recommended to order the CD version because it has proven itself to be a bit more reliable, and you will be sure to have all the required files at your disposal. For more information, visit `http://ieak.microsoft.com/`. You also can find documentation about IEAK on TechNet.

Troubleshooting Internet or Intranet Access Problems

Resolving Internet or intranet access-related problems is a two-step process. First, you must verify that your network connection is active. Second, you must verify that you are communicating properly with the remote host.

Verifying your network connection revolves around your physical network connection, the protocol in use, and authentication/logon parameters. If your Internet/intranet utilities are reporting that sites are inaccessible or timed-out, your network connection might be interrupted. To check this, open a command prompt (Start, Programs, Command Prompt) and issue a **PING** command (unless you are behind a proxy server or a firewall, in which case you'll need to perform this test from the machine hosting the proxy or firewall software). Use either a domain name (remote Internet host), a host name (local intranet host), or an IP address (either Internet or intranet host) as the PING object such as `PING_www.microsoft.com`. If you see the message `Destination Host Unreachable` or if no information is returned at all, you can suspect your network connection.

First, make sure the physical connections are secure. For modem users (this includes ISDN, ADSL, cable modems, and so on), verify that the modem has power, that it is properly connected or seated, and that all connection cables are securely fastened on both ends (such as the modem and the wall outlet). Inspect all connection cables for tight kinks, sharp bends, or exposed wiring (such as insulation that has been scraped off). Make sure the connectors on both ends are snug—loose connectors; otherwise, exposed wiring near the connectors can cause shorts and data loss. Replace all damaged wiring. Cycle the power on the modem device if external; reboot your system if internal. For network users, perform the same checks on your network interface cards and cabling. Include a check for proper termination, proper cable length, and maximum devices per segment restrictions. Also make sure all hubs and routers between you and the Internet are powered on and functioning properly.

Next, check your protocol installation. In most cases, you'll be using TCP/IP. Other protocols might be in use when a proxy server performs resource translation on the client's behalf. If you are connecting to an ISP, make sure the information provided by the ISP is exactly what is entered in the TCP/IP configuration (Network applet's Protocol tab, TCP/IP Properties dialog box). You might want to contact the ISP to verify that the configuration data you have is current and correct. If you are a network client, verify that the TCP/IP configuration matches that provided by your system administrator. At a minimum, it should include an IP address, a subnet mask, and a default gateway. You also might have one or more DNS servers. If you make any modifications to protocol settings, always reboot. In rare cases when the protocol driver files are corrupted, you might want to remove and reinstall TCP/IP.

If the problem is network related, you need to verify that you are properly authenticating with the logon system. This applies to systems connecting directly to an ISP as well as to clients on a network. Double-check the spelling and capitalization of your username, password, and domain name (when applicable).

Viewing TCP/IP Configuration

You also can view all TCP/IP configuration information by issuing the `IPCONFIG /ALL` command at the command prompt. This lists all the current TCP/IP information on the computer, which can be very helpful in troubleshooting.

If your problem is network-connection related, these actions should restore your communications. After each resolution step, retest to see whether your client software can access the remote/local site (or you can use another PING command).

If the communications themselves are at fault, several areas need inspection including your own client software, the path between your system and the remote host, and the remote host itself. Usually, you start with the remote host and work your way back to your local system. Just as with network problems, your first action should be to perform a PING command to see whether the remote system is even online. Don't just rely on a single PING to one host. Always test other systems located in the same general area (that is, inside your intranet, just outside your intranet, somewhere out there on the Internet, in this country, in other countries, and so on). It's difficult to know what hosts are located on the same router paths or even on the same major Internet segment. As long as you use a handful of hosts, however, you should be able to determine where the problem resides.

If you are unable to PING only a single host, you can deduct that the host is offline, that it does not respond to PINGs, or that the path to the host is interrupted. If multiple hosts—but not all—fail to PING, you can be sure a router somewhere is at fault or a serious network overload is occurring. If all hosts fail to PING, you should suspect your Internet connection if not your protocol stack (see the discussion about the network connection earlier in this section).

The second line of testing is using the TRACERT command. This tool lists each device encountered between your system and the remote host as well as the devices' response times. This tool often can inform you that your communication efforts are failing long before they reach the destination host or fail at the last step. Be sure to perform multiple trace routes against the suspect host and several other similar hosts. Again, you'll need to perform this test on the machine hosting firewall or proxy software. It will not work from behind a firewall or proxy.

If you have determined that the communication link fails outside your local computer or your attached network (or even the ISP to which you are connected), there is nothing you can do but wait until the problem is resolved by someone else.

If the problem seems to be closer to home, you've got more investigating to do. Your next step is to test communications between your system, other peer systems, and the ISP. These tests should be performed in both directions when possible (that is, use PING and TRACERT from your system to others and from other systems to yours). This should help track down the point of failure. At this level, if failure is pinpointed, it most likely will be a physical interruption or a network failure (such as protocol configuration or network overload).

TRACERT

TRACERT works by initially sending a PING packet with a Time To Live (TTL) of one. This packet will "die" after it crosses one router. The last router to handle it sends it back. TRACERT then reports this router's address, ups the TTL by one, and tries again. It keeps doing this until it either reaches the destination or exceeds the number of hops specified trying to read the target.

A final cause of problems is the client software itself. It is uncommon for client software to suddenly cease to function without cause; however, it often can seem as if this has occurred. After network connections and network communications are proven, you must suspect the client software. Verify that all configuration options are defined properly. In some cases, you might want to remove and reinstall the utility. In other cases, rebooting the system can restore the utility to operation. If not, consult the vendor's Web site for further troubleshooting advice. Common points of failure for client software include manual or automated patches or upgrades, changes to your system's protocol configuration, improper authentication with local or remote hosts, failed encryption synchronization, version mismatch, permitted use/trail use expiration, failed registration, required DLL or driver version change (due to installation of other software on the system), and file corruption (due to virus infection, fragmentation, drive errors, or read-write problems). In each case, the best order of action for resolution is to check configuration, reboot, contact the vendor, and then reinstall.

A related problem can occur if you access the Internet through a proxy server or a firewall. If the access permissions or configuration of these entities change, your capability to communicate with some types of information resources might be limited, restricted, or prohibited. Check with the administrator of these entities to determine whether any changes have been made that might be causing your communication problems. Restoring communication might require the original proxy/firewall settings to be restored, new and unique access capabilities to be defined for your user account, or special configuration changes to be made to your system or client software.

A Few More Third-Party Utilities Worth Mentioning

Internet Explorer can be enhanced to perform many Internet activities, especially if the activities focus or revolve around the Web. There are a few things, however, that Internet Explorer either cannot do or doesn't do that well. For these cases, there are some utilities from third-parties that you might find very worthwhile. Most of these tools are not directly Web related, but they seem to fit in this chapter better than elsewhere.

In our opinion, the best FTP utility out there is Ipswitch's WS_FTP Pro. With a wide range of features including an Explorer interface, support for firewalls and proxies, drag and drop support, auto re-get, file-version protection, and command-line support, this tool can perform any file transfer function you'll ever need. For a trial download and more information, visit `http://www.ipswitch.com/`.

If you are an avid newsgroup reader, you need to check out Forte's Agent Newsreader. This full-featured newsreader provides enhanced newsreading functionality; kill and watch filters; message sorting; search by author, heading, and body across multiple newsgroups; spell checking; support for MIME/Base 64 encoded attachments; customized storage folders; URL launching; and fully integrated email capabilities. For a download of Free Agent and more information, visit `http://www.forteinc.com/`.

If you enjoy conversing with strange and interesting people from across the globe, you'll want to check out mIRC. This is an Internet relay-chat client that brings a feature-rich GUI interface to this traditionally text-based communications medium. mIRC includes full support for CTCP, DCC, events handling, sounds, colors, programmable function keys, built-in Ident server, and more. You can download this utility and get more information at **http://www.mirc.com/**.

If you find yourself visiting the same site over and over but are discouraged with the throughput and response time of the site, you might want to look into Teleport Pro. This utility is a multifunctional resource-retrieval system. In the words of the vendor, "Teleport Pro is a fully automated, multithreaded, link-following, file-retrieving webspider. It will retrieve all the files you want—and only the files you want—from any part of the Internet. With Teleport Pro, you can schedule a complete download of an entire Web site or just the portions you want, granting you instant surfing access from your own hard drive." You can download this great tool from Tennyson Maxell Information Systems' Web site at **http://www.tenmax.com/**.

If you spend any time looking for information or performing any type of research on the Internet, you've probably collected a long list of search engines. Visiting a dozen search engines can become quite time consuming, so FerretSoft developed the Web Ferret. This single-interface utility employs more than two dozen predefined search engines (that are updated automatically) so you get all the links all at once. You'll never visit a single search engine again! FerretSoft has applied its technology to other resources including email addresses, files, IRCs, phone numbers, newsgroups, and more, each with their own ferret tool. You can download trial ferret utilities and get more information at **http://www.ferretsoft.com/**.

If you want to try other Web browsers, you do have a few options. Two of the most popular alternatives to Internet Explorer are Netscape Navigator and Opera. You might find that deploying only a single Web browser on your system prevents you from seeing some Web sites or some content that employs proprietary or browser-specific technologies not supported by Internet Explorer. We usually have Netscape Navigator and Opera present on our systems just in case IE doesn't cut the mustard on a particular Web site. We recommend keeping IE as your primary Web browser, but there's nothing like some healthy competition. Just think, you'll be re-enacting the Web browser wars right on your own desktop! Netscape Navigator was the industry leader until Microsoft stole the show a few years back with the success of IE 2.0. Opera is holding its own as a fast browser with a small system resource footprint. For more information and to download Netscape Navigator, visit **http://www.netscape.com/**. For more information and to download Opera, visit **http://www.operasoftware.com/**.

If you still have a hankering for more Internet software, you are in luck. The Internet itself offers numerous sites that host and offer a wide range of Internet software for your perusal and trial. Visit the following sites for enough utilities to choke a horse:

- C|Net's Download.COM: `http://www.download.com/`
- C|Net's Shareware.COM: `http://www.shareware.com/`
- TUCOWS: `http://www.tucows.com/`
- WinFiles.com Windows NT Shareware: `http://www.winfiles.com/apps/nt/`
- 32bit.com: `http://www.32bit.com/`
- FilePile: `http://filepile.com/`
- WUGNET: `http://www.wugnet.com/`

For More Information

- Chellis, James. *MCSE: Internet Explorer 4 Administration Kit Study Guide*. Sybex, 1998. ISBN: 0782123090.
- *Microsoft Internet Explorer Resource Kit (Microsoft Professional Editions)*. Microsoft Press, 1998. ISBN: 1572318422.
- Microsoft TechNet: `http://www.microsoft.com/technet/`
- Nelson, Stephen. *Microsoft Internet Explorer 4 Field Guide*. Microsoft Press, 1998. ISBN: 1572317418.
- *Windows NT Workstation Resource Kit*. Microsoft Press, 1996. ISBN: 1572313439.

25

Windows NT as an
Email Client

WITH THE FIERCELY COMPETITIVE ATMOSPHERE of today's business climate, the old adage "You have to stay in touch to be in touch" has never been more accurate. In the past few years, email has evolved from an alternative means of communication to an essential way of doing business. Simply put, email is everywhere.

This makes it critical for an email and collaboration client to possess a wide range of capabilities to keep up with ever-changing needs. A lot of third-party email and news programs are available for Windows NT, but Microsoft has several very good email and collaboration clients (which, in most cases, you can download for free).

In this chapter, we take a look at two of Microsoft's email clients: Outlook Express and Outlook 2000. We explain the strengths and weaknesses of each product in an attempt to help you evaluate which one is best for you. Then we step you through some of the difficult parts of setup and configuration of each product and show you a few tips and tweaks to make the products more efficient.

Similar Features

A lot of the tasks and features we describe are similar for all the different versions of Outlook. When they differ, we specify the differences or break the topic into separate sections.

Outlook 2000 and Outlook Express

Microsoft has developed the Outlook family of messaging and collaboration clients to serve the different needs of various users. Whereas the typical home user probably requires only simple and reliable Internet email and newsgroup functionality, business and power users need richer email functionality and tighter integration between email and tools for information management and collaboration.

The Microsoft Outlook family of email clients consists of not only Outlook 2000 and Outlook Express (which are available on Windows NT, Windows 2000, and other platforms), but also Outlook Web Access and Pocket Outlook for Windows CE. All of these products provide flexibility and power in key areas such as Internet functionality, security, integrated messaging, and information management. However, the feature sets and capabilities are adjusted to the individual platforms and target audiences.

The Windows NT products Outlook Express and Outlook 2000 support the key Internet standards, including POP3 (Post Office Protocol) and IMAP4 (Internet Messaging Access Protocol), LDAP (Lightweight Directory Access Protocol) for public address lookups, and S/MIME (Secure/Multipurpose Internet Mail Extensions) for security. In addition, each product allows you to compose messages using HTML and custom stationary. Both products also allow users with multiple mail accounts to consolidate email from multiple POP3 or IMAP4 mail servers into a single inbox. They also let you create rules that move incoming messages from different accounts into separate inbox folders.

Outlook Express

Compared to the previous versions of Microsoft Internet Mail and News, Microsoft Outlook Express provides more efficient and effective email and newsgroup services, enhanced security, and full support for Internet standards and technologies. Outlook Express is included with Internet Explorer 4.0 and later and is available from Microsoft as a free download.

Outlook Express is a scaled-down version of Microsoft's flagship email client, Outlook 2000. Whereas Outlook 2000 is a high-end mail/news client with a powerful PIM (Personal Information Manager) integrated into the package, Outlook Express concentrates strictly on Internet email and news. Even though Outlook Express is designed to be an entry-level product, it comes extremely close to matching Outlook 2000 feature for feature in terms of Internet email capabilities. The differences are a less-sophisticated Rules Wizard, an inability to create and send fax messages via a downloadable plug-in, and a few additional high-end mail features.

Microsoft Internet Main and News

If you're using one of the versions of Microsoft Internet Mail and News that was included with Microsoft Internet Explorer, you should immediately upgrade to one of the versions of Outlook. Because Outlook products are easy to use, have substantially more powerful mail management, and have an extensive list of additional features, the decision to upgrade should be a no brainer.

Although Outlook Express is less capable than Outlook 2000 in overall functionality, it's optimized for Internet mail and news functions and enjoys an edge in performance in every email area shared by the two clients. This makes Outlook Express suitable for use on 486s, slower Pentiums, and any machine with limited resources.

Outlook Express is seamlessly integrated with Internet Explorer 4.0 and later and is only available with Internet Explorer. It features a simple three-pane interface with separate panes for folders and message headers, as well as a preview window that displays the first few lines of a message before you actually open it. The folder and message header views are customizable, so you can change which fields are displayed. The toolbar has a row of large icons for accessing the most common features.

Tools and Wizards

Outlook Express is equipped with four tools/wizards that streamline the process of setting up and migrating from another mail or news client:

- The Address Book Import Tool
- The Import Messages Wizard
- The Import Mail Accounts Wizard
- The Import News Accounts Wizard

These wizards and tools are available for importing your existing messages, mail account settings, and news account settings. The Import Messages Wizard, Mail Accounts Wizard, and Address Book Import Tool automatically import your messages, address books, and mail account configuration from a variety of popular mail clients. At this time, the Import News Accounts Wizard only imports settings from Netscape Communicator. Although the wizards don't offer import capabilities for all mail and news clients, you can try to export your mail and configuration settings to a format that is supported by Outlook Express's import tools. Then you could try to import the data into Outlook. Importing is supported for the following email products:

- Eudora Light (through version 3.0)
- Eudora Pro (through version 3.0)
- Netscape Mail (version 2.0 or 3.0)
- Netscape Communicator
- Microsoft Exchange Client
- Microsoft Windows Messaging
- Microsoft Internet Mail and News

Importing from Another Email Client

After you import the information into Outlook, it's still available on your previous program if you want to use both packages.

Downloading Outlook Express

As was mentioned earlier, Outlook Express is part of the Internet Explorer 4.0 or later package. It can be obtained on CD, or it can be downloaded from the Internet Explorer download page at `http://www.microsoft.com/windows/ie/download/windows.htm`. The Web site automatically detects which version of Internet Explorer and Outlook Express, if any, you're running, and offers to download an update for you.

Basic System Requirements

As with all software products, your system must meet minimum requirements for Internet Explorer to be used with Outlook Express. The minimum requirements for a standard installation on Windows NT are outlined here:

- Processor: 486/66

- Memory requirements: 16MB RAM

- Hard disk: 47MB

- Disk space: 72MB

Outlook 2000

Outlook 2000 is the industrial-strength big brother of Outlook Express. Whereas the average user will find all the features he will ever need and more with Outlook Express, the serious power and/or business user will want to upgrade to the full version of Outlook 2000.

Microsoft Outlook 2000 provides users with tightly integrated email, calendar, and information management. The first version, Outlook 97, was introduced with the Microsoft Office 97 suite as a replacement for the Schedule+ and Exchange applications that were included in earlier versions of Microsoft Office.

Outlook 2000 includes most of the features of Outlook Express and adds to them by extending these features. In addition, Outlook 2000 adds a calendar, to-do list, journal, sticky notes, and a new module called Outlook Today, which displays unread messages, daily appointments, and tasks at a glance. Outlook 2000 also has far more powerful options for sorting and grouping email messages and a more flexible Rules Wizard. It also has the ability to support custom forms and applications that are designed around Outlook 2000. In addition to the major Internet standards supported by Outlook Express, Outlook 2000 includes support for vCalendar and iCalendar.

Like Outlook Express, Outlook 2000 imports your connection settings, email messages, and address books from your existing mail clients. Outlook 2000 also offers a similar import function for the PIM included as part of Outlook 2000. Currently, support is provided for ACT (Applied Computer Telephony), Ecco, Sidekick, Lotus Organizer, and Schedule+. Additional PIM import filters for Outlook 2000 are available separately from DataViz Inc. For more information, visit `http://www.dataviz.com`. A number of third-party companies also provide tools that allow users to synchronize Outlook data with hand-held devices.

Outlook 2000 System Requirements

To use Outlook 2000, you must have Microsoft Internet Explorer 4.01 installed on your machine. You're not required to use Internet Explorer as your Web browser, but Outlook 2000 does share the editing and rendering engine for HTML mail and some other components with Internet Explorer 4.01. The Outlook 2000 installation program automatically upgrades an older version of Internet Explorer to version 4.01.

Here are the requirements for installing Outlook 2000 on a Windows NT machine:

- Processor: 486/66
- Windows NT Service Pack 3 or later
- Memory requirements: 32MB RAM
- Disk space: Varies by features

Obtaining Outlook 2000

Outlook 2000 is available as part of Office 2000. This product can be purchased from your local software store or online. The online Microsoft purchase point is located at `http://www.microsoft.com/office/order/`.

Installing Outlook 2000

After you've obtained the CD, you'll have to make a choice about what version of Outlook 2000 to install. You have three choices:

- No E-Mail
- Internet Mail only
- Corporate/Workgroup

The No E-Mail option offers the most limited version of Outlook 2000. It is for either the user who has no use for any type of email communication or the user who is using another application for email. This version has all the PIM features of the Outlook client.

Internet Mail Only includes the PIM features and is a full-featured email client that is capable of sending and receiving messages with any POP3/SMTP or IMAP server. It also supports the vCalendar and iCalendar protocols for sending and accepting meeting requests, and publishing free/busy calendar information over the Internet. Also included is support for the vCard standard for sharing business card information.

The Corporate/Workgroup version adds a long list of features, most of which are fully supported only when Outlook is used with Microsoft Exchange Server. Some of these features are listed here:

- **Message Recall.** Allows you to unsend a message that has not yet been read.
- **Group Scheduling.** Allows you to schedule a meeting, check the free/busy times for all participants, have Outlook suggest a time if the originally scheduled time has too many conflicts, send out invitations, track the responses of attendees, and even reserve a meeting room and required A/V equipment.

- **Voting Buttons.** Allows a user to send a yes/no question to recipients and record their responses.

- **Assign Tasks.** Allows you to accept and/or decline task requests or delegate tasks to other users.

- **Full Schedule Visibility.** Lets you allow other users to view your full schedule instead of just your free and busy times.

- **Shared Contact Lists.** Allows you to share your entire contact list with other users; however, you can designate individual contacts as private.

- **Global Address List.** Contains a shared email address list that is available to all users and is stored and managed by Exchange Server.

- **Deferred Delivery.** Allows you to defer delivery of a message until a specified date and time.

- **Receipt and Read Notification.** Specifies whether you want to be notified when a sent message is received and/or opened.

Choosing the right version is easy. If you do not need email support, you would select No E-Mail; if you are connected to an Exchange Server or some type of mail server, you would select Corporate/Workgroup. If you will be using the Outlook email client for Internet use only, you will probably want to select the Internet Only version. However, this version is not MAPI compliant, so any function that requires MAPI support (including certain add-ons and Remote Mail) will not be available. On the other hand, the Internet Only version takes up less drive space, is noticeably faster, and is much easier to configure (the email configuration is exactly the same as Outlook Express), and you will not have the address book limitations that you have in the Corporate/Workgroup version.

Configuring Email Access

After you have decided on the version of Outlook Express or Outlook 2000 and installed it, it is time to get it configured for email access. Both versions of Outlook come with a tool called the Internet Connection Wizard (ICW), which walks you through the process of setting up your Internet account information. The ICW provides you with a step-by-step fill-in-the-blanks guide to setting up Outlook for use with either your Internet service provider (ISP) account(s) or on your POP3- or IMAP4-based local area network (LAN). The ICW is displayed automatically when you first enter Outlook. You can use it to set up your account information at that time, or you can set up your information later by choosing the Tools, Accounts command.

Before you start through the ICW, you should obtain the following information from your ISP:

- Internet email address (example: *jsmith@mail.com*)
- ISP telephone number

- Username and password
- Connection type (PPP, SLIP, or C-SLIP)
- Assigned IP (if necessary)
- DNS server (if necessary)
- Type of incoming mail server (POP3 or IMAP)
- Internet Mail logon or SPA
- POP3 server
- SMTP server
- LCP (Link Control Protocol) support (Yes/No)
- Logon script (if necessary)
- LDAP directories (if supported)

As you progress through the screens of the ICW, you will be prompted for all the information you need to set up your email and newsgroup accounts and Internet directories (also called LDAP directories). Before you start the Internet Configuration Wizard, you should have already installed and tested your modem (see Chapter 16). The steps of the ICW are outlined here:

1. Use the Your Name screen to provide the wizard with the name you want to show up in the From box of email messages you send to other people. This name can be up to 255 characters in length and can contain spaces. You can type your full name, a nickname, an alias, or any other name you want.

2. In the Internet EMail Address screen, enter the email address that was assigned to you by your ISP. This is the address that other people will use to send mail to you.

3. In the E-Mail Servers screen, enter the type (POP3 or IMAP) and the name of the incoming and outgoing email servers that handle your email. The addresses may be the same. This information is obtained from your ISP.

4. If your ISP does not use Secure Password Authentication (SPA)—most ISPs do not—click Log On Using and enter the email account name and password you use to log in to your ISP's mail server to send and receive email. Your email account name may also be referred to as User ID, Member ID, or User Name and is usually the name used to start your account. If your ISP uses SPA, click Log On Using Secure Password Authentication (SPA), and then click Next. You will then provide your email account name every time you log on to the mail server. This information is obtained from your ISP.

5. Select the first option if you have an account with an ISP and want to create a connection to that account using your modem and phone line. Select the second option if you want to connect to the Internet using a proxy server on your LAN or if your LAN is directly connected to the Internet. The third option is rarely used.

6. In the Dial-Up Connection screen, specify whether you want to create a new dial-up connection or use an existing one. If you are creating a new dial-up connection, enter the telephone number on this screen.

   This is the username and password that you have to enter when connecting to your ISP. This may or may not be the same as the username and password you use to log on to the mail server. This information is obtained from your ISP.

7. You may or may not need to change the Advanced Settings. Most ISPs use the default settings. Select No if the following statements are true:

   - Your ISP is not using PPP.
   - Your ISP did not assign you a fixed IP address.
   - Your ISP did not assign a DNS address.
   - Your ISP does not require LCP extensions to be disabled.
   - Your ISP does not require a logon script.

   If even one of these is not true, you need to select Yes and configure the screens that follow. This information is obtained from your ISP.

   Most ISPs support PPP, which is a newer connection protocol, but a few still support the older Serial Line Internet Protocol (SLIP) standard. This information is obtained from your ISP.

   Most ISPs either support LCP extensions or don't care one way or the other. This information is obtained from your ISP. Some ISPs require you to run a logon script when you connect. If it is needed, the ISP usually supplies it for you. This is where you enter the IP address if one is assigned by your ISP.

8. On the screen that follows, enter the IP address of the DNS server if it is specified by your ISP. If you were given two addresses, make sure you enter both of them. DNS servers get pretty busy, so it's always good to have an alternate if one goes down. On the next screen, enter a name for this dial-up connection. This is the friendly name that you assign to the dial-up configuration. It is usually the name of the ISP, but you can call it whatever you want.

At this point, you should be ready to connect to your ISP and start sending and receiving messages.

Multi-User Support

Because of the built-in security features of Windows NT, each user has a separate profile. This allows multiple users to use the same Outlook client and maintain separate mail stores, settings, and address books. As long as each user logs into Windows NT and Outlook, their mail, settings, and address book configuration information is stored in the %systemroot%\profiles\%username%\Application Data directory. Whenever a new user wants to log on, the current user simply logs off from the Start menu, and the new user logs on and automatically receives his or her personal mail folders, address books, mail, and news configuration.

In the No E-Mail and Internet Only versions of Outlook 2000, all data is stored in personal folders, files that are stored on your PC. In the Corporate/Workgroup version, if Exchange Server support is installed, all data is stored in your mailbox. The mailbox is physically located on the Exchange Server and is controlled by your Exchange Administrator.

You have the option to designate some or all of your working folders in your Exchange Server mailbox as offline folders. This enables you to still access the data in them, even when you are not connected to your Exchange Server. This feature is very handy for laptop and dial-up users. You can work with your data while offline, and when you reconnect, the information in the folders is automatically synchronized between the server and your machine. Also, you still have the option of adding personal folders to the Corporate/Workgroup version. This can be handy if you need to offload some of your data from your mailbox onto your PC. Just remember that although the contents of the mailbox is backed up and protected by your Exchange Administrator, after you move an item into a personal folder, it is your responsibility to protect it.

Encryption

Because Outlook 2000 stores most of your information in the personal folder (including your email, contacts list, calendars, and so on), there is an additional option that allows you to provide password protection for the personal mail folders. However, if you should forget your password, there is no way to recover the information in the file. This option can be set only during the initial configuration setup of the personal folders. If you need to change the options at a later time, you can install another set of personal folders with the desired options and then copy your data from the old folders to the new folders.

Secure Your File System
To add extra security for your personal mail folders, format your system drive with NTFS instead of FAT. This allows you to limit access to your %systemroot%\profiles\%username% directory.

Multiple Versions of Outlook
You can do a number of additional things with the Corporate/Workgroup version of Outlook 2000 attached to Exchange Server, but they are outside the scope of this book. For more information, see the resource list at the end of this chapter.

There are three encryption options for the personal folders:

- **No Encryption.** Does just what it says.
- **Compressible Encryption.** Encrypts the file in a format that allows compression if you are using NTFS disk compression.
- **Best Encryption.** Encrypts the file using a stronger encryption method. If you are using NTFS disk compression, the file can still be compressed, but to a lesser degree than is allowed by the Compressible Encryption option.

Moving Personal Folder Files

If you installed Outlook 2000 over an older Microsoft email client such as Exchange or Outlook 97/98, your personal folders might be stored in another directory (usually \Exchange). The name of the file also might be OUTLOOK.PST or USERNAME.PST, instead of the default MAIL.PST. If your personal folder file is not stored under the %systemroot%\profiles\%username% directory, it is probably not secure.

To move your Personal Folder file to another directory, follow these steps:

1. Exit Outlook 2000.
2. Before starting, make sure you have a backup of your ★.PST file.
3. Copy your ★.PST file to the desired directory.
4. Start Outlook 2000.
5. From the Outlook main menu, select Tools, Services.
6. Select Personal Folders, and then click Remove.
7. Click OK.
8. From the Outlook main menu, select Tools, Services.
9. Click Add.
10. Select Personal Folders, and then click OK.
11. From the Create, Open Personal Folders File window, navigate to the new location of your ★.PST file, and then click Open.
12. Make sure that all the options shown are correct, and then click OK.

Address Books

An address book is a list of names, usually with email addresses, from which you can select when addressing your email messages. Outlook Express stores all its addresses in the Windows Address Book. Each version of Outlook 2000 handles address books differently. You can have access to one or two address books in the Internet Only version, or you can access three or more in the Corporate/Workgroup version. Of the following four common address books, the last two are available only in the Corporate/Workgroup version.

- **Personal Address Book.** A holdover from the older Microsoft email clients. In MS Mail and Exchange, this was the only address book available. This address book is stored on your PC and is not installed by default during a new Outlook 2000 installation. If you are upgrading from an older Microsoft client, this feature is installed, and the old addresses will be available. If you need to use personal distribution lists, you have to store them here.

- **Contacts.** The default address book installed with the Internet Only and Corporate/Workgroup versions of Outlook. It includes all your contacts, even if they do not have an email or fax address. In the Internet Only version of Outlook, you can configure Groups, which is a form of distribution lists.

- **Outlook Address Book.** Available only in the Corporate/Workgroup version. It includes every contact in your Contacts address book that has an email or fax address.

- **Global Address List.** Available only to those Corporate/Workgroup users who have access to an MS Mail or Exchange server. This is a common address book that contains individual email addresses as well as distribution lists. It is typically maintained by the company mail administrator, and the average user cannot make changes to it.

The Windows Address Book that is used in Outlook Express is not directly accessible from Outlook 2000. To use it with any version of Outlook 2000, you must import the Outlook Express address book into one of Outlook 2000's address books. In addition, some other service providers such as CompuServe provide their own address books.

Address books can be a little tricky for users of the Corporate/Workgroup version of Outlook, mainly because there can potentially be so many choices. Just remember that the Global Address List is common to all users, whereas the Outlook Address Book is controlled by the individual user. For personal distribution lists, you must install the Personal Address Book.

LDAP

In addition to all the address book options available, you can search for users on the Internet using Directory Services. Directory Services are servers located on your network or on a public server on the Internet that you can use to locate someone if you know his or her name but do not know the email address. Directory Services follow the LDAP that defines a common format for electronic directories.

To locate someone in Outlook Express, from the main menu, select Edit, Find People. This opens the Find People window. From here, you can click the Look In field to select from your address books or one of the various LDAP servers that are preconfigured.

All the information available on the LDAP server is written into your address book. How much information you get varies; it could be limited to only a name and an email address, or it could include a street address, telephone number, and other miscellaneous information.

Customizing and Configuring Your Messages

The Outlook email clients provide a lot of flexibility in formatting your messages. Outlook Express supports both plain text and HTML; Outlook 2000 supports those options and adds support for RTF and Microsoft Word document formats. Different tools are available on the Format menu and the Formatting toolbar depending on what option you select.

You have the option of setting a default mode for all messages, which you can override for selected users by choosing the text-only option in the address book. Text-only and HTML give you the greatest degree of compatibility with other users on the Internet.

Selecting HTML opens up a lot of options for formatting email messages. You can use a background from your favorite Web site, or you can even create your own background using HTML. The HTML option also supports preconfigured stationery. Some sample stationery is included with all versions of Outlook, and many Internet sources offer more. To create a message using stationery, select Compose, New Message Using in Outlook Express, or choose Actions, New Mail Message Using in Outlook 2000.

The Word option requires that you have Microsoft Word installed on your machine, and for your messages to be read at the other end, the recipient also has to have it installed. To turn on the Word option, select Tools, Options from the main menu, and then select the Mail Format tab and change the Send in This Message Format option. Notice that this option is called WordMail and that there are additional options for selecting predefined templates for use with WordMail. When you turn on WordMail, a hidden copy of Word is run on your machine whenever you run Outlook 2000. If you have a slower machine, you probably won't want to enable this option.

Multiple Servers

You can add additional servers by using the Tools, Accounts command in either Outlook Express or the Internet Only version of Outlook 2000.

Enter the name you are looking for, and then click on Find Now. Notice that the search also returns names that are similar to what you were looking for. If you want to add the resulting name to your address book, select the desired name, and then click the Add to Address Book button.

Outlook Replies

All versions of Outlook reply to an incoming message in whatever format it was received, as long as that format is supported, and even if it is not the default for that user. For example, suppose John Doe is configured for plain text only, but you receive a message from him in HTML format. Your reply to him will be in HTML.

Managing and Searching Email Folders

All the features in Outlook are organized as folders, and like the folders that you work with in My Computer, they can be copied, moved, renamed, created, deleted, and viewed in different ways. This allows you to create a series of subfolders to organize your mail in various categories.

As is true of everything else in Windows NT, you have multiple choices for manipulating your folders in Outlook. You can highlight a folder and then right-click it to get a menu of options, or you can select File, Folder from the main menu to get options. Just as you do in My Computer to manipulate files, you can drag and drop messages to various folders.

The main folders of each version of Outlook cannot be moved, but they can be copied. The main folders include Inbox, Contacts, Calendar, Tasks, Notes, and Journal.

Searching Email Folders in Outlook Express

Although it's nice to have everything so well organized, it does not do you any good if you cannot find the information you so carefully stored when you really need it. No matter how well you try to stay organized, sometimes a message is going to be misplaced. With the Find Message tool in Outlook Express, you can search for a message in a folder and all its subfolders. You can look for a message using any of the following search criteria:

- Sender
- Recipient
- Subject or title of the message
- Text within the message
- Attachments
- Messages within a specified date range
- Messages in a specific folder and its subfolders

Searching Email Folders in Outlook 2000

Because Outlook 2000 is designed to store more data than Outlook Express, it comes with a more sophisticated search tool. Actually, two search utilities are included with Outlook 2000: Find, for quick, basic searches of the Inbox; and Advanced Find for the more sophisticated searches.

To use Find, select Tools, Find from the main menu. The search criteria is limited to information in the From and Subject fields or the message body of messages in the Inbox.

To use Advanced Find, select Tools, Advanced Find from the main menu. With this feature, the search criteria are virtually unlimited. You can search any type of Outlook 2000 data store for any text, condition, category, size, date, and so on.

Filtering Email

One of the most powerful features of the Outlook mail clients is the ability to filter incoming email. You can specify, by account, what rules you want applied to your incoming email. These rules let you sort, filter, redirect, and even delete mail before it arrives in your inbox.

Filtering Email in Outlook Express

Although the email filter that is included in Outlook Express is not as powerful as the Rules Wizard feature of Outlook 2000, it is still a very solid feature that's comparable with most other email clients.

Outlook Express uses a feature called the Inbox Assistant, which examines all incoming messages and processes them according to rules you configure. This allows you to have incoming messages that meet certain criteria sent to the folders you want. For example, you can specify that messages from all individuals using the same email account be delivered to their personal folders. Or maybe you want all mail from a certain person to be automatically routed to a specific folder. Incoming messages are examined for the following items:

- Recipient
- Carbon Copy (CC)
- Sender
- Subject
- Mail account message is being sent to
- Message size

You can even choose to have all messages rerouted. You can have any of the following actions performed on the selected messages:

- Move to a specific folder
- Copy to a specific folder
- Forward to a mail recipient or distribution list
- Reply to the sender with a file
- Do not download from server
- Delete from server

For example, you could identify spammers who add a user to email distribution lists without the user's permission and elect to have the spammers' messages automatically deleted from the server. These rules are not email-server specific, so any user of Outlook Express who has access to a POP3/IMAP server can use the Inbox Assistant.

You can specify multiple filters or rules for incoming messages. To change the priorities by which messages are sorted, click the Move Up or Move Down button in the Inbox Assistant dialog box.

Filtering Email in Outlook 2000

Although Outlook Express's Inbox Assistant is a pretty impressive feature, it simply can't match Outlook 2000's Rules Wizard when it comes to developing complex mail filters. The Outlook 2000 Rules Wizard is the most advanced email filtering system available and is a must-have for anyone who needs a multiple-level mail filter. The Rules Wizard has all the features of the Inbox Assistant in Outlook Express, along with the following capabilities:

- Operate on sent and received messages
- Automatically assign categories to messages
- Assign different colors and shading to messages
- Notify the user when a message of a certain priority arrives
- Filter with specific words, anywhere
- Filter with attachments
- Filter within a specific date range
- Use a predefined Junk Mail Senders list
- Use a predefined Adult Mail Senders list
- Right-click on an incoming message and add it to one of the predefined lists

Outlook 2000 also comes with a set of predefined rules you can use. There is also a file in the Program Files\Microsoft Office\Office directory called FILTERS.TXT that contains the text strings Outlook uses to identify spam. You can edit this file to add or change any of the filters. There are separate sections in this file for general spam and X-rated spam.

Of the several ways to create a new rule, one of the easiest is to start from the Organize window, as described here:

1. Highlight a message from a recipient that you want to work with.
2. From the drop-down list, select the folder you want to move to.
3. Click Create, and the rule is saved.

To edit the rule after it is saved, follow these steps:

1. Select Rules Wizard from the Organize window, or select Tools, Rules Wizard from the main menu.

2. From the Rules Wizard window, highlight the rule and select Modify.

3. Make any necessary changes. In this case, you are not creating a new rule or checking anything else, so click Next twice.

Because computer news ages fast, you might want to be notified, for example, if you didn't read a message for 10 days. To do so, you select Flag Message for Action in a Number of Days. At the bottom of the window, click Flag Message... and fill in the number of days and the flag in the dialog box.

Then click Next. Because there won't be any exceptions, click Next again. Now you can review the rule to make sure it is what you want. If it is, click Finish to save it.

Be careful how you use rules—even the predefined ones—especially when you choose automatic deletion. They are not 100% reliable and can sometimes filter out messages you want to receive.

Integrating Newsgroups and Mailing Lists

Both Outlook Express and Outlook 2000 use the Outlook Express Newsreader to access newsgroups. A newsgroup is like a public bulletin board (or a private one if a newsgroup is posted on your intranet). Users can post messages and download and read messages from other users. You configure the newsreader with the Internet Connection Wizard, and you will need most of the same information you used to configure your email account, with the addition of the name of the news server you want to connect to. (See the section "Configuring Email Access," earlier in this chapter.)

Newsgroups

After you have configured the Outlook newsreader and made your initial connection to the news server, you will be prompted to download the list of available Usenet groups. Literally thousands of groups are available, and more are added every day. The topics range from quantum physics to reruns of "Gilligan's Island." Microsoft, Symantec, Netscape, and other companies are setting up their own news servers to deliver tech support and service to customers.

If you want to find out what other people think of a product you're about to purchase, check the company's news server or one of the Usenet public newsgroups. To search the newsgroups for a specific topic, key your search argument into the Display Newsgroups Which Contain field. This is a case-insensitive search that finds the entered text in any part of the newsgroup name.

From the Newsgroup dialog box, you can subscribe or unsubscribe to newsgroups, review a list of your subscriptions, and view a list of new groups that have been added since the last time you downloaded the list. You can highlight a newsgroup and go directly to it by clicking the Go To button.

To view a newsgroup, double-click the newsgroup name in the left window. This downloads the message headers and displays them in the upper-right window. To view a message, double-click it, and it will be downloaded and displayed in the lower-right window. By default, the newsreader downloads only message headers, which can be a good thing because some of the newsgroups are heavily used, and the messages can get quite large. You then have the option of selecting one message at a time or marking a group to be downloaded.

The feature set in the newsgroup reader is similar to the Outlook Express email client. You are given the following options:

- Compose Messages
- Reply to Group
- Reply to Author of message
- Forward Message

The editor you use to compose responses is the editor you use for email, so it includes the same features (spell checker, HTML support, and so on). It also offers a Find Message feature and even a newsgroup filter so that you can block postings according to the following criteria:

- Newsgroup or server
- Sender
- Subject
- Message size
- Age of message

Unfortunately, when you post to a newsgroup, your email address is displayed. This is where some spammers get names to add to their mailing lists. They have computer programs that can pull your email address out of the messages you send. To make it more difficult for them, highlight your news server name and select Properties. Insert illegal characters or spaces in the email address field. If someone wants to reply to you, he will recognize what you have done and remove the extra characters; however, the automated programs can't do that. It doesn't provide a lot of extra protection from spam, but every little bit helps.

Mailing Lists

Mailing lists represent another informational offering available on the Internet. But, instead of you having to use your newsreader to sort through a newsgroup, a mailing list will deliver information directly to your inbox. This is how it works: Someone on the Internet sets up a program called a Listserver, which accepts subscription requests and sends updates to subscribed users at a predefined time, usually daily.

Here are a few common commands that you use with Listservers:

- To join, send a message with the word "Subscribe" in the body of the message.
- To leave, send a message with "Unsubscribe" or "Remove" in the body of the message.
- To list commands, send a message with "List" in the body of the message.

Like newsgroups, literally thousands of Listservers are available, covering every topic you can think of. Most Listservers use the common commands, but you must be aware of individual differences. Some Listservers allow you to contribute messages just like a newsgroup, whereas others are informational only.

To keep track of your subscriptions, create a folder in Outlook to store the mailing list introductory messages that you receive after joining a mailing list. This message tells you how to unsubscribe, contact the list administrator, and so on. On occasion, some Listservers lose their subscription lists, and you must subscribe again. Also, you might need to leave the list while you are on vacation, a business trip, and so on, or you might just lose interest after a while. Some of these lists can fill your inbox with a lot of information in a very short period of time. To obtain a list of some sample Listservers, go to `http://alabanza.com/kabacoff/Inter-Links/listserv.html`.

Creating Calendars

Up to this point, we have covered the email features in the two versions of Outlook available for the Windows NT platform. From here on, we start covering the features in Outlook 2000 that leave Outlook Express in the dust.

Most people think of Outlook as an email program only, and a surprising number of people use only the email features of Outlook. But they are ignoring a very powerful integrated Personal Information Manager (PIM), or as Microsoft prefers to call it, a Desktop Information Manager (DIM).

The heart of any good PIM (or DIM) is the calendar. In Outlook 2000, the look of the calendar program is pretty straightforward. It is designed to look similar to the pages in those paper planners most of us cannot live without. However if you want or need a different view, you can customize the calendar to look just about any way you want it to. The standard views for the calendar are to view your schedule by month, day, five-day week, or seven-day week. You can also create custom views to display your calendar with a week of any number of days, change the start day of your week, and adjust your workday. To configure these options, select Tools, Options, Preferences, Calendar Options.

The best feature of Outlook 2000 has to be the Outlook Today window. This is a default screen that brings up a summary of not only the day's schedule, but also other upcoming appointments and tasks. It also shows the importance flags, so you can see at a glance what you need to do and which items have priority. It also shows the number of unread messages in your inbox and provides a search field for locating your contacts.

Outlook treats holidays as all-day events or appointments. You have the option to show your time as busy or free. Outlook comes with a selection of predefined holidays that are specific to various countries or religious groups. To configure these options, choose Tools, Options, Preferences, Calendar Options, Add Holidays.

You can select more than one set of holidays if you want. However, if some of the holidays are the same in both sets (Christmas Day, for example), several identical events will show on the same day. To solve this, you can create your own set of holidays for Outlook to use.

Outlook stores the predefined calendar holidays in a plain text file called OUTLOOK.TXT that's located in the Program Files\Microsoft Office\Office directory. The OUTLOOK.TXT file lists holidays in the following format:

```
[Country] ###
Holiday description, yyyy/mm/dd
Holiday description, yyyy/mm/dd
```

In this format, ### is the total number of holidays listed for a particular country. Note that there is a space between the closing bracket and the number, as well as a carriage return at the end of the line. On each holiday line, there is a comma and a space between the holiday description and the date, as well as a hard return at the end of the line. For example, a file might look like this:

```
[United States] 3
Independence Day, 2000/07/04
Thanksgiving Day, 2000/11/24
Christmas Day, 2000/12/25
```

OUTLOOK.TXT is a read-only file, so before you start editing, make a backup copy and remove the read-only attribute. To minimize editing, it would probably be best to copy the section of the file that has the majority of the dates you need and then just add or subtract entries. Give the section a new name, update the number of entries, and you are done. The next time you run Outlook, you can add the new custom holidays to your calendar.

Handling Appointments

After you have created the calendar, you need to fill it with information. The calendar offers three major types of events: meetings, appointments, and events. An *event* is an all-day occurrence that does not have a set start time and during which you might be busy or not—such as a holiday or birthday. An *appointment* is something that you generally must attend, which has a scheduled start and end time between which your

528 Chapter 25 Windows NT as an Email Client

schedule will show you as busy by default. A *meeting* is similar to an appointment, but it is scheduled by a central person who sends out invitations and keeps track of the responses.

The procedures for creating events and appointments are similar:

1. From the Calendar view, select the month and day for which you want to schedule an appointment or event.

2. Double-click next to the time at which the appointment is scheduled to begin.

3. When the Untitled Appointment dialog box appears, fill in the information that identifies your appointment.

4. Select Save and Close, and the appointment will be posted to your calendar.

Pay close attention to the Appointment dialog box; you use the same window to enter meetings, appointments, and events. The only differences are the options you select. To make an appointment an event, click the All Day Event box. To make an appointment a meeting, select Attendee Availability and add the names of people you want to invite to the meeting. The calendar automatically sends an email message to the people you wish to include in your meeting. If you cancel the meeting, you can use this function to send a cancellation notice.

Outlook has a powerful but largely overlooked feature for converting one type of entry into another simply by dragging and dropping. For example, if someone sends you a message suggesting that you meet for lunch, you can drag that message and drop it on your calendar folder. It opens the Appointment dialog box with the subject filled in and the text of the message displayed. Just set the date and time details and save. In addition, it works the other way around: Dragging an appointment, task, or note to the Inbox creates a new message and inserts the subject and text for you.

Building Outlook Applications

Microsoft Outlook 2000 is a very powerful application. But Microsoft has made it extensible, in that you can build applications based on the Outlook engine. Outlook includes a form development environment that allows users to use the drag and drop capabilities of the environment to add custom fields to various forms.

Outlook also supports VBScript. VBScript is a subset of Visual Basic and allows Outlook developers to add custom functionality (such as accessing a database, hiding controls, and so on) to any Outlook form. Outlook events are exposed so developers can control Outlook forms and actions. Some events that Outlook supports include when an item opens, when an item is saved, when a user changes a property (such as subject or categories), and when an item is read. Microsoft Outlook also supports ActiveX controls in custom forms. This means developers can take advantage of thousands of third-party controls in their Outlook applications.

Instructions on how to build a full-blown Outlook application would fill a book, and quite a few books are already available. See the section titled "For More Information" at the end of this chapter for details. In this section, we make some small changes to an existing form to introduce you to the forms development environment of Outlook 2000.

Say, for example, that you want to build a small customer tracking system using Outlook, and the basic Outlook Contact form has some of the information you want but has more fields than you need. You can use the Contacts form as a base and modify it to suit your needs. To get into the development environment, from the main menu, select Tools, Form, Design a Form. Notice that you have the option of looking in several form libraries and all your Outlook folders. Select Contacts, and the form will be opened in design mode.

To get rid of the fields you don't want, select them and press the Delete key. To move around the remaining fields, just click to select them, and then drag and drop. You can also resize the fields by selecting and dragging the corners. To add additional fields, you can select predefined fields from the Field Chooser dialog box. You can also add text and other controls to the form from the Toolbox. To access the Toolbox, from the main menu, select Form, Control Toolbox.

When you have added and positioned everything as desired, save the new form. Then select Form, Run. You can fill in the form, and it will be saved in your Contacts list. You can also create a new Contacts folder in which to save all your custom forms

Troubleshooting Email Problems

Email is a great thing to have, but it's not so great if it doesn't work. This is a summary of some common email problems and the areas to check to fix them. The following sections list potential problems, followed by the best possible solutions to those problems.

Email Messages Stay in the Outbox

If you edit a message that is in the Outbox, you must explicitly click Send from within the message to send it. To check, note that messages that are queued to be sent are shown in italics. If an outgoing message is not italicized, open it and select Send again.

Make sure you have an address book entry for the recipient if the message was addressed to an alias. This should never happen, but sometimes it will sneak through. If only one message gets stuck, delete it and re-create it.

General Problems Sending Email

For general problems sending email, try the following solutions:

- Check your modem and phone line for proper operation (see Chapter 16).
- See if you can PING your email provider.
- Reboot your PC and your modem (if it's external). This seems simplistic, but sometimes it works.
- Send the problem email using another email program. If you are using Outlook 2000, try Outlook Express; or you can try Microsoft Internet Mail and News.
- Reinstall the current Windows NT service pack. This has fixed a lot of strange problems, and not just email related ones.
- Install the latest Outlook version or patches.
- If all else fails, uninstall and reinstall your version of Outlook.

Third-Party Email Tools

Although the various versions of Outlook are capable applications by themselves, you can always make a good thing better. Due to the popularity of Outlook, a number of add-on products are available. The following paragraphs list some of the better third-party email tools we've found.

Actioneer for Outlook 2000 places a small program in your taskbar that you can use to pop up a sticky-note style window. Type what ever you need to remember, and Auctioneer automatically places it in the appropriate area of Outlook (Calendar, Task, or Notes), categorizes it, links it to a contact, and places a due date and time on it. For more information or to download this program, visit `http://www.actioneer.com`.

Address Book Swapper is for use with Outlook Express. It allows you to switch between and add address books without having to restart Outlook. You can also open, view, and edit multiple books; drag and drop entries; and remove books when they are no longer needed. For more information or to download Address Book Swapper, visit `http://www.ofori-boateng.clara.net/ethereal`.

B-original is a small program that sits in the system tray and generates signature files for your email program. It generates a new one each minute, based on a database of quotations. You can add your own sayings or quotations to this database as well, and you can touch up the generic template for the actual signature file. For more information or to download B-original, visit `http://members.xoom.com/boriginal`.

CyberSecretary is a virtual office assistant that uses automation to control Outlook and perform various tasks, such as filing mail messages, taking phone messages or creating phone log entries, sending Internet URLs to the Inbox (or any mail recipient), getting stock prices, and much more. The CyberSecretary is controlled by scripts, which you can easily create. Scripts can be scheduled, can run on demand, or can run in response to more than two dozen Outlook events. CyberSecretary is an ActiveX component that developers can use to create applications sharing a common user interface. For more information or to download this program, visit `http://www.voicenet.com/~wheindl/cybersecretary.html`.

MAILJAIL is a spam filter program that comes with more than 400 preconfigured filters that look for telltale text and addresses that indicate spammers. Then the program deletes the suspected mail or sends it to a designated folder. It learns what you consider to be junk mail based on the messages you delete. For more information or to download MAILJAIL, visit `http://www.saberquest.com`.

MAIL SPY allows you to monitor your email for an important message without interrupting your work to check your Inbox. Tell this free utility how often to look, and it will dial up your mail server in the background, check for new mail, and notify you when new messages arrive. For more information or to download the program, visit `http://www.saberquest.com`.

MsgParse is a powerful utility for processing your email that allows you to transfer data from your email to other applications. It pulls data from email based on user-defined parameters and exports the messages to a plain file, configured to your wishes and ready to be imported into a spreadsheet, database, or other application. MsgParse supports multiple POP3 accounts or MAPI mail clients and features a template creation wizard for ease of use. For more information or to download MsgParse, visit `http://www.cypressnet.com`.

Outlook Express Mail Manager sets up and configures multiple Dial-Up Networking connections, address books, mailboxes, signature files and many other items used by Outlook Express. It allows you to easily manage multiple email accounts. For more information or to download it, visit `http://www.ofori-boateng.clara.net/ethereal`.

RPK InvisiMail is a standards-based email security add-in for POP3 email software. RPK InvisiMail is completely transparent, quietly monitoring your incoming and outgoing email messages and automatically encrypting and decrypting them using the appropriate public keys. You can add additional keys to your database as needed, and InvisiMail automatically adds the right key to each message you send. RPK InvisiMail uses worldwide strong encryption that is not subject to U.S. government regulation. For more information or to download this program, visit `http://www.invisimail.com`.

Talking Email is a utility that notifies you when you've received email and can then read the message to you. It supports plain text, HTML, and RTF formats. For more information or to download a demo, visit `http://www.4developers.com/talkmail/index.htm`.

WorldMerge is an electronic mail merge client that allows you to send personalized greetings to everyone on your email contact list. It also allows you to send customized messages to a large number of recipients, and it can import Access and ASCII files. For more information or to download WorldMerge, visit `http://www.saberquest.com`.

For More Information

For more information about Outlook Express and Outlook 2000, consult the following references:

- Microsoft Outlook Express Home Page:
  `http://www.microsoft.com/windows/ie/ie40/oe/`

- Microsoft Outlook Home Page: `http://www.microsoft.com/outlook/`

- Outlook Express Stationery by Wen: `http://members.tripod.com/~WenAnn/`

- Dyszel, Bill. *Microsoft Outlook 2000 for Windows for Dummies*. IDG Books Worldwide, 1999. ISBN: 0764504711.

- Mosher, Sue *The Microsoft Outlook: E-Mail and Fax Guide*. Duke Communications, 1998. ISBN: 1882419820.

- Neibauer, Alan R. *Running Microsoft Outlook 2000*. Microsoft Press, 1999. ISBN: 1572319399.

- Nelson, Stephen. *Microsoft Outlook 2000 at a Glance*. Microsoft Press, 1999. ISBN: 1572319488.

- Padwick, Gordon. *Using Outlook 2000*. Que, 1999. ISBN 0789719096.

- Byrne, Randy. *Building Applications with Microsoft Outlook 2000*. Microsoft Press, 1999. ISBN 0735605815.

26

Serving the Web from
Windows NT Workstation

W INDOWS NT WORKSTATION CAN function as a personal Web server and is able
to offer custom content to an intranet or the Internet. Although Windows NT
Workstation's Personal Web Server (PWS) is a fully functional Web server, the product
is limited to 10 simultaneous connections. The Windows NT Workstation 4.0 End
User License Agreement states: "You may install the software product on a single computer for use as interactive workstation software but not as server software. However,
you may permit a maximum of ten (10) computers to connect to the Workstation
Computer to access and use services of the software product such as file and print and
peer Web services." This means that PWS cannot legally support more than 10 visitors
at a time; this user connection limit is built into PWS and is not modifiable.

Windows NT Workstation running PWS can host a Web site, but due to its connection limitation, it is more commonly used as a development environment and test-
bed. This chapter discusses PWS along with basic Web creation, tools, and
troubleshooting.

Personal Web Server (PWS)

Personal Web Server is the version of Internet Information Server (IIS) designed for
use on Windows NT Workstation. PWS is primarily a Web and FTP server. This
means you can host Web pages and FTP sites that users elsewhere on the network can

access. Because PWS is hosted by a Windows NT Workstation system, you also can take advantage of the security and access controls inherent to Windows NT.

Some of the features, capabilities, and benefits of PWS 4.0 include:

- HTTP 1.1 support, which adds pipelining, persistent connections, chunked transfers, and proxy support to Web document distribution
- An integrated setup routine that installs PWS as part of Windows NT
- Flexible management and administration tools
- Content control based on users and groups
- 40-bit encryption
- Microsoft Management Console (MMC)
- Activity logging
- Content expiration settings
- Custom error messages

The following are some limitations to PWS not found in the Windows NT Server version of IIS:

- It can host only a single Web and FTP site.
- It has no bandwidth throttling.
- It has no access control based on IP addresses or domains.
- It does not support 128-bit encryption.
- It is limited to 10 simultaneous connections.

Microsoft specifically limited the design and capabilities of PWS to force Web site developers to use the Windows NT Server platform to host Web sites of consequence. Therefore, you'll find that PWS on Windows NT Workstation is useful for small intranets and site development, but it is not as useful as a Web host for Internet sites as the Windows NT Server version.

Windows NT Workstation's initial setup process enables you to install the version of PWS (2.0) included on the distribution CD. We recommend not installing version 2.0, however, and obtaining version 4.0 from the Windows NT 4.0 Option Pack (**http://www.microsoft.com/windows/downloads/**).

The Windows NT 4.0 Option Pack is a collection of software to be used on Windows NT 4.0 Server, Windows NT 4.0 Workstation, Windows 95, and Windows 98. It requires that Service Pack 3 and Internet Explorer 4.0 be installed first. We recommend installing the latest service pack available rather than the minimum requirement of Service Pack 3. You also should install the latest full version of Internet Explorer rather than just the minimum of Internet Explorer 4.0. For instructions on installing these items, consult their associated documentation, TechNet, or their related Microsoft Web areas.

PWS Management

PWS offers three built-in management and administration tools: Personal Web Manager, IIS MMC snap-in, and FrontPage Server Administrator. The Personal Web Manager is launched automatically when you start the HTTP service. It also is accessible through its tray icon or from the Start menu (Start, Programs, Windows NT 4.0 Option Pack, Microsoft Personal Web Server, Personal Web Manager). The Personal Web Manager is a simplified interface for Web administration that only grants access to basic administrative functions. If you are new to Web publishing, this is a great place to start. Otherwise, we suggest learning to use the IIS MMC snap-in because it offers access to all settings, not just basic functions. When first launched, the Personal Web Manager's main display window shows basic information and statistics about the Web site.

The Advanced display (accessed by clicking Advanced in the navigation bar on the left side) shows the Web site's folder hierarchy, the default document name(s), whether directory browsing is enabled, and whether an activity is logged. From this display, you can access folder properties to change path, alias, and access (read, execute, script).

The Web Site selection is a Web site creation wizard. It offers several selections to design a content-free structure for you to customize. You can use the Publish selection to transfer Web sites to a Web server (or from a development location to a publish location). The Tour selection offers a basic overview of the Personal Web Server's capabilities. The Microsoft Management Console (MMC) is a standardized administration interface that is reported to be an integral part of Windows 2000. Microsoft already has released the MMC with several products including the Windows NT Option Pack. MMC operates as a standard administration tool to which application-specific templates or plug-ins (also called *snap-ins*) are added for specific functions or controls. The IIS snap-in controls PWS management. You can access the IIS snap-in through the Start menu (Start, Programs, Windows NT 4.0 Option Pack, Microsoft Personal Web Server, Internet Service Manager).

You can use the Internet Service Manager (also called the MMC with the IIS snap-in) to create, manage, and administer both Web and FTP sites. You can manipulate the virtual structure of a Web or FTP site from this Explorer-like interface. The site as a whole or individual folders, virtual directories, and files can be individually managed by opening their associated Properties dialog boxes. (Select the item to be managed and then select Action, Properties or right-click Properties from the pop-up menu.)

The default settings for \wwwroot (the default Web site) are adequate for hosting any Web site off of Windows NT Workstation. If you are serious about hosting Web sites, you should upgrade to Windows NT Server where IIS offers a broader range of capabilities without the license restrictions.

The FrontPage Server Administrator is a GUI interface used to install, upgrade, verify, and uninstall FrontPage Server Extensions. FrontPage Server Extensions are not installed into PWS by default. This tool also is used to enable or disable Web publishing for certain users. (That is, it determines who can alter Web files.)

Setting Up a Web Site with PWS

PWS is an easy-to-use Web server. After it is installed, all you need to do is drop your Web documents into the proper directory, and they are instantly accessible to Web clients. The default PWS installation puts the main service files in the \Winnt\ System32\Inetsrv folder. You'll also find the remote administration Web documents in the \adminsamples subfolder in that location. The installation process creates a new root-level directory called \Inetpub. The following subfolders reside within this folder:

- **Ftproot.** The root directory for FTP access.
- **Iissamples.** A Web directory hosting a sample Web site.
- **Scripts.** The scripts directory also known as cgi-bin.
- **Webpub.** A directory used by the PWS publishing service to store published files.
- **Wwwroot.** The root directory for Web access.

The \wwwroot contains the following subfolders:

- **_private, _vti_bin, _vti_cnf, _vti_log, _vti_pvt, and _vti_txt.** These special FrontPage directories are only used if the FrontPage Server Extensions are installed on the Web server. The _private folder is used to house files that should be hidden from users but retained on the Web site. The _vti folders are all FPSE special use folders.
- **cgi-bin.** This is another scripts directory for the Web site.
- **Images.** This subfolder contains graphics used in the Web site.

You can employ the existing directory structure created by the installation routine, or you can use your own. If you create a custom layout, however, be sure to define the new layout in the MMC IIS snap-in tool. This mainly involves defining virtual directories to folders located outside of the \wwwroot folder.

Serving Web pages from PWS requires a TCP/IP network connection to an intranet or the Internet (or both). Because PWS can host only a single Web site, it automatically uses any or all IP addresses assigned to the host Windows NT Workstation system. Therefore, users accessing the Web site with a NetBIOS name, IP address, or even domain name (assuming DNS is present) will be able to access the Web site.

By default, anonymous Web access is enabled. Like IIS, PWS uses a special user account to grant anonymous access to hosted Web sites. The IUSR_<systemname> account is granted Read and Execute privileges to the wwwroot, ftproot, and scripts folders. To prevent anonymous access and to require enumerated user accounts to gain access to the Web site, you need to change the Web site's Authentication Methods configuration by clicking the top Edit button on the Directory Security tab of the Web site's Properties dialog box.

Serving Web pages from PWS is almost too simple. All you need to do is place the Web documents in the correct folders (content into \wwwroot, images into \wwwroot\images, and scripts into \scripts or \wwwroot\cgi-bin) and make sure the initial document name is correct (DEFAULT.HTM by default). That's it.

Obviously, more complex layouts and dynamic content creation require additional settings, administration, and add-on products. If you are going to deploy a Web site, you should deploy it on a Windows NT Server system and use PWS on Windows NT Workstation as a development platform (if at all). See Chapter 27, "Serving the Web from Windows NT Server," for information about IIS and its advanced capabilities.

Tools For Web Success

If you are sticking with PWS on Windows NT Workstation as your Web host, there are a handful of other Microsoft products you can employ in your Web development process. These products are examined in the following sections.

Microsoft Office

As a power user, you probably are very familiar with the Microsoft Office suite of productivity applications: Word, Excel, PowerPoint, Access, and Outlook. With the release of Microsoft Office 2000, Microsoft Office productive applications now include Internet capabilities. For the most part, this means you are able to export Microsoft Office data into a Web document–compatible form (typically .HTM files). This feature can enable non-HTML programmers to quickly publish Office documents to the Web with little more than using the Save As command.

Office documents need not be converted or saved to HTML format to be distributed on the Web. Internet Explorer 4.0 includes components that can read and display Office documents within its display window. Netscape Navigator supports several plug-ins that perform the same function. In addition, even if a visitor does not use a browser that can display Microsoft Office documents, Microsoft offers downloadable document viewers (`http://officeupdate.microsoft.com/index.htm`).

FrontPage 98

FrontPage 98 is a multifunctional Web site creation and management utility. It is considered to be an integral part of the Web-production environment from Microsoft that includes IIS or PWS and Microsoft Office. FrontPage 98 is a full-featured What You See Is What You Get (WYSIWYG) Web document editor that can modify existing materials or can create new documents and sites. In addition to Web document authoring, FrontPage 98 is a rich administration and management utility. It can be used to automate content creation, to verify hyperlinks, to integrate Web technologies, to create push channels, to track tasks for multiple authors, to remotely administer sites, to publish materials from development to production sites, and more.

FrontPage 98 is designed for the nonprogrammer as well as the Web expert and offers capabilities to simplify Web development and publishing on many levels. With the use of FrontPage Server Extensions, PWS and IIS (and other Web servers) can add several FrontPage-exclusive features to your Web sites.

Visual Studio

Visual Studio is Microsoft's premier developer tool suite for creating applications for intranet deployment. This professional programmer-grade suite includes Visual Basic, Visual C++, Visual FoxPro, Visual InterDev, Visual J++, Visual SourceSafe, and the Microsoft Developer Network (MSDN) Library. If you are creating a Microsoft network solution, this is the only programming suite you'll ever need. When combined with SQL Server and other Microsoft BackOffice products, there is nothing you can't accomplish.

Static Versus Dynamic Content

Content is the core of the Web. Without content, there would be no purpose for the Web to exist and no reason to visit it. Fortunately, there is content—lots and lots of content (often too much). The value of content lies in its applicability, its timeliness, and your ability to locate it. On a basic level, all content on the Web can be divided into two categories: static and dynamic. Static content does not change; dynamic content does change.

Static content includes Web documents (typically plain HTML) and their related objects (text files, graphics, sounds, movies, and so on) that do not change. By change, we mean that the information, data, or entertainment presented is hard-coded into the files and always is the same. The only way static content changes is if the author makes physical changes to the files or replaces the existing files with new ones. Static-content Web sites are the easiest to create and are the most common. They involve little beyond a basic knowledge of HTML and directory structures.

Dynamic content is any information, data, or entertainment that changes based on any number of variables. These variables might be the identity of the user, the browser type, the time, the date, the speed of connection, the level of security access, server load, user input, available database information, and so on. Anything and everything that could possibly be used as a variant to presented content can and is being used somewhere on the Web.

Dynamic Web sites are not always (and actually are fairly rarely) 100% dynamic. Most often, a dynamic object or component is added to a static document. Some common objects added include counters, time stamps, chat applications, tool-tip pop-up messages, and mouse-over animation. This is in addition to adding in forms, background CGIs, JavaScript flourishes, and Java applets. These are all just characteristics added to static documents to hide their staleness.

True dynamic content is created on-the-fly each time a user visits. A database often is used to provide content with ASP or CGI scripts used to manage layout. Creating a fully dynamic Web site is not a simple task. It requires extensive knowledge of Web communications, CGI scripts, databases, and programming (often in multiple programming languages—Perl, Active Server Pages (ASP), Dynamic HTML (DHTML), Cascading Style Sheets (CSS), Java, JavaScript, Visual Basic, Visual C++, and so on). The benefits of dynamic content are relevance, timeliness, and user-specific displays.

PWS can host both static and dynamic content. Some functions of dynamic content, however, require additional third-party products. Generally, dynamic Web sites are hosted from Windows NT Server using IIS 4.0 because it includes several more dynamic-oriented services such as Index Server, Site Server, and Certificate Server.

Push Versus Pull Publishing

A fairly new topic in Web publishing is push technology. *Push publishing* is a method of distributing content to users automatically. This is different from standard methods in which users must visit a site to obtain content (called *pull* when discussed with push). Push publishing focuses on reducing users' time spent locating relevant content by preloading their computers with data. The verdict is still out about whether this is the case. It is true, however, that often-visited sites are much easier to visit if they are sitting on your local hard drive instead of having to access them over a clogged Internet or a slow connection.

Push publishing comes in two forms. The first is a true push in which a Web site sends out data packets to subscribed users on a scheduled basis. The second is a quasi-push-pull method in which a user employs a client utility that automatically pulls data from a site on a scheduled basis. Either way, the end result is very similar—preloaded content.

With the ever-expanding content on the Internet and intranets, the concepts developed under the guise of push might evolve into a true timesaving technology. Until then, push offers Internet users with slow connections or limited connection time the capability to preload content during off-hours (such as overnight or while they are at work or home). Preloaded content offers the benefit of instant display, but it has the drawback of being out-of-date by hours or days, depending on the time lag between content download and user review. Any activated links to nonpreloaded content will employ the Internet connection to obtain new data. Preloaded content might not suit your needs if you often stray from the central topic or navigation path of a subscribed site.

Changing Channels

IE 5 does not include channels. If you install IE 5 over IE 4, IE 5 will keep them, but if you install it fresh, they will not be there.

Push is not limited to preloading Web sites. It also can be employed in virus update distribution, software installation, multimedia, user communications, scheduling, and more.

Push sites employ channels. A *channel* is a collection of topic-oriented content to which a user can subscribe. All of the channel's content is delivered to a user when the push site is updated. PWS offers you the capability to define channels from your Web sites to which users can subscribe. Details about channel creation are included later in this section.

As a Web surfer, you can use Internet Explorer 4.0 to subscribe to both push channels and nonpush channels. A nonpush channel is any Web site that you instruct Internet Explorer to download to your local drive on a regular basis. This feature is known as subscriptions. For complete usage details, view Internet Explorer Help files or the Internet Explorer Web site at `http://www.microsoft.com/ie/`.

Microsoft, along with several partners, has developed a standard for creating and distributing push content. It's called the Channel Definition Format (CDF) and is detailed at `http://www.microsoft.com/standards/cdf/default.asp`. Netscape, with other partners, is developing a rival standard that is not a new standard but a compilation of existing technologies. It's called NetCaster and is detailed at `http://sitesearch.netscape.com/communicator/netcaster/`. For more information about push, visit the Web sites of both Microsoft and Netscape to learn more and to find examples.

PWS can host push channels, but they must be created using FrontPage 98 or another tool. FrontPage 98 creates a subscription service for your Web site (or just a portion of the site) that is sent out regularly to subscribers. You can update and modify the Web site independently of the push channel definition. If your Web site hosts content that is updated regularly, offering a push channel to visitors might attract more visitors and doesn't involve much work.

Troubleshooting Personal Web Sites

Web site troubleshooting can be a very broad topic. Every unique technology incorporated into your Web site can be a point of failure. The more complex your design, the more possibilities for problems. Generally, PWS is fairly robust. One of the best ways to "flush out" a problem is to reboot the system. If this fails to resolve the issue, you can investigate the following items:

- Make sure the host computer can communicate with the network or Internet and vice versa. This can be done by using PING and TRACERT from the Web host and from various clients on the network.

- Check security permissions. If anonymous access is desired, it must be enabled. The IUSR account must be assigned at least Read permissions to the folders and files on the Web site.

- Make sure the IP address assigned to the Web site is either (All Unassigned) or a correct IP address.

- If DNS is in use, make sure the domain name is properly associated with the Web host's IP address.

- Make sure the TCP Port in use either is 80 (the default) or is included in the URL accessing the site (`http://www.mydomain.com:1892/`).

- If sessions fail before transactions are complete (such as when working with scripts or other dynamic components), check the Connection Timeout value and the HTTP Keep-Alives Enabled check box.

- If scripts will not execute, verify that the scripts folder is defined with Script or Execute permissions via the MMC IIS snap-in and that the NTFS-level permissions are set to Read and Execute for the IUSR account.

- If a Web site contains redirected links, virtual directories, or network share links, verify that the required network connections are active and enabled.

- If a list of the Web site's files are displayed instead of the introductory document, check to see whether Directory Browsing is enabled and whether the Default Documents are enabled and named correctly.

If these actions do not resolve the error, you have two other options: reinstall Windows NT Workstation and PWS (a very drastic solution that is not guaranteed to work and that causes your existing setup and configuration to be lost) or look at the coding of your Web documents and objects.

If you can eliminate PWS as the point of failure along with Windows NT Workstation, the remaining possibilities include the content or the viewer. Resolving viewer problems typically means testing different clients from different addresses and subnets. In some cases, updating the client browser or operating system can resolve the problem.

If content is the culprit, you'll need to perform a line-by-line or object-by-object inspection of your Web contents. If you are using plain HTML, you can employ one of the HTML validation tools found at `http://www.stars.com/Authoring/HTML/Validation/`. If you are using any programming language or advanced or dynamic HTML, you'll need to perform validation manually. Some programming languages offer debuggers or error logs to help locate problems. When all else fails, re-create the content from scratch checking yourself as you go.

Third-Party Personal Web Tools

Web tools available from non-Microsoft sources range from full-blown Web servers to content developers to site management and administration. There are so many tools around that it is nearly impossible to list them all. The following are a few of our favorites, and we've also included several archive sites to help you locate more on your own.

- Adobe PageMill: `http://www.adobe.com/`
- Alchemy Mindworks, Inc.'s GIF Construction Set: `http://www.mindworkshop.com/alchemy/gifcon.html`
- Floersch Enterprise's Search and Replace and Find String: `http://www.sky.net/~floersch/`
- InfoAccess, Inc.'s HTML Transit: `http://www.infoaccess.com/transit/`
- Jasc Inc.'s Paint Shop Pro: `http://www.jasc.com/`
- LView Pro: `http://www.lview.com/`
- Macromedia's Flash, Fireworks, Freehand, DreamWeaver, Director, and Generator: `http://www.macromedia.com/`
- MediaTech's LiveImage: `http://www.liveimage.com/`
- NetObjects Fusion: `http://www.netobjects.com/`
- O'Reilly & Associates' PolyForm: `http://polyform.ora.com/`
- O'Reilly & Associates' WebBoard: `http://webboard.ora.com/`
- Sausage Software's HotDog Professional: `http://www.sausage.com/`
- SoftQuad's HoTMetaL PRO: `http://www.sq.com/`
- Symantec's Visual Café: `http://www.symantec.com/`
- TetraNet's LinkBot: `http://www.linkbot.com/`

If what you want or need is not in this list, you can locate Web-related software on your own using the following sites. Remember, the more specific your keywords, the more likely you'll locate what you really want.

- `http://www.search.com/` is a database of more than 300 search engines. It's sure to have the right search for you.
- `http://www.metacrawler.com/` is a search engine that employs several other engines to do its dirty work.
- `http://www.webdeveloper.com/` is a Web Developer.
- `http://www.w3.org/pub/WWW/Tools/` is W3C's list of tools.
- `http://www.microsoft.com/sitebuilder/` is Microsoft SiteBuilder's tool list.

For More Information

If the information about PWS and general Web issues presented in this chapter has increased your desire to learn more, you can use several resources to obtain more knowledge. Note that PWS is not considered to be a mainline book or reference topic, so you'll need to consult IIS-related resources.

- Stewart, James Michael and Ramesh Chandak. *Exam Prep: IIS 4.* Coriolis, 1998. ISBN: 157610267X.

- Tulloch, Matt. *Administering Internet Information Server 4.* Osborne/McGraw-Hill, 1998. ISBN: 0070655367.

- Sheldon, Tom, et al. *Microsoft Internet Information Server 4: The Complete Reference.* Osborne/McGraw-Hill, 1998. ISBN: 0078824575.

- *Windows NT Workstation Resource Kit.* Microsoft Press, 1996. ISBN: 1572313439.

- Microsoft TechNet: `http://www.microsoft.com/technet/`

- If you need more general information about PWS, visit the IIS Web area on the Microsoft Web site: `http://www.microsoft.com/iis/`. There also is a scattering of information about PWS on TechNet.

- For more information about Microsoft Office and how it can be used in a Web production environment, visit the Microsoft Office Web area at `http://www.microsoft.com/office/`.

- For more information about FrontPage 98, visit the Microsoft FrontPage Web area at `http://www.microsoft.com/frontpage/`.

- For information about Visual Studio, visit the Visual Studio Web area at `http://msdn.microsoft.com/vstudio/`.

If you'd like more information about dynamic content, you need to decide what type of dynamic content you are interested in. The following are several resources you can use to find out more:

- The Web Developer's Virtual Library: `http://www.stars.com/`
- Microsoft's Site Builder Network: `http://www.microsoft.com/sitebuilder/`
- Internet.com: `http://www.internet.com/`
- World Wide Web Journal: `http://www.w3j.com/`
- XML.com: `http://www.xml.com/`
- WebReview.com: `http://www.webreview.com/`
- Perl: `http://www.perl.com/`
- Java: `http://java.sun.com/`
- JavaScript: `http://www.javascript.com/`
- HTML/Web site books written by LANWrights, Inc.: `http://www.lanw.com/html.htm`

27

Serving the Web from Windows NT Server

WINDOWS NT SERVER IS DESIGNED specifically to act as a service host for numerous clients. In fact, Microsoft has worked hard to make Windows NT Server a solid platform for hosting Internet information services such as Web and FTP (File Transfer Protocol). These efforts have resulted in a surprisingly versatile, robust, and feature-rich service platform. In this chapter, we discuss Windows NT Server as an Internet information services host.

This chapter on Windows NT Server is included in this Windows NT Workstation book to provide you with information about hosting unrestricted services. As discussed in the previous chapter, Windows NT Workstation is limited to 10 simultaneous connections. This severely restricts Windows NT Workstation from being deployed as an inexpensive Internet host. Microsoft implemented the restriction for a specific reason: Windows NT Workstation is designed as a client and does not include all the features and capabilities included with Windows NT Server. Windows NT Workstation is priced considerably lower than Windows NT Server because of these different capabilities.

The similarities between Windows NT Workstation and Windows NT Server are great. They basically share the same foundational architecture, design, layout, and interface. Therefore, in this chapter, you'll discover an overlap in the coverage of hosting Web and FTP sites on Windows NT Workstation and Windows NT Server systems.

IIS (Internet Information Server) 4.0

IIS (Internet Information Server) 4.0 is the latest revision of Microsoft's Internet information services application. IIS transforms a Windows NT Server system into a host for both Web and FTP sites with additional support for email handling and private discussion groups. The product distributed by Microsoft under the parent name Internet Information Server is actually a collection of several products that have been tightly integrated to offer a seamless, powerful Internet application design and publication environment.

IIS is designed to be hosted by Windows NT Server. Other versions with reduced capabilities are available for Windows NT Workstation and Windows 95/98. These versions are Peer Web Services and Personal Web Services, respectively. In fact, all three versions of the software are included on the distribution CD called the Windows NT 4.0 Option Pack (see the "Setup Integration" section later this chapter). The setup routing automatically determines which version to install based on the operating system it discovers. IIS is available as a free add-on for Windows NT Server, Windows NT Workstation, and Windows 95/98. You can download it for free, or you can order a CD for a moderate shipping and handling fee. The latter option is probably the better choice because the full Option Pack is more than 87MB. To order it, visit the Internet site at **http://www.microsoft.com/ntserver/nts/downloads/ recommended/NT4OptPk/**. The Option Pack is included in the Windows NT Server Enterprise Edition box, which is available from software distributors and the TechNet subscription service (see **http://www.microsoft.com/technet/**).

IIS is a fully standards-compliant Web and FTP server with additional support for several proprietary and experimental technologies developed or purchased/licensed by Microsoft. The collection of features within IIS enable you to perform a wide range of Web-related tasks, including Web application development, site publication, and remote administration. With IIS, you can create, develop, publish, and administer Internet content sites of any size, from personal hobby sites to interactive multimedia enterprise-level intranet/Intranet sites. IIS simplifies and enhances the processes involved in creating and maintaining such sites.

One of the most significant improvements of IIS 4.0 over its previous releases is the added support for HTTP (Hypertext Transfer Protocol) 1.1 while maintaining full backward compatibility with HTTP 1.0. HTTP 1.1 offers faster Web site response, improving user site experience for browsers supporting it (such as Internet Explorer 4.0). These performance benefits are realized through four key features of HTTP 1.1:

- **Pipelining.** This is a communications method in which the server does not wait for the completion of a resource transmission before sending the next resource. HTTP 1.0 requires that resources be sent one at a time in succession, waiting for one transmission to be complete before initiating another. Pipelining quickens document display by allowing multiple elements to be sent simultaneously.

- **Persistent connections.** This is a communication method in which multiple requests for resources are sent over a single communication link. HTTP 1.0 uses a different communication link for each resource request. This means that each element composing a Web page (such as graphics, Java applets, and so on) is sent to the browser separately. Persistent connections relieve the amount of communication overhead (establishment, maintenance, and tearing down of communication links), which results in higher throughput and faster response.

- **Chunked transfers.** This is a communications method that optimizes how variable length documents are transferred to the client. ASPs (Active Server Pages), which are created on-the-fly when requested by a client, vary in length each time they are created. HTTP 1.0 experienced difficulty transmitting such resources when the exact length of the resource was unknown at the start of the transmission. HTTP 1.1 employs a method of arbitrarily chunking the outbound resource as the resource is built. Thus, early chunk sizes are known, and only the final chunk requires a system-intensive function to determine its length.

- **Proxy support.** Caching information is built into HTTP 1.1 to maximize resource efficiency when handled by servers, clients, and proxies. HTTP 1.1 includes creation time, expiration dates, and other methods of determining the freshness of data that is used by proxies to properly cache resources.

In addition to performance benefits, several new tools and capabilities expand the functionality of IIS. These include new wizards, special administration tools, and improved access management, all of which are discussed in the following sections.

Setup Integration

IIS 4.0 is the central product on the Windows NT 4.0 Option Pack. It's no longer a stand-alone application; it's tightly integrated with other Web services and applications designed to improve and expand the Web development and publishing environment hosted by Windows NT Server. The other components on the Option Pack include:

- Index Server 2.0
- Certificate Server 1.0
- Site Server Express
- Transaction Server 2.0
- Message Queue Server Standard Edition
- Internet Connection Services for Microsoft RAS (Remote Access Service)
- SMTP Service (Simple Mail Transfer Protocol)
- NNTP Service (Network News Transfer Protocol)
- Windows NT Service Pack 3
- Internet Explorer 4.01

The Setup Wizard used by the Option Pack offers a single interface for installing all or only a select few of the available offerings. Therefore, simultaneous installation ensures proper integration and the presence of all required elements for a fully functional and diverse publishing system. One important fact to keep in mind is that before you can install IIS and the other Web server-related components, you must install Service Pack 3 (or greater) and Internet Explorer 4.01 (or greater). Whether you elect to install everything or just select components from the Option Pack, you can always add or remove components. This is true for both the distribution CD and the download version. However, it's recommended that you install all components simultaneously to ensure proper integration and prevent configuration loss caused by subsequent component installations.

Management Flexibility

IIS 4.0 has expanded and improved control and administration capabilities. These benefits offer site managers complete control locally and remotely over their content, the Web server, and all related Option Pack components. The Option Pack introduces the MMC (Microsoft Management Console) to Windows NT 4.0. This new standardized administrative interface was created for use in Windows NT 5.0 (or Windows 2000). It's included with IIS 4.0 because it provides a more exhaustive and intuitive administration and configuration interface than did the previous Internet Service Manager utility. MMC operates using a snap-in architecture. MMC itself offers no control mechanisms but rather a standardized interface into which application-specific modules are loaded to provide the actual administration controls.

IIS 4.0 also includes a full-featured, Web-based administrative interface that employs ASP (Active Server Pages) and JavaScript. Any Web browser can be used to remotely control your installation of IIS. The Web interface is disabled by default, and tight security can be maintained so only authorized users can actually alter your site.

Content Control

IIS 4.0 offers more ways to control, define, and restrict access than ever before. A fine-grained control offers Web administrators the ability to define settings on a server, Web, virtual directory, or individual file level. Therefore, complete control down to the single element is possible. Some of the benefits of this multi-level control capability include sectioned security, reduced log file size, and separated control tasks.

Through the use of SSL (Secure Sockets Layer) 3.0, IIS offers a secure environment for e-commerce or transfer of other sensitive data. SSL can also be applied on multiple levels of granularity.

Multiple Web Site Hosting

Unlike previous releases, IIS 4.0 is able to host distinctively individual Web sites from a single IP (Internet Protocol) address. With the use of HTTP 1.1 host headers, multiple

Web sites can be hosted over a single IP address. However, host headers are not supported by all browsers—only those supporting HTTP 1.1, such as Internet Explorer 4.0.

Network Bandwidth Control

If bandwidth usage is a concern, such as with a Web server hosting multiple popular Web sites or a Web server sharing an Internet link with other servers or an entire network, IIS offers the ability to limit or restrict how much bandwidth can actually be consumed by Web traffic on a server and individual Web site basis. Bandwidth throttling is used to define greater bandwidth access to popular sites, yet restrict overall usage by all Web sites hosted by IIS. It can also be used to ensure that low access sites or sites hosting resources with long transfer times always have enough bandwidth to operate adequately.

The Option Pack Components

The Option Pack is just that, a distribution of several applications that can be integrated into a development and publishing environment revolving around IIS 4.0. The elements in the Option Pack can be used independently of IIS, but they were originally designed with Web deployment in mind. The following sections provide a brief description of each Option Pack component.

Index Server 2.0

Index Server is an automated content indexing and search utility service used by IIS-hosted Web sites. With Index Server, the entire contents of a Web site and several non-HTML file formats, such as MS Office application formats (Word, Excel, PowerPoint), plain text, rich text format, and more, can be indexed and searched. With support for ASP, SQL (Structured Query Language) formatted queries, specialized content filters, multiple language support, and custom query and response forms, Index Server offers a rich document location service to users and administrators. Index Server is managed through both the MMC plug-in and a Web interface.

Certificate Server 1.0

Certificate Server brings the security and tracking capabilities of digital certificates to IIS. Digital certificates can be used to prove the identity of a Web site or verify the authenticity of a visitor. In both cases, certificates act as security currency. Before the release of Certificate Server, IIS-hosted Web sites had to rely solely upon the authentication services of third-party organizations (such as VeriSign). Now, anyone can provide his or her own internal site-specific authentication to track users or identify a Web site. Certificate Server supports X.509 digital certificates as well as both SSL and PCT (Private Communications Technology) protocols.

Site Server Express 2.0

Site Server Express is a Web site traffic and content analysis tool. It offers features such as IIS log translation, link verification, and site publishing. The Usage Import and Report Writer transforms the clunky IIS log files into human-readable summary documents. The resulting report shows you at a glance how many visitors interacted with a Web site, how long they stayed, how much data they retrieved, and more. The Content Analysis tool, previously known as the WebMapper from NetCarta, creates a graphical tree view of a Web site and pinpoints broken links and failed navigation. The Web Publishing Wizard simplifies the tasks required to move newly developed content out to a production Web server.

Transaction Server 2.0

Transaction Server brings true transaction and communication control, tracking, and administration to IIS. This application can be used to manage all transactions. A transaction is any communication between a client and a server or one server and another where data of any type is exchanged, such as e-commerce, database queries, files, resource requests, or even error messages. Transaction Server can watch each and every transaction to ensure that only complete, valid, and authorized data exchanges occur. This provides an environment in which security can be adequately maintained; performance is improved; the reliability of transmitted data is enhanced; and incomplete, invalid, and unauthorized transactions are not processed (which prevents bad data, data loss, or hung tasks). Transaction Server's capabilities can be employed over distributed applications where separate parts of the overall application are hosted by separate servers. Transaction Server can ensure that data exchanges take place only over active network links, and it allows for recovery of exchanged data when network communications are broken or interrupted.

Message Queue Server 1.0

As distributed applications become more commonplace, the need to improve and guarantee communications between distant servers is crucial. Message Queue Server provides just that service. This application hosts a message queue for local and remote servers, services, and applications. Using a system much like common email, messages are sent through the Message Queue Server to wait for the receiving application to request its messages. This form of communication enables tasks to operate even during network communication interruptions. Message Queue Server brings broad flexibility and communication fault tolerance to the IIS Web environment.

Internet Connection Services for Microsoft RAS 1.0

Since the release of Windows NT Server in August of 1996, Microsoft has sought to improve and widen the capabilities of its built-in RAS (Remote Access Service). The

ICS (Internet Connection Services) is an upgrade and extension for RAS, bringing Windows NT's remote communications many new capabilities. These new capabilities include custom client dialers, centrally managed phonebooks, support for RADIUS authentication, and a revamp of the RAS administration tools.

ICS is not required by stand-alone systems or by servers acting as a dial-out system; rather, ICS is an improvement of RAS servers acting as a dial-up host for remote users. ICS is a subset of the improvements available through the RRAS (Routing and Remote Access Service) Update. If you're deploying Windows NT Server as a dial-up host, you should obtain more information about ICS and RRAS from TechNet and visit the RRAS Web area at `http://www.microsoft.com/ntserver/nts/downloads/winfeatures/rras/rrasdown.asp` or `http://www.microsoft.com/NTServer/commserv/exec/feature/ICS.asp`.

SMTP Service

IIS includes an SMTP (Simple Mail Transfer Protocol) Service that brings basic email handling capabilities to Web sites. This service allows Web sites to send and receive email. Each Web site has a single inbound email deposit box where user feedback, error messages, and other email-related messages are placed. This box is not a standard POP (Post Office Protocol) email box; it's simply a holding tank for messages that must be read manually with a text editor. The primary use for the SMTP service is to send users email based on Web form-provided feedback or as a response to interacting with a particular Web application.

For full email capabilities, you need to investigate other solutions, such as Microsoft Exchange Server (`http://www.microsoft.com/exchange/`).

NNTP Service

IIS includes an NNTP Service to bring threaded discussion forums to Web sites. Although this service offers all the capabilities found on standard Internet newsgroups, it's not capable of true interaction with the public NNTP newsfeeds. Instead, the NNTP Service is used to host private, single-system discussion forums that operate in the same manner and with the same utilities as the public NNTP newsgroups. This allows both newsreader clients and Web-based interfaces to grant users access to the discussion groups. With the NNTP Service, you can host multiple moderated or unmoderated threaded discussion groups.

To interact with the public NNTP newsfeeds, you must deploy an application that fully supports NNTP, such as Microsoft Exchange Server (available at `http://www.microsoft.com/exchange/`).

Service Pack 3

SP3 (Service Pack 3) is included on the Option Pack CD. It was the latest release of a service pack for Windows NT at the time the option pack was created. IIS and related components require SP3 to be installed on a Windows NT system. SP3 is no longer the latest service pack. Please consult the Microsoft Web site or TechNet for details about the latest service pack release. If you install IIS on a system with Service Pack 4 or later, you will see a warning message stating that the option pack components have not been tested on systems hosting any service packs beyond SP3. Service Pack 4 has proven itself as a reliable service pack for deploying IIS. For more information on service packs, see Chapter 23, "Managing Windows NT System Security."

Internet Explorer 4.01

Internet Explorer 4.01 is included on the Option Pack CD. IIS and the other elements require Internet Explorer 4.01. Later versions of Internet Explorer may adequately support the Option Pack components, but you should consult the Option Pack Web area for more details. See Chapter 24, "Windows NT as a Web Client," for more information about Internet Explorer.

Setting Up a Web Site with IIS

IIS is an easy-to-use Web server. After it's installed, all you need to do is drop your Web documents into the proper directory, and they are instantly accessible to Web clients. The default installation location for the main IIS service files is \Winnt\System32\Inetsrv. You'll also find the remote administration Web documents at that location in the \adminsamples subfolder. The installation process creates a new root-level directory named \Inetpub. Within this folder are several subfolders:

- **Ftproot.** The root directory for FTP access.
- **Iissamples.** A Web directory hosting a sample Web site.
- **Scripts.** The scripts directory, also known as cgi-bin.
- **Webpub.** A directory used by the publishing service of IIS to store published files.
- **Wwwroot.** The root directory for Web access. Wwwroot also has several subfolders:
  - *_private, _vti_bin, _vti_cnf, _vti_log, _vti_pvt, and _vti_txt.* These are special FrontPage directories that are used only if the FrontPage Server Extensions are installed on the Web server. The _private folder is used to house files that should be hidden from users but retained in the Web site. The _vti folders are all FrontPage Server Extension special use folders.
  - *cgi-bin.* This is another scripts directory for the Web site.
  - *Images.* This folder contains graphics used in the Web site.

You can employ the existing directory structure created by the installation routine, or you can use your own. However, if you do create a custom layout, be sure to define the new layout in the MMC IIS snap-in tool. This mainly involves defining virtual directories to folders located outside of the \wwwroot folder.

Serving Web pages from IIS requires a TCP/IP (Transmission Control Protocol/Internet Protocol) network connection to either an intranet or the Internet (or both). IIS automatically uses any or all IP addresses assigned to the host Windows NT Server system. Therefore, users accessing the Web site with a NetBIOS name, IP address, or even domain name (assuming the DNS, or Domain Name Service, is present) will be able to access the Web site.

By default, Web access is anonymous. IIS uses a special user account to grant "anonymous" access to hosted Web sites. The IUSR_*<systemname>* account is granted Read and Execute privileges over the wwwroot, ftproot, and scripts folders. To prevent anonymous access and require enumerated user accounts to gain access to the Web site, you need to change the configuration of the Web site's Authentication Methods (click the top Edit button on the Directory Security tab of the Web site's Properties dialog box).

Serving Web pages from IIS is almost too simple. All you need to do is place the Web documents in the correct folders (content into \wwwroot, images into \www-root\images, and scripts into \scripts or \wwwroot\cgi-bin) and then make sure the initial document name is correct (DEFAULT.HTM, by default). That's it. Obviously, more complex layouts and dynamic content creation require additional settings, administration, and add-on products.

Tools for Web Success

You can use any one of a handful of other Microsoft products in your Web development process. Those products are discussed in the following sections.

Microsoft Office

Microsoft Office is a suite of productivity applications. You're probably already very familiar with them: Word, Excel, PowerPoint, Access, and Outlook. With the release of Office 97 and the soon-to-be-released Office 2000, Office productive applications include Internet capabilities. For the most part, this means they have the ability to export their document data into a Web document compatible form (typically, .htm files). This feature enables non-HTML programmers to quickly publish Office documents to the Web by using the Save As command.

Office documents don't have to be converted or saved to HTML format to be distributed on the Web. Internet Explorer 4.0 includes components that can read and display Office documents within its own display window. Netscape Navigator supports several plug-ins that can perform the same function. In addition, even if a visitor does not use a browser that can display Office documents, Microsoft offers downloadable document viewers (**http://officeupdate.microsoft.com/index.htm**).

FrontPage 98

FrontPage 98 is a multifunctional Web site creation and management utility. It's considered an integral part of the Web-production environment from Microsoft, which includes IIS and Microsoft Office. FrontPage 98 is a full-featured WYSIWYG Web document editor that can be used to modify existing materials or create new documents/sites. In addition to Web document authoring, FrontPage 98 is a rich administration and management utility. It can be used to automate content creation, verify links, integrate Web technologies, create push channels, track tasks for multiple authors, remotely administer sites, publish materials from development to production sites, and more. Designed for the nonprogrammer as well as the Web expert FrontPage 98 offers capabilities for simplifying Web development and publishing on many levels. With the use of FrontPage Server Extensions, IIS (or other Web servers) can add several FrontPage-exclusive features to your Web sites.

Visual Studio

Visual Studio is Microsoft's premier developer tool suite for creating applications for intranet deployment. This professional programmer grade suite includes Visual Basic, Visual C++, Visual FoxPro, Visual InterDev, Visual J++, Visual SourceSafe, and the MSDN Library. If you're creating a Microsoft network solution, this is the only programming suite you'll ever need. If you combine Visual Studio with SQL Server and other BackOffice products, there's nothing you can't accomplish.

Static Versus Dynamic Content

Content is the core of the Web. Without content there would be no purpose for the Web to exist and no reason to visit. Fortunately, there is content. Lots and lots of content (often too much). The value of content lies in its applicability and timeliness, and your ability to locate it. On a basic level, all content on the Web can be divided into two categories: static and dynamic. *Static content* is anything that does not change. *Dynamic content* is anything that does change.

Static content includes Web documents (typically, plain HTML) and their related objects (text files, graphics, sounds, movies, and so on) that do not change. What we mean by "change" is that the information, data, or entertainment they present is hard coded into the files and does not change. Static content changes only when the author makes physical changes to the files or replaces the existing files with new ones. A static content Web site is the easiest to create and the most common. It involves little beyond a basic knowledge of HTML and directory structures.

Dynamic content is any Web site with information, data, or entertainment that changes based on any one or a number of variables. These variables can be the identity of the user, browser type, time, date, speed of connection, level of security access, server load, user input, available database information, and so on. Anything and everything that could possibly be used as a variant to presented content can and is being used somewhere on the Web.

Dynamic Web sites are not always 100% dynamic (actually, they're fairly rare). Most often, a dynamic object or component is added to a static document. Some common dynamic objects you can add include counters, time stamps, chat applications, tooltip pop-up messages, and mouse-over animations. You can also add in forms, background CGIs (Common Gateway Interfaces), JavaScript flourishes, and Java applets. These are all just bandages you can add to static documents to hide their staleness.

True dynamic content is created on-the-fly each time a user visits. Often, a database is used to provide content, and ASP or CGI scripts are used to manage layout. Creating a fully dynamic Web site is not a simple task. It requires extensive knowledge of Web communications, CGI, databases, and programming (often in multiple programming languages, such as Perl, ASP, DHTML, Style Sheets, Java, JavaScript, Visual Basic, Visual C++, and so on). The benefits of dynamic content are relevance, timeliness, and user-specific display.

IIS can host both static and dynamic content. However, some functions of dynamic content require additional third-party products or other Option Pack or Microsoft components (such as Index Server, Site Server, and Certificate Server from the Option Pack, or Exchange Server or SQL Server).

If you'd like more information on dynamic content, you need to decide which type of dynamic content you're interested in. See the "For More Information" section at the end of this chapter.

Push Versus Pull Publishing

A fairly new topic in Web publishing is push. *Push publishing* is a method of distributing content to users automatically. This is different from standard methods in which users must visit a site to obtain content (called *pull* when discussed with push). Push publishing focuses on reducing the time it takes a user to locate relevant content by preloading the user's computer with data. The verdict is still out whether this is the case; however, it is true that frequently visited sites are much easier to visit if you can access them from your local hard drive instead of having to access them over a clogged Internet or slow connection.

Push publishing comes in two forms. First is true push in which a Web site sends out data packets to subscribed users on a scheduled basis. Second is a quasi-push-pull method in which a user employs a client utility that will automatically pull data from a site on a scheduled basis. Either way, the end result is very similar—preloaded content.

With the ever-expanding content on the Internet and intranets, the concepts developed under the guise of push may evolve into a true timesaving technology. Until then, push offers Internet users with slow connections or limited connection time the ability to preload content during off-hours (such as overnight or while they are at work or home). Preloaded content offers the benefit of instant display. However, it has the drawback of being hours to days out of date, depending on the timelag between content download and user review. Any activated links to non-preloaded content will employ the Internet connection to obtain new data. Preloaded content may not suit your needs if you often stray from the central topic or navigation path of a subscribed site.

Push is not limited to preloading Web sites. It can also be employed in virus update distribution, software installation, multimedia, user communications, scheduling, and more.

Push sites employ channels. A *channel* is a collection of topic-oriented content to which a user can subscribe. The entire content of a channel is delivered to a user when the push site is updated. IIS offers you the ability to define channels from your own Web sites to which users can subscribe.

As a Web surfer, you can use Internet Explorer 4.0 to subscribe to both push channels and non-push channels. A non-push channel is any Web site that you instruct Internet Explorer to download to your local drive on a regular basis. This feature is known as Subscriptions. For complete usage details, view the Internet Explorer help or the Internet Explorer Web site at **http://www.microsoft.com/ie/**.

Microsoft, along with several partners, has developed a "standard" for creating and distributing push content. Its called the CDF (Channel Definition Format) and you can find more information about it at **http://www.microsoft.com/standards/cdf/default.asp**. Netscape, with other partners, is developing a rival "standard" that is not a new standard, but a compilation of existing technologies. It's called NetCaster, and you can learn more about it at **http://sitesearch.netscape.com/communicator/netcaster/**. To learn more about and find examples of push publishing, we suggest you visit both the Microsoft and Netscape Web sites.

IIS can host push channels, but they must be created using FrontPage 98 or another tool. FrontPage 98 creates a subscription service for your Web site (or just a portion of the site) that is regularly sent out to subscribers. You can update and modify the Web site independently of the push channel definition. If your Web site hosts content that is updated regularly, offering a push channel to visitors may attract more visitors and doesn't involve much work.

Troubleshooting Web Sites

Web site troubleshooting can be a very broad topic. Every unique technology incorporated into your Web site can be a point of failure. Obviously, the more complex your design, the more possibilities there are for problems. Generally, IIS itself is fairly robust. One of the best ways to "flush out" a problem is to reboot the system. If this fails to resolve the issue, you should investigate several other items:

- Check to make sure the host computer can communicate with the network or Internet and vice versa. To do this, use PING and TRACERT from the Web host and from various clients on the network.

- Check security permissions. If anonymous access is desired, it must be enabled, and the IUSR account must be assigned at least Read permissions to the folders and files of the Web site.

- Confirm that the IP address assigned to the Web site is either "(All Unassigned)" or a correct and specific IP address.

- If DNS is being used, make sure the domain name is properly associated with the IP address of the Web host.

- Verify that the TCP Port in use is 80 (the default) or if not the default, that it's included in the URL accessing the site (**http://www.mydomain.com:1892/**).

- If sessions fail before transactions are complete (such as when you're working with scripts or other dynamic components), check the Connection Timeout value and the HTTP Keep-Alives Enabled check box.

- If scripts will not execute, verify that the folder is defined with Script or Execute permissions via the MMC IIS snap-in and that the NTFS-level permissions are set to Read and Execute for the IUSR account.

- If a Web site contains redirected links, virtual directories, or network share links, verify that the required network connections are active and enabled.

- If a listing of the Web site's files is displayed instead of the introductory document, check to see if Directory Browsing is enabled and if the Default Documents are enabled and named correctly.

If these actions do not resolve the error, you have two other options. You can reinstall Windows NT Server and IIS (a very drastic solution that is not guaranteed to work and causes your existing setup and configuration to be lost), or you can look at the coding of your Web documents and objects.

If you can eliminate IIS as the point of failure along with Windows NT Server, the remaining possibilities are the content and the viewer. Resolving viewer problems typically means testing different clients from different addresses and subnets. In some cases, updating the client browser or operating system can resolve the problem.

If content is the culprit, you need to perform a line-by-line or object-by-object inspection of your Web contents. If you're using plain HTML, you can employ one of the HTML validation tools found at **http://www.stars.com/Authoring/HTML/Validation/**. If you're using any programming language or advanced/Dynamic HTML, you need to perform validation manually. Some programming languages offer debuggers or error logs to help locate problems. When all else fails, re-create the content from scratch, checking yourself as you go.

Third-Party Web Tools

Web tools available from non-Microsoft sources range from full-blown Web servers to content developers to site management and administration. So many tools exist that it's nearly impossible to list them all. We've named a few of our favorites, but we've also included several archive sites to help you locate more on your own:

- Adobe PageMill, a Web page creation tool: `http://www.adobe.com/`
- Alchemy Mindworks, Inc.'s GIF Construction Set, an image creation application: `http://www.mindworkshop.com/alchemy/gifcon.html`
- InfoAccess, Inc.'s HTML Transit, a Web page creation tool: `http://www.infoaccess.com/transit/`
- Jasc Inc.'s Paint Shop Pro, an image manipulation utility: `http://www.jasc.com/`
- LView Pro, an image manipulation utility: `http://www.lview.com/`
- Macromedia's Flash, Fireworks, Freehand, DreamWeaver, Director, and Generator, a series of Web page and image tools: `http://www.macromedia.com/`
- MediaTech's LiveImage, an imagemap creation tool: `http://www.liveimage.com/`
- NetObjects Fusion, a Web page creation utility: `http://www.netobjects.com/`
- O'Reilly & Associates' PolyForm, a Web forms construction kit: `http://polyform.ora.com/`
- O'Reilly & Associates' WebBoard, Web conferencing software: `http://webboard.ora.com/`
- Sausage Software's HotDog Professional, an HTML authoring tool: `http://www.sausage.com/`
- SoftQuad's HoTMetaL PRO, a Web site creation tool: `http://www.sq.com/`
- Symantec's Visual Café, a visual programming environment for Java: `http://www.symantec.com/`
- TetraNet's LinkBot, an automated Web site testing tool: `http://www.linkbot.com/`

If what you want or need is not in this list, you can locate Web-related software on your own using the following sites (remember that the more specific your keywords are, the more likely you are to locate what you really want):

- `http://www.search.com/`   This is a database of more than 300 search engines, so it's sure to have the right search for you.
- `http://www.metacrawler.com/`   This search engine employs several other engines to do its dirty work.
- `http://www.webdeveloper.com/`   The *Web Developer* e-magazine provides tons of useful information for Web masters and novices alike.

- `http://www.w3.org/Tools/`   W3C lists numerous tools you can use for Web site creation and maintenance.

- `http://msdn.microsoft.com/default.asp`   This Microsoft developer site provides links to numerous Microsoft resources for Web developers.

For More Information

- For more information on Microsoft Office and how it can be used in a Web production environment, visit the Microsoft Office Web area at `http://www.microsoft.com/office/`.

- For more information about FrontPage 98, visit the Microsoft FrontPage Web area at `http://www.microsoft.com/frontpage/`.

- For information about Visual Studio, visit the Web area at `http://msdn.microsoft.com/vstudio/`.

- Stewart, James Michael and Ramesh Chandak. *Exam Prep: IIS 4.* Coriolis, 1998. ISBN: 157610267X.

- Tulloch, Matt. *Administering Internet Information Server 4.* McGraw-Hill, 1998. ISBN: 0070655367.

- Sheldon, Tom, et al. *Microsoft Internet Information Server 4: The Complete Reference.* McGraw-Hill, 1998. ISBN: 0078824575.

- *Windows NT Workstation Resource Kit.* Microsoft Press, 1996. ISBN: 1572313439.

- Microsoft TechNet: `http://www.microsoft.com/technet/`.

Here are several resources you can use to find out more about dynamic content:

- The Web Developer's Virtual Library: `http://www.stars.com/`

- Microsoft's Site Builder Network: `http://www.microsoft.com/sitebuilder/`

- Internet.com: `http://www.internet.com/`

- World Wide Web Journal: `http://www.w3j.com/`

- XML.com: `http://www.xml.com/`

- WebReview.com: `http://www.webreview.com/`

- Perl: `http://www.perl.com/`

- Java: `http://java.sun.com/`

- JavaScript: `http://www.javascript.com/`

- HTML/Web site books written by LANWrights, Inc.: `http://www.lanw.com/html.htm`

28

Other Windows NT Internet Services

Hosting Web services on a Windows NT Workstation or Windows NT Server system is only one of several information service options. The Windows NT platform offers a stable foundation for the delivery of many types of information services—to both intranet and Internet clients. The only catch is that most services worth deploying either require Windows NT Server's additional capabilities or are so popular it doesn't make sense to deploy them on Windows NT Workstation with its limit of 10 simultaneous uses. In this chapter, we look at several other Internet information services that can be deployed on the Windows NT platform.

In-the-Box Windows NT TCP/IP and Internet Services

In addition to IIS (Internet Information Server), Windows NT includes several TCP/IP (Transmission Control Protocol/Internet Protocol) services that we've only brushed over or barely mentioned elsewhere in this book. These included services that are add-ons or network services that can be installed directly from the distribution CD.

However, not all of these will operate on Windows NT Workstation; several of them require Windows NT Server. The following TCP/IP services are included with Windows NT:

- Simple TCP/IP Services
- TCP/IP Printing
- DNS (Domain Name Service)
- WINS (Windows Internet Name Service)
- DHCP (Dynamic Host Configuration Protocol)
- RAS and PPTP (Remote Access Service and Point-to-Point Tunneling Protocol)

Simple TCP/IP

Simple TCP/IP services bring to the Windows NT platform a handful of common TCP/IP utilities often found on UNIX systems. These include Character Generator, Daytime, Discard, Echo, and Quote of the Day. This service enables Windows NT to respond to and communicate with other TCP/IP systems that support these utilities. For more information about these tools, please refer to their respective RFCs: 864, 867, 863, 862, and 865 at `http://sunsite.auc.dk/RFC/`.

TCP/IP Printing

TCP/IP printing brings the Windows NT print system to non-Microsoft TCP/IP clients. This service brings the `LPD` (Line Printer Daemon) and `LPR` (Line Printer) commands to the Windows NT platform. `LPR` is used to send print jobs to TCP/IP printers. `LPD` accepts print jobs from `LPR` clients and sends them to Windows NT printers. Both `LPD` and `LPR` are compliant with the standards (RFC 1179) set for these tools. For more information, see Chapter 22, "Printing with Windows NT."

DNS

DNS (Domain Name Service) is a name resolution service hosted by Windows NT Server. DNS is used to resolve FQDNs (fully qualified domain names), such as `www.lanw.com`, into IP addresses. DNS can be hosted privately on an intranet or linked with Internet DNS servers. When employing human friendly FQDNs, DNS must be present to resolve the names into IP addresses used by the protocol for actual communication. DNS is manually configured. The Microsoft deployment of DNS is still complex, but it's much easier to use than its UNIX based counterpart, mainly because of its GUI (graphical user interface) and avoidance of kludgy command line controls. For more information about DNS, see Chapter 12, TechNet, or the DNS deployment guide, which is available from `http://www.microsoft.com/ntserver/nts/ deployment/planguide/dnswp.asp`.

WINS

WINS (Windows Internet Name Service) is a service similar to DNS except it resolves NetBIOS host names into IP addresses. WINS must be hosted by a Windows NT Server system. WINS is primarily deployed on an intranet to allow computer names to be used to access Internet information service resources. You can link WINS and DNS, so if WINS fails to resolve a name, it can pass the task to DNS. WINS dynamically maintains itself by tying into the NetBIOS service; therefore, as machines and shared resources enter and leave the domain, WINS is able to update its resolution table. For more information on WINS, please see Chapter 12, TechNet, or the WINS deployment guide, which is available at **http://www.microsoft.com/ntserver/nts/ techdetails/techspecs/winswp98.asp**.

DHCP

DHCP (Dynamic Host Configuration Protocol) is a service used to automatically configure the TCP/IP settings of clients as they boot into or connect to the network. DHCP must be deployed on a Windows NT Server system. DHCP can be used to serve transient clients that number greater than the available IP addresses. This is done by leasing IP addresses to clients for a limited amount of time and then reusing those addresses when the lease expires or the client goes offline. DHCP can provide clients with an IP address, subnet mask, default gateway, and addresses of WINS and DNS servers. For more information on DHCP, see Chapter 12, TechNet, or search the Microsoft Web site (**http://search.microsoft.com**), which offers a plethora of materials on DHCP.

RAS

RAS (Remote Access Service) is used to connect remote clients to a Windows NT network over telecommunication lines. This capability is not limited to the TCP/IP protocol; it can also support NWLink and NetBEUI clients. However, RAS does offer a unique service for remote clients employing the Internet as their connection medium. This is the ability to connect to a Windows NT network over the Internet, just as if they were connected by standard network cabling. Known as PPTP (Point-to-Point Tunneling Protocol), this service is fully encrypted and is supported by Windows NT Server, Windows NT Workstation, and Windows 95/98 as clients. A PPTP RAS server must be hosted by Windows NT Server. For more information on RAS and PPTP, please consult Chapter 16, TechNet, and the Understanding PPTP document, which is available from **http://www.microsoft.com/ntserver/commserv/ techdetails/prodarch/understanding_pptp.asp**.

The Great Galaxy of Internet Services

Internet information services encompass a broad and expanding collection of content or entertainment distribution services. In addition, these services are not restricted to Internet deployment; they can be deployed on an intranet. In fact, some services make more sense when operated in the restricted or limited environment of an intranet. As new technologies are developed, high bandwidth becomes more widely available, and as the distinction between the operating system and client utilities blur, more and more types of information services are being developed. It's hard to predict what will be dreamed up next. Just think, the Internet started as a network to distribute files and some text messages. It has since blossomed through revolutions of graphics, scripts, animation, interaction, streaming multimedia, and push.

Microsoft has not remained idle while the Internet has come of age. In fact, Microsoft has helped much of the growth by including information services' server and client support in its products. You've read about some of the Internet information services provided by the IIS Web services and Exchange's email support, but that's not where Microsoft's information services end. Many more are available through these and other products.

Working with FTP

IIS includes a full FTP service in addition to its Web services. FTP, or File Transfer Protocol, is the primary means by which files are transferred from one system to another over the Internet. The IIS FTP service is a standards-compliant, highly secure environment in which you have complete control over file access. When you combine Windows NT authentication with NTFS-level permissions based on users and group memberships, FTP becomes an extension of Windows NT's basic network services.

IIS-hosted FTP sites benefit from a wide range of capabilities, including anonymous and authenticated access, unique security on a folder and file basis, complete access logging, simultaneous user restrictions, bandwidth throttling, and more.

Most of the configuration guidelines and organizational structures employed against IIS Web sites can be directly applied to IIS FTP sites. For more information on the IIS FTP services, consult the IIS documentation, TechNet, Windows NT Resource Kits, and the Microsoft IIS Web area at `http://www.microsoft.com/iis/`.

Newsgroups

The term "newsgroups" is used to describe the threaded discussion forums that comprise Usenet. Usenet is a global Internet phenomenon similar to a BBS's (Bulletin Board System's) message center. Usenet is divided into topical groups that contain messages of similar interests, directions, or topics (this is a general observation and not a prescriptive fact). Currently, there are more than 50,000 newsgroups, ranging from the discussion of quilting, to building computers, to handling social problems, to distilling moonshine. If you can think of it, there's probably a newsgroup that discusses it.

There's really no way to explain Usenet without offering a narrow opinion and leaving out a lot of its fringes and extremes. You really need to experience Usenet directly to even begin to get a grip on what it is and what it contains. Get a newsreader, such as Internet Explorer or Forte's Agent (see Chapter 26, "Serving the Web from Windows NT Workstation"), and then jump in. You may want to pay particular attention to the `news.announce.newusers` group and other `news.announce.*` groups. In addition, be sure to look for a list of FAQs (Frequently Asked Questions) in any newsgroup before you attempt to post!

Most Usenet newsgroups are public, meaning they can be accessed by anyone with an NNTP-compliant (Network News Transport Protocol) newsreader. However, not all newsgroups can be freely posted to. *Posting* is the act of placing a message of your own into the discussion. Some groups are moderated. This means someone has been appointed or elected, or has taken responsibility (temporary insanity not withstanding) to read each post before actually releasing it to the newsgroup. Generally, the material in a moderated newsgroup is more focused and a bit more reliable. However, unmoderated groups often discuss related issues that might be important to you but outside the scope of the group's "charter or purpose." Most moderated groups regularly post FAQs about the group and the posting rules, regulations, and guidelines. We suggest that you always take the time to lurk in a group (which means you watch, read, and learn without posting a message) for a while to understand the "group norm" before attempting a post. Often, you will find that someone else has already posted your question or concern, and you can reap from the resulting discussion (or in many cases avoid the barrage of messages flaming the original poster or misdirected messages containing spurious data).

Usenet is not maintained or hosted on any single computer. Instead, it's a type of store-and-forward system in which each interconnected news server forwards posts to other news servers. Some systems retain messages for a few hours; others retain them for a few weeks. Some servers host only a few select groups, whereas others attempt to host every possible group available. Thus, it takes all the news servers across the Internet working together (in a limited, not real-time, interactive manner) to sustain Usenet.

Most ISPs (Internet service providers) have local newsgroup servers that locally store all or some of the available newsgroups. They might keep the newsgroups for a day or up to two weeks. The amount of data posted to Usenet is easily over 1GB per day (not including the binary attachments or postings—that's just the text). Therefore, it's very unlikely that your local ISP will host every newsgroup or retain messages for more than a few days. Our local ISP currently retains most messages for three days for just over 20,000 groups. This is maintained on a 9GB host drive that is quickly becoming too small for the task. You need to discuss with your ISP the length of time posts are maintained locally.

If you discover you're unable to locate a message or a topic by scouring the newsgroup messages from your local ISP, you should check out Deja News. This is a Web site service that maintains archives of Usenet postings for up to two years in a completely searchable database. We've used this tool to find information about new software products, to find details on repairing hardware, and even to find out how to remove melted wax from our carpet. Be sure to check out the Deja News Web site at `http://www.dejanews.com/`.

In most situations, as an individual user or even as a network administrator, you won't need to add yet another news server to the fray. If you need to access newsgroups, just deploy newsreaders on your Internet clients. If you need private discussion forums in the same format and styled as Usenet, employ the NNTP Service included with IIS 4.0. However, if you're destined to host and maintain a news server of your own, you can do so with Exchange Server.

Exchange Server is capable of fully interacting with the public NNTP Usenet newsfeed or maintaining private discussion groups without Internet interaction. In either case, you'll find that Exchange, as a product, is capable of performing all your newsgroup needs. You must supply it with a powerhouse computer with enormous storage capacity to obtain performance or message retention greater than that of your ISP.

You can obtain more information about Exchange Server from TechNet or the Microsoft Web site at `http://www.microsoft.com/exchange/`.

Exchange is not the only product from Microsoft that supports NNTP Usenet newsgroups. A commercial product called MCIS (Microsoft Commercial Internet System) contains an NNTP server designed for ISP or other large-scale Internet information service deployment. To learn more about MCIS, visit `http://www.microsoft.com/mcis/`.

Chat

Real-time chat has become a popular way to communicate with friends, relatives, co-workers, clients, associates, lovers, and new acquaintances next door or on the other side of the planet. It has not quite replaced the telephone conversation, but it's certainly more popular than visiting in person. There's no doubt that chat has become a popular technology-based communications method. Chat is really no more than engaging in conversations consisting of terse sentences with cryptic codes and symbols (such as :) for a smiley face).

Numerous chat systems are distributed across the Internet, including Microsoft's own MIC (Microsoft Internet Chat) Protocol. The most common or well-known chat system is IRC (Internet Relay Chat). However, even IRC is not a single distributed system like Usenet. There are chat nets that are interconnected IRC servers. Anyone on a chat net can communicate with any other individual on the same chat net, but not with users on other chat nets. On a chat net, users can join *channels*, similar to Usenet newsgroups, which are loosely based around a topic or purpose. Messages posted to a channel are seen by all members of that channel, but not by others on the same chat net who are not participating in that channel.

With Exchange Server, you can host your own chat service, which can connect to existing chat nets, or you can create a fully private net of your own. This Microsoft chat system brings several advanced functions to chat, including profanity filters, multi-language support, attack protection, transcripts/logs, SNMP (Simple Network Management Protocol) support, Web interface client, and performance counters. For more information about Exchange Server, visit `http://www.microsoft.com/exchange/`.

E-commerce

E-commerce (the new Internet term for *electronic commerce*, which refers to the ability to perform product and service purchase transactions over the Internet) is quickly becoming the way to purchase products when you don't want to go to a store. Dozens of commerce systems are available, but they don't offer the flexibility and integration with Windows NT as does Microsoft's own. Site Server Commerce Edition is a full-featured site management tool that offers a custom graphical online catalog, shopping cart, and monetary transaction system all in one.

Many well-known businesses have deployed the Microsoft Site Server Commerce Edition as their means of selling products to customers over the Internet. These companies include Dell, Starbucks, Merisel, 1-800-FLOWERS, CompUSA, Tower Records, and more.

You've probably seen the get-rich-quick infomercials that claim you can become an overnight Richie Rich just by hosting an e-commerce site—whether you have a product or not! Unfortunately, reaping money from the Internet is not that simple; however, it is possible. In most cases, a business that was strong locally will have a similar popularity on the Internet. The Microsoft Site Server Commerce Edition is a solid foundation for building an Internet store, but it has a hefty price tag of over $4,600.00 and allows for only 25 concurrent users.

Streaming Multimedia

Multimedia has become a difficult word to define. It previously meant the combination of two or more senses in a communication of content. But it has evolved to a broader and more exclusive term encompassing nearly anything that is not a static presentation. Multimedia can be any one or a combination of several of the following examples of communication types: audio, video, still graphics, text, chat, interactive applets, voice-overs, slide presentations, animations, and three-dimensional graphics. However, multimedia is even more than its component formats. New technologies allow large media files to be viewed by the client while the file is still being transferred. This is known as *streaming*. Streaming allows the viewer to watch or see the component while it's being transferred. A special buffering process pre-loads enough of the component before the display begins so the presentation of the content is not interrupted while transfer is completed. Streaming is most often used on live or continuous broadcasts where the content is being created as it's being transmitted.

Microsoft has maintained its place in the world of multimedia through its own streaming multimedia system. NetShow, Windows Media, and Streaming Media Services are all part of the multimedia delivery platform developed by Microsoft. With these tools, you can broadcast audio, video, and more to one or thousands of simultaneous viewers.

Proxy Services

Although not exactly an Internet information service, proxy services offer restricted, controlled, and protected Internet access to network clients. Many private networks host resources and information services that must remain confidential. Adding direct Internet access to such networks can pose a security risk. Employing a proxy server to restrict the flow of information, to hide the identities of internal systems, and to prevent external access to internal resources can eliminate the security risks of Internet access. Microsoft Proxy Server 2.0 is a multifaceted proxy system designed specifically for Windows NT domain networks.

Proxy Server uses three individual proxy services: Web, Winsock, and SOCKS. The Web proxy service deals with Web, FTP, and Gopher communication for most platforms. The Winsock proxy service supports Windows Sockets 1.1-compatible applications and service protocols, such as Telnet, RealAudio, SMTP, and VDOLive. The SOCKS proxy is used to support non-Winsock communications and to improve access for UNIX and Macintosh clients.

Proxy Server also boasts several other powerful features, including the following:

- Packet layer security (dynamic packet filtering)
- Circuit layer security
- Application layer security
- Reverse proxying
- Reverse hosting
- Server proxying
- Support for RRAS
- SSL security
- Array and hierarchical caching
- User/group access control
- Client auto-configuration
- IPX-to-IP (Internetwork Packet Exchange-to-Internet Protocol) gateway
- Auto-dial connections
- Custom protocol/service definitions

Gopher

Gopher is a text-only hyperlink menu system that was in its day before the Web became popular. Originally, Gopher servers were accessed through command-line text terminals or via shell accounts. Now, Internet Explorer and Netscape Navigator are the primary tools by which users access Gopher systems. There are a handful of Gopher-only client utilities, but because your Web browser includes support, there's no need for another single-purpose application.

IIS 3.0 included a Gopher server that enabled you to host your own Gopher site. However, since the Web has taken over the hyperlinked resource niche on the Internet, Microsoft dropped Gopher support when IIS 4.0 was released.

If you want to learn more about Gopher so you can interact with Gopher sites or deploy your own Gopher server, point your Web browser to the following gopher URL: `gopher://gopher.tc.umn.edu/`.

Third-Party IP Service Options

Windows NT is a popular platform for hosting Internet information services, but Microsoft is not the only source of Internet service products. Many vendors have developed services and delivery applications for Windows NT that can be used in collaboration with Microsoft products or even instead of a Microsoft product. The collection of products in the following list is not an exhaustive list—not even close. These are just some of the selections available to you.

- Chat system: Koz.com's ichat: `http://www.ichat.com/`
- Chat system: Lundeen and Associates' Web Crossing: `http://webcrossing.com/`
- Discussion forums: O'Reilly and Associates' WebBoard: `http://www.webboard.com/`
- E-commerce systems: Netscape's Commerce Solutions: `http://www.netscape.com/`
- E-commerce systems: The Vision Factory's Cat@log: `http://www.thevisionfactory.com/`
- Email services: Ipswitch's IMail Server: `http://www.ipswitch.com/`
- Email services: Seattle Labs' SLmail: `http://www.seattlelab.com/`
- Email services: Shelby Group Ltd's Lyris: `http://www.lyris.com/`
- Email services: URLabs' Mail-Gear: `http://www.urlabs.com/`
- FAX services: @fax Inc.'s FAXFree Server: `http://www.atfax.com/`
- FAX services: GFi's FAXmaker: `http://www.gfifax.com/`
- FAX services: Symantec's WinFax Pro: `http://www.symantec.com/`
- FTP server: Automated Programming Technologies' Beyond FTP: `http://www.aptnet.com/`

- FTP server: Frontier Technologies' SuperTCP Suite: `http://www.frontiertech.com/`
- FTP server: Ipswitch's WS FTP Server: `http://www.ipswitch.com/`
- Index and search system: Infoseek's Ultraseek Server: `http://software.infoseek.com/`
- Index and search system: ISYS/Odyssey Development's ISYS:web: `http://www.isysdev.com/`
- Index and search system: PC DOC's SearchServer: `http://www.pcdocs.com/`
- Mailing list server: L–Soft's ListServ: `http://www.lsoft.com/`
- Newsgroup server: MetaInfo's NewsChannel: `http://www.metainfo.com/`
- Newsgroup server: NetWin's DNEWS: `http://netwinsite.com/`
- Proxy server: Deerfield Communication's WinGate: `http://www.deerfield.com/`
- Proxy server: Netscape's Proxy Server: `http://www.netscape.com/`
- Proxy server: Ositis Software's WinProxy: `http://www.winproxy.com/`
- Push systems: BackWeb Technologies' BackWeb Infocenter: `http://www.backweb.com/`
- Push systems: PointCast's Intranet Broadcast Tools: `http://www.pointcast.com/`
- Push systems: Wireless Services Corp's NT Push Server: `http://www.airnote.net/`
- Streaming and interactive multimedia: Macromedia's Director, Flash, Fireworks, Freehand, DreamWeaver, and Generator: `http://www.macromedia.com/`
- Streaming audio and video multimedia: RealNetwork's RealSystem G2: `http://www.real.com/`
- Streaming audio and video multimedia: VDOnet's VDOLive: `http://www.vdo.net/`
- Streaming MPEG audio and video: Xing's StreamWorks: `http://www.xingtech.com/`
- Web server: Netscape Enterprise or FastTrack Servers: `http://www.netscape.com/`
- Web server: O'Reilly and Associates' Website Pro: `http://website.ora.com/`

If your desire for alternative solutions to Microsoft products is not saturated, you can look for additional products on your own. Here are several great places to start your search:

- *Windows NT* Magazine: `http://www.winntmag.com/`
- Internet.com: `http://www.internet.com/`; `http://ipw.internet.com/`; `http://serverwatch.internet.com/`
- Solutions Shopper: `http://www.winntsolutions.com/main.cfm`
- Server Xtras: `http://www.serverxtras.com/`
- *NT Systems* Magazine: `http://www.ntsystems.com/`
- Beverly Hills Software: `http://www.bhs.com/`
- Sunbelt Software: `http://www.sunbelt-software.com/`

If you think you may be interested in non-commercial software, you can always scour the shareware archives for Internet information service software:

- C|Net's Download.COM: `http://www.download.com/`
- C|Net's Shareware.COM: `http://www.shareware.com/`
- Slaughterhouse: `http://www.slaugherhouse.com/`
- TUCOWS: `http://www.tucows.com/`
- WinFiles.com Windows NT Shareware: `http://www.winfiles.com/apps/nt/`
- 32bit.com: `http://www.32bit.com/`
- FilePile: `http://filepile.com/`
- WUGNET: `http://www.wugnet.com/`

Interoperability

Before you rush out and obtain one of the third-party products mentioned in this chapter, you need to think about a few key issues. First, deploying a non-Microsoft product on Windows NT can introduce unique problems. Incompatibilities may crop up if you attempt to create a multivendor solution. It's important to test the functions and interactions of a multiproduct solution before putting it into production use. In some cases where incompatibilities do occur, Microsoft or another vendor may have a fix, patch, or workaround, so check the respective Web sites. Second, deploying products from multiple vendors can cause difficulty in getting technical support. This is especially true when determining the process responsible for the problem or failure is difficult or unclear. Third, as you maintain an up-to-date version of Windows NT by applying service packs and even hotfixes, you may introduce problems with third-party tools. Always test a new service pack before putting it into production.

Troubleshooting IP Service Delivery Problems

As with any network service or resource, you face the possibility of access failure or other problems related to delivering content to a user. Troubleshooting problems with Internet information service delivery varies from simple configuration corrections to complete system overhauls. The best method for locating and resolving problems is to take a step-by-step, systematic approach. This enables you to know which action resolved the problem and allows you to easily reverse any modifications that have no or negative effects.

Start at the Beginning

First, attempt to repeat the failure. This should be done from the location the problem was first detected as well as on other peers. You should employ the same user account context, then user peers, and finally an administration account. These basic tests will help you determine whether the problem is with the server, a particular client or group of clients, or if the problem is related to user access levels. If the problem is with only one client or just a few clients, use the troubleshooting steps from Chapter 24, "Windows NT as a Web Client," to resolve the issue. You may discover that the problem is not with the information server but with network communications or the client utility. If the problem is related to user access, double-check the permission settings on each folder and file associated with the information service and even the access configuration of the service, itself.

Protocol Troubleshooting

If the problem occurs from several clients and does not seem to be related to user access levels, you may have a protocol problem, a host problem, or an information service problem.

A protocol problem is a network issue, which means the information service is unable to interact with a client because of its inability to communicate over the network. This can be a result of a failed router or other network device. If this is the problem, you should notice problems with other network services or the inability to communicate with other network members. To check this, open a command prompt (choose Start, Programs, Command Prompt) and issue a *PING* command. Use either a domain name (remote Internet host), host name (local intranet host), or IP address (either Internet or intranet host) as the ping object, such as "ping www.lanw.com". If you see the message "destination host unreachable" or if no information at all is returned, you can suspect your network connection.

Next, check your protocol installation on the host server and all clients experiencing the problem. In most cases, you'll be using TCP/IP. Other protocols may be in use when a proxy server performs resource translation on the client's behalf. If the system is connected to an ISP, check to make sure the information provided to you by the

ISP is exactly what is entered in the TCP/IP configuration (access the Network applet's Protocol tab from the TCP/IP Properties dialog box). You may want to contact the ISP to verify that the configuration data you have is current and correct.

If you're a network client, verify that the TCP/IP configuration matches that provided to you by your system administrator. At a minimum, it should include an IP address, subnet mask, and default gateway. Use WINIPCFG or IPCONFIG to see what IP settings you are receiving from the DHCP server. If they do not seem to be correct, it can mean that TCP/IP needs to be reloaded. You may also have one or more DNS servers. If you make any modifications to protocol settings, always reboot. In rare cases when the protocol driver files are corrupted, you may want to remove and reinstall TCP/IP.

If the system is not connected to an ISP, you should verify that the setting used by the system is correct for its placement in the network and that it complies with the numbering and addressing scheme used on your network. This includes the IP address, subnet mask, and default gateway. If your network has deployed DNS servers or WINS servers, be sure to include these in your TCP/IP configuration. If you're not the system administrator for the network, you should verify the TCP/IP settings with the system administrator. If you are the system administrator, double-check your work.

Always Check the Cable

Check to see that the physical connections are secure on both the host server and all clients experiencing the problem. Verify that the network interface is properly connected or seated and that all connection cables are securely fastened on both ends. Include a check for proper termination, proper cable length, and maximum devices per segment restrictions. Inspect all connection cables for tight kinks, sharp bends, or exposed wiring (such as where the insulation has been scraped off). Make sure that the connectors on both ends are snug; loose connectors or exposed wiring near the connectors can cause shorts and data loss. Replace all damaged wiring. If you make any changes to the physical connections, reboot your system to force the system to restart its network components. Also, confirm that all hubs and routers between you, the Internet, and other network members are powered on and functioning properly.

If your problem was network connection related, these actions should restore your communications with the information service. After each resolution step, retest to see if your client software can access the information service, or you can use another *PING* command.

Troubleshoot the Software

If the communications themselves are at fault, several areas need to be inspected. These include your own server or client software and the path between the client and server. Usually you start with the host server and work your way back to the client. Just as with network problems, your first action should be to perform a **PING** command. Don't just rely on a single PING to one host. Always test other systems located in the same general area (inside your intranet, just outside your intranet, somewhere out there on the Internet, in this country, in other countries). It's difficult to know which hosts are located on the same router paths or even on the same major Internet segment, but if you use a handful of hosts, you should be able to determine where the problem resides. If you're unable to ping only one particular host, you can suspect that the host is either offline or does not respond to pings, or that the path to that host is interrupted. If multiple hosts, but not all of them, fail to ping, you can be sure that either a router somewhere is at fault or a serious network overload is occurring. If all hosts fail to ping, you should suspect your Internet connection or your protocol stack.

A second line of testing is to use the *TRACERT* command (see Chapter 12). This tool lists each device it encounters between your system and the remote host, along with the response time for each one. This tool can often inform you that your communication efforts are failing long before they reach the destination host or only fail at the last step. Be sure to perform multiple trace routes against the suspect host and several similar hosts.

If you are able to determine that the communication link fails outside your local computer or your attached network (or even the ISP to which you're connected), there's nothing you can do but wait until the problem is resolved by someone else.

If the problem seems to be closer to home, you've got more investigating to do. Your next step is to test communications between your system, other peer systems, and the ISP. These tests should be performed in both directions when possible (*PING* and *TRACERT* from your system to others and from other systems to yours). This should help further pinpoint the point of failure. At this level, if the point of failure is found, it will most likely be a physical interruption or a network failure (such as protocol configuration or network overload).

A host problem is a physical hardware problem or an operating system problem with the computer system hosting the information service. If a hardware problem is the culprit, you should notice problems with other services or applications attempting to use the same device. If the network interface is damaged, no communication with the network will occur. If a hard drive is at fault, reads and/or writes to that drive will fail. Other component problems, such as failing power supply, motherboard, memory, drive controller, or CPU, are often so serious they're impossible to miss (the system doesn't work). In the case of a device failure, you should replace the device and attempt to restore the system to operation. In the event of a drive failure, you need to either restore the data from a backup or reinstall the system.

An operating system error can occur in three instances: file corruption, version problems, or software incompatibility. File corruption can occur on failing hard drives when the system is overtaxed to the point that I/O tasks are interrupted or terminated prematurely, or when the system is infected by a virus. These issues are resolved by replacing the device, reducing system load or improving system capabilities, and employing virus protection and removal software, respectively. Version problems crop up when service packs, hotfixes, and other patches are applied to the foundational

operating system. It's easily possible to mix up driver versions and cause system insta-
bilities when working with multiple operating system fixes. File version problems can
also occur when an installed application replaces drivers and other files with older or
different versions.

Resolving file over-writes requires that a system backup be performed or that an
operating-specific uninstallation monitor tool be in use before the application installation. If the perpetrating application is a key element in your information services, you
need to contact Microsoft and the product's vendor to request a solution. A software
incompatibility shouldn't occur with a software product if it's labeled as designed for
Windows NT. However, as Windows NT evolves through service packs and add-ons
from other third-party vendors, incompatibilities may occur. In such cases, you need to
remove the assailant application. You may be able to deploy the application on a different system that has gone through a different evolution history or that hosts far fewer
non–Microsoft add-ons. In any case, resolving conflicts will inevitably require you to
contact the vendor for support.

An information service problem is an obstruction of content delivery caused by the
information service application or service itself. In much the same way as a client utility can prevent a user from accessing a resource when it's not properly configured, a
poorly configured information server will not distribute the content it's intended to
offer. You need to consult the manuals and setup instructions for each product to
ensure that you have properly configured all necessary elements. If you make any setting changes, be sure to reboot your system. Common points of fault that may not be
immediately obvious include the following:

- Mismatched protocol communication ports
- Improper setting of access permissions
- Incorrectly using the No Access setting
- Blanket access restrictions
- Minimal bandwidth requirements
- Misplacing content for delivery (the service is working properly, but it has noth-
  ing to send clients)

Check for product updates, patches, or fixes. Verify that your product is properly registered and not simply a limited or restricted trial version. If all else fails, you can
remove and reinstall the information service. This has shown some success in random
situations, but it's not recommended as a reliable resolution action except as a last
resort.

If clients are accessing the information service through a proxy or firewall, check to
ensure that the border patrol tool allows the protocol and service ports used by the
information service to traverse its barrier. Most borderware products have a default
setting of restrict all, so you may need to specifically enable service communications
manually on a product, application, protocol, and port basis. Furthermore, you need to
verify that users are granted access to interact with the information service over the
proxy or firewall.

For More Information

If the information about Internet information services issues presented in this chapter has sparked your desire to learn more, you can research several resources to obtain more knowledge:

- *Windows NT Workstation Resource Kit.* Microsoft Press, 1996. ISBN: 1572313439.

- Microsoft TechNet: `http://www.microsoft.com/technet/`

Because a wide range of topics are discussed in this chapter, we suggest you visit an online bookstore (such as the ones in the following list) and perform topic searches on the issues that concern you most:

- Amazon: `http://www.amazon.com/`

- Barnes and Noble: `http://www.barnesandnoble.com/`

- Computer Literacy Bookstores: `http://www.clbooks.com/`

- Acses: a comparison site for online book shoppers: `http://www.acses.com/`

- You can learn more about the Microsoft commerce system by visiting `http://www.microsoft.com/merchant/`.

- For more information about NetShow and the related server components and development kits, visit `http://www.microsoft.com/ntserver/mediaserv/`.

- For more information about Proxy Server, visit `http://www.microsoft.com/proxy/`.

VI

Appendixes

A

Windows NT Information Resources, Online and Off

T HERE ARE A GREAT NUMBER OF WINDOWS NT information resources on the Internet, and nearly as many in print. Here are the ones that we recommend—a collection of the best of the best.

Internet Resources

- 32bit.com: `http://www.32bit.com/`
- Windows NT FAQ: `http://www.ntfaq.com`
- System Internals: `www.sysinternals.com`
- ACTIS Windows NT Services UT Austin:
  `http://www.utexas.edu/cc/services/nt/`
- Alpha NT Source: `http://dutlbcz.lr.tudelft.nl/alphant/`
- Ask a Question of the Experts: `http://www.allexperts.com/software/nt.shtml`
- BHS Software: `http://www.bhs.com/`
- Bill Stout's Known NT Exploits:
  `http://www.emf.net/~ddonahue/NThacks/ntexploits.htm`
- C|Net's Download.COM: `http://www.download.com/`

- C|Net's Shareware.COM: `http://www.shareware.com/`
- ClieNT Server News: `http://www.computerwire.com/csnews/`
- Club NT: `http://www.clubnt.com/`
- Computerworld: `http://www.computerworld.com/`
- DejaNews (search all newsgroups for NT discussions back for two year): `http://www.dejanews.com/`
- ENT Magazine: `http://www.entmag.com/`
- Essential Windows NT Software on the Net: `http://www.cs.umd.edu/~rgc/nt.html`
- FilePile: `http://filepile.com/`
- Frank Condron's World O' Windows NT: `http://www.conitech.com/windows/winnt.html`
- Information NT: `http://www.informationnt.com/`
- InfoWorld: `http://www.infoworld.com/`
- Installing and Troubleshooting Windows NT: `http://tcp.ca/gsb/PC/NT-intro_ToC.html`
- l0pht: `http://www.l0pht.com/`
- Microsoft Certified Professional Magazine: `http://www.mcpmag.com/`
- Microsoft KnowledgeBase: `http://www.microsoft.com/kb/`
- Microsoft Security Advisor & Notification Service: `http://www.microsoft.com/security/`
- Microsoft Security reporting email: `secure@microsoft.com`
- Microsoft TechNet: `http://www.microsoft.com/technet/`
- Microsoft's Service Pack and hot fix FTP site: `ftp://ftp.microsoft.com/bussys/winnt/winnt-public/fixes/usa/nt40/`
- MSNEWS.MICROSOFT.COM – NNTP server: `microsoft.public.inetexplorer.ie4.security`
- NeoTech's Windows NT Help page: `http://www.geocities.com/SiliconValley/6591/`
- Net Admin Tools for NT: `http://www.netadmintools.com/`
- Netmation's Index of Windows NT Resources: `http://www.netmation.com/listnt.htm`
- Network Windows NT Server online course: `http://www.cit.ac.nz/smac/winnt/default.htm`
- NT Bugtraq: `http://www.ntbugtraq.com/`
- NT Explorer Magazine: `http://www.ntexplorer.com/`

- NT Professional Web Ring: `http://www.internexis.com/mcp/ring/`
- NT Professionals: `http://www.ntpro.org/indexIE.asp`
- NT Shop, NT Security News: `http://www.ntshop.net/`
- NTSecrets.com: `http://www.ntsecrets.com/`
- NTSecurity mailing list: `Majordomo@iss.net.` Type "subscribe ntsecurity" in the body of the message.
- NTsecurity.com: `http://www.ntsecurity.com/`
- NTWare.com: `http://www.ntware.com/`
- Paperbits' Support Center for Windows NT: `http://www.paperbits.com/`
- PC Webopedia: Windows NT: `http://webopedia.internet.com/TERM/W/Windows_NT.html`
- PCWatch: `http://www.pcwatch.com/`
- Richard Gamarra's NT World: `http://www.citi.net/home/richardg/nt.html`
- Robert Malmgren's NT Security FAQ: `http://www.it.kth.se/~rom/ntsec.html`
- SARC: Understanding Virus Behavior in the Windows NT Environment: `http://www.symantec.com/avcenter/reference/vbnt.html`
- SavillTech: `http://www.savilltech.com/`
- Security Bugware: `http://oliver.efri.hr/~crv/security/bugs/NT/nt.html`
- Security Mailing lists: `http://oliver.efri.hr/~crv/security/mlist/mlist.html`
- Server Xtras, Inc.: `http://www.ntxtras.com/`
- Slaughterhouse: `http://www.slaughterhouse.com/`
- Somarsoft: `http://www.somarsoft.com/`
- Sunbelt Software: `http://www.sunbelt-software.com/`
- TechWeb: `http://www.techweb.com/`
- Tek-Tips: `http://www.tek-tips.com/`
- The -NT- Registry: `http://www-personal.umd.umich.edu/~cwilli/`
- The Thin Net's Windows NT/2000 Links: `http://thethin.net/winnt.cfm`
- The Windows Mill: `http://www.mindspring.com/~ggking3/pages/windmill.htm`
- TipWorld: `http://www.tipworld.com/`
- TISC Security Web site: `http://tisc.corecom.com/`
- Trident's World of Windows NT: `http://www.ultranet.com/~trident/winnt/`
- TUCOWS: `http://www.tucows.com/`
- Web66: Windows NT Resource Center: `http://web66.umn.edu/WinNT/Default.html`

- Windows NT Enterprise Computing: `http://www.entmag.com/`
- Windows NT Fax Solutions: `http://www.stonecarver.com/ntfax-faq.html`
- Windows NT Interactive Archive: `http://www.winntia.com/`
- Windows NT Links Plus: `http://www.windowsnt-plus.com/`
- Windows NT Magazine: `http://www.winntmag.com/`
- Windows NT MegaSite: `http://www.nettaxi.com/citizens/vinods/`
- Windows NT Resource Center: `http://www.itlinks.com/download/`
- Windows NT Resource Site: `http://www.interlacken.com/winnt/default.htm`
- Windows NT Sites: `http://www.indirect.com/www/ceridgac/ntsite.html`
- Windows NT Systems Magazine: `http://www.ntsystems.com/`
- Windows NT Tips, Registry Hacks, and More:
  `http://www.jsiinc.com/reghack.htm`
- Windows NT Tips: `http://www.chami.com/tips/windows/`
- WinFiles.com Windows NT Shareware: `http://www.winfiles.com/apps/nt/`
- WINNT-INET – Windows NT on the Internet Mailing List:
  `http://www.neystadt.org/winnt/winnt.htm`
- WinPlanet: `http://www.winplanet.com/`
- Workstation NT: `http://personal.cfw.com/~tkprit/index.html`
- WUGNET: `http://www.wugnet.com/`
- X-Force's Computer Threats and Vulnerabilities:
  `http://www.iss.net/cgi-bin/xforce/xforce_index.pl`
- ZDNet: `http://www.zdnet.com/`

Publications

- Bisaillon, Teresa and Brad Werner. *TCP/IP with Windows NT Illustrated.*
  McGraw-Hill, 1998. ISBN: 0079136486.
- Carl-Mitchell, Smoot and John S. Quarterman. *Practical Internetworking with TCP/IP and UNIX.* Addison-Wesley, 1993. ISBN: 0201586290.
- Chapman, D. Brent and Elizabeth D. Zwicky. *Building Internet Firewalls.*
  O'Reilly & Associates, 1995. ISBN: 1565921240.
- Chellis, James. *MCSE: Internet Explorer 4 Administration Kit Study Guide.*
  Sybex, 1998. ISBN: 0782123090.
- Cheswick, William and Steven M. Bellovin. *Firewalls and Internet Security: Repelling the Wily Hacker.* Addison-Wesley, 1994. ISBN: 0201633574. New edition announced for 2000.

- Comer, Douglas E. *Internetworking with TCP/IP:* Principles, Protocols, and Architecture, vols. I–III. Prentice Hall, 1995, 1996, 1997. ISBNs: 0132169878, 0139738436, 0138487146.

- Cowart, Robert and Kenneth Gregg. *Windows NT Server 4.0 Administrator's Bible.* IDG Books Worldwide, 1996. ISBN 0764580094.

- Daily, Sean. *Optimizing Windows NT.* IDG Books, Foster City, CA, 1998. ISBN 0764531107.

- Edmead, Mark T. and Paul Hinsberg. *Windows NT Performance: Monitoring, Benchmarking, and Tuning.* New Riders Publishing, Indianapolis, IN, 1998. ISBN 1562059424.

- Edwards, Mark Joseph. *Internet Security with Windows NT.* Duke Press, 1998. ISBN 1882419626.

- Frisch, Aeleen. *Essential Windows NT System Administration.* O'Reilly and Associates, 1998. ISBN: 1565922743.

- Frisch, Aeleen. *Windows NT Desktop Reference.* O'Reilly & Associates, 1998. ISBN: 1565924371.

- Gardiner, Kenton. *Windows NT Performance Tuning & Optimization.* Osborne, New York, NY, 1998. ISBN 0078824966.

- Hilley, Valda. *Windows NT Server 4.0 Secrets.* IDG Books Worldwide, 1996. ISBN 1568847173.

- Iseminger, David. *Inside Rras: Remote Access Solutions for Windows NT.* John Wiley & Sons, 1998. ISBN: 0471251593.

- Ivens, Kathy. *Windows NT Troubleshooting* (Windows NT Professional Library). Osborne McGraw-Hill, 1998. ISBN: 0078824710.

- Marymee, J. D. and Sandy Stevens. *Novell's Guide to Integrating Intranetware and NT.* IDG Books Worldwide, 1998. ISBN: 076454523X.

- Meggitt, Ashley, et al. *Windows NT User Administration.* O'Reilly & Associates, 1997. ISBN: 1565923014.

- *Microsoft Internet Explorer Resource Kit* (Microsoft Professional Editions). Microsoft Press, Redmond, WA., 1998. ISBN: 1572318422.

- *Microsoft Windows NT Server 4.0 Enterprise Technologies Training Kit.* Microsoft Press, Redmond, WA., 1998. ISBN: 1572317108.

- *Microsoft Windows NT Server Resource Kit.* Microsoft Press, Redmond, WA. 1996. ISBN: 1572313447.

- *Microsoft Windows NT Technical Support Training Kit: Deluxe.* Microsoft Press, Redmond, WA., 1998. ISBN: 1572318333.

- *Microsoft Windows NT Workstation 4.0 Resource Kit.* Microsoft Press, Redmond, WA., 1996. ISBN: 1572313439.

■ Minasi, Mark, et al. *Mastering Windows NT Workstation 4*. Sybex, 1996. ISBN: 0782118887.

■ Minasi, Mark, et al. *Mastering Windows NT Server 4*, 6th ed. Sybex, 1999. ISBN: 0782124453.

■ Murphy, John. *NT Network Programming Toolkit*. Prentice Hall Computer Books, 1998. ISBN: 0130813249.

■ Murray, James. *Windows NT Event Logging*. O'Reilly & Associates, 1998. ISBN: 1565925149.

■ Nelson, Stephen. *Microsoft Internet Explorer 4 Field Guide*. Microsoft Press, 1998. ISBN: 1572317418.

■ Northrup, Anthony. *NT Network Plumbing: Routers, Proxies, and Web Services*. IDG Books Worldwide, 1998. ISBN: 076453209X.

■ Norton, Peter and John Mueller. *Peter Norton's Complete Guide to Windows NT Workstation 4* (Norton Series). Sams Publishing, 1998. ISBN: 0672313731.

■ Nowshadi, Farshad and Norman Buskell. *Managing Windows NT/NetWare Integration*. Addison-Wesley, 1998. ISBN: 0201177846.

■ Oliver, Robert, ed. *Building a Windows NT 4 Internet Server*. New Riders Publishing, 1997. ISBN: 1562056808.

■ Osborne, Sandra. *Windows NT Registry* (New Riders Professional Series). Macmillan Computer Company, 1998. ISBN: 1562059416.

■ Pearce, Eric, et al. *Windows NT in a Nutshell: A Desktop Quick Reference for System Administrators* (Nutshell Handbooks). O'Reilly & Associates, 1997. ISBN: 1565922514.

■ Robichaux, Paul. *Managing the Windows NT Registry*. O'Reilly & Associates, 1998. ISBN: 1565923782.

■ Rutstein, Charles. *Windows NT Security: A Practical Guide to Securing Windows NT Servers and Workstations.* Computing McGraw-Hill, 1997. ISBN: 0070578338

■ Sheldon, Tom, et al. *Microsoft Internet Information Server 4: The Complete Reference*. McGraw-Hill, 1998. ISBN: 0078824575.

■ Sheldon, Tom. *Windows NT Security Handbook*. Osborne McGraw-Hill, 1997. ISBN: 0078822408

■ Solomon, David. *Inside Windows NT*, Second Edition. Microsoft Press, 1998. ISBN: 1572316772.

■ Stevens, W. Richard. *TCP/IP Illustrated*, vols. I, II, and III. Addison-Wesley, 1994. ISBNs: 0201633469, 020163354X, 0201634953.

■ Stewart, James Michael and Ramesh Chandak. *Exam Prep: IIS 4*. Coriolis, 1998. ISBN: 157610267X.

- Sutton, Stephen. *Windows NT Security Guide.* Addison-Wesley, 1996. ISBN 0201419696.

- Thomas, Steven. *Windows NT 4.0 Registry: A Professional Reference* (McGraw-Hill NT Professional Reference Series). Computing McGraw-Hill, 1998. ISBN: 0079136559.

- Tittel, Ed, Christa Anderson, and David Johnson. *NT Workstation 4 Exam Prep.* Certification Insider Press, 1998. ISBN: 1576102386.

- Tittel, Ed, Kurt Hudson, and J. Michael Stewart. *MCSE NT Server 4 Exam Cram.* Certification Insider Press, 1997. ISBN: 1576101908.

- Tittel, Ed, Kurt Hudson, and J. Michael Stewart. *MCSE NT Server 4 in the Enterprise Exam Cram.* Certification Insider Press, 1997. ISBN: 1576101916.

- Tittel, Ed and Kurt Hudson, and J. Michael Stewart. *MCSE NT Workstation 4 Exam Cram.* Certification Insider Press, 1997. ISBN: 1576101932.

- Tittel, Ed, Kurt Hudson, and J. Michael Stewart. *MCSE TCP/IP 4 Exam Cram.* Certification Insider Press, 1998. ISBN: 1576101959.

- Tulloch, Matt. *Administering Internet Information Server 4.* McGraw-Hill, 1998. ISBN: 0070655367.

- Wilensky, Marshall and Candace Leiden. *TCP/IP for Dummies*, Second Edition. IDG Books Worldwide, Inc., 1997. ISBN: 0764500635.

- Hill, Tim. *Windows NT Shell Scripting.* Macmillan Technical Publishing, 1998. ISBN: 1578700477

- Strebe, Matthew and Charles Perkins. *MCSE: Internet Information Server 4.* Sybex, 1998. ISBN: 0782122485.

- Rozell, Erik, et al. *MCSE: Proxy Server 2.* Sybex, 1998. ISBN: 0782121942.

- Templeman, Julian. *Beginning Windows NT Programming.* Wrox Press, Inc., 1998. ISBN: 1861000170.

B

Comparing Windows NT Workstation and Server

Although both Windows NT Workstation and Windows NT Server share the same core system architecture, memory model, and security controls, there are real differences between them—chiefly as a result of the difference in their intended purposes. Windows NT Workstation is designed as an interactive desktop operating system; Windows NT Server is designed as a high-performance network server. Each of these roles requires a slightly different set of capabilities.

Both versions of Windows NT have the same look and feel and the same basic user operation interface. The interface is inherited from Windows 95 and has become the standard look for Windows operating systems. Windows NT Server and Windows NT Workstation both fully support Windows 32-bit applications, with backward-compatibility support for Windows 16-bit and MS-DOS applications. Both include minimal support for POSIX and OS/2 applications to meet government purchasing requirements.

Although both Windows NT Workstation and Windows NT Server can operate on Intel and RISC CPUs, their system requirements vary. Workstation requires only 12MB of RAM and 120MB of drive space, whereas Server requires at least 16MB of RAM and 160MB of drive space. These are the minimal requirements; we suggest 64MB or more of RAM and 1GB or more of drive space for both. Both versions of

Windows NT have multiprocessor capabilities, but Windows NT Workstation is limited to only two CPUs. Windows NT Server supports four CPUs out of the box, or 32 CPUs total. Special OEM versions of Windows NT Server are required for systems with more than four CPUs.

Windows NT Workstation has limited network capability; servers are limited to 10 simultaneous network connections, with only a single inbound RAS connection. It does not include support for hosting Microsoft DNS, WINS, or DHCP servers, although it can act as a client for these services. As an Internet information service host, Windows NT Workstation is restricted by the 10 simultaneous user license restrictions. In addition, Peer Web Services (Workstation's version of IIS) does not include Index Server or Transaction Server and can host only a single Web site.

Windows NT Workstation is further limited as a network server because it cannot host a number of important services, including Services for Macintosh, File and Print Services for NetWare, Gateway Services for NetWare, Directory Services Manager for NetWare, Remoteboot Service, and Routing and Remote Access Service. Windows NT Workstation cannot host any of the BackOffice products, such as SQL Server, SNA Server, SMS Server, Exchange Server, Proxy Server, and Site Server. In addition, Windows NT Workstation is unable to host the Network Monitor network packet capturing tool.

Windows NT Server is just what its name implies: a network service host. It has full support for all Microsoft network services and applications, including Services for Macintosh, File and Print Services for NetWare, Gateway Services for NetWare, Directory Services Manager for NetWare, Remoteboot Service, and Routing and Remote Access Service. The BackOffice product line is specifically designed to operate on Windows NT Server. You must be using Windows NT Server to deploy SQL Server, SNA Server, SMS Server, Exchange Server, Proxy Server, or Site Server. Furthermore, Network Monitor is a native tool for Server.

Both Windows NT Workstation and Windows NT Server support FAT and NTFS file systems. Both support 4GB (FAT) and 16GB (NTFS) volume and file sizes for these file systems; however, disk volume structure varies between the two applications. Windows NT Workstation does not include support for fault-tolerant drive volume constructs and is limited to disk striping without parity and multi-partition and multi-drive volumes. Windows NT Server supports several fault-tolerant drive volume constructs, including disk striping with parity, disk mirroring, and disk duplexing.

Windows NT Workstation includes some of the same management and administration tools as Windows NT Server, but they are restricted to local control and do not have domain interactive capabilities. The most prominent of these tools is User Manager. On Windows NT Workstation, User Manager can affect only local user accounts and local groups (including making global groups members of a local group). Windows NT Workstation is not completely excluded from network management, however. The user-installable remote server tools from the Windows NT Server CD allow a Windows NT Workstation system to be used as a remote management console for a Windows NT domain. These remote administration tools include DHCP Manager, Policy Editor, Remote Access Admin, Remote Boot Manager, Server Manager, User Manager for Domains, and WINS Manager, all of which are native to Windows NT Server.

With regard to general operations, Windows NT Workstation and Windows NT Server have different operational priorities. Workstation focuses on maximizing performance from the user's standpoint by boosting the foreground application's processing priority, granting applications the minimum amount of memory when launched, and by the Scheduler using small timeslices. CPU processing time is divided into very small timeslices on Windows NT Workstation to provide the highest level of responsiveness to the user. Small timeslices enable multiple tasks to be executed simultaneously and allow rapid task switching without noticeable delays. Windows NT Server focuses on maximizing network performance by maintaining processing priority for all network services, granting applications their requested maximum amount of memory, and by the Scheduler using larger timeslices. The use of larger timeslices allows the server to support network requests in a more reliable manner and prevents interruptions or timeouts.

Originally, Windows NT Workstation's retail price was $319 and Windows NT Server's was $809. Today, you can purchase Workstation for around $210 and Server for around $265 with five Client Access Licenses (CALs) or $550 with 25 CALs. (Check C|Net Shopper.com for these deals: **http://www.shopper.com**/.) For a standalone system, you can select either Server or Workstation as your main OS. However, for a computer connected to a network, it quickly becomes obvious that you should use Workstation as a desktop OS and Server to host network services.

For more information, visit the Microsoft Windows Web site at **http://www.microsoft.com/windows**/, consult the Windows NT Resource Kits, or review the TechNet CD (focusing on the article *Differences Between Windows NT Workstation 4.0 and Windows NT Server 4.0*).

C

Windows 2000 Overview

On October 27, 1998, Microsoft announced a name change for its top-of-the-line Windows products from Windows NT to Windows 2000. The name change was accompanied by the announcement of four new products in the Windows 2000 product family:

- **Windows 2000 Professional.** The replacement for Windows NT Workstation, this product is the desktop element of the new family.

- **Windows 2000 Server.** The replacement for Windows NT Server for small- to medium-sized enterprise application deployments, this product supports up to two CPUs. Existing Windows NT Server implementations with up to four CPUs can be upgraded to this product.

- **Windows 2000 Advanced Server.** The replacement for Windows NT Enterprise Server for departmental and application uses, this product supports up to four CPUs, large amounts of physical memory, and integrates clustering and load-balancing support. As the upgrade target for existing installations of Windows NT 4.0 Enterprise Server, existing Enterprise Server installations with up to eight CPUs can upgrade to this product.

- **Windows 2000 Datacenter Server.** This is a new addition to the Windows Server line and supports up to 16 CPUs and up to 64GB of RAM. Like Advanced Server, Datacenter Server includes clustering and load balancing services. This product is designed for extremely demanding, large-scale applications, such as data warehouses, complex simulations, and transaction processing.

Given the focus for this book, our overview covers primarily Windows 2000 Professional, with additional remarks about improving a desktop's reliability and manageability by combining the various Windows 2000 Server implementations with Windows 2000 Professional.

Windows 2000 Architecture

Windows 2000 involves no fundamental architectural changes in this operating system's organization or layout other than the addition of some new subsystems to augment existing Windows NT Executive Services modules. This is not to say that there's nothing new in Windows 2000—there certainly are a great many new tools, technologies, and terminology to master—but it indicates that Windows 2000 is an evolutionary development of Windows NT, rather than a revolutionary replacement.

This list sums up what's new and interesting about Windows 2000, particularly from the desktop perspective, and lays the foundation for the rest of this appendix. We'll explain in more detail what each of these new elements brings to the desktop:

- Windows 2000 incorporates "Best of Windows 98" features and functions, including customizable toolbars and menus, advanced Plug and Play support, plus numerous installation and configuration tools and wizards.

- This development of Windows NT includes significantly improved reliability, based in part on improvements to the Windows Installer. The improved Windows Installer can assist with installation, updates, repairs, and removal of most software and system components, and also supports IntelliMirror technology.

- Windows 2000 provides major ease-of-use and user-sensitivity enhancements, including the ability of configurations and profiles to roam with users, built-in support for disconnected and connected modes of operation, improved laptop support, and automatic recognition of recent user behavior.

- The introduction of Active Directory technology and of directory-enabled services and applications, makes it easier for users to locate and interact with network resources.

- The LAN Manager-based security model used in Windows NT 4.0 can be replaced with, or augmented by, a much more powerful security model built for Windows 2000. This model includes support for industry-standard Kerberos security and private key infrastructure services.

There's so much to say about Windows 2000 that Microsoft offers nearly a thousand pages of white papers and other documents on a variety of subjects, from Active Directory to Zero Administration.

The following sections provide some more information about the new elements Windows 2000 brings to the desktop. For more in-depth information, however, you'll need to go to the Microsoft Web site and download one or more of the many

Windows 2000 white papers. In particular, we recommend the white paper on Windows 2000 Professional that's currently available at `http://www.microsoft.com/windows/downloads/bin/ntw5/NTW5Beta2WhitePaper.exe`. There is more information about access to this material in the "For More Information" section at the end of this appendix.

Best of Windows Features

Windows 2000 Professional delivers broader support for software and hardware than Windows NT Workstation 4.0 does. Windows 2000 Professional's enhancements include the following improvements:

- **Support for more applications.** Microsoft has more than doubled the number of applications that it is testing with Windows 2000 Professional, compared to Windows NT Workstation 4.0. The applications being tested include the top 400 Win32 applications and the top 200 Win16- and MS-DOS-based applications. Windows 2000 is subject to requirements that legacy applications be "well-behaved" (that is, that they not attempt to address hardware directly or otherwise violate Windows 2000's security model). This makes Windows 2000 support for applications extremely robust and reliable.

- **Support for more hardware and devices.** Windows 2000 Professional supports more than 6,500 devices, including many devices and device types that are not supported by Windows NT Workstation 4.0. This is possible because Windows 98 and Windows 2000 use the same Windows Driver Model (WDM), which ensures that drivers developed for Windows 98 also work with Windows 2000. This makes installing and configuring Windows 2000 much easier than earlier Windows versions and allows the operating system to interact with more adapters and devices.

- **Support for next-generation hardware and devices.** Building on Windows 98 next-generation capabilities, Windows 2000 provides the most comprehensive level of Plug and Play support available, including support for Advanced Configuration and Power Interface (ACPI). Support for Dynamic Plug and Play (PnP) means that devices can be recognized as soon as they're plugged into a system. It also includes support for Universal Serial Bus (USB) and IEEE 1394 (FireWire) high-speed serial devices, the Accelerated Graphics Port (AGP), and a wide variety of removable storage devices and networking hardware. This support facilitates Windows 2000 installation and configuration and permits the operating system to use advanced, high-performance hardware and related functionality. Windows 2000 has also reduced from 42 to 7 the number of situations that require rebooting the operating system (compared to Windows NT 4.0).

- **Increased network access and connectivity.** Windows 2000 includes built-in connectivity for Windows NT Server and NetWare. It also includes an add-on called Windows 2000 Services for UNIX that supports easier access to UNIX services, such as NFS and scripting commands, and provides Telnet access to UNIX clients and r-utilities access to Professional and Server machines. Windows 2000 replaces the Network Neighborhood with an Explorer icon called Network Places that not only tracks areas that users visit, but that also maintains the same look and feel whether resources reside on Windows, NetWare, or UNIX servers.

All in all, Windows 2000 has much more powerful hardware and software support and enables easy incorporation of such system components during and after system installation.

Improved Reliability

Windows 2000 includes two major system reliability improvements. The Windows Installer technology has been significantly improved to include support not only for adding and removing software components, but also for repairing and updating such components. This makes it much easier to manage software on Windows 2000 throughout a system's and its software's life cycles.

Windows 2000 also includes support for IntelliMirror technology as long as there is access to a Windows 2000 Server platform somewhere on the network. IntelliMirror supports writing fromlocal copies of a system, applications and data to copies on a server elsewhere on the network, protecting users' desktops, applications, and data, even if their desktops fail or are otherwise unavailable.

IntelliMirror also supports user access to desktop settings, applications, and data even when users can't log on to their usual desktop machines. This technology permits users to log on to other Windows 2000 Professional machines on the network, and delivers on demand their desktop settings along with whatever applications and data they need. Changes or additions to user configurations are updated to the server automatically and will be copied to a user's usual desktop the next time he or she logs on to that machine.

IntelliMirror not only provides protection for user desktop machines, but also permits users' configurations to follow them around the network as necessary. This greatly improves the usability and reliability of Windows 2000 desktop machines.

Ease of Use

Window 2000 Professional includes numerous improvements and enhancements that make it significantly easier to use and that help to improve user productivity. These changes include a simplified user interface, improvements for laptop users, and Internet access.

On the user interface side, Windows 2000 helps to remove desktop clutter and simplifies the Start menu. It eliminates unnecessary desktop items and introduces the concept of *Personalized Menus*. These menus show only items that you actually reference, with additional symbols to permit you to invoke the entire related menu that shows up by default in Windows NT 4.0. Frequently used applications appear by default with Windows 2000, and other applications or menu entries are never more than a mouse-click away.

Windows 2000 includes improved search capabilities, allowing you to search local or remote directories, Internet locations, and documents. Windows 2000 also includes more useful and informative help files, with more details about everything from error messages to explanations of interface layouts, menu items, and commands.

For users who work with multiple languages, Windows 2000 can view and edit over 60 different language character sets on the same version of the operating system. This does away with language-specific versions of Windows and permits any application to view and interact with multiple languages, while permitting multiple languages to co-exist on a single platform or within a single application.

Windows 2000 also has new or improved wizards to facilitate configuration and set up, including the following:

- **Hardware Wizard.** The Hardware Wizard simplifies adding and configuring PC hardware.

- **Network Connection Wizard.** This wizard makes it easy to create and manage multiple dial-up connections for access to RAS and one or more ISPs, and to use Virtual Private Networking (VPN). The same wizard also supports serial or infrared connections between PCs for ongoing or temporary data transfers.

- **Add Printer Wizard.** The Printer Wizard has been extended to interact with Active Directory services and to provide better access to print services on the network by printer type and location.

In addition, Windows 2000 also has an Update facility (much like the ones already available for Internet Explorer and Windows 98) so that system components and services can be updated from the Internet at regular intervals or on demand. Administrators have the option of controlling or denying user access to this facility.

Windows 2000 Professional offers much better support for mobile and laptop users than do previous versions of Windows NT. It supports hot-swapping PC cards, battery and power management, and a broad range of offline and online operation modes that make it easy to operate while disconnected from a network, with automatic or manual synchronization of online and offline files as soon as a network connection becomes available. In addition, Windows 2000's Encrypting File System (EFS) makes it easier to protect sensitive data and applications when a machine is subject to the risks of loss or theft.

Windows 2000 Professional features tight integration between the operating system and Internet Explorer, so that Internet or intranet resources appear as an extension of local and networked resources. This makes it easier than ever before to search local, networked, and Internet information in a single pass and improves networking and Internet browsing for requested resources.

Active Directory

From an architecture perspective, Windows 2000 support for Active Directory (AD) and the Public Key Infrastructure (PKI) means there is an alternative to (or replacement for) the LAN Manager-based security components in earlier versions of Windows NT. Backward compatibility with LAN Manager-based security remains an option in Windows 2000, and LM security is not required on homogenous Windows 2000.

Active Directory brings a useful and flexible extension to the Windows NT domain concept. Microsoft continues to support domains in AD to ensure backward compatibility, while extending and expanding on the domain concept in a variety of ways:

- Domains remain a fundamental grouping concept in AD, where domain contains objects may be structured hierarchically using X.500-inspired Organizational Units (OUs).

- Organization Units permit any domain to be split into numerous, more manageable units based on a hierarchical structure. The OUs in AD correspond to X.500's OUs, but differ in several important ways.

- *Groups* act as collections of objects of the same type, as in Windows NT 4.0 domains. This provides Windows 2000 with a structure that helps maintain backward compatibility with Windows NT 4.0, while providing a useful container structure for addressing collections of objects with a single cognomen.

- *Objects* provide the lowest level information item in the AD environment. An object can be a user, a resource, a group, and so forth, as in Windows NT 4.0 domains.

- A *site* is a collection of machines treated as a single logical collection, usually on the same LAN at a single location. Microsoft uses this term frequently when describing AD solutions because the notion of a site is essential when designing and implementing data replication.

Beyond these fundamental building blocks, AD also introduces the concept of a *Global Catalog* that contains all the objects from all the domains in any given AD domain tree, along with part of the properties for each such object. The idea is to replicate the hierarchy of the domain tree and (as much of its contents as might be needed) in order to treat it as a kind of global address book when searching for objects, resources, users, and so on. The Global Catalog provides a local resource that users can search to locate other users and resources on demand.

From the perspective of trust relationships, AD greatly simplifies how multiple domains relate and share information by introducing the concept of a *transitive* trust. This means that if Domain A trusts Domain B and Domain B trusts Domain C, then Domain A automatically trusts Domain C. This greatly reduces the number of trust relationships that must be managed and makes it much easier to create and manage multi-domain environments for Windows 2000.

The introduction of AD with Windows 2000 provides two tremendous benefits. First, it means that users can search a single Global Catalog to locate and access resources that they have permission to access. Additionally, it means that applications written to Microsoft's Active Directory Services Interface (ADSI) can interrogate the same directory structures to locate and access resources automatically. Both of these capabilities simplify access to resources and make it possible for users to access resources and services more easily.

New Security Model

Windows 2000 includes support for a new security model, based on Kerberos and the Public Key Infrastructure. Kerberos replaces the older Windows NT LAN Manager authentication services and provides a new standard protocol for safe authentication of network users. PKI makes it easy to verify that a document's sender is indeed who he or she claims to be and also provides a so-called "digital signature" capability.

Kerberos was originally developed at MIT as a part of the Project Athena Network in the 1980s. Windows 2000 supports Kerberos version 5 as described in IETF RFC 1510, which is widely regarded as the most important security component in a Windows 2000-based networking environment. Analogous to the three-headed mythological creature after which it is named, Kerberos security uses a three-sided authentication process, with shared keys that enable network users to confirm their identities securely.

The client represents one leg of this tripod and represents the user who requests access to resources. The resource that the client requests must ensure that the client's request, and the client itself, is legitimate. A central repository, a *Key Distribution Center* (KDC) service, manages information about clients. The KDC database contains identities and passwords for all clients and servers that belong to a particular security domain (known in Kerberos terminology as a *realm*).

Kerberos uses the *Digital Encryption Standard* (DES) shared-key encryption to authenticate clients and all communication across the network is encrypted. Unless a recipient possesses a client's public or private key, the recipient won't be able to read requests for access or responses to such requests from the Kerberos service.

The fundamental item in Kerberos is called a *ticket*, which permits a user to set up a session with any particular server or service. In other words, a ticket is a kind of certificate that the KDC service issues to certify the establishment of a session between a requesting client and a responding server.

The key to permitting clients to request resources is a special kind of ticket called a *ticket-granting ticket*, or *TGT*. The TGT eliminates the need to request authentication from a server every time a client requests a resource by providing a one-time, session-specific private key that proves the client's identity as a part of any subsequent request. If a TGT is valid and adequate permissions exist, a client's request is granted. If either condition fails, the request is denied. The TGT also eliminates the necessity of sending passwords across the network because the user can decrypt the ticket using his or her own password as the key.

Experience has shown that Kerberos offers the best solution for creating a secure and manageable security and authentication system in networked environments, like those offered on Windows 2000-based networks. Kerberos is a great improvement over the NTLM (Windows NT/LAN Manager) authentication supported in Windows NT through version 4.0. Kerberos provides a method for clients to properly identify themselves and prove that a server has been properly identified, and provides a safe way to create session- and time-constrained access to a network. (The TGT is limited to a single session, but also has a fixed expiration time.) Kerberos can handle many more domains than NTLM authentication, is an industry standard mechanism, and is supported in a great many networking environments.

Public key encryption is a valuable alternative to Kerberos, especially when clients and servers belong to widely separated or disjointed networks and systems, which is why Microsoft also includes PKI support in Windows 2000. PKI offers a way to determine whether a document or other transmission indeed originates from a particular sender.

Public key technology works as follows:

1. A private key is issued only to a specific sender, and proof of identity and guaranteed delivery are used to ensure that the private key gets to its intended recipient. The private key is used to encrypt messages that originate with the sender.

2. A matching public key is issued at the same time as the private key. A complex mathematical relationship ensures that the public key can be used only to decrypt messages encrypted with the private key. (It has been proven that cracking such a key pair is computationally infeasible.) The public key enables any message recipient to be sure that any message it can decrypt originated with the holder of the private key.

This process can be reversed to send a message that only the private key holder can decrypt. In other words, the public key holder can encrypt a message that only the holder of the private key can decrypt. This ensures the confidentiality of data sent from someone with access to the public key and guarantees that its contents are available only to the private key's holder.

In Windows 2000, PKI permits users to obtain private keys, issue public keys, and work with certificate authorities to manage distribution and access to such keys. In other words, PKI provides a mechanism by which users can demonstrate their identities to obtain and use private-public key pairs to verify their identities (which act as digital signatures) and to ensure the confidentiality of information encrypted using the public key. This permits Windows 2000 users to interact securely not only with other Windows 2000-based users, but with any networked users that also support the standard PKI.

For Window 2000 Server, Kerberos is integrated with the operating system's domain controller functionality. There is no longer a distinction between primary and backup domain controllers in Windows 2000; they function as peers in a distributed controller environment to handle authentication and user identification. Existing services from the Security Reference Monitor and security identifier information in the domain database still provide object identification services and access controls continue to work as in previous versions of Windows NT. However, in Windows 2000, Kerberos and PKI combine to provide stronger proof of identity, more robust authentication services, and improved data confidentiality.

Other Miscellany

Windows 2000 also includes numerous other enhancements and improvements not mentioned elsewhere in this appendix. Among these are the following:

- **Support for FAT32 file systems.** Windows 2000 can create and manage volumes formatted using FAT32, as well as those formatted with FAT and NTFS. This makes it easier to dual-boot machines with Windows 98. It also provides the many benefits of FAT32 to Windows 2000 users, including support for more files, larger volume sizes, improved access to files, elimination of root directory restrictions, and improved file system performance.

- **Support for an Encrypted File System (EFS).** Individual files, folders, or entire volumes can be further protected against unauthorized access using state-of-the art encryption techniques.

- **Support for Distributed File Services (DFS).** Folders from multiple volumes on a network can be aggregated and treated as a single logical volume. Users don't have to worry about the actual locations of individual files and folders because they can access these resources from a single logical drive.

- **Improved content indexing for NTFS file systems.** Users can more easily locate files by name, type, or contents.

- **Easier access to unknown file types.** Users can more easily open unknown file types due to enhancements to the Open With menu entry that permits any program to be invoked to open a particular file type and to automatically create an association between that file type and the application used to open it.

- **Improved system, group, and user policies.** Users can more easily control which resources users can access, what applications they can install, and what elements of their working environments can follow them around a network.

- **Extended offline operation.** Users can identify files, folders, and URLs they wish to access while offline and performs necessary snapshot operations (creates a copy of those resources) for offline access, as well as necessary synchronization with online resources when network access is available.

- **Improvements to TCP/IP.** Improvements include support for large windows and selective acknowledgements, both of which help to improve data transfer and congestion management. Other improvements include the following:
  - More accurate estimates of round-trip time for packets and bandwidth allocation for media traffic

- Improved integration with client-side applications for better application performance in general
- Improved service for time-sensitive services, such as IP telephony, video conferencing, video streaming, and other bandwidth-intensive uses

- **Improvements to the Windows Scripting Host environment (WSH) and related task scheduling utilities.** Windows 2000 includes a Task Scheduler similar to the one in Windows 98 to make it easier to create and execute automated tasks and batch jobs.

- **Complete support for Y2K and the Euro currency reform.** Windows 2000 is set for use in the emerging global economy of the 21st century.

For More Information

For more information about Windows 2000, please consult the following references:

- Microsoft's announcement of its move to Windows 2000 family:
  `http://www.microsoft.com/windows/dailynews/102898.htm`
- Microsoft Windows 2000 Professional home page:
  `http://www.microsoft.com/WindowsNT5/Workstation/default.asp`
- The Microsoft Windows 2000 Server home page:
  `http://www.microsoft.com/ntserver/windowsnt5/default.asp`

D

Windows NT Performance Monitor Objects and Counters

THIS APPENDIX COVERS IN DETAIL SOME OF THE MOST IMPORTANT counters you should watch when monitoring performance including counters on hard drives, CPU, and memory. Each section highlights the counters that can be used to monitor the activity of a computer subsystem that might be causing a bottleneck. It's essential to check all possible culprits before deciding which subsystem needs improvement. It's possible, for example, for the CPU to operate at a high utilization level for an extended period of time because of a slow network interface. Always examine your entire system from several viewpoints before implementing any of our recommended bottleneck "cures." You must isolate the true cause to effect a real cure. After discussing the three most common areas of troubleshooting, a complete list of Performance Monitor counters is provided.

Hard Disk Counters

The hard drives inside your computer are more than just repositories for user data. They also contain all the files used by the operating system and the temporary paging file required to support virtual memory. The storage subsystem of Windows NT is one of the most important areas to fine-tune. A slow disk subsystem drags down the performance of your entire computer.

Enabling Storage Counters

Before you can monitor hard drive performance, you must turn on the counters that gather statistics for such devices. Because the very act of recording storage counters affects performance, they are not enabled by default. From the Run line or a command prompt, the following command enables disk counters:

```
diskperf -y
```

You'll need to restart the computer before these counters will activate. After you've completed your storage monitoring, be sure to disable these counters using the following command:

```
diskperf -n
```

Again, you'll need to reboot the machine to disable the counters. When disk counters are inactive, all counters for the PhysicalDisk and LogicalDisk objects always show zero values (0). This should occur only when the counters are inactive because even bootstrapping the operating system to start the machine creates substantial disk activity.

Identifying Storage Device Bottlenecks

By watching the following counters, you can pinpoint bottlenecks in your storage subsystem:

- **LogicalDisk: Disk Queue Length.** Tracks the number of system requests waiting for disk access. The number of queued requests should not exceed double the number of spindles in use. Most drives have only a single spindle, but RAID arrays have more (and Performance Monitor views RAID arrays as a single logical drive). A large number of waiting items indicates that a drive or an array is not operating fast enough to support the system's demands for I/O. When this occurs, you need a faster drive system.

- **LogicalDisk: % Disk Time.** Represents the percentage of time that the disk is actively handling read and write requests. It is not uncommon for this counter to regularly hit 100% on active servers. Sustained percentages of 90% or better, however, might indicate that a storage device is too slow. This most likely is true when its Disk Queue Length counter is constantly above 2 as well.

High levels of disk activity do not always indicate slow devices. Instead, they might be caused by too little physical RAM on a system. To decipher the amount of disk activity attributed to memory paging, perform the measurements and calculations shown in Table D.1.

Table D.1 **Calculating Disk Activity**

Line	Performance Counter or Calculation	Value
1	Memory: Pages/sec	_____
2	LogicalDisk: Avg. Disk sec/transfer	_____
3	Multiply line 1 by line 2	_____

If the value of line 3 is greater than 0.1 (10% of total disk activity), your system probably is suffering from a lack of RAM. After you add RAM to your computer, be sure to recheck the LogicalDisk counter to see if storage devices might be causing additional bottlenecks.

Disk Bottleneck Removal

If your system suffers from a storage-device bottleneck, the following are some methods to alleviate or lessen the performance degradation:

- Invest in faster drives with average seek times of 9ms or less. Drives search for data about 10 times as much as they actually transfer data; therefore, seek time is a crucial factor.

- Upgrade from IDE to SCSI, from SCSI-1 to SCSI-2, or from SCSI-2 to Fast SCSI-2 or Fast-Wide SCSI-2. IDE and EIDE drives should not be installed on a high-utilization server.

- Use a PCI bus mastering 32-bit SCSI controller card.

- Separate drives onto different controller cards.

- Use SCSI adapters that support asynchronous I/O. This enables multiple drives to operate in parallel, and it greatly improves performance of stripe sets and multiple paging files.

- Use RAID arrays to distribute drive load across multiple devices or add more drives to an existing array. (This requires the set to be broken and rebuilt if you use Windows NT's built-in disk stripe sets with parity.)

- Consider hardware RAID devices. Although they're more expensive, they offer considerably better performance.

- Use a disk defragmenter to decrease seek times. Symantec's Norton NT Tools (**http://www.symantec.com/**) and Executive Software's DiskKeeper (**http://www.execsoft.com/**) are excellent products.

- Verify that diskperf is turned off by executing the `diskperf -n` command and rebooting.

- If security is not an issue, FAT is faster than NTFS. By switching to FAT, however, you lose all capability to control access, most fault-tolerance support, and auditing.

- Don't use compression on files frequently accessed, especially any files within the Windows NT root directory and paging files.
- Place all swap files on fast drives or put your only swap file on a different drive than the one that includes the system files (the boot partition).

CPU Counters

The CPU is the brain of your computer. Nearly everything that goes on within the confines of your computer must pass through the CPU. Therefore, the CPU(s) can be a significant bottleneck.

Identifying CPU Bottlenecks

By watching the following counters, you can pinpoint CPU bottlenecks:

- **Processor: % Processor Time.** Indicates the amount of time the CPU spends on non-idle work. It's common for this counter to reach 100% during application launches or kernel-intensive operations (such as SAM synchronization). If this counter remains above 90% for an extended period, however, you should suspect a CPU bottleneck.
- **Processor: % Total Processor Time.** Applies only to multiprocessor systems. This counter should be used the same way as the single CPU counter. If any value remains consistently higher than 90%, at least one of your CPUs is a bottleneck.
- **System: Processor Queue Length.** Indicates the number of threads waiting for processor time. A sustained value of 2 or higher for this counter indicates processor congestion. Note that this counter is a snapshot of the time of measurement, not an average value over time.

CPU Bottleneck Removal

If your system suffers from a CPU bottleneck, the following are some methods to alleviate performance degradation:

- Add a second CPU (if your system supports it). This represents a greater increase in processing power than the total boost provided by adding processors 3 through 8.
- Alter or change priorities for non-kernel processes.
- Replace the current CPU with a faster chip (if your system supports it).
- Increase the L2, on-board, or secondary cache (if your system supports it).
- Remove all 3D or graphics-intensive screen savers.

- Move CPU-intensive applications to other machines.
- Replace the motherboard with a faster model, especially if its bus operates at only 33Mhz. (Upgrading to a motherboard that supports a 66Mhz bus offers a significant speed improvement.)

Memory Counters

The RAM in your computer is where data is stored before and after processing. Sufficient RAM enables your system to operate at peak efficiency. Insufficient RAM can cause severe performance degradation, I/O errors, and dropped network connections. Therefore, identifying and eliminating RAM bottlenecks is important.

Identifying Memory Bottlenecks

By watching the following counters, you can pinpoint memory bottlenecks:

- **Memory: Pages/sec.** Indicates the number of virtual memory page swaps that occur every second. If this value averages over 60, you probably need more RAM to obtain the best performance from your system.
- **Memory: Cache Faults/sec.** Indicates how frequently the system is unable to locate data in the cache and must search for it on disk. If this number grows steadily over time, your system is headed into constant thrashing. This means every bit of information required by the system must be retrieved directly from the disk.
- **Memory: Page Faults/sec.** Similar to cache faults, except that it also measures faults when a requested memory page is in use by another application. If this counter averages above 200 for low-end systems or above 600 for high-end systems, excess paging is occurring.
- **Memory: Available Bytes.** Indicates the amount of free memory available for use. If this number is less than 4MB, you do not have sufficient RAM on your system.
- **Paging File: % Usage Peak.** Indicates the level of paging file usage. If this number nears 100% during normal operations, the maximum size of your paging file is too small. If you have multiple drives with multiple paging files, be sure to view the _Total instance of this counter.

Memory Bottleneck Removal

If your system suffers from a memory bottleneck, the following are some methods to alleviate performance degradation:

- Add more RAM to your system. On most servers, it usually is most cost effective to fill all memory slots with the largest supported memory modules and to fully populate the motherboard with RAM.

- Increase the speed of your RAM. Purchase memory with a rating of 60ns or faster.
- Add faster hard drives to support the swap file or move the swap file to a faster drive.
- Increase the maximum size of the swap file.
- Split the swap file across multiple fast disks.
- Uninstall unneeded applications or Windows NT components to reduce memory usage.
- Add more cache to the motherboard.

Network Counters

Network performance monitoring is done on a protocol basis. You should examine each protocol separately to isolate individual performance characteristics. If you suspect one protocol might interfere with the operation of another, monitor related counters for both protocols simultaneously.

Identifying Network Bottlenecks

Network performance problems usually result from three different causes:

- **Server overload.** A system that attempts to handle more traffic than it can manage usually boils down to inadequate system resources such as memory capacity or speed, CPU capability, or NIC speed.
- **Network overload.** A network constantly at or near full capacity usually indicates that servers and workstations are trying to transmit data faster than the network architecture will allow.
- **Data loss.** Whenever data is lost outright, it usually indicates a network that contains one or more faulty devices or connections that are unable to deliver network packets properly.

To isolate protocol-specific issues, watch the error counters available for each protocol. Some error rate is to be expected, but sharp increases in error rates are a symptom of performance degradation. The only way to know when error counts are abnormal is to establish a regularly updated baseline for comparison purposes. You also can monitor demand for individual network resources that is larger than the demand for any or all other resources on or off the system. Such demand spikes also can help pinpoint bottlenecks.

To improve the odds of monitoring and isolating network-related slowdowns or bottlenecks, take the following preparatory steps:

- Install a fast (100MB), high-performance NIC in the server.
- Disable or uninstall all protocols and NICs not in use.

- Use more than one NIC if appropriate.

- Segment your network if appropriate.

Performance Monitor offers the following counters that do not focus on single protocols and instead act as general network identifiers:

- **Network Interface: Bytes Total/sec.** Indicates the rate at which data is sent to and received by a NIC (including framing characters). Compare this value with the expected capacity of the device. If the highest observed average is less than 75% of the expected value, communication errors or slowdowns might be occurring that limit the NIC's rated speed.

- **Network Interface: Current Bandwidth.** Estimates a NIC's current bandwidth, measured in bits per second (bps). This counter is useful only for NICs with variable bandwidth.

- **Network Interface: Output Queue Length.** Indicates the number of packets waiting to be transmitted by a NIC. If this averages above 2, you are experiencing delays.

- **Network Interface: Packets/sec.** Indicates the number of packets handled by a NIC. Watch this counter over a long interval of constant or normal activity. Sharp declines that occur while the Queue Length remains nonzero can indicate protocol-related or NIC-related problems.

Network Bottleneck Removal

If your system suffers from a network bottleneck, the following are some methods to mitigate performance degradation:

- Upgrade all NICs to 32-bit bus mastering cards.

- Make sure the NICs throughout your network are all the same speed.

- Add more RAM to your servers.

- Install only the protocols you actually use on your network.

- Adjust network binding to provide the fastest resolution of service selection. (That is, bind the most commonly used or fastest protocols first.)

- Adjust server parameters through the Network applet's Services tab:
  - Minimize Memory Used for 10 or fewer users
  - Balance for 10 to 64 users
  - Maximize Throughput for File Sharing for 64 or more users
  - Maximize Throughput for Network Applications for an application server

Windows NT provides a handful of protocol-specific Registry tuning controls, but we urge you to use caution when working with them. Editing the Registry is never something to be taken lightly. The following sections each list a tuning control, its location, and definitions of the available settings.

NetBEUI Frame

HKEY_LOCAL_MACHINE\SYSTEM\CurrentControlSet\Services\ NBF\Parameters

- **AddNameQueryTimeout.** Defines the length of time NBF waits for a private query response. The default is 500 milliseconds (.5 seconds). Increasing this value on busy or large networks offers additional time for the response to occur. Do not set this value above 10 seconds.

- **AddNameQueryResults.** Defines the maximum number of send retries for a private query. The default is 3. The minimum is 1. Setting this value lower on small or low-use networks can reduce wait time.

- **NBF Timer Parameters.** These should always have the relationship of T2 <= T1 <= Ti. These values offer performance improvements if slow computers or links are present on your network.

  - **DefaultT1Timeout.** This response timer indicates how long to wait before resending I-frames assumed to be lost due to no response. The default value is 600 milliseconds. Reducing this value to 250 might improve performance, but too low a setting forces unneeded retransmission.

  - **DefaultT2Timeout.** This acknowledgment timer indicates how long a sender should wait for a response I-frame before sending an ACK packet to force acknowledgment. The default is 150 milliseconds. This time can be lowered, but too low a value can cause unnecessary ACK packets to be sent.

  - **DefaultTiTimeout.** This inactivity timer determines whether a link to the receiver has failed. The default value is 30 seconds. A higher setting provides more time for successful acknowledgments and prevents the transmission of SESSION-ALIVE interrogation packets.

TCP/IP

HKEY_LOCAL_MACHINE\SYSTEM\CurrentControlSet\Services\ Tcpip\Parameters

- **TcpWindowSize.** This value determines the amount of data that can be transmitted by the system. The default is 32KB. Increasing this value might improve performance, especially if large files are continuously transmitted over the network.

- **TcpRecvSegmentSize** and **TcpSendSegmentSize.** These values control the minimum amount of data sent or received. The default for both is 1,460 bytes. Some adjustments higher or lower might improve performance. Results vary from network to network.

- **TcpKeepCnt** and **TcpKeepTries.** These values determine the length of time a TCP connection is sustained as active even without network traffic. A session is kept active for 40 minutes using the following default settings and formula:

TcpKeepCnt(120 seconds) × **TcpKeepTries**(20) = 40 minutes.

By reducing either or both values, inactive sessions will be terminated sooner, thereby reducing network overhead.

DLC

HKEY_LOCAL_MACHINE\SYSTEM\CurrentControlSet\Services\ DLC\Parameters

- **DefaultT1Timeout.** This response timer indicates how long to wait before resending I-frames assumed to be lost due to no response. The default value is 600 milliseconds. Reducing this value to 250 might improve performance, but too low a setting forces unneeded retransmission.
- **DefaultT2Timeout.** This acknowledgment timer indicates how long the sender should wait for a response I-frame before sending an ACK packet to force acknowledgment. The default is 150 milliseconds. This time can be reduced, but too low a setting can cause unnecessary ACK packets to be sent.
- **DefaultTiTimeout.** This inactivity timer determines whether the link to the receiver has failed. The default value is 30 seconds. A higher setting provides more time for a successful acknowledgment and prevents the transmission of SESSION-ALIVE interrogation packets.

Miscellaneous Counters

It's worth keeping an eye on the handful of other counters available for most networks. The following counters can identify symptoms of performance degradation, especially if monitored consistently over time:

- **Server: Sessions Errored Out.** Indicates the number of sessions terminated due to unexpected error conditions. This value lends insight to network problems that might cause dropped sessions on a server. If this cumulative counter exceeds 5 within a reasonable length of time, or if it displays a significant increase over time, you might have a network performance problem. The server must be rebooted to reset its value to zero (0).
- **Server: Work Item Shortages.** Indicates the number of times a work item was not available for allocation to an incoming request. A value of 3 or greater indicates a potential performance bottleneck. Adjusting the settings of the Server service properties might help alleviate the problem.

- **Server: Pool Paged Peak.** Indicates the number of bytes of memory allocated by the server to the page pool. If this value is equal or greater than the physical RAM in the machine, add more RAM.

- **Redirector: Network Errors/sec.** Indicates the number of errors that occur when a redirector and a server experience communication difficulties. Such an error also generates an entry in the system log (which you can view with the Event Viewer for details). A value of 5 or more errors per second is a call to action to locate and solve communication problems.

- **Redirector: Server Sessions Hung.** Identifies the existence of active sessions that have timed out because of communication failures. A value of 5 or more indicates network communication problems.

- **Redirector: Current Commands.** Indicates the number of requests queued for service. If this value stays above n, where $n = 2$ times the number of NICs in the server + 2, either the network or the server is causing a bottleneck.

For a complete list of all the default counters found in Performance Monitor, see the following resources:

- Windows NT Server Resource Kit Supplement 2—COUNTERS.HLP

- Using Tech Net, perform a search on "Performance Object and Counter Definitions." This search will lead you to Appendix C of the Windows NT Support workbook found in Microsoft's Windows NT Server Training box set.

AppleTalk Counters

The following Performance Monitor counters can help you troubleshoot problems with the AppleTalk protocol:

- **AppleTalk: AARP Packets/sec.** Indicates the number of AARP packets per second received by AppleTalk on this port.

- **AppleTalk: ATP ALO Response/sec.** Provides the number of ATP at-least-once transaction responses per second on this port.

- **AppleTalk: ATP Packets/sec.** Provides the number of ATP packets per second received by AppleTalk on this port.

- **AppleTalk: ATP Recvd Released/sec.** Indicates the number of ATP transaction release packets per second received on this port.

- **AppleTalk: ATP Response Timeouts.** Provides the number of ATP release timers that have expired on this port.

- **AppleTalk: ATP Retries Local.** Indicates the number of ATP requests retransmitted on this port.

- **AppleTalk: ATP Retries Remote.** Indicates the number of ATP requests retransmitted to this port.

- **AppleTalk: ATP XO Response/sec.** Indicates the number of ATP exactly-once transaction responses per second on this port.

- **AppleTalk: Average Time/AARP Packets.** Indicates the average time in milliseconds to process an AARP packet on this port.

- **AppleTalk: Average Time/ATP Packet.** Indicates the average time in milliseconds to process an ATP packet on this port.

- **AppleTalk: Average Time/DDP Packet.** Indicates the average time in milliseconds to process a DDP packet on this port.

- **AppleTalk: Average Time/NBP Packet.** Indicates the average time in milliseconds to process an NBP packet on this port.

- **AppleTalk: Average Time/RTMP Packet.** Indicates the average time in milliseconds to process an RTMP packet on this port.

- **AppleTalk: Average Time/ZIP Packet.** Indicates the average time in milliseconds to process a ZIP packet on this port.

- **AppleTalk: Bytes In/sec.** Provides the number of bytes received per second by AppleTalk on this port.

- **AppleTalk: Bytes Out/sec.** Provides the number of bytes sent per second by AppleTalk on this port.

- **AppleTalk: Current Nonpaged Pool.** Indicates the current amount of nonpaged memory resources used by AppleTalk.

- **AppleTalk: DDP Packets/sec.** Indicates the number of DDP packets per second received by AppleTalk on this port.

- **AppleTalk: NBP Packets/sec.** Provides the number of NBP packets per second received by AppleTalk on this port.

- **AppleTalk: Packets dropped.** Indicates the number of packets dropped due to resource limitations on this port.

- **AppleTalk: Packets In/sec.** Indicates the number of packets received per second by AppleTalk on this port.

- **AppleTalk: Packets Out/sec.** Indicates the number of packets sent per second by AppleTalk on this port.

- **AppleTalk: Packets Routed In/sec.** Indicates the number of packets routed in on this port.

- **AppleTalk: Packets Routed Out/sec.** Indicates the number of packets routed out on this port.

- **AppleTalk: RTMP Packets/sec.** Indicates the number of RTMP packets per second received by AppleTalk on this port.

- **AppleTalk: ZIP Packets/sec.** Indicates the number of ZIP packets per second received by AppleTalk on this port.

Browser Counters

The following Performance Monitor counters can help you troubleshoot problems with the Browser service:

- **Browser: Announcements Domain/sec.** Indicates the rate at which a domain has announced itself to the network.

- **Browser: Announcements Server/sec.** Indicates the rate at which the servers in this domain have announced themselves to this server.

- **Browser: Announcements Total/sec.** Indicates the sum of Announcements Server/sec and Announcements Domain/sec.

- **Browser: Duplicate Masters Announcements.** Indicates the number of times the master browser has detected another master browser on the same domain.

- **Browser: Election Packets/sec.** Indicates the rate at which browser election packets have been received by this workstation.

- **Browser: Enumerations Domain/sec.** Indicates the rate at which domain browse requests have been processed by this workstation.

- **Browser: Enumerations Other/sec.** Indicates the rate at which non-domain or server browse requests were processed by this workstation.

- **Browser: Enumerations Server/sec.** Indicates the rate at which server browse requests have been processed by this workstation.

- **Browser: Enumerations Total/sec.** Indicates the rate at which browse requests have been processed by this workstation. This is the sum of Enumerations Server, Enumerations Domain, and Enumerations Other.

- **Browser: Illegal Datagrams/sec.** Indicates the rate at which incorrectly formatted datagrams have been received by the workstation.

- **Browser: Mailslot Allocations Failed.** Indicates the number of times the datagram receiver has failed to allocate a buffer to hold a user mailslot write.

- **Browser: Mailslot Opens Failed/sec.** Indicates the rate at which mailslot messages to be delivered to mailslots not present on this workstation were received by the workstation.

- **Browser: Mailslot Receives Failed.** Indicates the number of mailslot messages that could not be received because of transport failures.

- **Browser: Mailslot Writes Failed.** Indicates the total number of mailslot messages that have been successfully received but were unable to be written to the mailslot.

- **Browser: Mailslot Writes/sec.** Indicates the rate at which mailslot messages have been successfully received.

- **Browser: Missed Mailslot Datagrams.** Indicates the number of mailslot datagrams that have been discarded because of configuration or allocation limits.

- **Browser: Missed Server Announcements.** Indicates the number of server announcements that have been missed because of configuration or allocation limits.

- **Browser: Missed Server List Requests.** Indicates the number of requests to retrieve a list of browser servers that were received by this workstation but could not be processed.

- **Browser: Server Announce Allocations Failed/sec.** Indicates the rate at which server (or domain) announcements that have failed because of lack of memory.

- **Browser: Server List Requests/sec.** Indicates the rate at which requests to retrieve a list of browser servers have been processed by this workstation.

Cache Counters

The following Performance Monitor counters can help you troubleshoot problems with the caching:

- **Cache: Async Copy Reads/sec.** Indicates the frequency of reads from cache pages that involve a memory copy of the data from the cache to the application's buffer. The application will regain control immediately even if you must access the disk to retrieve the page.

- **Cache: Async Data Maps/sec.** Indicates the frequency with which an application using a file system, such as NTFS or HPFS, maps a page of a file into the cache to read the page and does not want to wait for the cache to retrieve the page if it is not in main memory.

- **Cache: Async Fast Reads/sec.** Indicates the frequency of reads from cache pages that bypass the installed file system and retrieve the data directly from the cache. Usually, file I/O requests invoke the appropriate file system to retrieve data from a file, but this path permits direct retrieval of cache data without file system involvement if the data is in the cache. Even if the data is not in the cache, one invocation of the file system is avoided. If the data is not in the cache, the request (application program call) does not wait until the data has been retrieved from disk. It gets control immediately.

- **Cache: Async MDL Reads/sec.** Indicates the frequency of reads from cache pages using a Memory Descriptor List (MDL) to access the pages. The MDL contains the physical address of each page in the transfer, thus permitting Direct Memory Access (DMA) of the pages. If the accessed page(s) are not in the main memory, the calling application program does not wait for the pages to fault in from disk.

- **Cache: Async Pin Reads/sec.** Indicates the frequency of reading data into the cache preparatory to writing the data back to disk. Pages read in this fashion are pinned in memory at the completion of the read. The file system regains control immediately, even if the disk must be accessed to retrieve the page. While pinned, a page's physical address will not be altered.

- **Cache: Copy Read Hits %.** Indicates the percentage of cache Copy Read requests that hit the cache (for example, that did not require a disk read to provide access to the page in the cache). A Copy Read is a file read operation that is satisfied by a memory copy from a cache page to the application's buffer. The LAN Redirector uses this method for retrieving cache information, as does the LAN Server for small transfers. This is a method the disk file systems use as well.

- **Cache: Copy Reads/sec.** Indicates the frequency of reads from cache pages that involve a memory copy of the data from the cache to the application's buffer. The LAN Redirector uses this method for retrieving cache information, as does the LAN Server for small transfers. This method is used by the disk file systems as well.

- **Cache: Data Flush Pages/sec.** Indicates the number of pages the cache has flushed to disk as a result of a request to flush or to satisfy a write-through file write request. More than one page can be transferred on each flush operation.

- **Cache: Data Flushes/sec.** Indicates the frequency with which the cache has flushed its contents to disk as the result of a request to flush or to satisfy a write-through file write request. More than one page can be transferred on each flush operation.

- **Cache: Data Map Hits %.** Indicates the percentage of data maps in the cache that could be resolved without having to retrieve a page from the disk. (That is, the page was already in physical memory.)

- **Cache: Data Map Pins/sec.** Indicates the frequency of data maps in the cache that resulted in pinning a page in main memory, an action usually preparatory to writing to the file on disk. While pinned, a page's physical address in main memory and its virtual address in the cache will not be altered.

- **Cache: Data Maps/sec.** Indicates the frequency with which a file system, such as NTFS or HPFS, maps a page of a file into the cache to read the page.

- **Cache: Fast Read Not Possible/sec.** Indicates the frequency of attempts by an Application Programming Interface (API) function call to bypass the file system to get at cache data, which could not be honored without invoking the file system.

- **Cache: Fast Read Resource Misses/sec.** Indicates the frequency of cache misses necessitated by the lack of available resources to satisfy the request.

- **Cache: Fast Reads/sec.** Indicates the frequency of reads from cache pages that bypass the installed file system and retrieve the data directly from the cache. Usually, file I/O requests invoke the appropriate file system to retrieve data from a file, but this path permits direct retrieval of cache data without file system involvement if the data is in the cache. Even if the data is not in the cache, one invocation of the file system is avoided.

- **Cache: Lazy Write Flushes/sec.** Indicates the frequency with which the cache's Lazy Write thread has been written to disk. Lazy Writing is the process of updating the disk after the page has been changed in memory. The application making the change to the file does not have to wait for the disk writing to finish before proceeding. More than one page can be transferred on each write operation.

- **Cache: Lazy Write Pages/sec.** Indicates the frequency with which the cache's Lazy Write thread has been written to disk. Lazy Writing is the process of updating the disk after the page has been changed in memory. The application making the change to the file does not have to wait for the disk write to complete before proceeding. More than one page can be transferred on a single disk write operation.

- **Cache: MDL Read Hits %.** Indicates the percentage of cache Memory Descriptor List (MDL) Read requests that hit the cache That is, they did not require disk accesses to provide memory access to the page(s) in the cache.

- **Cache: MDL Reads/sec.** Indicates the frequency of reads from cache pages that use a Memory Descriptor List (MDL) to access the data. The MDL contains the physical address of each page involved in the transfer and therefore can employ a hardware Direct Memory Access (DMA) device to affect the copy. The LAN Server uses this method for large transfers out of the server.

- **Cache: Pin Read Hits %.** Indicates the percentage of cache Pin Read requests that hit the cache. That is, they did not require a disk read to provide access to the page in the cache. While pinned, a page's physical address in the cache will not be altered. The LAN Redirector uses this method for retrieving cache information, as does the LAN Server for small transfers. This usually is the method used by the disk file systems as well.

- **Cache: Pin Reads/sec.** Indicates the frequency of reading data into the cache preparatory to writing the data back to disk. Pages read in this fashion are pinned in memory at the completion of the read. While pinned, a page's physical address in the cache will not be altered.

- **Cache: Read Aheads/sec.** Indicates the frequency of cache reads in which the cache detects sequential access to a file. The read aheads permit the data to be transferred in larger blocks than those being requested by the application, thereby reducing the overhead per access.

- **Cache: Sync Copy Reads/sec.** Indicates the frequency of reads from cache pages that involve a memory copy of the data from the cache to the application's buffer. The file system will not regain control until the copy operation is complete, even if the disk must be accessed to retrieve the page.

- **Cache: Sync Data Maps/sec.** Counts the frequency with which a file system, such as NTFS or HPFS, maps a page of a file into the cache to read the page and wants to wait for the cache to retrieve the page if it is not in main memory.

- **Cache: Sync Fast Reads/sec.** Indicates the frequency of reads from cache pages that bypass the installed file system and retrieve the data directly from the cache. Usually, file I/O requests invoke the appropriate file system to retrieve data from a file, but this path permits direct retrieval of cache data without file system involvement if the data is in the cache. Even if the data is not in the cache, one invocation of the file system is avoided. If the data is not in the cache, the request (application program call) waits until the data has been retrieved from disk.

- **Cache: Sync MDL Reads/sec.** Indicates the frequency of reads from cache pages that use a Memory Descriptor List (MDL) to access the pages. The MDL contains the physical address of each page in the transfer, thus permitting Direct Memory Access (DMA) of the pages. If the accessed page(s) are not in main memory, the caller waits for the pages to fault in from the disk.

- **Cache: Sync Pin Reads/sec.** Indicates the frequency of reading data into the cache preparatory to writing the data back to disk. Pages read in this fashion are pinned in memory at the completion of the read. The file system does not regain control until the page is pinned in the cache, particularly if the disk must be accessed to retrieve the page. While pinned, a page's physical address in the cache will not be altered.

LogicalDisk Counters

The following Performance Monitor counters can help you troubleshoot problems with disk storage:

- **LogicalDisk: % Disk Read Time.** Indicates the percentage of elapsed time that the selected disk drive is busy servicing read requests.

- **LogicalDisk: % Disk Time.** Indicates the percentage of elapsed time that the selected disk drive is busy servicing read or write requests.

- **LogicalDisk: % Disk Write Time.** Indicates the percentage of elapsed time that the selected disk drive is busy servicing write requests.

- **LogicalDisk: % Free Space.** Indicates the ratio of the free space available on the logical disk unit to the total usable space provided by the selected logical disk drive.

- **LogicalDisk: Avg. Disk Bytes/Read.** Indicates the average number of bytes transferred from the disk during read operations.

- **LogicalDisk: Avg. Disk Bytes/Transfer.** Indicates the average number of bytes transferred to or from the disk during write or read operations.

- **LogicalDisk: Avg. Disk Bytes/Write.** Indicates the average number of bytes transferred to the disk during write operations.
- **LogicalDisk: Avg. Disk Queue Length.** Indicates the average number of both read and write requests that were queued for the selected disk during the sample interval.
- **LogicalDisk: Avg. Disk Read Queue Length.** Indicates the average number of read requests that were queued for the selected disk during the sample interval.
- **LogicalDisk: Avg. Disk sec/Read.** Indicates the average time in seconds of a read of data from the disk.
- **LogicalDisk: Avg. Disk sec/Transfer.** Indicates the time in seconds of the average disk transfer.
- **LogicalDisk: Avg. Disk sec/Write.** Indicates the average time in seconds of a write of data to the disk.
- **LogicalDisk: Avg. Disk Write Queue Length.** Indicates the average number of write requests that were queued for the selected disk during the sample interval.
- **LogicalDisk: Current Disk Queue Length.** Indicates the number of requests outstanding on the disk at the time the performance data is collected. It includes requests in service at the time of the snapshot. This is an instantaneous length, not an average over the time interval. Multispindle disk devices can have multiple requests active at one time, but other concurrent requests are awaiting service. This counter might reflect a transitory high or low queue length, but if there is a sustained load on the disk drive, it is likely that this will be consistently high. Requests are experiencing delays proportional to the length of this queue minus the number of spindles on the disks. This difference should average less than 2 for good performance.
- **LogicalDisk: Disk Bytes/sec.** Indicates the rate at which bytes are transferred to or from the disk during write or read operations.
- **LogicalDisk: Disk Read Bytes/sec.** Indicates the rate at which bytes are transferred from the disk during read operations.
- **LogicalDisk: Disk Reads/sec.** Indicates the rate of read operations on the disk.
- **LogicalDisk: Disk Transfers/sec.** Indicates the rate of read and write operations on the disk.
- **LogicalDisk: Disk Write Bytes/sec.** Indicates the rate at which bytes are transferred to the disk during write operations.
- **LogicalDisk: Disk Writes/sec.** Indicates the rate of write operations on the disk.
- **LogicalDisk: Free Megabytes.** Displays the unallocated space on the disk drive in megabytes. One megabyte = 1,048,576 bytes.

MacFile Server Counters

The following Performance Monitor counters can help you troubleshoot problems with MacFile Server objects:

- **MacFile Server: Current Files Open.** Indicates the number of internal files currently open in the MacFile Server. This count does not include files opened on behalf of Macintosh clients.

- **MacFile Server: Current Nonpaged Memory.** Displays the current amount of nonpaged memory resources used by the MacFile Server.

- **MacFile Server: Current Paged Memory.** Indicates the current amount of paged memory resources used by the MacFile Server.

- **MacFile Server: Current Queue Length.** Displays the number of outstanding work items waiting to be processed.

- **MacFile Server: Current Sessions.** Indicates the number of sessions currently connected to the MacFile Server and indicates current server activity.

- **MacFile Server: Current Threads.** Indicates the current number of threads used by the MacFile Server and indicates how busy the server is.

- **MacFile Server: Data Read/sec.** Indicates the number of bytes read from disk per second.

- **MacFile Server: Data Received/sec.** Indicates the number of bytes received from the network per second and indicates how busy the server is.

- **MacFile Server: Data Transmitted/sec.** Displays the number of bytes sent on the network per second and indicates how busy the server is.

- **MacFile Server: Data Written/sec.** Indicates the number of bytes written to disk per second.

- **MacFile Server: Failed Logons.** Indicates the number of failed logon attempts to the MacFile Server. Also can indicate whether password-guessing programs are being used to crack the security on the server.

- **MacFile Server: Max NonPaged Memory.** Indicates the maximum amount of nonpaged memory resources use by the MacFile Server.

- **MacFile Server: Max Paged Memory.** Displays the maximum amount of paged memory resources used by the MacFile Server.

- **MacFile Server: Maximum Files Open.** Displays the maximum number of internal files open at one time in the MacFile Server. This count does not include files opened on behalf of Macintosh clients.

- **MacFile Server: Maximum Queue Length.** Indicates the maximum number of outstanding work items waiting at one time.

- **MacFile Server: Maximum Sessions.** Indicates the maximum number of sessions connected at one time to the MacFile Server and indicates the usage level of the server.

- **MacFile Server: Maximum Threads.** Displays the maximum number of threads used by the MacFile server and indicates the peak usage level of the server.

Memory Counters

The following Performance Monitor counters can help you troubleshoot memory problems:

- **Memory: % Committed Bytes In Use.** Indicates the ratio of the committed bytes to the commit limit. This represents the amount of available virtual memory in use. Note that the commit limit might change if the paging file is extended. This is an instantaneous value, not an average.

- **Memory: Available Bytes.** Displays the size of the virtual memory currently on the zeroed, free, and standby lists. Zeroed and free memory is ready for use, with zeroed memory cleared to zeros. Standby memory is memory removed from a process's working set that is still available. Notice that this is an instantaneous count, not an average over the time interval.

- **Memory: Cache Bytes.** Measures the number of bytes currently in use by the system cache. The system cache is used to buffer data retrieved from disk or LAN. The system cache uses memory not in use by active processes in the computer.

- **Memory: Cache Bytes Peak.** Measures the maximum number of bytes used by the system cache. The system cache is used to buffer data retrieved from disk or LAN. The system cache uses memory not in use by active processes in the computer.

- **Memory: Cache Faults/sec.** Indicates the occurrence of cache faults. Such faults occur whenever the cache manager does not find a file's page in the immediate cache and must ask the memory manager to locate the page elsewhere in memory or on the disk so it can be loaded into the immediate cache.

- **Memory: Commit Limit.** Indicates the size (in bytes) of virtual memory that can be committed without having to extend the paging file(s). If the paging file(s) can be extended, this is a soft limit.

- **Memory: Committed Bytes.** Displays the size of virtual memory (in bytes) that has been committed (as opposed to simply reserved). Committed memory must have backing (that is, disk) storage available or must be assured never to need disk storage (because main memory is large enough to hold it.) Notice that this is an instantaneous count, not an average over the time interval.

- **Memory: Demand Zero Faults/sec.** Indicates the number of page faults for pages that must be filled with zeros before the fault is satisfied. If the zeroed list is not empty, the fault can be resolved by removing a page from the zeroed list.

- **Memory: Free System Page Table Entries.** Indicates the number of page table entries not currently in use by the system.

- **Memory: Page Faults/sec.** This is a count of the page faults in the processor. A page fault occurs when a process refers to a virtual memory page not in its working set in main memory. A page fault will not cause the page to be fetched from disk if that page is on the standby list (and hence, already in main memory) or if it is in use by another process with whom the page is shared.

- **Memory: Page Reads/sec.** Indicates the number of times the disk was read to retrieve pages of virtual memory necessary to resolve page faults. Multiple pages can be read during a disk read operation.

- **Memory: Page Writes/sec.** This is a count of the number of times pages have been written to the disk because they were changed since last retrieved. Each such write operation can transfer a number of pages.

- **Memory: Pages Input/sec.** Indicates the number of pages read from the disk to resolve memory references to pages not in memory at the time of the reference. This counter includes paging traffic on behalf of the system cache to access file data for applications. This is an important counter to observe if you are concerned about excessive memory pressure (that is, thrashing) and the excessive paging that can result.

- **Memory: Pages Output/sec.** This is a count of the number of pages written to disk because the pages have been modified in main memory.

- **Memory: Pages/sec.** Indicates the number of pages read from the disk or written to the disk to resolve memory references to pages not in memory at the time of the reference. This is the sum of Pages Input/sec and Pages Output/sec. This counter includes paging traffic on behalf of the system cache to access file data for applications. This value also includes the pages to/from noncached mapped memory files. This is the primary counter to observe if you are concerned about excessive memory pressure (that is, thrashing) and the excessive paging that can result.

- **Memory: Pool Nonpaged Allocs.** Indicates the number of calls to allocate space in the system nonpaged pool. The nonpaged pool is a system memory area where space is acquired by operating system components as they accomplish their appointed tasks. Nonpaged pool pages cannot be paged out to the paging file. Instead, they remain in main memory as long as they are allocated.

- **Memory: Pool Nonpaged Bytes.** Indicates the number of bytes in the nonpaged pool, a system memory area where space is acquired by operating system components as they accomplish their appointed tasks. Nonpaged pool pages cannot be paged out to the paging file. Instead, they remain in main memory as long as they are allocated.

- **Memory: Pool Paged Allocs.** Indicates the number of calls to allocate space in the system paged pool. The paged pool is a system memory area where space is acquired by operating system components as they accomplish their appointed tasks. Paged pool pages can be paged out to the paging file when not accessed by the system for sustained periods of time.

- **Memory: Pool Paged Bytes.** Indicates the number of bytes in the paged pool, a system memory area where space is acquired by operating system components as they accomplish their appointed tasks. Paged Pool pages can be paged out to the paging file when not accessed by the system for sustained periods of time.

- **Memory: Pool Paged Resident Bytes.** Indicates the size of paged pool resident in core memory. This is the actual cost of the paged pool allocation because it is actively in use and using real physical memory.

- **Memory: System Cache Resident Bytes.** Indicates the number of bytes currently resident in the global disk cache.

- **Memory: System Code Resident Bytes.** Indicates the number of bytes of System Code Total Bytes currently resident in core memory. This is the code working set of the pageable executive. In addition, there is another approximately 300,000 bytes of nonpaged kernel code.

- **Memory: System Code Total Bytes.** Indicates the number of bytes of pageable pages in NTOSKRNL.EXE, HAL.DLL, and the boot drivers and file systems loaded by ntldr/osloader.

- **Memory: System Driver Resident Bytes.** Indicates the number of bytes of System Driver Total Bytes currently resident in core memory. This number is the code working set of the pageable drivers. In addition, there is another approximately 700,000 bytes of nonpaged driver code.

- **Memory: System Driver Total Bytes.** Indicates the number of bytes of pageable pages in all other loaded device drivers.

- **Memory: Transition Faults/sec.** Indicates the number of page faults resolved by recovering pages in transition (that is, being written to disk at the time of the page fault). The pages were recovered without additional disk activity.

- **Memory: Write Copies/sec.** Indicates the number of page faults that have been satisfied by making a copy of a page when an attempt to write to the page is made. This is an economical way of sharing data because the copy of the page is made only on an attempt to write to the page. Otherwise, the page is shared.

NBT Counters

The following Performance Monitor counters can help you troubleshoot problems with NBT:

- **NBT Connection: Bytes Received/sec.** Indicates the rate at which bytes are received by the local computer over an NBT connection to some remote computer. All the bytes received by the local computer over the particular NBT connection are counted.

- **NBT Connection: Bytes Sent/sec**. Indicates the rate at which bytes are sent by the local computer over an NBT connection to some remote computer. All the bytes sent by the local computer over the particular NBT connection are counted.

- **NBT Connection: Total Bytes/sec.** Indicates the rate at which bytes are sent or received by the local computer over an NBT connection to some remote computer. All the bytes sent or received by the local computer over the particular NBT connection are counted.

NetBEUI Counters

The following Performance Monitor counters can help you troubleshoot problems with the NetBEUI protocol:

- **NetBEUI: Bytes Total/sec.** Indicates the sum of Frame Bytes/sec and Datagram Bytes/sec. This is the total rate of bytes sent to or received from the network by the protocol, but it only counts the bytes in frames (that is, packets) that carry data.

- **NetBEUI: Connection Session Timeouts.** Indicates the number of connections dropped due to a session timeout. This number is an accumulator and shows a running total.

- **NetBEUI: Connections Canceled.** Indicates the number of connections canceled. This number is an accumulator and shows a running total.

- **NetBEUI: Connections No Retries.** Indicates the total count of connections successfully made on the first try. This number is an accumulator and shows a running total.

- **NetBEUI: Connections Open.** Indicates the number of connections currently open for this protocol. This counter shows the current count only and does not accumulate over time.

- **NetBEUI: Connections With Retries.** Indicates the total count of connections made after retrying the attempt. A retry occurs when the first connection attempt fails. This number is an accumulator and shows a running total.

- **NetBEUI: Datagram Bytes Received/sec.** Indicates the rate at which datagram bytes are received by the computer. A datagram is a connectionless packet whose delivery to a remote computer is not guaranteed.

- **NetBEUI: Datagram Bytes Sent/sec.** Indicates the rate at which datagram bytes are sent from the computer. A datagram is a connectionless packet whose delivery to a remote computer is not guaranteed.

- **NetBEUI: Datagram Bytes/sec.** Indicates the rate at which datagram bytes are processed by the computer. This counter is the sum of datagram bytes sent as well as received. A datagram is a connectionless packet whose delivery to a remote is not guaranteed.

- **NetBEUI: Datagrams Received/sec.** Indicates the rate at which datagrams are received by the computer. A datagram is a connectionless packet whose delivery to a remote computer is not guaranteed.

- **NetBEUI: Datagrams Sent/sec.** Indicates the rate at which datagrams are sent from the computer. A datagram is a connectionless packet whose delivery to a remote computer is not guaranteed.

- **NetBEUI: Datagrams/sec.** Indicates the rate at which datagrams are processed by the computer. This counter displays the sum of datagrams sent and datagrams received. A datagram is a connectionless packet whose delivery to a remote is not guaranteed.

- **NetBEUI: Disconnects Local.** Indicates the number of session disconnections initiated by the local computer. This number is an accumulator and shows a running total.

- **NetBEUI: Disconnects Remote.** Indicates the number of session disconnections initiated by the remote computer. This number is an accumulator and shows a running total.

- **NetBEUI: Expirations Ack.** Indicates the count of T2 timer expirations.

- **NetBEUI: Expirations Response.** Indicates the count of T1 timer expirations.

- **NetBEUI: Failures Adapter.** Indicates the number of connections dropped due to an adapter failure. This number is an accumulator and shows a running total.

- **NetBEUI: Failures Link.** Indicates the number of connections dropped due to a link failure. This number is an accumulator and shows a running total.

- **NetBEUI: Failures No Listen.** Indicates the number of connections rejected because the remote computer was not listening for connection requests.

- **NetBEUI: Failures Not Found.** Indicates the number of connection attempts that failed because the remote computer could not be found. This number is an accumulator and shows a running total.

- **NetBEUI: Failures Resource Local.** Indicates the number of connections that failed because of resource problems or shortages on the local computer. This number is an accumulator and shows a running total.

- **NetBEUI: Failures Resource Remote.** Indicates the number of connections that failed because of resource problems or shortages on the remote computer. This number is an accumulator and shows a running total.

- **NetBEUI: Frame Bytes Received/sec.** Indicates the rate at which data bytes are received by the computer. This counter only counts the frames (packets) that carry data.

- **NetBEUI: Frame Bytes Rejected/sec.** Indicates the rate at which data bytes are rejected. This counter only counts the bytes in data frames (packets) that carry data.

- **NetBEUI: Frame Bytes Re-Sent/sec.** Indicates the rate at which data bytes are re-sent by the computer. This counter only counts the bytes in frames that carry data.

- **NetBEUI: Frame Bytes Sent/sec.** Indicates the rate at which data bytes are sent by the computer. This counter only counts the bytes in frames (packets) that carry data.

- **NetBEUI: Frame Bytes/sec.** Indicates the rate at which data bytes are processed by the computer. This counter is the sum of data frame bytes sent and received. This counter only counts the bytes in frames (packets) that carry data.

- **NetBEUI: Frames Received/sec.** Indicates the rate at which data frames are received by the computer. This counter only counts the frames (packets) that carry data.

- **NetBEUI: Frames Rejected/sec.** Indicates the rate at which data frames are rejected. This counter only counts the frames (packets) that carry data.

- **NetBEUI: Frames Re-Sent/sec.** Indicates the rate at which data frames (packets) are re-sent by the computer. This counter only counts the frames (packets) that carry data.

- **NetBEUI: Frames Sent/sec.** Indicates the rate at which data frames are sent by the computer. This counter only counts the frames (packets) that carry data.

- **NetBEUI: Frames/sec.** Indicates the rate at which data frames (or packets) are processed by the computer. This counter indicates the sum of data frames sent and data frames received. This counter only counts the frames (packets) that carry data.

- **NetBEUI: Packets Received/sec.** Indicates the rate at which packets are received by the computer. This counter counts all packets processed (that is, control as well as data packets).

- **NetBEUI: Packets Sent/sec.** Indicates the rate at which packets are sent by the computer. This counter counts all packets sent by the computer (that is, control as well as data packets).

- **NetBEUI: Packets/sec.** Indicates the rate at which packets are processed by the computer. This count is the sum of Packets Sent/sec and Packets Received/sec. This counter includes all packets processed (that is, control as well as data packets).

- **NetBEUI: Piggyback Ack Queued/sec.** Indicates the rate at which piggybacked acknowledgments are queued. Piggyback acknowledgments are acknowledgments of received packets to be included in the next outgoing packet to the remote computer.

- **NetBEUI: Piggyback Ack Timeouts.** Indicates the number of times a piggyback acknowledgment could not be sent because there was no outgoing packet to the remote on which to piggyback. A piggyback ack is an acknowledgment of a received packet sent along in an outgoing data packet to the remote computer. If no outgoing packet is sent within the time-out period, an ack packet is sent and the counter is incremented.

- **NetBEUI: Window Send Average.** Indicates the running average number of data bytes sent before waiting for an acknowledgment from the remote computer.

- **NetBEUI: Window Send Maximum.** Indicates the maximum number of data bytes sent before waiting for an acknowledgment from the remote computer.

NetBEUI Resources Counters

The following Performance Monitor counters can help you troubleshoot problems with NetBEUI resources:

- **NetBEUI Resources: Times Exhausted.** Indicates the number of times all the resources (buffers) were in use. The number in parentheses following the resource name is used to identify the resource in Event Log messages.

- **NetBEUI Resources: Used Average.** Indicates the current number of resources (buffers) in use at this time. The number in parentheses following the resource name is used to identify the resource in Event Log messages.

- **NetBEUI Resources: Used Maximum.** Indicates the maximum number of NetBEUI resources (buffers) in use at any point in time. This value is useful in sizing the maximum resources provided. The number in parentheses following the resource name is used to identify the resource in Event Log messages.

NWLink Counters

The following Performance Monitor counters can help you troubleshoot problems with the NWLink protocol:

- **NWLink IPX: Bytes Total/sec.** Indicates the sum of Frame Bytes/sec and Datagram Bytes/sec. This is the total rate of bytes sent to or received from the network by the protocol, but it only counts the bytes in frames (that is, packets) that carry data.

- **NWLink IPX: Connection Session Timeouts.** Indicates the number of connections dropped due to a session timeout. This number is an accumulator and shows a running total.

- **NWLink IPX: Connections Canceled.** Indicates the number of connections canceled. This number is an accumulator and shows a running total.

- **NWLink IPX: Connections No Retries.** Indicates the total count of connections successfully made on the first try. This number is an accumulator and shows a running total.

- **NWLink IPX: Connections Open.** Indicates the number of connections currently open for this protocol. This counter shows the current count only and does not accumulate over time.

- **NWLink IPX: Connections With Retries.** Indicates the total count of connections made after retrying the attempt. A retry occurs when the first connection attempt fails. This number is an accumulator and shows a running total.

- **NWLink IPX: Datagram Bytes Received/sec.** Indicates the rate at which datagram bytes are received by the computer. A datagram is a connectionless packet whose delivery to a remote computer is not guaranteed.

- **NWLink IPX: Datagram Bytes Sent/sec.** Indicates the rate at which datagram bytes are sent from the computer. A datagram is a connectionless packet whose delivery to a remote computer is not guaranteed.

- **NWLink IPX: Datagram Bytes/sec.** Indicates the rate at which datagram bytes are processed by the computer. This counter indicates the sum of datagram bytes sent as well as received. A datagram is a connectionless packet whose delivery to a remote is not guaranteed.

- **NWLink IPX: Datagrams Received/sec.** Indicates the rate at which datagrams are received by the computer. A datagram is a connectionless packet whose delivery to a remote computer is not guaranteed.

- **NWLink IPX: Datagrams Sent/sec.** Indicates the rate at which datagrams are sent from the computer. A datagram is a connectionless packet whose delivery to a remote computer is not guaranteed.

- **NWLink IPX: Datagrams/sec.** Indicates the rate at which datagrams are processed by the computer. This counter displays the sum of datagrams sent and datagrams received. A datagram is a connectionless packet whose delivery to a remote is not guaranteed.

- **NWLink IPX: Disconnects Local.** Indicates the number of session disconnections initiated by the local computer. This number is an accumulator and shows a running total.

- **NWLink IPX: Disconnects Remote.** Indicates the number of session disconnections initiated by the remote computer. This number is an accumulator and shows a running total.

- **NWLink IPX: Expirations Ack.** Indicates the count of T2 timer expirations.

- **NWLink IPX: Expirations Response.** Indicates the count of T1 timer expirations.

- **NWLink IPX: Failures Adapter.** Indicates the number of connections dropped due to an adapter failure. This number is an accumulator and shows a running total.

- **NWLink IPX: Failures Link.** Indicates the number of connections dropped due to a link failure. This number is an accumulator and shows a running total.

- **NWLink IPX: Failures No Listen.** Indicates the number of connections rejected because the remote computer was not listening for connection requests.

- **NWLink IPX: Failures Not Found.** Indicates the number of connection attempts that failed because the remote computer could not be found. This number is an accumulator and shows a running total.

- **NWLink IPX: Failures Resource Local.** Indicates the number of connections that failed because of resource problems or shortages on the local computer. This number is an accumulator and shows a running total.

- **NWLink IPX: Failures Resource Remote.** Indicates the number of connections that failed because of resource problems or shortages on the remote computer. This number is an accumulator and shows a running total.

- **NWLink IPX: Frame Bytes Received/sec.** Indicates the rate at which data bytes are received by the computer. This counter only counts the frames (packets) that carry data.

- **NWLink IPX: Frame Bytes Rejected/sec.** Indicates the rate at which data bytes are rejected. This counter only counts the bytes in data frames (packets) that carry data.

- **NWLink IPX: Frame Bytes Re-Sent/sec.** Indicates the rate at which data bytes are re-sent by the computer. This counter only counts the bytes in frames (packets) that carry data.

- **NWLink IPX: Frame Bytes Sent/sec.** Indicates the rate at which data bytes are sent by the computer. This counter only counts the bytes in frames (packets) that carry data.

- **NWLink IPX: Frame Bytes/sec.** Indicates the rate at which data bytes are processed by the computer. This counter is the sum of data frame bytes sent and received. This counter only counts the bytes in frames (packets) that carry data.

- **NWLink IPX: Frames Received/sec.** Indicates the rate at which data frames are received by the computer. This counter only counts the frames (packets) that carry data.

- **NWLink IPX: Frames Rejected/sec.** Indicates the rate at which data frames are rejected. This counter only counts the frames (packets) that carry data.

- **NWLink IPX: Frames Re-Sent/sec.** Indicates the rate at which data frames (packets) are re-sent by the computer. This counter only counts the frames or packets that carry data.

- **NWLink IPX: Frames Sent/sec.** Indicates the rate at which data frames are sent by the computer. This counter only counts the frames (packets) that carry data.

- **NWLink IPX: Frames/sec.** Indicates the rate at which data frames (packets) are processed by the computer. This counter is the sum of data frames sent and data frames received. This counter only counts the frames (packets) that carry data.

- **NWLink IPX: Packets Received/sec.** Indicates the rate at which packets are received by the computer. This counter counts all packets processed (that is, control as well as data packets).

- **NWLink IPX: Packets Sent/sec.** Indicates the rate at which packets are sent by the computer. This counter counts all packets sent by the computer (that is, control as well as data packets).

- **NWLink IPX: Packets/sec.** Indicates the rate at which packets are processed by the computer. This count is the sum of Packets Sent/sec and Packets Received/sec. This counter includes all packets processed (that is, control as well as data packets).

- **NWLink IPX: Piggyback Ack Queued/sec.** Indicates the rate at which piggybacked acknowledgments are queued. Piggyback acknowledgments are acknowledgments of received packets to be included in the next outgoing packet to the remote computer.

- **NWLink IPX: Piggyback Ack Timeouts.** Indicates the number of times a piggyback acknowledgment could not be sent because there was no outgoing packet to the remote on which to piggyback. A piggyback ack is an acknowledgment of a received packet sent along in an outgoing data packet to the remote computer. If no outgoing packet is sent within the timeout period, an ack packet is sent and the counter is incremented.

- **NWLink IPX: Window Send Average.** Indicates the running average number of data bytes sent before waiting for an acknowledgment from the remote computer.

- **NWLink IPX: Window Send Maximum.** Indicates the maximum number of data bytes sent before waiting for an acknowledgment from the remote computer.

NWLink NetBIOS Counters

The following Performance Monitor counters can help you troubleshoot NWLink NetBIOS problems:

- **NWLink NetBIOS: Bytes Total/sec.** Indicates the sum of Frame Bytes/sec and Datagram Bytes/sec. This is the total rate of bytes sent to or received from the network by the protocol, but it only counts the bytes in frames (packets) that carry data.

- **NWLink NetBIOS: Connection Session Timeouts.** Indicates the number of connections dropped due to a session timeout. This number is an accumulator and shows a running total.

- **NWLink NetBIOS: Connections Canceled.** Indicates the number of connections canceled. This number is an accumulator and shows a running total.

- **NWLink NetBIOS: Connections No Retries.** Indicates the total count of connections successfully made on the first try. This number is an accumulator and shows a running total.

- **NWLink NetBIOS: Connections Open.** Indicates the number of connections currently open for this protocol. This counter shows the current count only and does not accumulate over time.

- **NWLink NetBIOS: Connections With Retries.** Indicates the total count of connections made after retrying the attempt. A retry occurs when the first connection attempt fails. This number is an accumulator and shows a running total.

- **NWLink NetBIOS: Datagram Bytes Received/sec.** Indicates the rate at which datagram bytes are received by the computer. A datagram is a connectionless packet whose delivery to a remote computer is not guaranteed.

- **NWLink NetBIOS: Datagram Bytes Sent/sec.** Indicates the rate at which datagram bytes are sent from the computer. A datagram is a connectionless packet whose delivery to a remote computer is not guaranteed.

- **NWLink NetBIOS: Datagram Bytes/sec.** Indicates the rate at which datagram bytes are processed by the computer. This counter is the sum of datagram bytes sent as well as received. A datagram is a connectionless packet whose delivery to a remote is not guaranteed.

- **NWLink NetBIOS: Datagrams Received/sec.** Indicates the rate at which datagrams are received by the computer. A datagram is a connectionless packet whose delivery to a remote computer is not guaranteed.

- **NWLink NetBIOS: Datagrams Sent/sec.** Indicates the rate at which datagrams are sent from the computer. A datagram is a connectionless packet whose delivery to a remote computer is not guaranteed.

- **NWLink NetBIOS: Datagrams/sec.** Indicates the rate at which datagrams are processed by the computer. This counter displays the sum of datagrams sent and datagrams received. A datagram is a connectionless packet whose delivery to a remote is not guaranteed.

- **NWLink NetBIOS: Disconnects Local.** Indicates the number of session disconnections initiated by the local computer. This number is an accumulator and shows a running total.

- **NWLink NetBIOS: Disconnects Remote.** Indicates the number of session disconnections initiated by the remote computer. This number is an accumulator and shows a running total.

- **NWLink NetBIOS: Expirations Ack.** Indicates the count of T2 timer expirations.

- **NWLink NetBIOS: Expirations Response.** Indicates the count of T1 timer expirations.

- **NWLink NetBIOS: Failures Adapter.** Indicates the number of connections dropped due to an adapter failure. This number is an accumulator and shows a running total.

- **NWLink NetBIOS: Failures Link.** Indicates the number of connections dropped due to a link failure. This number is an accumulator and shows a running total.

- **NWLink NetBIOS: Failures No Listen.** Indicates the number of connections rejected because the remote computer was not listening for connection requests.

- **NWLink NetBIOS: Failures Not Found.** Indicates the number of connection attempts that failed because the remote computer could not be found. This number is an accumulator and shows a running total.

- **NWLink NetBIOS: Failures Resource Local.** Indicates the number of connections that failed because of resource problems or shortages on the local computer. This number is an accumulator and shows a running total.

- **NWLink NetBIOS: Failures Resource Remote.** Indicates the number of connections that failed because of resource problems or shortages on the remote computer. This number is an accumulator and shows a running total.

- **NWLink NetBIOS: Frame Bytes Received/sec.** Indicates the rate at which data bytes are received by the computer. This counter only counts the frames (packets) that carry data.

- **NWLink NetBIOS: Frame Bytes Rejected/sec.** Indicates the rate at which data bytes are rejected. This counter only counts the bytes in data frames (packets) that carry data.

- **NWLink NetBIOS: Frame Bytes Re-Sent/sec.** Indicates the rate at which data bytes are re-sent by the computer. This counter only counts the bytes in frames that carry data.

- **NWLink NetBIOS: Frame Bytes Sent/sec.** Indicates the rate at which data bytes are sent by the computer. This counter only counts the bytes in frames (packets) that carry data.

- **NWLink NetBIOS: Frame Bytes/sec.** Indicates the rate at which data bytes are processed by the computer. This counter is the sum of data frame bytes sent and received. This counter only counts the bytes in frames (packets) that carry data.

- **NWLink NetBIOS: Frames Received/sec.** Indicates the rate at which data frames are received by the computer. This counter only counts the frames (packets) that carry data.

- **NWLink NetBIOS: Frames Rejected/sec.** Indicates the rate at which data frames are rejected. This counter only counts the frames (packets) that carry data.

- **NWLink NetBIOS: Frames Re-Sent/sec.** Indicates the rate at which data frames (packets) are re-sent by the computer. This counter only counts the frames or packets that carry data.

- **NWLink NetBIOS: Frames Sent/sec.** Indicates the rate at which data frames are sent by the computer. This counter only counts the frames (packets) that carry data.

- **NWLink NetBIOS: Frames/sec.** Indicates the rate at which data frames (packets) are processed by the computer. This counter is the sum of data frames sent and data frames received. This counter only counts the frames (packets) that carry data.

- **NWLink NetBIOS: Packets Received/sec.** Indicates the rate at which packets are received by the computer. This counter counts all packets processed (that is, control as well as data packets).

- **NWLink NetBIOS: Packets Sent/sec.** Indicates the rate at which packets are sent by the computer. This counter counts all packets sent by the computer (that is, control as well as data packets).

- **NWLink NetBIOS: Packets/sec.** Indicates the rate at which packets are processed by the computer. This count is the sum of Packets Sent/sec and Packets Received/sec. This counter includes all packets processed (that is, control as well as data packets).

- **NWLink NetBIOS: Piggyback Ack Queued/sec.** Indicates the rate at which piggybacked acknowledgments are queued. Piggyback acknowledgments are acknowledgments of received packets to be included in the next outgoing packet to the remote computer.

- **NWLink NetBIOS: Piggyback Ack Timeouts.** Indicates the number of times a piggyback acknowledgment could not be sent because there was no outgoing packet to the remote on which to piggyback. A piggyback ack is an acknowledgment of a received packet sent along in an outgoing data packet to the remote computer. If no outgoing packet is sent within the timeout period, an ack packet is sent and the counter is incremented.

- **NWLink NetBIOS: Window Send Average.** Indicates the running average number of data bytes sent before waiting for an acknowledgment from the remote computer.

- **NWLink NetBIOS: Window Send Maximum.** Indicates the maximum number of data bytes sent before waiting for an acknowledgment from the remote computer.

NWLink SPX Counters

The following Performance Monitor counters can help you troubleshoot NWLink SPX problems:

- **NWLink SPX: Bytes Total/sec.** Indicates the sum of Frame Bytes/sec and Datagram Bytes/sec. This is the total rate of bytes sent to or received from the network by the protocol, but it only counts the bytes in frames (that is, packets) that carry data.

- **NWLink SPX: Connection Session Timeouts.** Indicates the number of connections dropped due to a session timeout. This number is an accumulator and shows a running total.

- **NWLink SPX: Connections Canceled.** Indicates the number of connections canceled. This number is an accumulator and shows a running total.

- **NWLink SPX: Connections No Retries.** Indicates the total count of connections successfully made on the first try. This number is an accumulator and shows a running total.

- **NWLink SPX: Connections Open.** Indicates the number of connections currently open for this protocol. This counter shows the current count only and does not accumulate over time.

- **NWLink SPX: Connections With Retries.** Indicates the total count of connections made after retrying the attempt. A retry occurs when the first connection attempt fails. This number is an accumulator and shows a running total.

- **NWLink SPX: Datagram Bytes Received/sec.** Indicates the rate at which datagram bytes are received by the computer. A datagram is a connectionless packet whose delivery to a remote computer is not guaranteed.

- **NWLink SPX: Datagram Bytes Sent/sec.** Indicates the rate at which datagram bytes are sent from the computer. A datagram is a connectionless packet whose delivery to a remote computer is not guaranteed.

- **NWLink SPX: Datagram Bytes/sec.** Indicates the rate at which datagram bytes are processed by the computer. This counter is the sum of datagram bytes sent as well as received. A datagram is a connectionless packet whose delivery to a remote is not guaranteed.

- **NWLink SPX: Datagrams Received/sec.** Indicates the rate at which datagrams are received by the computer. A datagram is a connectionless packet whose delivery to a remote computer is not guaranteed.

- **NWLink SPX: Datagrams Sent/sec.** Indicates the rate at which datagrams are sent from the computer. A datagram is a connectionless packet whose delivery to a remote computer is not guaranteed.

- **NWLink SPX: Datagrams/sec.** Indicates the rate at which datagrams are processed by the computer. This counter displays the sum of datagrams sent and datagrams received. A datagram is a connectionless packet whose delivery to a remote is not guaranteed.

- **NWLink SPX: Disconnects Local.** Indicates the number of session disconnections initiated by the local computer. This number is an accumulator and shows a running total.

- **NWLink SPX: Disconnects Remote.** Indicates the number of session disconnections initiated by the remote computer. This number is an accumulator and shows a running total.

- **NWLink SPX: Expirations Ack.** Indicates the count of T2 timer expirations.

- **NWLink SPX: Expirations Response.** Indicates the count of T1 timer expirations.

- **NWLink SPX: Failures Adapter.** Indicates the number of connections dropped due to an adapter failure. This number is an accumulator and shows a running total.

- **NWLink SPX: Failures Link.** Indicates the number of connections dropped due to a link failure. This number is an accumulator and shows a running total.

- **NWLink SPX: Failures No Listen.** Indicates the number of connections rejected because the remote computer was not listening for connection requests.

- **NWLink SPX: Failures Not Found.** Indicates the number of connection attempts that failed because the remote computer could not be found. This number is an accumulator and shows a running total.

- **NWLink SPX: Failures Resource Local.** Indicates the number of connections that failed because of resource problems or shortages on the local computer. This number is an accumulator and shows a running total.

- **NWLink SPX: Failures Resource Remote.** Indicates the number of connections that failed because of resource problems or shortages on the remote computer. This number is an accumulator and shows a running total.

- **NWLink SPX: Frame Bytes Received/sec.** Indicates the rate at which data bytes are received by the computer. This counter only counts the frames (packets) that carry data.

- **NWLink SPX: Frame Bytes Rejected/sec.** Indicates the rate at which data bytes are rejected. This counter only counts the bytes in data frames (packets) that carry data.

- **NWLink SPX: Frame Bytes Re-Sent/sec.** Indicates the rate at which data bytes are re-sent by the computer. This counter only counts the bytes in frames that carry data.

- **NWLink SPX: Frame Bytes Sent/sec.** Indicates the rate at which data bytes are sent by the computer. This counter only counts the bytes in frames (packets) that carry data.

- **NWLink SPX: Frame Bytes/sec.** Indicates the rate at which data bytes are processed by the computer. This counter is the sum of data frame bytes sent and received. This counter only counts the bytes in frames (packets) that carry data.

- **NWLink SPX: Frames Received/sec.** Indicates the rate at which data frames are received by the computer. This counter only counts the frames (packets) that carry data.

- **NWLink SPX: Frames Rejected/sec.** Indicates the rate at which data frames are rejected. This counter only counts the frames (packets) that carry data.

- **NWLink SPX: Frames Re-Sent/sec.** Indicates the rate at which data frames (packets) are re-sent by the computer. This counter only counts the frames or packets that carry data.

- **NWLink SPX: Frames Sent/sec.** Indicates the rate at which data frames are sent by the computer. This counter only counts the frames (packets) that carry data.

- **NWLink SPX: Frames/sec.** Indicates the rate at which data frames (or packets) are processed by the computer. This counter is the sum of data frames sent and data frames received. This counter only counts the frames (packets) that carry data.

- **NWLink SPX: Packets Received/sec.** Indicates the rate at which packets are received by the computer. This counter counts all packets processed (that is, control as well as data packets).

- **NWLink SPX: Packets Sent/sec.** Indicates the rate at which packets are sent by the computer. This counter counts all packets sent by the computer (that is, control as well as data packets).

- **NWLink SPX: Packets/sec.** Indicates the rate at which packets are processed by the computer. This count is the sum of Packets Sent/sec and Packets Received/sec. This counter includes all packets processed (that is, control as well as data packets).

- **NWLink SPX: Piggyback Ack Queued/sec.** Indicates the rate at which piggybacked acknowledgments are queued. Piggyback acknowledgments are acknowledgments of received packets to be included in the next outgoing packet to the remote computer.

- **NWLink SPX: Piggyback Ack Timeouts.** Indicates the number of times a piggyback acknowledgment could not be sent because there was no outgoing packet to the remote on which to piggyback. A piggyback ack is an acknowledgment of a received packet sent along in an outgoing data packet to the remote computer. If no outgoing packet is sent within the timeout period, an ack packet is sent and the counter is incremented.

- **NWLink SPX: Window Send Average.** Indicates the running average number of data bytes sent before waiting for an acknowledgment from the remote computer.

- **NWLink SPX: Window Send Maximum.** Indicates the maximum number of data bytes sent before waiting for an acknowledgment from the remote computer.

Objects Counters

The following Performance Monitor counters can help you troubleshoot problems with system objects:

- **Objects: Events.** Indicates the number of events in the computer at the time of data collection. This is an instantaneous count, not an average over the time interval. An event is used when two or more threads want to synchronize execution.

- **Objects: Mutexes.** Counts the number of mutexes in the computer at the time of data collection. This is an instantaneous count, not an average over the time interval. Mutexes are used by threads to make sure only one thread is executing some section of code.

- **Objects: Processes.** Indicates the number of processes in the computer at the time of data collection. This is an instantaneous count, not an average over the time interval. Each process represents the running of a program.

- **Objects: Sections.** Indicates the number of sections in the computer at the time of data collection. This is an instantaneous count, not an average over the time interval. A section is a portion of virtual memory created by a process for storing data. A process can share sections with other processes.

- **Objects: Semaphores.** Indicates the number of semaphores in the computer at the time of data collection. This is an instantaneous count, not an average over the time interval. Threads use semaphores to obtain exclusive access to data structures they share with other threads.

- **Objects: Threads.** Indicates the number of threads in the computer at the time of data collection. This is an instantaneous count, not an average over the time interval. A thread is the basic executable entity that can execute instructions in a processor.

Paging File Counters

The following Performance Monitor counters can help you troubleshoot paging file problems:

- **Paging File: % Usage.** Indicates the amount of the page file instance in use in percent (see also Process: Page File Bytes).

- **Paging File: % Usage Peak.** Indicates the peak usage of the page file instance in percent (see also Process: Page File Bytes Peak).

PhysicalDisk Counters

The following Performance Monitor counters can help you troubleshoot disk problems:

- **PhysicalDisk: % Disk Time.** Indicates the percentage of elapsed time that the selected disk drive is busy servicing read or write requests.

- **PhysicalDisk: % Disk Write Time.** Indicates the percentage of elapsed time that the selected disk drive is busy servicing write requests.

- **PhysicalDisk: Avg. Disk Bytes/Read.** Indicates the average number of bytes transferred from the disk during read operations.

- **PhysicalDisk: Avg. Disk Bytes/Transfer.** Indicates the average number of bytes transferred to or from the disk during write or read operations.

- **PhysicalDisk: Avg. Disk Bytes/Write.** Indicates the average number of bytes transferred to the disk during write operations.

- **PhysicalDisk: Avg. Disk Queue Length.** Indicates the average number of both read and write requests queued for the selected disk during the sample interval.

- **PhysicalDisk: Avg. Disk Read Queue Length.** Indicates the average number of read requests queued for the selected disk during the sample interval.

- **PhysicalDisk: Avg. Disk sec/Read.** Indicates the average time in seconds of a data read from the disk.

- **PhysicalDisk: Avg. Disk sec/Transfer.** Indicates the time in seconds of the average disk transfer.

- **PhysicalDisk: Avg. Disk sec/Write.** Indicates the average time in seconds of a data write to the disk.

- **PhysicalDisk: Avg. Disk Write Queue Length.** Indicates the average number of write requests queued for the selected disk during the sample interval.

- **PhysicalDisk: Current Disk Queue Length.** Indicates the number of requests outstanding on the disk at the time the performance data is collected. It includes requests in service at the time of the snapshot. This is an instantaneous length, not an average over the time interval. Multispindle disk devices can have multiple requests active at one time, but other concurrent requests are awaiting service. This counter might reflect a transitory high or low queue length, but if there is a sustained load on the disk drive, it is likely that this will be consistently high. Requests are experiencing delays proportional to the length of this queue minus the number of spindles on the disks. This difference should average less than two for good performance.

- **PhysicalDisk: Disk Bytes/sec.** Indicates the rate at which bytes are transferred to or from the disk during write or read operations.

- **PhysicalDisk: Disk Read Bytes/sec.** Indicates the rate at which bytes are transferred from the disk during read operations.

- **PhysicalDisk: Disk Reads/sec.** Indicates the rate of read operations on the disk.

- **PhysicalDisk: Disk Transfers/sec.** Indicates the rate of read and write operations on the disk.

- **PhysicalDisk: Disk Write Bytes.** Indicates the rate at which bytes are transferred to the disk during write operations.

- **PhysicalDisk: Disk Writes/sec.** Indicates the rate of write operations on the disk.

Process Counters

The following Performance Monitor counters can help you troubleshoot system process problems:

- **Process: % Privileged Time.** Indicates the percentage of elapsed time that this process's threads have spent executing code in Privileged mode. When a Windows NT system service is called, the service often runs in Privileged mode to gain access to system-private data. Such data is protected from access by threads executing in User mode. Calls to the system can be explicit, or they can be implicit such as when a page fault or an interrupt occurs. Unlike some early operating systems, Windows NT uses process boundaries for subsystem protection in addition to the traditional protection of User and Privileged modes. These subsystem processes provide additional protection. Therefore, some work done by Windows NT on behalf of your application might appear in other subsystem processes in addition to the privileged time in your process.

- **Process: % Processor Time.** Indicates the percentage of elapsed time that all the threads of this process used the processor to execute instructions. An instruction is the basic unit of execution in a computer, a thread is the object that executes instructions, and a process is the object created when a program is run. Code executed to handle certain hardware interrupts or trap conditions can be counted for this process.

- **Process: % User Time.** Indicates the percentage of elapsed time that this process's threads have spent executing code in User mode. Applications execute in User mode as do subsystems such as the Window Manager and the graphics engine. Code executing in User mode cannot damage the integrity of the Windows NT executive, kernel, and device drivers. Unlike some early operating systems, Windows NT uses process boundaries for subsystem protection in addition to the traditional protection of User and Privileged modes. These subsystem processes provide additional protection. Therefore, some work done by Windows NT on behalf of your application might appear in other subsystem processes in addition to the privileged time in your process.

- **Process: Elapsed Time.** Indicates the total elapsed time (in seconds) that this process has been running.

- **Process: Handle Count.** Provides the total number of handles currently open by this process. This number is the sum of the handles currently open by each thread in this process.

- **Process: ID Process.** Indicates the unique identifier of this process. ID process numbers are reused; therefore, they only identify a process for the lifetime of that process.

- **Process: Page Faults/sec.** Indicates the rate of page faults by the threads executing in this process. A page fault occurs when a thread refers to a virtual memory page not in its working set in main memory. This does not cause the page to be fetched from disk if it is on the standby list (and hence already in main memory) or if it is in use by another process with whom the page is shared.

- **Process: Page File Bytes.** Indicates the current number of bytes this process has used in the paging file(s). Paging files are used to store pages of memory used by the process that are not contained in other files. Paging files are shared by all processes, and lack of space in paging files can prevent other processes from allocating memory.

- **Process: Page File Bytes Peak.** Indicates the maximum number of bytes this process has used in the paging file(s). Paging files are used to store pages of memory used by the process that are not contained in other files. Paging files are shared by all processes, and lack of space in paging files can prevent other processes from allocating memory.

- **Process: Pool Nonpaged Bytes.** Indicates the number of bytes in the non-paged pool, a system memory area where space is acquired by operating system components as they accomplish their appointed tasks. Nonpaged pool pages cannot be paged out to the paging file. Instead, they remain in main memory as long as they are allocated.

- **Process: Pool Paged Bytes.** Indicates the number of bytes in the paged pool, a system memory area where space is acquired by operating system components as they accomplish their appointed tasks. Paged pool pages can be paged out to the paging file when not accessed by the system for sustained periods of time.

- **Process: Priority Base.** Indicates the current base priority of this process. Threads within a process can raise and lower their own base priority relative to the process's base priority.

- **Process: Private Bytes.** Indicates the current number of bytes this process has allocated that cannot be shared with other processes.

- **Process: Thread Count.** Indicates the number of threads currently active in this process. An instruction is the basic unit of execution in a processor, and a thread is the object that executes instructions. Every running process has at least one thread.

- **Process: Virtual Bytes.** Indicates the current size in bytes of the virtual address space the process is using. Use of virtual address space does not necessarily imply corresponding use of either disk or main memory pages. Virtual space is finite, however. By using too much, the process might limit its capability to load libraries.

- **Process: Virtual Bytes Peak.** Indicates the maximum number of bytes of virtual address space the process has used at any one time. Use of virtual address space does not necessarily imply corresponding use of either disk or main memory pages. Virtual space is finite, however. By using too much, the process might limit its capability to load libraries.

- **Process: Working Set.** Indicates the current number of bytes in the working set of this process. The working set is the set of memory pages touched recently by the threads in the process. If free memory in the computer is above a threshold, pages are left in the working set of a process even if they are not in use. When free memory falls below a threshold, pages are trimmed from working sets. If they are needed, they then will be soft-faulted back into the working set before they leave main memory.

- **Process: Working Set Peak.** Indicates the maximum number of bytes in the working set of this process at any point in time. The working set is the set of memory pages touched recently by the threads in the process. If free memory in the computer is above a threshold, pages are left in the working set of a process even if they are not in use. When free memory falls below a threshold, pages are trimmed from working sets. If they are needed, they then will be soft-faulted back into the working set before they leave main memory.

Processor Counters

The following Performance Monitor counters can help you troubleshoot processor problems:

- **Processor: % DPC Time.** Indicates the percentage of elapsed time that the processor spent in Deferred Procedure Calls. When a hardware device interrupts the processor, the Interrupt Handler might elect to execute the majority of its work in a DPC. DPCs run at lower priority than interrupts and permit interrupts to occur while DPCs execute. Deferred Procedure Calls are executed in Privileged mode, so this is a component of Processor: % Privileged Time. This counter can help determine the source of excessive time being spent in Privileged mode.

- **Processor: % Interrupt Time.** Indicates the percentage of elapsed time that the processor spent handling hardware interrupts. When a hardware device interrupts the processor, the Interrupt Handler executes to handle the condition, usually by signaling I/O completion and possibly by issuing another pending I/O request. Some of this work can be done in a Deferred Procedure Call (see % DPC Time). Time spent in DPCs, however, is not counted as time in interrupts. Interrupts are executed in Privileged mode, so this is a component of Processor: % Privileged Time. This counter can help determine the source of excessive time being spent in Privileged mode.

- **Processor: % Privileged Time.** Indicates the percentage of processor time spent in Privileged mode in non-idle threads. The Windows NT service layer, the executive routines, and the Windows NT kernel execute in Privileged mode. Device drivers for most devices other than graphics adapters and printers also execute in Privileged mode. Unlike some early operating systems, Windows NT uses process boundaries for subsystem protection in addition to the traditional protection of User and Privileged modes. These subsystem processes provide additional protection. Therefore, some work done by Windows NT on behalf of your application might appear in other subsystem processes in addition to the privileged time in your process.

- **Processor: % Processor Time.** Indicates the percentage of elapsed time that a processor is busy executing a non-idle thread. It can be viewed as a fraction of the time spent doing useful work. Each processor is assigned an idle thread in the idle process, which consumes unproductive processor cycles not used by any other threads.

- **Processor: % User Time.** Indicates the percentage of processor time spent in User mode in non-idle threads. All application code and subsystem code executes in User mode. The graphics engine, graphics device drivers, printer device drivers, and the Window Manager also execute in User mode. Code executing in User mode cannot damage the integrity of the Windows NT executive, kernel, and device drivers. Unlike some early operating systems, Windows NT uses process boundaries for subsystem protection in addition to the traditional protection of User and Privileged modes. These subsystem processes provide additional protection. Therefore, some work done by Windows NT on behalf of your application might appear in other subsystem processes in addition to the privileged Time in your process.

- **Processor: APC Bypasses/sec.** Indicates the rate at which kernel APC interrupts were short-circuited.

- **Processor: DPC Bypasses/sec.** Indicates the rate at which dispatch interrupts were short-circuited.

- **Processor: DPC Rate.** Indicates the average rate at which DPC objects are queued to this processor's DPC queue per clock tick.

- **Processor: DPCs Queued/sec.** Indicates the rate at which DPC objects are queued to this processor's DPC queue.

- **Processor: Interrupts/sec.** Indicates the number of device interrupts the processor is experiencing. A device interrupts the processor when it has completed a task or when it otherwise requires attention. Normal thread execution is suspended during interrupts. An interrupt might cause the processor to switch to another, higher-priority thread. Clock interrupts are frequent and periodic and create a background of interrupt activity.

Redirector Counters

The following Performance Monitor counters can help you troubleshoot redirector problems:

- **Redirector: Bytes Received/sec.** Indicates the rate at which bytes are coming into the Redirector from the network. It includes all application data as well as network protocol information (such as packet headers).

- **Redirector: Bytes Total/sec.** Indicates the rate at which the Redirector is processing data bytes. This includes all application and file data in addition to protocol information such as packet headers.

- **Redirector: Bytes Transmitted/sec.** Indicates the rate at which bytes are leaving the Redirector to the network. It includes all application data as well as network protocol information (such as packet headers and the like).

- **Redirector: Connects Core.** Counts the number of connections you have to servers running the original MS-Net SMB protocol including MS-Net itself and Xenix and Vax's.

- **Redirector: Connects LAN Manager 2.0.** Counts connections to LAN Manager 2.0 servers including LMX servers.

- **Redirector: Connects LAN Manager 2.1.** Counts connections to LAN Manager 2.1 servers including LMX servers.

- **Redirector: Connects Windows NT.** Counts connections to Windows NT computers.

- **Redirector: Current Commands.** Counts the number of requests to the Redirector currently queued for service. If this number is much larger than the number of network adapter cards installed in the computer, the network(s) or the server(s) being accessed is seriously bottlenecked.

- **Redirector: File Data Operations/sec.** Indicates the rate at which the Redirector is processing data operations. One operation includes (hopefully) many bytes. We say "hopefully" here because each operation has overhead. You can determine the efficiency of this path by dividing Bytes/sec by this counter to determine the average number of bytes transferred per operation.

- **Redirector: File Read Operations/sec.** Indicates the rate at which applications are asking the Redirector for data. Each call to a file system or similar Application programming interface (API) call counts as one operation.

- **Redirector: File Write Operations/sec.** Indicates the rate at which applications are sending data to the Redirector. Each call to a file system or similar Application programming interface (API) call counts as one operation.

- **Redirector: Network Errors/sec.** Counts serious unexpected errors that generally indicate that the Redirector and one or more servers are having serious communication difficulties. A Server Manager Block (SMB) protocol error, for example, generates a network error. This results in an entry in the system Event Log, so look there for details.

- **Redirector: Packets Received/sec.** Indicates the rate at which the Redirector is receiving packets (also called SMBs or Server Message Blocks). Network transmissions are divided into packets. The average number of bytes received in a packet can be obtained by dividing Bytes Received/sec by this counter. Some packets received might not contain incoming data. An acknowledgment to a write made by the Redirector, for example, would count as an incoming packet.

- **Redirector: Packets Transmitted/sec.** Indicates the rate at which the Redirector is sending packets (also called SMBs or Server Message Blocks). Network transmissions are divided into packets. The average number of bytes transmitted in a packet can be obtained by dividing Bytes Transmitted/sec by this counter.

- **Redirector: Packets/sec.** Indicates the rate at which the Redirector is processing data packets. One packet includes (hopefully) many bytes. We say "hopefully" here because each packet has protocol overhead. You can determine the efficiency of this path by dividing Bytes/sec by this counter to determine the average number of bytes transferred per packet. You also can divide this counter by Operations/sec to determine the average number of packets per operation, another measure of efficiency.

- **Redirector: Read Bytes Cache/sec.** Indicates the rate at which applications on your computer are accessing the cache using the Redirector. Some of these data requests can be satisfied by merely retrieving the data from the system cache on your own computer if it happened to be used recently and there was room to keep it in the cache. Requests that miss the cache cause a page fault (see Read Bytes Paging/sec).

- **Redirector: Read Bytes Network/sec.** Indicates the rate at which applications are reading data across the network. For one reason or another, the data was not in the system cache, and these bytes actually came across the network.

Dividing this number by Bytes Received/sec indicates the efficiency of data coming in from the network because all of these bytes are real application data (see Bytes Received/sec).

- **Redirector: Read Bytes Non-Paging/sec.** Indicates the bytes read by the Redirector in response to normal file requests by an application when they are redirected to come from another computer. In addition to file requests, this counter includes other methods of reading across the network such as named pipes and transactions. This counter does not count network protocol information, just application data.

- **Redirector: Read Bytes Paging/sec.** Indicates the rate at which the Redirector is attempting to read bytes in response to page faults. Page faults are caused by the loading of modules (such as programs and libraries), by a miss in the cache (see Read Bytes cache/sec), or by files directly mapped into the address space of applications (a high-performance feature of Windows NT).

- **Redirector: Read Operations Random/sec.** Counts the rate at which, on a file-by-file basis, reads are made that are not sequential. If a read is made using a particular file handle and then is followed by another read that is not immediately the contiguous next byte, this counter is incremented by one.

- **Redirector: Read Packets Small/sec.** Indicates the rate at which reads less than one-fourth of the server's negotiated buffer size are made by applications. Too many of these could indicate a waste of buffers on the server. This counter is incremented once for each read. It does not count packets.

- **Redirector: Read Packets/sec.** Indicates the rate at which read packets are being placed on the network. Each time a single packet is sent with a request to read data remotely, this counter is incremented by one.

- **Redirector: Reads Denied/sec.** Indicates the rate at which the server is unable to accommodate requests for raw reads. When a read is much larger than the server's negotiated buffer size, the Redirector requests a raw read. If granted, the raw read would permit the transfer of the data without lots of protocol overhead on each packet. To accomplish this, the server must lock out other requests, so the request is denied if the server is really busy.

- **Redirector: Reads Large/sec.** Indicates the rate at which reads more than two times the server's negotiated buffer size are made by applications. Too many of these could place a strain on server resources. This counter is incremented once for each read. It does not count packets.

- **Redirector: Server Disconnects.** Counts the number of times a server has disconnected your Redirector (see also Server Reconnects).

- **Redirector: Server Reconnects.** Counts the number of times your Redirector has had to reconnect to a server to complete a new active request. You can be disconnected by the server if you remain inactive for too long.

Locally, even if all your remote files are closed, the Redirector will keep your connections intact for (nominally) 10 minutes. Such inactive connections are called dormant connections. Reconnecting is expensive in time.

- **Redirector: Server Sessions.** Counts the total number of security objects the Redirector has managed. A logon to a server followed by a network access to the same server, for example, establishes one connection but two sessions.

- **Redirector: Server Sessions Hung.** Counts the number of active sessions timed out and unable to proceed due to a lack of response from the remote server.

- **Redirector: Write Bytes Cache/sec.** Indicates the rate at which applications on your computer are writing to the cache using the Redirector. The data might not leave your computer immediately. It might be retained in the cache for further modification before being written to the network. This saves network traffic. Each write of a byte into the cache is counted here.

- **Redirector: Write Bytes Network/sec.** Indicates the rate at which your applications are writing data across the network. Either the system cache was bypassed (as for named pipes or transactions) or the cache wrote the bytes to make room for other data. Dividing this counter by Bytes Transmitted/sec indicates the efficiency of data written to the network because all these bytes are real application data (see Transmitted Bytes/sec).

- **Redirector: Write Bytes Non-Paging/sec.** Indicates the rate of the bytes written by the Redirector in response to normal file outputs by an application when they are redirected to go to another computer. In addition to file requests, this counter includes other methods of writing across the network such as named pipes and transactions. This counter does not count network protocol information, just application data.

- **Redirector: Write Bytes Paging/sec.** Indicates the rate at which the Redirector is attempting to write bytes changed in the pages being used by applications. The program data changed by modules (such as programs and libraries) that were loaded over the network are "paged out" when no longer needed. Other output pages come from the cache (see Write Bytes cache/sec).

- **Redirector: Write Operations Random/sec.** Indicates the rate at which, on a file-by-file basis, writes are made that are not sequential. If a write is made using a particular file handle and then is followed by another write that is not immediately the next contiguous byte, this counter is incremented by one.

- **Redirector: Write Packets Small/sec.** Indicates the rate at which writes are made by applications that are less than one-fourth of the server's negotiated buffer size. Too many of these could indicate a waste of buffers on the server. This counter is incremented once for each write. It counts writes, not packets.

- **Redirector: Write Packets/sec.** Indicates the rate at which writes are being sent to the network. Each time a single packet is sent with a request to write remote data, this counter is incremented by one.

- **Redirector: Writes Denied/sec.** Indicates the rate at which the server is unable to accommodate requests for raw writes. When a write is much larger than the server's negotiated buffer size, the Redirector requests a raw write. If granted, the raw write would permit the transfer of the data without lots of protocol overhead on each packet. To accomplish this, the server must lock out other requests, so the request is denied if the server is really busy.

- **Redirector: Writes Large/sec.** Indicates the rate at which writes are made by applications that are more than two times the server's negotiated buffer size. Too many of these could place a strain on server resources. This counter is incremented once for each write. It counts writes, not packets.

Server Counters

The following Performance Monitor counters can help you troubleshoot problems with the server:

- **Server: Blocking Requests Rejected.** Indicates the number of times the server has rejected blocking SMBs due to insufficient count of free work items. Indicates whether the maxworkitem or minfreeworkitems server parameters need tuning.

- **Server: Bytes Received/sec.** Provides the number of bytes the server has received from the network and indicates how busy the server is.

- **Server: Bytes Total/sec.** Provides the number of bytes the server has sent to and received from the network. This value provides an overall indication of how busy the server is.

- **Server: Bytes/Transmitted/sec.** Indicates the number of bytes the server has sent on the network and indicates how busy the server is.

- **Server: Context Blocks Queued/sec.** Indicates the rate at which work context blocks had to be placed on the server's FSP queue to await server action.

- **Server: Errors Access Permissions.** Indicates the number of times that opens on behalf of clients have failed with STATUS_ACCESS_DENIED. Also can indicate whether somebody is randomly attempting to access files in hopes of getting at something that was not properly protected.

- **Server: Errors Granted Access.** Indicates the number of times accesses to files opened successfully were denied. Also can indicate attempts to access files without proper access authorization.

- **Server: Errors Logon.** Indicates the number of failed logon attempts to the server. Also can indicate whether password-guessing programs are being used to crack the security on the server.

- **Server: Errors System.** Indicates the number of times an internal server error was detected. Unexpected errors usually indicate a problem with the server.

- **Server: File Directory Searches.** Indicates the number of searches for files currently active in the server and indicates current server activity.

- **Server: Files Open.** Indicates the number of files currently opened in the server and indicates current server activity.

- **Server: Files Opened Total.** Indicates the number of successful open attempts performed by the server on behalf of clients. This is useful in determining the amount of file I/O, in determining overhead for path-based operations, and in determining the effectiveness of oplocks.

- **Server: Logon Total.** Includes all interactive logons, network logons, service logons, successful logon, and failed logons since the machine was last rebooted.

- **Server: Logon/sec.** Indicates the rate of all server logons.

- **Server: Pool Nonpaged Bytes.** Indicates the number of bytes of nonpageable computer memory the server is currently using. Also can help in determining good values for the maxnonpagedmemoryusage parameter.

- **Server: Pool Nonpaged Failures.** Indicates the number of times that allocations from nonpaged pool have failed. Also indicates that the computer's physical memory is too small.

- **Server: Pool Nonpaged Peak.** Indicates the maximum number of bytes of nonpaged pool the server has had in use at any one point. Also indicates how much physical memory the computer should have.

- **Server: Pool Paged Bytes.** Indicates the number of bytes of pageable computer memory the server is currently using. Also can help in determining good values for the maxpagedmemoryusage parameter.

- **Server: Pool Paged Failures.** Indicates the number of times that allocations from paged pool have failed. Also indicates that the computer's physical memory of page file is too small.

- **Server: Pool Paged Peak.** Indicates the maximum number of bytes of paged pool the server has had allocated. Also indicates the proper sizes of the page file(s) and physical memory.

- **Server: Server Sessions.** Displays the number of sessions currently active in the server and indicates current server activity.

- **Server: Sessions Errored Out.** Indicates the number of sessions that have been closed due to unexpected error conditions. Also indicates how frequently network problems cause dropped sessions on the server.

- **Server: Sessions Forced Off.** Displays the number of sessions that have been forced to log off. Also can indicate how many sessions were forced to log off due to logon time constraints.

- **Server: Sessions Logged Off.** Indicates the number of sessions that have terminated normally. This is useful in interpreting the Sessions Times Out and Sessions Errored Out statistics and allows percentage calculations.

- **Server: Sessions Timed Out.** Displays the number of sessions that have been closed due to idle time exceeding the autodisconnect parameter for the server. Also shows whether the autodisconnect setting is helping to conserve resources.

- **Server: Work Item Shortages.** Displays the number of times STATUS_DATA_NOT_ACCEPTED was returned at receive indication time. This occurs when no work items are available or can be allocated to service the incoming request. Also indicates whether the initworkitems or maxworkitems parameters need tuning.

Server Work Queues Counters

The following Performance Monitor counters can help you troubleshoot problems with the server work queues:

- **Server Work Queues: Active Threads.** Indicates the number of threads currently working on a request from the server client for this CPU. The system keeps this number as low as possible to minimize unnecessary context switching. This is an instantaneous count for the CPU, not an average over time.

- **Server Work Queues: Available Threads.** Indicates the number of server threads on this CPU not currently working on requests from a client. The server dynamically adjusts the number of threads to maximize server performance.

- **Server Work Queues: Available Work Items.** Indicates the instantaneous number of available work items for this CPU. Every request from a client is represented in the server as a "work item," and the server maintains a pool of available work items per CPU to speed processing. A sustained near-zero value indicates the need to increase the MinFreeWorkItems Registry value for the Server service. This value will always be 0 in the Blocking Queue instance.

- **Server Work Queues: Borrowed Work Items.** Indicates that the CPU has borrowed a free work item from another CPU. Every request from a client is represented in the server as a work item, and the server maintains a pool of available work items per CPU to speed processing. An increasing value of this running counter might indicate the need to increase the MaxWorkItems or MinFreeWorkItems Registry values for the Server service. This value will always be 0 in the Blocking Queue instance.

- **Server Work Queues: Bytes Received/sec.** Indicates the rate at which the server is receiving bytes from the network clients on this CPU. This value is a measure of how busy the server is.

- **Server Work Queues: Bytes Sent/sec.** Indicates the rate at which the server is sending bytes to the network clients on this CPU. This value is a measure of how busy the server is.

- **Server Work Queues: Bytes Transferred/sec.** Indicates the rate at which the server is sending and receiving bytes with the network clients on this CPU. This value is a measure of how busy the server is.

- **Server Work Queues: Context Blocks Queued/sec.** Indicates the rate that work context blocks had to be placed on the server's FSP queue to await server action.

- **Server Work Queues: Current Clients.** Indicates the instantaneous count of the clients being serviced by this CPU. The server actively balances the client load across all the CPUs in the system. This value will always be 0 in the Blocking Queue instance.

- **Server Work Queues: Queue Length.** Indicates the current length of the server work queue for this CPU. A sustained queue length greater than 4 might indicate processor congestion. This is an instantaneous count, not an average over time.

- **Server Work Queues: Read Bytes/sec.** Indicates the rate at which the server is reading data from files for the clients on this CPU. This value is a measure of how busy the server is.

- **Server Work Queues: Read Operations/sec.** Indicates the rate at which the server is performing file read operations for the clients on this CPU. This value is a measure of how busy the server is. This value will always be 0 in the Blocking Queue instance.

- **Server Work Queues: Total Bytes/sec.** Indicates the rate at which the server is reading and writing data to and from the files for the clients on this CPU. This value is a measure of how busy the server is.

- **Server Work Queues: Total Operations/sec.** Indicates the rate at which the server is performing file read and file write operations for the clients on this CPU. This value is a measure of how busy the server is. This value will always be 0 in the Blocking Queue instance.

- **Server Work Queues: Work Item Shortages.** Represents a work item. The server maintains a pool of available work items per CPU to speed processing. A sustained value greater than zero indicates the need to increase the MaxWorkItems Registry value for the Server service. This value will always be 0 in the Blocking Queue instance.

- **Server Work Queues: Write Bytes/sec.** Indicates the rate at which the server is writing data to files for the clients on this CPU. This value is a measure of how busy the server is.

- **Server Work Queues: Write Operations/sec.** Indicates the rate at which the server is performing file write operations for the clients on this CPU. This value is a measure of how busy the server is. This value will always be 0 in the Blocking Queue instance.

System Counters

The following Performance Monitor counters can help you troubleshoot problems with the system:

- **System: % Registry Quota in Use.** Indicates the percentage of the Total Registry Quota Allowed currently in use by the system.

- **System: % Total DPC Time.** Indicates the sum of the % DPC Time of all processors divided by the number of processors in the system (see Processor: % DPC Time).

- **System: % Total Interrupt Time.** Indicates the sum of the % Interrupt Time of all processors divided by the number of processors in the system (see Processor: % Interrupt Time).

- **System: % Total Privileged Time.** Indicates the average percentage of time spent in Privileged mode by all processors. On a multiprocessor system, if all processors are always in Privileged mode, the value is 100% If one-quarter of the processors are in Privileged mode, the value is 25%. When a Windows NT system service is called, the service often runs in Privileged mode to gain access to system-private data. Such data is protected from access by threads executing in User mode. Calls to the system might be explicit, or they might be implicit such as when a page fault or an interrupt occurs. Unlike some early operating systems, Windows NT uses process boundaries for subsystem protection in addition to the traditional protection of User and Privileged modes. These subsystem processes provide additional protection. Therefore, some work done by Windows NT on behalf of an application might appear in other subsystem processes in addition to the privileged time in the application process.

- **System: % Total Processor Time.** Indicates the average percentage of time that all the processors on the system are busy executing nonidle threads. On a multiprocessor system, if all processors are always busy, the value is 100% If half the processors are busy, the value is 50%. If one-quarter of the processors are busy, the value is 25%. This counter can be viewed as the fraction of time spent doing useful work. Each processor is assigned an idle thread in the idle process, which consumes unproductive processor cycles not used by any other threads.

- **System: % Total User Time.** Indicates the average percentage of time spent in User mode by all processors. Applications execute in User mode as do subsystems such as the Windows manager and the graphics engine. Code executing in User mode cannot damage the integrity of the Windows NT executive, kernel, and device drivers. Unlike some early operating systems, Windows NT uses process boundaries for subsystem protection in addition to the traditional protection of User and Privileged modes. These subsystem processes provide additional protection. Therefore, some work done by Windows NT on behalf of an application might appear in other subsystem processes in addition to the privileged time in the application process.

- **System: Alignment Fixups/sec.** Indicates the rate of alignment faults fixed by the system.

- **System: Context Switches/sec.** Indicates the rate of switches from one thread to another. Thread switches can occur either inside a single process or across processes. A thread switch can be caused either by one thread asking another for information or by a thread being preempted by another, higher-priority thread becoming ready to run. Unlike some early operating systems, Windows NT uses process boundaries for subsystem protection in addition to the traditional protection of User and Privileged modes. These subsystem processes provide additional protection. Therefore, some work done by Windows NT on behalf of an application might appear in other subsystem processes in addition to the privileged time in the application. Switching to the subsystem process causes one context switch in the application thread. Switching back causes another context switch in the subsystem thread.

- **System: Exception Dispatches/sec.** Indicates the rate of exceptions dispatched by the system.

- **System: File Control Bytes/sec.** Indicates an aggregate of bytes transferred for all file system operations that are neither reads nor writes. These operations usually include file system control requests or requests for information about device characteristics or status.

- **System: File Control Operations/sec.** Indicates an aggregate of all file system operations that are neither reads nor writes. These operations usually include file system control requests or requests for information about device characteristics or status.

- **System: File Data Operations/sec.** Indicates the rate at which the computer is issuing read and write operations to file system devices. It does not include file control operations.

- **System: File Read Bytes/sec.** Indicates an aggregate of the bytes transferred for all the file system read operations on the computer.

- **System: File Read Operations/sec.** Provides an aggregate of all the file system read operations on the computer.

- **System: File Write Bytes/sec.** Provides an aggregate of the bytes transferred for all the file system write operations on the computer.

- **System: File Write Operations/sec.** Provides an aggregate of all the file system write operations on the computer.

- **System: Floating Emulations/sec.** Indicates the rate of floating emulations performed by the system.

- **System: Processor Queue Length.** Indicates the instantaneous length of the processor queue in units of threads. This counter always is 0 unless you also are monitoring a thread counter. All processors use a single queue in which threads wait for processor cycles. This length does not include the threads currently executing. A sustained processor queue length greater than 2 generally indicates processor congestion. This is an instantaneous count, not an average over the time interval.

- **System: Systems Calls/sec.** Indicates the frequency of calls to Windows NT system service routines. These routines perform all the basic scheduling and synchronization of activities on the computer, and they provide access to non graphical devices, memory management, and name space management.

- **System: System Up Time.** Indicates the total time (in seconds) that the computer has been operational since it was last started.

- **System: Total APC Bypasses/sec.** Indicates the overall rate at which kernel APC interrupts were short-circuited across all processors.

- **System: Total DPC Bypasses/sec.** Indicates the overall rate at which dispatch interrupts were short-circuited across all processors.

- **System: Total DPC Rate.** Indicates the average rate at which DPC objects are queued to all processors' DPC queues per clock tick.

- **System: Total DPCs Queued/sec.** Indicates the rate at which DPC objects are queued to all processors' DPC queues per clock tick.

- **System: Total Interrupts/sec.** Indicates the rate at which the computer is receiving and servicing hardware interrupts. Some devices that might generate interrupts are the system timer, the mouse, data communication lines, network interface cards, and other peripheral devices. This counter provides an indication of how busy these devices are on a computer-wide basis (see Processor: Interrupts/sec).

Telephony Counters

The following Performance Monitor counters can help you troubleshoot problems with the telephony service:

- **Telephony: Active Lines.** Indicates the number of telephone lines serviced by this computer that are currently active.

- **Telephony: Active Telephones.** Displays the number of telephone devices currently being monitored.
- **Telephony: Client Apps.** Indicates the number of applications currently using telephony services.
- **Telephony: Current Incoming Calls.** Indicates the number of current incoming calls being serviced by this computer.
- **Telephony: Current Outgoing Calls.** Indicates the number of current outgoing calls being serviced by this computer.
- **Telephony: Incoming Calls/sec.** Indicates the rate of incoming calls answered by this computer.
- **Telephony: Lines.** Indicates the number of telephone lines serviced by this computer.
- **Telephony: Outgoing Calls/sec.** Indicates the rate of outgoing calls made by this computer.
- **Telephony: Telephone Devices.** Indicates the number of telephone devices serviced by this computer.

Thread Counters

The following Performance Monitor counters can help you troubleshoot problems with threads:

- **Thread: % Privileged Time.** Indicates the percentage of elapsed time that this thread has spent executing code in Privileged mode. When a Windows NT system service is called, the service often runs in Privileged mode to gain access to system-private data. Such data is protected from access by threads executing in User mode. Calls to the system might be explicit, or they might be implicit such as when a page fault or an interrupt occurs. Unlike some early operating systems, Windows NT uses process boundaries for subsystem protection in addition to the traditional protection of User and Privileged modes. These subsystem processes provide additional protection. Therefore, some work done by Windows NT on behalf of your application might appear in other subsystem processes in addition to the privileged time in your process.
- **Thread: % Processor Time.** Indicates the percentage of elapsed time that this thread used the processor to execute instructions. An instruction is the basic unit of execution in a processor, and a thread is the object that executes instructions. Code executed to handle certain hardware interrupts or trap conditions can be counted for this thread.
- **Thread: % User Time.** Indicates the percentage of elapsed time that this thread has spent executing code in User mode. Applications execute in User mode as do subsystems such as the Window Manager and the graphics engine. Code executing in User mode cannot damage the integrity of the Windows NT

executive, kernel, and device drivers. Unlike some early operating systems, Windows NT uses process boundaries for subsystem protection in addition to the traditional protection of User and Privileged modes. These subsystem processes provide additional protection. Therefore, some work done by Windows NT on behalf of your application might appear in other subsystem processes in addition to the privileged time in your process.

- **Thread: Context Switches/sec.** Indicates the rate of switches from one thread to another. Thread switches can occur either inside a single process or across processes. A thread switch can be caused either by one thread asking another for information or by a thread being preempted by another, higher-priority thread becoming ready to run. Unlike some early operating systems, Windows NT uses process boundaries for subsystem protection in addition to the traditional protection of User and Privileged modes. These subsystem processes provide additional protection. Therefore, some work done by Windows NT on behalf of an application might appear in other subsystem processes in addition to the privileged time in the application. Switching to the subsystem process causes one context switch in the application thread. Switching back causes another context switch in the subsystem thread.

- **Thread: Elapsed Time.** Indicates the total elapsed time (in seconds) that this thread has been running.

- **Thread: ID Process.** Indicates the unique identifier of this process. ID process numbers are reused; therefore, they only identify a process for the lifetime of that process.

- **Thread: ID Thread.** Indicates the unique identifier of this thread. ID thread numbers are reused; therefore, they only identify a thread for the lifetime of that thread.

- **Thread: Priority Base.** Indicates the current base priority of this thread. The system might raise the thread's dynamic priority above the base priority if the thread is handling user input, or it might lower it towards the base priority if the thread becomes computer bound.

- **Thread: Priority Current.** Displays the current dynamic priority of this thread. The system might raise the thread's dynamic priority above the base priority if the thread is handling user input, or it might lower it towards the base priority if the thread becomes compute bound.

- **Thread: Start Address.** Provides the starting virtual address for this thread.

- **Thread: Thread State.** Indicates the current state of the thread. The value is 0 for Initialized, 1 for Ready, 2 for Running, 3 for Standby, 4 for Terminated, 5 for Wait, 6 for Transition, and 7 for Unknown. A running thread is using a processor; a standby thread is about to use one. A ready thread wants to use a processor but is waiting because none are available. A thread in transition is waiting for a resource in order to execute such as waiting for its execution stack to be paged in from disk. A waiting thread has no use for the processor because it is waiting for a peripheral operation to complete or for a resource to become available.

- **Thread: Thread Wait Reason.** This is applicable only when the thread is in the waiting state (see Thread: Thread State). The value is 0 or 7 when the thread is waiting for the Executive, 1 or 8 for a Free Page, 2 or 9 for a Page In, 3 or 10 for a Pool Allocation, 4 or 11 for an Execution Delay, 5 or 12 for a Suspended Condition, 6 or 13 for a User Request, 14 for an Event Pair High, 15 for an Event Pair Low, 16 for an LPC Receive, 17 for an LPC Reply, 18 for Virtual Memory, 19 for a Page Out, 20 and higher are not assigned as of this writing. Event pairs are used to communicate with protected subsystems (see Thread: Context Switches).

E

Making Windows NT Y2K Ready

IT IS GETTING INCREASINGLY DIFFICULT to pick up a newspaper or a magazine or turn on the television and not run across something about the Y2K problem. Opinions vary widely about how much or how little this problem will impact the world as December 31, 1999 turns into January 1, 2000. Some pundits are calmly taking a wait-and-see approach, whereas others are stocking up on food, water, ammunition, and power generators in anticipation of complete anarchy when the computers that control so many aspects of our lives all shut down and leave us without food, utilities, and cable television.

What Exactly Is the Y2K Problem?

The Y2K issue is not a single problem; it is three separate programming issues: two-digit date storage, leap-year calculations, and special meanings for dates. Each of these needs to be addressed separately. Adding to the complications is the fact that the use of dates for calculations is not standardized and is pervasive throughout almost every computer system and software program.

Two-digit date storage is the most common Y2K issue and is the problem most often mentioned in the mainstream press. This refers to the convention of using only the last two of the four digits that indicate a particular year—for example, 11/25/49 rather than 11/25/1949. This convention was established early in the history of computing (apparently on the assumption that the century would always start with 19) and has been carried along into the present. In the early days, a mainframe with 16KB of main storage was considered a luxury. In such a limited memory environment, being able to save two bytes of precious storage meant a lot in terms of efficiency and speed.

Computers now assume that the century will always begin with 19, so calculations that include a date starting with some other number, such as 20, will either fail or produce incorrect results. Several centenarians, for example, recently received school enrollment forms in the mail. Their birth dates had the leading digits 18, which the computer either did not recognize or ignored. The computers assumed their birth years fell in the 1990s rather than the 1890s.

Furthermore, in the late 1950s and early '60s, the software running on most computers was incompatible with the software running on any other computer. This even applied to different models of computers built by the same manufacturer. Whenever a customer upgraded to a new computer, all the software had to be rewritten. This did not change until the mid-1960s when computer manufacturers finally responded to customer demand and made sure their new computers could run their old software.

By the mid-1960s, most programmers had gotten used to writing programs that were going to be completely rewritten in a few years, so they didn't bother planning for the future. Even after computer memory became relatively cheap and plentiful, programmers continued to use two-digit date storage, even as recently as the mid-1990s. In addition, there were (and still are) millions of lines of running code that originally were written in the 1960s and 1970s. Who could have guessed that some programs would survive for 35+ years?

Leap-year calculations are another aspect of the Y2K problem. Leap-year calculations are fairly simple except for certain special cases—and the year 2000 is a special case. Any year divisible by four is a leap year, for example, *except* when it also is divisible by 100. (A year divisible by 400 is a leap year.) Thus, the year 2000 is a special case that occurs only once every 400 years. For various reasons, a program that recognizes the leading digits 20 might not recognize the year 2000 as a leap year. If this is the case, date handling will be in serious difficulties on February 29, 2000.

The third aspect of the Y2K problem is special meanings for dates. In some applications, date fields are used as flags. It is common, for example, to use the date 9/9/99 to specify such things as "no expiration date" or "save this data item forever." It also might be used in a sort field to place an item at the beginning or end of a report.

The Y2K problem will not be easy to solve. It is difficult because no one really knows how widespread the problem is. Every piece of hardware and software, including embedded systems, must be checked and fixed or replaced as necessary. Everything from mission-critical central accounting systems to small convenience applications must be examined for date handling and how the dates affect the rest of the environment.

Y2K and the PC

Y2K can affect PC users in the areas of hardware, operating systems, and software applications. For a system to be fully Y2K compliant, all three of these areas must be in compliance. These areas have to be fixed in the stated order because the hardware provides the time to the operating system, which passes time information to the applications. This section briefly covers each of these areas and lists resources to help you identify and correct any problems.

Hardware

The date in your PC is controlled by a combination of the Basic Input/Output System (BIOS) and the Real Time Clock (RTC). The RTC is a battery-operated clock that is responsible for keeping track of the day and date, even when the machine is turned off. The BIOS is a software application usually embedded in a read-only memory (ROM) chip that acts as an interface between the operating system and the computer hardware. The RTC stores the year as two digits and relies on the BIOS to supply the century. When the operating system starts, it requests the date from the BIOS. In older machines, the century usually is hard-coded as 19. A Y2K-compliant BIOS assumes the century is 20.

The clock in your PC is potentially susceptible to both the two-digit date problem and the leap year problem. Some early Y2K-compliant BIOS chips fixed the two-digit date problem but ignored the leap year problem.

A noncompliant BIOS problem can be fixed in several ways. Some BIOS chips are read only (ROM) and need to be replaced, whereas others are flash ROM and can be upgraded using software. If no upgrade is available for your BIOS, you can replace the motherboard in your PC, but this can be expensive. Some software fixes will intercept the date passed from the BIOS and will pass a corrected date to the operating system. In addition, some ISA boards can act as a replacement BIOS.

Links to PC Vendors

The following is a list of links to some of the larger PC manufacturers and BIOS vendors that supply Y2K information about their products.

- Acer: `http://www.acer.com.tw/service/y2k`
- American Megatrends (AMI): `http://www.ami.com`
- Award: `http://www.award.com/tech/y2k.htm`
- Compaq: `http://www.compaq.com/year2000/`
- Dell Computer: `http://support.dell.com/support`
- Gateway 2000: `http://www.gateway.com/corp/y2k/y2k/default.html`
- Hewlett-Packard: `http://www.hp.com/year2000`
- IBM Corp.: `http://wwwyr2k.raleigh.ibm.com/`

- Micron: `http://support.micronpc.com`
- NEC: `http://www.nec.com/support/index.html`
- Packard Bell: `http://support.packardbell.com/year2000/default.asp`
- Phoenix: `http://www.phoenix.com`
- Toshiba: `http://www.y2k.toshiba.com`

Y2K Hardware Testers

If your PC vendor does not offer Y2K-compliance information for your machine, you can test it yourself. Many tools are available for checking your BIOS for Y2K compliance and several are free. There also are Y2K fix utilities that load themselves into your PC's memory and pass a corrected date to the operating system.

Check 2000 PC

This tester flags and fixes Year 2000 PC hardware problems. It also analyses and advises about Year 2000 PC software and data problems. Check 2000 PC also does the following:

- Scans your PC to perform a detailed hardware, software, and data audit to identify where any Year 2000 problems lie
- Compares audit results against the Greenwich Mean Time knowledge base to define PC Year 2000 status
- Performs all necessary BIOS checks and fixes hardware-level BIOS problems automatically
- Advises about the resolution of software- and data-level problems
- Ensures correct PC usage by showing you whether your operating system is set up for two- or four-digit years and steps you through the process of changing to four-digit years if necessary

For more information, visit `http://www.gmt-2000.com` or email `sales@gmt-2000.com`.

EZCheck2000

EZCheck 2000 is a small $15 utility from The About Time Group that checks your system BIOS for Year 2000 compatibility. For more information, visit `http://www.pcfix2000.com`.

PC Medic

PC Medic from Network Associates is a Windows 95 and Windows NT diagnostic utility that includes centralized administration and notification and can be configured to become transparent. If PC Medic discovers a hardware problem, a fix is applied that forces the PC to properly recognize the year 2000 by loading a Terminate and Stay Resident (TSR) program.

PC Medic diagnoses and repairs Year 2000 problems connected to your PC's hardware. PC Medic ensures that the RTC, the BIOS, DOS, and Windows successfully roll over from December 31, 1999 to January 1, 2000. It also verifies other important dates known to cause problems; for example, it checks to make sure your hardware is aware of February 29, 2000 and that your system will successfully roll over to the year 2001. PC Medic runs on Windows 95, Windows 98, and Windows NT 4.0. For more information, visit **http://www.nai.com**.

Norton 2000 BIOS Test/Fix

The Norton 2000 BIOS Test/Fix from Symantec is a small utility that tests your PC BIOS for Y2K compliance. It prompts you to create a special bootable disk that performs the actual test. The disk automatically launches the Test/Fix application on boot-up. (A full shutdown and boot is recommended.) The cycle consists of a simple date-rollover test and adds leap-year checking for compliance through the year 2015. The results of the tests indicate whether your PC is Y2K compliant and whether Norton 2000 is able to compensate for any problems found. For more information, visit **http://symantec.downloadstore.com/**.

PCfix 2000

PCfix 2000 from The About Time Group is a Y2K fix utility that loads itself on system boot, calculates the correct date, passes it to the operating system, and terminates. This frees up more memory for running applications as compared to fix utilities that stay loaded in memory. For more information, visit **http://www.pcfix2000.com**.

Prove It 2000

Prove It 2000 from Prove It 2000, Inc., is a test/fix package that tests for multiple Y2K-compliance issues. It also provides a TSR fix utility that can be loaded into the AUTOEXEC.BAT file. For more information, visit **http://www.proveit2000usa.com**.

Test2000.Exe and Y2K PC Pro

Test 2000.Exe is a free Year 2000 PC hardware diagnostic program; Y2K PC Pro is an inexpensive licensed product. Y2K PC Pro is a small memory resident program that installs in your machine's AUTOEXEC.BAT file, monitors the BIOS date for the 1999-to-2000 transition, and makes corrections when required. Both products are from The RighTime Clock Company, Inc. For more information, visit **http://www.rightime.com**.

YMark2000

YMark2000 from NSTL is a free, downloadable application that tests BIOS and RTC functionality. YMark2000 can be run on any IBM-compatible PC but can be run only from DOS. If your PC does not run DOS, you will need to boot the PC to DOS via disk. YMark2000 verifies real-time progression from December 31, 1999 to

January 1, 2000. If real-time support fails, the capability to set the date manually is checked. The program also verifies recognition and support for leap years from 2000 through 2009.

For more details about YMark2000 and Y2K-compliance issues, download NSTL's Year 2000 White Paper, *Year 2000 and the 'Industry Standard' Personal Computer*. For more YMark2000 information, visit `http://www.nstl.com/html/ymark_2000.html`.

Y2K Hardware Test

Y2K Hardware Test from SecureNet Technologies is a free, DOS-based diagnostic that performs two tests to determine Y2K compliance. The first test is a real-time BIOS rollover test that determines whether your system's BIOS can make the transition between 1999 and 2000 while the computer is up and running. The second test determines whether your system can accept a date beyond December 31, 2000 and whether the system will retain the date when restarted. For more information, visit `http://www.securenet.org/`.

Y2K Test

Y2K Test from SecureNet Technologies is a free DOS diagnostic utility that checks your system for year 2000 compatibility. It reboots your computer three times and performs a series of tests to determine whether your PC's RTC, BIOS, and operating system will be able to operate smoothly at one minute past midnight on December 31, 1999. When the process has finished, just rerun the program and view the test results. If your system fails the test, you can purchase Y2K Fix. A Windows version also is available. For more information, visit `http://www.securenet.org/`.

ZD Net Software Library

The ZD Net Software Library from Ziff-Davis is a selection of shareware and freeware software utilities to test your PC's CMOS and BIOS for year 2000 compliance. For more information, visit `http://www.zdnet.com/pcmag/pctech/download/swcol.y2k.html`.

Y2K Replacement BIOS Upgrades

If your system fails the Y2K tests and your BIOS is not upgradeable, you can purchase a BIOS extension card. These cards plug into any ISA slot and supplant your motherboard BIOS, even on a 80286. The following is a list of plug-in extension cards:

- **ATA PRO Flash.** From Phoenix Technologies. A BIOS extension card that not only updates your PC to Y2K compatibility, it also adds BIOS extensions for large hard drives, various boot options, and LS-120 disk drives. For more information, visit `http://www.firmware.com`.

- **Eurosoft fix2000.** From AIC Computer Devices Inc. An ISA add-on card that provides a replacement Y2K-compliant ROM. The product comes with a testing utility to ensure proper operation and installation. For more information, visit `http://www.hcdusa.com`.

- **MFI Flash 2000.** From Micro Firmware, Inc./Phoenix Technologies. An ISA add-on card that provides a ROM extension to correct problems with the system BIOS not correctly handling Y2K date rollover. The product comes with a testing utility to ensure proper operation and installation. For more information, visit **http://www.firmware.com**.

- **Millennium Pro.** A BIOS extension card manufactured by Unicore, a division of Award (one of the premier PC BIOS suppliers). For more information, visit **http://www.unicore.com**.

- **Year 2000 BIOS Enabler.** A BIOS extension card manufactured by American Megatrends (AMI), one of the premier PC BIOS suppliers. For more information, visit **http://www.ami.com/y2k**.

Operating Systems

For Windows NT 4.0 to be fully Y2K compliant, you have to install Service Pack 4. To find out the current status of Windows NT 4.0 Y2K compliance, go to the Microsoft Year 2000 Readiness Disclosure & Resource Center at **http://www.microsoft.com/technet/topics/year2k/product/product.htm**. This site will keep you informed about compliance, updates, and other information.

Applications

It can be extremely difficult to determine Y2K compliance for applications. In a most cases, the software manufacturer will advise you to upgrade to the latest version. For internally written applications, your best source of information is your programming tool vendor. The rest of this appendix is devoted to various resources that you might find helpful when dealing with any PC-related Y2K problems.

Y2K-Related Resources

Microsoft has a very extensive Y2K site that covers the large number of Microsoft applications and developers' tools. The Microsoft Year 2000 Resource Center contains a wealth of Y2K-related information about Microsoft commercial applications, operating systems, and programming tools.

Microsoft has published compliance information for its various products in the *Year 2000 Product Guide*, which is updated as new information becomes available. Microsoft lists its products in the guide with one of the following designations:

- **Compliant.** The product meets Microsoft's standards of compliance (although it might require a prerequisite service pack or patch).

- **Compliant with minor issues.** The product meets Microsoft's standards of compliance but has some "minor" outstanding issues without a fix or with a fix on the way that is not yet available.

- **Not compliant.** The product does not meet Microsoft's standards for compliance.

- **Testing yet to be completed.** The product is still undergoing testing.

- **Will not be tested.** The product is not scheduled to be tested for compliance.

Product information includes the version number, the language of release, the range of dates used for data, the product's release date, any prerequisites for compliance, and links to any necessary service packs or patches. You can check the product guide at `http://www.microsoft.com/year2000/`.

The Corel site provides Y2K information for Corel products, including WordPerfect. For more information, visit `http://www.corel.com/2000.htm`.

Intuit, the maker of Quicken and other financial software, has a list of products that are (and are not) Y2K compliant. Intuit also has a release schedule for patches required to bring supported products into compliance. For more information, visit `http://www.intuit.com/support/y2k_standard.html`.

The Lotus Y2K page provides information about the compliance of Lotus products. For more information, visit `http://www.lotus.com/home.nsf/tabs/y2k`.

Oracle lists supported products and how to bring them into Y2K compliance. For more information, visit `http://www.oracle.com/year2000`.

The Peachtree Software site provides Y2K-compliance patches for some of its older products. All current products are compliant. For more information, visit `http://www.peachtree.com`.

General Resources

This section points to resources that provide additional information about the Y2K problem and some potential fixes.

ZD NET

The ZD NET Anchordesk Year 2000 Briefing Center is an excellent resource with articles about various aspects of the Y2K problem. It also contains downloadable files and links to other Y2K sites. For more information, visit `http://www.zdnet.com/anchordesk/bcenter/bcenter_287.html`.

Consumer FAQ: How to Fix Windows Y2K Problems is another resource provided by Ziff Davis. It steps you through an online Y2K-compliance test. For more information, visit `http://www.zdnet.com/zdy2k/1998/11/5110.html`.

Countdown 2000

The Countdown 2000 site discusses software, books, and legal issues pertaining to the Y2K issue. It also features current Y2K news items. For more information, visit `http://www.countdown2000.com/`.

Data Fellows

The Data Fellows Hoax Warnings page specializes in debunking false virus warnings and has added a list of Y2K-related hoaxes. For more information, visit `http://www.datafellows.fi/news/hoax.htm`.

IBM Corp.

IBM offers a searchable database that outlines the compliance status of all IBM software and hardware. For more information, visit `http://wwwyr2k.raleigh.ibm.com/`.

ITAA

The Information Technology Association of America (ITAA) is recognized as the nation's leading trade association for year 2000 software conversion. Its Web site provides a wealth of Y2K-related information including white papers, press releases, case studies, and links to other Y2K sites. For more information, visit `http://www.itaa.org/year2000/index.htm`.

The Year 2000 Information Center

The Year 2000 Information Center is a comprehensive site that includes articles, white papers, current news, user groups, and links to other Y2K sites. For more information, visit `http://www.year2000.com/`.

Vendor 2000

This Web site, sponsored by EDS, contains an extensive database of compliance information from assorted vendors. For more information, visit `http://www.vendor2000.com/`.

Y2Kchaos

Y2Kchaos is the site for you if you expect the millennium bug to lead to total anarchy. It includes tips food storage, survival skills, firearm safety, and an extensive book list. For more information, visit `http://www.y2kchaos.com/`.

Y2K Help!

This site, sponsored by Comco Inc., contains a number of articles and breaking news pertaining to Y2K. For more information, visit `http://y2k.comco.org/`.

Y2Krun

This site is advertised as "Y2K for Ordinary People." It features articles and information geared toward people who are not technically inclined. Books and a free newsletter also are available. For more information, visit `http://www.y2krun.com/`.

Newsletters

The following is a list of some useful Y2K newsletters:

- *ITAA Outlook* is a periodic newsletter outlining current Y2K issues, breaking news, and case studies. To subscribe, visit `http://www.itaa.org/year2000/outlook.cfm`.

- *Millennium Today* publishes a newsletter that features breaking news, commentary, and events relating to Y2K. To subscribe, visit `http://www.countdown2000.com/The_Millennium_Fun_Page/the_millennium_fun_page.html`.

- *PC Week Y2K Watch* is an electronic newsletter that sends the latest Year 2000 news, reviews, and case studies directly to your inbox. You can subscribe at `http://www.zdnet.com/pcweek/newslet/`.

- *Y2K Newswire* provides daily Y2K news updates. The Web site has an extensive list of Y2K-related resources. You can subscribe at `http://www.y2knewswire.com`.

F

Windows NT Keyboard
Commands and Shortcuts

ALTHOUGH THE BENEFITS OF USING A MOUSE are obvious, there will always be times when you want to get things done without leaving the keyboard. The following tables summarize the shortcut keys we've found most useful. To help you navigate all the shortcuts, we've organized them in general categories. The following list gives a brief description of what's in each table.

- **Table G.1.** Shortcuts for the Desktop, Windows NT Explorer, Working with Windows, and Some Specialized Programs
- **Table G.2.** Shortcuts for when Icons or Items are Highlighted
- **Table G.3.** Shortcuts for Dialog Boxes and Other Places in Which You Can Make Selections
- **Table G.4.** Shortcuts for the Windows Key
- **Table G.5.** Shortcuts for Performance Monitor
- **Table G.6.** Shortcuts for Disk Administrator, Event Viewer, and User Manager
- **Table G.7.** Shortcuts for Standard Menu Commands
- **Table G.8.** Shortcuts for Microsoft Word and other Microsoft Office Applications

Table G.1 **Shortcuts for the Desktop, Windows NT Explorer, Working with Windows, and Some Specialized Programs**

To Do This	Command
Switch a DOS program (or prompt) between a window (if it can run in one) and a full screen. If an icon is highlighted, this is the same as a right-clicking then clicking Properties.	Alt+Enter
Cycle through the programs in the order in which they were started.	Alt+Esc
Close the current window or quit a program.	Alt+F4
Display the system (Control) menu for MDI programs or Open a document's System (Control) menu.	Alt+Hyphen (-)
Move backward to a previous view.	Alt+Left arrow
Copy an image of the active window to the Clipboard.	Alt+Print Screen (PrtSc)
Copy an image of the entire desktop to the Clipboard.	Print Screen
Move to a previous view.	Alt+Right arrow
Display the current window's System menu (sometimes referred to as the Control menu).	Alt+Spacebar
Cycle to the next window or program; such as Alt+Tab when the buttons are held, each press of the Tab key moves you forward. Alt+Shift+Tab starts in the opposite direction and automatically engages the cycling function.	Alt+Shift+Tab
Switch to the window you last used or switch to another window by holding down Alt while repeatedly pressing Tab.	Alt+Tab
Carry out a command on the menu.	Alt+*corresponding underlined letter on menu*
View the folder one level up.	Backspace
Select all items in the active window.	Ctrl+A
Display the Start menu.	Ctrl+Esc
Close the current window in MDI programs.	Ctrl+F4

To Do This	Command
Open the Task Manager.	Ctrl+Shift+Esc or Ctrl+Alt+Delete, then click Task Manager.
Display Help on the selected item in a dialog box or anywhere the Help function is available.	F1
Display Find: All Files in the active window.	F3
Refresh the active window.	F5
Switch between left and right (or top and bottom) panes (in any paned window).	F6
Activate the menu bar in programs.	F10
Bring up a context menu (equivalent to a right-click).	Shift+F10
Collapse the current selection if it is expanded, or select the parent folder.	Left arrow
Expand all folders below the current selection.	Num Lock, then asterisk (*)
Collapse the selected folder.	Num Lock, then minus sign (−)
Expand the selected folder.	Num Lock, then plus sign (+)
Expand the current selection if it is collapsed or select the first subfolder.	Right arrow
Close the selected folder and all its parent folders or close open windows and all parent windows.	Shift+Alt+F4, or Shift while clicking the Close button.

Table G.2   Shortcuts for when Icons or Items Are Highlighted

To Do This	Command
View an item's properties.	Alt+Enter, or Alt+double-click
Display an item's shortcut menu.	Application key or Shift+F10
Copy a file.	Ctrl while dragging the file
Create a shortcut.	Ctrl+Shift while dragging the file
Select a highlighted menu choice, activate the default button in a dialog box, or replace single left-click.	Enter

continues

Table G.2   **Continued**

To Do This	Command
Rename an item.	F2
Refresh the screen.	F5
Cancel highlighting (deselect icon).	F6
Bypass AutoPlay when inserting a compact disc.	Shift while inserting the CD-ROM
Delete an item immediately without moving it to the Recycle Bin.	Shift+Delete
Copy the highlighted selection.	Ctrl+C
Paste the contents of the Clipboard.	Ctrl+V
Cut the highlighted selection.	Ctrl+X
Display the shortcut menu for a selected item.	Shift+F10

Table G.3   **Shortcuts for Dialog Boxes and Other Places in Which You Can Make Selections**

To Do This	Command
Open a drop-down list.	Alt+Down arrow
Select a command.	Alt+*corresponding underlined letter*
Open a folder one level up when a folder is selected in the Save As or Open dialog box.	Backspace
Move backward through tabs.	Ctrl+Shift+Tab
Move forward through tabs.	Ctrl+Tab
Click the selected or default button or control.	Enter
Cancel the current task, or close a dialog box or drop-down menu without performing an action.	Esc
Open Save In or Look In in the Save As or Open dialog box.	F4
Refresh the Save As or Open dialog box.	F5
Move backward through menu options.	Shift+Tab

To Do This	Command
Select (click) a button when the current control is a button, or select or clear a checkbox when the current control is a checkbox, or click an option when the current control is an option button.	Spacebar
Move forward through options.	Tab

Table G.4   **Shortcuts for the Windows Key**

To Do This	Command
Display the Start menu.	Windows
Display the System Properties dialog box.	Windows+Break
Display Microsoft Windows NT Explorer in paned view.	Windows+E
Display Find: All Files.	Windows+F
Display Help.	Windows+F1
Minimize all windows.	Windows+M
Display the Run command.	Windows+R
Cycle through buttons on the taskbar.	Windows+Tab
Display Find: Computer.	Ctrl+Windows+F
Undo Minimize all Windows.	Shift+Windows+M

Table G.5   **Shortcuts for Performance Monitor**

To Do This	Command
Highlight current selection in legend.	Backspace, or Ctrl+H
Display or hide legend.	Ctrl+G
Switch to Alert view.	Ctrl+A
Create bookmark.	Ctrl+B
Switch to Chart view.	Ctrl+C
Open Time window.	Ctrl+E
Switch to Log view.	Ctrl+L
Display or hide menu and title bars.	Ctrl+M
Open Options dialog box.	Ctrl+O
Make selection Always on Top.	Ctrl+P
Switch to Report view.	Ctrl+R

continues

Table G.5 **Continued**

To Do This	Command
Display or hide status line.	Ctrl+S
Display or hide toolbar.	Ctrl+T
Manual Update Now.	Ctrl+U
Save Workspace.	Ctrl+W
Help.	F1
Save Settings As.	F12
Open file.	Ctrl+F12
Save settings.	Shift+F12
Add counter to (Chart, Alert, Log, or Report).	Tab +(or)– Ctrl+I

Table G.6 **Shortcuts for Disk Administrator, Event Viewer, and User Manager**

Menu	Option	Shortcut
Disk Administrator	Volume.	Ctrl+V
View menu	Disk Configuration.	Ctrl+D
Disk Administrator	Toolbar.	Ctrl+T
Options menu	Status bar.	Ctrl+S
Legend.	Ctrl+L	
Event Viewer	Find dialog box.	F3
View menu	Detail dialog box.Refresh window.	Enter F5
User Manager	Toggle between panes.	F6
User menu	Copy.	F8 Delete
	Delete.	Enter Shift+A
	Properties.	
	Highlight all users from the selected user to the top of the list.	

Table G.7 **Shortcuts for Standard Menu Commands**

Menu	Option	Shortcut
File Menu	Create new document	Ctrl+N
	Open the Open dialog box	Ctrl+O
	Save a document	Ctrl+S
	Print a document	Ctrl+P

Menu	Option	Shortcut
Edit Menu	Undo Typing	Ctrl+Z
	Redo Typing	Ctrl+Y
	Cut	Ctrl+X
	Copy	Ctrl+C
	Paste	Ctrl+V
	Clear	Delete
	Select All	Ctrl+A
	Find	Ctrl+F
	Replace	Ctrl+H
	Goto	Ctrl+G
Help Menu	Open Help dialog box	F1
	Open Context-specific help	Shift+F1

Table G.8 **Shortcuts for Microsoft Word and Other Microsoft Office Applications**

To Do This	Command
Access Macro dialog box.	Alt+F8
Access Visual Basic Editor.	Alt+F11
Move to the beginning of a document.	Ctrl+Home
Move to the end of a document.	Ctrl+End
Toggle between Preview and Regular view.	Ctrl+F2
Change to Windows view (same as clicking the Restore Windows button).	Ctrl+F5
Switch to the next open document (in Word or other Office applications, such as Excel).	Ctrl+F6
Insert paragraph formatting brackets ({}) at the cursor.	Ctrl+F9
Access Hyperlink dialog box.	Ctrl+K
Open the Open File dialog box.	Ctrl+O, or Ctrl+F12
Switch to the next open document (in Microsoft Office applications except Word).	Ctrl+Tab
Close document.	Ctrl+W or Ctrl+F4
Move to the end of a line.	End
Select an AutoText entry.	F3
Access Spelling and Grammar.	F7
Move to the beginning of a line.	Home
Access thesaurus.	Shift+F7

G

An Exhaustive Review of the Boot Partition

HERE IS AN EXHAUSTIVE REVIEW OF EVERY file found on a boot partition immediately after Windows NT Workstation is installed (this list includes hidden files). This list is useful for identifying the files that Windows NT installs on your system.

```
<drive root>:\pagefile.sys
<drive root>:\Program Files\Plus!
<drive root>:\Program Files\Windows NT
<drive root>:\Program Files\Plus!\Microsoft Internet
<drive root>:\Program Files\Plus!\Microsoft Internet\docs
<drive root>:\Program Files\Plus!\Microsoft Internet\iexplore.exe
<drive root>:\Program Files\Plus!\Microsoft Internet\secbasic.dll
<drive root>:\Program Files\Plus!\Microsoft Internet\docs\backgrnd.gif
<drive root>:\Program Files\Plus!\Microsoft Internet\docs\client.gif
<drive root>:\Program Files\Plus!\Microsoft Internet\docs\home.htm
<drive root>:\Program Files\Plus!\Microsoft Internet\docs\space.gif
<drive root>:\Program Files\Windows NT\Accessories
<drive root>:\Program Files\Windows NT\dialer.exe
<drive root>:\Program Files\Windows NT\hypertrm.exe
<drive root>:\Program Files\Windows NT\Pinball
<drive root>:\Program Files\Windows NT\Windows Messaging
<drive root>:\Program Files\Windows NT\Accessories\ImageVue
<drive root>:\Program Files\Windows NT\Accessories\mswd6_32.wpc
<drive root>:\Program Files\Windows NT\Accessories\wordpad.exe
<drive root>:\Program Files\Windows NT\Accessories\write32.wpc
```

```
<drive root>:\Program Files\Windows NT\Accessories\ImageVue\gotodlg.frm
<drive root>:\Program Files\Windows NT\Accessories\ImageVue\imgsamp.frm
<drive root>:\Program Files\Windows NT\Accessories\ImageVue\imgsampl.vbp
<drive root>:\Program Files\Windows NT\Accessories\ImageVue\wangimg.exe
<drive root>:\Program Files\Windows NT\Pinball\FONT.DAT
<drive root>:\Program Files\Windows NT\Pinball\PINBALL.DAT
<drive root>:\Program Files\Windows NT\Pinball\PINBALL.EXE
<drive root>:\Program Files\Windows NT\Pinball\PINBALL.MID
<drive root>:\Program Files\Windows NT\Pinball\PINBALL2.MID
<drive root>:\Program Files\Windows NT\Pinball\SOUND1.WAV
<drive root>:\Program Files\Windows NT\Pinball\SOUND104.WAV
<drive root>:\Program Files\Windows NT\Pinball\SOUND105.WAV
<drive root>:\Program Files\Windows NT\Pinball\SOUND108.WAV
<drive root>:\Program Files\Windows NT\Pinball\SOUND111.WAV
<drive root>:\Program Files\Windows NT\Pinball\SOUND112.WAV
<drive root>:\Program Files\Windows NT\Pinball\SOUND12.WAV
<drive root>:\Program Files\Windows NT\Pinball\SOUND13.WAV
<drive root>:\Program Files\Windows NT\Pinball\SOUND131.WAV
<drive root>:\Program Files\Windows NT\Pinball\SOUND136.WAV
<drive root>:\Program Files\Windows NT\Pinball\SOUND14.WAV
<drive root>:\Program Files\Windows NT\Pinball\SOUND16.WAV
<drive root>:\Program Files\Windows NT\Pinball\SOUND17.WAV
<drive root>:\Program Files\Windows NT\Pinball\SOUND18.WAV
<drive root>:\Program Files\Windows NT\Pinball\SOUND181.WAV
<drive root>:\Program Files\Windows NT\Pinball\SOUND19.WAV
<drive root>:\Program Files\Windows NT\Pinball\SOUND20.WAV
<drive root>:\Program Files\Windows NT\Pinball\SOUND21.WAV
<drive root>:\Program Files\Windows NT\Pinball\SOUND22.WAV
<drive root>:\Program Files\Windows NT\Pinball\SOUND24.WAV
<drive root>:\Program Files\Windows NT\Pinball\SOUND240.WAV
<drive root>:\Program Files\Windows NT\Pinball\SOUND243.WAV
<drive root>:\Program Files\Windows NT\Pinball\SOUND25.WAV
<drive root>:\Program Files\Windows NT\Pinball\SOUND26.WAV
<drive root>:\Program Files\Windows NT\Pinball\SOUND27.WAV
<drive root>:\Program Files\Windows NT\Pinball\SOUND28.WAV
<drive root>:\Program Files\Windows NT\Pinball\SOUND29.WAV
<drive root>:\Program Files\Windows NT\Pinball\SOUND3.WAV
<drive root>:\Program Files\Windows NT\Pinball\SOUND30.WAV
<drive root>:\Program Files\Windows NT\Pinball\SOUND34.WAV
<drive root>:\Program Files\Windows NT\Pinball\SOUND35.WAV
<drive root>:\Program Files\Windows NT\Pinball\SOUND36.WAV
<drive root>:\Program Files\Windows NT\Pinball\SOUND38.WAV
<drive root>:\Program Files\Windows NT\Pinball\SOUND39.WAV
<drive root>:\Program Files\Windows NT\Pinball\SOUND4.WAV
<drive root>:\Program Files\Windows NT\Pinball\SOUND42.WAV
<drive root>:\Program Files\Windows NT\Pinball\SOUND43.WAV
<drive root>:\Program Files\Windows NT\Pinball\SOUND45.WAV
<drive root>:\Program Files\Windows NT\Pinball\SOUND49.WAV
<drive root>:\Program Files\Windows NT\Pinball\SOUND49D.WAV
<drive root>:\Program Files\Windows NT\Pinball\SOUND5.WAV
<drive root>:\Program Files\Windows NT\Pinball\SOUND50.WAV
```

```
<drive root>:\Program Files\Windows NT\Pinball\SOUND528.WAV
<drive root>:\Program Files\Windows NT\Pinball\SOUND53.WAV
<drive root>:\Program Files\Windows NT\Pinball\SOUND54.WAV
<drive root>:\Program Files\Windows NT\Pinball\SOUND55.WAV
<drive root>:\Program Files\Windows NT\Pinball\SOUND560.WAV
<drive root>:\Program Files\Windows NT\Pinball\SOUND563.WAV
<drive root>:\Program Files\Windows NT\Pinball\SOUND57.WAV
<drive root>:\Program Files\Windows NT\Pinball\SOUND58.WAV
<drive root>:\Program Files\Windows NT\Pinball\SOUND6.WAV
<drive root>:\Program Files\Windows NT\Pinball\SOUND65.WAV
<drive root>:\Program Files\Windows NT\Pinball\SOUND68.WAV
<drive root>:\Program Files\Windows NT\Pinball\SOUND7.WAV
<drive root>:\Program Files\Windows NT\Pinball\SOUND713.WAV
<drive root>:\Program Files\Windows NT\Pinball\SOUND735.WAV
<drive root>:\Program Files\Windows NT\Pinball\SOUND8.WAV
<drive root>:\Program Files\Windows NT\Pinball\SOUND827.WAV
<drive root>:\Program Files\Windows NT\Pinball\SOUND9.WAV
<drive root>:\Program Files\Windows NT\Pinball\SOUND999.WAV
<drive root>:\Program Files\Windows NT\Pinball\table.bmp
<drive root>:\Program Files\Windows NT\Pinball\wavemix.inf
<drive root>:\Program Files\Windows NT\Windows Messaging\exchng32.exe
<drive root>:\Program Files\Windows NT\Windows Messaging\mapiwm.tpl
<drive root>:\Program Files\Windows NT\Windows Messaging\mlset32.exe
<drive root>:\Program Files\Windows NT\Windows Messaging\mlshext.dll
<drive root>:\Program Files\Windows NT\Windows Messaging\scanpst.exe
<drive root>:\WINNT\black16.scr
<drive root>:\WINNT\Blue Lace 16.bmp
<drive root>:\WINNT\Blue Monday 16.bmp
<drive root>:\WINNT\Blue Monday.bmp
<drive root>:\WINNT\clock.avi
<drive root>:\WINNT\Coffee Bean 16.bmp
<drive root>:\WINNT\Coffee Bean.bmp
<drive root>:\WINNT\Config
<drive root>:\WINNT\control.ini
<drive root>:\WINNT\Cursors
<drive root>:\WINNT\explorer.exe
<drive root>:\WINNT\FeatherTexture.bmp
<drive root>:\WINNT\Fiddle Head.bmp
<drive root>:\WINNT\FORMS
<drive root>:\WINNT\Furry Dog 16.bmp
<drive root>:\WINNT\Furry Dog.bmp
<drive root>:\WINNT\Geometrix.bmp
<drive root>:\WINNT\Gone Fishing.bmp
<drive root>:\WINNT\Greenstone.bmp
<drive root>:\WINNT\Hazy Autumn 16.bmp
<drive root>:\WINNT\Help
<drive root>:\WINNT\Hiking Boot.bmp
<drive root>:\WINNT\Leaf Fossils 16.bmp
<drive root>:\WINNT\Leather 16.bmp
<drive root>:\WINNT\Maple Trails.bmp
<drive root>:\WINNT\Media
```

```
<drive root>:\WINNT\network.wri
<drive root>:\WINNT\NOTEPAD.EXE
<drive root>:\WINNT\Petroglyph 16.bmp
<drive root>:\WINNT\Prairie Wind.bmp
<drive root>:\WINNT\printer.wri
<drive root>:\WINNT\Profiles
<drive root>:\WINNT\REGEDIT.EXE
<drive root>:\WINNT\repair
<drive root>:\WINNT\Rhododendron.bmp
<drive root>:\WINNT\River Sumida.bmp
<drive root>:\WINNT\Santa Fe Stucco.bmp
<drive root>:\WINNT\Seaside 16.bmp
<drive root>:\WINNT\Seaside.bmp
<drive root>:\WINNT\setup.old
<drive root>:\WINNT\setuplog.txt
<drive root>:\WINNT\Snakeskin.bmp
<drive root>:\WINNT\Soap Bubbles.bmp
<drive root>:\WINNT\Solstice.bmp
<drive root>:\WINNT\Swimming Pool.bmp
<drive root>:\WINNT\system
<drive root>:\WINNT\system.ini
<drive root>:\WINNT\system32
<drive root>:\WINNT\TASKMAN.EXE
<drive root>:\WINNT\TWAIN.LOG
<drive root>:\WINNT\Twain001.Mtx
<drive root>:\WINNT\Upstream 16.bmp
<drive root>:\WINNT\vmmreg32.dll
<drive root>:\WINNT\welcome.exe
<drive root>:\WINNT\WIN.INI
<drive root>:\WINNT\WINFILE.INI
<drive root>:\WINNT\WINHELP.EXE
<drive root>:\WINNT\winhlp32.exe
<drive root>:\WINNT\winnt.bmp
<drive root>:\WINNT\winnt256.bmp
<drive root>:\WINNT\winzip32.ini
<drive root>:\WINNT\Zapotec 16.bmp
<drive root>:\WINNT\Zapotec.bmp
<drive root>:\WINNT\_DEFAULT.PIF
<drive root>:\WINNT\Config\general.idf
<drive root>:\WINNT\Config\hindered.idf
<drive root>:\WINNT\Config\msadlib.idf
<drive root>:\WINNT\Cursors\3dgarro.cur
<drive root>:\WINNT\Cursors\3dgmove.cur
<drive root>:\WINNT\Cursors\3dgnesw.cur
<drive root>:\WINNT\Cursors\3dgno.cur
<drive root>:\WINNT\Cursors\3dgns.cur
<drive root>:\WINNT\Cursors\3dgnwse.cur
<drive root>:\WINNT\Cursors\3dgwe.cur
<drive root>:\WINNT\Cursors\3dsmove.cur
<drive root>:\WINNT\Cursors\3dsns.cur
<drive root>:\WINNT\Cursors\3dsnwse.cur
```

```
<drive root>:\WINNT\Cursors\3dwarro.cur
<drive root>:\WINNT\Cursors\3dwmove.cur
<drive root>:\WINNT\Cursors\3dwnesw.cur
<drive root>:\WINNT\Cursors\3dwno.cur
<drive root>:\WINNT\Cursors\3dwns.cur
<drive root>:\WINNT\Cursors\3dwnwse.cur
<drive root>:\WINNT\Cursors\3dwwe.cur
<drive root>:\WINNT\Cursors\appstar2.ani
<drive root>:\WINNT\Cursors\appstar3.ani
<drive root>:\WINNT\Cursors\appstart.ani
<drive root>:\WINNT\Cursors\banana.ani
<drive root>:\WINNT\Cursors\barber.ani
<drive root>:\WINNT\Cursors\coin.ani
<drive root>:\WINNT\Cursors\counter.ani
<drive root>:\WINNT\Cursors\cross.cur
<drive root>:\WINNT\Cursors\dinosau2.ani
<drive root>:\WINNT\Cursors\dinosaur.ani
<drive root>:\WINNT\Cursors\drum.ani
<drive root>:\WINNT\Cursors\fillitup.ani
<drive root>:\WINNT\Cursors\hand.ani
<drive root>:\WINNT\Cursors\handapst.ani
<drive root>:\WINNT\Cursors\handnesw.ani
<drive root>:\WINNT\Cursors\handno.ani
<drive root>:\WINNT\Cursors\handns.ani
<drive root>:\WINNT\Cursors\handnwse.ani
<drive root>:\WINNT\Cursors\handwait.ani
<drive root>:\WINNT\Cursors\handwe.ani
<drive root>:\WINNT\Cursors\harrow.cur
<drive root>:\WINNT\Cursors\hcross.cur
<drive root>:\WINNT\Cursors\hibeam.cur
<drive root>:\WINNT\Cursors\hmove.cur
<drive root>:\WINNT\Cursors\hnesw.cur
<drive root>:\WINNT\Cursors\hnodrop.cur
<drive root>:\WINNT\Cursors\hns.cur
<drive root>:\WINNT\Cursors\hnwse.cur
<drive root>:\WINNT\Cursors\horse.ani
<drive root>:\WINNT\Cursors\hourgla2.ani
<drive root>:\WINNT\Cursors\hourgla3.ani
<drive root>:\WINNT\Cursors\hourglas.ani
<drive root>:\WINNT\Cursors\hwe.cur
<drive root>:\WINNT\Cursors\lappstrt.cur
<drive root>:\WINNT\Cursors\larrow.cur
<drive root>:\WINNT\Cursors\lcross.cur
<drive root>:\WINNT\Cursors\libeam.cur
<drive root>:\WINNT\Cursors\lmove.cur
<drive root>:\WINNT\Cursors\lnesw.cur
<drive root>:\WINNT\Cursors\lnodrop.cur
<drive root>:\WINNT\Cursors\lns.cur
<drive root>:\WINNT\Cursors\lnwse.cur
<drive root>:\WINNT\Cursors\lwait.cur
<drive root>:\WINNT\Cursors\lwe.cur
```

```
<drive root>:\WINNT\Cursors\metronom.ani
<drive root>:\WINNT\Cursors\piano.ani
<drive root>:\WINNT\Cursors\rainbow.ani
<drive root>:\WINNT\Cursors\raindrop.ani
<drive root>:\WINNT\Cursors\sizenesw.ani
<drive root>:\WINNT\Cursors\sizens.ani
<drive root>:\WINNT\Cursors\sizenwse.ani
<drive root>:\WINNT\Cursors\sizewe.ani
<drive root>:\WINNT\Cursors\stopwtch.ani
<drive root>:\WINNT\Cursors\vanisher.ani
<drive root>:\WINNT\Cursors\wagtail.ani
<drive root>:\WINNT\Fonts\app850.fon
<drive root>:\WINNT\Fonts\arial.ttf
<drive root>:\WINNT\Fonts\arialbd.ttf
<drive root>:\WINNI\Fonts\arialbi.ttf
<drive root>:\WINNT\Fonts\ariali.ttf
<drive root>:\WINNT\Fonts\cga40850.fon
<drive root>:\WINNT\Fonts\cga40woa.fon
<drive root>:\WINNT\Fonts\cga80850.fon
<drive root>:\WINNT\Fonts\cga80woa.fon
<drive root>:\WINNT\Fonts\cour.ttf
<drive root>:\WINNT\Fonts\courbd.ttf
<drive root>:\WINNT\Fonts\courbi.ttf
<drive root>:\WINNT\Fonts\coure.fon
<drive root>:\WINNT\Fonts\courf.fon
<drive root>:\WINNT\Fonts\couri.ttf
<drive root>:\WINNT\Fonts\desktop.ini
<drive root>:\WINNT\Fonts\dosapp.fon
<drive root>:\WINNT\Fonts\ega40850.fon
<drive root>:\WINNT\Fonts\ega40woa.fon
<drive root>:\WINNT\Fonts\ega80850.fon
<drive root>:\WINNT\Fonts\ega80woa.fon
<drive root>:\WINNT\Fonts\l_10646.ttf
<drive root>:\WINNT\Fonts\lucon.ttf
<drive root>:\WINNT\Fonts\marlett.ttf
<drive root>:\WINNT\Fonts\modern.fon
<drive root>:\WINNT\Fonts\roman.fon
<drive root>:\WINNT\Fonts\script.fon
<drive root>:\WINNT\Fonts\serife.fon
<drive root>:\WINNT\Fonts\seriff.fon
<drive root>:\WINNT\Fonts\smalle.fon
<drive root>:\WINNT\Fonts\sserife.fon
<drive root>:\WINNT\Fonts\sseriff.fon
<drive root>:\WINNT\Fonts\symbol.ttf
<drive root>:\WINNT\Fonts\symbole.fon
<drive root>:\WINNT\Fonts\times.ttf
<drive root>:\WINT\Fonts\timesbd.ttf
<drive root>:\WINNT\Fonts\timesbi.ttf
<drive root>:\WINNT\Fonts\timesi.ttf
<drive root>:\WINNT\Fonts\vga850.fon
<drive root>:\WINNT\Fonts\vgafix.fon
```

```
<drive root>:\WINNT\Fonts\vgaoem.fon
<drive root>:\WINNT\Fonts\vgasys.fon
<drive root>:\WINNT\Fonts\wingding.ttf
<drive root>:\WINNT\FORMS\CONFIGS
<drive root>:\WINNT\FORMS\CONFIGS\MAPIF0.CFG
<drive root>:\WINNT\FORMS\CONFIGS\mapif0l.ico
<drive root>:\WINNT\FORMS\CONFIGS\mapif0s.ico
<drive root>:\WINNT\FORMS\CONFIGS\MAPIF1.CFG
<drive root>:\WINNT\FORMS\CONFIGS\mapif1l.ico
<drive root>:\WINNT\FORMS\CONFIGS\mapif1s.ico
<drive root>:\WINNT\FORMS\CONFIGS\MAPIF2.CFG
<drive root>:\WINNT\FORMS\CONFIGS\mapif2l.ico
<drive root>:\WINNT\FORMS\CONFIGS\mapif2s.ico
<drive root>:\WINNT\FORMS\CONFIGS\MAPIF3.CFG
<drive root>:\WINNT\FORMS\CONFIGS\mapif3l.ico
<drive root>:\WINNT\FORMS\CONFIGS\mapif3s.ico
<drive root>:\WINNT\FORMS\CONFIGS\MAPIF4.CFG
<drive root>:\WINNT\FORMS\CONFIGS\mapif4l.ico
<drive root>:\WINNT\FORMS\CONFIGS\mapif4s.ico
<drive root>:\WINNT\FORMS\CONFIGS\MAPIF5.CFG
<drive root>:\WINNT\FORMS\CONFIGS\mapif5l.ico
<drive root>:\WINNT\FORMS\CONFIGS\mapif5s.ico
<drive root>:\WINNT\Help\31users.hlp
<drive root>:\WINNT\Help\access.hlp
<drive root>:\WINNT\Help\acc_dis.cnt
<drive root>:\WINNT\Help\acc_dis.hlp
<drive root>:\WINNT\Help\common.hlp
<drive root>:\WINNT\Help\compstui.hlp
<drive root>:\WINNT\Help\dcomcnfg.hlp
<drive root>:\WINNT\Help\devapps.hlp
<drive root>:\WINNT\Help\dialer.cnt
<drive root>:\WINNT\Help\dialer.hlp
<drive root>:\WINNT\Help\exchng.cnt
<drive root>:\WINNT\Help\exchng.hlp
<drive root>:\WINNT\Help\hypertrm.cnt
<drive root>:\WINNT\Help\hypertrm.hlp
<drive root>:\WINNT\Help\iexplore.cnt
<drive root>:\WINNT\Help\iexplore.hlp
<drive root>:\WINNT\Help\int-mail.cnt
<drive root>:\WINNT\Help\int-mail.hlp
<drive root>:\WINNT\Help\joy.hlp
<drive root>:\WINNT\Help\mmdrv.hlp
<drive root>:\WINNT\Help\mouse.cnt
<drive root>:\WINNT\Help\mouse.hlp
<drive root>:\WINNT\Help\msfs.cnt
<drive root>:\WINNT\Help\msfs.hlp
<drive root>:\WINNT\Help\msnauth.cnt
<drive root>:\WINNT\Help\msnauth.hlp
<drive root>:\WINNT\Help\mspaint.cnt
<drive root>:\WINNT\Help\mspaint.hlp
<drive root>:\WINNT\Help\netcfg.hlp
```

```
<drive root>:\WINNT\Help\ntsecui.hlp
<drive root>:\WINNT\Help\ntshrui.hlp
<drive root>:\WINNT\Help\pinball.cnt
<drive root>:\WINNT\Help\pinball.hlp
<drive root>:\WINNT\Help\REGEDIT.CNT
<drive root>:\WINNT\Help\REGEDIT.HLP
<drive root>:\WINNT\Help\rtradmin.cnt
<drive root>:\WINNT\Help\rtradmin.hlp
<drive root>:\WINNT\Help\scanpst.hlp
<drive root>:\WINNT\Help\supp_ed.cnt
<drive root>:\WINNT\Help\supp_ed.hlp
<drive root>:\WINNT\Help\sysdm.hlp
<drive root>:\WINNT\Help\taskmgr.cnt
<drive root>:\WINNT\Help\taskmgr.hlp
<drive root>:\WINNT\Help\wangimg.cnt
<drive root>:\WINNT\Help\wangimg.hlp
<drive root>:\WINNT\Help\wangocx.cnt
<drive root>:\WINNT\Help\wangocx.hlp
<drive root>:\WINNT\Help\wangocxd.cnt
<drive root>:\WINNT\Help\wangocxd.hlp
<drive root>:\WINNT\Help\wangshl.cnt
<drive root>:\WINNT\Help\wangshl.hlp
<drive root>:\WINNT\Help\wordpad.cnt
<drive root>:\WINNT\Help\wordpad.hlp
<drive root>:\WINNT\inf\accessor.inf
<drive root>:\WINNT\inf\accessor.PNF
<drive root>:\WINNT\inf\apps.inf
<drive root>:\WINNT\inf\apps.PNF
<drive root>:\WINNT\inf\communic.inf
<drive root>:\WINNT\inf\communic.PNF
<drive root>:\WINNT\inf\display.inf
<drive root>:\WINNT\inf\display.PNF
<drive root>:\WINNT\inf\dispoem.inf
<drive root>:\WINNT\inf\dispoem.PNF
<drive root>:\WINNT\inf\font.inf
<drive root>:\WINNT\inf\font.PNF
<drive root>:\WINNT\inf\games.inf
<drive root>:\WINNT\inf\games.PNF
<drive root>:\WINNT\inf\iexplore.inf
<drive root>:\WINNT\inf\iexplore.PNF
<drive root>:\WINNT\inf\imagevue.inf
<drive root>:\WINNT\inf\imagevue.PNF
<drive root>:\WINNT\inf\intl.inf
<drive root>:\WINNT\inf\intl.PNF
<drive root>:\WINNT\inf\kbd.inf
<drive root>:\WINNT\inf\kbd.PNF
<drive root>:\WINNT\inf\keyboard.inf
<drive root>:\WINNT\inf\keyboard.PNF
<drive root>:\WINNT\inf\layout.inf
<drive root>:\WINNT\inf\LAYOUT.PNF
<drive root>:\WINNT\inf\mdm3com.inf
```

```
<drive root>:\WINNT\inf\mdm3com.PNF
<drive root>:\WINNT\inf\mdm3x.inf
<drive root>:\WINNT\inf\mdm3x.PNF
<drive root>:\WINNT\inf\mdmaceex.inf
<drive root>:\WINNT\inf\mdmaceex.PNF
<drive root>:\WINNT\inf\mdmadc.inf
<drive root>:\WINNT\inf\mdmadc.PNF
<drive root>:\WINNT\inf\mdmadtn.inf
<drive root>:\WINNT\inf\mdmadtn.PNF
<drive root>:\WINNT\inf\mdmairte.inf
<drive root>:\WINNT\inf\mdmairte.PNF
<drive root>:\WINNT\inf\mdmar1.inf
<drive root>:\WINNT\inf\mdmar1.PNF
<drive root>:\WINNT\inf\mdmarch.inf
<drive root>:\WINNT\inf\mdmarch.PNF
<drive root>:\WINNT\inf\mdmarcht.inf
<drive root>:\WINNT\inf\mdmarcht.PNF
<drive root>:\WINNT\inf\mdmarn.inf
<drive root>:\WINNT\inf\mdmarn.PNF
<drive root>:\WINNT\inf\mdmati.inf
<drive root>:\WINNT\inf\mdmati.PNF
<drive root>:\WINNT\inf\mdmatt.inf
<drive root>:\WINNT\inf\mdmatt.PNF
<drive root>:\WINNT\inf\mdmaus.inf
<drive root>:\WINNT\inf\mdmaus.PNF
<drive root>:\WINNT\inf\mdmblatz.inf
<drive root>:\WINNT\inf\mdmblatz.PNF
<drive root>:\WINNT\inf\mdmboca.inf
<drive root>:\WINNT\inf\mdmboca.PNF
<drive root>:\WINNT\inf\mdmbsb.inf
<drive root>:\WINNT\inf\mdmbsb.PNF
<drive root>:\WINNT\inf\mdmbsch.inf
<drive root>:\WINNT\inf\mdmbsch.PNF
<drive root>:\WINNT\inf\mdmcm28.inf
<drive root>:\WINNT\inf\mdmcm28.PNF
<drive root>:\WINNT\inf\mdmcmcm.inf
<drive root>:\WINNT\inf\mdmcmcm.PNF
<drive root>:\WINNT\inf\mdmcodex.inf
<drive root>:\WINNT\inf\mdmcodex.PNF
<drive root>:\WINNT\inf\mdmcom1.inf
<drive root>:\WINNT\inf\mdmcom1.PNF
<drive root>:\WINNT\inf\mdmcomm1.inf
<drive root>:\WINNT\inf\mdmcomm1.PNF
<drive root>:\WINNT\inf\mdmcommu.inf
<drive root>:\WINNT\inf\mdmcommu.PNF
<drive root>:\WINNT\inf\mdmcpi.inf
<drive root>:\WINNT\inf\mdmcpi.PNF
<drive root>:\WINNT\inf\mdmcpq.inf
<drive root>:\WINNT\inf\mdmcpq.PNF
<drive root>:\WINNT\inf\mdmcpqpr.inf
<drive root>:\WINNT\inf\mdmcpqpr.PNF
```

```
<drive root>:\WINNT\inf\mdmcpv.inf
<drive root>:\WINNT\inf\mdmcpv.PNF
<drive root>:\WINNT\inf\mdmcrtix.inf
<drive root>:\WINNT\inf\mdmcrtix.PNF
<drive root>:\WINNT\inf\mdmdefd.inf
<drive root>:\WINNT\inf\mdmdefd.PNF
<drive root>:\WINNT\inf\mdmdgitn.inf
<drive root>:\WINNT\inf\mdmdgitn.PNF
<drive root>:\WINNT\inf\mdmdicom.inf
<drive root>:\WINNT\inf\mdmdicom.PNF
<drive root>:\WINNT\inf\mdmdisco.inf
<drive root>:\WINNT\inf\mdmdisco.PNF
<drive root>:\WINNT\inf\mdmdsi.inf
<drive root>:\WINNT\inf\mdmdsi.PNF
<drive root>:\WINNT\inf\mdmdyna.inf
<drive root>:\WINNT\inf\mdmdyna.PNF
<drive root>:\WINNT\inf\mdmeiger.inf
<drive root>:\WINNT\inf\mdmeiger.PNF
<drive root>:\WINNT\inf\mdmelink.inf
<drive root>:\WINNT\inf\mdmelink.PNF
<drive root>:\WINNT\inf\mdmelpro.inf
<drive root>:\WINNT\inf\mdmelpro.PNF
<drive root>:\WINNT\inf\mdmelsa.inf
<drive root>:\WINNT\inf\mdmelsa.PNF
<drive root>:\WINNT\inf\mdmeric.inf
<drive root>:\WINNT\inf\mdmeric.PNF
<drive root>:\WINNT\inf\mdmetech.inf
<drive root>:\WINNT\inf\mdmetech.PNF
<drive root>:\WINNT\inf\mdmexp.inf
<drive root>:\WINNT\inf\mdmexp.PNF
<drive root>:\WINNT\inf\mdmeyp.inf
<drive root>:\WINNT\inf\mdmeyp.PNF
<drive root>:\WINNT\inf\mdmgal.inf
<drive root>:\WINNT\inf\mdmgal.PNF
<drive root>:\WINNT\inf\mdmgar.inf
<drive root>:\WINNT\inf\mdmgar.PNF
<drive root>:\WINNT\inf\mdmgatew.inf
<drive root>:\WINNT\inf\mdmgatew.PNF
<drive root>:\WINNT\inf\mdmgen.inf
<drive root>:\WINNT\inf\mdmgen.PNF
<drive root>:\WINNT\inf\mdmgv.inf
<drive root>:\WINNT\inf\mdmgv.PNF
<drive root>:\WINNT\inf\mdmgvc.inf
<drive root>:\WINNT\inf\mdmgvc.PNF
<drive root>:\WINNT\inf\mdmgvcd.inf
<drive root>:\WINNT\inf\mdmgvcd.PNF
<drive root>:\WINNT\inf\mdmhaeu.inf
<drive root>:\WINNT\inf\mdmhaeu.PNF
<drive root>:\WINNT\inf\mdmhaeus.inf
<drive root>:\WINNT\inf\mdmhaeus.PNF
<drive root>:\WINNT\inf\mdmhandy.inf
```

```
<drive root>:\WINNT\inf\mdmhandy.PNF
<drive root>:\WINNT\inf\mdmhay2.inf
<drive root>:\WINNT\inf\mdmhay2.PNF
<drive root>:\WINNT\inf\mdmhayes.inf
<drive root>:\WINNT\inf\mdmhayes.PNF
<drive root>:\WINNT\inf\mdmico.inf
<drive root>:\WINNT\inf\mdmico.PNF
<drive root>:\WINNT\inf\mdminfot.inf
<drive root>:\WINNT\inf\mdminfot.PNF
<drive root>:\WINNT\inf\mdminsys.inf
<drive root>:\WINNT\inf\mdminsys.PNF
<drive root>:\WINNT\inf\mdmintel.inf
<drive root>:\WINNT\inf\mdmintel.PNF
<drive root>:\WINNT\inf\mdmintpc.inf
<drive root>:\WINNT\inf\mdmintpc.PNF
<drive root>:\WINNT\inf\mdmitex.inf
<drive root>:\WINNT\inf\mdmitex.PNF
<drive root>:\WINNT\inf\mdmke.inf
<drive root>:\WINNT\inf\mdmke.PNF
<drive root>:\WINNT\inf\mdmkortx.inf
<drive root>:\WINNT\inf\mdmkortx.PNF
<drive root>:\WINNT\inf\mdmlasat.inf
<drive root>:\WINNT\inf\mdmlasat.PNF
<drive root>:\WINNT\inf\mdmlasno.inf
<drive root>:\WINNT\inf\mdmlasno.PNF
<drive root>:\WINNT\inf\mdmlce.inf
<drive root>:\WINNT\inf\mdmlce.PNF
<drive root>:\WINNT\inf\mdmlight.inf
<drive root>:\WINNT\inf\mdmlight.PNF
<drive root>:\WINNT\inf\mdmlngsh.inf
<drive root>:\WINNT\inf\mdmlngsh.PNF
<drive root>:\WINNT\inf\mdmmart.inf
<drive root>:\WINNT\inf\mdmmart.PNF
<drive root>:\WINNT\inf\mdmmcom.inf
<drive root>:\WINNT\inf\mdmmcom.PNF
<drive root>:\WINNT\inf\mdmmetri.inf
<drive root>:\WINNT\inf\mdmmetri.PNF
<drive root>:\WINNT\inf\mdmmhrtz.inf
<drive root>:\WINNT\inf\mdmmhrtz.PNF
<drive root>:\WINNT\inf\mdmmix.inf
<drive root>:\WINNT\inf\mdmmix.PNF
<drive root>:\WINNT\inf\mdmmoto.inf
<drive root>:\WINNT\inf\mdmmoto.PNF
<drive root>:\WINNT\inf\mdmmoton.inf
<drive root>:\WINNT\inf\mdmmoton.PNF
<drive root>:\WINNT\inf\mdmmotou.inf
<drive root>:\WINNT\inf\mdmmotou.PNF
<drive root>:\WINNT\inf\mdmmtd.inf
<drive root>:\WINNT\inf\mdmmtd.PNF
<drive root>:\WINNT\inf\mdmmts.inf
<drive root>:\WINNT\inf\mdmmts.PNF
```

```
<drive root>:\WINNT\inf\mdmmulog.inf
<drive root>:\WINNT\inf\mdmmulog.PNF
<drive root>:\WINNT\inf\mdmneuhs.inf
<drive root>:\WINNT\inf\mdmneuhs.PNF
<drive root>:\WINNT\inf\mdmniss.inf
<drive root>:\WINNT\inf\mdmniss.PNF
<drive root>:\WINNT\inf\mdmnokia.inf
<drive root>:\WINNT\inf\mdmnokia.PNF
<drive root>:\WINNT\inf\mdmnokno.inf
<drive root>:\WINNT\inf\mdmnokno.PNF
<drive root>:\WINNT\inf\mdmnova.inf
<drive root>:\WINNT\inf\mdmnova.PNF
<drive root>:\WINNT\inf\mdmnovfx.inf
<drive root>:\WINNT\inf\mdmnovfx.PNF
<drive root>:\WINNT\inf\mdmolic.inf
<drive root>:\WINNT\inf\mdmolic.PNF
<drive root>:\WINNT\inf\mdmolive.inf
<drive root>:\WINNT\inf\mdmolive.PNF
<drive root>:\WINNT\inf\mdmopt1.inf
<drive root>:\WINNT\inf\mdmopt1.PNF
<drive root>:\WINNT\inf\mdmoptn.inf
<drive root>:\WINNT\inf\mdmoptn.PNF
<drive root>:\WINNT\inf\mdmosi.inf
<drive root>:\WINNT\inf\mdmosi.PNF
<drive root>:\WINNT\inf\mdmpace.inf
<drive root>:\WINNT\inf\mdmpace.PNF
<drive root>:\WINNT\inf\mdmpbit.inf
<drive root>:\WINNT\inf\mdmpbit.PNF
<drive root>:\WINNT\inf\mdmpcsi.inf
<drive root>:\WINNT\inf\mdmpcsi.PNF
<drive root>:\WINNT\inf\mdmpctel.inf
<drive root>:\WINNT\inf\mdmpctel.PNF
<drive root>:\WINNT\inf\mdmphils.inf
<drive root>:\WINNT\inf\mdmphils.PNF
<drive root>:\WINNT\inf\mdmpn1.inf
<drive root>:\WINNT\inf\mdmpn1.PNF
<drive root>:\WINNT\inf\mdmpnb.inf
<drive root>:\WINNT\inf\mdmpnb.PNF
<drive root>:\WINNT\inf\mdmpp.inf
<drive root>:\WINNT\inf\mdmpp.PNF
<drive root>:\WINNT\inf\mdmprodm.inf
<drive root>:\WINNT\inf\mdmprodm.PNF
<drive root>:\WINNT\inf\mdmquant.inf
<drive root>:\WINNT\inf\mdmquant.PNF
<drive root>:\WINNT\inf\mdmracal.inf
<drive root>:\WINNT\inf\mdmracal.PNF
<drive root>:\WINNT\inf\mdmrfi.inf
<drive root>:\WINNT\inf\mdmrfi.PNF
<drive root>:\WINNT\inf\mdmrock.inf
<drive root>:\WINNT\inf\mdmrock.PNF
<drive root>:\WINNT\inf\mdmrock2.inf
```

```
<drive root>:\WINNT\inf\mdmrock2.PNF
<drive root>:\WINNT\inf\mdmrock3.inf
<drive root>:\WINNT\inf\mdmrock3.PNF
<drive root>:\WINNT\inf\mdmrock4.inf
<drive root>:\WINNT\inf\mdmrock4.PNF
<drive root>:\WINNT\inf\mdmrock5.inf
<drive root>:\WINNT\inf\mdmrock5.PNF
<drive root>:\WINNT\inf\mdmsecdy.inf
<drive root>:\WINNT\inf\mdmsecdy.PNF
<drive root>:\WINNT\inf\mdmsier.inf
<drive root>:\WINNT\inf\mdmsier.PNF
<drive root>:\WINNT\inf\mdmsimpl.inf
<drive root>:\WINNT\inf\mdmsimpl.PNF
<drive root>:\WINNT\inf\mdmsmart.inf
<drive root>:\WINNT\inf\mdmsmart.PNF
<drive root>:\WINNT\inf\mdmsmplt.inf
<drive root>:\WINNT\inf\mdmsmplt.PNF
<drive root>:\WINNT\inf\mdmsnit1.inf
<drive root>:\WINNT\inf\mdmsnit1.PNF
<drive root>:\WINNT\inf\mdmsnitn.inf
<drive root>:\WINNT\inf\mdmsnitn.PNF
<drive root>:\WINNT\inf\mdmsonix.inf
<drive root>:\WINNT\inf\mdmsonix.PNF
<drive root>:\WINNT\inf\mdmspq28.inf
<drive root>:\WINNT\inf\mdmspq28.PNF
<drive root>:\WINNT\inf\mdmsrt.inf
<drive root>:\WINNT\inf\mdmsrt.PNF
<drive root>:\WINNT\inf\mdmsupr3.inf
<drive root>:\WINNT\inf\mdmsupr3.PNF
<drive root>:\WINNT\inf\mdmsupra.inf
<drive root>:\WINNT\inf\mdmsupra.PNF
<drive root>:\WINNT\inf\mdmsuprv.inf
<drive root>:\WINNT\inf\mdmsuprv.PNF
<drive root>:\WINNT\inf\mdmtaicm.inf
<drive root>:\WINNT\inf\mdmtaicm.PNF
<drive root>:\WINNT\inf\mdmtdk.inf
<drive root>:\WINNT\inf\mdmtdk.PNF
<drive root>:\WINNT\inf\mdmtelbt.inf
<drive root>:\WINNT\inf\mdmtelbt.PNF
<drive root>:\WINNT\inf\mdmtelin.inf
<drive root>:\WINNT\inf\mdmtelin.PNF
<drive root>:\WINNT\inf\mdmtelnk.inf
<drive root>:\WINNT\inf\mdmtelnk.PNF
<drive root>:\WINNT\inf\mdmtexas.inf
<drive root>:\WINNT\inf\mdmtexas.PNF
<drive root>:\WINNT\inf\mdmtger.inf
<drive root>:\WINNT\inf\mdmtger.PNF
<drive root>:\WINNT\inf\mdmti.inf
<drive root>:\WINNT\inf\mdmti.PNF
<drive root>:\WINNT\inf\mdmtkr.inf
<drive root>:\WINNT\inf\mdmtkr.PNF
```

```
<drive root>:\WINNT\inf\mdmtorn.inf
<drive root>:\WINNT\inf\mdmtorn.PNF
<drive root>:\WINNT\inf\mdmtosh.inf
<drive root>:\WINNT\inf\mdmtosh.PNF
<drive root>:\WINNT\inf\mdmtripl.inf
<drive root>:\WINNT\inf\mdmtripl.PNF
<drive root>:\WINNT\inf\mdmtron.inf
<drive root>:\WINNT\inf\mdmtron.PNF
<drive root>:\WINNT\inf\mdmtrust.inf
<drive root>:\WINNT\inf\mdmtrust.PNF
<drive root>:\WINNT\inf\mdmucom.inf
<drive root>:\WINNT\inf\mdmucom.PNF
<drive root>:\WINNT\inf\mdmusrcr.inf
<drive root>:\WINNT\inf\mdmusrcr.PNF
<drive root>:\WINNT\inf\mdmusrf.inf
<drive root>:\WINNT\inf\mdmusrf.PNF
<drive root>:\WINNT\inf\mdmusrg.inf
<drive root>:\WINNT\inf\mdmusrg.PNF
<drive root>:\WINNT\inf\mdmusrsp.inf
<drive root>:\WINNT\inf\mdmusrsp.PNF
<drive root>:\WINNT\inf\mdmusrwp.inf
<drive root>:\WINNT\inf\mdmusrwp.PNF
<drive root>:\WINNT\inf\mdmvayrs.inf
<drive root>:\WINNT\inf\mdmvayrs.PNF
<drive root>:\WINNT\inf\mdmvdot.inf
<drive root>:\WINNT\inf\mdmvdot.PNF
<drive root>:\WINNT\inf\mdmvict.inf
<drive root>:\WINNT\inf\mdmvict.PNF
<drive root>:\WINNT\inf\mdmvv.inf
<drive root>:\WINNT\inf\mdmvv.PNF
<drive root>:\WINNT\inf\mdmwell.inf
<drive root>:\WINNT\inf\mdmwell.PNF
<drive root>:\WINNT\inf\mdmwhql0.inf
<drive root>:\WINNT\inf\mdmwhql0.PNF
<drive root>:\WINNT\inf\mdmwoer.inf
<drive root>:\WINNT\inf\mdmwoer.PNF
<drive root>:\WINNT\inf\mdmyorik.inf
<drive root>:\WINNT\inf\mdmyorik.PNF
<drive root>:\WINNT\inf\mdmzoom.inf
<drive root>:\WINNT\inf\mdmzoom.PNF
<drive root>:\WINNT\inf\mdmzyp.inf
<drive root>:\WINNT\inf\mdmzyp.PNF
<drive root>:\WINNT\inf\mdmzyxel.inf
<drive root>:\WINNT\inf\mdmzyxel.PNF
<drive root>:\WINNT\inf\mdmzyxld.inf
<drive root>:\WINNT\inf\mdmzyxld.PNF
<drive root>:\WINNT\inf\mdmzyxlg.inf
<drive root>:\WINNT\inf\mdmzyxlg.PNF
<drive root>:\WINNT\inf\mdmzyxln.inf
<drive root>:\WINNT\inf\mdmzyxln.PNF
<drive root>:\WINNT\inf\mmopt.inf
```

```
<drive root>:\WINNT\inf\mmopt.PNF
<drive root>:\WINNT\inf\msmail.inf
<drive root>:\WINNT\inf\msmail.PNF
<drive root>:\WINNT\inf\msmouse.inf
<drive root>:\WINNT\inf\msmouse.PNF
<drive root>:\WINNT\inf\multimed.inf
<drive root>:\WINNT\inf\multimed.PNF
<drive root>:\WINNT\inf\ntprint.inf
<drive root>:\WINNT\inf\ntprint.PNF
<drive root>:\WINNT\inf\optional.inf
<drive root>:\WINNT\inf\optional.PNF
<drive root>:\WINNT\inf\perms.inf
<drive root>:\WINNT\inf\perms.PNF
<drive root>:\WINNT\inf\pinball.inf
<drive root>:\WINNT\inf\pinball.PNF
<drive root>:\WINNT\inf\scsi.inf
<drive root>:\WINNT\inf\scsi.PNF
<drive root>:\WINNT\inf\syssetup.inf
<drive root>:\WINNT\inf\syssetup.PNF
<drive root>:\WINNT\inf\tape.inf
<drive root>:\WINNT\inf\tape.PNF
<drive root>:\WINNT\inf\wordpad.inf
<drive root>:\WINNT\inf\wordpad.PNF
<drive root>:\WINNT\Media\Bach's Brandenburg Concerto No. 3.RMI
<drive root>:\WINNT\Media\Beethoven's 5th Symphony.RMI
<drive root>:\WINNT\Media\Beethoven's Fur Elise.RMI
<drive root>:\WINNT\Media\canyon.mid
<drive root>:\WINNT\Media\chimes.wav
<drive root>:\WINNT\Media\chord.wav
<drive root>:\WINNT\Media\Dance of the Sugar-Plum Fairy.RMI
<drive root>:\WINNT\Media\Debussy's Claire de Lune.RMI
<drive root>:\WINNT\Media\ding.wav
<drive root>:\WINNT\Media\In the Hall of the Mountain King.RMI
<drive root>:\WINNT\Media\Jungle Asterisk.WAV
<drive root>:\WINNT\Media\Jungle Close.WAV
<drive root>:\WINNT\Media\Jungle Critical Stop.WAV
<drive root>:\WINNT\Media\Jungle Default.WAV
<drive root>:\WINNT\Media\Jungle Error.WAV
<drive root>:\WINNT\Media\Jungle Exclamation.WAV
<drive root>:\WINNT\Media\Jungle Maximize.WAV
<drive root>:\WINNT\Media\Jungle Menu Command.WAV
<drive root>:\WINNT\Media\Jungle Menu Popup.WAV
<drive root>:\WINNT\Media\Jungle Minimize.WAV
<drive root>:\WINNT\Media\Jungle Open.WAV
<drive root>:\WINNT\Media\Jungle Question.WAV
<drive root>:\WINNT\Media\Jungle Recycle.WAV
<drive root>:\WINNT\Media\Jungle Restore Down.WAV
<drive root>:\WINNT\Media\Jungle Restore Up.WAV
<drive root>:\WINNT\Media\Jungle Windows Exit.WAV
<drive root>:\WINNT\Media\Jungle Windows Start.WAV
<drive root>:\WINNT\Media\Mozart's Symphony No. 40.RMI
```

```
<drive root>:\WINNT\Media\Musica Asterisk.WAV
<drive root>:\WINNT\Media\Musica Close.WAV
<drive root>:\WINNT\Media\Musica Critical Stop.WAV
<drive root>:\WINNT\Media\Musica Default.WAV
<drive root>:\WINNT\Media\Musica Error.WAV
<drive root>:\WINNT\Media\Musica Exclamation.WAV
<drive root>:\WINNT\Media\Musica Maximize.WAV
<drive root>:\WINNT\Media\Musica Menu Command.WAV
<drive root>:\WINNT\Media\Musica Menu Popup.WAV
<drive root>:\WINNT\Media\Musica Minimize.WAV
<drive root>:\WINNT\Media\Musica Open.WAV
<drive root>:\WINNT\Media\Musica Question.WAV
<drive root>:\WINNT\Media\Musica Recycle.WAV
<drive root>:\WINNT\Media\Musica Restore Down.WAV
<drive root>:\WINNT\Media\Musica Restore Up.WAV
<drive root>:\WINNT\Media\Musica Windows Exit.WAV
<drive root>:\WINNT\Media\Musica Windows Start.WAV
<drive root>:\WINNT\Media\passport.mid
<drive root>:\WINNT\Media\ringin.wav
<drive root>:\WINNT\Media\ringout.wav
<drive root>:\WINNT\Media\Robotz Asterisk.WAV
<drive root>:\WINNT\Media\Robotz Close.WAV
<drive root>:\WINNT\Media\Robotz Critical Stop.WAV
<drive root>:\WINNT\Media\Robotz Default.WAV
<drive root>:\WINNT\Media\Robotz Error.WAV
<drive root>:\WINNT\Media\Robotz Exclamation.WAV
<drive root>:\WINNT\Media\Robotz Maximize.WAV
<drive root>:\WINNT\Media\Robotz Menu Command.WAV
<drive root>:\WINNT\Media\Robotz Menu Popup.WAV
<drive root>:\WINNT\Media\Robotz Minimize.WAV
<drive root>:\WINNT\Media\Robotz Open.WAV
<drive root>:\WINNT\Media\Robotz Question.WAV
<drive root>:\WINNT\Media\Robotz Recycle.WAV
<drive root>:\WINNT\Media\Robotz Restore Down.WAV
<drive root>:\WINNT\Media\Robotz Restore Up.WAV
<drive root>:\WINNT\Media\Robotz Windows Exit.WAV
<drive root>:\WINNT\Media\Robotz Windows Start.WAV
<drive root>:\WINNT\Media\tada.wav
<drive root>:\WINNT\Media\The Microsoft Sound.wav
<drive root>:\WINNT\Media\Utopia Asterisk.WAV
<drive root>:\WINNT\Media\Utopia Close.WAV
<drive root>:\WINNT\Media\Utopia Critical Stop.WAV
<drive root>:\WINNT\Media\Utopia Default.WAV
<drive root>:\WINNT\Media\Utopia Error.WAV
<drive root>:\WINNT\Media\Utopia Exclamation.WAV
<drive root>:\WINNT\Media\Utopia Maximize.WAV
<drive root>:\WINNT\Media\Utopia Menu Command.WAV
<drive root>:\WINNT\Media\Utopia Menu Popup.WAV
<drive root>:\WINNT\Media\Utopia Minimize.WAV
<drive root>:\WINNT\Media\Utopia Open.WAV
<drive root>:\WINNT\Media\Utopia Question.WAV
```

```
<drive root>:\WINNT\Media\Utopia Recycle.WAV
<drive root>:\WINNT\Media\Utopia Restore Down.WAV
<drive root>:\WINNT\Media\Utopia Restore Up.WAV
<drive root>:\WINNT\Media\Utopia Windows Exit.WAV
<drive root>:\WINNT\Media\Utopia Windows Start.WAV
<drive root>:\WINNT\Media\Windows NT Logoff Sound.wav
<drive root>:\WINNT\Media\Windows NT Logon Sound.wav
<drive root>:\WINNT\Profiles\Administrator
<drive root>:\WINNT\Profiles\All Users
<drive root>:\WINNT\Profiles\Default User
<drive root>:\WINNT\Profiles\Administrator\Application Data
<drive root>:\WINNT\Profiles\Administrator\Desktop
<drive root>:\WINNT\Profiles\Administrator\Favorites
<drive root>:\WINNT\Profiles\Administrator\NTUSER.DAT
<drive root>:\WINNT\Profiles\Administrator\ntuser.dat.LOG
<drive root>:\WINNT\Profiles\Administrator\Personal
<drive root>:\WINNT\Profiles\Administrator\SendTo
<drive root>:\WINNT\Profiles\Administrator\Start Menu
<drive root>:\WINNT\Profiles\Administrator\Desktop\Files named @.exe.fnd
<drive root>:\WINNT\Profiles\Administrator\Desktop\My Briefcase
<drive root>:\WINNT\Profiles\Administrator\Recent\rasread.txt.lnk
<drive root>:\WINNT\Profiles\Administrator\Recent\setuplog.txt.lnk
<drive root>:\WINNT\Profiles\Administrator\Recent\Swimming Pool.bmp.lnk
<drive root>:\WINNT\Profiles\Administrator\Recent\text.txt.lnk
<drive root>:\WINNT\Profiles\Administrator\Recent\trace.txt.lnk
<drive root>:\WINNT\Profiles\Administrator\Recent\trace1.txt.lnk
<drive root>:\WINNT\Profiles\Administrator\Recent\winword.doc.lnk
<drive root>:\WINNT\Profiles\Administrator\Recent\Zapotec.bmp.lnk
<drive root>:\WINNT\Profiles\Administrator\SendTo\3« Floppy (A).lnk
<drive root>:\WINNT\Profiles\Administrator\SendTo\Mail Recipient.lnk
<drive root>:\WINNT\Profiles\Administrator\SendTo\My Briefcase.lnk
<drive root>:\WINNT\Profiles\Administrator\Start Menu\Programs
<drive root>:\WINNT\Profiles\Administrator\Start Menu\Programs\Accessories
<drive root>:\WINNT\Profiles\Administrator\Start Menu\Programs\Command Prompt.lnk
<drive root>:\WINNT\Profiles\Administrator\Start Menu\Programs\Startup
<drive root>:\WINNT\Profiles\Administrator\Start Menu\Programs\
➥Windows Messaging.lnk
<drive root>:\WINNT\Profiles\Administrator\Start Menu\Programs\
➥Windows NT Explorer.lnk
<drive root>:\WINNT\Profiles\Administrator\Start Menu\Programs\
➥Accessories\Calculator.lnk
<drive root>:\WINNT\Profiles\Administrator\Start Menu\Programs\
➥Accessories\Character Map.lnk
<drive root>:\WINNT\Profiles\Administrator\Start Menu\Programs\Accessories\Chat.lnk
<drive root>:\WINNT\Profiles\Administrator\Start Menu\Programs\
➥Accessories\Clipboard Viewer.lnk
<drive root>:\WINNT\Profiles\Administrator\Start Menu\Programs\
➥Accessories\Clock.lnk
<drive root>:\WINNT\Profiles\Administrator\Start Menu\Programs\
➥Accessories\Dial-Up Networking.lnk
<drive root>:\WINNT\Profiles\Administrator\Start Menu\Programs\Accessories\Games
```

```
<drive root>:\WINNT\Profiles\Administrator\Start Menu\Programs\
➥Accessories\Hyperterminal
<drive root>:\WINNT\Profiles\Administrator\Start Menu\Programs\
➥Accessories\Imaging.lnk
<drive root>:\WINNT\Profiles\Administrator\Start Menu\Programs\
➥Accessories\Multimedia
<drive root>:\WINNT\Profiles\Administrator\Start Menu\Programs\
➥Accessories\Notepad.lnk
<drive root>:\WINNT\Profiles\Administrator\Start Menu\Programs\
➥Accessories\Object Packager.lnk
<drive root>:\WINNT\Profiles\Administrator\Start Menu\Programs\
➥Accessories\Paint.lnk
<drive root>:\WINNT\Profiles\Administrator\Start Menu\Programs\
➥Accessories\Phone Dialer.lnk
<drive root>:\WINNT\Profiles\Administrator\Start Menu\Programs\
➥Accessories\System Tools
<drive root>:\WINNT\Profiles\Administrator\Start Menu\Programs\
➥Accessories\Telnet.lnk
<drive root>:\WINNT\Profiles\Administrator\Start Menu\Programs\
➥Accessories\WordPad.lnk
<drive root>:\WINNT\Profiles\Administrator\Start Menu\Programs\
➥Accessories\Games\Freecell.lnk
<drive root>:\WINNT\Profiles\Administrator\Start Menu\Programs\
➥Accessories\Games\Minesweeper.lnk
<drive root>:\WINNT\Profiles\Administrator\Start Menu\Programs\
➥Accessories\Games\Pinball.lnk
<drive root>:\WINNT\Profiles\Administrator\Start Menu\Programs\
➥Accessories\Games\Solitaire.lnk
<drive root>:\WINNT\Profiles\Administrator\Start Menu\Programs\
➥Accessories\Hyperterminal\AT&T Mail.ht
<drive root>:\WINNT\Profiles\Administrator\Start Menu\Programs\
➥Accessories\Hyperterminal\CompuServe.ht
<drive root>:\WINNT\Profiles\Administrator\Start Menu\Programs\
➥Accessories\Hyperterminal\HyperTerminal BBS.ht
<drive root>:\WINNT\Profiles\Administrator\Start Menu\Programs\
➥Accessories\Hyperterminal\HyperTerminal.lnk
<drive root>:\WINNT\Profiles\Administrator\Start Menu\Programs\
➥Accessories\Hyperterminal\MCI Mail.ht
<drive root>:\WINNT\Profiles\Administrator\Start Menu\Programs\
➥Accessories\Hyperterminal\Microsoft BBS.ht
<drive root>:\WINNT\Profiles\Administrator\Start Menu\Programs\
➥Accessories\Multimedia\CD Player.lnk
<drive root>:\WINNT\Profiles\Administrator\Start Menu\Programs\
➥Accessories\Multimedia\Media Player.lnk
<drive root>:\WINNT\Profiles\Administrator\Start Menu\Programs\
➥Accessories\Multimedia\Sound Recorder.lnk
<drive root>:\WINNT\Profiles\Administrator\Start Menu\Programs\
➥Accessories\Multimedia\Volume Control.lnk
<drive root>:\WINNT\Profiles\Administrator\Start Menu\Programs\
➥Accessories\System Tools\Inbox Repair Tool.lnk
<drive root>:\WINNT\Profiles\All Users\Desktop
```

```
<drive root>:\WINNT\Profiles\All Users\Start Menu
<drive root>:\WINNT\Profiles\All Users\Start Menu\Programs
<drive root>:\WINNT\Profiles\All Users\Start Menu\Programs\
➡Administrative Tools (Common)
<drive root>:\WINNT\Profiles\All Users\Start Menu\Programs\Startup
<drive root>:\WINNT\Profiles\All Users\Start Menu\Programs\
➡Administrative Tools (Common)\Backup.lnk
<drive root>:\WINNT\Profiles\All Users\Start Menu\Programs\
➡Administrative Tools (Common)\Disk Administrator.lnk
<drive root>:\WINNT\Profiles\All Users\Start Menu\Programs\
➡Administrative Tools (Common)\Event Viewer.lnk
<drive root>:\WINNT\Profiles\All Users\Start Menu\Programs\
➡Administrative Tools (Common)\Performance Monitor.lnk
<drive root>:\WINNT\Profiles\All Users\Start Menu\Programs\
➡Administrative Tools (Common)\Remote Access Admin.lnk
<drive root>:\WINNT\Profiles\All Users\Start Menu\Programs\
➡Administrative Tools (Common)\User Manager.lnk
<drive root>:\WINNT\Profiles\All Users\Start Menu\Programs\
➡Administrative Tools (Common)\Windows NT Diagnostics.lnk
<drive root>:\WINNT\Profiles\Default User\Application Data
<drive root>:\WINNT\Profiles\Default User\Desktop
<drive root>:\WINNT\Profiles\Default User\Favorites
<drive root>:\WINNT\Profiles\Default User\NTUSER.DAT
<drive root>:\WINNT\Profiles\Default User\Personal
<drive root>:\WINNT\Profiles\Default User\SendTo
<drive root>:\WINNT\Profiles\Default User\Start Menu
<drive root>:\WINNT\Profiles\Default User\SendTo\3« Floppy (A).lnk
<drive root>:\WINNT\Profiles\Default User\SendTo\Mail Recipient.lnk
<drive root>:\WINNT\Profiles\Default User\Start Menu\Programs
<drive root>:\WINNT\Profiles\Default User\Start Menu\Programs\Accessories
<drive root>:\WINNT\Profiles\Default User\Start Menu\Programs\Command Prompt.lnk
<drive root>:\WINNT\Profiles\Default User\Start Menu\Programs\Startup
<drive root>:\WINNT\Profiles\Default User\Start Menu\Programs\Windows Messaging.lnk
<drive root>:\WINNT\Profiles\Default User\Start Menu\Programs\
➡Windows NT Explorer.lnk
<drive root>:\WINNT\Profiles\Default User\Start
Menu\Programs\Accessories\Calculator.lnk
<drive root>:\WINNT\Profiles\Default User\Start Menu\Programs\
➡Accessories\Character Map.lnk
<drive root>:\WINNT\Profiles\Default User\Start Menu\Programs\
➡Accessories\Chat.lnk
<drive root>:\WINNT\Profiles\Default User\Start Menu\Programs\
➡Accessories\Clipboard Viewer.lnk
<drive root>:\WINNT\Profiles\Default User\Start Menu\Programs\
➡Accessories\Clock.lnk
<drive root>:\WINNT\Profiles\Default User\Start Menu\Programs\
➡Accessories\Dial-Up Networking.lnk
<drive root>:\WINNT\Profiles\Default User\Start Menu\Programs\
➡Accessories\Games
<drive root>:\WINNT\Profiles\Default User\Start Menu\Programs\
➡Accessories\Hyperterminal
```

```
<drive root>:\WINNT\Profiles\Default User\Start Menu\Programs\
➥Accessories\Imaging.lnk
<drive root>:\WINNT\Profiles\Default User\Start Menu\Programs\
➥Accessories\Multimedia
<drive root>:\WINNT\Profiles\Default User\Start Menu\Programs\
➥Accessories\Notepad.lnk
<drive root>:\WINNT\Profiles\Default User\Start Menu\Programs\
➥Accessories\Object Packager.lnk
<drive root>:\WINNT\Profiles\Default User\Start Menu\Programs\Accessories\Paint.lnk
<drive root>:\WINNT\Profiles\Default User\Start Menu\Programs\
➥Accessories\Phone Dialer.lnk
<drive root>:\WINNT\Profiles\Default User\Start Menu\Programs\
➥Accessories\System Tools
<drive root>:\WINNT\Profiles\Default User\Start Menu\Programs\
➥Accessories\Telnet.lnk
<drive root>:\WINNT\Profiles\Default User\Start Menu\Programs\
➥Accessories\WordPad.lnk
<drive root>:\WINNT\Profiles\Default User\Start Menu\Programs\
➥Accessories\Games\Freecell.lnk
<drive root>:\WINNT\Profiles\Default User\Start Menu\Programs\
➥Accessories\Games\Minesweeper.lnk
<drive root>:\WINNT\Profiles\Default User\Start Menu\Programs\
➥Accessories\Games\Pinball.lnk
<drive root>:\WINNT\Profiles\Default User\Start Menu\Programs\
➥Accessories\Games\Solitaire.lnk
<drive root>:\WINNT\Profiles\Default User\Start Menu\Programs\
➥Accessories\Hyperterminal\AT&T Mail.ht
<drive root>:\WINNT\Profiles\Default User\Start Menu\Programs\
➥Accessories\Hyperterminal\CompuServe.ht
<drive root>:\WINNT\Profiles\Default User\Start Menu\Programs\
➥Accessories\Hyperterminal\HyperTerminal BBS.ht
<drive root>:\WINNT\Profiles\Default User\Start Menu\Programs\
➥Accessories\Hyperterminal\HyperTerminal.lnk
<drive root>:\WINNT\Profiles\Default User\Start Menu\Programs\
➥Accessories\Hyperterminal\MCI Mail.ht
<drive root>:\WINNT\Profiles\Default User\Start Menu\Programs\
➥Accessories\Hyperterminal\Microsoft BBS.ht
<drive root>:\WINNT\Profiles\Default User\Start Menu\Programs\
➥Accessories\Multimedia\CD Player.lnk
<drive root>:\WINNT\Profiles\Default User\Start Menu\Programs\
➥Accessories\Multimedia\Media Player.lnk
<drive root>:\WINNT\Profiles\Default User\Start Menu\Programs\
➥Accessories\Multimedia\Sound Recorder.lnk
<drive root>:\WINNT\Profiles\Default User\Start Menu\Programs\
➥Accessories\Multimedia\Volume Control.lnk
<drive root>:\WINNT\Profiles\Default User\Start Menu\Programs\
➥Accessories\System Tools\Inbox Repair Tool.lnk
<drive root>:\WINNT\repair\autoexec.nt
<drive root>:\WINNT\repair\config.nt
<drive root>:\WINNT\repair\default._
<drive root>:\WINNT\repair\ntuser.da_
```

```
<drive root>:\WINNT\repair\sam._
<drive root>:\WINNT\repair\security._
<drive root>:\WINNT\repair\setup.log
<drive root>:\WINNT\repair\software._
<drive root>:\WINNT\repair\system._
<drive root>:\WINNT\ShellNew\amipro.sam
<drive root>:\WINNT\ShellNew\excel.xls
<drive root>:\WINNT\ShellNew\excel4.xls
<drive root>:\WINNT\ShellNew\lotus.wk4
<drive root>:\WINNT\ShellNew\powerpnt.ppt
<drive root>:\WINNT\ShellNew\presenta.shw
<drive root>:\WINNT\ShellNew\quattro.wb2
<drive root>:\WINNT\ShellNew\winword.doc
<drive root>:\WINNT\ShellNew\winword2.doc
<drive root>:\WINNT\ShellNew\wordpfct.wpd
<drive root>:\WINNT\ShellNew\wordpfct.wpg
<drive root>:\WINNT\system\AVICAP.DLL
<drive root>:\WINNT\system\AVIFILE.DLL
<drive root>:\WINNT\system\COMMDLG.DLL
<drive root>:\WINNT\system\KEYBOARD.DRV
<drive root>:\WINNT\system\LZEXPAND.DLL
<drive root>:\WINNT\system\MCIAVI.DRV
<drive root>:\WINNT\system\MCISEQ.DRV
<drive root>:\WINNT\system\MCIWAVE.DRV
<drive root>:\WINNT\system\MMSYSTEM.DLL
<drive root>:\WINNT\system\MMTASK.TSK
<drive root>:\WINNT\system\MOUSE.DRV
<drive root>:\WINNT\system\MSVIDEO.DLL
<drive root>:\WINNT\system\OLECLI.DLL
<drive root>:\WINNT\system\OLESVR.DLL
<drive root>:\WINNT\system\setup.inf
<drive root>:\WINNT\system\SHELL.DLL
<drive root>:\WINNT\system\SOUND.DRV
<drive root>:\WINNT\system\SYSTEM.DRV
<drive root>:\WINNT\system\TAPI.DLL
<drive root>:\WINNT\system\TIMER.DRV
<drive root>:\WINNT\system\VER.DLL
<drive root>:\WINNT\system\VGA.DRV
<drive root>:\WINNT\system\WFWNET.DRV
<drive root>:\WINNT\system\WINSPOOL.DRV
<drive root>:\WINNT\system32\$winnt$.inf
<drive root>:\WINNT\system32\3c90xcfg.dll
<drive root>:\WINNT\system32\3nicdiag.exe
<drive root>:\WINNT\system32\3nicdiag.hlp
<drive root>:\WINNT\system32\3varaddr.txt
<drive root>:\WINNT\system32\access.cpl
<drive root>:\WINNT\system32\acledit.dll
<drive root>:\WINNT\system32\advapi32.dll
<drive root>:\WINNT\system32\alrsvc.dll
<drive root>:\WINNT\system32\amddlg.dll
<drive root>:\WINNT\system32\amdncdet.dll
```

```
<drive root>:\WINNT\system32\ansi.sys
<drive root>:\WINNT\system32\append.exe
<drive root>:\WINNT\system32\appwiz.cpl
<drive root>:\WINNT\system32\ARP.EXE
<drive root>:\WINNT\system32\at.exe
<drive root>:\WINNT\system32\atsvc.exe
<drive root>:\WINNT\system32\attrib.exe
<drive root>:\WINNT\system32\audiocdc.hlp
<drive root>:\WINNT\system32\autochk.exe
<drive root>:\WINNT\system32\autoconv.exe
<drive root>:\WINNT\system32\AUTOEXEC.NT
<drive root>:\WINNT\system32\autolfn.exe
<drive root>:\WINNT\system32\avicap.dll
<drive root>:\WINNT\system32\avicap32.dll
<drive root>:\WINNT\system32\avifil32.dll
<drive root>:\WINNT\system32\avifile.dll
<drive root>:\WINNT\system32\backup.cnt
<drive root>:\WINNT\system32\backup.exe
<drive root>:\WINNT\system32\backup.hlp
<drive root>:\WINNT\system32\basesrv.dll
<drive root>:\WINNT\system32\bios1.rom
<drive root>:\WINNT\system32\bios4.rom
<drive root>:\WINNT\system32\bootok.exe
<drive root>:\WINNT\system32\bootvrfy.exe
<drive root>:\WINNT\system32\BROWSER.DLL
<drive root>:\WINNT\system32\cacls.exe
<drive root>:\WINNT\system32\calc.cnt
<drive root>:\WINNT\system32\calc.exe
<drive root>:\WINNT\system32\calc.hlp
<drive root>:\WINNT\system32\cards.dll
<drive root>:\WINNT\system32\cdplayer.cnt
<drive root>:\WINNT\system32\cdplayer.exe
<drive root>:\WINNT\system32\cdplayer.hlp
<drive root>:\WINNT\system32\cfgmgr32.dll
<drive root>:\WINNT\system32\charmap.cnt
<drive root>:\WINNT\system32\charmap.exe
<drive root>:\WINNT\system32\charmap.hlp
<drive root>:\WINNT\system32\chcp.com
<drive root>:\WINNT\system32\chkdsk.exe
<drive root>:\WINNT\system32\clb.dll
<drive root>:\WINNT\system32\clipbrd.cnt
<drive root>:\WINNT\system32\clipbrd.exe
<drive root>:\WINNT\system32\clipbrd.hlp
<drive root>:\WINNT\system32\clipsrv.exe
<drive root>:\WINNT\system32\clock.exe
<drive root>:\WINNT\system32\cmc.dll
<drive root>:\WINNT\system32\cmd.exe
<drive root>:\WINNT\system32\cmos.ram
<drive root>:\WINNT\system32\cnvfat.dll
<drive root>:\WINNT\system32\comctl32.dll
<drive root>:\WINNT\system32\comdlg32.dll
```

```
<drive root>:\WINNT\system32\comm.drv
<drive root>:\WINNT\system32\command.com
<drive root>:\WINNT\system32\commdlg.dll
<drive root>:\WINNT\system32\comp.exe
<drive root>:\WINNT\system32\compact.exe
<drive root>:\WINNT\system32\compobj.dll
<drive root>:\WINNT\system32\compstui.dll
<drive root>:\WINNT\system32\config
<drive root>:\WINNT\system32\CONFIG.NT
<drive root>:\WINNT\system32\CONFIG.TMP
<drive root>:\WINNT\system32\console.cpl
<drive root>:\WINNT\system32\control.exe
<drive root>:\WINNT\system32\control.hlp
<drive root>:\WINNT\system32\convert.exe
<drive root>:\WINNT\system32\country.sys
<drive root>:\WINNT\system32\crtdll.dll
<drive root>:\WINNT\system32\csrsrv.dll
<drive root>:\WINNT\system32\csrss.exe
<drive root>:\WINNT\system32\ctl3dv2.dll
<drive root>:\WINNT\system32\ctype.nls
<drive root>:\WINNT\system32\c_10000.nls
<drive root>:\WINNT\system32\c_1250.nls
<drive root>:\WINNT\system32\c_1251.nls
<drive root>:\WINNT\system32\c_1252.nls
<drive root>:\WINNT\system32\c_1253.nls
<drive root>:\WINNT\system32\c_1254.nls
<drive root>:\WINNT\system32\c_1255.nls
<drive root>:\WINNT\system32\c_1256.nls
<drive root>:\WINNT\system32\c_1257.ns
<drive root>:\WINNT\system32\c_1258.nls
<drive root>:\WINNT\system32\c_20261.nls
<drive root>:\WINNT\system32\c_20866.nls
<drive root>:\WINNT\system32\c_28592.nls
<drive root>:\WINNT\system32\c_437.nls
<drive root>:\WINNT\system32\c_775.nls
<drive root>:\WINNT\system32\c_850.nls
<drive root>:\WINNT\system32\dc21x4.hlp
<drive root>:\WINNT\system32\dciman32.dll
<drive root>:\WINNT\system32\dcomcnfg.exe
<drive root>:\WINNT\system32\ddeml.dll
<drive root>:\WINNT\system32\ddeshare.cnt
<drive root>:\WINNT\system32\ddeshare.exe
<drive root>:\WINNT\system32\ddeshare.hlp
<drive root>:\WINNT\system32\ddhelp.exe
<drive root>:\WINNT\system32\ddraw.dll
<drive root>:\WINNT\system32\debug.exe
<drive root>:\WINNT\system32\defddi.hlp
<drive root>:\WINNT\system32\defea.dll
<drive root>:\WINNT\system32\defpa.dll
<drive root>:\WINNT\system32\desk.cpl
<drive root>:\WINNT\system32\devapps.cpl
```

```
<drive root>:\WINNT\system32\dhcp
<drive root>:\WINNT\system32\DHCPCSVC.DLL
<drive root>:\WINNT\system32\DHCPSAPI.DLL
<drive root>:\WINNT\system32\digsig.dll
<drive root>:\WINNT\system32\diskcomp.com
<drive root>:\WINNT\system32\diskcopy.com
<drive root>:\WINNT\system32\diskcopy.dll
<drive root>:\WINNT\system32\diskperf.exe
<drive root>:\WINNT\system32\dlcapi.dll
<drive root>:\WINNT\system32\docprop.dll
<drive root>:\WINNT\system32\doshelp.hlp
<drive root>:\WINNT\system32\doskey.exe
<drive root>:\WINNT\system32\dosx.exe
<drive root>:\WINNT\system32\dplay.dll
<drive root>:\WINNT\system32\dpserial.dll
<drive root>:\WINNT\system32\dpwsock.dll
<drive root>:\WINNT\system32\drivers
<drive root>:\WINNT\system32\drmon
<drive root>:\WINNT\system32\drmonnt.inf
<drive root>:\WINNT\system32\drwatson.exe
<drive root>:\WINNT\system32\drwtsn32.cnt
<drive root>:\WINNT\system32\drwtsn32.exe
<drive root>:\WINNT\system32\drwtsn32.hlp
<drive root>:\WINNT\system32\dsound.dll
<drive root>:\WINNT\system32\dtaapi.dll
<drive root>:\WINNT\system32\edit.com
<drive root>:\WINNT\system32\edit.hlp
<drive root>:\WINNT\system32\edlin.exe
<drive root>:\WINNT\system32\ega.cpi
<drive root>:\WINNT\system32\eventlog.dll
<drive root>:\WINNT\system32\eventvwr.cnt
<drive root>:\WINNT\system32\eventvwr.exe
<drive root>:\WINNT\system32\eventvwr.hlp
<drive root>:\WINNT\system32\exe2bin.exe
<drive root>:\WINNT\system32\expand.exe
<drive root>:\WINNT\system32\fastopen.exe
<drive root>:\WINNT\system32\fc.exe
<drive root>:\WINNT\system32\find.exe
<drive root>:\WINNT\system32\findstr.exe
<drive root>:\WINNT\system32\FINGER.EXE
<drive root>:\WINNT\system32\fmifs.dll
<drive root>:\WINNT\system32\fontext.dll
<drive root>:\WINNT\system32\fontview.exe
<drive root>:\WINNT\system32\forcedos.exe
<drive root>:\WINNT\system32\format.com
<drive root>:\WINNT\system32\framebuf.dll
<drive root>:\WINNT\system32\freecell.cnt
<drive root>:\WINNT\system32\freecell.exe
<drive root>:\WINNT\system32\freecell.hlp
<drive root>:\WINNT\system32\FTP.EXE
<drive root>:\WINNT\system32\ftsrch.dll
```

```
<drive root>:\WINNT\system32\gdi.exe
<drive root>:\WINNT\system32\gdi32.dll
<drive root>:\WINNT\system32\glmf32.dll
<drive root>:\WINNT\system32\glossary.hlp
<drive root>:\WINNT\system32\glu32.dll
<drive root>:\WINNT\system32\gorilla.bas
<drive root>:\WINNT\system32\graftabl.com
<drive root>:\WINNT\system32\graphics.com
<drive root>:\WINNT\system32\graphics.pro
<drive root>:\WINNT\system32\grpconv.exe
<drive root>:\WINNT\system32\hal.dll
<drive root>:\WINNT\system32\halftone.hlp
<drive root>:\WINNT\system32\hardware.inf
<drive root>:\WINNT\system32\help.exe
<drive root>:\WINNT\system32\himem.sys
<drive root>:\WINNT\system32\HOSTNAME.EXE
<drive root>:\WINNT\system32\hpscan32.dll
<drive root>:\WINNT\system32\hticons.dll
<drive root>:\WINNT\system32\htui.dll
<drive root>:\WINNT\system32\hwaccess.dll
<drive root>:\WINNT\system32\hypertrm.dll
<drive root>:\WINNT\system32\iccvid.dll
<drive root>:\WINNT\system32\ICMP.DLL
<drive root>:\WINNT\system32\ifsutil.dll
<drive root>:\WINNT\system32\imaadp32.acm
<drive root>:\WINNT\system32\imagehlp.dll
<drive root>:\WINNT\system32\imgadmin.ocx
<drive root>:\WINNT\system32\imgedit.ocx
<drive root>:\WINNT\system32\imgscan.ocx
<drive root>:\WINNT\system32\imgthumb.ocx
<drive root>:\WINNT\system32\imm32.dll
<drive root>:\WINNT\system32\indicdll.dll
<drive root>:\WINNT\system32\inetcpl.cpl
<drive root>:\WINNT\system32\inetins.exe
<drive root>:\WINNT\system32\INETMIB1.DLL
<drive root>:\WINNT\system32\internat.exe
<drive root>:\WINNT\system32\intl.cpl
<drive root>:\WINNT\system32\iologmsg.dll
<drive root>:\WINNT\system32\IPCONFIG.EXE
<drive root>:\WINNT\system32\IPINFO.INF
<drive root>:\WINNT\system32\ipxcfg.dll
<drive root>:\WINNT\system32\ir32_32.dll
<drive root>:\WINNT\system32\iso88591.trn
<drive root>:\WINNT\system32\joy.cpl
<drive root>:\WINNT\system32\jpeg1x32.dll
<drive root>:\WINNT\system32\jpeg2x32.dll
<drive root>:\WINNT\system32\kb16.com
<drive root>:\WINNT\system32\kbddll.dll
<drive root>:\WINNT\system32\KBDUS.DLL
<drive root>:\WINNT\system32\kernel32.dll
<drive root>:\WINNT\system32\keyb.com
```

```
<drive root>:\WINNT\system32\keyboard.drv
<drive root>:\WINNT\system32\keyboard.sys
<drive root>:\WINNT\system32\kmddsp.tsp
<drive root>:\WINNT\system32\krnl386.exe
<drive root>:\WINNT\system32\label.exe
<drive root>:\WINNT\system32\lanman.drv
<drive root>:\WINNT\system32\legacy.inf
<drive root>:\WINNT\system32\lights.exe
<drive root>:\WINNT\system32\linkinfo.dll
<drive root>:\WINNT\system32\LMHSVC.DLL
<drive root>:\WINNT\system32\LMREPL.EXE
<drive root>:\WINNT\system32\loadfix.com
<drive root>:\WINNT\system32\loadperf.dll
<drive root>:\WINNT\system32\locale.nls
<drive root>:\WINNT\system32\localmon.dll
<drive root>:\WINNT\system32\localspl.dll
<drive root>:\WINNT\system32\LOCATOR.EXE
<drive root>:\WINNT\system32\lodctr.exe
<drive root>:\WINNT\system32\logon.scr
<drive root>:\WINNT\system32\lsasrv.dll
<drive root>:\WINNT\system32\lsass.exe
<drive root>:\WINNT\system32\lz32.dll
<drive root>:\WINNT\system32\lzexpand.dll
<drive root>:\WINNT\system32\l_except.nls
<drive root>:\WINNT\system32\l_intl.nls
<drive root>:\WINNT\system32\main.cpl
<drive root>:\WINNT\system32\mapi.dll
<drive root>:\WINNT\system32\mapi32.dll
<drive root>:\WINNT\system32\mapirpc.reg
<drive root>:\WINNT\system32\mapisp32.exe
<drive root>:\WINNT\system32\mapisrvr.exe
<drive root>:\WINNT\system32\mapisvc.inf
<drive root>:\WINNT\system32\mapiu.dll
<drive root>:\WINNT\system32\mapiu32.dll
<drive root>:\WINNT\system32\mapix.dll
<drive root>:\WINNT\system32\mapix32.dll
<drive root>:\WINNT\system32\mcd32.dll
<drive root>:\WINNT\system32\mcdsrv32.dll
<drive root>:\WINNT\system32\mciavi.drv
<drive root>:\WINNT\system32\mciavi32.dll
<drive root>:\WINNT\system32\mcicda.dll
<drive root>:\WINNT\system32\mciole16.dll
<drive root>:\WINNT\system32\mciole32.dll
<drive root>:\WINNT\system32\mciseq.dll
<drive root>:\WINNT\system32\mciseq.drv
<drive root>:\WINNT\system32\mciwave.dll
<drive root>:\WINNT\system32\mciwave.drv
<drive root>:\WINNT\system32\mdgncdet.dll
<drive root>:\WINNT\system32\mdisp.tlb
<drive root>:\WINNT\system32\mdisp32.exe
<drive root>:\WINNT\system32\mdisp32.reg
```

```
<drive root>:\WINNT\system32\mdisp32.tlb
<drive root>:\WINNT\system32\mem.exe
<drive root>:\WINNT\system32\mf3216.dll
<drive root>:\WINNT\system32\mfc40.dll
<drive root>:\WINNT\system32\mfc40u.dll
<drive root>:\WINNT\system32\mfc42.dll
<drive root>:\WINNT\system32\mfc42u.dll
<drive root>:\WINNT\system32\mfcuix.hlp
<drive root>:\WINNT\system32\midimap.cfg
<drive root>:\WINNT\system32\midimap.dll
<drive root>:\WINNT\system32\minet32.dll
<drive root>:\WINNT\system32\ml3xec16.exe
<drive root>:\WINNT\system32\mlcfg32.cpl
<drive root>:\WINNT\system32\mmdriver.inf
<drive root>:\WINNT\system32\mmdrv.dll
<drive root>:\WINNT\system32\MMFMIG32.DLL
<drive root>:\WINNT\system32\mmsys.cpl
<drive root>:\WINNT\system32\mmsystem.dll
<drive root>:\WINNT\system32\mmtask.tsk
<drive root>:\WINNT\system32\mode.com
<drive root>:\WINNT\system32\modem.cpl
<drive root>:\WINNT\system32\modemui.dll
<drive root>:\WINNT\system32\money.bas
<drive root>:\WINNT\system32\monitor.inf
<drive root>:\WINNT\system32\more.com
<drive root>:\WINNT\system32\moricons.dll
<drive root>:\WINNT\system32\mouse.drv
<drive root>:\WINNT\system32\mplay32.exe
<drive root>:\WINNT\system32\mplayer.cnt
<drive root>:\WINNT\system32\mplayer.hlp
<drive root>:\WINNT\system32\mpnotify.exe
<drive root>:\WINNT\system32\mpr.dll
<drive root>:\WINNT\system32\mprui.dll
<drive root>:\WINNT\system32\msacm.dll
<drive root>:\WINNT\system32\msacm32.dll
<drive root>:\WINNT\system32\msacm32.drv
<drive root>:\WINNT\system32\msadp32.acm
<drive root>:\WINNT\system32\msafd.dll
<drive root>:\WINNT\system32\msaudite.dll
<drive root>:\WINNT\system32\mscdexnt.exe
<drive root>:\WINNT\system32\msfs32.dll
<drive root>:\WINNT\system32\msg711.acm
<drive root>:\WINNT\system32\msgina.dll
<drive root>:\WINNT\system32\msgsm32.acm
<drive root>:\WINNT\system32\msgsvc.dll
<drive root>:\WINNT\system32\msjt3032.dll
<drive root>:\WINNT\system32\msncdet.dll
<drive root>:\WINNT\system32\msnsspc.dll
<drive root>:\WINNT\system32\msobjs.dll
<drive root>:\WINNT\system32\mspaint.exe
<drive root>:\WINNT\system32\msprivs.dll
```

```
<drive root>:\WINNT\system32\mspst32.dll
<drive root>:\WINNT\system32\msrle32.dl
<drive root>:\WINNT\system32\msv1_0.dll
<drive root>:\WINNT\system32\msvcirt.dll
<drive root>:\WINNT\system32\msvcrt.dll
<drive root>:\WINNT\system32\msvcrt20.dll
<drive root>:\WINNT\system32\msvcrt40.dll
<drive root>:\WINNT\system32\msvfw32.dll
<drive root>:\WINNT\system32\msvidc32.dll
<drive root>:\WINNT\system32\msvideo.dll
<drive root>:\WINNT\system32\mswsock.dll
<drive root>:\WINNT\system32\musrmgr.cnt
<drive root>:\WINNT\system32\musrmgr.exe
<drive root>:\WINNT\system32\musrmgr.hlp
<drive root>:\WINNT\system32\nbinfo.inf
<drive root>:\WINNT\system32\NBTSTAT.EXE
<drive root>:\WINNT\system32\ncpa.cpl
<drive root>:\WINNT\system32\ncparam.inf
<drive root>:\WINNT\system32\ncpashel.inf
<drive root>:\WINNT\system32\nddeagnt.exe
<drive root>:\WINNT\system32\nddeapi.dll
<drive root>:\WINNT\system32\nddeapir.exe
<drive root>:\WINNT\system32\nddenb32.dll
<drive root>:\WINNT\system32\net.exe
<drive root>:\WINNT\system32\net.hlp
<drive root>:\WINNT\system32\net1.exe
<drive root>:\WINNT\system32\netapi.dll
<drive root>:\WINNT\system32\netapi32.dll
<drive root>:\WINNT\system32\netbond.inf
<drive root>:\WINNT\system32\netcfg.dll
<drive root>:\WINNT\system32\netdde.exe
<drive root>:\WINNT\system32\netdefs.inf
<drive root>:\WINNT\system32\NetDefs.PNF
<drive root>:\WINNT\system32\netdtect.dll
<drive root>:\WINNT\system32\netdtect.inf
<drive root>:\WINNT\system32\netevent.dll
<drive root>:\WINNT\system32\netflx.dll
<drive root>:\WINNT\system32\neth.dll
<drive root>:\WINNT\system32\netlogon.dll
<drive root>:\WINNT\system32\netmsg.dll
<drive root>:\WINNT\system32\netoemdh.inf
<drive root>:\WINNT\system32\NetOemDh.PNF
<drive root>:\WINNT\system32\netrap.dll
<drive root>:\WINNT\system32\netsetup.dll
<drive root>:\WINNT\system32\NETSTAT.EXE
<drive root>:\WINNT\system32\netui0.dll
<drive root>:\WINNT\system32\netui1.dll
<drive root>:\WINNT\system32\netui2.dll
<drive root>:\WINNT\system32\network.hlp
<drive root>:\WINNT\system32\nibbles.bas
<drive root>:\WINNT\system32\nlsfunc.exe
```

```
<drive root>:\WINNT\system32\norweg.trn
<drive root>:\WINNT\system32\notepad.cnt
<drive root>:\WINNT\system32\notepad.exe
<drive root>:\WINNT\system32\notepad.hlp
<drive root>:\WINNT\system32\NSLOOKUP.EXE
<drive root>:\WINNT\system32\nt.fnt
<drive root>:\WINNT\system32\nt2.fnt
<drive root>:\WINNT\system32\ntbackup.exe
<drive root>:\WINNT\system32\ntcmds.hlp
<drive root>:\WINNT\system32\ntctl3d.dll
<drive root>:\WINNT\system32\ntdll.dll
<drive root>:\WINNT\system32\ntdos.sys
<drive root>:\WINNT\system32\ntio.sys
<drive root>:\WINNT\system32\ntlanman.dll
<drive root>:\WINNT\system32\ntlanui.dll
<drive root>:\WINNT\system32\ntlanui2.dll
<drive root>:\WINNT\system32\ntlmssps.dll
<drive root>:\WINNT\system32\ntlsapi.dll
<drive root>:\WINNT\system32\ntoskrnl.exe
<drive root>:\WINNT\system32\ntprint.dll
<drive root>:\WINNT\system32\ntshrui.dll
<drive root>:\WINNT\system32\ntvdm.exe
<drive root>:\WINNT\system32\nwcfg.dll
<drive root>:\WINNT\system32\odbcjt32.dll
<drive root>:\WINNT\system32\oemnad0.inf
<drive root>:\WINNT\system32\oemnadam.inf
<drive root>:\WINNT\system32\oemnadap.inf
<drive root>:\WINNT\system32\oemnadar.inf
<drive root>:\WINNT\system32\oemnadd1.inf
<drive root>:\WINNT\system32\oemnadd2.inf
<drive root>:\WINNT\system32\oemnadd3.inf
<drive root>:\WINNT\system32\oemnadd4.inf
<drive root>:\WINNT\system32\oemnadde.inf
<drive root>:\WINNT\system32\oemnaddf.inf
<drive root>:\WINNT\system32\oemnaddi.inf
<drive root>:\WINNT\system32\oemnadds.inf
<drive root>:\WINNT\system32\oemnaddt.inf
<drive root>:\WINNT\system32\oemnade1.inf
<drive root>:\WINNT\system32\oemnade2.inf
<drive root>:\WINNT\system32\oemnade3.inf
<drive root>:\WINNT\system32\oemnadee.inf
<drive root>:\WINNT\system32\oemnadem.inf
<drive root>:\WINNT\system32\oemnaden.inf
<drive root>:\WINNT\system32\oemnadep.inf
<drive root>:\WINNT\system32\oemnadfd.inf
<drive root>:\WINNT\system32\oemnadim.inf
<drive root>:\WINNT\system32\oemnadin.inf
<drive root>:\WINNT\system32\oemnadlb.inf
<drive root>:\WINNT\system32\oemnadlm.inf
<drive root>:\WINNT\system32\oemnadlt.inf
<drive root>:\WINNT\system32\oemnadma.inf
```

```
<drive root>:\WINNT\system32\oemnadn1.inf
<drive root>:\WINNT\system32\oemnadn2.inf
<drive root>:\WINNT\system32\oemnadne.inf
<drive root>:\WINNT\system32\oemnadnf.inf
<drive root>:\WINNT\system32\oemnadni.inf
<drive root>:\WINNT\system32\oemnadnm.inf
<drive root>:\WINNT\system32\oemnadnp.inf
<drive root>:\WINNT\system32\oemnadp3.inf
<drive root>:\WINNT\system32\oemnadp9.inf
<drive root>:\WINNT\system32\oemnadpm.inf
<drive root>:\WINNT\system32\oemnadt2.inf
<drive root>:\WINNT\system32\oemnadtk.inf
<drive root>:\WINNT\system32\oemnadtm.inf
<drive root>:\WINNT\system32\oemnadub.inf
<drive root>:\WINNT\system32\oemnadum.inf
<drive root>:\WINNT\system32\oemnadwd.inf
<drive root>:\WINNT\system32\oemnadwm.inf
<drive root>:\WINNT\system32\oemnadzz.inf
<drive root>:\WINNT\system32\oemnsvbh.inf
<drive root>:\WINNT\system32\oemnsvcu.inf
<drive root>:\WINNT\system32\oemnsvin.inf
<drive root>:\WINNT\system32\oemnsvnb.inf
<drive root>:\WINNT\system32\oemnsvnw.inf
<drive root>:\WINNT\system32\oemnsvra.inf
<drive root>:\WINNT\system32\oemnsvrp.inf
<drive root>:\WINNT\system32\oemnsvrr.inf
<drive root>:\WINNT\system32\oemnsvsa.inf
<drive root>:\WINNT\system32\oemnsvsn.inf
<drive root>:\WINNT\system32\oemnsvsp.inf
<drive root>:\WINNT\system32\oemnsvsv.inf
<drive root>:\WINNT\system32\oemnsvtp.inf
<drive root>:\WINNT\system32\oemnsvwk.inf
<drive root>:\WINNT\system32\oemnxpdl.inf
<drive root>:\WINNT\system32\oemnxpip.inf
<drive root>:\WINNT\system32\oemnxpnb.inf
<drive root>:\WINNT\system32\oemnxppp.inf
<drive root>:\WINNT\system32\oemnxpsm.inf
<drive root>:\WINNT\system32\oemnxpst.inf
<drive root>:\WINNT\system32\oemnxptc.inf
<drive root>:\WINNT\system32\oiadm400.dll
<drive root>:\WINNT\system32\oicom400.dll
<drive root>:\WINNT\system32\oidis400.dll
<drive root>:\WINNT\system32\oifil400.dll
<drive root>:\WINNT\system32\oigfs400.dll
<drive root>:\WINNT\system32\oiprt400.dll
<drive root>:\WINNT\system32\oislb400.dll
<drive root>:\WINNT\system32\oissq400.dll
<drive root>:\WINNT\system32\oitwa400.dll
<drive root>:\WINNT\system32\oiui400.dll
<drive root>:\WINNT\system32\ole2.dll
<drive root>:\WINNT\system32\ole2disp.dll
```

```
<drive root>:\WINNT\system32\ole2nls.dll
<drive root>:\WINNT\system32\ole32.dll
<drive root>:\WINNT\system32\oleaut32.dll
<drive root>:\WINNT\system32\olecli.dll
<drive root>:\WINNT\system32\olecli32.dll
<drive root>:\WINNT\system32\olecnv32.dll
<drive root>:\WINNT\system32\oledlg.dll
<drive root>:\WINNT\system32\olepro32.dll
<drive root>:\WINNT\system32\olesvr.dll
<drive root>:\WINNT\system32\olesvr32.dll
<drive root>:\WINNT\system32\olethk32.dll
<drive root>:\WINNT\system32\opengl32.dll
<drive root>:\WINNT\system32\os2
<drive root>:\WINNT\system32\os2.exe
<drive root>:\WINNT\system32\os2srv.exe
<drive root>:\WINNT\system32\os2ss.exe
<drive root>:\WINNT\system32\other.inf
<drive root>:\WINNT\system32\pacecfg.cpl
<drive root>:\WINNT\system32\pacecfg.hlp
<drive root>:\WINNT\system32\packager.cnt
<drive root>:\WINNT\system32\packager.exe
<drive root>:\WINNT\system32\packager.hlp
<drive root>:\WINNT\system32\panmap.dll
<drive root>:\WINNT\system32\pax.exe
<drive root>:\WINNT\system32\pbrush.exe
<drive root>:\WINNT\system32\pcl.sep
<drive root>:\WINNT\system32\pcnet.hlp
<drive root>:\WINNT\system32\pcomdrv.sys
<drive root>:\WINNT\system32\pentnt.exe
<drive root>:\WINNT\system32\perfc009.dat
<drive root>:\WINNT\system32\perfctrs.dll
<drive root>:\WINNT\system32\perfh009.dat
<drive root>:\WINNT\system32\perfmon.cnt
<drive root>:\WINNT\system32\perfmon.exe
<drive root>:\WINNT\system32\perfmon.hlp
<drive root>:\WINNT\system32\pifmgr.dll
<drive root>:\WINNT\system32\PING.EXE
<drive root>:\WINNT\system32\pjlmon.dll
<drive root>:\WINNT\system32\plustab.dll
<drive root>:\WINNT\system32\pmspl.dll
<drive root>:\WINNT\system32\ports.cpl
<drive root>:\WINNT\system32\portuas.exe
<drive root>:\WINNT\system32\posix.exe
<drive root>:\WINNT\system32\prflbmsg.dll
<drive root>:\WINNT\system32\print.exe
<drive root>:\WINNT\system32\printui.dll
<drive root>:\WINNT\system32\probrep.txt
<drive root>:\WINNT\system32\prodspec.ini
<drive root>:\WINNT\system32\profext.dll
<drive root>:\WINNT\system32\progman.cnt
<drive root>:\WINNT\system32\progman.exe
```

```
<drive root>:\WINNT\system32\progman.hlp
<drive root>:\WINNT\system32\pscript.sep
<drive root>:\WINNT\system32\psxdll.dll
<drive root>:\WINNT\system32\psxss.exe
<drive root>:\WINNT\system32\qbasic.exe
<drive root>:\WINNT\system32\qbasic.hlp
<drive root>:\WINNT\system32\ras
<drive root>:\WINNT\system32\rasadmin.cnt
<drive root>:\WINNT\system32\rasadmin.exe
<drive root>:\WINNT\system32\rasadmin.hlp
<drive root>:\WINNT\system32\rascfg.dll
<drive root>:\WINNT\system32\rasfil32.dll
<drive root>:\WINNT\system32\rasmon.exe
<drive root>:\WINNT\system32\rasphone.cnt
<drive root>:\WINNT\system32\rasphone.exe
<drive root>:\WINNT\system32\rasphone.hlp
<drive root>:\WINNT\system32\rassapi.dll
<drive root>:\WINNT\system32\rassetup.cnt
<drive root>:\WINNT\system32\rassetup.hlp
<drive root>:\WINNT\system32\rasshell.dll
<drive root>:\WINNT\system32\RCP.EXE
<drive root>:\WINNT\system32\rdisk.cnt
<drive root>:\WINNT\system32\rdisk.exe
<drive root>:\WINNT\system32\rdisk.hlp
<drive root>:\WINNT\system32\readme.wri
<drive root>:\WINNT\system32\recover.exe
<drive root>:\WINNT\system32\redir.exe
<drive root>:\WINNT\system32\regedt32.cnt
<drive root>:\WINNT\system32\regedt32.exe
<drive root>:\WINNT\system32\regedt32.hlp
<drive root>:\WINNT\system32\registry.inf
<drive root>:\WINNT\system32\remline.bas
<drive root>:\WINNT\system32\Repl
<drive root>:\WINNT\system32\replace.exe
<drive root>:\WINNT\system32\restore.exe
<drive root>:\WINNT\system32\REXEC.EXE
<drive root>:\WINNT\system32\riched20.dll
<drive root>:\WINNT\system32\riched32.dll
<drive root>:\WINNT\system32\rnr20.dll
<drive root>:\WINNT\system32\ROUTE.EXE
<drive root>:\WINNT\system32\rpcltc1.dll
<drive root>:\WINNT\system32\rpcltc8.dll
<drive root>:\WINNT\system32\rpcltccm.dll
<drive root>:\WINNT\system32\rpclts1.dll
<drive root>:\WINNT\system32\rpclts8.dll
<drive root>:\WINNT\system32\rpcltscm.dll
<drive root>:\WINNT\system32\rpcns4.dll
<drive root>:\WINNT\system32\rpcrt4.dll
<drive root>:\WINNT\system32\rpcss.exe
<drive root>:\WINNT\system32\rsabase.dll
<drive root>:\WINNT\system32\RSH.EXE
```

```
<drive root>:\WINNT\system32\rshx32.dll
<drive root>:\WINNT\system32\rundll32.exe
<drive root>:\WINNT\system32\runonce.exe
<drive root>:\WINNT\system32\s3.dll
<drive root>:\WINNT\system32\samlib.dll
<drive root>:\WINNT\system32\samsrv.dll
<drive root>:\WINNT\system32\savedump.exe
<drive root>:\WINNT\system32\schannel.dll
<drive root>:\WINNT\system32\scrnsave.scr
<drive root>:\WINNT\system32\secsspi.dll
<drive root>:\WINNT\system32\security.dll
<drive root>:\WINNT\system32\serialui.dll
<drive root>:\WINNT\system32\services.exe
<drive root>:\WINNT\system32\setup.exe
<drive root>:\WINNT\system32\setupapi.dll
<drive root>:\WINNT\system32\setupdll.dll
<drive root>:\WINNT\system32\setver.exe
<drive root>:\WINNT\system32\sfmatcfg.dll
<drive root>:\WINNT\system32\sfmutil.dll
<drive root>:\WINNT\system32\share.exe
<drive root>:\WINNT\system32\shcompui.dll
<drive root>:\WINNT\system32\shell.dll
<drive root>:\WINNT\system32\shell32.dll
<drive root>:\WINNT\system32\shmgrate.exe
<drive root>:\WINNT\system32\shscrap.dll
<drive root>:\WINNT\system32\skdll.dll
<drive root>:\WINNT\system32\skeys.exe
<drive root>:\WINNT\system32\smss.exe
<drive root>:\WINNT\system32\sndrec32.exe
<drive root>:\WINNT\system32\sndvol32.cnt
<drive root>:\WINNT\system32\sndvol32.exe
<drive root>:\WINNT\system32\sndvol32.hlp
<drive root>:\WINNT\system32\SNMPAPI.DLL
<drive root>:\WINNT\system32\softpub.dll
<drive root>:\WINNT\system32\sol.cnt
<drive root>:\WINNT\system32\sol.exe
<drive root>:\WINNT\system32\sol.hlp
<drive root>:\WINNT\system32\sort.exe
<drive root>:\WINNT\system32\sortkey.nls
<drive root>:\WINNT\system32\sorttbls.nls
<drive root>:\WINNT\system32\sound.drv
<drive root>:\WINNT\system32\soundrec.cnt
<drive root>:\WINNT\system32\soundrec.hlp
<drive root>:\WINNT\system32\spinit.exe
<drive root>:\WINNT\system32\spool
<drive root>:\WINNT\system32\SPOOLSS.DLL
<drive root>:\WINNT\system32\SPOOLSS.EXE
<drive root>:\WINNT\system32\sprestrt.exe
<drive root>:\WINNT\system32\srvmgr.cpl
<drive root>:\WINNT\system32\srvsvc.dll
<drive root>:\WINNT\system32\ss3dfo.scr
```

```
<drive root>:\WINNT\system32\ssbezier.scr
<drive root>:\WINNT\system32\ssflwbox.scr
<drive root>:\WINNT\system32\ssmarque.scr
<drive root>:\WINNT\system32\ssmaze.scr
<drive root>:\WINNT\system32\ssmyst.scr
<drive root>:\WINNT\system32\sspipes.scr
<drive root>:\WINNT\system32\ssstars.scr
<drive root>:\WINNT\system32\sstext3d.scr
<drive root>:\WINNT\system32\stdole.tlb
<drive root>:\WINNT\system32\stdole2.tlb
<drive root>:\WINNT\system32\stdole32.tlb
<drive root>:\WINNT\system32\storage.dll
<drive root>:\WINNT\system32\subroutn.inf
<drive root>:\WINNT\system32\subst.exe
<drive root>:\WINNT\system32\swedish.trn
<drive root>:\WINNT\system32\syncapp.exe
<drive root>:\WINNT\system32\synceng.dll
<drive root>:\WINNT\system32\syncui.dll
<drive root>:\WINNT\system32\sysdm.cpl
<drive root>:\WINNT\system32\sysedit.exe
<drive root>:\WINNT\system32\sysprint.sep
<drive root>:\WINNT\system32\syssetup.dll
<drive root>:\WINNT\system32\system.drv
<drive root>:\WINNT\system32\systray.exe
<drive root>:\WINNT\system32\t1instal.dll
<drive root>:\WINNT\system32\tapi.dll
<drive root>:\WINNT\system32\tapi32.dll
<drive root>:\WINNT\system32\tapiperf.dll
<drive root>:\WINNT\system32\tapisrv.exe
<drive root>:\WINNT\system32\taskman.exe
<drive root>:\WINNT\system32\taskmgr.exe
<drive root>:\WINNT\system32\tcpcfg.dll
<drive root>:\WINNT\system32\tcpip.cnt
<drive root>:\WINNT\system32\tcpip.hlp
<drive root>:\WINNT\system32\TCPSVCS.EXE
<drive root>:\WINNT\system32\telephon.cpl
<drive root>:\WINNT\system32\TELNET.CNT
<drive root>:\WINNT\system32\telnet.exe
<drive root>:\WINNT\system32\TELNET.HLP
<drive root>:\WINNT\system32\TFTP.EXE
<drive root>:\WINNT\system32\timedate.cpl
<drive root>:\WINNT\system32\timer.drv
<drive root>:\WINNT\system32\toolhelp.dll
<drive root>:\WINNT\system32\TRACERT.EXE
<drive root>:\WINNT\system32\tree.com
<drive root>:\WINNT\system32\tsd32.dll
<drive root>:\WINNT\system32\tssoft32.acm
<drive root>:\WINNT\system32\typelib.dll
<drive root>:\WINNT\system32\ufat.dll
<drive root>:\WINNT\system32\ulib.dll
<drive root>:\WINNT\system32\umpnpmgr.dll
```

```
<drive root>:\WINNT\system32\unicode.nls
<drive root>:\WINNT\system32\unimdm.tsp
<drive root>:\WINNT\system32\unlodctr.exe
<drive root>:\WINNT\system32\untfs.dll
<drive root>:\WINNT\system32\ups.cpl
<drive root>:\WINNT\system32\ups.exe
<drive root>:\WINNT\system32\ureg.dll
<drive root>:\WINNT\system32\url.dll
<drive root>:\WINNT\system32\usascii.trn
<drive root>:\WINNT\system32\user.exe
<drive root>:\WINNT\system32\user32.dll
<drive root>:\WINNT\system32\userenv.dll
<drive root>:\WINNT\system32\userinit.exe
<drive root>:\WINNT\system32\utility.inf
<drive root>:\WINNT\system32\v7vga.rom
<drive root>:\WINNT\system32\vcdex.dll
<drive root>:\WINNT\system32\vdmdbg.dll
<drive root>:\WINNT\system32\vdmredir.dll
<drive root>:\WINNT\system32\ver.dll
<drive root>:\WINNT\system32\version.dll
<drive root>:\WINNT\system32\vga.dll
<drive root>:\WINNT\system32\vga.drv
<drive root>:\WINNT\system32\vga256.dll
<drive root>:\WINNT\system32\vga64k.dll
<drive root>:\WINNT\system32\viewers
<drive root>:\WINNT\system32\wangcmn.dll
<drive root>:\WINNT\system32\wangshl.dll
<drive root>:\WINNT\system32\wdl.trm
<drive root>:\WINNT\system32\wfwnet.drv
<drive root>:\WINNT\system32\wgpoadmn.dll
<drive root>:\WINNT\system32\wgpocpl.cpl
<drive root>:\WINNT\system32\win.com
<drive root>:\WINNT\system32\win32k.sys
<drive root>:\WINNT\system32\win32spl.dll
<drive root>:\WINNT\system32\win87em.dll
<drive root>:\WINNT\system32\winchat.cnt
<drive root>:\WINNT\system32\winchat.exe
<drive root>:\WINNT\system32\winchat.hlp
<drive root>:\WINNT\system32\windisk.cnt
<drive root>:\WINNT\system32\windisk.exe
<drive root>:\WINNT\system32\windisk.hlp
<drive root>:\WINNT\system32\windows.cnt
<drive root>:\WINNT\system32\windows.hlp
<drive root>:\WINNT\system32\winfile.cnt
<drive root>:\WINNT\system32\winfile.exe
<drive root>:\WINNT\system32\winfile.hlp
<drive root>:\WINNT\system32\winhelp.hlp
<drive root>:\WINNT\system32\winhlp32.cnt
<drive root>:\WINNT\system32\winhlp32.exe
<drive root>:\WINNT\system32\winhlp32.hlp
<drive root>:\WINNT\system32\winlogon.exe
```

```
<drive root>:\WINNT\system32\winmine.cnt
<drive root>:\WINNT\system32\winmine.exe
<drive root>:\WINNT\system32\winmine.hlp
<drive root>:\WINNT\system32\winmm.dll
<drive root>:\WINNT\system32\winmsd.exe
<drive root>:\WINNT\system32\winnt.hlp
<drive root>:\WINNT\system32\winoldap.mod
<drive root>:\WINNT\system32\wins
<drive root>:\WINNT\system32\winsock.dll
<drive root>:\WINNT\system32\winspool.drv
<drive root>:\WINNT\system32\winspool.exe
<drive root>:\WINNT\system32\winsrv.dll
<drive root>:\WINNT\system32\winstrm.dll
<drive root>:\WINNT\system32\wintrust.dll
<drive root>:\WINNT\system32\WinTrust.hlp
<drive root>:\WINNT\system32\winver.exe
<drive root>:\WINNT\system32\WKSSVC.DLL
<drive root>:\WINNT\system32\wmsfr32.dll
<drive root>:\WINNT\system32\wmsui32.dll
<drive root>:\WINNT\system32\wow32.dll
<drive root>:\WINNT\system32\wowdeb.exe
<drive root>:\WINNT\system32\wowexec.exe
<drive root>:\WINNT\system32\wowfax.dll
<drive root>:\WINNT\system32\wowfaxui.dll
<drive root>:\WINNT\system32\write.exe
<drive root>:\WINNT\system32\ws2help.dll
<drive root>:\WINNT\system32\ws2_32.dll
<drive root>:\WINNT\system32\wshisn.dll
<drive root>:\WINNT\system32\wshnetbs.dll
<drive root>:\WINNT\system32\wshtcpip.dll
<drive root>:\WINNT\system32\wsock32.dll
<drive root>:\WINNT\system32\xactsrv.dll
<drive root>:\WINNT\system32\xcopy.exe
<drive root>:\WINNT\system32\xfilexr.dll
<drive root>:\WINNT\system32\~GLH0033.TMP
<drive root>:\WINNT\system32\config\AppEvent.Evt
<drive root>:\WINNT\system32\config\default
<drive root>:\WINNT\system32\config\default.LOG
<drive root>:\WINNT\system32\config\default.sav
<drive root>:\WINNT\system32\config\SAM
<drive root>:\WINNT\system32\config\SAM.LOG
<drive root>:\WINNT\system32\config\SecEvent.Evt
<drive root>:\WINNT\system32\config\SECURITY
<drive root>:\WINNT\system32\config\SECURITY.LOG
<drive root>:\WINNT\system32\config\software
<drive root>:\WINNT\system32\config\software.LOG
<drive root>:\WINNT\system32\config\software.sav
<drive root>:\WINNT\system32\config\SysEvent.Evt
<drive root>:\WINNT\system32\config\system
<drive root>:\WINNT\system32\config\SYSTEM.ALT
<drive root>:\WINNT\system32\config\system.LOG
```

```
<drive root>:\WINNT\system32\config\system.sav
<drive root>:\WINNT\system32\config\userdiff
<drive root>:\WINNT\system32\drivers\afd.sys
<drive root>:\WINNT\system32\drivers\aha154x.sys
<drive root>:\WINNT\system32\drivers\atapi.sys
<drive root>:\WINNT\system32\drivers\atdisk.sys
<drive root>:\WINNT\system32\drivers\beep.sys
<drive root>:\WINNT\system32\drivers\cdaudio.sys
<drive root>:\WINNT\system32\drivers\cdfs.sys
<drive root>:\WINNT\system32\drivers\cdrom.sys
<drive root>:\WINNT\system32\drivers\changer.sys
<drive root>:\WINNT\system32\drivers\class2.sys
<drive root>:\WINNT\system32\drivers\disk.sys
<drive root>:\WINNT\system32\drivers\diskdump.sys
<drive root>:\WINNT\system32\drivers\diskperf.sys
<drive root>:\WINNT\system32\drivers\dtadrv.sys
<drive root>:\WINNT\system32\drivers\EL90x.SYS
<drive root>:\WINNT\system32\drivers\etc
<drive root>:\WINNT\system32\drivers\fastfat.sys
<drive root>:\WINNT\system32\drivers\floppy.sys
<drive root>:\WINNT\system32\drivers\fs_rec.sys
<drive root>:\WINNT\system32\drivers\ftdisk.sys
<drive root>:\WINNT\system32\drivers\hpscan16.sys
<drive root>:\WINNT\system32\drivers\i8042prt.sys
<drive root>:\WINNT\system32\drivers\kbdclass.sys
<drive root>:\WINNT\system32\drivers\ksecdd.sys
<drive root>:\WINNT\system32\drivers\modem.sys
<drive root>:\WINNT\system32\drivers\mouclass.sys
<drive root>:\WINNT\system32\drivers\msfs.sys
<drive root>:\WINNT\system32\drivers\mup.sys
<drive root>:\WINNT\system32\drivers\ndis.sys
<drive root>:\WINNT\system32\drivers\NETBIOS.SYS
<drive root>:\WINNT\system32\drivers\NETBT.SYS
<drive root>:\WINNT\system32\drivers\netdtect.sys
<drive root>:\WINNT\system32\drivers\npfs.sys
<drive root>:\WINNT\system32\drivers\ntfs.sys
<drive root>:\WINNT\system32\drivers\null.sys
<drive root>:\WINNT\system32\drivers\parallel.sys
<drive root>:\WINNT\system32\drivers\parport.sys
<drive root>:\WINNT\system32\drivers\parvdm.sys
<drive root>:\WINNT\system32\drivers\pcmcia.sys
<drive root>:\WINNT\system32\drivers\qic117.sys
<drive root>:\WINNT\system32\drivers\RDR.SYS
<drive root>:\WINNT\system32\drivers\s3.sys
<drive root>:\WINNT\system32\drivers\scsiport.sys
<drive root>:\WINNT\system32\drivers\scsiprnt.sys
<drive root>:\WINNT\system32\drivers\scsiscan.sys
<drive root>:\WINNT\system32\drivers\serial.sys
<drive root>:\WINNT\system32\drivers\sermouse.sys
<drive root>:\WINNT\system32\drivers\sfloppy.sys
<drive root>:\WINNT\system32\drivers\SRV.SYS
```

```
<drive root>:\WINNT\system32\drivers\streams.sys
<drive root>:\WINNT\system32\drivers\tape.sys
<drive root>:\WINNT\system32\drivers\TCPIP.SYS
<drive root>:\WINNT\system32\drivers\tdi.sys
<drive root>:\WINNT\system32\drivers\vga.sys
<drive root>:\WINNT\system32\drivers\videoprt.sys
<drive root>:\WINNT\system32\drivers\etc\HOSTS
<drive root>:\WINNT\system32\drivers\etc\LMHOSTS.SAM
<drive root>:\WINNT\system32\drivers\etc\NETWORKS
<drive root>:\WINNT\system32\drivers\etc\PROTOCOL
<drive root>:\WINNT\system32\drivers\etc\SERVICES
<drive root>:\WINNT\system32\os2\dll
<drive root>:\WINNT\system32\os2\oso001.009
<drive root>:\WINNT\system32\os2\dll\doscalls.dll
<drive root>:\WINNT\system32\os2\dll\netapi.dll
<drive root>:\WINNT\system32\ras\modem.inf
<drive root>:\WINNT\system32\ras\pad.inf
<drive root>:\WINNT\system32\ras\ras.ico
<drive root>:\WINNT\system32\ras\rasread.txt
<drive root>:\WINNT\system32\ras\switch.inf
<drive root>:\WINNT\system32\Repl\Export
<drive root>:\WINNT\system32\Repl\Import
<drive root>:\WINNT\system32\Repl\Export\Scripts
<drive root>:\WINNT\system32\Repl\Import\Scripts
<drive root>:\WINNT\system32\spool\drivers
<drive root>:\WINNT\system32\spool\PRINTERS
<drive root>:\WINNT\system32\spool\prtprocs
<drive root>:\WINNT\system32\spool\drivers\w32x86
<drive root>:\WINNT\system32\spool\drivers\w32x86\2
<drive root>:\WINNT\system32\spool\prtprocs\w32x86
<drive root>:\WINNT\system32\spool\prtprocs\w32x86\winprint.dll
<drive root>:\WINNT\system32\viewers\debmp.dll
<drive root>:\WINNT\system32\viewers\dehex.dll
<drive root>:\WINNT\system32\viewers\demet.dll
<drive root>:\WINNT\system32\viewers\dess.dll
<drive root>:\WINNT\system32\viewers\dewp.dll
<drive root>:\WINNT\system32\viewers\msviewut.dll
<drive root>:\WINNT\system32\viewers\quikview.exe
<drive root>:\WINNT\system32\viewers\sccview.dll
<drive root>:\WINNT\system32\viewers\vsasc8.dll
<drive root>:\WINNT\system32\viewers\vsbmp.dll
<drive root>:\WINNT\system32\viewers\vsdrw.dll
<drive root>:\WINNT\system32\viewers\vsexe.dll
<drive root>:\WINNT\system32\viewers\vsexe2.dll
<drive root>:\WINNT\system32\viewers\vsmp.dll
<drive root>:\WINNT\system32\viewers\vsmsw.dll
<drive root>:\WINNT\system32\viewers\vspp.dll
<drive root>:\WINNT\system32\viewers\vsqp6.dll
<drive root>:\WINNT\system32\viewers\vsrtf.dll
<drive root>:\WINNT\system32\viewers\vstiff.dll
<drive root>:\WINNT\system32\viewers\vsw6.dll
```

```
<drive root>:\WINNT\system32\viewers\vswks.dll
<drive root>:\WINNT\system32\viewers\vswmf.dll
<drive root>:\WINNT\system32\viewers\vsword.dll
<drive root>:\WINNT\system32\viewers\vswork.dll
<drive root>:\WINNT\system32\viewers\vswp5.dll
<drive root>:\WINNT\system32\viewers\vswp6.dll
<drive root>:\WINNT\system32\viewers\vswpf.dll
<drive root>:\WINNT\system32\viewers\vsxl5.dll
```

Windows NT Service Pack 5 Overview

Windows NT 4.0 originally was released in August 1996. In the years since, several updates have been released to correct coding problems, security holes, poor applications, defective drivers, and other bugs. The result is a Windows NT environment that is much more stable and reliable than its right-off-the-CD version. Microsoft regularly releases service packs to provide customers with the most recent updates for its products. The current service pack for Windows NT 4.0 is Service Pack 5 (SP5), which was released in April 1999.

Service Packs Overview

A *service pack* is a collection of hundreds of individual fixes, corrections, and code patches that install as a single process. Service packs previously were released on a sporadic basis only when the number of hotfixes became unreasonable. Recently, Bill Gates announced a commitment by Microsoft to release service packs every quarter (three months).

A *hotfix* is a software patch that addresses only a single problem or error. Hotfixes are released to quickly offer a correction for a problem. A service pack is a collection of all hotfixes and any other patches not released as hotfixes. Usually, a hotfix is less than 2MB in size because it corrects only a single problem. Service packs often are many MB in size. SP5 is 33MB in size for Intel; the Alpha version is 44MB.

The differences between service packs and hotfixes go way beyond their size. Hotfixes are not supported by Microsoft. This means that, if you apply a hotfix, you are removing yourself from the umbrella of Microsoft support. Hotfixes are released to appease the masses without indemnifying Microsoft. In addition, hotfixes often can cause other difficulties with their crude method of patching problems, and they often cannot be uninstalled. It is therefore recommended that you only apply a hotfix if you are experiencing the specific problem it was designed to eliminate or if the hotfix offers a significant security improvement.

Service packs, on the other hand, are more thoroughly tested, are fully supported by Microsoft, provide an uninstall path, and rarely cause additional problems. In addition to guaranteeing a quarterly release, Microsoft recently promised to improve its testing of service packs. Information about current service packs is available on the Microsoft Web site. Typically, a link to service packs can be found on the product's page. Because the Microsoft Web site changes so frequently, you might have to search for it.

Service packs are cumulative releases. Each service pack includes its immediate predecessor plus all hotfixes released since the last SP. Service Pack 5 (SP5), for example, includes SP4 and all post-SP4 hotfixes. Only the most recent service pack needs to be installed along with any required post-SP hotfixes.

Without a doubt, you should apply Service Pack 4 immediately after installing Windows NT 4.0. It contains nearly 1,000 bug fixes and dozens of memory leak corrections. It also brings Windows NT into Y2K compliance. SP4 is indispensable in sustaining an operational and secure operating system. Although SP4 is not the most recent service pack, it definitely is the most important. If SP5 solves problems you think are important (see "The Details of Service Pack 5" later in this appendix), go ahead and install SP5. Before installing any service pack or hotfix, take the following precautions:

- Back up all important data and the Registry (if not your entire system).

- Update your Emergency Repair Disk (`rdisk /s`).

- Reboot the system.

- If you have installed a previous service pack, move the previous SP's uninstall directory from %SystemRoot%\$NTServicePackUninstall$\ to another safe location. This enables you to retain the previous SP's capability to be uninstalled if you ever uninstall SP5. Note that the installation of SP5 will overwrite the existing data in the default uninstall directory.

- Verify that you have enough free drive space on the boot partition for the extraction of the temporary files performed by the installation routine. If you chose to save uninstall information, 80MB is required; otherwise, only 40MB is needed. After the installation, the uninstall data will consume about 40MB. The temporary files will be removed after the setup process, and the 40MB used will once again be free space.

- Terminate all applications, stop all unnecessary services, stop all debugging activities, and terminate all remote control sessions before applying the service pack.
- Make sure to stop all third-party services that require disk access, especially virus-protection utilities and disk defragmenters.
- Take time to review the documentation and Knowledge Base documents associated with the service pack and hotfix.

After you install a service pack or hotfix, many key system files will have been changed. Attempting to install additional services or components from the original distribution CD might cause system failures or other strange problems. You should install everything you need from the distribution CD before applying a service pack. The following is a general step-by-step procedure:

1. Install Windows NT.
2. Install all protocols, drivers, and services required.
3. Configure the network, RAS, and other connections.
4. Install the Service Pack.
5. Install any necessary hotfixes.
6. Install applications.
7. Reapply the service pack.
8. Reapply hotfixes.

If you add new applications in the future, you should reapply the service pack and hotfixes again. If you discover an application that does not work with the service pack–altered system files, you should contact the application's vendor for a workaround, a patch, or another solution.

You can determine which service pack (if any) has been applied to your system by doing one of the following:

- Issuing the `WINVER` command from a command prompt
- Issuing the Help, About command from any Windows NT native application (such as Windows NT Explorer)
- Viewing the CSDVersion value in the HKEY_LOCAL_MACHINE\ SOFTWARE\Microsoft\WindowsNT\CurrentVersion Registry key

The Microsoft Web site contains cursory information about service packs and absolutely nothing about hotfixes. Several third parties maintain great knowledge sites that collect tons of useful information about hotfixes and service packs. It is highly recommended that you keep an eye on these sites because Microsoft releases many hotfixes without informing the general public.

- The Windows NT FAQ: `http://www.ntfaq.com`
- NT Bug Traq Web site: `http://www.ntbugtraq.com/`
- Paperbits Web site: `http://www.paperbits.com/`

The documentation associated with service packs and hotfixes typically is Knowledge Base documents. These are technical papers written by Microsoft technicians that are assigned a Q reference number. You can search for Knowledge Base documents by using this Q number (remember to always include the Q) at the following locations:

- Microsoft support and Knowledge Base Web site:
  `http://support.microsoft.com/`

- TechNet CD or online: `http://technet.microsoft.com/`

- Microsoft Network or CompuServe: **GO MICROSOFT**

Applying the latest service pack is important because it resolves many security issues. Without the service pack, your system is vulnerable to all the well-known and well-published system attacks. Your computer can easily be broken into, data can be stolen, or computers can be flooded with packets so that it cannot function properly. If you are serious about maintaining a secure environment, you must deploy the latest service pack release. Even with user account restrictions and service packs, however, Windows NT is not an impregnable fortress.

The Details of Service Pack 5

Service Pack 5 combines all the patches, updates, and enhancements for Windows NT 4.0 from its release in August 1996 through April 1999. This means it includes Service Pack 4 and all hotfixes released since SP4. This section discusses all the new items appearing in Service Pack 5 that were not part of any previous service pack. If you are interested in components included in Service Pack 4 or earlier, consult the Knowledge Base, TechNet, and the documentation accompanying the service pack or hotfix.

Service Pack 5 includes more than 200 corrections, updates, and enhancements for Windows NT 4. Instead of discussing all these items one by one, we will leave that to the plethora of Knowledge Base documents associated with SP5. Several key improvements and security enhancements, however, are well worth discussing in more detail. The following sections highlight several areas of corrections contained in Service Pack 5.

Security Enhancements

The security issues in SP5 are not as significant as those in SP4, but they do correct and address several important issues ranging from several denial-of-service vulnerabilities for Windows NT Servers connected to the Internet to improper handling of security barriers associated with logon and authentication.

Base Operating System Enhancements

The bulk of the corrections in SP5 apply to the core operating system. Most of these corrections are minor and only affect systems performing specific operations in unique environments, but your system might be the one in a thousand that fits the bill. The base OS corrections include API repairs, file system problems, memory leaks, various STOP error triggers, cluster server functions, and various third-party software products that introduce operational problems.

Year 2000 Enhancements

Service Pack 5 builds on the Y2K compliance of previous service packs and works in cooperation with the tools available from the Microsoft Year 2000 Resource Site (**http://www.microsoft.com/y2k/**). A handful of BIOS and command line date-related issues are corrected in SP5.

Networking Enhancements

Another significant section of corrections in Service Pack 5 deals with networking issues. Most of the issues are client-, technology-, or service-specific problems. These problems include shared-resource failures, NetWare client interaction, RAS and DUN connectivity, WINS and DNS services, and DHCP automatic client configuration.

For more information about the fixes, corrections, and enhancements provided for Windows NT 4 by Service Pack 5, you can consult any of the following:

- The link to Knowledge Base documents, which is included at the end of this appendix.
- The Release Notes included with SP5.
- TechNet.
- The Microsoft Web site's Windows NT and service pack areas.

Obtaining Service Pack 5

In the past, service packs have been difficult to locate and obtain. Microsoft has since provided many more avenues to obtain service packs, and numerous third-party Web sites host links to the Microsoft resource locations. The primary means by which service packs are obtained is through the Microsoft Web site. By following links from the main Windows NT Workstation or Windows NT Server areas, you eventually will arrive at **http://www.microsoft.com/support/winnt/** or a similar page. From there, you can select to download the 40-bit or 128-bit versions of the latest service pack. The 128-bit version is restricted for domestic U.S. deployment. You must prove that you currently are within the United States when downloading and must virtually sign an agreement that you will not export the service pack after it is downloaded.

In addition to the Web page interface, you can obtain the 40-bit version of SP5 directly from the Microsoft FTP site. You can use either Internet Explorer or an FTP client to access this anonymous FTP site at **ftp://ftp.microsoft.com/bussys/ winnt/winnt-public/fixes/usa/nt40/**. The service packs are within a subdirectory labeled "ussp5" for U.S. Service Pack 5. The hotfixes can be found in the "hotfixes-postsp5" directories.

If you don't want to spend the time required to download the bulk of the service pack data, you can order a CD containing the 40-bit or 128-bit version of SP5. The CD costs $14.95 plus $5 for shipping and handling. The CD can be ordered by phone, fax, snail mail, or online. For details, visit **http://www.microsoft.com/ntserver/nts/ downloads/recommended/sp5/ordercd.asp** or follow the Order SP5 CD links from the main Windows NT areas.

Important SP5 Caveats

After SP5 is installed, you might encounter situations in which the presence of SP5 can actually cause problems. Many of these situations are detailed in the Release Notes included with SP5. Several are discussed in this section, but we highly recommend that you review the Release Notes document in its entirety before installing SP5. The Release Notes can be viewed online at **http://www.microsoft.com/ntserver/nts/ downloads/recommended/sp5/readme.asp**.

If you ever perform an ERD repair that requires the distribution CD, you must reapply SP5. This caveat assumes you updated the ERD following the installation of SP5; otherwise, using a pre-SP5 ERD will result in a system that might not even boot. If a post-SP5 ERD is used and materials from the distribution CD are copied to the system, you will need to reapply SP5. In some cases, the repair process will mix SP5 materials with distribution CD materials in such a fashion that the system will not function. Therefore, it is important to maintain a current backup in the event of an error that requires a repair which might or might not restore the system to proper operation. Microsoft has stated that a re-release of Windows NT incorporating all service pack updates is forthcoming. Until then, the ERD repair process is capable of causing as much damage as the problem requiring it to be performed.

Because Service Pack 5 makes changes to key system components, drivers, and other important files, you need to reapply SP5 after installing any new application or service. This includes utilities, drivers, and services from the Windows NT distribution CD. Then, if possible, point the Installation dialog box path to an expanded version of the service pack before pulling material from the distribution CD. This keeps the version problems to a minimum, which decreases the risk of a system failure.

SP5 has a handful of problems with various software. Consult the Release Notes for details about problems encountered with the following hardware:

- Number Nine Visual Technologies Imagine 2 video card
- Dell Latitude portable computer with Softex Advanced Power Management and PC Card Controller services version 1.0
- Softex PC Card Controller or Phoenix CardExecutive for Windows NT
- Softex Power Management Controller or Phoenix APM for Windows NT
- Softex Docking Controller or Phoenix NoteDock for Windows NT
- Softex DeskPower Controller or Phoenix DeskAPM for Windows NT
- SCSI logical units above eight
- SystemSoft Card Wizard

I

Contents of the CD-ROM

THIS APPENDIX DESCRIBES EACH PIECE of software on the CD-ROM that accompanies this book. For more information or support for a particular product, visit the software manufacturer's Web site.

AutoPilot

http://www.sunbelt-software.com

Sunbelt Software's AutoPilot is a real-time tuner for Windows NT. It dynamically speeds up performance by automatically detecting and eliminating bottlenecks. AutoPilot is a great tool for Windows NT machines that are hammered with high CPU and/or memory loads. The more applications you have open and the busier your machine is, the more AutoPilot will benefit you.

Beyond FTP

http://www.aptnet.com/

Automated Programming Technologies, Inc. created Beyond FTP specifically for the Internet and corporate intranets. This tool is the latest generation in the automation of file distribution and data collection. Beyond FTP is extremely easy to use with a drag-and-drop interface. Beyond FTP is the first Internet/intranet file transfer tool that has combined automation, scheduling, encryption, compression, and assured delivery into one product. A Beyond FTP client can communicate with either generic FTP servers or a Beyond FTP server.

BQMS

`http://www.advsyscon.com`

BQMS, the Batch Queue Management System, from Advanced Systems Concepts, Inc., is an advanced, fully distributed batch job management and scheduling system. BQMS allows clients to submit batch jobs for execution on the same or other systems across the network using the security of the submitting user. BQMS' advanced scheduling capabilities allow jobs to be run on a user-defined schedule or as required. BQMS has powerful features, such as load balancing, and performs job restart via job check-pointing.

Diskeeper Lite for Windows NT 4.0

`http://www.executive.com`

Diskeeper Lite for Windows NT, from Executive Software, is a high-speed manual disk defragmenter. It increases system performance by consolidating fragmented files on the disk.

DNEWS

`http://netwinsite.com/`

The DNEWS News Server, from Netwin Ltd., is an advanced news server. This tool makes it easy for you to provide users fast access to Internet (Usenet) newsgroups. You can install your own local news, which gives you complete control to create your own private or public discussion forums for enhanced communications across your organization or over the Internet. The DNEWS News Server has an advanced design that outperforms other news server software and provides a large set of features. This server works excellently with Free Agent as a client on the other side.

e-Lock PKI

`http://www.elock.com`

e-Lock PKI, from E-Lock Technologies, reduces the hackers stealing, viewing, and/or tampering with confidential documents and communications on the Internet. e-Lock uses PKI technology, which is emerging as an effective and secure method of offering security to organizations. e-Lock PKI provides the only Public Key Infrastructure that works with MS CryptoAPI and Microsoft Certificate Server, which simplifies the deployment of PKI technologies for the administrator, network manager, and end-user.

e-Lock PKI adds to the Microsoft Certificate system by adding its own e-Lock CSP. Making it easy to use and providing for tighter methods of preserving keys, e-Lock PKI proves to be a cost effective way of managing an organization's keys and certificates.

FAT 32 for Windows NT
http://www.winternals.com
FAT32, from Winternals, allows Windows NT to access FAT32 partitions just as it does regular FAT and NTFS volumes. Once installed, FAT32 drives on your system will be fully accessible as native Windows NT volumes. Performance of FAT32 volumes is comparable to your existing FAT volumes.

File Rescue
http://www.sunbelt-software.com
Sunbelt Software's File Rescue allows for full retrieval of files after they have been removed from the Recycle Bin, or if you have deleted them from the command line or a shared directory. All you have to do is load File Rescue, and it will find all your deleted files. Once you undelete, you can restore the file right back to the same directory it was deleted from. This product supports Windows 95, 98, NT, and 2000.

Hyena
http://www.sunbelt-software.com
Hyena, from Sunbelt Software, is an administration tool for Windows NT 3.51 and 4.0 systems. Hyena has added integrated event viewing into the latest V2.0 release, plus lots more. Hyena provides a single, centralized interface for nearly all system management functions. Whether your organization has one or more domains, Hyena can simplify your Windows NT administration tasks.

IMail Server
http://www.ipswitch.com/
IMail Server, from Ipswitch, Inc., is a lightweight but powerful email server for network administrators in companies of any size who need a flexible, Web-accessible, standards-based, and spam-resistant mail server for Windows NT. Version 5.0 adds a Web mail interface that is configurable, ODBC database connections, and improved SMTP security. Furthermore, it has expanded its mail delivery rules and includes LDAP 3.0 support. IMail server supports multiple domains on a single machine, remote administration, and you can use a Web browser to read and send mail. It also gives you list server capabilities, supports anti-spamming measures, and includes an email-to-pager/beeper gateway.

Linkbot Pro

`http://www.tetranet.com`

Linkbot Pro 4.1, created by Tetranet Software, is the industry's most complete Web site testing solution. Benchmark your Web site against the best. Linkbot Pro now includes the Site Quality Rating Report, allowing you to quickly compare your Web site against your peers, competitors, and the Fortune 500.

LISTSERV

`http://www.lsoft.com/`

LISTSERV, from L-Soft International, is a software product that allows you to create, manage, and control electronic mailing lists on your corporate network or on the Internet. Since its inception in 1986, LISTSERV has been continually improved and is available on Windows NT but also on VM, VMS, 13 flavors of UNIX, and the MAC. If you want to host lists on your Windows NT Server, this tool provides you with a number of advanced functions to both list moderators and list subscribers. Some of those functions include an algorithm called DISTRIBUTE, which can dramatically reduce the bandwidth cost of bulk mail delivery, automated digests, and indexes; subscription options customizable on a per-subscriber basis; SCAN command; and an automatic delivery error monitoring system to simplify processing of delivery errors. It also has a "Spam" detector, shielding LISTSERV lists from unsolicited advertisements.

Lyris

`http://www.lyris.com`

Lyris, from Lyris Technologies, is an email list server program for hosting Internet email mailing lists, such as open discussions, moderated forums, announcement lists, auto-responders and DocBots. Features include a Web interface for members and administrators, failsafe unsubscribing, automatic error mail handling, multiple security roles, and a newsgroup interface to all the lists hosted on the server.

Mail-Gear

`http://www.urlabs.com/`

Mail-Gear, from URLabs, is a full-featured mail server that supports all popular email client programs such as Eudora, Netscape, and Microsoft Outlook. Mail-Gear also includes the Mail-Gear Web Client so no client-based software other than a common Web browser needs to be installed to access email. If you are a Windows NT user who must control email connections and content, and if you need "roaming user" support, Mail-Gear is a good solution.

Metabot Pro

http://www.tetranet.com

Metabot Pro 1.0, available from Tetranet Software, is the industry's first automated Metatag creation, insertion, and testing tool. Using a familiar spreadsheet-style interface, Metabot Pro makes it simple to generate and manage Metadata for HTML documents.

NetObjects Fusion

http://www.netobjects.com/

NetObjects Fusion 4.0, from NetObjects, Inc., is a fast and easy way to build your business Web site. You can create, manage, and update your sites quickly and efficiently with the Fusion WYSIWYG environment. It has powerful site management capabilities. You can build and update your site structure quickly in the drag-and-drop SiteStructure Editor. You are able to place objects precisely where you want them in the Layout Editor. You can also add e-commerce on your site with dynamic database access site without programming.

NetObjects ScriptBuilder

http://www.netobjects.com

ScriptBuilder, from NetObjects, Inc., is a tool that helps you write dynamic client- and server-side scripts for Web sites. You can enhance your code-writing productivity and reduce errors with this script development environment.

Set Owner

http://www.sunbelt-software.com

Sunbelt Software's Set Owner allows you to change file ownership on directories and files. You can also set ownership for a complete path or directory.

SPQuery

http://www.sunbelt-software.com

SPQuery, from Sunbelt Software, allows you to determine which service pack is installed on your Windows NT system, as well as what hotfixes are already applied. Version 3.0 shows you this information on all your machines in all domains. The SPQuery Single Machine License allows the query of all the machines on the network and generates a full report for you. You can use this information to keep track of all the networked machines configuration data.

Storage Utility Pak

`http://www.sunbelt-software.com`

Sunbelt Software's Storage Utility Pak is a set of Storage Management reports that are executed from the command line. Reports are Large Files, New Files, Aged Files, Detailed Summary, Duplicates, Directory Usage, Usage By User, and Files Last Accessed.

SuperTCP Suite

`http://www.frontiertech.com/`

The SuperTCP Suite, from Frontier Technologies, is a flexible connectivity solution you can use to hook up any Windows 3.x, Windows 95, or Windows NT machine to the Internet via the TCP/IP protocol. SuperTCP Suite's smart install creates a small footprint by loading *only* the application you need for the correct Windows operating system. This product claims to be the only connectivity solution that allows administrators to easily maintain your current legacy information technology while allowing you to take advantage of new intranet/Internet tools. SuperTCP was rated "A" by *PC Week* for usability and capacity.

Ultrabac

`http://www.ultrabac.com`

Ultrabac, from BEI Corporation, provides backup and disaster recovery features for Windows NT.

WinGate Pro

`http://www.deerfield.com/`

WinGate Pro 3.0, from Derfield.com, allows multiple network users to share a single Internet connection through dial-up, ISDN modems, DSL and cable modems, as well as dedicated Internet connections and satellite connections. It is available in three flavors: Home, Standard, and Pro. WinGate Home, a new version in WinGate 3.0, is specifically designed for home users and emerging home network environments, allowing easy sharing of Internet access in the home and the ability to monitor Internet usage throughout the home. It operates on both Windows 95 and Windows NT platforms. WinGate 3.0 also features a robust firewall component that allows you to protect your networks from outside intrusion.

This Trial License is valid for 255 concurrent users, and will expire 30 days after the date of installation. It is recommended that you purchase a WinGate license prior to this date in order to avoid an interruption in use of the software.

To purchase WinGate, select the Register/Online link from the Help menu within the GateKeeper interface. Alternatively, a WinGate license can be purchased at `http://www.wingate.com/purchase.htm` or from one of the Authorized Deerfield.com Resellers listed at `http://www.securecc.com/windealers/index.cfm`. The License name and License key must be entered into the GateKeeper interface under "System Info" or during the installation process *exactly* as they appear as follows. Your License name is MacMillan Computer Publishing. Your License key is 02AD44202A1ED034149CF627.

Wisebot Pro
`http://www.tetranet.com`
Wisebot Pro 2.0, created by Tetranet Software, is an application dedicated to creating intelligent Web site navigation solutions. Wisebot Pro provides a cost-effective tool to manage your Web site structure as well as enhance its usability to potential customers in finding the information they require.

WS_FTP Pro
`http://www.ipswitch.com/`
This is the client side of the two WS_FTP components from Ipswitch. Of course it will download and upload to any FTP server on the Internet. The latest version comes with an option: You can use the classic interface or the new Explorer-type interface that is fully Windows standards-compliant. The drag-and-drop interface is intuitive and simple to use.

WS FTP Server
`http://www.ipswitch.com/`
WS_FTP Server, from Ipswitch, is a full-featured FTP server for your Windows NT system. It's the server side software that complements WS_FTP Pro, the world's most popular FTP client for Windows. With WS_FTP Server, you can create an FTP site that makes files and folders on your Windows NT Server or Workstation available to users anywhere on the Internet. WS_FTP Server has a full feature set and an easy-to-use graphical interface.

XLNT
`http://www.advsyscon.com`
XLNT, the Enterprise Command and Scripting Language from Advanced System Concepts, Inc., is perfect for accessing Windows NT components to implement the repetitive tasks of System Administration and/or Application Development, without reliance on traditional programming languages and development tools. XLNT's unique and powerful command shell provides extensive commands that eliminate unnecessary script statements and simplify complex scripting tasks.

Index

Symbols

@ (at sign character), REGINI.EXE, 166
@fax Inc. Web site, 569
\ (backslash character), REGINI.EXE, 164
$ (dollar sign), 213
. (periods), booting process, 92
? (question mark) parameter, 55
; (semicolon character), REGINI.EXE, 164
_ (underscore), 96
4 Firewalls Web site, 258
9/9/99 (Y2K), 656
10-Base100 cables, 323
10-BaseT cables, 323
16K D-channel (data channel) ISDN, 319
128K ISDNs, 320
32bit.com Web site, 502, 571, 579
33.6K modems, 316
56K v.90 modems, 315
64K B-channels (bearer channels)
   ISDN, 319
3270 emulators, 276

A

A (address) DNS record type, 306
A class IP addresses, 246
A:Drive, 365
AAAA (address) DNS record type, 306
AARP Packets/sec counter (Performance
   Monitor), 610
About command (Help menu), 715
About Time Group (PCfix 2000), 659
access, 311
   FTP, 256
   granting (User Manager), 27
   Internet. *See* Internet access
   NTFS partitions, 30
   page files, 435
   permissions, troubleshooting, 460
   Registry security, 138-139
   remote access. *See* remote access
   remote control, 311-312
   restrictions, Registry, 137

access control, IIS (Internet Information
   Server), 548
Access Control Lists. *See* ACLs
AccessData Web site, 483
Accessories directory, 41
Account Operators group, 230
Account policy, 465-466
accounts. *See also* groups
   copying (User Manager), 26
   deleting (User Manager), 26
   disabling (User Manager), 26
   domain networks, single master domain
      networks, 225
   granting access (User Manager), 27
   groups, 464
   Guest accounts, 231
   IUSR_<systemname>, 536
   memberships (User Manager), 26
   NetWare Migration tools, duplicate
      names, 279
   synchronization, domain networks, 221
   users, 464
Accounts command (Tools menu), 520
Acer Y2K problem Web site, 657
ACLs (Access Control Lists), 466
   CACLS.EXE (Change ACLs), 45
   DumpACL tool (Somarsoft), 27
   Everyone groups, 466-467
   numbers, 165
Acrobat Reader, 501
Acses Web site, 576
Actioneer Web site, 530
ACTIS Windows NT Services Web
   site, 579
Active Desktop, 496-497
Active Directory (AD), 596-597
Active Directory Services Interface
   (ADSI), 597
Active Lines counter (Performance
   Monitor), 651
active partitions, 84
Active Telephones counter (Performance
   Monitor), 652

B

G

S

Windows 2000 Answers

Selected Windows 2000 Titles from New Riders Publishing

Updated edition of New Riders' best-selling *Inside Windows NT 4 Server*. Taking the author-driven, no-nonsense approach we pioneered with our Windows NT *Landmark* books, New Riders proudly offers something unique for Windows 2000 administrators—an interesting and discriminating book on Windows 2000 Server, written by someone in the trenches who can anticipate your situation and provide answers you can trust.

Windows 2000 Server

William Boswell

Windows 2000 ESSENTIAL REFERENCE

Architected to be the most navigable, useful, and value-packed reference for Windows 2000, this book uses a creative "telescoping" design that you can adapt to your style of learning. Written by Steve Tate, key Windows 2000 partner and developer of Microsoft's W2K Training Program, it's a concise, focused quick reference for Windows 2000.

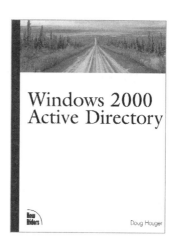

Windows 2000 Active Directory

Doug Houger

Windows 2000 Active Directory is just one of several new Windows 2000 titles from New Riders' acclaimed Landmark series. Focused, no-nonsense advice on planning, implementing, and managing the Active Directory in your business.

Advanced Information on Windows Technologies

New Riders Books Offer Advice and Experience

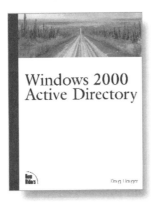

LANDMARK
Rethinking Computer Books

The *Landmark* series from New Riders targets the distinct needs of the working computer professional by providing detailed and solution-oriented information on core technologies. We begin by partnering with authors who have unique depth of experience and the ability to speak to the needs of the practicing professional. Each book is then carefully reviewed at all stages to ensure it covers the most essential subjects in substantial depth, with great accuracy, and with ease of use in mind. These books speak to the practitioner: they offer accurate information and trustworthy advice at the right depth and at an attractive value.

ESSENTIAL REFERENCE
Smart, Like You

The *Essential Reference* series from New Riders provides answers when you know what you want to do but need to know how to do it. Each title skips extraneous material and assumes a strong base of knowledge. These are indispensable books for the practitioner who wants to find specific features of a technology quickly and efficiently. Avoiding fluff and basic material, these books present solutions in an innovative, clean format—and at a great value.

MCSE CERTIFICATION
Engineered for Test Success

New Riders offers a complete line of test preparation materials to help you achieve your certification. With books like *MCSE Training Guides*, *TestPrep*, and *Fast Track*, and software like the acclaimed *MCSE Complete*, *Top Score*, and the revolutionary *ExamGear* suite, New Riders offers comprehensive products built by experienced professionals who have passed the exams and instructed hundreds of candidates.

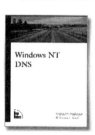

Windows NT Performance Monitoring Benchmarking and Tuning

By Mark Edmead
and Paul Hinsberg
1st Edition
288 pages, $29.99
ISBN: 1-56205-942-4

Performance monitoring is a little like preventive medicine for the administrator: No one enjoys a checkup, but it's a good thing to do on a regular basis. This book helps you focus on the critical aspects of improving the performance of your NT system, showing you how to monitor the system, implement benchmarking, and tune your network. The book is organized by resource components, which makes it easy to use as a reference tool.

Windows NT Terminal Server and Citrix MetaFrame

By Ted Harwood
1st Edition
416 pages, $29.99
ISBN: 1-56205-944-0

It's no surprise that most administration headaches revolve around integration with other networks and clients. This book addresses these types of real-world issues on a case-by-case basis, giving tools and advice on solving each problem. The author also offers the real nuts and bolts of thin client administration on multiple systems, covering relevant issues such as installation, configuration, network connection, management, and application distribution.

Windows NT Security

By Richard Puckett
1st Edition Fall 1999
600 pages, $29.99
ISBN: 1-56205-945-9

Swiss cheese. That's what some people say Windows NT security is like. And they might be right because they only know what the NT documentation says about implementing security. Who has the time to research alternatives; to play around with the features, service packs, hot fixes and add-on tools; and to figure out what makes NT rock solid? Well, Richard Puckett does. He has been researching Windows NT security for the University of Virginia for a while now, and he has pretty good news. He's going to show you how to make NT secure in your environment, and we mean secure.

Windows NT Network Management: Reducing Total Cost of Ownership

By Anil Desai
1st Edition Spring 1999
400 pages, $34.99
ISBN: 1-56205-946-7

Administering a Windows NT network is kind of like trying to herd cats—an impossible task characterized by constant motion, exhausting labor, and lots of hairballs. Author Anil Desai knows all about it; he's a consulting engineer for Sprint Paranet who specializes in Windows NT implementation, integration, and management. So we asked him to put together a concise manual of the best practices, a book of tools and ideas that other administrators can turn to again and again in managing their own NT networks.

Planning for Windows 2000
By Eric K. Cone, Jon Boggs, and Sergio Perez
1st Edition Spring 1999
400 pages, $29.99
ISBN: 0-73570-048-6

Windows 2000 is poised to be one of the largest and most important software releases of the next decade, and you are charged with planning, testing, and deploying it in your enterprise. Are you ready? With this book, you will be. *Planning for Windows 2000* lets you know what the upgrade hurdles will be, informs you how to clear them, guides you through effective Active Directory design, and presents you with detailed rollout procedures. Eric K. Cone, Jon Boggs, and Sergio Perez give you the benefit of their extensive experiences as Windows 2000 Rapid Deployment Program members, sharing problems and solutions they've encountered on the job.

MCSE Core NT Exams Essential Reference
By Matthew Shepker
1st Edition
256 pages, $19.99
ISBN: 0-7357-0006-0

You're sitting in the first session of your Networking Essentials class, the instructor starts talking about RAS, and you have no idea what that means. You think about raising your hand to ask, but you reconsider—you'd feel foolish asking a question in front of all these people. You turn to your handy *MCSE Core NT Exams Essential Reference* and find a quick summary on Remote Access Services. Question answered. It's a couple months later, and you're taking your Networking Essentials exam the next day. You're reviewing practice tests and keep forgetting the maximum lengths for the various commonly used cable types. Once again, you turn to the *MCSE Core NT Exams Essential Reference* and find a table on cables, including all the characteristics you need to memorize in order to pass the test.

BackOffice Titles

Implementing Exchange Server
By Doug Hauger, Marywynne Leon, and William C. Wade III
1st Edition
400 pages, $29.99
ISBN: 1-56205-931-9

If you're interested in connectivity and maintenance issues for Exchange Server, this book is for you. Exchange's power lies in its capability to be connected to multiple email subsystems to create a "universal email backbone." It's not unusual to have several different and complex systems all connected via email gateways, including Lotus Notes or cc:Mail, Microsoft Mail, legacy mainframe systems, and Internet mail. This book covers all of the problems and issues associated with getting an integrated system running smoothly and addresses troubleshooting and diagnosis of email problems with an eye toward prevention and best practices.

Exchange System Administration

By Janice K. Howd
1st Edition Spring 1999
400 pages, $34.99
ISBN: 0-7357-0081-8

Okay, you've got your Exchange Server installed and connected; now what? Email administration is one of the most critical networking jobs, and Exchange can be particularly troublesome in large, heterogeneous environments. Janice Howd, a noted consultant and teacher with over a decade of email administration experience, has put together this advanced, concise handbook for daily, periodic, and emergency administration. With in-depth coverage of topics like managing disk resources, replication, and disaster recovery, this is the one reference book every Exchange administrator needs.

SQL Server System Administration

By Sean Baird, Chris Miller, et al.
1st Edition
352 pages, $29.99
ISBN: 1-56205-955-6

How often does your SQL Server go down during the day when everyone wants to access the data? Do you spend most of your time being a "report monkey" for your coworkers and bosses? *SQL Server System Administration* helps you keep data consistently available to your users. This book omits introductory information. The authors don't spend time explaining queries and how they work. Instead, they focus on the information you can't get anywhere else, like how to choose the correct replication topology and achieve high availability of information.

Internet Information Server Administration

By Kelli Adam, et. al.
1st Edition Fall 1999
300 pages, $29.99
ISBN: 0-73570-022-2

Are the new Internet technologies in Internet Information Server giving you headaches? Does protecting security on the Web take up all of your time? Then this is the book for you. With hands-on configuration training, advanced study of the new protocols in IIS, and detailed instructions on authenticating users with the new Certificate Server and implementing and managing the new e-commerce features, *Internet Information Server Administration* gives you the real-life solutions you need. This definitive resource also prepares you for the release of Windows 2000 by giving you detailed advice on working with Microsoft Management Console, which was first used by IIS.

SMS Administration

By Darshan Doshi
and Michael Lubanski
1st Edition Winter 1999
350 pages, $34.99
ISBN: 0-7357-0082-6

Microsoft's new version of its Systems Management Server (SMS) is starting to turn heads. Although complex, it allows administrators to lower their total cost of ownership and more efficiently manage clients, applications, and support operations. So if your organization is using or implementing SMS, you'll need some expert advice. Darshan Doshi and Michael Lubanski can help you get the most bang for your buck, with insight, expert tips, and real-world examples. Darshan and Michael are consultants specializing in SMS, having worked with Microsoft on one of the most complex SMS rollouts in the world, involving 32 countries, 15 languages, and thousands of clients.

UNIX/Linux Titles

Solaris Essential Reference
By John Mulligan
1st Edition Spring 1999
350 pages, $19.99
ISBN: 0-7357-0230-7

Looking for the fastest, easiest way to find the Solaris command you need? Need a few pointers on shell scripting? How about advanced administration tips and sound, practical expertise on security issues? Are you looking for trustworthy information about available third-party software packages that will enhance your operating system? Author John Mulligan— creator of the popular Unofficial Guide to Solaris Web site (sun.icsnet.com)— delivers all that and more in one attractive, easy-to-use reference book. With clear and concise instructions on how to perform important administration and management tasks and key information on powerful commands and advanced topics, *Solaris Essential Reference* is the book you need when you know what you want to do and only need to know how.

Linux System Administration
By M Carling
1st Edition Summer 1999
450 pages, $29.99
ISBN: 1-56205-934-3

As an administrator, you probably feel that most of your time and energy is spent in endless firefighting. If your network has become a fragile quilt of temporary patches and work-arounds, this book is for you. For example, have you had trouble sending or receiving email lately? Are you looking for a way to keep your network running smoothly with enhanced performance? Are your users always hankering for more storage, more services, and more speed? *Linux System Administration* advises you on the many intricacies of maintaining a secure, stable system. In this definitive work, the author addresses all the issues related to system administration, from adding users and managing file permissions, to Internet services and Web hosting, to recovery planning and security. This book fulfills the need for expert advice that will ensure a trouble-free Linux environment.

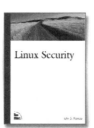

Linux Security
By John S. Flowers
1st Edition Spring 1999
400 pages, $29.99
ISBN: 0-7357-0035-4

New Riders is proud to offer the first book aimed specifically at Linux security issues. Although a host of general UNIX security books exist, we thought it was time to address the practical needs of the Linux network. In this definitive work, author John Flowers takes a balanced approach to system security by discussing topics like planning a secure environment, setting up firewalls, and utilizing security scripts.

With comprehensive information on specific system compromises and advice on how to prevent and repair them, this is one book that every Linux administrator should have on the shelf.

Developing Linux Applications with GTK+ and GDK
By Eric Harlow
1st Edition
400 pages, $34.99
ISBN: 0-7357-0214-7

We all know that Linux is one of the most powerful and solid operating systems in existence. And as the success of Linux grows, there is an increasing interest in developing applications with graphical user interfaces that take advantage of the power of Linux. In this book, software developer Eric Harlow gives you an indispensable development handbook focusing on the GTK+ toolkit. More than an overview of the elements of application or GUI design, this is a hands-on book that delves deeply into the technology. With in-depth material on the various GUI programming tools and loads of examples, this book's unique focus will give you the information you need to design and launch professional-quality applications.

Linux Essential Reference
By David "Hacksaw" Todd
1st Edition Summer 1999
400 pages, $19.99
ISBN: 0-7357-0852-5

This book is all about getting things done as quickly and efficiently as possible by providing a structured organization to the plethora of available Linux information. We can sum it up in one word—value. This book has it all: concise instructions on how to perform key administration tasks, advanced information on configuration, shell scripting; hardware management, systems management, data tasks, automation, and tons of other useful information. All of this coupled with an unique navigational structure and a great price. This book truly provides groundbreaking information for the growing community of advanced Linux professionals.

Lotus Notes and Domino Titles

Domino System Administration
By Rob Kirkland
1st Edition Fall 1999
500 pages, $39.99
ISBN: 1-56205-948-3

Your boss has just announced that you will be upgrading to the newest version of Notes and Domino when it ships. As a Premium Lotus Business Partner, Lotus has offered a substantial price break to keep your company away from Microsoft's Exchange Server. How are you supposed to get this new system installed, configured, and rolled out to all your end users? You understand how Lotus Notes works—you've been administering it for years. What you need is a concise, practical explanation of the new features and how to make some of the advanced stuff work smoothly. You need answers and solutions from someone like you, who has worked with the product for years and understands what you need to know. *Domino System Administration* is the answer—the first book on Domino that attacks the technology at the professional level, with practical, hands-on assistance to get Domino running in your organization.

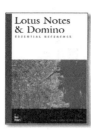

Lotus Notes and Domino Essential Reference
By Dave Hatter
and Tim Bankes
1st Edition Spring 1999
500 pages, $24.99
ISBN: 0-7357-0007-9

You're in a bind because you've been asked to design and program a new database in Notes for an important client that will keep track of and itemize a myriad of inventory and shipping data. The client wants a user-friendly interface without sacrificing speed or functionality. You are experienced (and could develop this application in your sleep) but feel that you need to take your talents to the next level. You need something to facilitate your creative and technical abilities, something to perfect your programming skills. The answer is waiting for you: *Lotus Notes and Domino Essential Reference*. It's compact and simply designed. It's loaded with information. All of the objects, classes, functions, and methods are listed. It shows you the object hierarchy and the relationship between each one. It's perfect for you. Problem solved.

Networking Titles

Cisco Router Configuration & Troubleshooting
By Pablo Espinosa and
Mark Tripod
1st Edition
300 pages, $34.99
ISBN: 0-7357-0024-9

Want the real story on making your Cisco routers run like a dream? Why not pick up a copy of *Cisco Router Configuration and Troubleshooting* and see what Pablo Espinosa and Mark Tripod have to say? They're the folks responsible for making some of the largest sites on the Net scream, like Amazon.com, Hotmail, USAToday, Geocities, and Sony. In this book, they provide advanced configuration issues, sprinkled with advice and preferred practices. You won't see a general over-view on TCP/IP. They talk about more meaty issues, like security, monitoring, traffic management, and more. In the troubleshooting section, the authors provide a unique methodology and lots of sample problems to illustrate. By providing real-world insight and examples instead of rehashing Cisco's documentation, Pablo and Mark give network administrators information they can start using today.

Implementing Virtual Private Networks: A Practitioner's Guide
By Tina Bird and Ted Stockwell
1st Edition Spring 1999
300 pages, $29.99
ISBN: 0-73570-047-8

Understanding Data Communications, Sixth Edition
By Gilbert Held
6th Edition Summer 1999
500 pages, $39.99
ISBN: 0-7357-0036-2

Tired of looking for decent, practical, up-to-date information on virtual private networks? *Implementing Virtual Private Networks: A Practitioner's Guide*, by noted authorities Dr. Tina Bird and Ted Stockwell, finally gives you what you need—an authoritative guide on the design, implementation, and maintenance of Internet-based access to private networks. This book focuses on real-world solutions, demonstrating how the choice of VPN architecture should align with an organization's business and technological requirements. Tina and Ted give you the information you need to determine whether a VPN is right for your organization, select the VPN that suits your needs, and design and implement the VPN you have chosen.

Updated from the highly successful Fifth Edition, this book explains how data communications systems and their various hardware and software components work. Not an entry-level book, it approaches the material in textbook format, addressing the complex issues involved in internetworking today. A great reference book for the experienced networking professional, this offering was written by the noted networking authority Gilbert Held.

Other Books By New Riders Press

We Want to Know What You Think

To better serve you, we would like your opinion on the content and quality of this book. Please complete this card and mail it to us or fax it to 317-581-4663.

Name _____

Address _____

City_____State_____Zip _____

Phone _____

Email Address _____

Occupation _____

Operating system(s) that you use _____

What influenced your purchase of this book?
- ❏ Recommendation
- ❏ Table of Contents
- ❏ Magazine Review
- ❏ New Riders' Reputation
- ❏ Cover Design
- ❏ Index
- ❏ Advertisement
- ❏ Author Name

How would you rate the contents of this book?
- ❏ Excellent
- ❏ Good
- ❏ Below Average
- ❏ Very Good
- ❏ Fair
- ❏ Poor

How do you plan to use this book?
- ❏ Quick Reference
- ❏ Classroom
- ❏ Self-Training
- ❏ Other

What do you like most about this book?
Check all that apply.
- ❏ Content
- ❏ Accuracy
- ❏ Listings
- ❏ Index
- ❏ Price
- ❏ Writing Style
- ❏ Examples
- ❏ Design
- ❏ Page Count
- ❏ Illustrations

What do you like least about this book?
Check all that apply.
- ❏ Content
- ❏ Accuracy
- ❏ Listings
- ❏ Index
- ❏ Price
- ❏ Writing Style
- ❏ Examples
- ❏ Design
- ❏ Page Count
- ❏ Illustrations

What would be a useful follow-up book to this one for you?_____

Where did you purchase this book? _____

Can you name a similar book that you like better than this one, or one that is as good? Why?

_____

_____

How many New Riders books do you own? _____

What are your favorite computer books?_____

What other titles would you like to see us develop? _____

Any comments for us? _____

_____

_____

_____

Windows NT Power Toolkit 0-7357-0922X

www.newriders.com • Fax 317-581-4663

Fold here and tape to mail

New Riders Publishing
201 W. 103rd St.
Indianapolis, IN 46290

New Riders How to Contact Us

Visit Our Web Site

www.newriders.com

On our Web site you'll find information about our other books, authors, tables of contents, indexes, and book errata. You can also place orders for books through our Web site.

Email Us

Contact us at this address:

newriders@mcp.com

- If you have comments or questions about this book
- To report errors that you have found in this book
- If you have a book proposal to submit or are interested in writing for New Riders
- If you would like to have an author kit sent to you
- If you are an expert in a computer topic or technology and are interested in being a technical editor who reviews manuscripts for technical accuracy

international@mcp.com

- To find a distributor in your area, please contact our international department at this address.

pr@mcp.com

- For instructors from educational institutions who wish to preview New Riders books for classroom use. Email should include your name, title, school, department, address, phone number, office days/hours, text in use, and enrollment in the body of your text, along with your request for desk/examination copies and/or additional information.

Write to Us

New Riders Publishing

201 W. 103rd St.

Indianapolis, IN 46290-1097

Call Us

Toll-free (800) 571-5840 + 9 +4557

If outside U.S. (317) 581-3500. Ask for New Riders.

Fax Us

(317) 581-4663

URLabs Software License Agreement and Limited Warranty

READ THIS DOCUMENT CAREFULLY. THIS IS A LEGAL AGREEMENT BETWEEN YOU AND UNIFIED RESEARCH LABORATORIES, INC. ("URLABS"). BY USING THIS SOFTWARE ("SOFTWARE") AND THE DOCUMENTATION ACCOMPANYING THIS SOFTWARE ("DOCUMENTATION"), YOU ARE AGREEING TO BE BOUND BY THE TERMS AND CONDITIONS OF THIS AGREEMENT, INCLUDING WITHOUT LIMITATION THE DISCLAIMER OF WARRANTIES AND LIMITATION OF LIABILITY CONTAINED HEREIN. IF YOU ARE NOT WILLING TO BE BOUND BY THE TERMS OF THIS AGREEMENT, DO NOT USE THIS SOFTWARE AND PROMPTLY RETURN IT TO THE PLACE WHERE OR TO THE PERSON FROM WHOM YOU PURCHASED IT.

The enclosed Software and Documentation are licensed, not sold, to you by URLabs. You shall inform all users of the Software of the terms and conditions of this Software License Agreement.

1. GRANT OF LICENSE; USE RESTRICTIONS. URLabs grants you a personal, nontransferable, and nonexclusive right to install the Software on a single server for your own internal use. You shall not permit any other party to use the Software or process or permit to be processed the data of any other party; provided, however, that if you are an "Internet Service Provider," as hereinafter defined, you may install the Software on a single server to provide "ISP Services," as hereinafter defined.

   You are an "Internet Service Provider" if you are a firm, company, or organization that provides for a fee Internet access or services to your subscribers, none of whom are under your immediate employ or the employ of any parent, subsidiary, or affiliate firm, company, or organization.

   "ISP Services" means content-managed Internet access service and/or electronic mail service provided by you as an Internet Service Provider to your subscribers using the Software.

   You agree that you shall not disassemble, reverse compile, reverse engineer, decrypt, reproduce, adapt, modify, translate, distribute, duplicate, copy, transfer possession of, loan, rent, lease, sublicense, resell for profit, create derivative works based upon, or make any attempt to discover the source code of, the Software or any portion thereof.

   The Documentation may be used for your internal use only. You may not duplicate, copy, or otherwise reproduce the Documentation nor may you distribute the Documentation to any third party.

Prior to disposing of any media or apparatus containing the Software or Documentation, you will ensure that any Software or Documentation contained on such media or stored in such apparatus has been completely erased or otherwise destroyed.

2. OWNERSHIP. You agree that no title to the Software or the Documentation, or to the intellectual property in any of the Software or Documentation or in any copy of the Software or Documentation, is transferred to you, and that all rights not expressly granted to you hereunder are reserved by URLabs.

3. LIMITED WARRANTY. URLabs warrants that the media on which the Software is distributed will be free from defects for a period of sixty (60) days from the date of delivery of the Software to you. Your sole remedy in the event of a breach of this warranty will be that URLabs will replace any defective media returned to URLabs within the warranty period. This Limited Warranty is void if failure of the Software media has resulted from accident, abuse, or misuse of the media. URLabs does not warrant that the Software will meet your requirements or that operation of the Software will be uninterrupted or that the Software will be error-free.

4. DISCLAIMER OF WARRANTIES. THE ABOVE WARRANTY IS EXCLUSIVE AND IN LIEU OF ALL OTHER WARRANTIES, WHETHER EXPRESS OR IMPLIED, INCLUDING WITHOUT LIMITATION ANY WARRANTIES OF MERCHANTABILITY, FITNESS FOR PARTICULAR PURPOSE, OR NONINFRINGEMENT. THE ENTIRE RISK AS TO THE QUALITY AND PERFORMANCE OF THE SOFTWARE IS WITH YOU.

5. LIMITATION OF LIABILITY. IN NO EVENT SHALL URLABS BE LIABLE TO YOU FOR ANY DAMAGES WHATSOEVER, INCLUDING WITHOUT LIMITATION LOSS OF DATA, USE, PROFITS, OR GOODWILL, OR INDIRECT, SPECIAL, INCIDENTAL, EXEMPLARY, PUNITIVE, OR CONSEQUENTIAL DAMAGES, ARISING FROM ANY CAUSE AND ON ANY THEORY OF LIABILITY INCLUDING WITHOUT LIMITATION CONTRACT, WARRANTY, STRICT LIABILITY, NEGLIGENCE, OR OTHER TORT, BREACH OF ANY STATUTORY DUTY, PRINCIPLES OF INDEMNITY, THE FAILURE OF ANY LIMITED REMEDY TO ACHIEVE ITS ESSENTIAL PURPOSE, OR OTHERWISE, EVEN IF URLABS HAS BEEN NOTIFIED OF THE POSSIBILITY OF SUCH DAMAGES. THESE LIMITATIONS SHALL APPLY NOTWITHSTANDING THE FAILURE OF THE ESSENTIAL PURPOSE OF ANY LIMITED REMEDY, AND REGARDLESS OF WHETHER YOU ACCEPT THE SOFTWARE.

6. EXPORT RESTRICTIONS. You agree that you shall not directly or indirectly export the Software.

7. TERMINATION. This license is terminated if you fail to perform or observe any covenant, condition, or term to be performed or observed under this Agreement. URLabs, at its sole option, may provide written notification of the termination of the License for any reason, and in addition to any other rights or remedies available to URLabs, you shall promptly return to URLabs the original and all copies of the Software and Documentation in your possession, in whole or in part, in any form, including partial copies or modifications, and within two weeks after any such termination you shall certify in writing to URLabs that you have done so through your best efforts and to the best of your knowledge.

8. U.S. GOVERNMENT RESTRICTED RIGHTS. U.S. GOVERNMENT RESTRICTED RIGHTS LEGEND. Use, duplication, or disclosure by the Government is subject to restrictions as set forth in the Commercial Computer Software-Restricted Rights clause at FAR 52.227-19(c)(1) and (2) or subparagraph (c)(1) of the Rights in Technical Data and Computer Software clause at DFARS 252.227-7013 and/or in similar or successor clauses in the FAR, or the DOD or NASA FAR Supplement, as applicable. Unpublished rights reserved under the Copyright Laws of the United States. Contractor/manufacturer is Unified Research Laboratories, Inc., 303 Butler Farm Road, Suite 106, Hampton, VA 23666.

9. LAWS GOVERNING WARRANTIES AND LIABILITY. Some U.S. states do not allow the limitation or exclusion of liability for incidental or consequential damages, or allow the exclusion of implied warranties, so the above limitation and exclusion may not apply to you, and you may have other rights which vary from state to state. In any event, URLabs' liability shall not exceed the purchase price actually paid for the Software.

10. GENERAL. This Agreement shall be governed by and interpreted in accordance with the laws of the State of Virginia. You hereby submit to the jurisdiction of the District and Circuit courts for the city of Hampton, Virginia, and the U.S. District Court for the Eastern District of Virginia, Newport News Division, and agree that these shall be the sole fora to resolve all disputes arising under this Agreement or connected in any way with the Software. You agree to pay all costs associated with any such action or suit, including URLabs' costs and attorney's fees. This Agreement may only be modified by a written document which has been signed by both you and URLabs. If any provision of this Agreement is deemed invalid by a court of competent jurisdiction, it is to that extent to be deemed omitted, unless the court can modify said provision to make it valid and enforceable, in which case the provision shall be so modified. The remainder of the Agreement shall be valid and enforceable to the maximum extent possible.

This Trial License is valid for 255 concurrent users, and will expire 30 days after the date of installation. It is recommended that you purchase a WinGate license prior to this date to avoid an interruption in use of the software. To purchase WinGate, select the Register, Online link from the Help menu within the GateKeeper interface. Alternatively, a WinGate license can be purchased at **http://www.wingate.com/ purchase.htm** or from one of the Authorized Deerfield.com Resellers listed at **http://www.securecc.com/windealers/index.cfm**.

The License name and License key must be entered into the GateKeeper interface under "System Info," or during the installation process, EXACTLY as they appear below. We recommend that you copy and paste this information into the license dialog box.

Your License name is: MacMillan Computer Publishing

Your License key is: 02AD44202A1ED034149CF627

The License type you selected to evaluate is: WinGate Pro For pre-sales support, please refer to the WinGate Help or Support Pages. Each contains links to many valuable resources, such as our Support Forums, the WinGate Knowledge Base, various articles of interest, and more.

Help Page—**http://www.wingate.com/help.htm**

Support Page—**http://www.wingate.com/support.htm**

Purchase Page—**http://www.wingate.com/purchase.htm**

Locate an Authorized Deerfield.com Reseller—
http://www.securecc.com/windealers/index.cfm